Women's Human Rights

Pennsylvania Studies in Human Rights

Bert B. Lockwood, Jr., Series Editor

A complete list of books in the series is available from the publisher.

Women's Human Rights

The International and Comparative Law Casebook

Susan Deller Ross

PENN

University of Pennsylvania Press

Philadelphia

Published by
University of Pennsylvania Press
Philadelphia, Pennsylvania 19104-4112

Printed in the United States of America on acid-free paper
10 9 8 7 6 5 4 3 2 1
Library of Congress Cataloging-in-Publication Data
Ross, Susan Deller
  Women's human rights : The international and comparative law casebook / Susan Deller Ross
      p.   cm.—(Pennsylvania studies in human rights)
    ISBN: 978-0-8122-2091-9
    Includes bibliographical references and index.
    1. Sex discrimination against women—Law and legislation.   2. Women (International law).
3. Women's rights—International cooperation.   4. Human rights.   I. Title
K3243.R67   2008
341.4′858—dc22   2008018607

*To the Global Advocates for
Women's Human Rights*

Summary of Contents

Contents

CHAPTER 2
Equality Doctrines and Gender Discrimination:
The Evolving Jurisprudence of the UN Human Rights
Committee and the U.S. Supreme Court

CHAPTER 4
Conflicting Human Rights Under International Law: Freedom of Religion Versus Women's Equality Rights

CHAPTER 5

Enforcing Women's International Human Rights Under Regional Treaties: The American Convention on Human Rights and the African Charter on Human and Peoples' Rights

CHAPTER 6
Enforcing Women's International Human Rights Under Regional Treaties: The [European] Convention for the Protection of Human Rights and Fundamental Freedoms

CHAPTER 7

**Economic Empowerment and Employment Discrimination:
Europe and the United States Compared**

CHAPTER 9
CEDAW in Practice

CHAPTER 10
Enforcing Women's International Rights at Home:
International Law in Domestic Courts

A Case Study in Human Rights Litigation for African Girls and
Women

CHAPTER 11
Strategies to Combat Domestic Violence

CHAPTER 13
Gender and Polygyny: Religion, Culture, and Equality in Marriage

CHAPTER 14
Women's Reproductive Rights

Preface

This book is the first human rights casebook for law students to focus specifically on women's human rights. It does so for several reasons. Many human rights advocates still do not see women's rights as human rights. Why? Perhaps because they do not understand the breadth and depth of the laws, practices, customs, and cultural and religious norms that condemn women to a deeply inferior status in so many locations around the globe. Such advocates might conceive of human rights as involving torture, extrajudicial killings, cruel and degrading treatment—all clearly in violation of international human rights. But, they think, those are not issues women face. Yet is female genital mutilation, practiced on millions of young girls and even infants, not torture? When a daughter flouts some family notion of honor—being seen in public with an unrelated man, for example—and her father orders a family member to kill her knowing that the murderer will benefit from judicial impunity, is that not an extrajudicial killing violating her rights to life, liberty, and security? When a husband rapes or savagely beats his wife, knowing the legal authorities will take no action to protect her, is that not cruel and degrading treatment?

Human rights advocates rightly condemn racial apartheid: it deprives persons, solely on the basis of their race, of equal rights to land, housing, schools, work and travel. But when state codes and customary or religious laws deny women, solely on the basis of their sex, their equal rights to own land and housing, attend school, work outside the home, and travel when and where they want, these same advocates do not decry sexual apartheid. After all, when such laws force women to remain in the home, that is just their "natural condition"—to be wives and mothers without the rights and freedoms men have. Women, it is confidently thought, have no desire to lead more complex lives. Not for them the rights to liberty of movement and freedom of association. Not for them the right to own property or to express or receive opinions and ideas.

Protecting people's health and human rights has rightly become a mantra for change. Yet how many focus on the fact that women are now disproportionately the victims of HIV/AIDS and that laws help put them in this situation? In sub-Saharan Africa, women are nearly 60 percent of all victims; among young people aged 15–24 the statistics are worse—for example, girls in South Africa are four times more likely to be infected with HIV (17%) than boys (4.4%). It is the accepted wisdom that effective prevention requires promoting sexual fidelity between two partners as an ideal. Yet there seems to be a global taboo about discussing two sets of laws that promote men's sexual infidelity. Polygamy laws permit men to have several wives, and adultery laws excuse married men if they sleep with unmarried women. Any married man who exercises these rights cannot, by definition, be faithful to one woman; thus, even a sexually faithful wife or unmarried woman with whom he sleeps is exposed through him to any virus he may have acquired from one of his multiple partners. Surely this violates women's rights to health and life, yet the Joint United Nations Programme on HIV/AIDS (UNAIDS), the World Health Organization (WHO), and international human rights organizations fail even to mention the topic.

In the "War on Terror," many human rights advocates rightly denounce the killing of innocent civilians and prisoners as a violation of their right to life. But when women die due to unsafe and illegal abortions—and about 70,000 to 80,000 women do die each year from this cause—how many see the anti-abortion laws as violating women's right to life? Most would see a religious or moral issue, not a human rights violation.

And so, this book's first purpose is to introduce law students to the realities of women's lives and an understanding of how states deny women their most fundamental human rights and freedoms. Its second purpose is to give future lawyers the legal tools to change that reality. By studying how international human rights law can be implemented at the domestic level through local courts and legislatures, lawyers will understand how to call upon these newly-articulated rights to help gain legislation, court decisions, and executive action that protect women from human rights violations. They will also understand how to take complaints to international and regional human rights treaty bodies that can hold States parties to their treaty obligations.

This book is also designed for a broader audience. Because the book contains many inter-disciplinary materials, it can be used for advanced undergraduate courses in women's studies, anthropology and sociology, international relations and politics, and regional, comparative, and interdisciplinary studies. Human rights reports describe the impact on human beings of the Afghanistan Taliban's rule and governmental indifference to "honor" killings. Medical studies and news accounts provide a vivid account of the physical effects of FGM and breast implants, thus permitting rich discussion of cultural relativism. An anthropological report about how rural women in Tanzania experience polygyny and a theoretical overview of the subject by a noted law and economics scholar offer sharply divergent perspectives that will enhance student discussion. Specialists in anthropology and in sociology and demographics contribute articles with contrasting approaches to the ethical, policy, and human rights concerns posed by sex-selective abortions.

Regional studies will be enhanced by a rich variety of materials from Africa, Latin America, Asia, and Europe. Political scientists can learn in detail how the regional human rights mechanisms function in practice and weigh their impact on changing law and culture. International scholars can broaden their understanding of international law and the different kinds of work human rights bodies conduct. Comparative specialists will find materials and questions to permit students to make comparisons between the approaches of different countries and human rights bodies to such subjects as land and inheritance rights, marriage and divorce law, religious fundamentalism, discrimination in employment, violence against women, female genital mutilation, polygyny, abortion, and child marriage.

Another even broader audience is that found in any Anglophone country. Lawyers, judges, legislators, and executive branch officials can use this book as a resource for applying national, regional, and international human rights law in their work. International law requires the three branches of government to apply its principles in their work. If they do not, they—as state officials—put the country in the position of violating its binding treaty obligations. This book will help them accomplish the mission of bringing their nations into compliance with treaty commitments to advance women's human rights, rather than the reverse.

Similarly, law professors in many different countries can use this book to start new courses in the subject. Many graduate students from Africa, Asia, Europe, Latin America, and the Middle East who have taken my course in this subject have expressed a desire to teach the subject at home. But lack of materials make that difficult to do. It is my hope that this book can help fill the gap.

Using This Book

This casebook features a website (http://www.RossRights.com) that contains the full text of all the treaties and other international and regional documents studied in the course. It also contains additional resources, such as maps and information on countries discussed in the casebook. This will enable students to quickly access any of these documents while reading the book in order to enhance their understanding of the information.

In order to differentiate between footnotes by the author, Susan Deller Ross, and the footnotes by authors of excerpted materials, the book uses the footnote numbers (1, 2, 3) for the excerpted materials and capital letters (A, B, C) to indicate the Ross footnotes.

Citations in excerpted material are omitted without ellipses. Moreover, ellipses are not used at the beginnings or ends of excerpts.

Acknowledgments

I acknowledge and thank the many teaching colleagues and students who so generously gave their time, ideas, and suggestions for materials. They include Johanna E. Bond, Naomi R. Cahn, Tamar Ezer, Anne Tierney Goldstein, Courtney W. Howland, Tzili Mor, Shannon M. Roesler, and Merle Weiner; their many contributions greatly enriched this volume. Anne Tierney Goldstein made especially valuable contributions. During 1992–1998, while we were co-teaching the course for which this book is designed, she suggested using many of the cases and articles in the book; while changed since then, her initial research and vision proved invaluable. Georgetown Law's international and foreign law librarians Marci Hoffman, Marylin J. Raisch, and Mabel Shaw provided invaluable help with international and comparative research. Many students provided excellent research assistance, including Greg Burns, Alexandra Caplazi, Cora Guffey, Amy Lewis, Kalsoom Khalid Malik, Daniel McLaughlin, Uriel Mendieta, Cherine Smith, Melysa Sperber, Rebekah Stafford, Katherine Volovsky, Daniel Widdison, and Jennifer Woodson. Anna Selden, Dianne McDonald, and Jennifer Lindner also provided very helpful technical support in formatting and producing the final manuscript. Georgetown Law Deans Judith C. Areen and T. Alexander Aleinikoff were likewise generous in supporting my work through summer writing grants. I would also like to thank the many people I worked with at the University of Pennsylvania Press, including Peter Agree, Alison Anderson, Chris Bell, Sandra Haviland, and Chris Hu.

Special thanks go to Bert Lockwood who encouraged me to pursue this effort and provided invaluable support. His belief in the project meant so much to me. Finally, I want to thank my family for their continued support of my work on behalf of women's human rights over the years.

Chapter 1
Women's Status and CEDAW

I. Women's Human Rights: An Introduction

Throughout human history women have faced discrimination and violence and, despite significant progress, still do. But today, it is possible to help change that reality through the international human rights system that arose from the ashes of World War II. Lawyers can use international treaties and lessons from comparative law to create new domestic legal structures to advance women's rights in every country around the globe. To do so, they must understand the interlocked elements of women's subordination and the ways that law can be used either to deny or grant women equality and freedom from violence.

This chapter will explore women's status at the beginning of the 21st century and introduce you to the Convention on the Elimination of All Forms of Discrimination Against Women (CEDAW).[1] The Convention is the most comprehensive international treaty on women's issues and therefore our starting point. Later chapters will introduce other major human rights treaties and explore how advocates can use them to advance women's legal status by proposing new laws in their legislatures or starting test cases in their domestic courts. If they lose at the national level, advocates can then turn for help to the regional or international bodies that monitor the human rights treaties.

The book also examines and compares the legal approaches of different countries and human rights systems to many specific women's rights problems, such as domestic violence, marital rape, female genital mutilation, polygamy, and unequal rights in marriage, divorce, and inheritance. Discriminatory employment practices and laws deprive women of access to jobs and equal pay and promotion; women also suffer sexual harassment on the job and unequal treatment when they are pregnant or give birth. Other laws and practices prevent women from owning land and other property, an issue of key importance to women in the developing world. Tax codes and laws regulating military service, police and fire departments, citizenship, social security

---

[1] Convention on the Elimination of All Forms of Discrimination Against Women, G.A. res. 34/180, 34 U.N. GAOR Supp. (No. 46), at 193, U.N. Doc. A/34/46, *entered into force* Sept. 3, 1981.

programs, jury service, and education treat women differently from men. Many laws and practices expose women to increased risk for HIV/AIDS and prevent them from making reproductive decisions about how many children to have and when to have them.

Comparative analysis also extends to procedural, remedial, and enforcement issues. A litigator must analyze these factors and the substantive likelihood of winning in planning a test case and choosing the forum most likely to yield a favorable decision. A non-governmental organization (NGO) or legislator must understand the range of options available in order to craft the most effective human rights statutes, constitutions and treaties.

The reader will necessarily confront key philosophical questions in studying these materials. How should the conflict between women's human rights and cultural relativism be resolved? Should religious rights trump women's human rights? What is the best way to address the conflict between work and family issues—in laws providing benefits to women alone or to both men and women? Should abortion be allowed in no case, in some cases, or when a woman herself makes the choice?

II. Women's Status Around the World

NAOMI NEFT & ANNE D. LEVINE, WHERE WOMEN STAND: AN INTERNATIONAL REPORT ON THE STATUS OF WOMEN IN 140 COUNTRIES, 1997–1998
(1998)

Women throughout the world today live longer, healthier lives, are better educated, enjoy more job opportunities, and earn higher salaries than ever before. In many countries around the globe there are more women than men in college and more women than ever in top-level leadership roles, both in business and in public life. The past several decades have witnessed tremendous improvements in women's literacy, longevity, education and employment opportunities, and general standard of living. And as women's lives have gotten better, their families have become better educated, better nourished, healthier, and more productive. Where women thrive, communities and nations thrive.

Global Gender Gaps

Yet progress has not always been even, and some parts of the world have suffered recent reversals. There are many places in the world where women's average life expectancy is less than 50 years and where the great majority of women can neither read nor write. And in country after country, women constitute the majority of the poor, accounting for more than 70% of the world's 1.3 billion people living in poverty.

Despite having made many great strides in attaining women's rights and improving their lives, all too often girls and women find that their access to education, employment, health care, political influence, and sometimes even food or life itself is limited solely because of their gender. In some parts of the world, it is not uncommon for a fetus to be aborted or a baby killed for no other reason than because she is female. Around the world, millions of women live in societies where centuries-old social and religious laws, customs, and traditions have created insurmountable barriers to education, jobs, and health care, as well as depriving women of most of their political and civil rights. And where women have limited access to schooling, health care, and economic opportunities, their families tend to be larger, poorer, less educated, and debilitated by malnutrition and disease.

Although Female Enrollment in School is Higher than Ever and Literacy Rates Are Rising:

- Women make up nearly two-thirds of the world's 960 million illiterates.
- In primary school, enrollment rates for girls are about equal to boys', yet girls' dropout rates are higher and girls account for two-thirds of the 100 million children who drop out of primary school in the first four years.
- Female students are still enrolled mostly in the courses traditionally regarded as suitable for women: home economics, humanities, education, and the arts.
- Women teachers predominate in preschools and primary schools, are a minority in colleges and universities, and rarely attain the rank of full professor.

Although More Women Than Ever Are Working Outside the Home and Make Up One-Third of the World's Labor Force They:

- Are concentrated in the least skilled and the lowest paying jobs.
- Occupy less than 6% of top management positions.
- Work overwhelmingly more in part-time jobs than men and are thus often not eligible for maternity, health insurance, and other benefits.
- Generally earn one-half to three-quarters of men's wages.
- Usually have higher unemployment rates than men and take longer to find new jobs.
- Tend to be the last ones hired, the first ones fired.

Although Most Women Have the Right to Marry Whom They Choose and Have Legal Access to Divorce and Inheritance Rights, There are Still Parts of the World Where:

- A husband is the legal head of the household, with complete authority over his wife and children.
- A married woman cannot work, obtain a passport, buy or sell property, secure a bank loan, or open a bank account without her husband's permission.
- A widow is entitled to only a small fraction of her husband's estate, and customary law may even award the entire estate to the husband's family, leaving her destitute.

- Adultery is defined differently for women and men (a woman may be guilty if she has been unfaithful only once, a man only if he keeps a mistress).

Although Women Throughout the World are Healthier than Ever and their Life Expectancy Rates are Rising:

- In some countries, particularly where sons are favored over daughters, it is not unusual for baby girls to die of neglect or even to be killed by their parents.
- Over half a million women around the world die from pregnancy-related causes every year, while another 15 million suffer serious long-term complications.
- 70,000 to 200,000 women, including teenage girls, die every year as a result of unsafe, illegal abortions.
- Women now account for nearly half of all new cases of HIV infection.

Although Many Countries Have Enacted Laws Specifically Aimed at Prohibiting Acts of Violence Against Women:

- In some societies, physical abuse of wives is an accepted part of marriage.
- In most countries, marital rape is not considered a crime.
- The great majority of rapes and other assaults are never reported, let alone prosecuted, and when convictions do occur, sentences are often light.
- In some Islamic countries, women are beaten and sometimes even killed for not wearing the traditional Muslim head covering.
- In war-torn countries around the globe, thousands of women and girls are victims of mass rape and torture.
- Only five countries, all in Europe, have national legislatures with 30% or more female members.
- Sweden is the only country with more women than men in its cabinet.
- Only five countries currently have women leaders.

Where Today's Women Live

While women outlive men almost everywhere, there are 39 countries where males outnumber females. . . .

The relatively few countries where men outnumber women . . . [include] Afghanistan, Bangladesh, China, India, Pakistan, and many Middle Eastern countries. . . . And in those countries that also favor sons over daughters, this natural sex imbalance is skewed even further by the abortion of a disproportionate number of female fetuses and higher death rates among female infants and young girls. Among the countries with such "missing" girls are Bangladesh, China, India, Pakistan, and to a lesser extent Egypt, Nepal, South Korea, and Turkey.

Women's Rights

Throughout history there has never been a time or place where women enjoyed complete equality with men. Since ancient times women have been considered men's inferiors—physically, morally, and intellectually. In most parts of the world women have traditionally been considered men's property to be handed over from fathers to husbands. Over the years laws and customs concerning women's rights have been shaped by a variety of Greek, Roman, and other ancient legal systems, as well as by Christian, Jewish, Hindu, Islamic, and other religious laws and traditions.

Women in the Ancient World

In most ancient societies women were considered legal minors, under the control of either their fathers or husbands. They were seldom allowed to own property or manage their own finances. Yet the earliest known code of law, the 18th-century B.C. Babylonian Code of Hammurabi, afforded women some measure of economic independence. They were entitled to dowries, could pass land and other possessions down to their children, and shared equal authority with their husbands over their children. In ancient Egypt women were considered equal to their husbands in law and business, and they could dispose of their own property.

Throughout most of ancient Greece and Rome, women enjoyed very few rights. Marriages were arranged; usually the bride was in her early teens and the groom was 15 years or more her senior. A wife had no control over her property or children, and if the family produced no male heirs, an adult male might be adopted to marry one of the daughters. The Greek colony of Sparta was the exception: women enjoyed great freedom, and girls were entitled to the same education as boys.

In ancient China the yin and yang philosophy of nature reinforced the notion of women's inferiority; the yang (male) principle always dominated the yin (female). China also devised one of the most repressive and painful customs for women—foot binding—which arose in the 10th century. Limited at first to the wealthy upper class, by the 14th century the practice had become widespread. A young girl, between the ages of four and seven, would have all four little toes bent under and bound to make her foot narrower. At the same time, her big toe was pulled toward the heel so that the arch rose and broke, ideally shortening the foot to about three inches. Only the heel could bear any weight, and she could not walk unassisted. For the rest of her life she was generally confined to her chambers, totally dependent on family and servants.

Under ancient Hebrew law a woman could inherit property, but her contracts could be invalidated by her father or husband. If a widow had no children, she was required to marry her husband's brother to continue the dead husband's lineage. In both Hebrew and Islamic law, polygamy was allowed and divorce was legal, but according to Islam, divorce was the sole prerogative of the husband. In Jewish law, a woman could not be divorced against her will, but neither could she obtain a divorce decree without her husband's consent. Islamic women were expected to remain secluded in the home, and when going out had to be covered from head to toe.

Among some North American Indian tribes, too, a girl was kept secluded in the company of other females, rarely seeing even her brothers, and it was not unusual for a man to have more than one wife. Among the Aztecs of ancient Mexico, daughters could inherit their parents' property, and women gained honor and respect by bearing children. A woman who died in childbirth was revered as a goddess.

Although Christian doctrine preached equality of all souls before God, it held that women were inferior to men and taught women to be obedient to their husbands. According to the Hindu laws of Manu, women were subservient to all male relatives. Only a husband could initiate a divorce, and disobedience was just cause. In addition, a widow could not remarry, and the law sanctioned *sati*, the burning alive of a widow on her husband's funeral pyre.

Women in the Middle Ages

Over the centuries, as traditional patriarchal customs and laws became more deeply entrenched, women's lives became more restricted and their rights more limited. During the Middle Ages most women were still denied an education, and their lives generally revolved around managing their homes and caring for their families. Women in rural areas often worked alongside their husbands in the fields, while those in towns and cities sometimes assisted their husbands in a trade or craft.

Beginning in the 15th century, women in Europe slowly started gaining some rights and freedoms. During the Renaissance, learning was considered a virtue, and many girls as well as boys were taught to read. The invention of the printing press in Germany in the mid-15th century made books and other printed materials readily available, and the burgeoning Protestant sects encouraged women to read the Bible and conduct religious services at home. However, church leaders were still preaching that the subjugation of women was God's law and that because women were weaker than men, they were subject to male control. In 1533 the Protestant Reformation leader Martin Luther explained, ''Girls begin to talk and to stand on their feet sooner than boys because weeds always grow up more quickly than good crops.''

Emergence of Modern Feminism

By the 17th century a few women had started speaking out for women's rights, especially for educational opportunities, but it was not until the 18th century that the seeds of modern feminism were sown. With the intellectual movement known as the Enlightenment came many democratic ideas and values, including the rights of the individual. Yet most women were untouched by the social, political, and economic rights that the Enlightenment conferred on men. Even as feudalism disintegrated as a social system, feudal relations of power persisted in marriage: wives were still regarded as the property of their husbands.

The first major feminist work was Mary Wollstonecraft's *A Vindication of the Rights of Woman*, published in Britain [in] 1792. It argued for increased educational opportunities for women as well as political equality with men. Gradually, women in many countries started to organize to advance their own concerns, which usually included such issues as educational opportunities, the right to work, and laws pertaining to divorce and child custody.

The Struggle to Vote

Over the next two centuries women made tremendous strides toward equality with men. The single most important and most arduous struggle during this period was the fight for women's suffrage, which originated in western Europe and spread, ironically, largely through colonization, around the globe.

In many countries, women attained the right to vote only after years of difficult struggle. In most Western countries, the women's suffrage movement grew out of decades of women's increasing public involvement in social issues, such as the abolition of slavery and the temperance movement. By the mid-1800s many of the women who had been active in these movements started banding together in a campaign for women's rights, especially the right to vote. In Britain and the United States, as the movement for suffrage gained momentum, it sometimes grew militant and even violent.

Despite these efforts, by the dawn of the 20th century only one country had granted its female citizens the right to vote. In 1893 New Zealand granted women equal voting rights with men. It took nearly a decade for the next country to follow suit: in 1902 Australia granted women the right to vote in federal elections, even though some states still barred them from voting in local elections. Finland (1906), Norway (1913), Denmark (1915), and a host of other European countries followed in quick succession.

In 1918 Canada became the first North American country to extend the franchise to women, followed by the United States in 1920. Ecuador, in 1928, was the first South American country to grant women's suffrage, and in 1931 Sri Lanka became the first Asian country to do so, followed by Thailand in 1932. The first African country to grant women the right to vote was Senegal in 1945. Cameroon and Liberia followed in 1946.

Following World War II the process greatly accelerated, and today practically every woman in the world has the right to vote. In only a small handful of countries— Bahrain, Brunei, Kuwait, Oman, Qatar, Saudi Arabia, and United Arab Emirates—are women still denied access to the ballot box. However, it should be noted that in all of these countries except Kuwait, men cannot vote either. And in Kuwait, for many years voting was strictly limited to literate, native-born males whose families had lived in the country since 1920. It was not until the mid-1990s, that the government extended voting rights to naturalized male citizens and their sons. Although a separate law granting women the right to vote was under consideration at the same time, it was never adopted.

In a few countries, including Russia and China, women's suffrage was adopted practically overnight as part of a national revolution that granted equal political rights to women and men. Elsewhere, suffrage was often achieved only after many years of struggle, and sometimes it came in stages. In several countries women were first allowed to vote in local elections, later on a national level. In Chile, for example, women could vote in municipal elections as early as 1931 but had to wait until 1949 to cast their ballots in legislative and presidential elections.

In other countries, voting rights were first limited to certain groups of women, defined by age, education, or other criteria. The United Kingdom, for example, first extended voting rights to women in 1918, but only to women over the age of 30. It was not until 1928 that the franchise was extended to all women over 21, finally giving them complete voting equality with men. In Belgium a 1919 law granted national voting rights to widows or mothers of servicemen and civilians killed during World War I, as well as to women who had been political prisoners. Only in 1948 was the franchise extended to all women. In Portugal a 1931 law gave voting rights to women who had completed secondary or higher education, whereas men were required only to know how to read and write. It was not until 1976 that full equality was achieved. In South Africa voting rights were granted to white women in 1930, to Indian and colored women and men in 1983, and to African women and men in 1994.

New Wave of Feminism

In many countries, once suffrage was attained, women's movements began diminishing in strength as well as size, and it was not until the 1960s that a new wave of feminism emerged. By this time several factors—lower infant mortality rates, rising life expectancy, and the introduction of modern contraceptives—had given women more control over their lives and greater freedom from childbearing responsibilities.

At the same time, rising inflation was propelling more women into the labor force, and by 1970 women constituted 40% or more of the work force in more than a dozen developed countries, among them Canada, Denmark, France, the United Kingdom, and the United States. The blatant discrimination these women encountered reinvigorated the older feminist organizations; it also inspired a new generation of women's groups that were concerned largely with women's rights in general and employment discrimination in particular. In the United States and parts of Europe, this resurgence became known as the women's liberation movement, and much attention was given to consciousness raising, that is, making women more aware of their common problems.

Today's Issues

As the feminist movement gained momentum in many countries, it grew stronger, earned greater acceptance, and broadened its scope to encompass a wider range of issues. Today almost every country has a wide array of women's organizations—some dealing with the broad issue of women's rights, others focusing on specific concerns such as abortion, sexual harassment, violence against women, or the problems of immigrant or minority women. In poorer countries women's groups concentrate more on obtaining adequate food and health care; gaining legal rights and educational opportunities; and improving their economic status, for example through gaining easier access to credit.

Although progress on many fronts has been fairly steady over the past several decades, the recent marked growth of religious fundamentalism has begun to pose a serious threat to women's rights in many countries. While fundamentalist movements within Catholicism, evangelical Protestantism, Judaism, and Hinduism have had serious repercussions in some parts of the world, none has had such a far-reaching effect on women as the worldwide resurgence of the various forms of Islamic fundamentalism. One of the most militant and repressive of these movements has taken hold in Afghanistan, where a fundamentalist force known as Taliban has imposed strict Islamic law. . . . [The Taliban was overthrown in 2001, following the publication of this report.] Militant Islamic groups have also emerged in Algeria, Egypt, Iran, Somalia, and Turkey, where they have attacked and even killed women who were not wearing the traditional head covering. They have also closed shelters for battered women and revised schoolbooks to emphasize their interpretation of Islamic teachings, including those aspects that restrict women.

In some of the Eastern European countries that have recently undergone a transition from communism to democracy, a resurgence of the Roman Catholic Church has been a critical factor in curtailing women's access to abortion. In Poland in 1993, the church lobbied successfully to greatly restrict the country's liberal abortion law and keep sex education out of the classroom. Three years later a revised law reinstated sex education and somewhat liberalized the country's abortion rules although it was still far from the abortion-on-demand policy that existed under communism.

Other setbacks for women, especially in the area of employment, are evident in those parts of the world currently suffering drastic economic downturns. Women are bearing the brunt of these crises, suffering high levels of unemployment coupled with cutbacks in child care and other government services. And in the many war-torn nations of the world, such as Bosnia, Cambodia, Croatia, Liberia, Peru, Rwanda, Somalia, and Uganda, it is estimated that women and children account for about 70% of all civilian fatalities. Whether a conflict is with another country or an internal ethnic, religious, or civil war, women and girls are often prime targets, and those who survive suffer the many devastating effects of armed conflict: torture, mass rape, broken families, and the loss of homes and property.

Women in Politics

Despite the fact that women make up half or sometimes more than half of the electorates in most countries, there are only a handful of women who serve as heads of states throughout the world and there is not a single country where women enjoy the same political status, access, or influence as men do. In no country do women even come close to constituting half the national legislature or other major elected political body.

Women Political Leaders

The first woman ever elected to lead a country was Sirimavo Bandaranaike, who became prime minister of Sri Lanka (then called Ceylon) in 1960. By 1970 two other countries, India and Israel, were led by women, and in 1988, Benazir Bhutto became the first woman to head a Muslim country when she was elected Pakistan's prime minister. By 1997 five countries were headed by women. One of these women was Sirimavo Bandaranaike, serving her third term as prime minister of Sri Lanka, this time appointed by her daughter, Chandrika Kumaratunga, Sri Lanka's president.

Women in National Legislatures

Overall, the percentage of women in national legislatures has been declining somewhat in recent years, largely because the quotas formerly allotted to women in the former Soviet Union and socialist states of Eastern Europe were abolished when these governments turned to democracy. Elsewhere the proportion of women legislators has been rising. In fact, some countries have adopted quotas to ensure a minimum representation of women.

Five countries—all in Europe—have now [1998] crossed the 30% threshold, the minimum proportion of women in national legislatures recommended in 1990 by the United Nations Commission on the Status of Women. Sweden, with 41%, has the world's largest proportion of women legislators as well as the highest percentage of women in the cabinet, 52%. Other countries that have crossed the critical 30% threshold of women in their national legislatures include Norway, with 39%; Finland, with 34%; Denmark, with 33%; and the Netherlands, with 30%.

Women in International Parliaments

Among some European countries, women are better represented in delegations to the European Parliament than in their national legislatures. The European Parliament is the only body of the European Union whose members are directly elected by the citizens of its 15 member states. Of the Parliament's total 626 members, 173 (28%) are women. Finland has by far the largest female representation, followed by Sweden and Denmark. The countries with the smallest percentages of female delegates are the United Kingdom, Greece, Italy, and Portugal. Only one woman has ever been elected president of the European Parliament: Simone Veil of France, who served from 1979 to 1982.

The Central American Parliament, or Parlacen, created in 1987, consists of representatives of its six member nations: Costa Rica, El Salvador, Guatemala, Honduras, Nicaragua, and Panama. As of 1996, only El Salvador, Honduras, and Panama had elected representatives to this body, and approximately 10% of them were women. Only one woman has ever served as president of the Parlacen: Ilsa Diaz Zelaya of Honduras, who was elected in 1993.

NOTES

Women in Politics: An Update. Since the publication of WHERE WOMEN STAND in 1998, the number of women in positions of political leadership across the world has increased.[B] From 1998 to May 2007 the number of countries having legislatures composed of at least 30% women in a single-house parliament or in both houses of a bicameral parliament grew from five to twelve with one subtraction and the addition of the following countries: Burundi, Mozambique, Rwanda, South Africa, and Tanzania in Africa; Belgium and Iceland in Europe; Argentina, Costa Rica, and Cuba in Latin America; and New Zealand. The Netherlands dropped from the list (36.7% in lower house, but 29.3 percent in upper house). Rwanda (48.4% lower house; 34.6 upper house), Sweden (47.3% unicameral), and Argentina (35% lower house; 43.1% upper house) have the highest percentages of women in Parliament. The United States ranks 68th in the world, with women at 16.3% of the House of Representatives and 16% of the Senate. Women also gained strength in the European and Central American Parliaments.

In that same time period, nine countries elected women presidents, including: Switzerland, Latvia, and Panama in 1999; Finland in 2000; the Philippines and Indonesia in 2001; Chile and Liberia in 2006; and Bosnia-Hercegovina in 2007. Twelve nations—New Zealand in 1999; Senegal in 2001; Finland and Peru in 2003; Mozambique in 2004; Germany, Liberia, Sao Tome and Principe, and Ukraine in 2005; Jamaica and South Korea in 2006; and Switzerland in 2007—elevated women to prime minister.

In addition, women have gained the right to vote in several countries, including Bahrain in 2001 and Qatar and Oman in 2003. In October 2003, Saudi Arabia announced that it will hold municipal elections without explicitly banning women from voting. Eventually the ruling family decided that women would not be allowed to participate in the elections. Evan Osnos, *A Question of Democracy*, Chicago Tribune, Mar. 13, 2005, at C1. In May 2005, Kuwait granted women the right to vote. Hassan M. Fattah, *Kuwait Grants Political Rights to Its Women*, New York Times, May 17, 2005, at A9.

Ancient and Medieval? Many laws and practices identified as occurring in ancient times still govern women in many parts of the world. Which would you place in that category? Consider, in reading the chapters that follow, what else you would add to that list.

The authors describe foot binding, seclusion, and *sati*. How might these and similar practices have benefited others?

III. The Convention on the Elimination of All Forms of Discrimination Against Women

CEDAW is one among many international human rights treaties that require nations to end sex-based discrimination and insure equality between men and women. It did not become law until 1981, long after the United Nations Charter of 1945 first called for the "equal rights of men and women."[C] But it is CEDAW that women activists around the globe have seized as a vehicle for demanding equal rights now.

[B] *See* the Inter-Parliamentary Union website link at www.RossRights.com (RossRights).
[C] U.N. Charter pmbl., cl. 2.

Elizabeth Evatt describes its history, broad outlines and functions. She served on the Committee on the Elimination of Discrimination Against Women [the CEDAW Committee], the human rights body that oversees country compliance with CEDAW norms, from 1984 to 1992 and as its Chair from 1989 to 1990.

Elizabeth Evatt, *Finding a Voice for Women's Rights: The Early Days of CEDAW*
34 Geo. Wash. Int'l L. Rev. 515 (2002)

B. The United Nations Takes Up Women's Rights

From time to time the question is raised whether women's rights should be treated separately or integrated into the broader field of human rights. When the United Nations (U.N.) was founded in 1945, however, the female delegates had no doubt that there should be a permanent body in the U.N. to deal with women's rights. They got their way, and the Commission on the Status of Women (CSW) was established [in 1946]. Among its activities, the CSW drafted several conventions and declarations, including the Declaration on the Elimination of Discrimination Against Women in 1967. CSW promoted International Women's Year in 1975, the Women's Decade that followed, and the major women's conferences, held at Mexico [1975], Copenhagen [1980], . . . Nairobi [1985, and Beijing 1995].

C. The Convention on the Elimination of All Forms of Discrimination Against Women

The impetus from the Mexico Conference and the Women's Decade carried forward work on the draft Convention on the Elimination of All Forms of Discrimination Against Women (Women's Convention or Convention). The Women's Convention was adopted in 1979 and came into force on September 3, 1981. Within ten years there were 110 States as parties. . . . The Convention is now the second most widely ratified human rights treaty, after the Convention on the Rights of the Child.

There were already three major U.N. human rights instruments in force in 1976: (1) the Convention on the Elimination of All Forms of Racial Discrimination of 1965 (CERD); (2) the International Covenant on Civil and Political Rights (ICCPR); and (3) the International Covenant on Economic, Social and Cultural Rights (ICESCR). The Women's Convention was in part a response to the perception of women that those instruments had failed to deal effectively with women's rights. The Covenants were, in any event, directed mainly at actions by public agencies, whereas discrimination against women occurs in the private as well as the public arena.

1. What the Convention Does

Following the model of CERD, the Women's Convention is directed against both public and private discrimination and calls for affirmative action. The Convention defines discrimination [against women] as:

any distinction, exclusion or restriction made on the basis of sex which has the effect or purpose of impairing or nullifying the recognition, enjoyment or exercise by women irrespective of their marital status, on a basis of equality of men and women, of human rights and fundamental freedoms in the political, economic, social, cultural, civil or any other field [Article 1].

The principal obligation of States parties under Article 2 is to "condemn discrimination against women in all its forms, [and] to pursue by all appropriate means and without delay a policy of elimination of discrimination against women." Articles 2, 3, and 4 set out the kinds of legal, administrative, and other measures to be taken by States, all of which promote the equal enjoyment of rights by women.

Article 5 calls on States to "modify the social and cultural patterns of conduct," in order to eliminate traditional attitudes, prejudices, and practices concerning the status and role of women and men and to promote the sharing of parental responsibility. Article 6 calls for the suppression of traffic in women and the "exploitation of prostitution." The other substantive Articles, 7 through16, set out in some detail the obligations of States to eliminate discrimination in particular fields.[14]

Some of the provisions were quite controversial during the drafting of the Convention. Some States saw Articles 5 and 16 as posing a threat to cultural and religious values. Many States made reservations to the Convention; some of these specifically invoked Shari'a [Islamic] law. . . .

2. CEDAW: The Monitoring Body

The Convention establishes an independent monitoring body (CEDAW or Committee) composed of twenty-three elected experts. CEDAW's primary function is to receive and consider reports from State parties, explaining what they have done to give effect to the Convention, and the difficulties they have encountered in fulfilling their obligations.

CEDAW was modeled on the monitoring bodies established by other U.N. human rights treaties and has similar functions. Although they have similar functions, CEDAW was subject to its own particular restrictions. Unlike CERD and the ICCPR, the Women's Convention originally made no provision for an individual complaints procedure, thus limiting access by women and opportunities for CEDAW to develop jurisprudence. Another limitation was that CEDAW would "normally" meet for only two weeks annually, which put enormous pressure on the Committee as the number of State parties and reports to be considered increased.

The States parties elect the members of CEDAW. . . . The elected members are to be of "high moral standing and competence in the field covered by the Convention." The experts serve in their personal capacity for terms of four years, half being elected at two year intervals.

In electing the members, States are to give consideration to equitable geographical

---

14 Such obligations include: political and public life (Article 7); international representation (Article 8); nationality (Article 9); education (Article 10); employment (Article 11); health care (Article 12); economic and social life (Article 13); rural women (Article 14); equality before the law (Article 15); marriage and family (Article 16).

distribution and representation of the different forms of civilization and principal legal systems. This is not an enforceable requirement, and its implementation depends to some extent on who is nominated, as well as on the balance among the States parties.

3. Effectiveness of the Monitoring System

The impact of the U.N. human rights treaties and their monitoring committees (treaty bodies) depends on many interrelated factors. The most important of these is the commitment by State parties to give effect to the obligations they have undertaken in their domestic laws and policies. Commitment is especially important because although the treaties are legally binding in international law, there are no effective sanctions. Some States have, of course, amended their laws and reviewed their policies in regard to women as a consequence of ratifying the Convention. Some had done so beforehand. Other States have taken little action, perhaps viewing that ratification was enough. As mentioned, reservations reduced the impact of the Convention in some States.

As the views, conclusions, and recommendations of treaty bodies such as CEDAW are not legally binding, the potential of those bodies to "add value" to the instruments they monitor depends on whether they can influence the State parties to give full effect to their obligations. The treaty bodies also need to influence the State parties to support them in their work by ensuring that they have competent members and adequate resources. For CEDAW to succeed in these rather contradictory aims, it must win respect for its work from the States and from civil society. The CEDAW must accomplish three tasks: (1) demonstrate its competence and its understanding of the key issues affecting women's equality rights in States of different legal and cultural backgrounds; (2) interpret the relevant instrument in a coherent and consistent manner; and (3) apply it to those issues.

Other factors which are relevant to the effectiveness and impact of the treaty bodies include access to adequate sources of information and data, opportunities for discussing and reflecting on issues, and adoption of efficient methods of operation. Additionally, it is important for information about the instruments and the work of the treaty bodies to be widely disseminated, and to be known and understood by the communities whose rights are at issue.

4. Functions and Challenges

The functions of CEDAW, its tools in adding value to the Convention, are

- to consider progress made in the implementation of the Convention;
- to consider the reports of States Parties;
- to report annually, through the Economic and Social Council, to the General Assembly on its activities;
- to "make suggestions and general recommendations based on the examination of reports and information received from the States Parties;" and

• to invite the [UN] specialized agencies to submit reports on the implementation of the Convention in areas falling within the scope of their activities. . . .

NOTES

CEDAW Improvements. CEDAW now has an individual complaints procedure and increased meeting time, thanks to intensive lobbying by women's human rights groups and other NGOs. *See* the Optional Protocol to the Convention on the Elimination of All Forms of Discrimination against Women, G.A. res. 54/4, 54 U.N. GAOR Supp. (No. 49) at 5, U.N. Doc. A/54/49 (Vol. 1) (2000), *entered into force* Dec. 22, 2000, *available at* www.RossRights.com (RossRights). As of August 7, 2007, eighty-eight states had ratified or acceded to the protocol, thus becoming state parties to the Protocol and bound by it. An additional seventy-seven states had taken an initial step toward becoming a state party by signing it.

The Complaints Procedure. Article 2 of the Protocol permits "communications . . . by or on behalf of individuals or groups of individuals" to the CEDAW Committee. Where a person or group submits "on behalf" of others, the victims must give consent "unless the author can justify acting on their behalf without such consent." The individual complaints procedure allows individuals to bring a complaint against their own governments for violating their CEDAW treaty obligations, although only after exhausting all possible domestic remedies for the violation. Article 8 further authorizes the Committee to investigate "grave or systematic violations." For the Committee's Rules of Procedure, *see* RossRights. Other international human-rights monitoring bodies have issued decisions on such complaints. They are not binding, but most states comply.

Declarations Versus Treaties. The UN General Assembly can vote to adopt a declaration or treaty. A declaration is not legally binding but can often lead to binding human-rights treaties. For example, the non-binding 1967 Declaration on the Elimination of Discrimination Against Women helped build pressure for adoption of the binding Convention on the Elimination of All Forms of Discrimination Against Women.

Convention on the Elimination of All Forms of Discrimination Against Women

U.N. Doc. A/34/46, *entered into force* Sept. 3, 1981, *available at* RossRights

Part I

Article 1

For the purposes of the present Convention, the term "discrimination against women" shall mean any distinction, exclusion or restriction made on the basis of sex which has the effect or purpose of impairing or nullifying the recognition, enjoyment or exercise by women, irrespective of their marital status, on a basis of equality of men and women, of human rights and fundamental freedoms in the political, economic, social, cultural, civil or any other field.

Article 2

States Parties condemn discrimination against women in all its forms, agree to pursue by all appropriate means and without delay a policy of eliminating discrimination against women and, to this end, undertake:

(a) To embody the principle of the equality of men and women in their national constitutions or other appropriate legislation if not yet incorporated therein and to ensure, through law and other appropriate means, the practical realization of this principle;

(b) To adopt appropriate legislative and other measures, including sanctions where appropriate, prohibiting all discrimination against women;

(c) To establish legal protection of the rights of women on an equal basis with men and to ensure through competent national tribunals and other public institutions the effective protection of women against any act of discrimination;

(d) To refrain from engaging in any act or practice of discrimination against women and to ensure that public authorities and institutions shall act in conformity with this obligation;

(e) To take all appropriate measures to eliminate discrimination against women by any person, organization or enterprise;

(f) To take all appropriate measures, including legislation, to modify or abolish existing laws, regulations, customs and practices which constitute discrimination against women;

(g) To repeal all national penal provisions which constitute discrimination against women.

Article 3

States Parties shall take in all fields, in particular in the political, social, economic and cultural fields, all appropriate measures, including legislation, to ensure the full development and advancement of women, for the purpose of guaranteeing them the exercise and enjoyment of human rights and fundamental freedoms on a basis of equality with men.

Article 4

1. Adoption by States Parties of temporary special measures aimed at accelerating de facto equality between men and women shall not be considered discrimination as defined in the present Convention, but shall in no way entail as a consequence the maintenance of unequal or separate standards; these measures shall be discontinued when the objectives of equality of opportunity and treatment have been achieved.

2. Adoption by States Parties of special measures, including those measures contained in the present Convention, aimed at protecting maternity shall not be considered discriminatory.

Article 5

States Parties shall take all appropriate measures:

(a) To modify the social and cultural patterns of conduct of men and women, with a view to achieving the elimination of prejudices and customary and all other practices which are based on the idea of the inferiority or the superiority of either of the sexes or on stereotyped roles for men and women;
(b) To ensure that family education includes a proper understanding of maternity as a social function and the recognition of the common responsibility of men and women in the upbringing and development of their children, it being understood that the interest of the children is the primordial consideration in all cases.

Article 6

States Parties shall take all appropriate measures, including legislation, to suppress all forms of traffic in women and exploitation of prostitution of women.

Part II

Article 7

States Parties shall take all appropriate measures to eliminate discrimination against women in the political and public life of the country and, in particular, shall ensure to women, on equal terms with men, the right:

(a) To vote in all elections and public referenda and to be eligible for election to all publicly elected bodies;
(b) To participate in the formulation of government policy and the implementation thereof and to hold public office and perform all public functions at all levels of government;
(c) To participate in non-governmental organizations and associations concerned with the public and political life of the country.

Article 8

States Parties shall take all appropriate measures to ensure to women, on equal terms with men and without any discrimination, the opportunity to represent their Governments at the international level and to participate in the work of international organizations.

Article 9

1. States Parties shall grant women equal rights with men to acquire, change or retain their nationality. They shall ensure in particular that neither marriage to an

alien nor change of nationality by the husband during marriage shall automatically change the nationality of the wife, render her stateless or force upon her the nationality of the husband.

2. States Parties shall grant women equal rights with men with respect to the nationality of their children.

Part III

Article 10

States Parties shall take all appropriate measures to eliminate discrimination against women in order to ensure to them equal rights with men in the field of education and in particular to ensure, on a basis of equality of men and women:

(a) The same conditions for career and vocational guidance, for access to studies and for the achievement of diplomas in educational establishments of all categories in rural as well as in urban areas; this equality shall be ensured in pre-school, general, technical, professional and higher technical education, as well as in all types of vocational training;

(b) Access to the same curricula, the same examinations, teaching staff with qualifications of the same standard and school premises and equipment of the same quality;

(c) The elimination of any stereotyped concept of the roles of men and women at all levels and in all forms of education by encouraging coeducation and other types of education which will help to achieve this aim and, in particular, by the revision of textbooks and school programmes and the adaptation of teaching methods;

(d) The same opportunities to benefit from scholarships and other study grants;

(e) The same opportunities for access to programmes of continuing education, including adult and functional literacy programmes, particulary those aimed at reducing, at the earliest possible time, any gap in education existing between men and women;

(f) The reduction of female student drop-out rates and the organization of programmes for girls and women who have left school prematurely;

(g) The same opportunities to participate actively in sports and physical education;

(h) Access to specific educational information to help to ensure the health and well-being of families, including information and advice on family planning.

Article 11

1. States Parties shall take all appropriate measures to eliminate discrimination against women in the field of employment in order to ensure, on a basis of equality of men and women, the same rights, in particular:

    (a) The right to work as an inalienable right of all human beings;

(b) The right to the same employment opportunities, including the application of the same criteria for selection in matters of employment;

(c) The right to free choice of profession and employment, the right to promotion, job security and all benefits and conditions of service and the right to receive vocational training and retraining, including apprenticeships, advanced vocational training and recurrent training;

(d) The right to equal remuneration, including benefits, and to equal treatment in respect of work of equal value, as well as equality of treatment in the evaluation of the quality of work;

(e) The right to social security, particularly in cases of retirement, unemployment, sickness, invalidity and old age and other incapacity to work, as well as the right to paid leave;

(f) The right to protection of health and to safety in working conditions, including the safeguarding of the function of reproduction.

2. In order to prevent discrimination against women on the grounds of marriage or maternity and to ensure their effective right to work, States Parties shall take appropriate measures:

(a) To prohibit, subject to the imposition of sanctions, dismissal on the grounds of pregnancy or of maternity leave and discrimination in dismissals on the basis of marital status;

(b) To introduce maternity leave with pay or with comparable social benefits without loss of former employment, seniority or social allowances;

(c) To encourage the provision of the necessary supporting social services to enable parents to combine family obligations with work responsibilities and participation in public life, in particular through promoting the establishment and development of a network of child-care facilities;

(d) To provide special protection to women during pregnancy in types of work proved to be harmful to them.

3. Protective legislation relating to matters covered in this article shall be reviewed periodically in the light of scientific and technological knowledge and shall be revised, repealed or extended as necessary.

Article 12

1. States Parties shall take all appropriate measures to eliminate discrimination against women in the field of health care in order to ensure, on a basis of equality of men and women, access to health care services, including those related to family planning.

2. Notwithstanding the provisions of paragraph 1 of this article, States Parties shall ensure to women appropriate services in connection with pregnancy, confinement and the post-natal period, granting free services where necessary, as well as adequate nutrition during pregnancy and lactation.

Article 13

States Parties shall take all appropriate measures to eliminate discrimination against women in other areas of economic and social life in order to ensure, on a basis of equality of men and women, the same rights, in particular:

(a) The right to family benefits;
(b) The right to bank loans, mortgages and other forms of financial credit;
(c) The right to participate in recreational activities, sports and all aspects of cultural life.

Article 14

1. States Parties shall take into account the particular problems faced by rural women and the significant roles which rural women play in the economic survival of their families, including their work in the non-monetized sectors of the economy, and shall take all appropriate measures to ensure the application of the provisions of the present Convention to women in rural areas.
2. States Parties shall take all appropriate measures to eliminate discrimination against women in rural areas in order to ensure, on a basis of equality of men and women, that they participate in and benefit from rural development and, in particular, shall ensure to such women the right:
    (a) To participate in the elaboration and implementation of development planning at all levels;
    (b) To have access to adequate health care facilities, including information, counselling and services in family planning;
    (c) To benefit directly from social security programmes;
    (d) To obtain all types of training and education, formal and non-formal, including that relating to functional literacy, as well as, inter alia, the benefit of all community and extension services, in order to increase their technical proficiency;
    (e) To organize self-help groups and co-operatives in order to obtain equal access to economic opportunities through employment or self employment;
    (f) To participate in all community activities;
    (g) To have access to agricultural credit and loans, marketing facilities, appropriate technology and equal treatment in land and agrarian reform as well as in land resettlement schemes;
    (h) To enjoy adequate living conditions, particularly in relation to housing, sanitation, electricity and water supply, transport and communications.

Part IV

Article 15

1. States Parties shall accord to women equality with men before the law.

2. States Parties shall accord to women, in civil matters, a legal capacity identical to that of men and the same opportunities to exercise that capacity. In particular, they shall give women equal rights to conclude contracts and to administer property and shall treat them equally in all stages of procedure in courts and tribunals.
3. States Parties agree that all contracts and all other private instruments of any kind with a legal effect which is directed at restricting the legal capacity of women shall be deemed null and void.
4. States Parties shall accord to men and women the same rights with regard to the law relating to the movement of persons and the freedom to choose their residence and domicile.

Article 16

1. States Parties shall take all appropriate measures to eliminate discrimination against women in all matters relating to marriage and family relations and in particular shall ensure, on a basis of equality of men and women:
   (a) The same right to enter into marriage;
   (b) The same right freely to choose a spouse and to enter into marriage only with their free and full consent;
   (c) The same rights and responsibilities during marriage and at its dissolution;
   (d) The same rights and responsibilities as parents, irrespective of their marital status, in matters relating to their children; in all cases the interests of the children shall be paramount;
   (e) The same rights to decide freely and responsibly on the number and spacing of their children and to have access to the information, education and means to enable them to exercise these rights;
   (f) The same rights and responsibilities with regard to guardianship, wardship, trusteeship and adoption of children, or similar institutions where these concepts exist in national legislation; in all cases the interests of the children shall be paramount;
   (g) The same personal rights as husband and wife, including the right to choose a family name, a profession and an occupation;
   (h) The same rights for both spouses in respect of the ownership, acquisition, management, administration, enjoyment and disposition of property, whether free of charge or for a valuable consideration.
2. The betrothal and the marriage of a child shall have no legal effect, and all necessary action, including legislation, shall be taken to specify a minimum age for marriage and to make the registration of marriages in an official registry compulsory.

NOTES

Gaps in CEDAW Coverage? Consider whether CEDAW requires states to eliminate domestic violence or to allow women access to safe and legal abortions. Does it permit states to draft and send into combat only men? Consider the Article 1 definition of discrimination in answering the question. Article 10 permits sex-segregated schools. Is that a form of discrimination?

International Treaties. Treaties have traditionally been defined as agreements between nation states that create legally binding obligations governing states in their actions as states toward the other state party or parties. International law did not countenance one state interfering with another state's treatment of its own subjects. That was a matter of sovereignty, within the state's sole control.

In the aftermath of World War II and the horrors of genocide, international human rights treaties added a new dimension. They overrode state sovereignty and gave each state party a legal interest in the other state's treatment of its own citizens. In adhering to such a treaty, a ratifying state asserts that it will take the measures required in the treaty to protect its own citizens. CEDAW's Article 2 defines these obligations. What legal actions does Article 2 require of states parties' legislatures? Of their courts? Of the executive bodies? Substantive Articles 6–16 require states parties to eliminate discrimination by many private actors. Who are they?

International Law Terms. International law has developed its own body of legal terminology. In order to assist readers new to the study of international law, the book includes notes throughout such as this to define important terms.

Treaties and Customary International Law. Today, most international law is set through treaties between two or more states parties. *See* the Vienna Convention on the Law of Treaties, 1155 U.N.T.S. 331, *entered into force* January 27, 1980 (Vienna Convention), *available at* RossRights, for the "codification and progressive development" of the law of treaties. Prior to codification, this law took the form of international customary law—that is, the practice of states—and customary law remains in force for those legal issues not governed by the Vienna Convention or by other conventions. International human rights are primarily derived from multi-state treaties such as CEDAW. Some international human rights, e.g., the right not to be tortured, are so widely accepted, however, that they are considered customary law. In the rare case where a country might not have ratified the Torture Convention, advocates in that state could resort to customary international law to assert that state torture violates victims' rights. Thus, treaties are the main source of international law, but customary law remains an important back-up source.

Adoption. Adoption is the process by which the parties drafting a treaty agree to its text and thereby open the treaty for ratification or accession by potential states parties. *See* Article 9 of the Vienna Convention. The UN General Assembly adopted CEDAW on December 18, 1979, through UN General Assembly Resolution 34/180. On July 2, 1980, Sweden became the first state to ratify CEDAW.

Signature and Ratification. "Where the signature is subject to ratification, acceptance or approval, the signature does not establish the consent to be bound. However, it is a means of authentication and expresses the willingness of the signatory state to continue the treaty-making process. The signature qualifies the signatory state to proceed to ratification, acceptance or approval. It also creates an obligation to refrain, in good faith, from acts that would defeat the object and the purpose of the treaty." *Treaty Reference Guide*, U.N. Treaty Collection (Treaty Guide), *available at* RossRights.

Ratification usually follows after signature and "defines the international act whereby a state indicates its consent to be bound to a treaty if the parties intended to show their consent by such an act." *Id.* For an example of the difference between signature and ratification, U.S. President Carter signed CEDAW on July 17, 1980; however, since the U.S. Senate has not yet ratified CEDAW (by a 2/3 vote as required by U.S. Const. art. II, § 2, cl. 2), the U.S. is not a party to CEDAW. Therefore, as a signatory, the U.S. must refrain from acts that would defeat CEDAW's object and purpose, but it is not bound as a party to take positive action to fulfill CEDAW's mandates. The processes by which states ratify international treaties vary between states; some states, such as the U.S., require approval by both the executive and legislative branches for ratification, while other states require approval from only the executive.

Accession. "Accession is the act whereby a state accepts the offer or the opportunity to become a party to a treaty already negotiated and signed by other states. It has the same legal effect as ratification. Accession usually occurs after the treaty has entered into force. The Secretary-General of the United Nations, in his function as depositary, has also accepted accessions to some conventions before their entry into force." *Id.* As with ratification, states have different processes for acceding to treaties. The difference between ratification and accession is that the first involves an initial signature by a state official while the second does not.

Entry into force. A treaty enters into force and becomes a legally binding document on all states parties when the relevant treaty conditions are satisfied. Vienna Convention, art. 24, para. 1. Article 27 of CEDAW provides that it "shall enter into force on the thirtieth day after the date of deposit with the Secretary-General of the United Nations of the twentieth instrument of ratification or accession." CEDAW entered into force on September 3, 1981, after St. Vincent and the Grenadines acceded to CEDAW on August 4, 1981, thereby becoming the twentieth state party.

Reservation. A reservation is "a unilateral statement, however phrased or named, made by a State, when signing, ratifying, accepting, approving or acceding to a treaty, whereby it purports to exclude or to modify the legal effect of certain provisions of the treaty in their application to that State." Vienna Convention, art. 2, para. 1(d). A state cannot enter a reservation that is "incompatible with the object and purpose of the treaty." *Id.*, art. 19, para. c. As discussed below, 33% of states parties have entered reservations to CEDAW, an unusually high number.

CEDAW Ratifications and Reservations. As of August 7, 2007, 185 countries had ratified or acceded to CEDAW. States that became parties in the twenty-first century include Saudi Arabia in 2000; Democratic People's Republic of Korea and Mauritania in 2001; Bahrain and the Solomon Islands in 2002; Afghanistan, San Marino, Sao Tome and Principe, Syrian Arab Republic, and Timor-Leste in 2003; Kiribati, Micronesia, and Swaziland in 2004; Monaco in 2005; and Brunei Darussalem, Cook Islands, Marshall Islands, Montenegro, and Oman in 2006. The United States remains the one country which has signed the Convention but has failed to take the steps necessary to ratify it.

By July 2007, sixty-two of the states parties still had in place one or more CEDAW reservations or declarations. The original number was higher but many states had withdrawn their reservations by then. The procedure for making reservations to CEDAW differs from that of other international human rights treaties. For example, the International Convention on the Elimination of All Forms of Racial Discrimination requires that two-thirds of states parties approve a proposed reservation before the reservation is entered; a reservation to CEDAW, however, requires no such approval. As a result, CEDAW is one of the most heavily reserved human rights treaties.

States parties have made numerous reservations to Articles 2, 9, 15, and 16, which are of critical importance to the successful enforcement of the Convention. Thirty-six countries have continued reservations to at least one of these articles and five countries (Algeria, Bahrain, Morocco, Syrian Arab Republic, and the United Arab Emirates) reserve to all four. Many states assert that CEDAW provisions contradict Islamic religious law (Shari'a); these countries include Bahrain, Bangladesh, Brunei Darussalem, Egypt, Iraq, Kuwait, Libyan Arab Jamahiriya, Malaysia, Maldives, Mauritania, Morocco, Oman, Pakistan, Saudi Arabia, Syrian Arab Republic, and the United Arab Emirates. *See* Rebecca J. Cook, *Reservations to the Convention on the Eliminations of All Forms of Discrimination against Women*, 30 Va. J. Int'l L. 643 (1990) for a more comprehensive discussion. Read CEDAW Articles 9, 15, and 16 and identify the discriminatory laws that reserving states seek to retain. Read Article 2 to understand the enforcement measures they are unwilling to take.

IV. Case Study: Afghanistan

Afghanistan is best known today as the state where the Taliban oppressed women on taking power in 1996, supported Osama bin Laden, and lost power after September 11, 2001. The Soviet Union invasion in 1979 led to a decade of communist rule and continuing civil war. The first excerpt below describes women's traditional status and the laws in place by 1991. The second provides a statistical portrait of women's position as of 1980—the latest time for which this information is available—and more detail about the laws described in the first excerpt. The third excerpt describes women's lives under the Taliban and discusses the changes over time in women's legal status during the 20th century. The notes that follow discuss the changes that have occurred since the fall of the Taliban in 2001.

The following excerpt was written by an Afghan man in 1991. While the wording of the piece might suggest that some of the practices described occurred in the past, many of them are still current.

Wali M. Rahimi, Status of Women: Afghanistan
6–14, 62–65 (1991)

The Status of Women in Historical Perspective

The position of women in Afghanistan has traditionally been inferior to that of men. This position has varied according to age, socio-cultural norms, and ethnicity. In fact,

Afghan women, even until the beginning of [the] 20th century were the slaves of their father, husband, father-in-law, and elder brother. Her most valued characteristic was silence and obedience. The essence of [the Afghan] attitude towards women could be clearly seen in the relationship of the family after the birth of a female baby. Such a birth was considered and judged as an unpleasant event and unfortunate for the entire family, both in a settled and a nomadic population. The birth of a female baby, particularly in those cases where the mother gave birth to several girls, was, and still is, the main cause of contracting a second marriage. Girls were usually raised to be good mothers and tolerant housewives. . . . They were married to young and even to very old men, in most cases wealthy ones, between the ages of 13 and 16, and in certain cases between the ages of 10 and 12, if their parents desired. They were exchanged for what is called "Toyana" or marriage price. . . . Early marriage was the main cause of suffering for girls in Afghan society. Such marriages were both physically and psychologically unhealthy, and often resulted in sickness and psycho-neurotic diseases. Many young mothers died during delivery because of physiological reasons and early motherhood.

Divorce was an easy act if the husband wanted it. Afghan women did not have the right to ask for divorce. It was a slur for both families. Occasionally, wives were deprived of their rights and claims on their own children.

Polygamy was damaging for the personality of women and caused contempt. This practice changed women into slaves and furthermore led to an unpleasant and unhealthy atmosphere of hatred and conflict among wives. . . .

Economically, women do not own as much as men. Legally, daughters inherit only half the amount compared to the sons. Often, however, because of socio-cultural reasons they would leave even this sum to their brothers.

Besides inheritance, there is another main source of women's property called *Mahr*. It is the amount of money assigned to a wife by her husband at the time of the marriage contract. Since women are completely supported by men, they seldom claim *Mahr*. They claim it only at the time of seeking divorce which happens very rarely, even if men are proven to be impotent, suffering from an incurable disease or insanity, either of which is a main reason according to Islamic laws for women to seek divorce. . . .

With respect to tradition, women, in general, are not supposed to earn a living. This has been true for all women of all ages and of all ethnicities. Earning a living by a woman is considered to be a reflection on the husband and even on his family. Only helpless widows can work to feed their orphans. Women have total economic dependence on men.

As has been noted, women receive half of a man's share according to "Sharia" or Islamic law, in the case of inheritance. Combined with the fact that two female witnesses are equivalent to one male witness in courts, there exists the notion that one man is equal to two women. This implies that women are regarded intellectually inferior to men. They are thought to be weak by nature. For this reason, they are not allowed to seek positions outside the home or take part in the development of the society. Common people use the word "woman" to insult opponents simply by calling him "Zun", the "woman". The same word is used for cowards too. . . .

Women usually did not receive an education in the past. Only some upper class women received informal education at home in order to be able to read, mainly the Holy Koran. That is why this group of women was able only to read and not to write. Formal education for women started with the opening of the first girls' school in Kabul in 1919.

Women were mainly occupied with rearing children, cooking, sewing, milking, weaving, spinning, and other similar houseworks. For those who could afford servants, their servants freed them from the burden of home duties. Women took part in social occasions and family entertainments, but were separate from men. On all occasions where both sexes took part, they remained separated. According to Scharmann, the division of men and women into two separate worlds is pronounced in Afghan society. In entering the world outside their homes, women were to veil themselves. They usually tried to hide their faces from men, calling them "Namahram", though the exception was for women in upper class families, the number of which was very small.

It is interesting to note that the seclusion of women historically has been more pronounced in urban areas than in rural areas. Among Pashtuns they were less secluded. The Uzbiks [sic] kept their wives out of view. Nuristani women neither were secluded nor were veiled. It is said that these women had more freedom in terms of establishing social relations with others. But their condition, as the condition of women in other ethnic groups was deplorable; they were overworked and underfed. . . .

In rural communities, beautiful girls get married earlier and to rich persons regardless of their ages. There are many elders who have two, three or four wives, and they all live together in one household or camp. On the other hand, there are also a large number of adults who are celibate, as they are not able to pay the marriage price to the bride's family.

Since Afghanistan is a patriarchal society, common household decisions are mostly made by men. A man decides about residence, and the children's education, and gives permission for women to work. A man is chief of the household because he feeds the household members. A man is allowed to punish his wife, sometimes to death if she attempts adulterous actions.

Age of marriage also shows distinction between the status of a man and a woman. When a girl reaches puberty, she is to be married, while a male does not marry until he has reached adulthood.

Afghans spend a great amount of money on the education of their boys, and even some of them are sent abroad for further studies. But this is not true with the girls; since they are not considered to be the persons who will feed and support the family in the future. Some families even wait for a girl's dismissal from the family. . . .

Let us consider the effects of national languages. A nation's language reflects its social relations. People in both rural and urban areas do not like to give their wives names. It is considered shameful. They are called for example, the mother of children, the mother of X, the daughter of Y or simply, woman . . . .

Legal Status of Women

1. Marriage

Marriage among the Afghans is a relationship established between a man and one or more women.

A Muslim girl cannot marry a non-Muslim boy; but on the contrary, a Muslim boy is legally permitted to marry a non-Muslim girl. If a girl wants to marry a man from another Muslim nationality, she needs an official permit from the government.

With respect to premarital relationship between boys and girls, there is no dating system among Afghans, whether rural or urban. A minor suspicion of [a] love affair between a boy and a girl may endanger their lives. It must, therefore, be kept secret until they are engaged or married.

Marriage is arranged by the parents. The process may begin with the sending of a go-between and then commence by a visit from the mother or an aunt of the boy to the house of the girl's parents. The girl's mother reports the case first to her husband and, if the agreement is reached, to other close relatives afterwards. If all is agreed upon, the prospective bride's and groom's fathers and other close male relatives meet to discuss the final terms of marriage. A formal deputation, *Rooybar*, is sent to ask the girl's hand in marriage. All conditions for marriage including the amount of bride-price, *Walwer* or *Mahr* are proposed by the girl's family or her guardian, *Wali*. If these are acceptable to the other party, then a formal day for engagement is fixed.

The amount of the bride-price is fixed in the laws of Afghanistan and Islamic Sharia and amounts to 300 Afs [Afghan shillings]. The uneducated section of the population and some of the rural people are still asking for an extraordinary amount for the bride-price. In some parts of the country it is more than 700,000 Afs, and in other parts, not less than 50,000 Afs. Modern and educated families do not ask for a bride-price, but they expect the bridegroom to invite all the relatives of the bride and his own to a very glorious and magnificent marriage ceremony. The groom is also expected to purchase expensive jewelry and other ornaments made of gold and other precious stones for his wife. All these may not be less than 200,000 Afs to 300,000 Afs. Among most Afghan families, the bridegroom is also expected to purchase some gifts for his mother-in-law, father-in-law and some other close relatives of the bride.

The parents are the decision makers in all aspects of the marriage of their girls in Afghanistan particularly if the bride and groom are not from the same community. While making their decision, the bridegroom's parents consider several qualifications which are expected to be met by the girl, such as good health, acceptable manners and character, education and skill, good family background, proper statuesque and well-proportioned organs, i.e., her fingers should be long, and her eyes, wide and large; her skin must be soft, and she should have a small mouth and white teeth.

According to Islamic principles and Afghan customs, after the engagement the bridegroom is allowed to visit his fiancee in her father's house. But most Afghans, particularly in rural areas, do not approve of the idea of visiting the bride by the bridegroom in her house before the marriage ceremony. Therefore, some brides, for the first time, see their husbands after their marriage ceremony when they are taken to their husband's house.

Based upon Islamic law and Afghan traditions, premarital sexual relationships are absolutely prohibited. The penalty for adultery is death. Virginity is therefore highly valued in Afghanistan. The roots of this strict custom and tradition lie in its latent function. Among those people who are mostly uneducated and are unaware of the means and methods of birth control this custom is developed to control the population growth in a meager habitat which cannot support a dense population. This practice also helps prevent promiscuous behaviour and the possibility of venereal diseases, especially among youth. The attempts of parents to marry their daughters and sons at an early age is to prohibit premarital sexual relationships. There are other reasons for such early marriages such as honour, power, and family size.

2. Polygamous Marriage

In principle, all Afghan ethnic groups are polygynous. Islamic laws and Afghan traditions, customs and norms permit a man to have simultaneously four wives. Although it is difficult to trace the origin of polygyny in Afghan society, history tells us that at the dawn of Islam, when several of the Arabs and other Muslims were killed, many women were widowed. Being aware of the situation, Mohammed permitted and even encouraged his companions, Shabas, to have more than one wife but not more than four. It is not congenial for two or more wives to live in one household under the guardianship of one man. The terms *Ben* and *Unbaq* [co-wife] in Pashtu and Dari, respectively, indicate extreme hostility in both of these national languages.

Two types of other marriages are also present. When one brother dies, his wife is married to his next brother, technically called junior levirate. Also, when a woman dies, her husband can marry her sister, i.e., the practice of sororate.

3. Divorce

Although Islamic principles and Sharia permit separation, in practice, expelling a wife from the family is strongly disapproved. An Afghan ethnographer who studied the Almara villagers in southern Afghanistan was not able to find even a single case of divorce there. A divorced man and woman cannot live in their natal community, because a divorce not only damages a husband's and a wife's status, but brings shame to their ancestors and successors as well as to their whole tribe. In a national demographic study of Afghanistan, only 0.1 per cent divorce is shown for the total population of the country.

4. Women's Inheritance

Based on Islamic laws, theoretically wives, husbands, daughters, mothers, fathers, sons, sisters, and other relatives inherit a certain portion of the property left after the death of their close relatives. In practice, except for the educated section of the population, Afghans, particularly rural and highly traditional people, distribute the property left after the death of their close relatives only among the deceased's close male heirs. Asking for one's wife's inheritance share, for example, after her father's death is regarded as socially, not legally, unacceptable.

Although uncommon, cases of divorce do happen in urban areas more than rural areas. According to the Afghan customary law and tradition, after divorce the father gets custody of the children, but this is not always the case according to Sharia. Even so, the ages of children and the causes of conflict resulting in divorce determine who should get the custody of the children. Customarily babies and very young children are kept in the custody of their mothers. Fathers have to pay for all their expenses. If the mother remarries very soon, she loses the right to keep the children from her first marriage. In that case, the close relatives of the father will look after them until he remarries. In extreme cases the state has the responsibility of guarding such children.

According to the Civil Law in Afghanistan, [the] marriage contract [—] and all rights and duties of both parties of the contract for the legitimacy of the relations of man and woman and the formation of family by them . . . [—] determine the alimony of the wife, her inheritance right, parentage proof [for their children], and reverence.

Problems Associated with Marriage . . .

2. Polygamy

The Civil Law Article 86, clearly allows polygamy under specific conditions. However, later articles in the law allow women to seek divorce through court if the husband does not observe the conditions laid down by traditional and legal laws and brings harm to them.

There are, however, some legal conditions that prohibit polygamy. But in practice, people do not take them into consideration. Such behaviour violates the equality of woman to man. Also keeping many wives in one residence is not lawful, but there are many people who violate this law, and do not provide equal rights and privileges to all their wives.

3. Divorce

The termination of marriage according to Article 121 of the Civil Law takes place on the ground of dissolution, divorce, disposition and separation under conditions specified by law.

Divorce takes place by using words which precisely convey the meaning of divorce. With the exception of the insane and mentally ill persons, the husband has complete freedom to divorce his wife. He not only asks for her divorce in writing or in spoken words but by common gestures used in the culture which convey the meaning of divorce. The same is true with divorce by means of absence of the husband which is a kind of one way imposition. This is done without any prior knowledge and without legal status. This practice terminates marriage contract in many families, and many women face a painful fate.

In "Khola", the dissolution of a marriage takes place after payment by the wife to the husband. Also, the request for separation by the wife can be realized under certain conditions such as husband being affected by incurable diseases or long term diseases; intercourse with the husband being harmful to the wife; or long absence of the husband (i.e., three years or more). Since, according to Sharia, divorce is considered to be unacceptable, the realization of the equality of women's rights with regard to divorce can only be achieved through providing equal rights and freedom to seek divorce under certain conditions set by the law.

The true realization of the equality of the rights of women to men would lead to the solution of yet another major problem caused by the dissolution of marriage. It is the guardianship of children which, according to Article 236 of the Civil Law, is the protection, socialization and education of children during the period which the child needs a mother's care and attention. This period, according to Articles 249 and 250 of the Law, is seven years for boys and nine for girls, which may be extended for two more years by a court decision. This period is not a sufficient time for either sex to determine where and to whom to go after the period is over. This shortcoming has ill psychological effects on children and has become a major source of complexes and maladjustment in children.

4. Property Rights

Inheritance . . . is based on marriage bond and relationships. According to the Civil Law (Article 2207), the husband, in the case of having no children, receives half of the property and in the [case] of having children one-fourth of the property. But the wife in the first case gets one-fourth and in the second case, one-eighth of the property left after the death of the husband.

According to Islamic Sharia, a woman's main sources of property are trade, industry, agriculture, inheritance and Mahr. It is their right to have property through those sources, to manage it, to have control over it, to have legal possession of it, and to use it freely.

Women have the right to make contracts according to the Civil Law and are allowed to open bank accounts.

NOTES

Afghan Marriage, Divorce, and Inheritance Laws. As seen in Wali Rahimi's 1991 book, even after a decade of Communist rule, Afghan civil law based on Shari'a concepts permitted men to be married to several wives at once, allowed men but not women to divorce a spouse at will and without going to court, and limited women to a one-half share of men's inheritance rights. The law also permitted a wife to stipulate her right to divorce her husband if he takes another wife when she registers her marriage. Do Afghan laws concerning polygamy violate any subsection of CEDAW Articles 15 (equality before the law) or 16 (equality in marriage)? The divorce law? The inheritance law? Note that Article 2(f) requires ratifying states "to modify or abolish existing laws . . . which constitute discrimination against women."

In order to make ratification a meaningful act, equal-rights advocates must use ratification as a tool for persuading courts and legislatures to bring their laws into compliance with CEDAW. A country that ratifies CEDAW but refuses to change its sex-based laws on marriage and inheritance makes an inviting target for test-case litigation in domestic courts based on equality principles. State courts might not rule in favor of women's rights advocates. For example, they might rule that religious rights require the laws or that wives consent to the existing marriage laws. And of course many states have entered reservations as to Articles 15 and 16. You will, however, encounter many examples of the successful results of equality litigation in the chapters that follow, and they illustrate how turning to the courts can force state legislatures to comply with CEDAW's mandates. Chapter 10 will illustrate how advocates can sue in national courts using CEDAW provisions in support of their cases.

Civil Code Governing Marriage and Divorce. Mr. Rahimi mentions two specific provisions of the Civil Code: Article 86 on marriage, and Article 2207 on inheritance. The excerpt below, from SISTERHOOD IS GLOBAL: THE INTERNATIONAL WOMEN'S MOVEMENT ANTHOLOGY 38–39 (Robin Morgan, ed., Feminist Press 1996) (1984), more fully describes the relevant provisions of the Civil Code Articles:

Based on . . . the Hanafi school of law in Islamic jurisprudence, the 1976 Civil Code set the legal marriage age at 16 for females (15 with paternal consent) and 18 for males. Polygyny is legal; a man may marry more than 1 wife if 1) there is no injustice to any wife, 2) the husband is financially able to provide necessities for all the wives (food, clothing, housing, and health care), and 3) a lawful reason exists for the second marriage (e.g., the first wife is barren or seriously ill). In inheritance matters . . . a female inherits 1/2 the share of a male. . . . Among the Shi'ite Moslems, fixed-period "temporary marriages" or *mut'a* . . . are still practiced in some nomadic communities. . . .

The 1976 Civil Code (Article 135, Section 2) allows a man to divorce his wife verbally (*talaq*) or in writing. A wife can divorce her husband only by judicial process, on the grounds that her husband has an incurable illness, if she is compromised while living with her husband, if he refuses or is unable to support her financially, or if he is imprisoned for 10 years or more— whereby she can demand separation after the first 5 years of his imprisonment. In addition, Article 183 of the Code allows a wife to divorce whether or not she can prove the existence of prejudice or harm if arbitration fails to reconcile the couple. Article 88 of the Code allows a wife to stipulate in writing (when she registers her marriage) her right to divorce if her husband takes a second wife; Article 89 grants a woman divorce if her husband has hidden the existence of another wife. . . .

The Current Situation of Women in Afghanistan. Women still do not enjoy an equal status with men. Human Rights Watch reports that of students enrolled in primary school, only 34% are women while 66% are men. A mere 9% of those women proceed on to secondary school. Only 14% of women are literate compared to 43% of men and only 41% of registered voters are women. 57% of girls are married before age 16. *See* HUMAN RIGHTS WATCH, THE STATUS OF WOMEN IN AFGHANISTAN, OCTOBER 2004 (2004), *available at* RossRights. Women also face tremendous hurdles in the area of reproductive rights. UNICEF reports that the maternal mortality rate in 2000 was

1,900 per 100,000 live births, the second-highest in the world. Throughout their lifetime, Afghan women have a one in six chance of dying during childbirth. *See* UNICEF, AFGHANISTAN: STATISTICS, *available at* RossRights.

PHYSICIANS FOR HUMAN RIGHTS, THE TALIBAN'S WAR ON WOMEN: A HEALTH AND HUMAN RIGHTS CRISIS IN AFGHANISTAN[D]
(1998), *available at* RossRights

I. Executive Summary

This report documents the results of a three-month study of women's health and human rights concerns and conditions in Afghanistan by Physicians for Human Rights (PHR). The extent to which the Taliban regime has threatened the human rights of Afghan women is unparalleled in recent history. Taliban policies of systematic discrimination against women seriously undermine the health and well-being of Afghan women. Such discrimination and the suffering it causes constitute an affront to the dignity and worth of Afghan women, and humanity as a whole. . . .

In November 1994, a new group named "Taliban" emerged as a military and political force. Taliban, which means "students of Muslim religious studies," are poorly educated rural Pashtun youths mostly recruited from refugee camps and religious schools ("*madrasas*") in neighboring Pakistan. This movement, led by Mullah Mohammed Omar, a 31-year-old religious leader, claims to be restoring peace and security through the imposition of a strict Islamic order. With no functioning judicial system, many municipal and provincial authorities use the Taliban's interpretation of *Shari'a* (Islamic law) and traditional tribal codes of justice.

The Taliban is the first faction laying claim to power in Afghanistan that has targeted women for extreme repression and punished them brutally for infractions. To PHR's knowledge, no other regime in the world has methodically and violently forced half of its population into virtual house arrest, prohibiting them on pain of physical punishment from showing their faces, seeking medical care without a male escort, or attending school.

After taking control of the capital city of Kabul on September 26, 1996, the Taliban

---

[D] The data in this report reflect data collected during the Taliban era. PHR now recognizes that the situation was more complex than originally presented, and that the data and stories did not reflect the position of rural women. In particular, many rural women used the *burqa* before the Taliban era. Email from Barbara Ayotte, Director of Communications, PHR, to Susan Deller Ross, Professor of Law, Georgetown University Law Center (July 24, 2003) (on file with author). PHR also issued an update of this report in 2001. The format of the update was slightly different from the original survey: while the original survey included responses from women only, the updated survey included responses from both women and men. However, the findings of the updated survey were substantially similar to those of the original: both surveys found that the large majority of Afghan citizens who were questioned did not support the policies of the Taliban. *See* PHYSICIANS FOR HUMAN RIGHTS, WOMEN'S HEALTH AND HUMAN RIGHTS IN AFGHANISTAN: A POPULATION-BASED ASSESSMENT (2001).

issued edicts[2] forbidding women to work outside the home, attend school, or to leave their homes unless accompanied by a husband, father, brother, or son. In public, women must be covered from head to toe in a *burqa*. . . . Women are not permitted to wear white (the color of the Taliban flag) socks or white shoes, or shoes that make noise while they are walking. Also, houses and buildings in public view must have their windows painted over if females are present in these places.

Furthermore, in January 1997, Taliban officials announced a policy of segregating men and women into separate hospitals. This regulation was not strictly enforced until September 1997 when the Ministry of Public Health ordered all hospitals in Kabul to suspend medical services to the city's half million women at all but one, poorly-equipped hospital for women. Female medical workers also were banned from working in Kabul's 22 hospitals. . . . An international uproar ensued, and in November 1997, after two months of negotiations with the International Committee of the Red Cross, the Taliban partially rescinded its directive and agreed to reopen some of the hospitals and make available limited beds therein. Despite the reversal, however, Taliban gender restrictions—preventing women from moving freely and prohibiting women from working—continue to interfere with the delivery of health services and humanitarian assistance to women and girls. . . .

On June 16, 1998, the Taliban ordered the closing of more than 100 privately funded schools where thousands of young women and girls were receiving training in skills that would have helped them support their families. . . .

Taliban policies that restrict women's rights and deny basic needs are often brutally and arbitrarily enforced by the "religious police" (Department for the Propagation of Virtue and the Suppression of Vice) usually in the form of summary, public beatings. In addition, Afghan staff members of international organizations have reportedly faced threats, harassment, beating and arrest in the course of conducting their professional duties.

PHR's researcher when visiting Kabul in 1998, saw a city of beggars—women who had once been teachers and nurses now moving in the streets like ghosts under their enveloping *burqas*, selling every possession and begging so as to feed their children. It is difficult to find another government or would-be government in the world that has deliberately created such poverty by arbitrarily depriving half the population under its control of jobs, schooling, mobility, and health care. Such restrictions are literally life threatening to women and to their children. . . .

Afghanistan's history of civil war and particularly the period of anarchy between 1992 and 1995 following the collapse of the Communist regime has contributed to the perception outside Afghanistan that while the Taliban is repressive, at least it has stopped the war and ended violent crime in the capital.

Physicians for Human Rights rejects this assessment of Afghanistan under the Taliban. For nearly twenty years, the Afghan people have suffered the health consequences of armed conflict and human rights violations. That Taliban officials now claim to be "restoring peace" to Afghanistan is perhaps one of the cruelest ironies of

---

[2] *See* Appendices A, B, and C.

our time, as they have virtually imprisoned Afghan women in their homes and threatened their very survival. The "peace" imposed on that portion of the country under Taliban rule is the peace of the *burqa*, the quiet of women and girls cowering in their homes, and the silence of a citizenry terrorized by the Taliban's violent and arbitrary application of their version of *Shari'a* law.

Methods of Investigation. . .

The three components of the study included:

1) a women's health and human rights survey of 160 Afghan women,
2) forty case testimonies of Afghan women, and
3) interviews with 12 humanitarian assistance providers, health personnel or other experts.

In addition, the direct observations of PHR's investigator have enhanced the documentation. The domains of inquiry for each study component included Afghan women's:

1) physical health status and access to health care,
2) mental health status, . . .
4) experiences of abuse by Taliban officials, and
5) attitudes toward women's human rights.

The information included in this report was collected during a three month period in the beginning of 1998. Women who participated in the health and human rights survey and case testimonies were from all walks of life, ethnic groups, educational levels and economic backgrounds. The participants included women currently living in Kabul and Afghan women who recently migrated to Pakistan. All participants lived in Kabul for most of their lives and for at least one year after the Taliban took control of Kabul in September 1996. . . .

Summary of Findings

The results of the survey of 160 Afghan women indicated that the extension of the Taliban's authority in Afghanistan has had debilitating consequences for women's health and human rights there. 71% of participants reported a decline in their physical health over the past two years. The majority of respondents (77%) reported poor access to health care services in Kabul over the past year of residence there; an additional 20% reported no access. Both the access to care and the quality of health care services in Kabul were deemed "much worse" over the past year compared with two years prior by a majority of the participants (62% and 58%, respectively). In addition, fifty-three percent of women described occasions in which they were seriously ill and unable to seek medical care. 28% of the Afghan women reported inadequate control over their own reproduction.

The women interviewed by PHR consistently described high levels of poor health, multiple specific symptoms, and a significant decline in women's physical condition since the beginning of the Taliban occupation. Sixty-six percent of women interviewed described a decline in their physical condition over the past two years. An Afghan physician described declining nutrition in children, an increasing rate of tuberculosis, and a high prevalence of other infectious diseases among women and children.

PHR visited the Rabia Balkhi Hospital, previously the only facility in Kabul open to women, and found that it [had only 35 beds and] lacked basic medical supplies and equipment such as X-ray machines, suction and oxygen, running water, and medications. Women housed there said they had received no medical attention; one had not been attended to for ten days.

At the only maternity hospital in Kabul, Maiwand, there were seven or eight beds to a room and, in one room, two patients shared one bed. One woman was losing her child because of RH incompatibility and no available antigen. Some of the women interviewed by PHR were experiencing abnormal bleeding during pregnancy. Some were given a prescription but they had not bought it because they couldn't afford it; other women had been at the hospital for days and had received no treatment at all.

Yet even these poor facilities are not available to many women who seek treatment for themselves or their children. In the semi-structured interviews with 40 Afghan women [different from the 160 woman survey discussed above], PHR explored the reasons for decreased access to health care services. Of the 40 women interviewed, 87% (33 of 38) reported a decrease in their access to health services. The reasons given included: no chaperone available (27%), restrictions on women's mobility (36%), hospital refused to provide care (21%), no female doctor available (48%), do not own a *burqa* (6%), and economics (61%).

Male doctors' access to sick children within women's hospitals is also severely curtailed, leading to unnecessary death. A female physician reported that a female child died of the measles because the authorities didn't allow a male doctor to visit the children's ward, which is located within a designated female ward of a local hospital. . . .

The requirement, reiterated in June 1998, that physicians may not treat women unaccompanied by close male relatives, has caused particular problems for the many women in Kabul and elsewhere who do not have male relatives to play this role. In Kabul alone, there are more than 30,000 widows. . . .

Male physicians cannot properly examine women patients because of prohibitions on touching them or looking at their bodies. A dentist said he only examined a woman's teeth if a lookout was posted at the door while he lifted her veil. He noted that if he were caught treating a woman, he and his patient would be beaten, and the authorities would likely close his office and throw him in jail.

Women's fear of being publicly beaten or arrested by the Taliban for being on the street discourages many of them from even attempting to seek health care. PHR interviewed homeless, displaced women occupying an abandoned school with their children. One woman was mourning the recent death of her 20-year-old daughter, who had suffered from stomach pains for days but could not be taken out because her mother did not possess a *burqa*. The women gathered there begged the PHR researcher to send them some *burqas* from the United States so that they could go out on the street. They didn't possess the garment, and had no money to pay for it . . . .[25]

Participants in the health and human rights survey also reported extraordinarily high levels of mental stress and depression. 81% of participants reported a decline in their mental condition. A large percentage of respondents (42%)[28] met the diagnostic criteria for post traumatic stress disorder (PTSD) (based on the *Diagnostical and Statistical Manual of Mental Disorders, Fourth Edition)* and major depression (97%), and also demonstrated significant symptoms of anxiety (86%). Twenty-one percent of the participants indicated that they had suicidal thoughts "extremely often" or "quite often". It is clear from PHR's forty interviews with Afghan women that the general climate of cruelty, abuse, and tyranny that characterizes Taliban rule has had a profound affect on women's mental health. Ninety-five percent of women interviewed described a decline in their mental condition over the past two years.

The denial of education also contributes to Afghan women's deteriorating mental health. All of the women interviewed by PHR indicated that they had become unemployed due to Taliban policies, and 74% indicated that they are now unemployed as well. The interviews revealed that women attributed the anxiety and depression that affects the vast majority of them to their fear of limited opportunities for their children, specifically denial of education to girl children. Poor and uneducated women spoke with particular urgency of their desire to obtain education for children, and saw health care, schooling, and protection of human rights as a key towards achieving a better future.

Humanitarian assistance providers have played a critical role in meeting the basic needs of the Afghan people. However, in striking contrast to published reports indicating the successful disbursement of humanitarian assistance, only 6% of respondents reported receiving any form of humanitarian assistance while living in Kabul. In addition to reported corruption in the distribution of aid, Taliban gender restrictions inevitably interfere with the delivery of humanitarian assistance to women. A Taliban decree dated July 20, 1997, for example, stated that women could not pick up food or other aid from distribution centers themselves. A male relative had to pick up and deliver the aid to the women. Widows are particularly vulnerable to exclusion by such requirements.

The Taliban's claim that its policy of gender segregation is rooted in Afghan history

---

[25] Before the Taliban, few urban dwellers owned a *burqa*, as it was not typically worn in Afghanistan. In Kabul, a very cheap *burqa* costs approximately $9.00 US, which is much more than most Afghan women can now afford.

[28] Even higher percentages reported significant intrusive (94%) and arousal (95%) symptoms of PTSD.

and culture is invalidated by the experience and views of Afghan women themselves. Afghan women have a long history of participation in Afghan society and in political and economic life, including employment as health professionals, teachers, and in government offices. PHR's interviews with 160 women represented a diverse sample of Afghan women living or having recently lived in Kabul under Taliban rule [and these women did not agree with Taliban views]. . . .

PHR's health and human rights survey demonstrates that harassment and physical abuse of Afghan women and their family members by Taliban officials is extremely common in Kabul. Sixty-nine percent of women reported that they or a family member had been detained in Kabul by Taliban religious police or security forces. Twenty-two percent of women reported a total of 43 separate incidents in which they were detained and abused. Of these incidents 72% followed non-adherence to the Taliban's dress code for women.[33] The majority (35/43, 81%) of detentions lasted less than one hour; however, 36 (84%) resulted in public beatings and one (2%) in torture. . . .[34]

The atmosphere of fear created by the Taliban laws and their harsh imposition has exacerbated the multiple traumas related by the women PHR interviewed. PHR gained firsthand knowledge of those experiences while in Kabul.[37] Every Friday, the Taliban terrorizes the city of Kabul by publicly punishing alleged wrongdoers in the Kabul sports stadium and requiring public attendance at the floggings, shootings, hangings, beheadings, and amputations.[38]

On one occasion, PHR's [female] researcher . . . witnessed the public execution (stabbing and beheading) of two men convicted of murder by the Taliban *Shari'a* court at the sports stadium, and another day saw the amputation of an alleged thief's

---

[33] [Two of these cases involved] disabled women (leg amputees from rocket blast injuries) [who] were detained and beaten for entering through a designated male entrance in a public building.

[34] In this report, the term "torture" is defined according to the United Nations Convention Against Torture; that is, "any act by which severe pain or suffering, whether physical or mental, is intentionally inflicted on a person for such purposes as obtaining from him or a third person information or a confession, punishing him for an act he or a third person has committed or is suspected of having committed, or intimidating or coercing him or a third person for any reason based on discrimination of any kind, when such pain or suffering is inflicted by or at the instigation of or with the consent or acquiescence of a public official or other person acting in an official capacity." *See* the definition by The Committee Against Torture (CAT), UN Document A/48/44/Add. I, ¶ 58. Torture is considered to be "systematic" in this report when: "it is apparent that the torture cases reported have not occurred fortuitously in a particular place or at a particular time, but are seen to be habitual, widespread and deliberate in at least a considerable part of the territory of the country. . . ."

[37] The organization's researcher herself narrowly escaped a beating when she was pursued by a young member of the security forces brandishing a whip, as he screamed at her for exposing her wrists and for being alone in public.

[38] Amnesty International reported on March 13, 1998, that over 30,000 spectators (made up of women and boys) were summoned by loudspeaker to gather at Kabul's sports stadium to watch the father and brother of a murdered man shoot an alleged murderer who had been sentenced to death by a Taliban *Shari'a* court.

hand and the flogging of an eighteen-year-old girl who was accused of having a romantic relationship. Witnesses told PHR that another young woman died a few days after being subjected to a public flogging for a similar charge. Reportedly, she either committed suicide or was killed by her father because of the embarrassment and shame of the punishment. The researcher said that before, during, and after the execution and punishments, the stadium was filled with women and children crying and pleading with the authorities not to carry out the sentences, albeit in vain.[39]

Recommendations

In recent years, Physicians for Human Rights and many leaders in public health have argued that health, defined as "a state of complete physical, mental and social well-being and not merely the absence of disease or infirmity," requires the protection and promotion of human rights. In Afghanistan, Taliban restrictions on Afghan women's freedom of expression, association, and movement deny women full participation in society, and consequently, from effectively securing equal opportunities for work, education, and access to health. Furthermore, such exclusion of women from employment and education jeopardizes their capacity to survive and participate in society. The health and human rights concerns of Afghan women identified in this study illustrate that the promotion of Afghan women's health is inseparable from the protection and promotion of human rights.

Afghanistan has been the focus of extensive efforts by the United Nations [UN] for two decades. A Special Rapporteur to monitor human rights is in place and has issued many detailed reports. A Special Envoy to the Secretary General visits regularly, and a Special Mission for Afghanistan has been established. The General Assembly has passed numerous resolutions calling upon all parties to cease their violations of human rights, and UN interlocutors have been attempting to mediate the conflict for the past six years. Hundreds of millions of dollars worth of humanitarian aid have been spent both within Afghanistan and in Pakistan to support Afghan refugees. Yet Afghanistan today is a monument to the avarice of the warring parties that brought it to this point, to the international and Afghan actors who promoted the Taliban, and to the United Nations' failure.[43]

II. Introduction. . .

Status of Women in Afghanistan

Male Afghan leaders have publicly acknowledged the need for reform on the status of women for the past one hundred years. At the end of the 19th century, Amir Abdur

---

[39] The researcher saw a number of women who were apparently family members on the field at the execution site. The executions were carried out in front of them; following the beheadings, the women, shrouded in *burqa,* continued crouching next to the bodies.

[43] In *Fundamentalism Reborn? Afghanistan and the Taliban* (1998) author William Maley cites the U.N. itself on the failure of its mission in Afghanistan: ". . . it could be argued that . . . the role of the United Nations in Afghanistan is little more than that of an alibi to provide cover for the inaction—or worse—of the international community at large."

Rahman introduced a series of laws in an attempt to align customary social practices with the prescriptions of Islam. Using the dictates of the *Qur'an*, he prohibited child marriages, forced marriages, exorbitant bride prices and marriage gifts, and ruled that women could seek divorce.

Constitutions from 1923 onwards guaranteed equal rights for men and women. Women were automatically enfranchised by the 1964 Constitution which guaranteed all Afghans "dignity, compulsory education and freedom to work." Article 27 of the 1977 Constitution stated, "The entire people of Afghanistan, women and men, without discrimination have equal rights and obligations before the law."

In 1959, new policies called for expanded roles for women regarding education and career opportunities, the voluntary removal of the veil and the end to the expectation that women should remain in their homes. In 1964, Afghanistan recognized the right of women to vote. Education and work opportunities for women were concentrated primarily in urban areas. By the late 1970s, women students outnumbered male students in Kabul. The progress of modern development in Afghanistan was measured by the emancipation of the Afghan woman and the attraction such policies would exert on rural populations. The status of the women embodied the pride of the urban elite and the bitterness of rural women.

During the 1980s, the Communist government legally ensured equal rights of women with men. Over subsequent years, increasing numbers of educated women worked in government and business, in industry, as hairdressers and diplomats, in the police and in the army, as entertainers and parliamentarians. No career was closed to them. Attitudes toward the role of women changed dramatically as education for girls and employment in public areas for women became more and more acceptable to wider segments of society.

The status of Afghan women changed in April 1992 when the Islamic State of Afghanistan was installed in Kabul. . . .

III. Women's Health and Rights Survey. . .

Attitudes Toward Women's Human Rights

Nearly all study participants were in agreement on the issues of women's human rights listed in Table 6. More than 95% of respondents agreed that women should have equal access to education, equal work opportunities, freedom of expression, freedom of association, freedom of movement, control over the number and spacing of children, legal protection for women's human rights, and participation in government. More than 95% disagreed with Taliban dress codes and believed that the teachings of Islam do not inherently impose restrictions on women's human rights. In assessing future recommendations, 150 (94%) of study participants believed that the health of women in Afghanistan would be improved by involving women in the United Nations peace process in Afghanistan, ending armed conflict in Afghanistan, and changing the political control in the country.

Table 6. Majority Opinions[1] on Women's Human Rights

- Strict dress codes for women are not appropriate.
- Women should have equal access to education.
- Women should have equal work opportunities.
- Women should be able to express themselves freely.
- Women should be able to associate with people of their choosing.
- Women should be able to move about in society without restriction.
- Women should be able to control the number and spacing of their children.
- There should be legal protections for the rights of women.
- Women should be able to participate in government.
- The teachings of Islam do not inherently restrict women's human rights.

Comments on Survey Findings

Human rights are founded on principles that all members of the human family are equal in dignity and rights. However, where discrimination against women exists, women are often excluded from effective participation in identifying and securing their rights. In Afghanistan, Taliban restrictions on women's participation in society make it nearly impossible for women to represent their health and human rights interests.

This study was designed to survey women who would otherwise not have the opportunity for effective representation, to enable them to identify the health and human rights problems they have experienced in recent years under Taliban rule, and to convey their attitudes regarding women's human rights. PHR's purpose was to understand better the nature and extent of human right abuses in Afghanistan and the impact on women's physical and mental health. . . .

Nearly all of the women surveyed supported women's human rights. Given their support for women's human rights in this study, it appears that Taliban policies regarding the role of women in society do not represent the interests of the individuals they claim to serve. Taliban repression combines restrictions regarding minute details of its residents' personal lives justified in the name of their interpretation of Islamic law, with violent and often arbitrary enforcement.

IV. Interviews with Afghan Women and Health Experts . . .

Prohibition on Work and the Impoverishment of Women

With the exception of a small percentage of positions available as health workers and as surveyors with international aid organizations, Afghan women are not permitted to work. This prohibition exists notwithstanding the dim circumstances of hundreds of thousands of women widowed by wars lasting two decades and a long tradition of work, including professionalism, among Afghan women. Before the Taliban, women

---

[1] Opinions shared by more than 95% of all respondents.

worked as teachers, nurses, physicians, pharmacists, and held other essential jobs in society. Now, most are relegated to unemployment and destitution, and begging is, for many, the only option. PHR's researcher saw many women begging on the streets of Kabul.

One widow explained her plight:

Women are literally forced to beg on the streets. For most widows who have nobody close to look after them, begging is the only way to feed their children.

Another woman reported:

I have economic problems, mental distress, loneliness and a lot of health problems. Five months after my husband's death, my younger brother was injured by another rocket attack in Kabul city. In the last two years, my sufferings have doubled due to the harsh and strict policies of Taliban on people in Kabul, in particular on women. As a widow, I have no support system in this society and I am about to lose my mind . . . it is worse than two years ago. The high cost of living is depressing; you can't even afford to buy wheat, flour, cooking oil, etc. . . . I need to work to support myself and family, but there are no jobs for women. With no husband, no job, no other source of income, the economic situation is bad for me. I barely survive without any support and income. There are beatings for showing up in public without a male chaperone or showing your face. Worst of all is not being allowed to work. How can a widow survive like this?

Another woman described her economic hopelessness:

We are ten times worse off than we were two years ago. We are without jobs, and don't have a regular income. And with the high prices for food and any household goods, we are in a terrible economic situation. We prefer the rocket attacks and the fighting to the current situation under Taliban. A rocket or a bomb may kill all members of a family at once, but this is a slow death, which is more painful. . . .

For many, economic deprivation comes atop the suffering of having lost husbands to war. An Afghan widow who finally fled to Pakistan described her effort to survive in Kabul after the death of her husband:

He was sitting in his office when a bullet passed through the window and hit him in his heart. After his death our home was destroyed by a rocket, and we moved to a different part of the city. I suffered a lot from the loss of my husband. My children were young when their father was killed. The pressure was too much on me: I had to be a father and a mother for them. I was working two jobs, and we had an okay living until 1996 when another disaster happened. The Taliban took me out of work and my daughters out of school. This was unbearable and sickening for me and my entire family. I almost lost my sanity, and I did not have anyone to support me financially. . . . Without a source of income and with the dramatic rise in prices, I didn't have a way to support my family. If I hadn't left, I would have gone crazy. . . .

Restrictions on the Education of Girls and Women

Before the Taliban took control of Kabul, schools were coeducational and women accounted for seventy percent of all teachers, about fifty percent of civil servants, and forty percent of medical doctors. One of the first edicts issued by the Taliban regime when it rose to power was to prohibit girls and women from attending school. Humanitarian groups initiated projects to replace through philanthropy what prior governments had afforded as a right to both sexes.[201] Hundreds of girls' schools were established in private homes, and thousands of women and girls were taught to sew and weave. On June 16, 1998, the Taliban ordered the closing of more than 100 privately funded schools where thousands of young women and girls were receiving training in skills that would have helped them support their families. The Taliban issued new rules for non-governmental organizations providing the schooling: education must be limited to girls up to the age of eight, and restricted to the *Qur'an*.

One young woman explained the situation:

The quality of education is obviously changed for females. Women are not allowed to start or complete their education. Two years ago I graduated from Kabul University, but now the university door is closed to all female students—Afghan women have no rights today. They are all walking deads.

The despair that afflicts women prevented from working thus extends to girls equally trapped in hopelessness and confinement in the home. Mothers suffer as well. One mother stated, "Both of my daughters were locked at home and not allowed to continue their college educations. We had to cover our windows and stay at home all day long. No radio, no television, no music—my daughters were about to go crazy." . . . As one physician put it, "Thousands of young girls and women are hopeless, sitting at home with an incomplete education. And this is not because of the teachings of Islam, it is what Taliban are imposing on people."

Restrictions on Freedom of Movement and Physical Abuse for Non-Compliance

Afghan women are virtual prisoners in their homes [due to the edicts requiring a *burqa* and a male chaperone]. . . .

The *burqa is* no ordinary garment. It is a heavy envelopment covering the entire body, with a narrow slit covered by mesh for the eyes to see through. Some women choose to wear a *burqa* or wear one to satisfy their husband. For others it is suffocating. It is certainly the case that there are areas of conservatism in Afghanistan where women have traditionally worn the veil. But a draconian dress code has never before been imposed by the authorities and punishment for violations has never been imposed by the state.

One Afghan woman complained:

---

[201] Historically, Afghan women had an illiteracy rate of over 80%, but it was not based on legal prohibitions on their attendance in school. Afghanistan had free public education for all before the Taliban, but facilities for schooling of both boys and girls were poor and scarce in rural areas. And conservative families often restricted girls' access to public education.

Taliban are violating our rights completely. . . . I must wear a *burqa* when going outside the house. I have a baby to carry with me, and it is very difficult to do that with a burqa covering your face. . . .

Another woman explained how her father's life became in danger because she was not wearing a *burqa*:

I was inside a taxi with my sick father taking him to the hospital. I didn't have a *burqa* on, since I did not even own one. The Taliban police stopped the taxi and almost beat my sick father and the driver. The taxi driver begged them to let us go, since he had a sick man in his car. They verbally insulted me and told me to go home and cover my face before taking my father to the hospital. I had to go home and borrow a neighbor's *burqa*. Only then could I take my father to the hospital. I don't have a brother and my only uncle is an amputee. Thus, I have to be the one to take my father to the doctor.

The feeling that wearing the *burqa* is injurious to health is not mere opinion. Two physicians described the danger. An Afghan pediatrician explained:

Walking in a *burqa* is hard; it has so many heath hazards. It causes poor vision, impaired hearing, skin rashes, headaches, itching of the scalp and loss of hair. Wearing a *burqa* also causes depression in women. You can't see well and there is a risk of falling or getting hit by a car. Shopping is problematic for women, since we can't see the items very well from under the *burqa*. Also, for women with asthma and hypertension, wearing a *burqa* is very unhealthy.

The penalty for not wearing a *burqa* is a beating. The women of Afghanistan know this very well, often through cruel experience—and it is terrifying:

We can't go out shopping, we can't go to the doctor, we can't leave home without head to toe cover. Any slight divergence from the dress code results in beating—we live in terror.

Another woman described the experience of her mother-in-law:

I was with my mother-in-law shopping at a fabric store. A Taliban police walked in and hit my mother-in-law with his stick. The reason? She had her face uncovered. She was trying to look at the quality of the material she was going to buy. It is very difficult to see from under a *burqa* the color and quality of anything you may want to purchase. The Taliban militia man then threatened both of us, ordered us to leave the store, and verbally insulted both of us.

Even young girls and old women do not escape the violence inflicted on them for not wearing a burqa. One woman interviewed described an incident involving her eight-year-old-sister, who was beaten by the Taliban religious police for not wearing a *burqa*:

She was frightened by that incident and now she experiences psychological distress. For example, she is afraid of leaving the house, she has bad dreams, and she is very upset and depressed.

Another described what happened to her great aunt:

My mother's aunt, an elderly woman, was flogged by a Taliban militia member because her ankle was showing. She was beaten with a metal cable, and her leg was broken. She is here in Pakistan now for treatment. . . .

Afghan women can no longer walk the streets unaccompanied by a man. . . . One woman described her life:

My activity is restricted, but little in comparison to those women who use[d] to work outside the home. I didn't work before. However I now follow the strict dress code when going outside the house and the most difficult thing for me is having to have a male chaperone every time I go out.

The constant fear of what awaits them on the street for the slightest offense—or perceived offense—perpetuates the feeling of imprisonment:

I have now restricted my activity in public quite a bit since the Taliban issued these edicts. Before, I was able to go out freely, but now I worry about getting beaten by the religious police. . . .

Another Afghan woman summarized the impact of Taliban edicts on her:

We undergo public beatings, we have no right to express our opinions, and we have no right to employment, or freedom of movement. Women and girls are not allowed to go to school due to Taliban edicts. I have changed my activities quite a bit. I am stuck at home, with no job and no social life. I don't have a male chaperone and when I need to go someplace it is very difficult for me to leave the house knowing that I might get detained and beaten for appearing in public alone. I don't like to leave the house unless it is necessary. . . .

V. Application of Relevant International Law

International Human Rights Law . . .

A wide array of international treaties, declarations and resolutions govern aspects of women's health-related rights. The weight and status of these instruments vary under international law. For example, treaties are legally binding upon parties while declarations and resolutions carry only moral force. . . .

Status of Afghanistan's International Legal Obligations

Under international law the Taliban is responsible for adherence to human rights law Afghanistan has ratified, notwithstanding the fact that its leadership does not recognize the validity of these to the extent that they depart from the Taliban's particular interpretation of *Shari'a*. Moreover, that the Taliban does not possess all of the attributes of a functioning and recognized government does not relieve it of accountability for the human rights violations it has committed.

Under previous governments, Afghanistan became a party to a large number of human rights treaties without substantive reservations. For example, Afghanistan was among the first countries to accede to the Convention on the Political Rights of Women in 1966. Afghanistan acceded to the ICCPR [International Covenant on Civil and Political Rights] and the ICESCR [International Covenant on Economic, Social and

Cultural Rights] on January 24, 1983 without reservations.[303] It ratified the CAT [Convention against Torture] on April 1, 1987. As noted above, Afghanistan has even signed—although is not a party to—the Women's Convention [Convention on the Elimination of All Forms of Discrimination against Women].[304]

After the expulsion of the Soviet-backed regime in 1992, the *mujaheddin* groups [of freedom fighters] in power in Afghanistan and subsequently the Taliban adopted a different attitude toward human rights treaties. On the one hand, Afghanistan ratified the CRC [Convention on the Rights of the Child] on March 28, 1994, which . . . contains many provisions affecting women, the organization of the family and girl-children. However, in so doing it made a general reservation to the effect that: "the Government of the Republic of Afghanistan reserves the right to express, upon ratifying the Convention, reservations on all provisions of the Convention that are incompatible with the laws of Islamic *Shari'a* and the local legislation in effect."[305]

Declarations and reservations based on religious objection must generally be respected; however, local customs and legislation cannot be used as an excuse for failing to attempt compliance with the treaty.[306] That is, under international law, reservations—whether based on religion or any other objection—must be narrowly tailored, rather than sweeping justifications for abdication. Article 51(2) of the CRC specifically prohibits reservations that are "incompatible with the object and purpose of the treaty;" under the terms of the CRC as well as international law generally, such reservations are not permissible and not given legal effect. Broadly-worded reservations that attempt to excuse the Taliban from responsibility for upholding fundamental human rights principles, such as non-discrimination, as well as specific obligations central to the promotion of children's well-being and development, such as to health care and education, are clearly contrary to the object and purpose of the CRC.

It is important to note that the *Shari'a* is not one single law, but rather is derived from multiple sources. As discussed below, "[d]ifferent and often conflicting laws make up the totality of what is collectively known as the *Shari'a*." Indeed, the *Shari'a* is often cited as expounding the fundamental equality among races and between the sexes. For example, the Committee on the Elimination of Discrimination Against Women (CEDAW), which is charged with the monitoring [of] the Women's Conven-

---

[303] Some treaties place conditions upon which States may become Parties through ratification. Under international law, accession equally indicates the consent of a given State to be bound by the provisions of the treaty. *See Vienna Convention*, Articles 11, 12, 14(1).

[304] Afghanistan signed the Women's Convention on August 14, 1980.

[305] A reservation is a unilateral statement by a ratifying state which "purports to exclude or to modify the legal effect of certain provisions of the treaty in their application to that state." A "declaration" in contrast specifies the state's understanding or interpretation of a given provision or set of provisions in the treaty. Although nominally a "declaration," Afghanistan's "declaration" attempts to amend the CRC *pro tanto*, in order to change future obligations among itself and the other parties and is therefore treated as a reservation by the United Nations. *See Vienna Convention*, Article 2(d).

[306] *See* Venkatraman, B. A., *Islamic States and the United Nations Convention on the Elimination of All Forms of Discrimination Against Women: Are the Shari'a and the Convention Compatible?*, 44 Am. U. L. Rev. 1949, 2008 (1995).

tion, has specifically stated in observations that "[t]he Shariah itself gave equality to women, but the problem that had to be overcome was that of interpretation." CEDAW has urged governments to undertake efforts "to proceed to an interpretation of the Shariah that was permissible and did not block the advancement of women." CEDAW has forcefully declared that reservations based on the *Shari'a* "that were not compatible with the goals of the [Women's] Convention were not acceptable."

While the CRC was ratified by the government of President Burhanuddin Rabbani, the Taliban rejects the validity of not only treaty—but also Charter-based international human rights obligations.[312] In so doing, the Taliban employs two often inconsistent arguments: incompatibility with the *Shari'a*, and inability to perform. Neither is valid.

First, Mr. Choong-Hyun Paik, the UN Special Rapporteur for Afghanistan, reports that in meetings with the Taliban-designated Attorney General, this official "indicated that if a promise, convention, treaty or other instrument, even if it was in the Charter of the United Nations, was contrary to *Shari'a*, they would not fulfil it or act on it":

We accept *Shari'a*, our God's convention . . . . If someone is drinking in public, even if the Covenant or the United Nations Charter says they should not be punished, we will. The core of our action and our policy is the law of God, as contained in the *Qur'an*. We do not follow individuals, or people of other countries. We follow the law of God. We adhere strictly to what the *Qur'an* is telling us. Therefore, we invite all people in the world to follow the *Qur'an*. Any laws that negate the *Qur'an* or the law of God, we don't accept that.

The Special Rapporteur's report also notes that the Taliban authorities indicated that although they were willing to accept human rights conventions, "the concept and meaning of human rights were totally dependent on God's will." The Governor of Kabul told the UN Special Rapporteur that "The provisions of international human rights instruments could not be applied if they conflicted with God's law. [Our] domestic interpretation of human rights [is] not based on individual rights."

As stated above, the Taliban is not free to disregard all international law that is not in accordance with their particular interpretation of *Shari'a*. It is a fundamental tenet of modern international human rights law that certain principles that govern the way a state or quasi-state may treat its subjects transcend domestic legislation and customs. This principle, which allowed for judgment of the crimes against humanity committed in Nazi Germany and ultimately prevailed in the dismantling of racial apartheid in South Africa, applies equally to the situation of gender apartheid in Afghanistan under the Taliban.

Second, at times, the Taliban does not base its non-compliance on religious grounds at all, but rather claims "impossibility of performance" with respect to its human rights obligations, arguing that they are waiting to achieve political stability before the Taliban can establish the conditions for women's basic rights, such as education and employment.[318] For example, the Special Rapporteur's 1997 report notes:

---

[312] Charter-based obligations are assumed by virtue of being members in the United Nations. [The UN Charter created the United Nations, and is itself a treaty.]

[318] That is, under international law, the fact that the government of Afghanistan has changed since accession or signature of these treaties does not terminate or suspend the State's treaty

The most frequent responses by representatives of the Taliban authorities regarding the resumption of female employment and education have been: "we are in an emergency situation", "when security conditions are restored", "we are in a situation of war and want to restore peace and a centralized government", "until there is peace and stability", the latest one being "when we are in control".

Not only, as the Special Rapporteur notes, does this appear "to be at odds with the affirmation of most officials that peace and security have been brought to all areas under their control," but it also underlines the political nature of the Taliban's claims—at times invoking religion and tradition and at times justifying their conduct on the grounds of incapacity. . . .

NOTE: The following document[s A, B, and C are appendices] to the *Final report on the situation of human rights in Afghanistan*, submitted by Mr. Choong Hyun Paik, Special Rapporteur, in accordance with Commission on Human Rights resolution 1996/75. . . .

Appendix A

Notice of Department for enforcement of right Islamic way and prevention of evils:

The Department for enforcement of right Islamic way and prevention of evils for the implementation of legal Islamic orders and prophet Mohamad [sic] tradition in order to prevent evils which cause serious dangers and problems for Islamic society requests from all pious sisters and brothers to seriously follow 8 articles mentioned below to prevent occurrence of evils:

1. No exit and traveling of sisters without escort of legal close relative (*Mahram*).
2. Those sisters are coming out of their homes with legal escort should use veil (*burqa*) or similar things to cover the face.
3. Sitting of sisters in the front seat of cart (*gadi*) and Jeep (vehicle) without legal relative is forbidden. In the case of appearance serious measures will be carried out against the vehicle and cart rider/driver.
4. Shopkeepers do not have right to buy or sell things with those women without covered face, otherwise the shopkeeper is guilty and has no right to complain.
5. Cars are strictly forbidden to be covered with flowers for wedding ceremony and also is [sic] not allowed to drive around the city.
6. Women's invitations in hotels and wedding party in hotels are forbidden.
7. Sisters without legal close relative with them can not use taxis, otherwise the taxi driver is responsible.
8. The person who is in charge of collecting fares (money) for sisters in buses, minibuses and jeeps should be under 10 years old.

---

obligations, even if States Parties to the treaty have suspended diplomatic relations and do not recognize the Taliban as the legitimate government of Afghanistan. Only a fundamental change in circumstances justifies the termination of or withdrawal from a treaty only under circumstances of impossibility of performance *(rebus sic standibus)*. *See Vienna Convention,* Articles 54, 57[,] 61(2).

The professional delegates of this department are in charge to punish violators according to Islamic principles.

Appendix B . . .

Taliban Islamic Movement of Afghanistan Rules of work for the State hospitals and private clinics based on *Shari'a* principles

1. Female patients should go to female physicians. In case a male physician is needed, the female patient should be accompanied by her close relatives (*mahram*).
2. During examination, the female patients and male physicians both should be dressed with Islamic *Hijab.*
3. Male physicians should not touch or see the other parts of female patients except the affected part.
4. Waiting rooms for female patients should be safely covered.
5. The person who regulates turns for female patients should be a female.
6. During night duty, in the rooms where female patients are hospitalized, a male doctor without the call of patient is not allowed to enter the room.
7. Sitting and speaking between male and female doctors are not allowed. If there be need for discussion, it should be done with *hejab.*
8. Female doctors should wear simple clothes, they are not allowed to wear stylish clothes or use cosmetics and makeup.
9. Female doctors and nurses are not allowed to enter the rooms where male patients are hospitalized.
10. Hospital staff should pray in the mosque on time. The director of hospital is bound to assign a place and appoint a priest (*mullah*) for prayer.
11. Staff of (Amri Bel Maroof Wa Nai Az Munkar) Department are allowed to go for control at any time and nobody can prevent them. Anybody who violates the order will be punished as per Islamic regulations.

—Amirul-Mominin Mullah Mohamma
Omer Mujahed

—Mofti Mohammad Masoom Afghani
Acting Minister of Public Health

Appendix C

Islamic State of Afghanistan
General Presidency of Amr Bil Marof Wa Nai Az Munkir
(religious police)
Administration Department
To: The received letter from the Cultural and Social Affairs Department of General Presidency of Islamic State of Afghanistan dated [December 16, 1996] states that:

The role and regulation of Amr Bil Marof Wa Nai Az Munkir is to be distributed via your office to all whom it may concern for implementation.

1. To prevent sedition and uncovered females (be hejab): No drivers are allowed to pick up females who are using Iranian burqa. In the case of violation the driver will be imprisoned. If such kinds of female are observed in the street, their houses will be found and their husbands punished. If the women use stimulating and attractive cloth and there is no close male relative with them, the drivers should not pick them up.
2. To prevent music. . . .
3. To prevent beard shaving and its cutting. . . .
4. To prevent not praying and order gathering prayer at the bazaar. . . .
5. To prevent keeping pigeons and playing with birds. . . .
6. To eradicate the use of addiction and its users [through imprisonment of sellers and users]. . . .
7. To prevent kite flying. . . .
8. To prevent idolatry. . . .
9. To prevent gambling. . . .
10. To prevent British and American hairstyles. . . .
11. To prevent interest charges on loans, charges on changing small denomination notes and charges on money orders. . . .
12. To prevent washing clothes by young ladies along the water streams in the city: It should be announced in all mosques and the matter should [be] monitored. Violator ladies should be picked up with respectful Islamic manner, taken to their houses and their husbands severely punished.
13. To prevent music and dances in wedding parties. . . .
14. To prevent the playing of music drums. . . .
15. To prevent sewing ladies' cloth and taking female body measures by tailors: If women or fashion magazines are seen in the shop the tailor should be imprisoned.
16. To prevent sorcery: All the related books should be burnt and the magician should be imprisoned until his repentance.

The above issues are stated and you are requested, according to your job responsibilities, to implement and inform your related organizations and units.
Regards,
Mawlavi Enayatullah Baligh
Deputy Minister
General Presidency of Amr Bil Marof Wa Nai Az Munkir

NOTES

Afghanistan Ratifies CEDAW and Adopts a New Constitution. On January 4, 2004, the Loya Jirga, a forum of tribal elders—of whom 1000 were elected and 500 appointed—unanimously passed a new Constitution. The provisions below all affect women's rights. Where relevant, both the draft article presented at the beginning of the Loya Jirga debate on December 14, 2003, and the final article adopted in January, are shown. As you read the Articles below, consider how much they conform to CEDAW's requirements. Afghanistan signed CEDAW in August 1980 after the Soviet takeover. It did not ratify until March 2003, but ratified without reservations.

Article 3.
Draft: In Afghanistan, no law can be contrary to the sacred religion of Islam and the values of this Constitution.
Final: In Afghanistan, no law can be contrary to the beliefs and provisions of the sacred religion of Islam.

Article 7.
The state shall abide by the UN Charter, international treaties, international conventions that Afghanistan has signed, and the Universal Declaration of Human Rights. . . .

Article 17.
The state shall adopt necessary measures for promotion of education in all levels, development of religious education, organizing and improving the conditions of mosques, *madrasas* and religious centers.

Article 22.
Draft: Any kind of discrimination between and privilege among the citizens of Afghanistan is prohibited. The citizens of Afghanistan have equal rights and duties before the law.
Final: Same first sentence. The citizens of Afghanistan—whether man or woman—have equal rights and duties before the law.

Article 43.
Education is the right of all citizens of Afghanistan and shall be provided up to the level of the B.A. . . . , free of charge.

Article 44.
The state shall devise and implement effective programs for balancing and promoting education for women. . . .

Article 48.
Work is the right of every Afghan. Working hours, paid holidays, right of employment and employee, and other regulated affairs are regulated by law. Choice of occupation and craft is free within the limits of law.

Article 121.
The Supreme Court upon request of the Government or the Courts can review compliance with the Constitution of laws, legislative decrees, international treaties, and international conventions, and interpret them, in accordance with the law.

Article 130.
While processing the cases, the courts apply the provisions of this Constitution and other laws. When there is no provision in the Constitution or other laws regarding ruling on an issue, the courts' decisions shall be within the limits of this Constitution in accord with the Hanafi jurisprudence [of the Sunni 80% majority] and in a way to serve justice in the best possible manner.

Article 131.
Courts shall apply Shia school of law in cases dealing with personal matters involving the followers of Shia Sect [the 20% minority] in accordance with the provisions of law. . . .

Article 149.
The provision of adherence to the fundamentals of the sacred religion of Islam and the regime of the Islamic Republic cannot be amended. . . .

How well does the Constitution protect women from new legislation modeled on the Taliban decrees? How well does it protect women from the Shari'a provisions on polygamous marriage, divorce, and women's inheritance ("personal" law) set forth in the excerpts from WALI M. RAHIMI, STATUS OF WOMEN: AFGHANISTAN and from SISTERHOOD IS GLOBAL?

A CEDAW Roleplay. Assume that you are a staff lawyer for the Minister for Women's Affairs in the new Afghanistan government. Under CEDAW's Article 19, the state must submit a report to the CEDAW Committee within one year of ratification and every four years thereafter. It describes the state's "legislative, judicial, administrative or other measures" taken to comply with CEDAW. The Committee issues Concluding Comments after reviewing the state report. The Committee Comments to Afghanistan will note positive points, areas for concern, and recommended changes.

The Minister asks you to develop the Afghanistan report to the CEDAW Committee. It should highlight both strengths in the new Constitution and areas of concern. The Minister has to walk a fine line between adhering to government policy and bringing to the Committee's attention women's rights problems in the new Constitution. Develop arguments that she can use on both points.

The Status of Women in Post-Taliban Afghanistan. As detailed by the Physicians for Human Rights report, women suffered extensive human rights abuses under the rule of the Taliban. After the fall of the Taliban regime in November 2001, important steps were taken to improve the situation of women living in Afghanistan. A 2003 report from the Secretary-General to the Commission on the Status of Women documents these developments:

Afghanistan's emergence from 24 years of conflict has led to significant achievements and progress for women who went from complete marginalization and denial of rights to participation in several key institutions for the reconstruction of their country, including the Emergency Loya Jirga, the Afghan Transitional Administration, the Ministry of Women's Affairs, the Afghan Independent Human Rights Commission and Judicial and Constitutional Drafting Commissions. One of the major changes has been the re- emergence of women in urban areas with relatively better access to employment, health care and education. Although women's participation in civil society continues to be limited, the re-emergence of media, the re-opening of academic institutions and the formation of professional associations are increasingly affecting women's role in society. Over 3 million girls and boys have returned to school since March 2002; and over 1.7 million refugees have returned from neighboring countries.[E]

In particular, political participation of women has increased dramatically:

The Independent Commission for the convening of the Emergency Loya Jirga included 3 women out of 21 commissioners, including one vice-chair of the Commission. Women from all

---

[E] *The Situation of Women and Girls in Afghanistan: Report of the Secretary-General,* U.N. Commission on the Status of Women, 47th Sess., Provisional Agenda Item 3(a), at 4, U.N. Doc. E/CN.6/ 2003/4 (2003).

segments of society, across ethnic and religious communities accounted for 200 delegates to the Loya Jirga, or 12.5 per cent. One woman was elected vice-chair of the Loya Jirga; and another, Massouda Jalal, ran for the position of President and received the second largest number of ballots.[F]

While the situation of Afghan women has improved significantly since the Taliban were removed from power, large obstacles remain. Of particular importance is the limited presence of security forces throughout much of Afghanistan. The interim government in Afghanistan has enacted measures intended to protect its female citizens; however, as the Secretary-General's report reveals, such measures are meaningless without the means by which to enforce them:

Women's progress is . . . determined by post-conflict characteristics and complexities of Afghan society with patriarchal values and traditions which are deeply ingrained. In the absence of an effective national force, the lack of security across the country continues to impede progress in the rehabilitation of Afghanistan and the advancement of women. Women are reported to restrict their participation in public life to avoid being targets of violence by armed factions and elements seeking to enforce the repressive edicts of the previous regime. Despite positive developments regarding women's rights, intimidation and violence by regional and local commanders against women continue unabated. In rural areas, especially in the more conservative tribal belt, the situation of women has not changed to any great extent since the removal of the Taliban. The prevalence of conservative attitudes limits the full, equal and effective participation of women in civil, cultural, economic, political and social life throughout the country at all levels of society.[G]

Six months after enactment of the new Constitution, the Secretary-General's report remained an accurate description of the situation of Afghan women. In the province of Herat, women undergo examinations for signs of recent intercourse if they are seen with men who are not close relatives.[H] In this province, as well as many others, the number of women who have committed suicide through self-immolation is on the rise. Forced marriages, domestic violence, and lack of freedom and access to education have contributed to the increasing numbers.[I]

Though women have a constitutional right to receive an education, women face many difficulties in attending schools. Several girls' schools have been burnt down, and violence against women continues to occur, such as the poisoning of three schoolgirls in the town of Khost in April 2004.[J] In addressing complaints by women members, the chairperson of the Loya Jirga further illustrated the societal bias women face:

[F] *Id.* at 6.

[G] *Id.* at 4. For additional information on the impact that the lack of security forces has had on the women of Afghanistan, *see Between Hope and Fear: Intimidation and Attacks against Women in Public Life in Afghanistan*, Human Rights Watch Briefing Paper (October 2004).

[H] Stuart MacFarlane, *Taliban's brutal legacy lives on, says Afghan activist*, CANBERRA TIMES, Apr. 30, 2004, at A9.

[I] Golnaz Esfandiari, *Self-Immolation Of Women On The Rise In Western Provinces*, RFE/FL, Mar. 4, 2004.

[J] *Afghan Schoolgirls Poisoned*, AFP via Bloomberg, Apr. 30, 2004.

"Do not try to put yourself on a level with men. Even God has not given you equal rights because under his decision two women are counted equal to one man."[K]

Is International Human Rights Law Effective? PHR points out that Afghanistan had ratified many human rights treaties (to be studied in subsequent chapters) before the Taliban took power—all of them guaranteeing women equal treatment with men. Yet it took a war launched for other reasons to stop the Taliban's war on women. What conclusions do you draw?

Human Rights Groups and Reports. Activists have formed many human rights organizations (HROs) since the human rights era began. Well-known examples include Amnesty, the Center for Reproductive Rights, Human Rights Watch, and Global Rights (known before 2004 as the International Human Rights Law Group). These bodies often select particular issues on which to focus. Physicians for Human Rights, for example, highlights health and human rights. The early human rights organizations did not focus on women's human rights as such. Only after pressure from women activists did they begin examining the whole range of issues women faced.

One of the key ways HROs have influenced world public opinion is through investigation and reporting. The PHR report is one such example. When the report was published, newspapers responded with articles on the subject, and that in turn spurred activists to do more. PHR also increased its audience by placing the report on its website, a common practice among HROs. The HRO reports provide an invaluable source of information concerning human rights abuses.

[K] Amy Waldman, *Meeting on New Constitution, Afghan Women Find Old Attitudes*, NEW YORK TIMES, Dec. 16, 2003, Foreign Desk.

Chapter 2
Equality Doctrines and Gender Discrimination: The Evolving Jurisprudence of the UN Human Rights Committee and the U.S. Supreme Court

This chapter begins an examination of the way different state courts and international and regional human rights bodies decide whether a statute treating women and men differently violates provisions guaranteeing women equal rights and equal protection of the law. Many state constitutions and international and regional treaties make these guarantees. Advocates can turn to those bodies in seeking to invalidate sex-discriminatory laws. In doing so, they need to know which body is most likely to rule in their favor and how to argue that the body should adopt a more probing review if it is overly deferential to the state law. Thus, in this and many following chapters we will be closely comparing the bodies' different approaches to deciding equality issues.

We begin our evaluation by comparing the jurisprudence of the UN Human Rights Committee under the equality provisions of the International Covenant on Civil and Political Rights with that of the U.S. Supreme Court under the Constitution's Fourteenth Amendment guaranteeing all persons the "equal protection of the law." Both bodies have changed their approaches over time, dramatically so in the case of the Supreme Court. The chapter opens, however, with a brief discussion of the international origins for women's equality rights.

I. Early International Sources of Women's Human Rights

The modern human rights system started with the formation of the United Nations after World War II. From its first beginnings it gave women important rights although few were aware of that fact. Indeed, early HROs such as Amnesty International and Human Rights Watch paid scant attention until the early 1990s to the profound discrimination and violence that pervaded women's lives.

The key foundational documents were the United Nations Charter and the International Bill of Rights: the Universal Declaration of Human Rights (UDHR); the International Covenant of Civil and Political Rights (ICCPR); and the separate International Covenant of Economic, Social and Cultural Rights (ICESCR). CEDAW came later and covered the combined topics of the International Covenants, but in much greater detail. Its definition of discrimination required equality between men and women as to "human rights and fundamental freedoms, in the political, economic, social, cultural, civil or any other field." Inspired by the new Women's Convention and the First World Conference on Women, held in Mexico in 1975, women's rights activists and NGOs developed a powerful international women's human rights movement dedicated to changing the status of women around the globe. By the end of the 20th century, these players had created a network of international, regional, and state human rights laws that gave women unprecedented protection against the discrimination and violence they encountered in their daily lives. The task of the 21st century will be to enforce these rights and make them a living reality for all.

A. The Charter of the United Nations

The Charter establishing the United Nations entered into force on October 24, 1945. Its many provisions regarding women's rights were revolutionary at a time when law and culture subordinated women in every country around the globe. In the Preamble, the ratifying governments asserted their determination "to reaffirm faith in fundamental human rights, in the dignity and worth of the human person, [and] in the equal rights of men and women. . . ." The Charter's core purposes included "promoting and encouraging respect for human rights and for fundamental freedoms for all without distinction as to race, sex, language, or religion. . . ." *See* Article 1(3), *available at* RossRights. The United Nations pledged to "promote . . . universal respect for, and observance of, human rights and fundamental freedoms for all without distinction as to race, sex, language, or religion." Member states agreed "to take joint and separate action in cooperation with the Organization" to achieve those purposes. *See* Articles 55 and 56, *id.*

The Charter also created constituent UN bodies empowered to work toward these goals. The most relevant bodies for their impact on women's rights include the General Assembly, the Economic and Social Council, specialized agencies (such as the International Labour Organization (ILO)) and human rights commissions established by the Council (Articles 13, 57, 62, and 68). Finally, Article 8 states that "[t]he United Nations shall place no restrictions on the eligibility of men and women to participate in any capacity and under conditions of equality in its principal and subsidiary organs."

B. The Universal Declaration of Human Rights (UDHR) and the International Bill of Rights

In June 1946, the UN Economic and Social Council established the Commission on Human Rights and a separate Commission on the Status of Women. The Human Rights Commission started work the following January and completed drafting the UDHR by December 1948. The eighteen-member body had only two women—India's

Hansa Mehta and the United States's Eleanor Roosevelt, serving as Chair—but they were extremely powerful advocates for women's rights. As a result, the UDHR provided the world's first comprehensive articulation of women's rights to equality both in general and in marriage. *See* MARY ANN GLENDON, A WORLD MADE NEW: ELEANOR ROOSEVELT AND THE UNIVERSAL DECLARATION OF HUMAN RIGHTS (2001), for a comprehensive history of the UDHR and the roles of these remarkable women.

The UN General Assembly voted to approve the UDHR on December 10, 1948, by a vote of 48 in favor, eight abstentions and none opposed.[A] Since it was a Declaration approved by the U.N. General Assembly, and not a treaty between states, it was not legally binding. But its principles were subsequently embodied in binding multilateral treaties: the ICCPR and the ICESCR. Collectively, the UDHR, the ICCPR, and the ICESCR are known as the International Bill of Rights.

II. The UN Human Rights Committee: Its Role and Function

A. The International Covenant on Civil and Political Rights and Its Optional Protocol

The International Covenant on Civil and Political Rights entered into force on March 23, 1976. Provisions concerning the ICCPR women's equality rights are found in the Preamble (first paragraph) and Articles 2(1), 3, 23(4), 24, and 26, *available at* RossRights. Read those provisions and compare them to the predecessor concepts in the UDHR, Articles 1, 2, 7, and 16(1), *available at* RossRights. How do the ICCPR provisions expand and give meaning to the UDHR provisions?

The Human Rights Committee has the same basic functions as the CEDAW Committee. But the HR Committee had jurisdiction from the beginning to consider individual complaints against states parties, provided they had ratified the ICCPR Optional Protocol, *available at* RossRights, a separate treaty that also entered into force on March 23, 1976. Optional Protocol Article 1 allows the "Committee to receive and consider communications from individuals subject to its jurisdiction who claim to be victims of a violation by that State Party of any of the rights set forth in the Covenant." Compare this provision to the CEDAW Optional Protocol provision, *available at* RossRights and quoted in the Chapter One Note, "Complaints Procedure." How do they differ? As with the CEDAW Optional Protocol, the ICCPR Protocol requires that complainants first exhaust their domestic remedies and that the "same matter is not being examined under another procedure of international investigation or settlement. . . ." Art. 5(2)(a) and (b). The Committee holds closed meetings to examine such complaints and written information submitted by the two parties, and then forwards its "views" to both. Art. 5, *id.*

The Committee has developed an extensive body of decisions. Most scholars would say that its "views" are not legally binding, but the Committee has acted increasingly

---

[A] The Soviet bloc countries, South Africa, and Saudi Arabia abstained. The other Muslim states all voted yes, including Pakistan and Syria. GLENDON, A WORLD MADE NEW, at 169–70.

like a court and has strongly suggested that its views *are* binding. For example, in *Bradshaw v. Barbados,*[B] the Committee reacted to a state court decision that it would execute a criminal defendant before the Committee could issue its views on the ICCPR issues raised against the state party. It requested that Barbados not do so, and stated:

By ratifying the Covenant and the Optional Protocol, Barbados has undertaken to fulfil its obligations thereunder and has recognized the Committee's competence to receive and consider communications from individuals. . . . While [under governing domestic law] the Covenant is not part of the domestic law of Barbados which can be applied directly by the courts, the State party has nevertheless accepted the legal obligation to make the provisions of the Covenant effective. To this extent, it is an obligation for the State party to adopt appropriate measures to give legal effect to the views of the Committee as to the interpretation and application of the Covenant in particular cases. . . . This includes the Committee's views . . . on the desirability of interim measures of protection to avoid irreparable damage to the victim of the alleged violation.[C]

Many of the Committee decisions have concerned women's equality issues, and are therefore an important source of equality jurisprudence. As you read its decisions in this and the next chapter, consider how the Committee decides whether a statute explicitly based on sex violates equality and equal protection norms.

B. The Committee's Equality Jurisprudence: Challenges to Gender-Based State Limitations on Women's Roles

1. *Gender-Based Right to Sue Concerning Matrimonial Property*

Ato del Avellanal v. Peru
(U.N. Human Rights Committee)
Communication No. 202/1986 (28 October 1988), U.N. Doc. Supp. No. 40 (A/44/ 40) at 196 (1988), *available at* RossRights

1.   The author of the communication (initial letter dated 13 January 1986 . . .) is Graciela Ato del Avellanal, a Peruvian citizen born in 1934, employed as professor of music and married to Guillermo Burneo, currently residing in Peru. . . . It is claimed that the Government of Peru has violated articles 2, paragraphs 1 and 3,[D]

[B] No. 489/1992, U.N. GAOR, Hum. Rts. Comm., 49th Sess., Supp. No. 40, Annex, at 305, 307, 309, U.N. Doc. A/49/40 (1994).

[C] *See generally,* LOUIS HENKIN ET AL., HUMAN RIGHTS 504–505 (1999), quoting the Barbados decision and Fausto Pocar, *Legal Value of the Human Rights Committee's Views,* 1991–92 CANADIAN HUM. RTS. Y.B. 119.

[D] Article 2 of the ICCPR provides:

"(1) Each State Party to the present Covenant undertakes to respect and to ensure to all individuals within its territory and subject to its jurisdiction the rights recognized in the present Covenant, without distinction of any kind, such as race, color, sex, language, religion, political or other opinion, national or social origin, property, birth or other status. . . .

(3) Each State Party to the present Covenant undertakes:

(a) To ensure that any person whose rights or freedoms as herein recognized are violated shall have an effective remedy, notwithstanding that the violation has been committed by persons acting in an official capacity;

(b) To ensure that any person claiming such a remedy shall have his right thereto deter-

16,[E] 23, paragraphs 4[F] and 26[G] of the Covenant, because the author has been alleg-edly discriminated against only because she is a woman.

2.1   The author is the owner of two apartment buildings in Lima, which she acquired in 1974. It appears that a number of tenants took advantage of the change in ownership to cease paying rent for their apartments. After unsuccessful attempts to collect the overdue rent, the author sued the tenants on 13 September 1978. The court of first instance found in her favour and ordered the tenants to pay her the rent due since 1974. The Superior Court reversed the judgement on 21 November 1980 on the procedural ground that the author was not entitled to sue, because, according to article 168 of the Peruvian Civil Code, when a woman is married only the husband is entitled to represent matrimonial property before the Courts. . . . On 10 December 1980 the author appealed to the Peruvian Supreme Court, submitting *inter alia* that the Peruvian Constitution now in force abolished discrimination against women and that article 2 (2) of the Peruvian Magna Carta provides that "the law grants rights to women which are not less than those granted to men". However, on 15 February 1984 the Supreme Court upheld the decision of the Superior Court. Thereupon, the author interposed the recourse of *amparo* [petition requesting the protection of rec-ognized civil and political rights] on 6 May 1984, claiming that in her case article 2(2) of the Constitution had been violated by denying her the right to litigate before the courts only because she is a woman. The Supreme Court rejected the recourse of *amparo* on 10 April 1985. . . .

3.   . . .[T]he Working Group of the Human Rights Committee transmitted the communication . . . to the State party concerned, requesting information and obser-vations relevant to the question of the admissibility of the communication in so far as it may raise issues under articles 14, paragraph 1,[H] 16 and 26 in conjunction with articles 2 and 3 of the Covenant. . . .

7.   On 9 July 1987 the Human Rights Committee . . . decided that the communi-cation was admissible, in so far as it raised issues under articles 14, paragraph 1, and 16 in conjunction with articles 2, 3 and 26 of the Covenant. . . .

---

mined by competent judicial, administrative or legislative authorities, or by any other compe-tent authority provided for by the legal system of the State, and to develop the possibilities of judicial remedy;

(c) To ensure that the competent authorities shall enforce such remedies when granted."

[E] Article 16 of the ICCPR provides: "Everyone shall have the right to recognition everywhere as a person before the law."

[F] Article 23 (4) of the ICCPR provides: "States Parties to the present Covenant shall take appropriate steps to ensure equality of rights and responsibilities of spouses as to marriage, dur-ing marriage and at its dissolution. . . ."

[G] Article 26 of the ICCPR provides: "All persons are equal before the law and are entitled without any discrimination to the equal protection of the law. In this respect, the law shall pro-hibit any discrimination and guarantee to all persons equal and effective protection against dis-crimination on any ground such as race, colour, sex, language, religion, political or other opinion, national or social origin, property, birth or other status."

[H] Article 14 (1) of the ICCPR provides: "All persons shall be equal before the courts and tribunals. . . ."

9.1   . . . [T]he facts of the case . . . have not been contested by the State party.

9.2   In formulating its views, the Committee takes into account the failure of the State party to furnish certain information and clarifications, in particular with regard to the allegations of discrimination of which the author has complained. It is not sufficient to forward the text of the relevant laws and decisions, without specifically addressing the issues raised in the communication. It is implicit in article 4, paragraph 2,[1] of the Optional Protocol that the State party has the duty to investigate in good faith all allegations of violation of the Covenant made against it and its authorities, and to furnish to the Committee all relevant information. In the circumstances, due weight must be given to the author's allegations.

10.1   With respect to the requirement set forth in article 14, paragraph 1, of the Covenant that "all persons shall be equal before the courts and tribunals", the Committee notes that the court of first instance decided in favour of the author, but the Superior Court reversed that decision on the sole ground that according to article 168 of the Peruvian Civil Code only the husband is entitled to represent matrimonial property, i.e. that the wife was not equal to her husband for purposes of suing in Court.

10.2   With regard to discrimination on the ground of sex the Committee notes further that under article 3 of the Covenant State parties undertake "to ensure the equal right of men and women to the enjoyment of all civil and political rights set forth in the present Covenant" and that article 26 provides that all persons are equal before the law and are entitled to the equal protection of the law. The Committee finds that the facts before it reveal that the application of article 168 of the Peruvian Civil Code to the author resulted in denying her equality before the courts and constituted discrimination on the ground of sex.

11.   The Human Rights Committee . . . is of the view that the events of this case, in so far as they continued or occurred after 3 January 1981 (the date of entry into force of the Optional Protocol for Peru), disclose violations of articles 3, 14, paragraph 1 and 26 of the Covenant.

12.   The Committee, accordingly, is of the view that the State party is under an obligation, in accordance with the provisions of article 2 of the Covenant, to take effective measures to remedy the violations suffered by the victim. In this connection the Committee welcomes the State party's commitment, expressed in articles 39 and 40 of Law No. 23506, to co-operate with the Human Rights Committee, and to implement its recommendations.

N O T E S

A Switch in Articles. The Committee decision is based on its interpretation of Articles 3, 14(1) and 26. Graciela, however, did not rely on 14(1) and focused instead on

---

[1] Article 4 (2) of the ICCPR Protocol provides: "Within six months, the receiving State shall submit to the Committee written explanations or statements clarifying the matter and the remedy, if any, that may have been taken by that State."

Articles 16 (recognition as person before the law) in combination with Articles 2(1), 3, and 26. She also relied on Article 23(4) (equal rights and responsibilities of husband and wife in marriage). Why might the Committee have switched?

Denying Wives the Right to Sue. Such laws are common around the world, whatever the legal system. Peru is in South America and derives its law from the Spanish civil-law system. But common-law jurisdictions such as Great Britain, the United States, Australia, and the Commonwealth states in Africa and Asia once had such laws on the books and many still do. These laws were developed in the 18th and 19th centuries by the all-male legislatures that ruled before women got the vote. These men undoubtedly felt protective toward women. How might they have justified such laws? What arguments can be made against them?

The Committee's Approach. One reading of the Committee's views is that if a state party fails to defend, it will lose the case. Yet the Committee did offer a very simple reason in paragraph 10.2 for its holding. What was it?

Exhaustion of Remedies and the Decision on Admissibility. Note that Graciela exhausted her domestic remedies by starting her case in Peru's trial court and appealing to the Superior Court and then the Supreme Court, with an additional final petition to the Supreme Court. The Committee must first decide whether a case is admissible before proceeding to a separate merits decision. Failure to exhaust will, in most cases, result in a decision of inadmissibility. It is not enough to appeal to one court without exhausting all possible appeals beyond that level.

It would also be advisable to rely on the ICCPR (or other relevant treaty) provisions in the state court cases in addition to the state laws and constitutional provisions. Most judges will not have studied human rights laws. Advocates can simultaneously teach them new sources of law and persuade them to apply it in their courts—a subject we will explore in more depth in Chapter Ten. Ultimately, the treaties are most effective if enforced domestically. Human rights bodies typically do not have the resources to handle large dockets but state courts do. If ICCPR advocates do not prevail in the domestic courts, they still have the option to proceed to the HR Committee and bring global attention to the state's human rights violations.

2. Gender-Based Nationality Laws

Shirin Aumeeruddy-Cziffra and 19 Other Mauritian Women v. Mauritius
(U.N. Human Rights Committee)
Communication No. 35/1978 (9 April 1981), U.N. Doc. CCPR/C/OP/1 at 67 (1984),
   available at RossRights

1.1   The authors of this communication . . . claim that the enactment of the Immigration (Amendment) Act, 1977, and Deportation (Amendment) Act, 1977, by Mauritius constitutes discrimination based on sex against Mauritian women, violation of the right to found a family and home, and removal of the protection of the courts of law, in breach of articles 2,[J] 3,[K] . . . 17,[L] 23,[M] 25[N] and 26[O] of the International Covenant on Civil and Political Rights. . . .

1.2   The authors state that prior to the enactment of the laws in question, alien men and women married to Mauritian nationals enjoyed the same residence status, that is to say, by virtue of their marriage, foreign spouses of both sexes had the right, protected by law, to reside in the country with their Mauritian husbands or wives. The authors contend that, under the new laws, alien husbands of Mauritian women lost their residence status in Mauritius and must now apply for a "residence permit" which may be refused or removed at any time by the Minister of Interior. The new laws, however, do not affect the status of alien women married to Mauritian husbands who retain their legal right to residence in the country. The authors further contend that under the new law alien husbands of Mauritian women may be deported under a ministerial order which is not subject to judicial review. . . .

5.1   In its submission . . . , the State party explains . . . [b]oth Acts were passed following certain events in connection with which some foreigners (spouses of Mauritian women) were suspected of subversive activities. . . .

5.2   The State party admits that the two statutes in question do not guarantee similar rights of access to residence in Mauritius to all foreigners who have married Mauritian nationals, and it is stated that the "discrimination", if there is any, is based on the sex of the spouse. The State party further admits that foreign husbands of Mauritian citizens no longer have the right to free access to Mauritius and immunity from deportation therefrom, whereas prior to 12 April 1977, this group of persons had the right to be considered, de facto, as residents of Mauritius. They now must apply to the Minister of the Interior for a residence permit and in case of refusal of the permit they have no possibility to seek redress before a court of law.

5.3   The State party, however, considers that this situation does not amount to a

---

J *See* Article 2(1) (barring sex distinctions in ICCPR rights) in footnote D.

K Article 3 of the ICCPR provides: "The States Parties to the present Covenant undertake to ensure the equal right of men and women to the enjoyment of all civil and political rights set forth in the present covenant."

L Article 17 of the ICCPR provides:

"1. No one shall be subjected to arbitrary or unlawful interference with his privacy, family, home or correspondence, nor to unlawful attacks on his honour and reputation.

2. Everyone has the right to the protection of the law against such interference or attacks."

M Article 23 (1) of the ICCPR provides: "The family is the natural and fundamental group unit of society and is entitled to protection by society and the State."

N Article 25 of the ICCPR provides: "Every citizen shall have the right and the opportunity, without any of the distinctions mentioned in article 2 and without unreasonable restrictions:

(a) To take part in the conduct of public affairs, directly or through freely chosen representatives;

(b) To vote and to be elected at genuine periodic elections which shall be by universal and equal suffrage and shall be held by secret ballot, guaranteeing the free expression of the will of the electors;

(c) To have access, on general terms of equality, to public service in his country."

O *See* Article 26 (granting equal protection of the law) in footnote G.

violation. . . . The State party concludes that if the right "to enter, reside in and not to be expelled from" Mauritius is not one guaranteed by the Covenant, the authors cannot claim that there has been any violation of articles 2(1), 2(2), 3, . . . or 26 of the Covenant on the grounds that . . . exclusion of their husbands or prospective husbands may be an interference in their private and family life.

5.4   As far as the allegation of a violation of article 25 [right to participate in public affairs] of the Covenant is concerned, the State party argues that if a citizen of Mauritius chooses to go and live abroad with her husband because the latter is not entitled to stay in Mauritius, she cannot be heard to say that she is thus denied the right to take part in the conduct of public affairs and to have access on general terms of equality to public service in her country. The State party claims that nothing in the law prevents the woman, as such, from exercising the rights guaranteed by article 25, although she may not be in a position to exercise the said rights as a consequence of her marriage and of her decision to live with her husband abroad. The State party mentions, as an example of a woman who has married a foreign husband and who is still playing a prominent role in the conduct of public affairs in Mauritius, the case of Mrs. Aumeeruddy-Cziffra, one of the leading figures of the Mouvement Militant Mauricien opposition party.

5.5   The State party further argues that nothing in the laws of Mauritius denies any citizen the right to marry whomever he may choose and to found a family. Any violation of articles 17 and 23 is denied by the State party which argues that this allegation is based on the assumption that "husband and wife are given the right to reside together in their own countries and that this right of residence should be secure." . . .

5.7   The State party is of the opinion that if the exclusion of a non-citizen is lawful (the right to stay in a country not being one of the rights guaranteed by the provisions of the Covenant), then such an exclusion (based on grounds of security or public interest) cannot be said to be an arbitrary or unlawful interference with the family life of its national in breach of article 17 of the Covenant.

6.1   In their additional information and observations . . . , the authors argue that the two Acts . . . are discriminatory in themselves in that the equal rights of women are no longer guaranteed. The authors emphasize that they are not so much concerned with the unequal status of spouses of Mauritian citizens—to which the State party seems to refer—but they allege that Mauritian women who marry foreigners are themselves discriminated against on the basis of sex. . . .

6.2   . . . They allege:

(a) That female citizens do not have an unrestricted right to married life in their country if they marry a foreigner, whereas male citizens have an unrestricted right to do so;

(b) That the law, being retroactive, had the effect of withdrawing from the female citizens the opportunity to take part in public life and restricted, in particular, the right of one of the authors in this respect;

(c) That the "choice" to join the foreign spouse abroad is only imposed on Mauritian women and that only they are under an obligation to "choose" between exercising their political rights guaranteed under article 25 of the Covenant, or to live with their foreign husbands abroad.

(d) That the female citizen concerned may not be able to leave Mauritius and join her husband in his country of origin for innumerable reasons (health, long-term contracts of work, political mandate, incapacity to stay in the husband's country of origin because of racial problems, as, for example, in South Africa);

(e) That by rendering the right of residence of foreign husbands insecure, the State party is tampering with the female citizens' right to freely marry whom they choose and to found a family. . . .

[The Committee first dismissed the claims of the 17 unmarried women for lack of standing, finding that the risk of being affected by the legislation was only a "theoretical possibility." It then turned to the claims of the three married women.]

9.2 (b) 1   The Committee will . . . examine that part of the communication which relates to the effects of the laws of 1977 on the family life of the three married women. . . .

9.2 (b) 2 (i) 1   First, their relationships to their husbands clearly belong to the area of "family" as used in article 17 (1). . . . They are therefore protected against what that article calls "arbitrary or unlawful interference" in this area.

9.2 (b) 2 (i) 2   The Committee takes the view that the common residence of husband and wife has to be considered as the normal behaviour of a family. Hence, . . . the exclusion of a person from a country where close members of his family are living can amount to an interference within the meaning of article 17. In principle, article 17 (1) applies also when one of the spouses is an alien. Whether the existence and application of immigration laws affecting the residence of a family member is compatible with the Covenant depends on whether such interference is either "arbitrary or unlawful" as stated in article 17 (1), or conflicts in any other way with the State party's obligations under the Covenant.

9.2 (b) 2 (i) 3   In the present cases, not only the future possibility of deportation, but the existing precarious residence situation of foreign husbands in Mauritius represents . . . an interference by the authorities of the State party with the family life of the Mauritian wives and their husbands. The statutes in question have rendered it uncertain for the families concerned whether and for how long it will be possible for them to continue their family life by residing . . . in Mauritius. Moreover, . . . even the delay for years, and the absence of a positive decision granting a residence permit, must be seen as a considerable inconvenience, among other reasons because the granting of a work permit, and hence the possibility of the husband to contribute to supporting the family, depends on the residence permit, and because deportation without judicial review is possible at any time.

9.2 (b) 2 (i) 4   Since, however, this situation results from the legislation itself, there can be no question of regarding this interference as "unlawful" within the meaning of article 17 (1) in the present cases. It remains to be considered whether it is "arbitrary" or conflicts in any other way with the Covenant.

9.2 (b) 2 (i) 5   The protection owed to individuals in this respect is subject to the principle of equal treatment of the sexes which follows from several provisions of the

Covenant. It is an obligation of the State parties under article 2 (1) generally to respect and ensure the rights of the Covenant "without distinction of any kind, such as . . . (inter alia) sex", and more particularly under article 3 "to ensure the equal right of men and women to the enjoyment" of all these rights, as well as under article 26 to provide "without any discrimination" for "the equal protection of the law."

9.2 (b) 2 (i) 6   The authors who are married to foreign nationals are suffering from the adverse consequences of the statutes discussed above only because they are women. The precarious residence status of their husbands affecting their family life as described, results from the 1977 laws which do not apply the same measures of control to foreign wives. In this connection the Committee has noted that under section 16 of the Constitution of Mauritius sex is not one of the grounds on which discrimination is prohibited.

9.2 (b) 2 (i) 7   In these circumstances, it is not necessary . . . to decide in the present case how far such or other restrictions on the residence of foreign spouses might conflict with the Covenant if applied without discrimination of any kind.

9.2. (b) 2 (i) 8   The Committee considers that it is also unnecessary to say whether the existing discrimination should be called an "arbitrary" interference with the family within the meaning of article 17. Whether or not the particular interference could as such be justified if it were applied without discrimination does not matter here. Whenever restrictions are placed on a right guaranteed by the Covenant, this has to be done without discrimination on the ground of sex. Whether the restriction in itself would be in breach of that right regarded in isolation, is not decisive in this respect. It is the enjoyment of the rights which must be secured without discrimination. Here it is sufficient, therefore, to note that in the present position an adverse distinction based on sex is made, affecting the alleged victims in their enjoyment of one of their rights. No sufficient justification for this difference has been given. The Committee must then find that there is a violation of articles 2 (1) and 3 of the Covenant, in conjunction with article 17 (1).

9.2 (b) (2) (ii) 1   At the same time each of the couples concerned constitutes also a "family" within the meaning of article 23 (1). . . . They are therefore as such "entitled to protection by society and the State" as required by that article, which does not further describe that protection. The Committee is of the opinion that the legal protection or measures a society or a State can afford to the family may vary from country to country and depend on different social, economic, political and cultural conditions and traditions.

9.2 (b) 2 (ii) 2   Again, however, the principle of equal treatment of the sexes applies by virtue of articles 2(1), 3 and 26, of which the latter is also relevant because it refers particularly to the "equal protection of the law". Where the Covenant requires a substantial protection as in article 23, it follows from those provisions that such protection must be equal, that is to say not discriminatory, for example on the basis of sex.

9.2 (b) 2 (ii) 3   It follows that also in this line of argument the Covenant must lead to the result that the protection of a family cannot vary with the sex of the one or the other spouse. Though it might be justified for Mauritius to restrict the access of aliens to their territory and to expel them therefrom for security reasons, the Committee is of the view that the legislation which only subjects foreign spouses of Mauritian women to those restrictions, but not foreign spouses of Mauritian men, is discriminatory with respect to Mauritian women and cannot be justified by security requirements.

9.2 (b) 2 (ii) 4   The Committee therefore finds that there is also a violation of articles 2(1), 3 and 26 of the Covenant in conjunction with the right of the three married co-authors under article 23(1).

9.2 (c) 1   It remains to consider the allegation of a violation of article 25 of the Covenant, which provides that every citizen shall have the right and the opportunity without any of the distinctions mentioned in article 2 (inter alia as to sex) and without unreasonable restrictions, to take part in the conduct of public affairs, as further described in this article. . . .

9.2 (c) 2   The Committee considers that restrictions established by law in various areas may prevent citizens in practice from exercising their political rights, i.e. deprive them of the opportunity to do so, in ways which might in certain circumstances be contrary to the purpose of article 25 or to the provisions of the Covenant against discrimination, for example if such interference with opportunity should infringe the principle of sexual equality.

9.2 (c) 3   However, there is no information before the Committee to the effect that any of this has actually happened in the present cases. . . .

10.1   Accordingly, the Human Rights Committee . . . is of the view that the facts . . . disclose violations of the Covenant, in particular of articles 2 (1), 3 and 26 in relation to articles 17 (1) and 23 (1) with respect to the three co-authors who are married to foreign husbands, because the coming into force of the Immigration (Amendment) Act, 1977, and the Deportation (Amendment) Act, 1977, resulted in discrimination against them on the ground of sex. . . .

11.   The Committee, accordingly, is of the view that the State party should adjust the provisions of the Immigration (Amendment) Act, 1977 and of the Deportation (Amendment) Act, 1977 in order to implement its obligations under the Covenant, and should provide immediate remedies for the victims of the violations found above.

NOTES

A Gender-Neutral Hypothetical. Assume that Mauritius prevented future violations by amending the Immigration and Deportation Acts to provide that all foreign spouses, whether male or female, would have no automatic right to enter or reside in Mauritius and would be subject to deportation at any time. Would the amended Acts violate Mauritian citizens' rights under Articles 17 or 23 of the ICCPR? What arguments could be made by either party to such a challenge?

A New Test. The Committee adds one further element to the test it applies to determine whether a sex-based distinction violates the equality provisions as compared to its decision in the Peru decision above. *See* paragraph 9.2 (b) 2 (i) 8. What is the new element? Consider whether it would provide useful guidance to state court judges seeking to apply HR Committee jurisprudence in their state courts or to lawyers litigating further cases before the Committee.

Who Is the Victim of Sex Discrimination—the Foreign Husband or the Citizen Wife? The state argues for the first, the Mauritian women for the second. Why do they care? Describe the stereotypes about husbands and wives that support the sex distinction. Many states make such distinctions.

CEDAW's Article 9. Article 9 of CEDAW provides:

1. States Parties shall grant women equal rights with men to acquire, change or retain their nationality. They shall ensure in particular that neither marriage to an alien nor change of nationality by the husband during marriage shall automatically change the nationality of the wife, render her stateless or force upon her the nationality of the husband.
2. States Parties shall grant women equal rights with men with respect to the nationality of their children.

Do the Mauritian laws in question violate this article?

State Responses to Committee Views. The Human Rights Committee is increasingly respected. States often, though not always, follow its recommendations. The next step in the Mauritian case demonstrates an effective state response.

Shirin Aumeeruddy-Cziffra and 19 Other Mauritian Women v. Mauritius
(U.N. Human Rights Committee)
Communication No. 35/1978 (9 April 1981), U.N. Doc. CCPR/C/OP/2 at 226 (1990), *available at* RossRights

Response, dated 15 June 1983, of the Government of Mauritius to the Committee's Views
   1. The Ministry of External Affairs, Tourism, and Emigration . . . has the honour to refer to the views expressed by the Human Rights Committee . . . .
   3. [T]he Committee expressed the view that Mauritius, as a State party to the Covenant, should adjust the provisions of those laws so as to remedy the situation.
   4. The Ministry . . . has the honour to request the Secretary-General to inform the Human Rights Committee that the two impugned Acts have now been amended by the [I]mmigration (Amendment) Act of 1983 (Act No. 5 of 1983) and the Deportation (Amendment) Act of 1983 (Act. No. 6 of 1983) which were passed by Parliament on Women's Day, 8 March 1983, so as to remove the discriminatory effects of those laws on grounds of sex.

Section 5(1)(c) of the amended Immigration Act provides that ". . . any person, not being a citizen, shall have the status of a resident for the purposes of this act where . . . he is the spouse of a citizen. . . ." Section 6(2) further provides that such a person ". . . shall cease to be a resident 6 months after the termination of the marriage to the citizen." Similarly, section 3 of the amended Deportation Act states that:

(1) This Act shall not apply to persons who belong to Mauritius.
(2) [F]or the purposes of subsection (1) a person shall belong to Mauritius where . . . (c) he is the spouse of a citizen.

III. Equality Doctrines, Gender, and the United States Supreme Court: A Comparative Standard

In a 1971 case entitled *Reed v. Reed*, 404 U.S. 71 (1971), the U.S. Supreme Court began the process of completely reversing its prior approach to sex-discrimination cases. Its initial approach began when the country ratified the Fourteenth Amendment to the Constitution in 1868, shortly after the end of the Civil War. Section 1 of the Fourteenth Amendment provides:

All persons born or naturalized in the United States and subject to the jurisdiction thereof, are citizens of the United States and of the State wherein they reside. No State shall make or enforce any law which shall abridge the privileges or immunities of citizens of the United States; nor shall any State deprive any person of life, liberty, or property, without due process of law; nor deny to any person within its jurisdiction the equal protection of the laws.

In the next hundred years, women fought against many sex-discriminatory laws by bringing test cases to challenge their constitutional legitimacy under the Fourteenth Amendment. The Court upheld every law it reviewed. It was permissible, the Court ruled, to deny women the vote, the right to practice law, the right to earn a living by working more than 40 hours a week, the right to work as a bartender and the right to serve on juries.

But in 1971, the tide shifted. As women litigators brought new cases, they persuaded the Court to adopt a more stringent approach to deciding whether sex-discriminatory law denied equal protection of the law to women. By 1996, the Court had turned 180 degrees. The following decision represents the culmination of that turning. Justice Ruth Bader Ginsburg wrote the opinion. She was well acquainted with the issues, having been a lead litigator in *Reed v. Reed*, and in many cases that followed.

As you read the opinions, define the various tests the Court has used and consider how they have differed. As you will see, they are far more complex than the initial approach of the Human Rights Committee.

United States v. Virginia
(United States Supreme Court)
518 U.S. 515 (1996), *available at* RossRights

JUSTICE GINSBURG delivered the opinion of the Court [in which STEVENS, O'CONNOR, KENNEDY, SOUTER, and BREYER, JJ., joined]

Virginia's public institutions of higher learning include an incomparable military college, Virginia Military Institute (VMI). The United States maintains that the Constitution's equal protection guarantee precludes Virginia from reserving exclusively to men the unique educational opportunities VMI affords. We agree.

I

Founded in 1839, VMI is today the sole single-sex school among Virginia's 15 public institutions of higher learning. VMI's distinctive mission is to produce "citizen-soldiers," men prepared for leadership in civilian life and in military service. VMI pursues this mission through pervasive training of a kind not available anywhere else in Virginia. Assigning prime place to character development, VMI uses an "adversative method" modeled on English public schools and once characteristic of military instruction. VMI constantly endeavors to instill physical and mental discipline in its cadets and impart to them a strong moral code. The school's graduates leave VMI with heightened comprehension of their capacity to deal with duress and stress, and a large sense of accomplishment for completing the hazardous course.

VMI has notably succeeded in its mission to produce leaders; among its alumni are military generals, Members of Congress, and business executives. The school's alumni overwhelmingly perceive that their VMI training helped them to realize their personal goals. VMI's endowment reflects the loyalty of its graduates; VMI has the largest per-student endowment of all undergraduate institutions in the Nation.

Neither the goal of producing citizen-soldiers nor VMI's implementing methodology is inherently unsuitable to women. And the school's impressive record in producing leaders has made admission desirable to some women. Nevertheless, Virginia has elected to preserve exclusively to men the advantages and opportunities a VMI education affords.

II

A . . .

VMI today enrolls about 1,300 men as cadets. Its academic offerings in the liberal arts, sciences, and engineering are also available at other public colleges and universities in Virginia. But VMI's mission is special. It is the mission of the school

"'to produce educated and honorable men, prepared for the varied work of civil life, imbued with love of learning, confident in the functions and attitudes of leadership, possessing a high sense of public service, advocates of the American democracy and free enterprise system, and ready as citizen-soldiers to defend their country in time of national peril.'" . . .

VMI produces its "citizen-soldiers" through "an adversative, or doubting, model of education" which features "physical rigor, mental stress, absolute equality of treatment, absence of privacy, minute regulation of behavior, and indoctrination in desirable values." . . .

VMI cadets live in spartan barracks where surveillance is constant and privacy nonexistent; they wear uniforms, eat together in the mess hall, and regularly participate in drills. Entering students are incessantly exposed to the rat line, "an extreme form of the adversative model," comparable in intensity to Marine Corps boot camp. Tormenting and punishing, the rat line bonds new cadets to their fellow sufferers and, when they have completed the 7-month experience, to their former tormentors.

VMI's "adversative model" is further characterized by a hierarchical "class system" of privileges and responsibilities, a "dyke system" for assigning a senior class mentor to each entering class "rat," and a stringently enforced "honor code," which prescribes that a cadet "'does not lie, cheat, steal nor tolerate those who do.'"

VMI attracts some applicants because of its reputation as an extraordinarily challenging military school, and "because its alumni are exceptionally close to the school." . . . "[W]omen have no opportunity anywhere to gain the benefits of [the system of education at VMI]."

B

In 1990, prompted by a complaint of a female high-school student seeking admission to VMI, the United States sued the State Commonwealth of Virginia and VMI, alleging that VMI's exclusively male admission policy violated the Equal Protection Clause of the Fourteenth Amendment [to the Constitution]. . . .

In the two years preceding the lawsuit, the District Court noted, VMI had received inquiries from 347 women, but had responded to none of them. "[S]ome women, at least," the court said, "would want to attend the school if they had the opportunity." The court further recognized that, with recruitment, VMI could achieve at least 10% female enrollment"—"a sufficient 'critical mass' to provide the female cadets with a positive educational experience." . . . And it was also established that "some women are capable of all of the individual activities required of VMI cadets." In addition, experts agreed that if VMI admitted women, "the VMI ROTC experience would become a better training program from the perspective of the armed forces, because it would provide training in dealing with a mixed-gender army."

The District Court ruled in favor of VMI, however. . . .

The District Court reasoned that education in "a single-gender environment, be it male or female," yields substantial benefits. VMI's school for men brought diversity to an otherwise coeducational Virginia system, and that diversity was "enhanced by VMI's unique method of instruction." If single-gender education for males ranks as an important governmental objective, it becomes obvious, the District Court concluded, that the only means of achieving the objective "is to exclude women from the all-male institution—VMI."

"Women are [indeed] denied a unique educational opportunity that is available only at VMI," the District Court acknowledged. But "[VMI's] single-sex status would be lost, and some aspects of the [school's] distinctive method would be altered" if women were admitted . . .

The Court of Appeals for the Fourth Circuit disagreed . . . [holding]: "The Commonwealth of Virginia has not . . . advanced any state policy by which it can justify its determination, under an announced policy of diversity, to afford VMI's unique type of program to men and not to women." . . .

C

In response to the Fourth Circuit's ruling Virginia proposed a parallel program for women: Virginia Women's Institute for Leadership (VWIL). The 4-year, state-sponsored undergraduate program would be located at Mary Baldwin College, a private liberal arts school for women, and would be open, initially, to about 25 to 30 students. Although VWIL would share VMI's mission—to produce "citizen-soldiers"—the VWIL program would differ, as does Mary Baldwin College, from VMI in academic offerings, methods of education, and financial resources.

The average combined SAT score of entrants at Mary Baldwin is about 100 points lower than the score for VMI freshmen. Mary Baldwin's faculty holds "significantly fewer Ph.D.'s than the faculty at VMI," and receives significantly lower salaries. While VMI offers degrees in liberal arts, the sciences, and engineering, Mary Baldwin, at the time of trial, offered only bachelor of arts degrees. A VWIL student seeking to earn an engineering degree could gain one, without public support, by attending Washington University in St. Louis, Missouri for two years, paying the required private tuition. . . .

VWIL students would participate in ROTC programs and a newly established, "largely ceremonial" Virginia Corps of Cadets but the VWIL House would not have a military format, and VWIL would not require its students to eat meals together or to wear uniforms during the school day. In lieu of VMI's adversative method, the VWIL Task Force favored "a cooperative method which reinforces self-esteem." In addition to the standard bachelor of arts program offered at Mary Baldwin, VWIL students would take courses in leadership, complete an off-campus leader externship, participate in community service projects, and assist in arranging a speaker series. . . .

D

[The District Court approved the proposed remedial plan.] [T]he "controlling legal principles," the District Court decided, "do not require the Commonwealth to provide a mirror image VMI for women." The court anticipated that the two schools would "achieve substantially similar outcomes." It concluded: "If VMI marches to the beat of a drum, then Mary Baldwin marches to the melody of a fife and when the march is over, both will have arrived at the same destination."

A divided Court of Appeals affirmed. . . . This time, the appellate court determined to give "greater scrutiny to the selection of means than to the [State's] proffered objective." The official objective or purpose the court said, should be reviewed deferentially. Respect for the "legislative will," the court reasoned, meant that the judiciary should take a "cautious approach," inquiring into the "legitima[cy]" of the governmental objective and refusing approval for any purpose revealed to be "pernicious."

"Providing the option of a single-gender college education may be considered a legitimate and important aspect of a public system of higher education," the appeals court observed . . . ; that objective, the court added, is "not pernicious." Moreover, the court continued, the adversative method vital to a VMI education "has never been tolerated in a sexually heterogeneous environment." The method itself "was not designed to exclude women," the court noted, but women could not be accommodated in the VMI program [because] female participation in VMI's adversative training "would destroy . . . any sense of decency that still permeates the relationship between the sexes." . . .

Having determined, deferentially, the legitimacy of Virginia's purpose, the court considered the question of means. Exclusion of "men at Mary Baldwin College and women at VMI," the court said, was essential to Virginia's purpose, for without such exclusion, the State could not "accomplish [its] objective of providing single-gender education."

The court recognized that, as it analyzed the case, means merged into end, and the merger risked "bypassing any equal protection scrutiny." The court therefore added another inquiry, a decisive test it called "substantive comparability." The key question, the court said, was whether men at VMI and women at VWIL would obtain "substantively comparable benefits at their institution or through other means offered by the [S]tate." Although the appeals court recognized that the VWIL degree "lacks the historical benefit and prestige" of a VMI degree, it nevertheless found the educational opportunities at the two schools "sufficiently comparable." . . .

III

The cross-petitions in this case present two ultimate issues. First, does Virginia's exclusion of women from the educational opportunities provided by VMI—extraordinary opportunities for military training and civilian leadership development—deny to women "capable of all of the individual activities required of VMI cadets," the equal protection of the laws guaranteed by the Fourteenth Amendment? Second, if VMI's "unique" situation—as Virginia's sole single-sex public institution of higher education—offends the Constitution's equal protection principle, what is the remedial requirement?

IV

We [reiterate] the core instruction of this Court's pathmarking decisions in *J. E. B. v. Alabama ex rel. T. B.*, 511 U.S. 127 (1994), and *Mississippi Univ. for Women* [*v. Hogan*], 458 U.S. [718] [(1982)]: Parties who seek to defend gender-based government action must demonstrate an "exceedingly persuasive justification" for that action.

Today's skeptical scrutiny of official action denying rights or opportunities based on sex responds to volumes of history. As a plurality of this Court acknowledged a generation ago, "our Nation has had a long and unfortunate history of sex discrimination." *Frontiero v. Richardson*, 411 U.S. 677 (1973). Through a century plus three decades and more of that history, women did not count among voters composing "We the People";[5] not until 1920 did women gain a constitutional right to the franchise. And for a half century thereafter, it remained the prevailing doctrine that government, both federal and state, could withhold from women opportunities accorded men so long as any "basis in reason" could be conceived for the discrimination. *See, e.g., Goesaert v. Cleary*, 335 U.S. 464 (1948) (rejecting challenge of female

---

[5] As Thomas Jefferson stated the view prevailing when the Constitution was new: "Were our State a pure democracy . . . there would yet be excluded from their deliberations . . . women, who, to prevent depravation of morals and ambiguity of issue, should not mix promiscuously in the public meetings of men."

tavern owner and her daughter to Michigan law denying bartender licenses to females—except for wives and daughters of male tavern owners; Court would not "give ear" to the contention that "an unchivalrous desire of male bartenders to . . . monopolize the calling" prompted the legislation).[P]

In 1971, for the first time in our Nation's history, this Court ruled in favor of a woman who complained that her State had denied her the equal protection of its laws. *Reed v. Reed,* 404 U.S. 71. . . . Since *Reed,* the Court has repeatedly recognized that neither federal nor state government acts compatibly with the equal protection principle when a law or official policy denies to women, simply because they are women, full citizenship stature—equal opportunity to aspire, achieve, participate in and contribute to society based on their individual talents and capacities. *See, e.g., Kirchberg v. Feenstra,* 450 U.S. 455 (1981) (affirming invalidity of Louisiana law that made husband "head and master" of property jointly owned with his wife, giving him unilateral right to dispose of such property without his wife's consent); *Stanton v. Stanton,* 421 U.S. 7 (1975) (invalidating Utah requirement that parents support boys until age 21, girls only until age 18).

Without equating gender classifications, for all purposes, to classifications based on race or national origin,[6] the Court, in post-*Reed* decisions, has carefully inspected official action that closes a door or denies opportunity to women (or to men). *See J. E. B.* (Kennedy, J., concurring in judgment) (case law evolving since 1971 "reveal[s] a strong presumption that gender classifications are invalid"). To summarize the Court's current directions for cases of official classification based on gender: Focusing on the differential treatment or denial of opportunity for which relief is sought, the reviewing court must determine whether the proffered justification is "exceedingly

---

[P] In fact, the Bartenders Union had a long history of excluding women from bartending. During World War II women did become bartenders as male bartenders left to fight in the war. After World War II, the Bartenders' official journal, CATERING INDUSTRY EMPLOYEE, described the Union's pre-war policy of excluding women from bartending jobs and from the union because the Union had "persistently held and proclaimed that the bartenders' work was a cloister for the male gender." *Bartending Must Revert to Bartenders, Says the G.E.B.* 4–5 (April 12, 1946). The article also noted that California, Ohio, and Pennsylvania had already enacted anti-barmaid legislation and urged union members to work to restore the union's "traditional principle" that "bartending is a man's job!" Three years later, the Union reported: "You will recall receiving from the International Union in December a survey in which it was revealed that 17 states have some form of law banning employment of women behind the bar, and how at the same moment the United States Supreme Court declared that such laws are quite constitutional and are not discriminatory within the meaning of the 14th Amendment. Thereupon in Arizona, New Mexico, Washington, Montana, Colorado, Missouri, Ohio, New York and perhaps other states, our people went to work to mobilize support for similar measures." BARBARA ALLEN BAB-COCK, ANN E. FREEDMAN, ELEANOR HOLMES NORTON, AND SUSAN [DELLER] ROSS, SEX DISCRIMINATION AND THE LAW: CAUSES AND REMEDIES 280 (1975) (quoting report of Fred Sweet, Director, Anti-Prohibition Dept., Proceedings of the Thirty-Second General Convention of Hotel and Restaurant Employees and Bartenders International Union 54 (April 25–29, 1949)).

[6] The Court has thus far reserved most stringent judicial scrutiny for classifications based on race or national origin, but last Term observed that strict scrutiny of such classifications is not inevitably "fatal in fact." *Adarand Constructors, Inc. v. Peña,* 515 U.S. 200 (1995).

persuasive." The burden of justification is demanding and it rests entirely on the State. *See Mississippi Univ. for Women.* The State must show "at least that the [challenged] classification serves 'important governmental objectives and that the discriminatory means employed' are 'substantially related to the achievement of those objectives.'" *Ibid.* (quoting *Wengler v. Druggists Mutual Ins. Co.,* 446 U.S. 142 (1980)). The justification must be genuine, not hypothesized or invented *post hoc* in response to litigation. And it must not rely on overbroad generalizations about the different talents, capacities, or preferences of males and females. *See Weinberger v. Wiesenfeld,* 420 U.S. 636 (1975); *Califano v. Goldfarb,* 430 U.S. 199 (1977) (Stevens, J., concurring in judgment).

The heightened review standard our precedent establishes does not make sex a proscribed classification. Supposed "inherent differences" are no longer accepted as a ground for race or national origin classifications. *See Loving v. Virginia,* 388 U.S. 1 (1967). Physical differences between men and women, however, are enduring: "[T]he two sexes are not fungible; a community made up exclusively of one [sex] is different from a community composed of both." *Ballard v. United States,* 329 U.S. 187 (1946).

"Inherent differences" between men and women, we have come to appreciate, remain cause for celebration, but not for denigration of the members of either sex or for artificial constraints on an individual's opportunity. Sex classifications may be used to compensate women for particular economic disabilities [they have] suffered," *Califano v. Webster,* 430 U.S. 313 (1977), to "promot[e] equal employment opportunity," *see California Federal Sav. & Loan Assn. v. Guerra,* 479 U.S. 272 (1987), to advance full development of the talent and capacities of our Nation's people.[7] But such classifications may not be used, as they once were, *see Goesaert,* to create or perpetuate the legal, social, and economic inferiority of women.

Measuring the record in this case against the review standard just described, we conclude that Virginia has shown no "exceedingly persuasive justification" for excluding all women from the citizen-soldier training afforded by VMI. We therefore affirm the Fourth Circuit's initial judgment, which held that Virginia had violated the Fourteenth Amendment's Equal Protection Clause. Because the remedy proffered by Virginia—the Mary Baldwin VWIL program—does not cure the constitutional violation, i.e., it does not provide equal opportunity, we reverse the Fourth Circuit's final judgment in this case.

---

[7] Several amici have urged that diversity in educational opportunities is an altogether appropriate governmental pursuit and that single-sex schools contribute importantly to such diversity. Indeed, it is the mission of some single-sex schools "to dissipate, rather than perpetuate, traditional gender classifications." *See Brief for Twenty-Six Private Women's Colleges as Amici Curiae* 5. We do not question the State's prerogative evenhandedly to support diverse educational opportunities. We address specifically and only an educational opportunity recognized by the District Court and the Court of Appeals as "unique," . . . an opportunity available only at Virginia's premier military institute, the State's sole single-sex public university or college. *Cf. Mississippi Univ. for Women* ("Mississippi maintains no other single-sex public university or college. Thus, we are not faced with the question of whether States can provide 'separate but equal' undergraduate institutions for males and females.")

V. . . .

Virginia . . . asserts two justifications in defense of VMI's exclusion of women. First, the Commonwealth contends, "single-sex education provides important educational benefits," . . . and the option of single-sex education contributes to "diversity in educational approaches." . . . Second, the Commonwealth argues, "the unique VMI method of character development and leadership training," the school's adversative approach, would have to be modified were VMI to admit women. We consider these two justifications in turn.

A

Single-sex education affords pedagogical benefits to at least some students, Virginia emphasizes, and that reality is uncontested in this litigation.[8] Similarly, it is not disputed that diversity among public educational institutions can serve the public good. But Virginia has not shown that VMI was established, or has been maintained, with a view to diversifying, by its categorical exclusion of women, educational opportunities within the State. In cases of this genre, our precedent instructs that "benign" justifications proffered in defense of categorical exclusions will not be accepted automatically; a tenable justification must describe actual state purposes, not rationalizations for actions in fact differently grounded. *See Wiesenfeld* ("mere recitation of a benign [or] compensatory purpose" does not block "inquiry into the actual purposes" of government-maintained gender-based classifications); *Goldfarb* (rejecting government-proffered purposes after "inquiry into the actual purposes").

Mississippi Univ. for Women is immediately in point. There the State asserted, in justification of its exclusion of men from a nursing school, that it was engaging in "educational affirmative action" by "compensat[ing] for discrimination against women." Undertaking a "searching analysis," the Court found no close resemblance between "the alleged objective" and "the actual purpose underlying the discriminatory classification." Pursuing a similar inquiry here, we reach the same conclusion.

Neither recent nor distant history bears out Virginia's alleged pursuit of diversity through single-sex educational options. In 1839, when the State established VMI, a range of educational opportunities for men and women was scarcely contemplated.

---

[8] . . . "Both men and women can benefit from a single-sex education," the District Court recognized, although "the beneficial effects" of such education, the court added, apparently "are stronger among women than among men." The United States does not challenge that recognition. *Cf.* C. JENCKS & D. RIESMAN, THE ACADEMIC REVOLUTION (1968): "The pluralistic argument for preserving all-male colleges is uncomfortably similar to the pluralistic argument for preserving all-white colleges. . . . The all-male college would be relatively easy to defend if it emerged from a world in which women were established as fully equal to men. But it does not. It is therefore likely to be a witting or unwitting device for preserving tacit assumptions of male superiority—assumptions for which women must eventually pay."

Higher education at the time was considered dangerous for women;[9] reflecting widely held views about women's proper place, the Nation's first universities and colleges—for example, Harvard in Massachusetts, William and Mary in Virginia—admitted only men. *See* E. Farello, A History of the Education of Women in the United States (1970). VMI was not at all novel in this respect: in admitting no women, VMI followed the lead of the State's flagship school, the University of Virginia, founded in 1819. . . .

"[N]o struggle for the admission of women to a state university," a historian has recounted, "was longer drawn out, or developed more bitterness, than that at the University of Virginia." T. Woody, 2 A History of Women's Education in the United States (1929) (2 History of Women's Education). In 1879, the State Senate resolved to look into the possibility of higher education for women, recognizing that Virginia "'has never, at any period of her history,'" provided for the higher education of her daughters, though she "'has liberally provided for the higher education of her sons.'" *Ibid.* (quoting 10 Educ. J. Va. 212 (1879)). Despite this recognition, no new universities were instantly open to women.[10]

Virginia eventually provided for several women's seminaries and colleges. Farmville Female Seminary became a public institution in 1884. Two women's schools, Mary Washington College and James Madison University, were founded in 1908; another, Radford University, was founded in 1910. By the mid-1970's, all four schools had become coeducational.

Debate concerning women's admission as undergraduates at the main university continued well past the century's midpoint. Familiar arguments were rehearsed. If women were admitted, it was feared, they "would encroach on the rights of men; there would be new problems of government, perhaps scandals; the old honor system would have to be changed; standards would be lowered to those of other coeducational schools; and the glorious reputation of the university, as a school for men, would be trailed in the dust." 2 History of Women's Education.

---

[9] Dr. Edward H. Clarke of Harvard Medical School, whose influential book, Sex in Education, went through 17 editions, was perhaps the most well-known speaker from the medical community opposing higher education for women. He maintained that the physiological effects of hard study and academic competition with boys would interfere with the development of girls' reproductive organs. *See* E. Clarke, Sex in Education (1873); ("identical education of the two sexes is a crime before God and humanity, that physiology protests against, and that experience weeps over"); *see also* H. Maudsley, Sex in Mind and in Education (1874) ("It is not that girls have not ambition, nor that they fail generally to run the intellectual race [in coeducational settings], but it is asserted that they do it at a cost to their strength and health which entails life-long suffering, and even incapacitates them for the adequate performance of the natural functions of their sex."); C. Meigs, Females and Their Diseases (1848) (after five or six weeks of "mental and educational discipline," a healthy woman would "lose . . . the habit of menstruation" and suffer numerous ills as a result of depriving her body for the sake of her mind).

[10] Virginia's Superintendent of Public Instruction dismissed the coeducational idea as "'repugnant to the prejudices of the people'" and proposed a female college similar in quality to Girton, Smith, or Vassar. 2 History of Women's Education (quoting Dept. of Interior, 1 Report of Commissioner of Education, H. R. Doc. No. 5, 58th Cong., 2d Sess. (1904)).

Ultimately, in 1970, "the most prestigious institution of higher education in Virginia," the University of Virginia, introduced coeducation and, in 1972, began to admit women on an equal basis with men. *See Kirstein v. Rector and Visitors of Univ. of Virginia*, 309 F. Supp. 184 (ED Va. 1970). . . .[Q]

Virginia describes the current absence of public single-sex higher education for women as "an historical anomaly." But the historical record indicates action more deliberate than anomalous: First, protection of women against higher education; next, schools for women far from equal in resources and stature to schools for men; finally, conversion of the separate schools to coeducation. The state legislature, prior to the advent of this controversy, had repealed "[a]ll Virginia statutes requiring individual institutions to admit only men or women." And in 1990, an official commission, "legislatively established to chart the future goals of higher education in Virginia," reaffirmed the policy "of affording broad access" while maintaining "autonomy and diversity." Significantly, the [Virginia Commission on the University of the 21st Century] reported: "'Because colleges and universities provide for students to develop values and learn from role models, it is extremely important that they deal with faculty, staff, and students without regard to sex, race, or ethnic origin." . . .

Our 1982 decision in *Mississippi Univ. for Women* prompted VMI to reexamine its male-only admission policy. Virginia relies on that reexamination as a legitimate basis for maintaining VMI's single-sex character. A Mission Study Committee, appointed by the VMI Board of Visitors, studied the problem from October 1983 until May 1986, and in that month counseled against "change of VMI status as a single-sex college." Whatever internal purpose the Mission Study Committee served—and however well-meaning the framers of the report—we can hardly extract from that effort any state policy evenhandedly to advance diverse educational options. As the District Court observed, the committee's analysis "primarily focuse[d] on anticipated difficulties in attracting females to VMI," and the report, overall, supplied "very little indication of how th[e] conclusion was reached.". . . .

That court also questioned "how one institution with autonomy, but with no authority over any other state institution, can give effect to a state policy of diversity among institutions." A purpose genuinely to advance an array of educational options, as the Court of Appeals recognized, is not served by VMI's historic and constant plan—a plan to "affor[d] a unique educational benefit only to males." However "liberally" this plan serves the State's sons, it makes no provision whatever for her daughters. That is not *equal* protection.

B

Virginia next argues that VMI's adversative method of training provides educational benefits that cannot be made available, unmodified, to women. Alterations to accommodate women would necessarily be "radical," so "drastic," Virginia asserts, as to

---

[Q] In fact, the University only admitted women as a result of the U.S. District Court ruling ordering it to do so.

transform, indeed "destroy," VMI's program. Neither sex would be favored by the transformation, Virginia maintains: Men would be deprived of the unique opportunity currently available to them; women would not gain that opportunity because their participation would "eliminat[e] the very aspects of [the] program that distinguish [VMI] from other institutions of higher education in Virginia."

The District Court forecast from expert witness testimony, and the Court of Appeals accepted, that coeducation would materially affect "at least these three aspects of VMI's program—physical training, the absence of privacy, and the adversative approach." And it is uncontested that women's admission would require accommodations, primarily in arranging housing assignments and physical training programs for female cadets. It is also undisputed, however, that "the VMI methodology could be used to educate women." The District Court even allowed that some women may prefer it to the methodology a women's college might pursue. "[S]ome women, at least, would want to attend [VMI] if they had the opportunity," the District Court recognized; . . . and "some women," the expert testimony established, "are capable of all of the individual activities required of VMI cadets." The parties, furthermore, agree that "*some* women can meet the physical standards [VMI] now impose[s] on men." . . . In sum, as the Court of Appeals stated, "neither the goal of producing citizen-soldiers," VMI's *raison d'être*, "nor VMI's implementing methodology is inherently unsuitable to women."

In support of its initial judgment for Virginia . . . , the District Court made "findings" on "gender-based developmental differences." These "findings" restate the opinions of Virginia's expert witnesses, opinions about typically male or typically female "tendencies." For example, "[m]ales tend to need an atmosphere of adversativeness," while "[f]emales tend to thrive in a cooperative atmosphere." "I'm not saying that some women don't do well under [the] adversative model," VMI's expert on educational institutions testified, "undoubtedly there are some [women] who do"; but educational experiences must be designed "around the rule," this expert maintained, and not "around the exception."

The United States does not challenge any expert witness estimation on average capacities or preferences of men and women. Instead, the United States emphasizes that time and again since this Court's turning point decision in *Reed* . . . , we have cautioned reviewing courts to take a "hard look" at generalizations or "tendencies" of the kind pressed by Virginia and relied upon by the District Court. State actors controlling gates to opportunity, we have instructed, may not exclude qualified individuals based on "fixed notions concerning the roles and abilities of males and females." *Mississippi Univ. for Women, see J. E. B.* (equal protection principles, as applied to gender classifications, mean state actors may not rely on "overbroad" generalizations to make "judgments about people that are likely to . . . perpetuate historical patterns of discrimination").

It may be assumed, for purposes of this decision, that most women would not choose VMI's adversative method. As Fourth Circuit Judge Motz observed, however, in her dissent from the Court of Appeals' denial of rehearing en banc, it is also probable that "many men would not want to be educated in such an environment." (On that point, even our dissenting colleague might agree.) Education, to be sure, is not a "one size fits all" business. The issue, however, is not whether "women—or men—should be forced to attend VMI"; rather, the question is whether the State can constitutionally deny to women who have the will and capacity, the training and attendant opportunities that VMI uniquely affords.

The notion that admission of women would downgrade VMI's stature, destroy the adversative system and, with it, even the school,[11] is a judgment hardly proved,[12] a prediction hardly different from other "self-fulfilling prophec[ies]," *see Mississippi Univ. for Women*, once routinely used to deny rights or opportunities. When women first sought admission to the bar and access to legal education, concerns of the same order were expressed. For example, in 1876, [a common pleas court] explained why women were thought ineligible for the practice of law. Women train and educate the young, the court said, which

"forbids that they shall bestow that time (early and late) and labor, so essential in attaining to the eminence to which the true lawyer should ever aspire. It cannot therefore be said that the opposition of courts to the admission of females to practice . . . is to any extent the outgrowth of . . . 'old fogyism[.]' . . . [I]t arises rather from a comprehension of the magnitude of the responsibilities connected with the successful practice of law, and a desire to *grade up* the profession." *In re Application of Martha Angle Dorsett to Be Admitted to Practice as Attorney and Counselor at Law* (Minn. C. P. Hennepin Cty. 1876) . . . (*emphasis added*).

A like fear, according to a 1925 report, accounted for Columbia Law School's resistance to women's admission, although

"[t]he faculty . . . never maintained that women could not master legal learning. . . . No, its argument has been . . . more practical. If women were admitted to the Columbia Law School, [the faculty] said, then the choicer, more manly and red-blooded graduates of our great universities would go to the Harvard Law School! . . ." THE NATION.

Medical faculties similarly resisted men and women as partners in the study of medicine. *See* E. Clarke, *Medical Education of Women*, 4 BOSTON MED. & SURG. J. 345 (1869)

---

[11] . . . Forecasts of the same kind were made regarding admission of women to the federal military academies. *See e.g.,* (statement of Lt. Gen. A.P. Clark, Superintendent of U.S. Air Force Academy) ("It is my considered judgement that the introduction of female cadets will inevitably erode the vital atmosphere."); (statement of Hon. H.H.. Callaway, Secretary of the Army) ("Admitting women to West Point would irrevocably change the Academy. . . . The Spartan atmosphere—which is so important to producing the final products—would be diluted, and would in all probability disappear.").

[12] *See* 766 F. Supp. at 1413 (describing testimony of expert witness David Riesman: "[I]f VMI were to admit women, it would eventually find it necessary to drop the adversative system altogether, and adopt a system that provides more nurturing and support for the students."). Such judgments have attended, and impeded, women's progress toward full citizenship stature throughout our Nation's history. Speaking in 1879 in support of higher education for females, for example, Virginia State Senator C. T. Smith of Nelson recounted that legislation proposed to protect the property rights of women had encountered resistance. A Senator opposing the measures . . . "depicted in burning eloquence the terrible consequences such laws would produce." The legislation passed, and a year or so later, its sponsor, C. T. Smith, reported that "not one of [the forecast "terrible consequences"] has or ever will happen even unto the sounding of Gabriel's trumpet."

("God forbid that I should ever see men and women aiding each other to display with the scalpel the secrets of the reproductive system. . . .") More recently, women seeking careers in policing encountered resistance based on fears that their presence would "undermine male solidarity"; deprive male partners of adequate assistance; and lead to sexual misconduct. Field studies did not confirm these fears.

Women's successful entry into the federal military academies,[13] and their participation in the Nation's military forces, indicate that Virginia's fears for the future of VMI may not be solidly grounded.[15] The State's justification for excluding all women from "citizen-soldier" training for which some are qualified, in any event, cannot rank as "exceedingly persuasive," as we have explained and applied that standard.

Virginia and VMI trained their argument on "means" rather than "end," and thus misperceived our precedent. Single-sex education at VMI serves an "important governmental objective," they maintained, and exclusion of women is not only "substantially related," it is essential to that objective. By this notably circular argument, the "straightforward" test *Mississippi Univ. for Women* described was bent and bowed.

The Commonwealth's misunderstanding and, in turn, the District Court's is apparent from VMI's mission to produce "citizen-soldiers," individuals

"'imbued with love of learning, confident in the functions and attitudes of leadership, possessing a high sense of public service, advocates of the American democracy and free enterprise system, and ready . . . to defend their country in time of national peril.'" 766 F. Supp. (quoting Mission Study Committee of the VMI Board of Visitors, Report, May 16, 1986).

Surely that goal is great enough to accommodate women, who today count as citizens in our American democracy equal in stature to men. Just as surely, the State's great goal is not substantially advanced by women's categorical exclusion, in total disregard of their individual merit, from the State's premier "citizen-soldier" corps."[16] Virginia, in sum, "has fallen far short of establishing the 'exceedingly persuasive justification,'" that must be the solid base for any gender-defined classification.

VI

In the second phase of the litigation, Virginia presented its remedial plan—maintain VMI as a male-only college and create VWIL as a separate program for women. The

---

[13] Women cadets have graduated at the top of the class at every federal military academy. *See Brief for Lieutenant Colonel Rhonda Cornum et al. as Amici Curiae.*

[15] Inclusion of women in settings where, traditionally, they were not wanted inevitably entails a period of adjustment. As one West Point cadet squad leader recounted: "[T]he classes of '78 and '79 see the women as women, but the classes of '80 and '81 see them as classmates."

[16] VMI has successfully managed another notable change. The school admitted its first African-American cadets in 1968. *See* THE VMI STORY (students no longer sing "Dixie," salute the Confederate flag or the tomb of General Robert E. Lee at ceremonies and sports events). As the District Court noted, VMI established a Program on "retention of black cadets" designed to offer academic and social-cultural support to "minority members of a dominantly white and

plan met District Court [and Fourth Circuit] approval. . . . Inspecting the VMI and VWIL educational programs to determine whether they "afford[ed] to both genders benefits comparable in substance, [if] not in form and detail," the Court of Appeals concluded that Virginia had arranged for men and women opportunities "sufficiently comparable" to survive equal protection evaluation.

A

A remedial decree, this Court has said, must closely fit the constitutional violation; it must be shaped to place persons unconstitutionally denied an opportunity or advantage in "the position they would have occupied in the absence of [discrimination.]" The constitutional violation in this case is the categorical exclusion of women from an extraordinary educational opportunity afforded men. A proper remedy for an unconstitutional exclusion . . . aims to "eliminate [so far as possible] the discriminatory effects of the past" and to "bar like discrimination in the future". . . .

Having violated the Constitution's equal protection requirement, Virginia was obliged to show that its remedial proposal "directly address[ed] and relate[d] to" the violation, i.e., the equal protection denied to women ready, willing, and able to benefit from educational opportunities of the kind VMI offers. Virginia described VWIL as a "parallel program," and asserted that VWIL shares VMI's mission of producing "citizen-soldiers" and VMI's goals of providing "education, military training, mental and physical discipline, character . . . and leadership development." . . . If the VWIL program could not "eliminate the discriminatory effects of the past," could it at least "bar like discrimination in the future"? A comparison of the programs said to be "parallel" informs our answer. . . .

VWIL affords women no opportunity to experience the rigorous military training for which VMI is famed. Instead, the VWIL program "deemphasize[s]" military education . . . and uses a "cooperative method" of education "which reinforces self-esteem."

VWIL students participate in ROTC and a "largely ceremonial" Virginia Corps of Cadets, but Virginia deliberately did not make VWIL a military institute. The VWIL House is not a military style residence and VWIL students need not live together throughout the 4-year program, eat meals together, or wear uniforms during the school day. VWIL students thus do not experience the "barracks" life "crucial to the VMI experience," the spartan living arrangements designed to foster an "egalitarian ethic." "[T]he most important aspects of the VMI educational experience occur in the barracks," the District Court found, yet Virginia deemed that core experience nonessential, indeed inappropriate, for training its female citizen-soldiers.

VWIL students receive their "leadership training" in seminars, externships, and speaker series, . . . episodes and encounters lacking the "physical rigor, mental

---

tradition-oriented student body." The school maintains a "special recruitment program for blacks" which, the District Court found, "has had little, if any, effect on VMI's method of accomplishing its Mission."

stress, . . . minute regulation of behavior, and indoctrination in desirable values" made hallmarks of VMI's citizen-soldier training. Kept away from the pressures, hazards, and psychological bonding characteristic of VMI's adversative training, VWIL students will not know the "feeling of tremendous accomplishment" commonly experienced by VMI's successful cadets.

Virginia maintains that these methodological differences are "justified pedagogically," based on "important differences between men and women in learning and developmental needs," "psychological and sociological differences" Virginia describes as " 'real" and "not stereotypes." The Task Force charged with developing the leadership program for women, drawn from the staff and faculty at Mary Baldwin College, "determined that a military model and, especially VMI's adversative method, would be wholly inappropriate for educating and training *most women*."

As earlier stated, generalizations about "the way women are," estimates of what is appropriate for *most women*, no longer justify denying opportunity to women whose talent and capacity place them outside the average description. Notably, Virginia never asserted that VMI's method of education suits *most men*. It is also revealing that Virginia accounted for its failure to make the VWIL experience "the entirely militaristic experience of VMI" on the ground that VWIL "is planned for women who do not necessarily expect to pursue military careers." By that reasoning, VMI's "entirely militaristic" program would be inappropriate for men in general or as *a group*, for "[o]nly about 15% of VMI cadets enter career military service."

In contrast to the generalizations about women on which Virginia rests, we note again these dispositive realties: VMI's "implementing methodology" is not "inherently unsuitable to women" . . . ; "some women . . . do well under [the] adversative model," . . . ; "some women, at least, would want to attend [VMI] if" they had the opportunity, . . . ; "some women are capable of all of the individual activities required of VMI cadets," . . . and "can meet the physical standards [VMI] now impose[s] on men." . . . It is on behalf of these women that the United States has instituted this suit, and it is for them that a remedy must be crafted,[19] a remedy that will end their exclusion from a state-supplied educational opportunity for which they are fit, a decree that will bar like discrimination in the future."

B

In myriad respects other than military training, VWIL does not qualify as VMI's equal. VWIL's student body, faculty, course offerings, and facilities hardly match VMI's. Nor can the VWIL graduate anticipate the benefits associated with VMI's 157-year history, the school's prestige, and its influential alumni network. . . .

For physical training, Mary Baldwin has "two multipurpose fields" and "[o]ne gymnasium." . . . VMI has "an NCAA competition level indoor track and field facility;

---

[19] Admitting women to VMI would undoubtedly require alterations necessary to afford members of each sex privacy from the other sex in living arrangements, and to adjust aspects of the physical training programs. Experience shows such adjustments are manageable.

a number of multi-purpose fields; baseball, soccer and lacrosse fields; an obstacle course; large boxing, wrestling and martial arts facilities; an 11-laps-to-the-mile indoor running course; an indoor pool; indoor and outdoor rifle ranges; and a football stadium that also contains a practice field and outdoor track."

Although Virginia has represented that it will provide equal financial support for in-state VWIL students and VMI cadets, and the VMI Foundation has agreed to endow VWIL with $5.4625 million, the difference between the two schools' financial reserves is pronounced. Mary Baldwin's endowment, currently about $19 million, will gain an additional $35 million based on future commitments; VMI's current endowment, $131 million—the largest per-student endowment in the Nation—will gain $220 million.

The VWIL student does not graduate with the advantage of a VMI degree. Her diploma does not unite her with the legions of VMI "graduates who have distinguished themselves" in military and civilian life. "[VMI] alumni are exceptionally close to the school," and that closeness accounts, in part, for VMI's success in attracting applicants. A VWIL graduate cannot assume that the "network of business owners, corporations, VMI graduates and non-graduate employers . . . interested in hiring VMI graduates" . . . will be equally responsive to her search for employment.

Virginia, in sum, while maintaining VMI for men only, has failed to provide any "comparable single-gender women's institution." Instead, the Commonwealth has created a VWIL program fairly appraised as a "pale shadow" of VMI. . . .

Virginia's VWIL solution is reminiscent of the remedy Texas proposed 50 years ago, in response to a state trial court's 1946 ruling that . . . African Americans could not be denied a legal education at a state facility. *See Sweatt v. Painter*, 339 U.S. 629 (1950). Reluctant to admit African Americans to its flagship University of Texas Law School, the State set up a separate school for Herman Sweatt and other black law students. . . .

Before this Court considered the case, the new school had gained "a faculty of five full-time professors; a student body of 23; a library of some 16,500 volumes serviced by a full-time staff; a practice court and legal aid association; and one alumnus who ha[d] become a member of the Texas Bar." This Court contrasted resources at the new school with those at the school from which Sweatt had been excluded. The University of Texas Law School had a full-time faculty of 16, a student body of 850, a library containing over 65,000 volumes, scholarship funds, a law review, and moot court facilities.

More important than the tangible features, the Court emphasized, are "those qualities which are incapable of objective measurement but which make for greatness" in a school, including "reputation of the faculty, experience of the administration, position and influence of the alumni, standing in the community, traditions and prestige. Facing the marked differences reported in the *Sweatt* opinion, the Court unanimously ruled that Texas had not shown "substantial equality in the [separate] educational opportunities" the State offered. . . . Accordingly, the Court held, the Equal Protection Clause required Texas to admit African Americans to the University of Texas Law School. In line with *Sweatt*, we rule here that Virginia has not shown substantial equality in the separate educational opportunities the State supports at VWIL and VMI.

C

When Virginia tendered its VWIL plan, the Fourth Circuit did not inquire whether the proposed remedy, approved by the District Court, placed women denied the VMI advantage in "the position they would have occupied in the absence of [discrimination]."

The Fourth Circuit acknowledged that "the VWIL degree from Mary Baldwin College lacks the historical benefit and prestige of a degree from VMI." . . . Nevertheless, the appeals court declared the substantially different and significantly unequal program satisfactory. The court reached that result by revising the applicable standard of review. . . .

We have earlier described [in Part II.D.] the deferential review in which the Court of Appeals engaged, a brand of review inconsistent with the more exacting standard our precedent requires. . . . [T]he Court of Appeals candidly described its own analysis as one capable of checking a legislative purpose ranked as "pernicious," but generally according "deference to [the] legislative will." . . . Recognizing that it had extracted from our decisions a test yielding "little or no scrutiny of the effect of a classification directed at [single-gender education]," the Court of Appeals devised another test, a "substantive comparability" inquiry . . . and proceeded to find that new test satisfied.

The Fourth Circuit plainly erred in exposing Virginia's VWIL plan to a deferential analysis. . . . Valuable as VWIL may prove for students who seek the program offered, Virginia's remedy affords no cure at all for opportunities and advantages withheld from women who want a VMI education and can make the grade.[20] In sum, Virginia's

---

[20] Virginia's prime concern, it appears, is that "plac[ing] men and women into the adversative relationship inherent, in the VMI program . . . would destroy, at least for that period of the adversative training, any sense of decency that still permeates the relationship between the sexes. It is an ancient and familiar fear. *Compare In re Lavinia Goodell,* 39 Wis. 232 (1875) (denying female applicant's motion for admission to the bar of its court, Wisconsin Supreme Court explained: "Discussions are habitually necessary in courts of justice, which are unfit for female ears. The habitual presence of women at these would tend to relax the public sense of decency and propriety."), *with* Levine, *Closing Comments,* 6 LAW & INEQUALITY 41 (1988). . . . : "Plato questioned whether women should be afforded equal opportunity to become guardians, those elite Rulers of Platonic society. Ironically, in that most undemocratic system of government, the Republic, women's native ability to serve as guardians was not seriously questioned. The concern was over the wrestling and exercise class in which all candidates for guardianship had to participate, for rigorous physical and mental training were prerequisites to attain the exalted status of guardian. And in accord with Greek custom, those exercise classes were conducted in the nude. Plato concluded that their virtue would clothe the women's nakedness and that Platonic society would not thereby be deprived of the talent of qualified citizens for reasons of mere gender." . . .

Virginia, not bound to ancient Greek custom in its "rigorous physical and mental training" programs, could more readily make the accommodations necessary to draw on "the talent of [all] qualified citizens." . . .

remedy does not match the constitutional violation; the State has shown no "exceedingly persuasive justification" for withholding from women qualified for the experience premier training of the kind VMI affords.

VII . . .

Commencing in 1970, Virginia opened to women "educational opportunities at the Charlottesville campus that [were] not afforded in other [State-operated] institutions. . . .

A prime part of the history of our Constitution . . . is the story of the extension of constitutional rights and protections to people once ignored or excluded.[21] VMI's story continued as our comprehension of "We the People" expanded. There is no reason to believe that the admission of women capable of all the activities required of VMI cadets would destroy the Institute rather than enhance its capacity to serve the "more perfect Union." . . .

JUSTICE THOMAS took no part in the consideration or decision of this case. [His son was enrolled at VMI.]

CHIEF JUSTICE REHNQUIST, concurring in judgment. . . .

While I agree with [the Court's] conclusions, I disagree with [its] analysis. . . .

Two decades ago in *Craig v. Boren*, 429 U.S. 190 (1976), we announced that "[t]o withstand constitutional challenge, . . . classifications by gender must serve important governmental objectives and must be substantially related to achievement of those objectives. We have adhered to that standard of scrutiny ever since. . . . While the majority adheres to this test today, it also says that the State must demonstrate an "exceedingly persuasive justification" to support a gender-based classification. . . .

While terms like "important governmental objective" and "substantially related" are hardly models of precision, they have more content and specificity than does the phrase "exceedingly persuasive justification." That phrase is best confined, as it was first used, as an observation on the difficulty of meeting the applicable test, not as a formulation of the test itself. . . .

Our cases dealing with gender discrimination also require that the proffered purpose for the challenged law be the actual purpose. It is on this ground that the Court rejects the first of two justifications Virginia offers for VMI's single-sex admissions policy, namely, the goal of diversity among its public educational institutions. . . .

---

[21] R. MORRIS, THE FORGING OF THE UNION, 1781–1789 (1987); *see id.*, setting out letter to a friend from Massachusetts patriot (later second President) John Adams, on the subject of qualifications for voting in his home state: "[I]t is dangerous to open so fruitful a source of controversy and altercation as would be opened by attempting to alter the qualifications of voters; there will be no end of it. New claims will arise; women will demand a vote; lads from twelve to twenty-one will think their rights not enough attended to; and every man who has not a farthing, will demand an equal voice with any other, in all acts of state. It tends to confound and destroy all distinctions, and prostrate all ranks to one common level." Letter from John Adams to James Sullivan (May 26, 1776), in 9 WORKS OF JOHN ADAMS (C. Adams ed. 1854).

I agree with the Court that there is scant evidence in the record that [diversity] was the real reason that Virginia decided to maintain VMI as men only. But, unlike the majority, I would consider only evidence that postdates our decision in [*Mississippi Univ. for Women v.*] *Hogan,* and would draw no negative inferences from the State's actions before that time. I think that after *Hogan,* the Commonwealth was entitled to reconsider its policy with respect to VMI, and not to have earlier justifications, or lack thereof, held against it. . . .

By defining the [constitutional] violation [as "the categorical exclusion of women from an extraordinary educational opportunity afforded to men"], and by emphasizing that a remedy for a constitutional violation must place the victims of discrimination in " 'the position they would have occupied in the absence of [discrimination],' " the Court necessarily implies that the only adequate remedy would be the admission of women to the all-male institution. . . . I would not define the violation in this way; it is not the "exclusion of women" that violates the Equal Protection Clause, but the maintenance of an all-men school without providing any—much less a comparable—institution for women. . . .

An adequate remedy in my opinion might be a demonstration by Virginia that its interest in educating men in a single-sex environment is matched by its interest in educating women in a single-sex institution. To demonstrate such, the State does not need to create two institutions with the same number of faculty Ph.D.'s, similar SAT scores, or comparable athletic fields. Nor would it necessarily require that the women's institution offer the same curriculum as the men's . . . it would be a sufficient remedy, I think, if the two institutions offered the same quality of education and were of the same overall caliber.

If a state decides to create single-sex programs, the state would, I expect, consider the public's interest and demand in designing curricula. And rightfully so. But the state should avoid assuming demand based on stereotypes; it must not assume *a priori,* without evidence, that there would be no interest in a women's school of civil engineering, or in a men's school of nursing.

In the end, the women's institution Virginia proposes, VWIL, fails as a remedy, because it is distinctly inferior to the existing men's institution and will continue to be for the foreseeable future.

JUSTICE SCALIA, dissenting. . . .

I . . .

It is my view that, whatever abstract tests we may choose to devise, they cannot supersede—and indeed ought to be crafted *so as to reflect*—those constant and unbroken national traditions that embody the people's understanding of ambiguous constitutional texts. More specifically, it is my view that "when a practice not expressly prohibited by the text of the Bill of Rights bears the endorsement of a long tradition of open, widespread, and unchallenged use that dates back to the beginning of the Republic, we have no proper basis for striking it down." The same applies

. . . to a practice asserted to be in violation of the post-Civil War Fourteenth Amendment.

The all-male constitution of VMI comes squarely within such a governing tradition. . . . For almost all of VMI's more than a century and a half of existence, its single-sex status reflected the uniform practice for government-supported military colleges. . . . [A]ll the federal military colleges . . . admitted only males for most of their history. Their admission of women in 1976 . . . came not by court decree, but because the people, through their elected representatives, decreed a change. . . .

II

To reject the Court's disposition today, however, it is not necessary to accept my view that the Court's made-up tests cannot displace longstanding national traditions as the primary determinant of what the Constitution means. It is only necessary to apply honestly the test the Court has been applying to sex-based classifications for the past two decades. . . .

Although the Court . . . recites the test . . . which asks whether the State has demonstrated "that the classification serves important governmental objectives and that the discriminatory means employed are substantially related to the achievement of those objectives . . . [it] never answers the question in anything resembling that form. When it engages in analysis, the Court instead prefers the phrase "exceedingly persuasive justification". . . . The Court's nine invocations of that phrase . . . would be unobjectionable if the Court acknowledged that whether a "justification" is "exceedingly persuasive" must be assessed by asking "whether the classification serves important governmental objectives and whether the discriminatory means employed are substantially related to the achievement of those objectives." Instead, however, the Court proceeds to interpret "exceedingly persuasive justification" in a fashion that contradicts the reasoning of *Hogan* and our other precedents. . . .

Only the amorphous "exceedingly persuasive justification" phrase, and not the standard elaboration of intermediate scrutiny, can be made to yield th[e] conclusion that VMI's single-sex composition is unconstitutional because there exist several women (or, one would have to conclude under the Court's reasoning, a single woman) willing and able to undertake VMI's program. Intermediate scrutiny has never required a least-restrictive-means analysis but only a "substantial relation" between the classification and the state interests that it serves. . . . There is simply no support in our cases for the notion that a sex-based classification is invalid unless it relates to characteristics that hold true in every instance.

[Moreover,] the Court purports to reserve the question whether, even in principle, a higher standard (i.e., strict scrutiny) should apply. . . . But [this is] misleading, insofar as [it] suggest[s] that we have not already categorically *held* strict scrutiny to be inapplicable to sex-based classifications. *See, e.g., Heckler v. Mathews*, 465 U.S. 728 (1984) (*upholding* state action after applying only intermediate scrutiny) . . .

[I]f the question of the applicable standard of review for sex-based classifications were to be regarded as an appropriate subject for reconsideration, the stronger argument would be . . . for reducing it to rational-basis review. . . . Whereas no majority of the Court has ever applied strict scrutiny in a case involving sex-based classifications, we routinely applied rational-basis review until the 1970's. . . . And of course normal rational-basis review of sex-based classifications would be much more in accord with the genesis of heightened standards of judicial review, the famous footnote in *United States v. Carolene Products Co.*, 304 U.S. 144 (1938), which said (intimatingly) that we did not have to inquire in the case at hand

"whether prejudice against discrete and insular minorities may be a special condition, which tends seriously to curtail the operation of those political processes ordinarily to be relied upon to protect minorities, and which may call for a correspondingly more searching judicial inquiry." *Id.*

It is hard to consider women a "discrete and insular minorit[y]" unable to employ the "political processes ordinarily to be relied upon," when they constitute a majority of the electorate. And the suggestion that they are incapable of exerting that political power smacks of the same paternalism that the Court so roundly condemns. . . . Moreover, a long list of legislation proves the proposition false. *See, e.g.*, Equal Pay Act of 1963; Title VII of the Civil Rights Act of 1964; Title IX of the Education Amendments of 1972; Women's Business Ownership Act of 1988; Violence Against Women Act of 1994.

<h2 style="text-align:center">III . . .</h2>

B . . .

The Court's analysis at least has the benefit of producing foreseeable results. Applied generally, it means that whenever a State's ultimate objective is "great enough to accommodate women" (as it always will be), then the State will be held to have violated the Equal Protection Clause if it restricts to men even one means by which it pursues that objective—no matter how few women are interested in pursuing the objective by that means, no matter how much the single-sex program will have to be changed if both sexes are admitted, and no matter how beneficial that program has theretofore been to its participants.

The Court argues that VMI would not have to change very much if it were to admit women. The principal response to that argument is that it is irrelevant: If VMI's single-sex status is substantially related to the government's important educational objectives, as I have demonstrated above . . . , that concludes the inquiry. . . .

But if such a debate were relevant, the Court would certainly be on the losing side. . . . Changes that the District Court's detailed analysis found would be required include new allowances for personal privacy in the barracks, . . . [and] changes in the physical training program, which would reduce "[t]he intensity and aggressiveness of the current program". . . .

IV . . .

A . . .

[T]he rationale of today's decision is sweeping: for sex-based classifications, a redefinition of intermediate scrutiny that makes it indistinguishable from strict scrutiny. . . . Indeed, the Court indicates that if any program restricted to one sex is "uniqu[e]," it must be opened to members of the opposite sex "who have the will and capacity" to participate in it. I suggest that the single-sex program that will not be capable of being characterized as "unique" is not only unique but nonexistent. . . .

B

There are few extant single-sex public educational programs. The potential of today's decision for widespread disruption of existing institutions lies in its application to private single-sex education. Government support is immensely important to private educational institutions. . . . Charitable status under the tax laws is also highly significant for private educational institutions, and it is certainly not beyond the Court that rendered today's decision to hold that a donation to a single-sex college should be deemed contrary to public policy and therefore not deductible if the college discriminates or the basis of sex. . . . *See* . . . *Bob Jones Univ. v. United States,* 461 U.S. 574 (1983). . . .

The issue will be not whether government assistance turns private colleges into state actors, but whether the government itself would be violating the Constitution by providing state support to single-sex colleges.

NOTES

Sex-Segregated Schools. Does the Court conclude that all single-sex public schools or colleges would violate the equal protection clause? Notice that CEDAW's Article 10 permits such schools. *See* Chapter One. Would it save VMI's policy?

The Bitter Fight to the End. The facts show how long and hard VMI fought to stave off allowing women to attend. Indeed, it spent millions defending the policy. Meanwhile, within the women's rights movement, feminists themselves were split. Some wanted to preserve all-women's schools and colleges in order to provide protected space for girls and women to serve in leadership positions and develop their self-confidence. They asserted women would learn better in an all-female environment. These advocates feared the influence of aggressive boys and men who might dominate class discussions and take all the leadership positions. Other advocates thought the problem was teacher and male student bias, and that the solution was to persuade them to change rather than to exclude female students. They doubted that women learned better without men around. Were that so, logic would require educating all girls in single-sex schools. Where do you stand on these issues and why do people have such intense feelings on the subject?

**The Four Tests: Rational Basis; Intermediate Review; Skeptical Scrutiny; Strict Scru-

tiny. The Court has taken these four distinct approaches to analyzing whether a sex-based law denies equal protection of the law to women. The opinion identifies *Goesaert v. Cleary* as typical of the rational basis approach and *Mississippi University for Women* as representing intermediate review. *Loving v. Virginia* represents the strict scrutiny approach to race-based classifications. *VMI* seems to reflect a new heightened "skeptical"scrutiny standard. How do the four standards differ in the Court's description? *See* the text paragraph containing note 5 and the three paragraphs which follow.

Pre-*VMI* equal protection scholars have long noted that the Court asks two basic equal protection questions: what is the state's purpose; and how closely are the sex-based or race-based classifications related to achieving that purpose. For rational basis review, the purpose must be "legitimate;" for intermediate review, "important;" and for strict scrutiny, "compelling." Similarly, the use of a sex-based or race-based statute to achieve the purpose must be "rationally related" at the lowest level; "substantially related" for intermediate scrutiny; and "necessary" to achieve the purpose for strict scrutiny.

The lowest level permits substantial sex stereotyping by relying on group averages to permit different treatment, despite the fact that many men and women do not fit the group average but are forced to act as though they did. If a higher percentage of young men (aged 18–20) have driving accidents after consuming beer than do young women, then a statute can deny all young men but no young women the right to purchase and consume beer. Rational basis review permits this because of young men's higher average accident rate than young women's—for example, two percent of men versus one eighteenth of one percent of women. Intermediate scrutiny says only two percent of young men have such accidents, so let the ninety-eight percent of young men who don't have accidents purchase the beer and strike down the statute. *See Craig v. Boren*, 429 U.S. 190 (1976). In essence, such a statute is highly overinclusive in achieving its purpose as to young men (dragging in the vast majority who do not create traffic safety problems) and mildly underinclusive concerning young women (of whom a tiny percentage do pose a problem). Strict scrutiny would permit no stereotyping by requiring that every excluded person of one sex should be unqualified (all young men drink and drive), while every included person of the other sex should be qualified (no young women drink and drive). If that were the case, the sex-based classification would indeed be "necessary" to achieve the state purpose of preventing traffic accidents among young drivers.

Justice Scalia accuses the majority of requiring a *de facto* strict scrutiny. Has the Court done so? The majority opinion gives examples where it would be permissible to use a legislative sex-based category. What are they and what constraints does the Court put on their use? Are those uses consistent with strict scrutiny? *See* note 6.

VMI is actually a consolidation of two cases. In the first, VMI appealed from a decision striking down the sex-based classification for violating women's right to equal protection. In the second, the United States appealed from a different and later decision permitting VMI to continue to exclude women on the ground that another college provided a separate program for women. Part V deals with the first case and Part VI with the second. In Part V.A., the Court examines the asserted state purpose of "diversifying" state education options. What does it find about this purpose? In Part V.B., the Court examines the assertion that it is "necessary" to exclude women (language suggesting strict scrutiny), because their entrance would require changing VMI's unique and valuable adversative education methods. The Court describes the argument as "circular." What makes it so? Why does the Court reject this argument?

In Part VI, the Court examines the Fourth Circuit's finding that the VMI and VWIL programs were "sufficiently comparable" to provide a remedy for the excluded women. Why does the Court reject that finding in Parts VI.A. and VI.B.? In Part VI.C. the Court rejects the lower court's "deferential" standard of review, described earlier in Part II.D. How had the Fourth Circuit changed the standard of review? That changed standard illustrates one of the ways litigators try to win cases: they assert new review standards under which they can win and try to get courts to accept the standard. It almost worked here, convincing the Fourth Circuit but not the Supreme Court. Human rights advocates can use that insight as they prepare equal protection lawsuits in different countries. They can argue that the courts should use the standard that will best help them win their cases and then apply that standard to the facts at issue to demonstrate why the statute should be struck down.

Chapter 3
The Interrelationship of the ICCPR and the ICESCR; and the Human Rights Committee's Evolving Equal Protection Doctrine

I. The International Covenant on Economic, Social and Cultural Rights (ICESCR)

A. The ICESCR and the ICCPR—Similarities and Differences

The International Covenant on Economic, Social and Cultural Rights (ICESCR) shares many features with the ICCPR. Both entered into force in 1976. As of August 7, 2007, the ICESCR had 156 States Parties, while the ICCPR had 160. The Committee on Economic, Social and Cultural Rights (ESC Committee) monitors state compliance with the treaty through a reporting process, as does the Human Rights Committee (and the CEDAW Committee). Each body issues General Comments which provide States Parties with detailed guidance on the meaning of the treaty articles, recommendations for further action, and guidelines for preparing state reports.[A]

The reporting mechanism requires States Parties to file periodic reports with the monitoring body describing the "measures" they have adopted for, and "progress made" in, achieving Covenant rights. *See* ICCPR, Art. 40(1) and ICESCR, Art. 16(1), *available at* RossRights. Both Committees have used the reporting process to good effect, as has the CEDAW Committee. After the relevant Committee receives the state report, it meets the state representative for discussion, clarification, and questions. Subsequently, it issues Concluding Observations to the state which focus on positive aspects, factors and difficulties impeding implementation, principal subjects of concern, and suggestions and recommendations for the future.[B] Together, the reports and concluding observations provide a wealth of information about laws and practices in countries around the globe and the Committees' concerns about non-compliance. Since both Committees have become quite concerned about women's rights, the reports and observations repeatedly speak to these issues.

The two treaties also differ in many respects. The ICCPR provides for civil rights

---

[A] *See* RossRights for website links to each committee's General Comments.
[B] *See* RossRights for website links to concluding observations and state reports.

such as equality, due process, free speech, freedom of religion, and political rights such as the right to vote or stand for election. In contrast, the ICESCR provides for economic, social and cultural rights. The treaty requires States Parties to provide assistance enabling everyone to have access to employment opportunities (Arts. 6–8), social security insurance (Art. 9), family protection (Art. 10), adequate food and housing (Art. 11), good health (Art. 12), education (Arts. 13–14), and cultural, scientific, copyright, and patent protections (Art. 15). Ratifying states cannot immediately provide such assistance because of the enormous expense. Accordingly, ICESCR Article 2(1) requires a State Party "to **take steps** . . . to the **maximum of its available resources,** with a view to **achieving progressively** the full realization of the rights recognized in the present Covenant. . . ." Compare this to ICCPR Article 2(1), which requires a State Party "to **respect** and to **ensure** to all individuals . . . the rights recognized in the present Covenant. . . ."

Thus, the time period for implementing the two treaties is quite different. On the other hand, both require the immediate provision of equality rights. ICESCR Article 2(2) provides that States Parties "**guarantee** that the rights enunciated in the present Covenant will be exercised without discrimination of any kind [such] as . . . sex. . . ." Similarly, ICCPR Article 2(1) requires States Parties "to **respect** and **ensure** . . . Covenant [rights] . . . without distinction of any kind, such as . . . sex. . . ." In the same vein, Article 3 of each treaty requires that the "States Parties to the present Covenant undertake to **ensure** the equal right of men and women to the enjoyment of all [either 'civil and political' or 'economic, social, and cultural'] rights set forth in the present Covenant."

There are two other significant differences. First, there is no individual complaint procedure under the ICESCR, although efforts are well under way to establish one. The ESC Committee concluded considering a draft optional protocol during its 15th session in November and December 1996. The Committee sent its report, U.N. Doc. E/CN.4/1997/105, to the Commission on Human Right for the Commission's 53rd session in March and April 1997.

Second, the original monitoring bodies differed in make-up. The ICESCR did not establish its own monitoring body. Instead, Article 16(2) required States Parties to report through the UN Secretary General to a UN Charter body, the Economic and Social Council (ECOSOC). This proved unsatisfactory, and in 1985 ECOSOC established the ESC Committee. ECOSOC elected the new Committee, composed of 18 experts serving in their personal capacity, and the Committee met for the first time in 1987.

B. The ICCPR and the ICESCR—Interrelated and Interdependent, or Stand Alone Covenants?

Some human rights advocates and scholars have proclaimed that the ICCPR, deemed by them the first generation of rights, is largely irrelevant to women, and that only the ICESCR, the second generation of rights, speaks to women's most serious concerns in the developing world: poverty, lack of adequate food and housing, access to clean water, and land ownership rights. Consider the impact of the following two cases on those issues. Can the ICCPR be used to advance women's economic rights?

Both cases concern different forms of social security insurance. These are government benefit payments financed by taxes that replace some of workers' lost wages when they are unable to work for various reasons. The payments prevent such employees from falling into deep poverty because they can no longer earn a living. Unemployment benefits replace wages when employers dismiss employees; they are not available to workers who are fired for cause. Disability benefits replace wages when an employee can no longer work due to disabilities. For example, an employee might suffer a stroke which either prevents the worker from working full-time or from working at all. Other common forms of such social security insurance include retirement benefits and survivors' benefits for dependents after a wage-earner's death.

The *Broeks* case that follows concerns unemployment insurance. Article 9 of the ICESCR requires that "States Parties . . . recognize the right of everyone to social security, including social insurance."

Broeks v. The Netherlands
(U.N. Human Rights Committee)
Communication No. 172/1984, U.N. Doc. Supp. No. 40 (A/42/40) at 139 (1987), *available at* RossRights

1.   The author of the communication (initial letter dated 1 June 1984 . . .) is Mrs. S.W.M. Broeks, a Netherlands citizen born on 14 March 1951 and living in the Netherlands. . . .

2.1   Mrs. Broeks, who was married at the time when the dispute in question arose . . . was employed as a nurse from 7 August 1972 to 1 February 1979, when she was dismissed for reasons of disability. She had become ill in 1975, and from that time she benefited from the Netherlands social security system until 1 June 1980 (as regards disability and as regards unemployment), when unemployment payments were terminated in accordance with Netherlands law [which denied unemployment benefits to a married woman—but not a married man—who was neither a breadwinner nor permanently separated from her/his spouse].

2.2   Mrs. Broeks contested the decision of the relevant Netherlands authorities to discontinue unemployment payments to her and in the course of exhausting domestic remedies invoked article 26 of the International Covenant on Civil and Political Rights, claiming that the relevant Netherlands legal provisions were contrary to the right to equality before the law and equal protection of the law without discrimination guaranteed by article 26[c] of the International Covenant on Civil and Political Rights. Legal counsel submits that domestic remedies were exhausted on 26 Novem-

---

[c] Article 26 of the ICCPR provides: "All persons are equal before the law and are entitled without any discrimination to the equal protection of the law. In this respect, the law shall prohibit any discrimination and guarantee to all persons equal and effective protection against discrimination on any ground such as race, colour, sex, language, religion, political or other opinion, national or social origin, property, birth or other status."

ber 1983, when the appropriate administrative authority, the Central Board of Appeal, confirmed a decision of a lower municipal authority not to continue unemployment payments to Mrs. Broeks.

2.3   Mrs. Broeks claims that, under . . . [the] Unemployment Benefits Act [section 13, subsection 1(1)] an unacceptable distinction has been made on the grounds of sex and status. She bases her claim on the following: if she were a man, married or unmarried, the law in question would not deprive her of unemployment benefits. Because she is a woman, and was married at the time in question, the law excludes her from continued unemployment benefits. This, she claims, makes her a victim of a violation of article 26 of the Covenant on the grounds of sex and status. She claims that article 26 of the ICCPR was meant to give protection to individuals beyond the specific civil and political rights enumerated in the Covenant. . . .

4.1   In its submission . . . the State party underlined, *inter alia*, that:

(a) "The principle that elements of discrimination in the realization of the right to social security are to be eliminated is embodied in article 9 [recognizing everyone's right to social security] in conjunction with articles 2 [barring States Parties from using sex-based distinctions in ensuring ICESCR rights] and 3 [requiring states to ensure the equal right of men and women to ICESCR rights] of the International Covenant on Economic, Social and Cultural Rights [hereinafter ICESCR];

(b) "The Government of the Kingdom of the Netherlands has accepted to implement this principle under the terms of the ICESCR. Under these terms, States parties have undertaken to take steps to the maximum of their available resources with a view to achieving progressively the full realization of the rights recognized in that Covenant (art.2, para. 1);

(c) "The process of gradual realization to the maximum of available resources is well on its way in the Netherlands. Remaining elements of discrimination in the realization of the rights are being and will be gradually eliminated;

(d) "The ICESCR has established its own system for international control of the way in which States parties are fulfilling their obligations. To this end States parties have undertaken to submit to the Economic and Social Council reports on the measures they have adopted and the progress they are making. The Government of the Kingdom of the Netherlands to this end submitted its first report in 1983."

4.2   The State party then posed the question whether the way in which the Netherlands was fulfilling its obligations under article 9 in conjunction with articles 2 and 3 of the ICESCR, could become, by way of article 26 of the ICCPR, the object of an examination by the Human Rights Committee. . . .

4.5   The State party also indicated that a change in legislation had been adopted recently in the Netherlands, eliminating [the] article [of the Unemployment Benefits Act], which was the subject of the author's claim. This is the Act of 29 April 1985, having a retroactive effect to 23 December 1984. . . .

5.1   In a memorandum dated 5 July 1985, the author commented on the State party's submission. . . .

5.2   First, the author stated that in the preambles to the ICESCR and the ICCPR an explicit connection was made between an individual's exercise of his civil and political rights and his economic, social and cultural rights. The fact that those different kinds of rights had been incorporated into two different covenants did not detract from their interdependence. It was striking, the author submitted, that in the ICCPR, apart from article 26, there were specific references on numerous occasions to the principle of equality or non-discrimination. She listed them as follows:

article 2, paragraph 1: non-discrimination with reference to the rights recognized in the Covenant;

article 3: non-discrimination on the grounds of sex with reference to the rights recognized in the Covenant;

article 14: equality before the courts;

article 23, paragraph 4: equal rights of spouses;

article 24, paragraph 1: equal rights of children to protective measures;

article 25, and under (c): equal right to vote and equal access to government service.

5.3   Further, the author stated that article 26 of the Covenant was explicitly not confined to equal treatment with reference to certain rights, but stipulated a general principle of equality. . . .

5.4   The author recalled that during the discussion by the Human Rights Committee, at its fourteenth session, of the Netherlands report submitted in compliance with article 40 of the Covenant . . . it had been assumed by the Netherlands Government that article 26 of the Covenant also applied in the field of economic, social and cultural rights. . . . [The representative] had stated . . . that by virtue of national, constitutional law "direct application of article 26 in the area of social, economic and cultural rights depended on the character of the regulations or policy. . . . [I]n his opinion, article 26 of the Covenant was applicable to those rights and the only relevant question in terms of internal, constitutional law in the Netherlands (sects. 93 and 94 of the Constitution) was whether in such instances article 26 was self-executing and could be applied by the courts. . . .

5.5   The author further stated that in various national constitutional systems of countries which have acceded to the Covenant, generally formulated principles of equality could be found which were also regarded as being applicable in the field of economic, social and cultural rights. Thus, in the Netherlands Constitution, partly inspired, the author submitted, by article 26 of the Covenant, a generally formulated prohibition of discrimination (sect. 1) was laid down which was irrefutably regarded in the Netherlands as being applicable to economic, social and cultural rights as well. The only reason, she submitted, why the present issue had not been settled at a national level by virtue of section 1 of the Constitution was because the courts were forbidden to test legislation, such as that being dealt with currently, against the Constitution (sect. 120 of the Constitution). The courts, she stated, were allowed to test legislation against self-executing provisions of international conventions.

5.6   The author submitted that judicial practice in the Netherlands had been consistent in applying article 26 of the Covenant also in cases where economic, social and cultural rights had been at stake, for example:

(a) Afdeling Rechtspraak van de Raad van State (Judicial Division of the Council of State), 29-1-1981. This case involved discrimination on the grounds of sex with reference to housing. An appeal under article 26 of the Covenant in conjunction with article 11, paragraph 1, of the ICESCR was founded.

(b) Gerechtschof's Gravenhage (Court of Appeal at the Hague), 17 June 1982. Again with regard to housing, an appeal was made under article 26 of the Covenant and was granted. . . .

(d) Centrale Raad van Beroep (Central Board of Appeal), 1 November 1983. In this case, which constitutes the basis for the petition to the Human Rights Committee, the Central Board of Appeal considered "that article 26 is not applicable only to the civil and political rights which are recognized by the Covenant". The appeal under article 26 was subsequently rejected for other reasons.

(e) Board of Appeal, Groningen, 2 May 1985. On the basis of article 26 of the Covenant among other things a discriminatory provision in the General Disablement Benefits Act was declared null and void.

5.7   The author further submitted that the question of equal treatment in the field of economic, social and cultural rights was not fundamentally different from the problem of equality with regard to freedom to express one's opinion or the freedom of association, in other words with regard to civil and political rights. The fact was, she argued, that in both cases it was not a question of the level at which social security had been set or the degree to which freedom of opinion was guaranteed, but purely and simply whether equal treatment or the prohibition of discrimination was respected. . . . The only relevant question, she submitted, was whether unequal treatment was compatible with article 26 of the Covenant. A contrary interpretation of article 26, the author argued, would turn that article into a completely superfluous provision, for then it would not differ from article 2, paragraph 1[D], of the Covenant. . . .

5.9   The author further recalled that the State party was of the opinion that the alleged violation could also fall under article 9 of the ICESCR in conjunction with articles 2 and 3 of the same Covenant. Although that question was not relevant in the case in point, the author submitted, it was obvious that certain issues were related to provisions in both Covenants. Although civil and political rights on the one hand and economic and social and cultural rights on the other had been incorporated for technical reasons into two different Covenants, it was a fact, the author submitted, that those rights were highly interdependent. That interdependence, she argued, had not only emerged in the preamble to both Covenants, but was also once again underlined in General Assembly resolution 543 (VI), in which it had been decided to draw up two covenants: "the enjoyment of civic and political freedoms and of economic, social and cultural rights are interconnected and interdependent". . . .

5.10   In her opinion, the author added, the State party seemed to wish to say that the Human Rights Committee was not competent to take note of the present com-

---

[D] Article 2(1) of the ICCPR provides: "Each State Party to the present Covenant undertakes to respect and to ensure to all individuals within its territory and subject to its jurisdiction the rights recognized in the present Covenant, without distinction of any kind, such as race, colour, sex, language, religion, political or other opinion, national or social origin, property, birth or other status."

plaint because the matter could also be brought up as part of the supervisory [reporting] procedure under the ICESCR (*see* art. 16–22). That assertion, the author contended, was not valid because the reporting procedure under the ICESCR could not be regarded as "another procedure of international investigation or settlement" in the sense of article 5, paragraph 2 (a) of the Optional Protocol . . . .[E]

8.2   In discussing the merits of the case, the State party elucidates first the factual background as follows:

When Mrs. Broeks applied for [unemployment] benefits in February 1980, section 13, subsection 1 (1), was still applicable. This section laid down that [unemployment] benefits could not be claimed by married women who were neither breadwinners nor permanently separated from their husbands. . . . Whether a married woman was deemed to be a breadwinner depended, *inter alia*, on the absolute amount of the family's total income and on what proportion of it was contributed by the wife. That the conditions for granting benefits laid down in section 13, subsection 1 (1) applied solely to married women and not to married men is due to the fact that the provision in question corresponded to the then prevailing views in society in general concerning the roles of men and women within marriage and society. Virtually all married men who had jobs could be regarded as their family's breadwinner, so that it was unnecessary to check whether they met this criterion for the granting of benefits upon becoming unemployed. These views have gradually changed in later years.

The Netherlands is a member State of the European Economic Community[F] (EEC). On 19 December 1978 the Council of the European Communities issued a directive on the progressive implementation of the principle of equal treatment for men and women in matters of social security (79/7/EEC), giving member States a period of six years, until 23 December 1984, within which to make any amendments to legislation which might be necessary in order to bring it into line with the directive. Pursuant to this directive the Netherlands Government examined the criterion for the granting of benefits laid down in section 13, subsection 1 (1), in the light of the principle of equal treatment of men and women and in the light of the changing role patterns of the sexes in the years since about 1960.

Since it could no longer be assumed as a matter of course in the early 1980s that married men with jobs should always be regarded as "breadwinners," the Netherlands amended [section 13, subection 1 (1)] to meet its obligations under the EEC directive. . . . [I]t became possible for married women who were not breadwinners to claim [unemployment] benefits. . . .

In view of changes in the status of women—and particularly married women—in recent decades, the failure to award Mrs. Broeks [unemployment] benefits in 1979 is explicable in historical terms. If she were to apply for such benefits now, the result would be different.

8.3   With regard to the scope of article 26 of the Covenant, the State party argues, inter alia, as follows:

The Netherlands Government takes the view that article 26 of the Covenant does entail an obligation to avoid discrimination, but that this article can only be invoked under the Optional Protocol to the Covenant in the sphere of civil and political rights, not necessarily limited to those civil and political rights that are embodied in the Covenant. The Government could, for

---

[E] Article 5(2) of the Optional Protocol provides: "The Committee shall not consider any communication from an individual unless it is ascertained that . . . [t]he same matter is not being examined under another procedure of international investigation or settlement. . . ."

[F] The EEC was a predecessor to the European Community (EC), which forms part of the European Union (EU).

instance, envisage the admissibility under the Optional Protocol of a complaint concerning discrimination in the field of taxation. But it cannot accept the admissibility of a complaint concerning the enjoyment of economic, social and cultural rights. The latter category of rights is the object of a separate United Nations Covenant. Mrs. Broeks' complaint relates to rights in the sphere of social security, which fall under the ICESCR. Articles 2 [prohibiting discrimination of any kind in realization of ICESCR rights], 3 [requiring states to ensure equal right of men and women to ICESCR rights] and 9 [recognizing universal right to social security] of that Covenant are of particular relevance here. That Covenant has its own specific system and its own specific organ for international monitoring of how State parties meet their obligations and deliberately does not provide for an individual complaints procedure. . . .

The Netherlands Government reports to the Economic and Social Council on matters concerning the way it is fulfilling its obligations with respect to the right to social security, in accordance with the relevant rules of the ICESCR. . . .

If article 26 of the ICCPR were deemed applicable to complaints concerning discriminatory elements in national legislation in the field of [other] conventions [such as CEDAW], this could surely not be taken to mean that a State party would be required to have eliminated all possible discriminatory elements from its legislation in those fields at the time of ratification of the Covenant. Years of work are required in order to examine the whole complex of national legislation in search of discriminatory elements. The search can never be completed, either, as distinctions in legislation which are justifiable in the light of social views and conditions prevailing when they are first made may become disputable as changes occur in the views held in society. . . .

8.4   With regard to the principle of equality laid down in article 26 of the Covenant in relation to section 13, subsection 1 (1), in its unamended form, the State party explains the legislative history of [the Unemployment Benefits Act] and in particular the social justification of the "breadwinner" concept. . . . [W]ith the "breadwinner" concept,

a proper balance was achieved between the limited availability of public funds (which makes it necessary to put them to limited, well-considered and selective use) on the one hand and the Government's obligation to provide social security on the other. The Government does not accept that the 'breadwinner' concept as such was 'discriminatory' in the sense that equal cases were treated in an unequal way by law.

Moreover, it is argued that the provisions of [the Unemployment Benefits Act]

are based on reasonable social and economic considerations which are not discriminatory in origin. The restriction making the provision in question inapplicable to men was inspired not by any desire to discriminate in favour of men and against women but by the *de facto* social and economic situation which existed at the time when the Act was passed and which would have made it pointless to declare the provision applicable to men. At the time when Mrs. Broeks applied for unemployment benefits the *de facto* situation was not essentially different. There was therefore no violation of article 26 of the Covenant. This is not altered by the fact that a new social trend has been growing in recent years, which has made it undesirable for the provision to remain in force in the present social context . . . .

8.5   With reference to the decision of the Central Board of Appeal of 26 November 1983, which the author criticizes, the State party contends that:

The observation of the Central Board of Appeal that the Covenants employ different international control systems is highly relevant. Not only do parties to the Covenants report to different United Nations bodies but, above all, there is a major difference between the Covenants as regards the possibility of complaints by States or individuals, which exists only under the ICCPR. The contracting parties deliberately chose to make this difference in international monitoring systems, because the nature and substance of social, economic and cultural rights make them unsuitable for judicial review of a complaint lodged by a State party or an individual.

9.1   In her comments, dated 19 June 1986, the author reiterates that "article 26 [o]f the Covenant is explicitly not confined to equal treatment with reference to certain rights, but stipulates a general principle of equality."

9.2   With regard to the State party's argument that it would be incompatible with the aims of both the Covenants and the Optional Protocol if an individual complaint with respect to the rights of social security, as referred to in article 9 of the ICESCR[,] could be dealt with by the Human Rights Committee, the author contends that this argument is ill-founded, because she is not complaining about the level of social security or other issues relating to article 9 of the ICESCR, but rather she claims to be a victim of unequal treatment prohibited by article 26 of the ICCPR. . . .

10.   The Human Rights Committee [finds] . . . [t]he facts of the case are not in dispute.

11.   Article 26 of the Covenant on Civil and Political Rights provides:

All persons are equal before the law and are entitled without any discrimination to the equal protection of the law. In this respect, the law shall prohibit any discrimination and guarantee to all persons equal and effective protection against discrimination on any ground such as race, colour, sex, language, religion, political or other opinion, national or social origin, property, birth or other status.

12.1   The State party contends that there is considerable overlapping of the provisions of article 26 with the provisions of article 2[G] of ICESCR. The Committee is of the view that the ICCPR would still apply even if a particular subject-matter is referred to or covered in other international instruments, for example, . . . the ICESCR. Notwithstanding the interrelated drafting history of the two Covenants, it remains necessary for the Committee to apply fully the terms of the ICCPR. . . .

12.2   The Committee has also examined the contention of the State party that article 26 of the ICCPR cannot be invoked in respect of a right which is specifically

---

[G] Article 2 of the ICESCR provides:

"1. Each State Party to the present Covenant undertakes to take steps, individually and through international assistance and co-operation, especially economic and technical, to the maximum of its available resources, with a view to achieving progressively the full realization of the rights recognized in the present Covenant by all appropriate means, including particularly the adoption of legislative measures.

2. The States Parties to the present Covenant undertake to guarantee that the rights enunciated in the present Covenant will be exercised without discrimination of any kind as to race, colour, sex, language, religion, political or other opinion, national or social origin, property, birth or other status.

3. Developing countries, with due regard to human rights and their national economy, may determine to what extent they would guarantee the economic rights recognized in the present Covenant to non-nationals."

provided for under article 9 of the ICESCR (social security, including social insurance). In so doing, the Committee has perused the relevant *travaux préparatoires* of the ICCPR, namely, the summary records of the discussions that took place in the Commission on Human Rights in 1948, 1949, 1950 and 1952 and in the Third Committee of the General Assembly in 1961, which provide a "supplementary means of interpretation" (art. 32 of the Vienna Convention on the Law of Treaties).[H] The discussions, at the time of drafting, concerning the question whether the scope of article 26 extended to rights not otherwise guaranteed by the Covenant, were inconclusive and cannot alter the conclusion arrived at by the ordinary means of interpretation referred to in paragraph 12.3 below.

12.3   For the purpose of determining the scope of article 26, the Committee has taken into account the "ordinary meaning" of each element of the article in its context and in the light of its object and purpose (art. 31 of the Vienna Convention on the Law of Treaties). The Committee begins by noting that article 26 does not merely duplicate the guarantees already provided for in article 2. It derives from the principle of equal protection of the law without discrimination, as contained in article 7 of the Universal Declaration of Human Rights, which prohibits discrimination in law or in practice in any field regulated and protected by public authorities. Article 26 is thus concerned with the obligations imposed on States in regard to their legislation and the application thereof.

12.4   Although article 26 requires that legislation should prohibit discrimination, it does not of itself contain any obligation with respect to the matters that may be provided for by legislation. Thus it does not, for example, require any State to enact legislation to provide for social security. However, when such legislation is adopted in the exercise of a State's sovereign power, then such legislation must comply with article 26 of the Covenant.

12.5   The Committee observes in this connection that what is at issue is not whether or not social security should be progressively established in the Netherlands but whether the legislation providing for social security violates the prohibition against discrimination contained in article 26 of the ICCPR and the guarantee given therein to all persons regarding equal and effective protection against discrimination.

13.   The right to equality before the law and to equal protection of the law without any discrimination does not make all differences of treatment discriminatory. A differentiation based on reasonable and objective criteria does not amount to prohibited discrimination within the meaning of article 26.

14.   It therefore remains for the Committee to determine whether the differentiation in Netherlands law at the time in question and as applied to Mrs. Broeks constituted discrimination within the meaning of article 26. The Committee notes that in Netherlands law the provisions of articles 84 and 85 of the Netherlands Civil Code impose equal rights and obligations on both spouses with regard to their joint income. Under section 13, subsection 1 (1), of the Unemployment Benefits Act, a

---

[H] The French term *travaux préparatoires*, meaning "preparatory works," is the international law term equivalent to the use of "legislative history" in the domestic law context.

married woman, in order to receive [unemployment] benefits, had to prove that she was a "breadwinner"—a condition that did not apply to married men. Thus a differentiation which appears at one level to be one of status is in fact one of sex, placing married women at a disadvantage compared with married men. Such a differentiation is not reasonable; and this seems to have been effectively acknowledged even by the State party by the enactment of a change in the law on 29 April 1985, with retroactive effect to 23 December 1984.

15.   The circumstances in which Mrs. Broeks found herself at the material time and the application of the then valid Netherlands law made her a victim of a violation, based on sex, of article 26 of the ICCPR, because she was denied a social security benefit on an equal footing with men.

16.   The Committee notes that the State party had not intended to discriminate against women and further notes with appreciation that the discriminatory provisions in the law applied to Mrs. Broeks have, subsequently, been eliminated. Although the State party has thus taken the necessary measures to put an end to the kind of discrimination suffered by Mrs. Broeks at the time complained of, the Committee is of the view that the State party should offer Mrs. Broeks an appropriate remedy.

NOTES

The Breadwinner Test. In paragraph 8.2, the breadwinner test is described as depending "on the absolute amount of the family's total income and on what proportion of it was contributed by the wife." Typically, such tests require that the wife produce at least 75% of the family's income. For example, if the total family income were $24,000, she would have to earn at least $18,000 and her husband no more than $6000. The government asserted that almost all married men were family breadwinners so it was "unnecessary to check whether they met this criterion." *Id.* But contrary to the stereotype, men often do not meet this standard. The U.S. Supreme Court has found numerous state and federal laws using the same breadwinner test a violation of the Fourteenth Amendment guarantee of the "equal protection of the law." It invalidated these provisions and required the relevant government to extend the benefit to the women employees disqualified by the test or to the deceased working wives' survivors. *See Frontiero v. Richardson*, 411 U.S. 677 (1973) (female air force lieutenant earning more than 50% of family income but not 75% granted enhanced housing allowance and medical benefits automatically provided to married men; U.S. government administrative convenience rationale for not applying the breadwinner test to air force husbands was not sufficiently "important" to justify the sex-based distinction); *Califano v. Goldfarb*, 430 U.S. 199 (1977) (automatic Social Security surviving spouse benefit for all married male workers but only for married women earning 75% of family income; actual cost to government of not screening male workers for test was $750,000,000 per year extra paid to surviving widows who were **not** dependent on their deceased working husbands' incomes, far more than the amount saved by not screening male workers as a matter of "administrative convenience"); *Wengler v. Druggists Mut. Ins. Co.*, 446 U.S. 142 (1980) (same as to state benefit). In *Wengler*, the Court noted that the Missouri worker's compensation statute discriminated "against working women" and "against men who survive their employed wives dying in work-related accidents." Consider your own life situation. Do you earn more than 75% of family income? Does your spouse?

The Dutch government made the argument that as of 1980, when Mrs. Broeks applied for her benefits, it was "unnecessary" to check male workers with the breadwinner test. Seen in light of the *Goldfarb* facts, that seems unlikely. *Goldfarb* also demonstrates the importance of solid litigation preparation for equal protection litigation. Lawyers used civil discovery procedures to learn from the government the actual cost of the extra payments to non-dependent surviving wives. The facts they discovered gave strength to their argument and disclosed that the government's cost hypothesis, based on stereotypical images of breadwinner husbands and dependent wives, was actually false.

Using Article 26 of the ICCPR to Advance Women's Economic Status. Because the HR Committee decided that Article 26 can be applied to **any** state law that discriminates on the basis of sex, it can be an invaluable tool for helping women gain greater economic resources. In *Broeks*, a large group of working women gained valuable unemployment benefits. What economic rights did women gain in *Ato del Avellanal v. Peru*, Chapter Two?

Advancing Women's Equal Right to Housing and Land. Notice that another key economic issue was at stake in the Dutch national litigation discussed in paragraph 5.6. Article 11 of the ICESCR requires that "States Parties . . . recognize the right of everyone to an adequate standard of living for himself [or herself] and his [or her] family, including adequate food, clothes and housing. . . ." Many other laws deprive women of equal access to important economic rights. For example, many African and Asian countries have laws denying women the right to own or inherit land. Seen in this light, the ICCPR can be used to help women gain "second-generation" rights. Indeed, the distinction between generations of rights seems more academic than real.

The Committee's Test. *See* paragraphs 13 and 14 for yet another formulation of the Committee's test for equal protection analysis. What is new? How is it applied in this case? What is the decisive factor? Would you find it helpful as a litigator trying to decide how to frame an argument? Or as a judge trying to apply the text to another law based on sex?

The Committee's General Comment 18 and the *VMI* test. This General Comment was adopted in 1989. Read articles 6–8, 10, 12, and 13, *available at* RossRights. In article 13, yet another test is proposed. This is the final HR Committee test. How does it compare with the *VMI* test, Chapter Two? If you were to apply the *VMI* test to the *Broeks* hypothetical, what questions would you ask and how would you answer them? How do the other General Comment 18 assigned articles compare to the *VMI* test?

CEDAW. If the Committee had considered CEDAW, which provisions could it have used? Which would be most persuasive?

Self-Executing Treaties. Paragraphs 5.4 and 5.5 discuss the question of whether Article 26 of the ICCPR is self-executing. A treaty that is self-executing can be used by national courts without having a new law passed to implement the treaty. A treaty that is non-self-executing requires the legislature to first enact an implementing law before the courts may use the treaty, via the new statute. Whether a treaty is self-executing or not depends on domestic law. Although many state ratifying bodies (the executive, the legislature, or both) make statements concerning whether the treaty is self-executing or not as part of the process of issuing reservations or declarations to the ratification document, ultimately it is the national courts which decide the issue. Chapter Ten will discuss this issue in more depth.

Notice again the importance of litigation preparation. The lawyer's research demonstrated that national courts had already applied Article 26 as a self-executing provision, greatly strengthening the argument. *See* paragraph 5.6.

II. Applying Equal Protection to Different Sex-Based Statutes.

A. Disability and Surviving Widow Benefits

Vos v. The Netherlands
(U.N. Human Rights Committee)
Communication No. 218/1986, U.N. Doc. Supp. No. 40 (A/44/40) at 232 (1989), *available at* RossRights

1.   The author of the communication (initial letter dated 23 December 1986 . . .) is Hendrika S. Vos, a citizen of the Netherlands, residing in that country. She claims to be a victim of a violation of article 26 [equal protection of the law] of the International Covenant on Civil and Political Rights by the Government of the Netherlands. . . .

2.1   The author states that since 1 October 1976 she had received an allowance . . . under the General Disablement Benefits Act [Disability Act], but that in May 1979, following the death of her ex-husband (from whom she had been divorced in 1957), payment of the disability allowance was discontinued . . . because she then became entitled to a payment under the General Widows and Orphans Act [Widows Act]. Under the latter, she receives some 90 guilders per month less than she had been receiving under [the Disability Act]. . . . [Before the Netherlands courts, Vos unsuccessfully challenged the cut-off of her disability allowance.]

2.3   The author had argued before the Netherlands Courts that, whereas a disabled man whose (former) wife dies retains the right to a disability allowance, article 32 of [the Disability Act] makes an improper distinction according to sex, in that a disabled woman whose (former) husband dies does not retain the right to a disability allowance. Section 1 (b) of this article provides:

1. The employment disability benefit will be withdrawn when: . . .
    (b) a woman, to whom this benefit has been granted, becomes entitled to a widow's pension or a temporary widow's benefit in compliance with the General Widows and Orphans Law.

In her specific case she claimed that the application of the law was particularly unjust because she had been divorced from her husband for 22 years and had been providing for her own support when she became disabled. Thus she claims that she should be treated primarily as a disabled persons and not as a widow. . . .

2.5   The author claims that the [Netherlands] Central Appeals Court incorrectly interpreted the scope of article 26 of the International Covenant on Civil and Political Rights and asks the Committee to find that the cessation of the payment of her [disability] allowance was a form of discrimination based on sex and marital status in contravention of article 26 of the Covenant. . . .

8.2   . . . [T]he State party elucidates . . . the relevant Netherlands legislation as follows:

8.3   ". . . The aim of national insurance schemes is to insure all residents of the Netherlands against the financial consequences of certain contingencies. The national insurance schemes concerning survivors, old age and long-term disability guarantee payment of a benefit related to the statutory minimum wage. The entitlements concerned . . . are set at such a level that, after tax and social insurance premiums have been deducted from them, net benefits are sufficient to enable the beneficiary to subsist."

8.4   "The [1975 Disability Act] created a national insurance scheme concerning long-term disability; under the terms of the Act, anybody who has been disabled for longer than one year is entitled to a basic benefit. If the beneficiary was employed full-time before becoming unfit for work, full benefit is paid (equivalent to the subsistence minimum). . . .

8.5   "The [1956 Widows Act] created a national insurance scheme which entitles widows and orphans to receive benefit related to the statutory minimum wage if their husband or father dies. The rationale underlying the Act is that after a married man dies his widow may well have insufficient means of subsistence. At the time when the Act was passed, it was felt that, if there were good reasons why the widow should not be expected to earn her own living (for example, because she still had children to look after, or because she was too old), it was desirable to pay her benefit. In some cases, women are eligible for the [Widows] benefit even if they have been divorced from the deceased."

8.6   "At the time when the General Widows and Orphans Act was passed, it was customary for husbands to act as bread-winners for their families, and it was therefore desirable to make financial provision for dependents in the event of the bread-winner's premature death. In recent years more married women have been going out to work and households consisting of unmarried people have increasingly been granted the same status as traditional families. This being so, the Government has been studying since the early 1980s ways of amending the [Widows Act]; one of the questions being examined is whether the privileged position enjoyed by women under the Act is still justified nowadays."

8.7   "It is too early to say what provisions future Surviving Dependants Acts will contain. As the Netherlands is a member of the European Community, it will in all events comply with the obligations arising from a European Community Directive which is currently in preparation concerning sexual equality with regard to provision for survivors; it is expected to be many years before the directive enters force. However, it is possible that the Netherlands Government may make proposals for new legislation on survivors before the European Community directive is finalized."

8.8   "In a social security system, it is necessary to ensure that individuals do not qualify for more that one benefit simultaneously under different social insurance acts, when each such benefit is intended to provide a full income at subsistence level. . . . The legislature had to decide whether claimants who were entitled to benefits under both the [Disability Act] and the [Widows Act] should receive benefits under the one or under the other, and it was decided that in such cases the [Widows Act] benefit should be paid. The decision to opt for a rule on concurrence as laid down in [the Widows Act] is based, *inter alia*, on practical considerations with a view to the implementation of the legislation. It is necessary, for example, to avoid the necessity of entering the person concerned in the records of two different bodies responsible for paying benefits and to avoid having to levy income tax in arrears on income from two separate sources."

8.9   "From the point of view of widows, it is generally speaking, more advantageous to receive [the Widows Act benefit] than [the Disability Act benefit]; if the legislature had decided that the [Disability Act] benefit should have precedence over the [Widows Act] benefit, many widows would have been worse off, because in most cases the [Widows Act] benefit exceeds the [Disability Act] benefit payable to married women. This is because most married women have worked part-time and therefore receive only a partial [disability] benefit in the event of long-term disability. This is not to say that the rule on concurrence which gives precedence to the [Widows Act] is always advantageous to all widows: it merely benefits the majority of them. Cases are conceivable in which the award of the [Widows Act] benefit instead of the [Disability Act] benefit leads to a slight fall in income. This is evidently so in the case of Mrs. Vos."

8.10   "However, the fact that in a particular case, the application of article 23, subsection 1 (b), of [the Disability Act] leads to a disadvantageous result for a particular individual is irrelevant for purposes of assessing whether a form of discrimination has occurred which is prohibited by article 26 of the International Covenant on Civil and Political Rights. . . ."

9.1   With regard to the author's specific complaint in relation to article 26 of the Covenant, the State party contests the contention of Mrs. Vos

that [the Disability Act] discriminates unjustifiably between the sexes because a disabled man whose wife (divorced or otherwise) dies retains his right to disablement benefit whereas a disabled woman whose husband (divorced or otherwise) dies forfeits hers. The difference in position between a disabled widow and a disabled widower can be explained as follows. The provision which is made for survivors is not available to men, and the problem of overlapping of benefits therefore does not arise. Precisely on account of the fact that a disabled man cannot be eligible for [Widows Act] benefit and that the death of his wife therefore does not affect his [Disability Act] benefit, it is impossible to compare the rules of concurrence.

9.2   "By way of illustration of the relative discrimination in favour of women which is inherent in the [Widows Act], the Netherlands Government would observe that the favourable treatment which women receive in the Netherlands under [the Widows Act] has led some people to suggest that the Act discriminates against men. This is one of the reasons why a review of the [Widows Act] is under consideration. . . ."

11.3   The Committee . . . observes that . . . the right to equality before the law and to equal protection of the law without any discrimination does not make all differences of treatment discriminatory. A differentiation based on reasonable and objective criteria does not amount to prohibited discrimination within the meaning of article 26. Further, differences in result of the uniform application of laws do not *per se* constitute prohibited discrimination.

12.   It remains for the Committee to determine whether the disadvantageous treatment complained of by the author resulted from the application of a discriminatory statute and thus violated her rights under article 26 of the Covenant. In the light of the explanations given by the State party with respect to the legislative history, the purpose and application of the General Disablement Benefits Act and the General Widows and Orphans Act, the Committee is of the view that the unfavourable result complained of by Mrs. Vos follows from the application of a uniform rule to avoid overlapping in the allocation of social security benefits. This rule is based on objective and reasonable criteria, especially bearing in mind that both statutes under which Mrs. Vos qualified for benefits aim at ensuring to all persons falling thereunder subsistence level income. Thus the Committee cannot conclude that Mrs. Vos has been a victim of discrimination within the meaning of article 26 of the Covenant.

13.   The Human Rights Committee . . . is of the view that the facts as submitted do not disclose a violation of any article of the International Covenant on Civil and Political Rights.

Appendix

Individual opinion: submitted by MESSRS. FRANCISCO AGUILAR URBINA and BERTIL WENNERGREN. . . .

4.   . . . The State party contends that the legislature had to decide whether claimants who were entitled to benefits under both the [Disability Act] and the [Widows Act] should receive benefits under the one or the other. This is conceivable, but it is not justifiable that this necessarily should be solved by the introduction of a clause which does not allow for a modicum of flexibility in its implementation. An exception should, in our opinion, be made with regard to women who enjoy full [disability] benefits, if such benefits exceed [widows] benefits. By failing to make such an exception, the legislature has created a situation in which disabled women with full [disability] benefits who become widows can no longer be treated on par with other women who enjoy full [disability] benefits. The case cannot be considered as affecting only Mrs. Vos, but rather an intermediate group of persons who fall in the category of disabled women entitled to full disability pensions. Moreover, the intention of the legislator to grant maximum protection to those in need would be violated every time the law is applied in the strict formal sense as it has been applied in Mrs. Vos's case. The increasing number of cases such as this one can be inferred from the asser-

tion made by the State party that it has seen the need to change the legislation since the early 1980s.

5.   A differentiation with regard to full [disability] benefits among disabled women on the sole ground of marital status as widows cannot be said to be based on reasonable and objective criteria. It therefore constitutes prohibited discrimination within the meaning of article 26. We note that a review of [the Widows Act] is under consideration and hope that the discriminatory elements will be eliminated and compensation given to those who have been the victims of unequal treatment.

N O T E S

Purpose and Fit. What would you identify as the Dutch government's purpose in providing these benefits? How can one figure out what a government's purpose is? In what ways are the laws over-inclusive or under-inclusive in achieving their purposes?

Can One Discrimination Justify Another? It is not nature that places men and women in different places with regard to the cutoff of disability benefits. Rather, the legislature has placed them in different situations by providing survivors' benefits only to surviving female spouses. What are your reactions?

The Committee's Test, CEDAW, and *VMI*. How is the Committee's test applied in this case? *See* paragraphs 11.3 and 12. What could CEDAW contribute? How would the analysis proceed under *VMI*?

Discrimination Against Men. Should discrimination against men be prohibited? Is it under the ICCPR? CEDAW? *VMI*? Does discrimination against men hurt women?

B. Civic Duty: Challenges to Sex-Based Exclusions from Jury Service

Ponsamy Poongavanam v. Mauritius
(U.N. Human Rights Committee)
Communication No. 567/1993, U.N. Doc. CCPR/C/51/D/567/1993 (1993), *available at* RossRights

The Human Rights Committee . . . adopts the following:

Decision on Admissibility

1.   The author of the communication is Ponsamy Poongavanam, a citizen of Mauritius currently detained at the prison of Beau Bassin, Mauritius. He claims to be a victim of violations by Mauritius of articles 2 [barring sex distinctions in ICCPR rights], 3 [equal ICCPR rights for men and women], . . . 25(c) [equal access to participate in public service] and 26 [equal protection of the law] of the International Covenant on Civil and Political Rights.

The Facts as Submitted by the Author:

2.1   On 28 March 1987, the author was convicted of murder and sentenced to death in the Assizes Court of Mauritius. He was tried before a judge and a jury of nine men, whose verdict was unanimous. He appealed to the Court of Appeal of Mauritius. . . .

2.2 The author then applied for leave to appeal to the Judicial Committee of the Privy Council; leave was granted . . . on a ground . . . that the author's conviction should have been quashed because the trial was unconstitutional, having regard to the composition of the jury, which had been composed of men only. On 6 April 1992, the Judicial Committee dismissed the author's petition on its merits.

2.3 The author subsequently requested the President of Mauritius to exercise his prerogative of mercy. On 29 April 1992, the death sentence was commuted to 20 years' imprisonment, without possibility of parole. Leave was granted to apply to the Supreme Court of Mauritius for constitutional redress. On 16 March 1993, the author's constitutional motion was dismissed. With this, the author submits, all available domestic remedies have been exhausted.

The Complaint:

3.1 The author challenges the compatibility with the Covenant of Section 42(2) of the Courts Act and Section 2 of the Jury Act (as they applied prior to 1990). At the time of conviction (March 1987), the Jury Act provided as follows:

Every male citizen of Mauritius who has resided in Mauritius at any time at least one full year, and who is between the ages of 21 and 65, shall be qualified and liable to serve as a juror. . . .

In 1990, the Jury Act, was amended to allow women to have access to trial juries. The Courts Act has not been amended in the same way.

3.2 The author claims that Section 42 of the Courts Act, which provides for a jury "consisting of nine men qualified as provided in the Jury Act" violates article 3[1] of the Covenant, as it is discriminatory *vis-à-vis* women, who remain in practice excluded from jury service.

3.3 It is further submitted that article 25(c) of the Covenant was violated, as Mauritian women did not and in practice do not have access, on general terms of equality, to public service, service in a trial jury being interpreted as constituting public service.

3.4 The author contends that the State party violated article 26 of the Covenant, as the exclusion of women from jury service in fact means that their equality before the law is not guaranteed. . . .

3.6 . . . As to the representativity of the jury, the Judicial Committee carefully analyzed the applicable common law and United States jurisprudence on the subject. It concluded that there was ". . . no basis for concluding that before the enactment of the legislative change in 1990 . . . (which appears to have been promoting rather

---

[1] Article 3 of the ICCPR provides: "The States parties to the present Convention undertake to ensure the equal right of men and women to the enjoyment of all civil and political rights set forth in the Covenant."

than following a change in public opinion on the matter) the exclusion of women from juries in Mauritius had ceased to have objective justification." . . .

Issues and Proceedings Before the Committee:

4.1   Before considering any claims contained in a communication, the Human Rights Committee must . . . decide whether or not it is admissible under the Optional Protocol to the Covenant.

4.2   The Committee has noted the author's claim that he is a victim of violations by Mauritius of articles 3, 25(c) and 26, because women were excluded from jury service at the time of his trial. The author has failed to show, however, how the absence of women on the jury actually prejudiced the enjoyment of his rights under the Covenant. Therefore, he cannot claim to be a "victim" within the meaning of article 1 of the Optional Protocol. . . .

5.   The Human Rights Committee therefore decides:

(a) that the communication is inadmissible under articles 1, 2 and 3 of the Optional Protocol;

(b) that this decision shall be transmitted to the author of the communication and, for information, to the State party.

N O T E

Women's Absence from Juries. Do you agree that the victim suffered no harm from women's absence on the jury? Do women suffer harm from being excluded from juries? Consider CEDAW, Article 5. If the Committee considered that article, would it change the Committee's views? In 1961, the U.S. Supreme Court upheld the effective exclusion of women from Florida juries under a Florida statute. The case involved a battered wife convicted of murdering her husband by an all-male jury. *Hoyt v. Florida,* 368 U.S. 57 (1961). Over 30 years later, the Court reversed itself and ruled that the Equal Protection Clause protected the right of both men and women not to be discriminated against in jury selection. *J.E.B. v. Alabama ex rel. T.B.,* 511 U.S. 127 (1994), involved a woman who became pregnant after an affair with a married man who had promised to marry her but jilted her instead. A local prosecutor sought child support for her and systematically removed all but one man from the jury pool through peremptory challenges (dismissal without having to give reasons). While the defense attorney struck women, the jury that emerged was 100% female and it found the man liable for support. He appealed on the ground that striking men from the jury denied him equal protection. The Court rejected the man's claim that women jurors would be inherently more sympathetic to the woman as "the very stereotype the law condemns." But the Court ruled that sex-based exclusion "from participation in the jury process" must be condemned because citizens will not perceive the system as fair, but will think "the deck has been stacked" in favor of one side. "Striking individual jurors on the assumption that they hold particular views simply because of their gender" also injured the juror's "dignity." Justice Sandra Day O'Connor concurred but wrote,

"[O]ne need not be a sexist to share the intuition that in certain cases a person's gender and resulting life experience will be relevant to his or her view of the case."

Do you agree that it was unfair for women to be excluded from the all-male jury that convicted Gwendolyn Hoyt of murdering her husband? Or for men to be excluded from the all-female jury that found a man liable for child support? If the Committee had applied the *J.E.B.* standard in *Ponsamy Poongavanam v. Mauritius*, how would it have ruled?

C. Civic Duty: Challenges to Gender-Based Exclusions from Taxation

J.H.W. v. The Netherlands
(U.N. Human Rights Committee)
Communication No. 501/1992, U.N. Doc.CCPR/C/48/D/501/1992 (1993),
available at RossRights

Decision on Admissibility

1.   The author of the communication, dated 5 May 1992, is J.H.W., a Dutch citizen born on 3 October 1919, presently residing in Wassenaar, the Netherlands. He claims to be a victim of a violation by the Netherlands of article 26 [equal protection of the law] . . . [in conjunction with] article 2, paragraph 3 [requiring states to ensure adequate remedies for violation of ICCPR rights], of the International Covenant on Civil and Political Rights. He is represented by Counsel.

The Facts as Submitted by the Author:

2.1   The author states that, under the General Child Benefit Act contributions are levied on the same basis as wage and income tax. These contributions are used to fund the benefits payable under the Act to assist parents in the maintenance of their children. Contributions have to be paid up to the age of 65, regardless whether one will ever apply for a benefit under the Act or not. However, an exemption was made . . . for unmarried childless women over the age of 45. The exemption was based on the expectation that these women would be childless. No similar exemption was made for unmarried childless men over the age of 45. The exemption for women was subsequently withdrawn in 1989.

2.2   On 30 August 1986, the author received notice of the assessment concerning his contributions under several social security acts, including the Child Benefit Act, covering the period from 1 January 1984 to 3 October 1984. He objected to the assessment, whereupon the tax inspector decided to reduce his assessed contributions. An amount (10,160 guilders in total) remained to be paid, however. The author appealed. . . . The Supreme Court considered that the distinction made in the Act was reasonable, taking into account the physical differences between men and women.

The Complaint:

3.1   The author claims that he is a victim of discrimination based on sex, since he has been denied an exemption which he would have enjoyed if he had been a woman. He argues that then there is no objective, reasonable and proportionate justification for the distinction made in the Child Benefit Act between men and women. He refers in this connection to a statement of the Dutch Government in 1988 to the effect that an exemption for women only was no longer acceptable, following developments in present-day society. The author argues that this was not acceptable in 1984 either. He submits in this context that the Covenant should be interpreted in the light of present-day developments, and that views prevalent at a time when the legislation was introduced cannot be decisive when applying the Covenant to his case. In this connection the author refers to the Views of the Committee in . . . *Broeks v. the Netherlands.* . . .

3.2   Moreover, the author argues that it is not correct to expect that women aged over 45 will not have children. In this connection, he refers to the regulation in the Child Benefit Act according to which an applicant can receive benefits for foster-children He further submits that, even if the distinction between men and women could be based on objective data, showing that women over 45 are less likely to beget children than men, this would still not justify the distinction. According to the author, the small difference in possibility did not justify such an absolute distinction. In this connection, the author contends that the statistical frequency of a man over the age of 45 to father a child is not more than few per thousand. The author therefore concludes that the necessary proportionality between the distinction and the aim of the exemption is lacking. . . .

Issues and Proceedings Before the Committee:

5.1   Before considering any claim contained in a communication, the Human Rights Committee must . . . decide whether or not it is admissible under the Optional Protocol to the Covenant.

5.2   The Committee notes that the State party does not object to the admissibility of the communication. Nevertheless, it is the Committee's duty to ascertain whether the admissibility criteria laid down in the Optional Protocol have been met. In this context the Committee notes that the State party, in 1989, adopted measures to abolish the exemption at issue in the present communication. The Committee considers, taking into account social security legislation and its application usually lag behind socio-economic developments in society, and that the purpose of the abrogated exemption was at its time not considered discriminatory, that the issue which the author raises in his communication is moot and that he has no claim under article 2ʲ of the Optional Protocol.

ʲ Article 2 of the Optional Protocol provides: "Subject to the provisions of article 1, individuals who claim that any of their rights enumerated in the Covenant have been violated and who have exhausted all available domestic remedies may submit a written communication to the Committee for consideration."

6.   The Human Rights Committee therefore decides:

(a) that the communication is inadmissible under article 2 of the Optional Protocol;

(b) that this decision shall be communicated to the State party, to the author and to his Counsel.

NOTES

The Proposed Test. Note the complainant's use of a new test, in paragraph 3. He introduces the term "proportionate" justification, and proceeds to show how the law is both over-inclusive (very few men in the older age group will become fathers) and under-inclusive (some women in the older age group will become mothers). Do you find the argument convincing?

The Effect of Changing the Sex-Based Law to a Gender-Neutral One. In *Broeks,* paragraph 14, the Committee used the fact that the law had been changed to show that the sex- based law at issue was not "reasonable." Here it uses that fact to show that the issue is "moot" and that the victim has no admissible case—an issue not even raised by the government. Do you have any theories as to what could have caused this shift?

III. Case Study: Philippine Family Law

The 1986 Philippine Constitution provides that "no person shall be deprived of life, liberty, or property without due process of law nor shall any person be denied the equal protection of the law." (Art. III sec. 1). It also provides that "[t]he State recognizes the role of women in nation-building, and shall ensure the fundamental equality before the law of women and men." (Art. XI, sec. 14)

In its first compliance report to the Human Rights Committee, the Philippines made the following representations as to the ICCPR's enforceability in Philippine courts:

The Provisions of the Covenant can be invoked before and directly enforced by Philippine courts, other tribunals or administrative authorities. . . . They do not have to be transformed into Philippine internal laws or administrative regulations to be enforced by Philippine courts or administrative authorities concerned. Under section 2, article II of the 1987 Constitution, "The Philippines . . . adopts the generally accepted principles of international law as part of the law of the land and adheres to the policy of peace, equality, justice, freedom, co-operation and amity with all nations." . . . Since the International Covenant on Civil and Political Rights was ratified by the Philippine Government and is, therefore, binding upon it, its provisions can be invoked before, and directly enforced by, Philippine courts, tribunals and administrative authorities, under the afore recited provisions of the 1987 Constitution. Any doubt is dispelled by section 18(8), article XIII thereof which provides that "the Commission on Human Rights shall monitor the Philippine Government's compliance with international treaty obligations on human rights."[K]

[K] Consideration of Reports Submitted by States Parties Under Article 40 of the Covenant, *Initial Reports of States Parties due in 1988: Philippines,* U.N. Doc. No. CCPR/C/50 Add.1/Rev.1 (1989).

In 1987, the Philippines passed the Philippine Family Code of 1987, eliminating most sex-discriminatory provisions of its prior law.[L] The following provisions are from the revised Family Code:

Art. 211. The father and the mother shall jointly exercise parental authority over the persons of their common children. In case of disagreement the father's decision shall prevail, unless there is a judicial order to the contrary.

Children shall always observe respect and reverence toward their parents and are obliged to obey them as long as the children are under parental authority. . . .

Art. 213. In case of separation of the parents, parental authority shall be exercised by the parent designated by the court. The court shall take into account all relevant considerations, especially the choice of the child over seven years of age, unless the parent chosen is unfit.

No child under seven years of age shall be separated from the mother unless the court finds compelling reasons to order otherwise. . . .

Art. 225. The father and the mother shall . . . jointly exercise legal guardianship over the property of their unemancipated common child without the necessity of a court appointment. In case of disagreement, the father's decision shall prevail, unless there is a judicial order to the contrary.[M]

NOTES

Questions for Discussion. Do Articles 211, 213, or 225 violate the Equal Protection clauses of the Philippine Constitution and the ICCPR? What test would you apply?

What are the arguments on each side? Why do you suppose each provision was enacted?

What effect do you think the challenged provisions have on the beliefs or behavior of Philippine parents? Philippine children? In addition to the ICCPR, the Philippines is also a party to CEDAW. What provisions of CEDAW do you think the three Articles violate?

Consider the following opinion from a 1995 Philippine Supreme Court case,[N] describing family law prior to the 1987 reforms:

It is a historical fact that for over three centuries, the Philippines had been colonized by Spain, a conservative, Catholic country which transplanted to our shores the Old World culture, mores, attitudes and values. Through the imposition on our government of the Spanish Civil Code . . . the people, both men and women, had no choice but to accept such concepts as the husband's being the head of the family and the wife's subordination to his authority. In such role, his was the right to make vital decisions for the family. . . . Because he is made responsible for the support of the wife and the rest of the family, he is also empowered to be the administrator of the conjugal property, with a few exceptions. . . . As regards the property pertaining to the children under parental authority, the father is the legal administrator and only in his absence may the mother assume his powers. Demeaning to the wife's dignity are certain stric-

---

[L] *See generally* M. Feliciano, *Law, Gender, and the Family in the Philippines,* 28 LAW & SOCIETY REV. 547 (1994).

[M] 14 United Nations Population Fund & Harvard Law School, *Annual Review of Population Law: 1987,* 422–23 (1990).

[N] *Imelda Romualdez-Marcos v. Commission on Elections,* Separate opinion of Romero, J., as reported in THE LAWYERS REVIEW, November 30, 1995.

tures on her personal freedoms, practically relegating her to the position of minors and disabled persons. To illustrate a few: The wife cannot, without the husband's consent, acquire any property by gratuitous title, except from her ascendants, descendants, parents in-law, and collateral relatives within the fourth degree. With respect to her employment, the husband wields . . . veto power in case the wife exercises her profession or occupation or engages in business, provided his income is sufficient for the family, according to its social standing and his opposition is founded on serious and valid grounds. Most offensive, if not repulsive to the liberal-minded is the effective prohibition upon a widow to get married till after three hundred days following the death of her husband, unless, in the meantime, she has given birth to a child. The mother who contracts a subsequent marriage loses the parental authority over her children unless the deceased husband, father of the latter, has expressly provided in his will that his widow might marry again, and has ordered that in such cases she should keep and exercise parental authority over their children. Again, an instance of a husband's overarching influence from beyond the grave.

All these indignities and disabilities suffered by Filipino wives for hundreds of years evoked no protest from them until the concept of human right and equality between and among nations and individuals found hospitable lodgement in the United Nations Charter of which the Philippines was one of the original signatories. . . . (*Imelda Romualdez-Marcos v. Commission on Elections*, Separate opinion of Romero, J., as reported in *The Lawyers Review*, November 30, 1995.)

The Human Rights Committee's General Comment 28 (2000). Skim General Comment 28, *available at* RossRights. What paragraphs could you use to determine whether Articles 211, 213, or 225 of the new Philippine Family Code violate the Equal Protection Clause? What do they say?

This General Comment represents a major improvement in the Committee's approach to women's rights over the 1989 General Comment 18. For its new discussion of equal protection concepts under Article 26, *see* paragraphs 30 and 31. How has the Committee's view of Article 26's reach expanded?

Chapter 4
Conflicting Human Rights Under International Law: Freedom of Religion Versus Women's Equality Rights

When freedom of religion conflicts with women's right to equality and the question is which should take precedence, many would intuitively respond that the right to religious freedom should prevail. Perhaps this is because religion is seen as "sacred" and therefore something that cannot be questioned under international law. We have already seen how Islamic beliefs shaped Afghanistan law both before the Taliban and during its rule. Similarly, we have seen how Catholic beliefs shaped Spanish law which then influenced laws in the Philippines and Peru. This chapter explores the role of these religions and others—Buddhism, Hinduism, and Judaism—in forming laws that discriminate against women, particularly regarding their role within the family. It then explores the UN Treaty, the UDHR, the ICCPR, and CEDAW and their perspectives on each of these rights. Do they provide any resolution of this most basic conflict?

I. A Comparison of Religious Fundamentalist Norms in Five Religions

Courtney W. Howland, *The Challenge of Religious Fundamentalism to the Liberty and Equality Rights of Women: An Analysis Under the United Nations Charter* [A]
35 Colum. J. Transnat'l L. 271, 274–79, 282–324 (1997)

The use of the term "fundamentalism" to describe a religious movement evokes high emotion. Whatever the preferred term, however, the movement thus identified is an important reality recognized by women from many diverse backgrounds and religions throughout the world. The term "religious fundamentalism" is particularly meaningful for many religious women as representing a movement within religion that they understand to be oppressive of women.[4] Women have recognized the phe-

---

[A] Hereinafter, Courtney W. Howland, *The Challenge of Religious Fundamentalism.*

[4] Religious women fighting fundamentalism come from a wide variety of religions and races and many of them lay stress on their cultural origins and attachments. Although an outsider's critique of a religion and culture may well be as valid as that of an insider, most of these religious

nomenon and movement of fundamentalism and have formed groups around the world specifically to fight fundamentalism. For example, Women Against Fundamentalism is a group composed of Catholics, Protestants, Hindus, Sikhs, Muslims and Jews, all of various origins (Afro-Caribbean, English, Asian, Indian, Iranian, Irish, and others) whose activities are aimed at curbing fundamentalism across a wide range of religions and countries.

Acting in a quite different context, academic scholars too have observed the modern phenomenon defined as religious fundamentalism. Some scholars have expressed concern or given apologias about defining the phenomenon of fundamentalism cross-culturally or using the term "fundamentalism" itself. . . . Nonetheless, there has developed an extensive academic discipline that uses the term, even if uneasily, because these scholars have "felt the cumulative force of a series of 'family resemblances' as [they] move from one militantly antimodern religious group to another tradition by tradition, and culture by culture."[8] These family resemblances have prompted scholars to endeavor to set out definitional criteria and determine the various sociological causes and effects of the phenomenon. These scholars come from a variety of religions, races and nations and work in various disciplines.

Although these two groups (religious women engaged in political struggle and academic scholars) are not always explicit or precise in defining fundamentalism, my analysis of their work shows plainly that the two groups generally agree on the broad criteria that define a religious group as fundamentalist. These are that the group: believes that the group and society need to be rescued from the secular state; rejects Enlightenment norms, particularly individual rights and secularism; is committed to the authority of ancient scripture; holds a total world view such that religious beliefs are inseparable from politics, law and culture; relies on an idealized past; is selective in drawing from the past for religious traditions and orthodox practice; centers that idealized past in a patriarchal framework mandating separate gender spheres and a "pristine morality"; rejects outsiders and the concept of pluralism; and is committed to activism and fighting for changed social, political and legal order.

Fundamentalism thus defined exists within many religions, ethnic groups and countries, and takes different forms within these various contexts. Nevertheless, these fundamentalist movements share in common the feature that they are effecting political, legal and social changes that are highly detrimental to women's rights. For most

---

women generally confine their critique to their own respective religion and culture and so do not raise the issue of outsider critique. Religious women may analyze fundamentalist groups as violating their own religious norms of dignity and respect as well as Western norms. Thus, it is improper to dismiss them—as some fundamentalists are wont to do—as representing only a Western, white or Christian perspective. Indeed, a number of the women find themselves in the dilemma of wanting to fight both the West and fundamentalism. The fact that women from different religions, perspectives, and a great variety of cultures recognize these religious movements as detrimental to women demonstrates that this recognition is cross-cultural and supports the cross-cultural legitimacy of defining and critiquing fundamentalism.

[8] [John S. Hawley & Wayne Proudfoot, *Introduction, in* FUNDAMENTALISM AND GENDER 1, 5 (John S. Hawley, ed., 1994).] . . . .

academic writers, this is merely one aspect of the general political activism that characterizes the movement. However, women, and especially religious women, engaged in political struggle against the movement emphasize that the central aim of its social and political activism is to restrict women to a narrowly defined role and exercise control over them within the patriarchal family structure.[23] They also see fundamentalism's militant activism in changing social and legal structures of society as inextricably linked with its appeal to selected traditional beliefs encompassing separate-spheres ideology for men and women. . . .

Nonfundamentalist religious groups may argue that fundamentalism misinterprets the religious texts or doctrines, or even that it wrongly asserts non-religious views as religious doctrine, but these internal theological disputations are irrelevant to my analysis. The point is that religious fundamentalists believe in and assert their interpretations as religious doctrine, and raise claims of religious freedom for their actions based upon these doctrines.

III. Religious Fundamentalist Laws Requiring the Obedience of Women

In this Part, I focus on a particular religious fundamentalist legal norm that I call the obedience rule. This states that a wife is required to submit to the authority of her husband—to be obedient to her husband. In addition to being subordinating in and of itself, this rule serves as a basic general norm justifying a variety of religious rules that limit women's independence and autonomy, and ensure women's subordinate position to men.

I focus on this rule of obedience for two main reasons: first, the rule is such a gross manifestation of the subordination of women that there can be little good faith argument that the rule promotes the equality of women; and second, the effect of the rule on women's lives is profound since it ramifies into laws regarding education and employment. Thus, the obedience rule serves as a clear example of a rule designed to maintain women in a subordinate position, and as such it brings the conflict between rights of religious freedom and women's rights of equality and liberty into sharp relief. . . .

A. Women's Religious Duty of Submission and Obedience to Men

In this Section, I discuss the background to the obedience rule and explore how subordination inevitably follows from a relationship based on obedience. I also consider religious fundamentalists' rationalizations for such subordination.

Religious fundamentalist legal structures regard women's sexuality as potentially evil and destructive of men. The legal structures of fundamentalist marriage and

---

[23] . . . An Iranian woman in exile states "Fundamentalism is about absolute control over the female body and mind. It is about segregation and exclusion of women. The regime in Iran is founded on sexual apartheid. . . ." Maryam Poya, *Double Exile: Iranian Women and Islamic Fundamentalism,* in REFUSING HOLY ORDERS 141, 159 [(Gita Sahgal & Nira Yuval-Davis eds., 1992)]. . . .

divorce and modesty codes[31] serve as enforcement mechanisms to maintain women's chastity and control their sexuality. The principle underlying these structures is that women are to be submissive to men in general, and in particular that a wife must submit and be obedient to her husband.

In a fundamentalist regime, girls first learn obedience to their fathers and marriages may be arranged for them at a young age in order to protect their chastity. The marriage ceremony or marriage contract gives the husband the right to his wife's submission and obedience. Moreover, her obligation to submit and obey is also regarded as her own duty of religious practice and worship. If she disobeys her husband, she is thus guilty of a double violation: of her husband's right to her obedience and of her own religious duties.

The obedience rule means that a husband has the right of sexual access to his wife at any time, the final say in reproductive decisions, the right to forbid his wife to work and the right to forbid his wife to continue her education. A wife's submission to her husband has no time limit, but continues through the rest of her life. Moreover, it is generally legitimate for men to enforce the obedience rule through physical punishment. As a result, women may be subject to beatings and physical violence for disobedience. The obedience rule places a crippling physical burden on women. Under religious fundamentalist doctrine there is general insistence on the hierarchical relations between women and men, with men having a divine mandate to exercise authority over women with little restriction.

Fundamentalists do not deny that women have less rights than men under the obedience rule. Some argue that this structure is appropriate because women are inferior. Others, often in response to international disapproval of a doctrine of inferiority of women and to claims of religious women that religious fundamentalism is not treating them equally, have argued that women and men are equal before the deity but have natural and different—rather than unequal—rights and duties under religious law. According to this latter argument the entire religious fundamentalist social structure justifies women having less rights in certain areas, including the obedience rule. Thus, fundamentalists claim that a wife's duty of submission and obedience is an equal exchange for the duty of "protection" that her husband owes to her, in the form of an obligation to provide basic material and financial support—food, shelter and clothing. Wives are assigned the role of having children and caring for them in the private sphere of home, while the public sphere of employment and government belongs to men.

This "protection," however, does not alleviate the wife's subordination, but rather enhances it by increasing her financial dependence on her husband, making her more vulnerable in the event of divorce or widowhood. This is particularly dangerous in this fundamentalist context where it is generally much easier for a husband than a wife to obtain a divorce. In addition, the wife may lose her right to maintenance during marriage or be divorced if she is disobedient or "rebellious." Thus, if women do

---

[31] Modesty codes require the segregation of women from men in general, and demand that women stay primarily in their homes, act modestly, and dress with their entire body covered. . . .

not obey their husbands' wishes their very survival is in danger. The wife is particularly vulnerable in the event of the husband's death, as she is unlikely to have accumulated any property during her child-bearing years because of her dependence upon her husband, and is also unlikely to have any training to be able to earn wages. Some fundamentalist structures will not permit her to work in any event. If she is lucky, she may become dependent upon a son or other male relative, to whom she now owes her duty of submission.

Fundamentalists' substantive arguments fail to provide a credible defense for the obedience rule, and fail to demonstrate that the obedience rule supports women's equality or is necessary for women's equality. It is thus difficult to credit these *ad hoc* different-but-equal arguments with good faith since they support the same hierarchy of relations between genders as is supported by traditional fundamentalist (and conservative) religious doctrines that, in turn, are explicitly based on the natural inferiority of women.

B. Five Major Religions

The following five sections deal with the respective religious contexts of Buddhism, Christianity, Hinduism, Islam, and Judaism. In each section, the first part identifies the fundamentalist religious-legal doctrine concerning the obedience rule and the second part reviews the success of the political activity of fundamentalists in conforming the law in their respective states to their religious-legal doctrine.

1. Buddhism

Buddhist fundamentalism is found in several parts of the Buddhist world. This section deals primarily with fundamentalist movements in Theravada Buddhism in Sri Lanka and Thailand, and in the New Religions of Japan.

a. The Religious-Legal Doctrine

Various fundamentalist groups support notions of a traditional family and morality that, in turn, serve as the basis for separate roles and spheres of activities for women and men. A central doctrine underlying separate-spheres ideology is that women are unable to control their dangerous sexuality which is potentially destructive of men. To deal with this problem, marriages are arranged for women at young ages before their chastity is in danger, at which point they enter the realm of their husband's authority. According to traditional doctrine, embraced in Theravada movements, every woman must bear three kinds of subordination: "to her father when young, to her husband while married, and to her son when old."[50] In the New Religions of Japan, "[w]omen are urged to be meek and submissive and to build up the husband's ego by performing elaborate gestures of deference and respect, simultaneously indi-

---

[50] Rita M. Gross, Buddhism After Patriarchy: A Feminist History, Analysis, and Reconstruction of Buddhism 42 & n.* (1993). . . .

cating self-effacement and humility on their part."[51] Thus, being a good wife and mother is not only the proper role for women, but is imbued with religious significance. The New Religions unabashedly assert men's superiority over women: "[i]t's men who are superior, and the women who are behind all the trouble in the world."[53] Modesty codes also require that a woman have humility in all things, particularly in relation to men.

The doctrine of a woman's submission and obedience to her husband goes beyond rhetoric; it is enforced by the threat and reality of sanctions. A woman who does not conform to this approved role may experience stigmatization and devaluation. Moreover, violence to enforce obedience to the husband is also a constant threat. In Thailand, for example, where many people consider that "a husband is entitled to 'discipline' his wife," battered women often believe that their situation is due to bad "karma," in accordance with the Buddhist belief that the accumulation of good or bad deeds in the past may influence one's present life.[55] Fundamentalists are also concerned that as a woman's economic independence increases, she will be less committed to the patriarchal family. Consequently, they regard employment outside the home as interfering with her role as wife and mother. Thus, the requirement that wives submit to husbands has the additional impact of limiting a woman's earning possibilities.

b. Political Activity to Conform State Law to Religious-Legal Doctrine

A great deal of fundamentalist political activity is devoted to maintaining and enlarging the requirement of women's submission. A number of the Japanese New Religions are lobbying to bring back the *"ie"* model of patriarchal family life by reinstating the relevant parts of the prewar Meiji Civil Code. The *ie* model of family consisted of the "househead, wife-of-househead, successor, successor's wife, and the unmarried children of the successor generation."[58] The eldest male was the head of the family, and normally he was succeeded by his eldest son. The househead had authority over all *ie* property. Women could not own real property other than in very exceptional circumstances, and any other property a woman brought to the marriage belonged to her husband for him to dispose of without her consent. Men could divorce women for, among other reasons, adultery or failure to produce a male child and the divorced wife had no automatic entitlement to financial assistance. Women could only initiate divorce under rare circumstances (not including adultery). The husband obtained custody of children as members of his *ie*. The Meiji Civil Code also strictly forbade contraception and education about contraception. The repeal of the Meiji Civil Code brought many legal reforms for women in the areas of marriage, divorce and prop-

---

[51] [HELEN HARDACRE, LAY BUDDHISM IN CONTEMPORARY JAPAN 47 (1984).] . . . .

[53] [Helen Hardacre, *Japanese New Religions: Profiles in Gender, in* FUNDAMENTALISM & GENDER, *supra* note [8],] at 111 (quoting sermon of religious leader).

[55] Women's Information Centre, [*Shelter for Battered Women in Thailand, in* THIRD WORLD/SECOND SEX (vol. 2) 205, 206–7 (Miranda Davies ed., 1987).] . . .

[58] Hardacre, *Japanese New Religions, supra* note [53], at 121.

erty, and consequently increased their power in postwar Japan. A number of the New Religions desire to reverse these reforms.

2. Christianity

Fundamentalisms in Christianity exist in traditional branches such as the Roman Catholic Church (RCC), the Orthodox Church and Protestantism, and have also developed in other Christian sects or offshoots. The vast array of Christian fundamentalist groups is spread over strikingly diverse geographic locations: from the United States to Latin and Central America, and from Britain to India. I draw examples from this wide range of Christian fundamentalist groups with particular emphasis on fundamentalist groups within American Protestantism such as sect fundamentalists and Reconstructionists, and from fundamentalist groups within the RCC. The RCC groups rely heavily on traditional conservative doctrine, with some groups fully endorsing RCC interpretations of doctrine.

a. The Religious-Legal Doctrine

Many of these various Christian fundamentalist groups perceive Western culture to be in a desperate state due to the decline of what they perceive to be the basic unit of society, the "traditional family." They regard women's sexuality as potentially dangerous and destructive of men. Fundamentalists look back with nostalgia to the nineteenth century construct of a middle-class family or even to a seventeenth century construct. Fundamentalists define "traditional" family to mean a legally married man and woman with children, where the man is the head of the family and preferably is the sole financial supporter of the group. They strongly support a separate-spheres gender ideology, which they base on a religious requirement that women be submissive and subordinate to men. Some read the scriptures as calling for the headship of man and the subordination of woman. Others, steeped in the belief that the Bible is infallible and that it condones women's subordination, come to view the hierarchy of men over women as somehow "natural." All agree that a girl grows up subject to the authority of her father, who then delivers her in marriage to her husband's authority. The father, as leader of the family, exercises discipline with absolute authority over his wife and children. He is the chief, if not sole, breadwinner and the protector and provider of his wife and family. In return, the wife is to submit to her husband and serve the needs of her husband and children. She is also subject to a modesty code in matters of behavior and dress.

Fundamentalist Protestants' model for marriage is thus based on an exchange of protection for obedience and submission. A wife who does not obey is termed "rebellious," and she is admonished to treat her husband as a "high priest and prophet of God."[88] This is particularly oppressive since modern studies show a high incidence of

---

[88] [MARGARET L. BEDROTH, FUNDAMENTALISM AND GENDER: 1875 TO THE PRESENT 103 (1993).]

spousal abuse in fundamentalist Christian homes.[89] "[W]here wives are taught to submit blindly to their husbands' every word and deed, . . . such teachings provide a good covering for abuse under the guise of bringing one's wife 'into subjection.' Thus the batterer does not consider his actions abusive; he is simply fulfilling his God-given responsibilities."[90] Many women whose husbands enforce obedience through physical violence are counseled by Christian religious advisors to stay in these battering relationships, and convinced that they themselves are in the wrong.[91]

The requirement of submission and obedience detracts from the possibility of a woman achieving any economic independence or autonomy, since her husband may exercise his authority by limiting or forbidding her from working outside the home. Fundamentalists regard a woman's economic independence as undesirable since it will reduce her commitment to patriarchy.

b. Political Activity to Conform State Law to Religious-Legal Doctrine

Christian fundamentalists are increasingly active in the political arena to enact their vision of Christian society into law. For example, in the United States, they hope to pose a direct threat to the secular state and to establish the United States as a Christian country. Not surprisingly, their particular goal is to establish the legal structure of the patriarchal family and women's subordinate role in it. Thus, Christian fundamentalists strongly opposed the Equal Rights Amendment to the U.S. Constitution as preventing women from serving their proper submissive role as wives and mothers, and are credited with its defeat. They have also worked to prevent passage of statutes or to repeal already-enacted statutes that protect abused children and abused wives because the statutes interfere with the husband's disciplinary rights to enforce obedience.

Catholic fundamentalist groups have also politically supported "traditional" family laws and opposed laws that did not fit the patriarchal family model.[99] The RCC itself is always heavily involved in political activity, including the political lobbying of individual states. A recent Vatican success was lobbying China to ban reformist Catholic groups from the 1995 United Nations Conference on Women's Rights in Beijing. Thus, these groups, which have long fought for women's equality, were excluded

---

[89] Christian fundamentalist (Protestant and Catholic) emphasis on women's self-sacrifice and the glorification of their suffering and victimization make women particularly vulnerable to accepting battering relationships. Generally, such abuse is common in families with rigid sex roles and gross inequities in power distribution.

[90] [JAMES ALSDURF & PHYLLIS ALSDURF, BATTERED INTO SUBMISSION: THE TRAGEDY OF WIFE ABUSE IN THE CHRISTIAN HOME 18 (1989).]

[91] Under traditional religious law of the Orthodox Church a husband had a right to beat his wife, but if a wife raised her hand against her husband she could be divorced. Although civil law rather than religious law now applies, the religious attitudes are unchanged.

[99] *See* Zadra, *supra* note 72 (discussing CL's promotion of traditional family legal structures and its lobbying against divorce and abortion). [Communione e Liberazione (CL) is an organization founded in Italy which "claims divine authority for the RCC and aims to bring back the 'expelled Church' and papal state to Italy and reassert 'Catholic hegemony.'"]

from the debate on formulating international legal policy on women's equality, whereas the Vatican, which has historically and consistently opposed women's equality, even including women's fight for suffrage, participated in the debate.

3. Hinduism

There are several Hindu fundamentalist movements, with the main movements located in India and focused on making India a Hindu state. The most important is Rashtriya Swayamsevak Sangh (RSS), a combined religious and cultural organization whose political manifestation is the Bharatiya Janata Party (BJP) (The Indian People's Party) and whose affiliate Vishva Hindu Parishad (VHP) (World Hindu Society) is responsible for promoting religious and cultural aspects of Hindu fundamentalism.

a. The Religious-Legal Doctrine

The RSS-VHP-BJP ideology embraces selected traditional and conservative practices of Hinduism that correspond to its view of an idealized past, particularly the glory of India and the glorification of male warriors. Its rhetoric centers on certain mythological epics of Hinduism that it seeks to make relevant to contemporary times. It vigorously promotes the epic Ramayana as grounded in historical fact, representative of Hindu truths and providing a moral foundation for contemporary India. The epic is the story of Lord Rama, the human incarnation of the god Vishnu, and his wife, Sita. Sita sacrifices her life to prove her chastity to her doubting husband and thereby uphold his honor.[111] Throughout Hindu fundamentalism in India, Rama is considered admirable and represents the ideal Hindu man, a warrior, while Sita is considered to be the ideal wife, chaste, obedient and self-sacrificing. These role models reinforce strong gender ideologies that require separate and distinct roles for each sex.

Hindu fundamentalism reaffirms these divine role models in another epic myth that constitutes important rhetoric for the movement: the story of the god Siva and his consort the goddess Sati, whose name means chastity or virginity.[114] Like Sita, Sati sacrifices herself to save the honor of her husband. Along with Sita, Sati represents

---

[111] In the *Ramayana*, a demon abducts Sita, but refrains from raping her. Rama wages war and rescues Sita, but doubts her chastity (for which she, although abducted, is plainly responsible) and publicly disowns her. Sita defends her virtue by a test of fire, and the god of fire rescues her and testifies to her virtue and chastity. Rama and Sita return home and live in peace until further rumors surface, questioning Sita's chastity during the abduction. As a result, Rama banishes the pregnant Sita who soon thereafter gives birth to two sons. Rama then recalls her and requires her to undergo a second test of fire for his people. Sita chooses to defend her virtue by dying, announcing publicly that she will thereby remove Rama's grief, shame and dishonor, and asserts her loyalty to him by stating that she hopes he will be her husband in her next rebirth. For an account of this epic as related here, *see* LEIGH MINTURN, SITA'S DAUGHTERS: COMING OUT OF PURDAH 170–73 (1993).

[114] In the myth, Sati becomes an ascetic like Siva and thereby wins him in marriage. Sati's father, disapproving of Siva as an unkempt ascetic hermit, holds an important sacrifice to which he invites all the top divinities except Siva. Sati confronts her father about this insult, but is ignored, and so she kills herself to protest the insult to her husband. . . .

the Hindu ideal woman, whose devotion to her husband constitutes "the fire of her inner truth (sat) . . . [that] bursts forth in flames" and consumes her.[117] Sati is thus the name given to a woman who is burned to death on her husband's funeral pyre, with this ultimate sacrifice for her husband's honor representing the ideal of virtuous and honorable womanhood. The RSS holds strongly to the view that women are best able to serve the Hindu nation by following this deepest tradition of the role of women in Hindu society as manifested by Sita and Sati.[119]

Thus, the primary religious role for Hindu women as promoted by the RSS family of organizations is to be a devoted wife and mother. However, Hinduism views women as possessed of a dangerous sexuality that constantly threatens to destroy their virtue, and that they cannot themselves control. Consequently, women must be subject to external controls to maintain their virtue. The girl or young woman is first controlled by her father or male guardian. If, despite this control, she loses, or is perceived to have lost her virtue, she disgraces her family and her male relatives are therefore "obliged to execute her."[124]

The woman's marriage reduces her potential to disgrace her family.[125] Consequently, a family is always anxious to marry off daughters, and will pay for the privilege in the form of dowry.[126] Dowry as practiced in Hinduism reinforces the view of women as objects that men control and dispose of like chattels, and this is sufficient reason to justify the Indian government's prohibition of dowry.[128]

Marriage transfers the woman from the control of her father to the control of her husband. "After her marriage, her husband is for her in the position of god. . . . The

---

[117] [*See* John S. Hawley, *Hinduism:* Sati *and Its Defenders, in* FUNDAMENTALISM AND GENDER, *supra* note [8], at 79, 82.]

[119] Fundamentalists argue that Hinduism is not based on individual rights and personal freedoms, but on community responsibilities. Thus, women who follow in Sita's or Sati's steps are oriented to the community, not selfishly concerned with their independent freedoms. However, Hindu fundamentalists consistently require self-sacrifice and selflessness primarily from women for the benefit of men, and not the other way around. In this way, even the attractive concept of community responsibility is mustered in support of subordinating women.

[124] MINTURN, *supra* note 111, at 221. . . .

[125] Marriages are arranged for daughters at young ages, preferably before menstruation, to prevent premarital affairs. The Hindu Marriage Act 1955 and Hindu Minority and Guardianship Act 1956, which raised minimum marriage ages to 18 for women and 21 for men, have generally been ignored. . . . [T]he Health Minister . . . of Uttar Pradesh in India admitted that there were a number of villages in Uttar Pradesh where all the girls over age eight were married.

[126] Dowry is a gift of property from the bride's family. Although ostensibly made to the bride, it is in reality a payment to the groom and groom's family as a condition for performance of the marriage. The amount of dowry depends upon the relative value (or, rather, lack of value) placed upon the girl, with detriments in her looks, education and age "outweighed by an unusually high dowry." Dowry was originally a Brahmanical religious practice. With the spread of fundamentalism and reaffirmation of Hindu values through "Sanskritization" and Brahmanical values, dowry has been reinforced as an appropriate religious practice, and has expanded into more communities and castes.

[128] The Dowry Prohibition Act of 1961 was amended in 1984 and made giving or receiving dowry a substantive offense.

husband of a married woman is her 'lord' and master. . . ."[129] The highest religious duty of a woman is to be "devotional and conjugal" to this her personal god.[130] This role requires her absolute obedience, and indeed the RSS describes the duty of absolute obedience that RSS members owe to the leader as that found in an "ideal Hindu family."[132]

Hindu fundamentalists prescribe or legitimate a number of social mechanisms for ensuring the wife's obedience and maintaining the husband's control. The religious modesty laws of *purdah* require a woman to stay indoors and segregated from men, effectively keeping women isolated and submissive.[133]

It is also accepted practice that the husband may enforce his wife's duty of obedience by beatings and other violence. Since he is the sole judge of whether she is obedient, this further condones his being violent if she displeases him in any way. His displeasure commonly finds expression in complaints of inadequate dowry that escalate into beatings, torture and murder. Such murders are known as "dowry deaths" or "bride-burnings" and, despite their illegality, they occur frequently and regularly in Hindu society in India, and are on the increase.[135] Most dowry deaths take the form

---

[129] [Sanjukta Gupta, *Women in the Saiva/Sakta Ethos*, in ROLES AND RITUALS FOR HINDU WOMEN 193, 194–95 (Julia Leslie ed., 1991).]

[130] *See* [LINA M. FRUZZETTI, THE GIFT OF A VIRGIN: WOMEN, MARRIAGE AND RITUAL IN BENGALI SOCIETY 13 (1982).] There is no apparent exception for the wife, as devotee, to refuse sex. Some authors argue that wives should agree with husbands in sexuality, but they acknowledge that, in practice, if a wife refuses sexual relations her husband may beat her or elder woman of house may make sure the wife becomes more obedient and accessible to her husband. MINTURN, *supra* note 111, at 209–11.

[132] [Ainslie T. Embree, *The Function of the Rashtriya Swayamsevak Sangh: To Define the Hindu Nation*, in 4 THE FUNDAMENTALISM PROJECT: ACCOUNTING FOR FUNDAMENTALISMS 617, 625–26 (Martin E. Marty & R. Scott Appleby eds., 1994).]

[133] *Purdah* is the cloistering of women by high-caste Hindus, with some aspects now popularized among other classes by "Sanskritization" and fundamentalism. Strict *purdah* requires a woman to cover her face in front of her husband and older men. *Purdah* also restricts a woman's travel alone which otherwise would "contaminate" her character.

[135] The Dowry Prohibition Act of 1961 was amended in 1984 and 1986 to make dowry death illegal. But dowry deaths continue to increase year by year. A typical week's newspaper reports about eight deaths of women that the authorities have evidence to link with dowry. Three typical examples . . . are:

"Haryana official victim of dowry": Mrs . . . Dala, a senior officer of the Haryana Government, died of burns in her in-laws' house on Tuesday night. . . . Her husband . . . was arrested on a charge of abetment to suicide. In her dying declaration, she stated she had been tortured by her husband and in-laws for not bringing enough dowry. (Statesman, 6 June 1986).

"Commits Suicide": A 28-year-old woman allegedly burnt herself to death because she could not stand the harassment by her husband. . . . The police have registered a case of abetment to suicide against the husband, an employee of the New Delhi government. (Times of India, 6 June 1986).

"Burnt for a Refrigerator": A young life was lost because of the rapacity of the in-laws. It began when the newly married Nirmal (24 years old) was unable to bring a refrigerator as part of her dowry. Nirmal was burnt to death. (Statesman, 11 June 1986).

The government now estimates that in the decade since [1992] . . . dowry deaths have increased 170 percent, with 6,200 recorded last year.

of the husband setting the wife on fire and then claiming that the burning was a kitchen accident or that the wife committed suicide in a good derivation of the *sati* tradition. As a result, the police often classify dowry deaths as accident or suicide, and consequently there are few prosecutions. Some wives, in the Sita and Sati tradition, do commit suicide, often as a result of great harassment, beatings and torture from their husbands.

The greatest and most spectacular demonstration of loyalty, obedience and submission is made by the wife who becomes a *sati* for her husband's benefit. The religious practice of becoming a *sati* was outlawed by the British in 1829 and has remained illegal, although it has continued to occur. However, it was not until Roop Kanwar became a *sati* in 1987 that the religious practice created a furore in India. The 18-year-old Roop Kanwar had been married eight months to a twenty-four year old man when he died. Some eyewitnesses said that she mounted his funeral pyre voluntarily, whereas others claimed that she was drugged by her in-laws, tried nevertheless to escape, but was pushed back on to the pyre to burn.

This *sati* prompted Hindu fundamentalists, including the Hindu religious political parties such as the BJP, to rally to support the institution and practice of becoming a *sati*, particularly against the government law. All the major actors in this movement were men: men served in the religious roles of the *sati sthal* [the site of the sati], men ran the Committee for defending the *sati*, men organized the rallies to support the *sati*, men gave the speeches to support the *sati*, and men have been combing the religious and historical texts to justify the *sati*. However, these fundamentalist men ignored the fact that not every *sati* acts voluntarily: many are pushed onto the pyre.[146] Even absent immediate physical coercion, a widow in Indian Hindu society is regarded as so inauspicious and burdensome and faces such a bleak prospect that she may well yield to social pressure to become a *sati* as the path of least resistance.[147]

In 1974 the Indian government Committee on the Status of Women issued a report, *Towards Equality*, which concluded that Hinduism was one of the critical determinants in women's inferior status in India. The report observed that a woman in orthodox Hinduism "is called fickle-minded, sensual, seducer of men, given to falsehood, trickery, folly, greed, impurity and thoughtless action; root of all evil; inconsistent and cruel. . . . In childhood a woman must be subject to her father, in youth to her husband, and when her lord is dead to her sons. A woman must never be

---

[146] There are economic reasons why a family might want its widowed daughter-in-law to become a *sati*. This prevents her from inheriting her husband's property, which used to be prohibited under religious law, but is now allowed under civil law. Also, families make money from visitors to *sati* shrines.

[147] . . . Widow remarriage was made legal in India, but it is rare for widows to remarry because remarriage is still regarded as highly dubious. Ironically, this religious prohibition against remarriage to protect the woman's chastity and dead husband's honor has encouraged young widows into prostitution as their only economic source of survival. Despite legal reforms concerning remarriage, widows' position in society has actually worsened in recent times. Widowers, however, suffer no detriment due to their status and have always been expected to remarry. There is not even a Hindi word for a widowed man.

independent.''[149] But despite legal reforms in the last twenty years since *Towards Equality*, the rise of Hindu fundamentalism has brought an increase in dowry deaths, an increased acceptance of *purdah*, *sati*, and the general dependency of women.

b. Political Activity to Conform State Law to Religious-Legal Doctrine

The RSS-VHP-BJP family, flush with power from its 1996 electoral gains, continues its intense political activity pushing for legal reforms that correspond to its notion of a Hindu state. In furtherance of this goal, Hindu fundamentalists call for repeal of the Hindu Marriage Act of 1955 and the Hindu Succession Act of 1956 that reformed Hindu religious practices by giving women more rights in marriage, banning polygamy, allowing for widow remarriage, giving women statutory bases for divorce, and giving women some rights in inheritance where they formerly had none.[152] Their nationalist aim for a Hindu state is enhanced by cutting back on women's rights, as was already clear at the time of the passage of the Hindu Marriage Act and Hindu Succession Act when fundamentalist opponents of the bills called them "anti-Hindu and anti-Indian" and declared that they would put "religion in danger."

4. Islam

In Islam, fundamentalist groups are found among both the Sunni and Shi'ite Muslims in a broad range of geographic locations. I draw examples from a wide variety of groups with particular emphasis on three representative groups: the Muslim Brotherhood; the Jama'at-i-Islami; and the Ayatollah Khomeini's Islamic movement in Iran and its related groups. Despite great diversity within Muslim fundamentalism and with regard to the interpretation of orthodox practices, the movements are strikingly similar in certain doctrines and goals.

a. The Religious-Legal Doctrine

A central doctrine throughout Muslim fundamentalism is that women harbor the seeds of destruction of all society and that to avoid this they and their sexuality must be carefully controlled.[158] Fundamentalists blame women's uncontrolled sexuality for the modern Western "sensate culture" represented by selfishness, greed and immorality. Unless women adhere strongly to their "natural" role as childbearers they will

---

[149] GOVERNMENT OF INDIA, [MINISTRY OF EDUCATION AND SOCIAL WELFARE, TOWARDS EQUALITY: REPORT OF THE COMMITTEE ON THE STATUS OF WOMEN IN INDIA 40–41 (1974).]

[152] Family laws in India are divided along religious lines, with Hindus covered by the civil Hindu laws, and Muslims and Christians each covered by their own respective religious laws.

[158] . . . Marriages are arranged for girls at young ages in order to protect their chastity and honor. In a number of Islamic-law states, the minimum age for girls for marriage is on average about 15. One of the first acts of the post-Revolutionary Iranian government was lowering the age for marriage for girls in the aim of protecting their chastity. In rural areas the average age of brides is between 13 and 15, but in certain parts of Iran 80% of wives had been married between the ages of 9 and 16.

become unchaste and immoral and bring down the rest of society. To avoid these consequences, Muslim fundamentalists support traditional notions of morality with emphasis on separate gender spheres. Their separate-spheres ideology requires segregation of the sexes so that women's alluring sexuality does not morally undermine men. Under this ideology, the place for the woman is confined at home caring for her family, of which the man is indisputably head. A man must be head of the family in order to maintain control over the dangerous sexuality of the women in the family, and because women are considered unsuited to any role of authority by virtue of their submissive nature and periodic instability.[163]

Indeed, a number of Islamic fundamentalists explicitly declare men to be superior to women, which places men in control of women and requires that women be obedient to men. The requirement of obedience to the male head of household extends through every woman's entire life, but is particularly compelling for a married woman in respect of her husband. Obedience requires submission to her husband in all things, including sexual and social matters. Furthermore, fundamentalist doctrine allows men to enforce this duty of obedience through violence. If a wife is disobedient a proper husband is first to "appeal to her good sense, and if she does not improve, then he may abandon her in her marital bed. Thereafter, it is permissible for him to give her a good, but gentle, beating."[169]

Muslim fundamentalists also utilize the modesty doctrine of *hejab* for ensuring the wife's obedience and reinforcing the husband's control, particularly his economic control. *Hejab* (as interpreted by fundamentalists) requires segregation of women and men and dictates that women are not to leave their houses unless absolutely necessary, and if they do go out, they should be fully covered, often including veiling the face. *Hejab* sets up barriers against a woman working outside the home, and makes it very difficult for her to achieve economic independence. This accords with fundamentalist doctrine disallowing a woman to earn money like a man and forbidding her to work without her husband's permission. Fundamentalists disfavor any economic independence for a woman because it would "ma[k]e her free of the authority of the father and husband."[173] A woman's inheritance rights are also very limited.[174] A woman who nevertheless succeeds in living outside male control is

---

[163] . . . [W]omen are naturally "submissive and impressionable" and . . . "[i]n order to maintain the family system and save it from confusion some one must be entrusted with necessary authority. . . . Such a one can only be the man. For the member whose mental and physical state becomes unstable time and again during menstruation and pregnancy cannot be expected to use such authority with wisdom and discretion. . . . To maintain this division [of labor between husband and wife] there must be some safeguards provided in the social system. . . ."[ABUL A 'LA MAUDUDI, PURDAH AND THE STATUS OF WOMAN IN ISLAM 121–23 (Al-Ash 'ari trans. ed., 1972).]

[169] [Andrea B. Rugh, *Reshaping Personal Relations in Egypt*, in 2 THE FUNDAMENTALISM PROJECT: FUNDAMENTALISMS AND SOCIETY 151, 170 (Martin E. Marty & R. Scott Appleby eds., 1993).] . . . .

[173] [ABUL A 'LA MAUDUDI, PURDAH AND THE STATUS OF WOMEN IN ISLAM 14–15, 68 (Al-Ash 'ari trans. ed., 1972.)] . . . .

[174] For example, a daughter inherits half the share of a son.

regarded as a threat to the good morality of society, and as such is in constant mortal danger.

b. Political Activity to Conform State Law to Religious-Legal Doctrine

Fundamentalist political activity has pressed for enactment of family and personal status laws as part of state legal systems, and this has succeeded in a number of states.[176] In most cases, fundamentalists owe this success not to any vote of confidence in their viewpoint but rather to their use of violence to intimidate people into silent compliance with their actions, which is especially effective where the populace is already intimidated by corrupt, oppressive and undemocratic government.

Fundamentalist success is reflected in the enactment of state laws requiring the obedience of women: marriage and divorce laws, and *hejab.* The marriage laws of various Islamic states provide that marriage transfers a woman from the control of her father to the protection and control of her husband.[179] As a wife, her duty of obedience to her husband may be statutorily explicit or implicit through the concept of *nashiz.* A *nashiz is* a disobedient or rebellious wife,[181] and this may include a woman who acts superior to her husband, disobeys his orders, leaves her marital home without legitimate reason or her husband's permission, works outside the home without his permission, or uses contraception without permission. For example, Shi'ite Muslim fundamentalists specifically define a *nashiz* to include a wife who denies her husband his conjugal rights, even temporarily, and a wife who borrows money without the permission of a judge or of her husband.

A *nashiz* loses her right to protection under the marriage contract for as long as she is disobedient. This protection is the right to maintenance—food, clothing and housing—as long as "she places or offers to place herself in the husband's power so as to allow him free access to herself at all lawful times . . . and . . . obeys all his lawful commands for the duration of the marriage."[185] This is a serious threat to a woman who is made financially dependent on the husband and may not work without his permission. Moreover, a husband may obtain an obedience order from a court against his wife, and "[i]f she still persists, he is entitled to divorce her and, because she has violated his rights, he is under no obligation whatsoever to provide maintenance for her."[187]

---

[176] [Howland cites Algeria, Bangladesh, Egypt, Iran, Iraq, Pakistan, and Sudan.] . . . .

[179] The extent of the father's control is particularly clear in his role as marriage guardian (*wali*). If the father is dead, another male relative, or if there is none a judge (who is male) becomes marriage guardian. Under guardianship laws, a woman cannot contract her own marriage, even if she possesses full legal capacity.

[181] This concept of "rebellious" wife is similar to the Christian concept and the Jewish concept. However, there are greater legal ramifications and punishments for women based on the concept of a "rebellious" wife in present-day Islam and Judaism.

[185] [JAMIL J. NASIR, THE STATUS OF WOMEN UNDER ISLAMIC LAW AND UNDER MODERN ISLAMIC LEGISLATION 64–65 (2d. ed., 1994).] . . . .

[187] [Wael B. Hallaq, Islamic Response to Contraception-Fact Pattern VI.B., *Symposium on Religious Law: Roman Catholic, Islamic, and Jewish Treatment of Familial Issues, Including Education, Abor-*

The ultimate act of disobedience by a wife is adultery. In 1990 Iran decreed that according to its fundamentalist ideology, men were allowed to kill their womenfolk for adultery.[189] Since the killing is based on the husband's (not a court's) assessment of the situation it may easily occur if the adultery is merely feared or suspected rather than real. Kurdistan has recently passed a law absolving a man for murder of his wife if he can prove she was morally disobedient.[190]

A further threat is that a man may divorce his wife at will or whim.[191] After a divorce an ex-wife is entitled to maintenance in some circumstances during the three-month period of *iddat* which is intended to determine whether she is pregnant. After this she is not entitled to maintenance regardless of the number of years of marriage and her financial dependence on her husband. The fear of unilateral divorce and no financial support strongly encourages obedience. It is also important to note that during the period of *iddat* the husband may unilaterally revoke the divorce,[193] and is thereupon entitled to "resume the conjugal relationship with the wife without her consent."[194]

Finally, fundamentalists have succeeded in enforcing their interpretation of *hejab* by public laws specifically requiring the dress of *hejab*. In Sudan the fundamentalist military regime has required that "women should dress in loose long dresses and

---

tion, In Vitro *Fertilization, Prenuptial Agreements, Contraception, and Marital Fraud,* 16 Loy. L.A. Int'l & Comp. L.J. 80 (1993)]. . . .

[189] Stoning to death is a punishment for women's adultery under fundamentalist interpretation of the *Hudd* punishments [a category of punishment given for certain crimes in the Qur'an]. In Iran there is a law that regulates the size of the stone with which the woman is to be killed. It should not be too large because then she would be killed too quickly, nor too small because then she would not be killed. Amnesty International reported on the stoning of Saraya in Iran: "Saraya was buried up to her shoulders. . . . The stones were flying, her head and her chest were reduced to raw flesh. Using all of his strength, the man hits her skull many times, her brain is scattered on the ground, and a big cry of joy arises, 'Allah o Akbar.' [God is Great.]"

[190] [T]his law was passed by the "autonomous Kurdistan government" and . . . "550 women have been murdered since the establishment of the new government." . . . [8 IWRAW, The Women's Watch 4 (no.3) (Dec. 1994)].

[191] In general, husbands may divorce their wives at will and without court order (the right of *talaq*). *Talaq* is the unilateral declaration of a husband divorcing and repudiating his wife and can be performed by word of mouth or in writing. It is legally binding. . . . Other Muslim states incorporate Shari'ah law with its provisions of *talaq*. Fundamentalists have interpreted these to allow the husband to make an *unwitnessed* declaration of repudiation, with no evidence that he has repudiated other than his own word. If the woman divorced by unwitnessed repudiation now remarries, her ex-husband, either for revenge or financial reasons, may later deny he pronounced *talaq*, at which point the woman can be tried for adultery (with the new husband) for which she risks being stoned to death. . . .

A wife may be able to get a divorce if she can get her husband's consent by giving him consideration (*khula*) for her freedom. Often this amounts to the wife forfeiting the dowry due to her on marriage. Otherwise, the grounds of divorce for a wife are very narrow and limited.

[193] The husband may make the *talaq* irrevocable by making his pronouncement of repudiation three times with three *iddat* periods.

[194] [Jamil J. Nasir, The Status of Women Under Islamic Law and Under Modern Islamic Legislation 112 (2d. ed., 1994).]

cover their heads,"[195] and when their dress is inappropriate they are now subject to amputation of hands and feet, hanging, stoning to death or hanging followed by crucifixion of the body. Khomeini's Islamic regime quickly passed a law making it mandatory for women to wear the "Islamic veil" in public. Violation brings a woman 74 lashes and internment for rehabilitation, with her family being compelled to pay her internment expenses. In Iran, police may now beat women on the streets and otherwise harass them if they are not veiled, and women have been tried and even executed for failure to observe *hejab*. *Hejab* also serves to justify other limitations on women. For example, in . . . Saudi Arabia, women are not allowed to drive, in Kuwait, women do not have the right to vote, and in Algeria, fundamentalist law has now delegated women's right to vote to men.

This treatment of women under state laws is designed to make them submissive and obedient. The violence inflicted by husbands, religious men in the streets and Shari'ate jurists is designed to keep women in their subordinate place, obedient and dependent. Indeed, the success of Islamization throughout the Muslim world has primarily been measured in terms of either the repeal of laws that granted women more rights or the codification of fundamentalist interpretation of Shari'ah personal status and family laws that support the institution of the patriarchal family.

5. Judaism

I draw examples of Jewish fundamentalism from a wide variety of groups, with particular emphasis on groups known as *haredim* (Ultra-Orthodox Jews)[203] who are primarily anti-Zionist, and the Zionist group, Gush Emunim (GE). Each group follows its own interpretation of Jewish religious laws *(halakhah)*, but their interpretations are quite similar in certain doctrines due to their sharing of many Ultra-Orthodox norms.

a. The Religious-Legal Doctrine

Jewish fundamentalists reject modernity, which for them means decadent contemporary Western culture. They see the sexual licentiousness of modernity as a consequence of women straying from their proper role as wife and mother, and their ideology strongly endorses separate gender spheres and segregation of the sexes. All of the groups require a degree of submissiveness and obedience of women to men, most particularly in marriage.[208]

---

[195] [Asma Mohamed Abdel Halim, *Challenges to the Application of International Women's Human Rights in the Sudan, in* HUMAN RIGHTS OF WOMEN 397, 401 (Rebecca J. Cook ed., 1994).] . . . .

[203] The term *haredim* has come to denote essentially the radical segment of Orthodox Jews (Ultra-Orthodox), where "Orthodox" denotes Jews who observe the Torah and its commandments, and interpret those commandments to require a traditional way of life punctiliously attached to ritual. . . .

[208] Although doctrine formally requires a woman's consent to marriage, in practice most girls in fundamentalist communities have their marriages arranged at an early age. Early arranged marriages help protect a girl's chastity. This concern is reflected in marriage contracts, which normally provide for higher alimony for a virgin bride than for a non-virgin bride [in case the couple should later divorce].

Although fundamentalist Judaism does not explicitly declare that a wife must be submissive and obedient to her husband, the overall structure of marriage and divorce laws delegates such a degree of authority and power to the husband as to allow him effectively to coerce his wife's obedience. The assumption is "that authority over her was transferred from her father to her husband."[210] Fundamentalist norms of marriage oblige the husband to provide for the wife's basic physical needs, and normally impose on him a financial obligation in the event of divorce. In return, the wife is obliged to care for the home and children.[212] In this context, the husband's coercive power is established by three fundamentalist *halakhah* norms: first during the life of the marriage, the husband has rights to his wife's earnings, the produce of all property she owned prior to the marriage, and inheritance of her property upon her death; second, the husband retains the exclusive power of divorce; and third, the husband may obtain a divorce on the ground of the wife being "rebellious."

Under fundamentalist law, no divorce may take place unless the husband consents and gives his wife a divorce writ (*get*).[216] Until he does so the marriage continues in existence and he continues to exercise control over her earnings and income from her property. Thus, she remains economically dependent on the marriage and without financial resources to leave. His price for agreeing to end the marriage may be a beneficial financial settlement.[217] The husband's unilateral power with respect to divorce

---

[210] [Blu Greenberg, *Female Sexuality and Bodily Functions in the Jewish Tradition, in* WOMEN, RELIGION AND SEXUALITY 1, 9 (Jeanne Becher ed., First Trinity Press Int'l 1991) (1990).]

[212] In practice, the Jewish Israeli marriage pattern across cultural and social lines conforms to the religious one as childcare is almost exclusively the wife's concern, except for discipline of children, which is left to the husband, and the husband, as head of the family, controls the family budget.

[216] Divorce requires a proceeding in a rabbinical court which either party may initiate. If the court finds appropriate ground for divorce it will recommend that the marriage be terminated, and this gives the husband a right to give his wife a *get*. However, he has no obligation to give a *get*, even if the court recommended the divorce on one of the few grounds available for the wife. The husband generally has more grounds than his wife for divorce. For example, "[a] married woman commits adultery when she has sexual relations with any other man than her husband, while a married man is legally an adulterer only when he becomes sexually involved with another man's wife." [Paula Hyman, *The Other Half: Women in the Jewish Tradition, in* THE JEWISH WOMAN 105, 110 (Elizabeth Koltun ed., 1976).] If a woman's marriage is dissolved due to her adultery, she is not allowed to be married either to her former partner or her partner in adultery, whereas a man may divorce his wife and marry his adulterous partner or remarry his wife. Occasionally, rabbinical courts in Israel have ordered a husband to give a *get*, and on rare occasions his failure then to do so has triggered civil penalties, even imprisonment. However, current practice in Israeli rabbinical courts declines to issue such orders, on the ground that a *get* that a husband issues against his free will is of doubtful validity. For certain Ashkenazic communities, a wife's consent to divorce is now theoretically needed, but a rebellious wife's consent is not necessary. "Rebellious" may be defined so broadly in this context as to eviscerate any requirement of the wife's consent. A husband may remarry despite not having his wife's consent to divorce, and his remarriage is not defined as bigamous. However, if a wife fails to obtain a *get*, she may not remarry without committing bigamy.

[217] In the United States, civil courts have just begun to penalize husbands for withholding the religious divorce writ in order to obtain financial concessions from the wife. . . .

is further enhanced by the concept of the rebellious wife (*moredet*) which may serve him as a ground for divorce. If a wife refuses sexual relations or fails to do housework without valid reason, her husband may deem her rebellious and divorce her, whereupon she forfeits her divorce settlement. In Israel, there have been cases of women being declared "rebellious" for refusing to sew buttons on their husband's shirts or perform other domestic chores, and in consequence being denied maintenance in the divorce.

By vesting these powers in the husband, fundamentalist Judaism gives him coercive force to ensure that his wife is submissive and obedient and behaves as he wishes. Jewish fundamentalists, however, are not clear as to whether a husband may beat his wife. Some rabbis interpret the *halakhah* as giving the wife grounds for divorce if she is beaten, although of course the divorce still requires her husband's consent. Under other interpretations of the *halakhah* a wife who leaves her husband because of a beating may be termed rebellious and thereby made to forfeit the divorce settlement. In any event, physical abuse of the wife in fundamentalist families, by her sons as well as her husband, is a serious problem.

The *halakhah* norms of modesty reinforce a woman's dependency on men, particularly her husband. The purpose of the modesty laws is to guard women's chastity and to prevent women from "tempting" men into adultery. The modesty laws require segregation of the sexes in all public areas: at the synagogue, at school, in government, and in entertainment. The rules restrict women's dress, movement, employment and independence. Modesty laws also require women to be generally quiet because a woman's voice is regarded as seductive. They further require that a woman should stay in her home if possible, and in any event within the confines of her fundamentalist community. Some sects do not allow women to drive.

The modesty laws operate as gate-keepers. By confining women to their homes, performing housework and childcare, these laws generally aid in legitimating women's submission to the authority of their husbands. By confining women to their community, these laws ensure that women do not hear new ideas that might allow them to reevaluate their subordinate position. By preventing women from working outside the house, these laws ensure women's economic dependency.[230] In sum, under fundamentalist legal structures, the modesty, marriage, and divorce laws ensure women's obedience to their husbands and confine them to the role of wife and mother.

b. Political Activity to Conform State Law to Religious-Legal Doctrine

Jewish fundamentalists are politically active in Israel. Many a fundamentalist group has its own political party, while other fundamentalist groups join together for political representation. The resulting small parties wield great influence in Israel because neither of the two major political parties is generally able to form a government without forming an alliance with these religious parties. As a result, these religious parties

---

[230] . . . [C]omputers and modems may be important to *haredi* women who wish to be employed without needing to leave their homes. . . .

have a history of being able to extract concessions and financial benefits from the Israeli government. Some fundamentalist political effort is directed at maintaining and extending the force of their doctrine within their own communities. Other political efforts are aimed at replacing the secular state with a religious state that acknowledges the *halakhah* as its exclusive law. For example, GE has a "Proposed Torah Constitution for the State of Israel," and seeks to "institute the ancient system of law and justice" of the *halakhah*.[235]

Fundamentalists have succeeded in making *halakhah* norms part of state law in several crucial areas. The religious courts have exclusive jurisdiction in marriage, divorce and ancillary matters, and concurrent jurisdiction (with consent of the parties) in personal status and property disputes between spouses. Other religious norms have been enacted as Israeli law. Moreover, fundamentalists fight to broaden Rabbinate jurisdiction in general, and specifically to empower the religious courts to nullify marriage or divorce proceedings outside Israel. The fundamentalist focus on marriage and divorce and modesty laws is of particular concern to women because of the disproportionately negative impact that these laws have on women. Jewish fundamentalists are engaged in political activity aimed to ensure that the laws of the state implement their vision of woman's proper role as wife and mother, and to make sure that women occupy no legitimate place in the public life of the polity.

II. The UN Charter and Universal Declaration of Human Rights

This section explores the lessons that can be drawn from international documents concerning the rights to freedom of religion and women's equality with men. Part II.A. presents the relevant excerpts from the UN Charter and the Universal Declaration of Human Rights. Consider how each affects your views as to the conflict between religious freedom and women's equality rights.

A. The International Instruments

The Charter of the United Nations
59 Stat. 1031, *entered into force* Oct. 24, 1945, *available at* RossRights

Preamble

WE THE PEOPLES OF THE UNITED NATIONS DETERMINED
to save succeeding generations from the scourge of war, which twice in our lifetime
  has brought untold sorrow to mankind, and
to reaffirm faith in fundamental human rights, in the dignity and worth of the human
  person, in the equal rights of men and women and of nations large and small, and
to establish conditions under which justice and respect for the obligations arising
  from treaties and other sources of international law can be maintained, and

---

[235] [Gideon Aran, *Jewish Zionist Fundamentalism, The Bloc of the Faithful in Israel (Gush Emunim)*, *in* 1 THE FUNDAMENTALISM PROJECT: FUNDAMENTALISMS OBSERVED 265, 319 (Martin E. Marty & R. Scott Appleby eds., paperback ed. 1994 (1991).] . . . .

to promote social progress and better standards of life in larger freedom. . . .
HAVE RESOLVED TO COMBINE OUR EFFORTS TO ACCOMPLISH THESE AIMS
Accordingly, our respective Governments, through representatives assembled in the
city of San Francisco, who have exhibited their full powers found to be in good and
due form, have agreed to the present Charter of the United Nations and do hereby
establish an international organization to be known as the United Nations.

Article 1

The Purposes of the United Nations are: . . .
3. To achieve international cooperation in solving international problems of an
economic, social, cultural, or humanitarian character, and in promoting and encouraging respect for human rights and for fundamental freedoms for all without distinction as to race, sex, language, or religion. . . .

Article 55

With a view to the creation of conditions of stability and well-being which are necessary for peaceful and friendly relations among nations based on respect for the principle of equal rights and self-determination of peoples, the United Nations shall
promote:
a. higher standards of living, full employment, and conditions of economic and
social progress and development;
b. solutions of international economic, social, health, and related problems; and
international cultural and educational co-operation; and
c. universal respect for, and observance of, human rights and fundamental freedoms for all without distinction as to race, sex, language, or religion.

Article 56

All Members pledge themselves to take joint and separate action in co-operation with
the Organization for the achievement of the purposes set forth in Article 55. . . .

Article 103

In the event of a conflict between the obligations of the Members of the United
Nations under the present Charter and their obligations under any other international
agreement, their obligations under the present Charter shall prevail.

Universal Declaration of Human Rights
U.N. Doc A/810 at 71 (1948), *available at* RossRights

Article 2

Everyone is entitled to all the rights and freedoms set forth in this Declaration, without distinction of any kind, such as race, colour, sex, language, religion, political or
other opinion, national or social origin, property, birth or other status. . . .

Article 3

Everyone has the right to life, liberty and security of person. . . .

Article 7

All are equal before the law and are entitled without any discrimination to equal protection of the law. All are entitled to equal protection against any discrimination in violation of this Declaration and against any incitement to such discrimination. . . .

Article 16

1. Men and women of full age, without any limitation due to race, nationality or religion, have the right to marry and to found a family. They are entitled to equal rights as to marriage, during marriage and at its dissolution.
2. Marriage shall be entered into only with the free and full consent of the intending spouses.
3. The family is the natural and fundamental group unit of society and is entitled to protection by society and the State. . . .

Article 18

Everyone has the right to freedom of thought, conscience and religion; this right includes freedom to change his religion or belief, and freedom, either alone or in community with others and in public or private, to manifest his religion or belief in teaching, practice, worship and observance. . . .

Article 29 . . .

2. In the exercise of his rights and freedoms, everyone shall be subject only to such limitations as are determined by law solely for the purpose of securing due recognition and respect for the rights and freedoms of others and of meeting the just requirements of morality, public order and the general welfare in a democratic society.
3. These rights and freedoms may in no case be exercised contrary to the purposes and principles of the United Nations.

NOTES

The UN Charter. The Charter is a treaty, binding on all States Parties. What arguments can you make, based on Charter language, about how to resolve the conflict between women's rights and religious freedom?

Article 2 of the UDHR. How does Article 2 of the Universal Declaration of Human Rights affect Article 7? Article 16? Article 18?

Article 18. Article 18 provides that everyone has the right to "manifest his religion or belief in teaching, practice, worship and observance." What do the last three terms mean?

Article 29. This article permits limitations of a person's rights and freedoms if certain conditions are met. What are they?

B. A Historical Analogy: Race and Religion

In the following excerpt from Howland's article, she analyzes the religious beliefs that historically justified both slavery and racial apartheid. She then explores the meaning of UDHR Article 29(2)'s "due recognition" standard for permitting limits on UDHR rights and freedoms. In other words, can limits be imposed on an asserted religious right to practice slavery in order to secure "due recognition and respect" for a person's right to freedom from slavery?

Courtney W. Howland, *The Challenge of Religious Fundamentalism*
35 COLUM. J. TRANSNAT'L L. 271, 349, 358–65 (1997)

2. Religious Fundamentalist Laws Analyzed Under [*Article 29 of*] *the Universal Declaration* . . .

[I]nternational jurisprudence has worked out the limits beyond which recognition of a religion is not due in the context of racial discrimination. The major jurisprudential developments have taken place in the international approaches to slavery and apartheid. In these contexts, gross and systematic discrimination was not accepted for the sake of giving due recognition to religion. As discussed, this demonstrates that the standard of due recognition for religion may not be interpreted without consideration of the due recognition of minimum basic norms of human dignity and freedom of other protected groups.

The major religions historically supported and justified slavery, with the three religions that rely on the Old Testament finding justification within it.[374] Religious justifi-

---

[374] Slavery was justified under traditional Buddhism and was considered legitimate under Hindu law. . . . Christianity, Islam, and Judaism . . . relied on Genesis 9:24–25 where Noah awakens from his drunkenness and curses Ham, his youngest son, that Canaan (Ham's son) be a "servant of servants" of his brethren, and Leviticus 25:44–46 where God tells Moses that Hebrews should not sell their own brethren but should buy their slaves "of the nations that are around you." By the Middle Ages, Jewish, Muslim and Christian writers all separately identified the curse of Noah on Canaan as referring specifically to the "black children of Ham" understood to be black Africans, although they justified the institution in general and did not limit it to black Africans. Christianity and Islam also justified taking infidels and captives of war as slaves, and consequently each enslaved prisoners of war taken from the other, a practice that continued for six centuries including through the Crusades and Jihads in the eleventh, twelfth and thirteenth centuries. . . .

cation supported the Christian and Islamic role in the North Atlantic slave trade and slavery in the New World. The New World Christian doctrine preached to slaves was that: slaves should accept their servile position as part of the divine plan; they were spiritually equal even if not equal in the world; their religious duty was one of obedience to their master; they should feel happy and content with their position; and they should accept discipline and correction since it was for their sins, and in any event their reward for bearing their punishments patiently was to be in heaven. Moreover, "Christianizing" slaves was regarded as good practice since it would increase the likelihood of their being obedient to their masters. Despite some Christian sects' change in the nineteenth century to a new theological position mandating the abolition of slavery, other Christians continued to justify slavery on the basis of the Old Testament and fought its abolition. Moreover, the underlying doctrine that Christianity was good for black African heathens served to feed ideologies of racial inferiority that justified institutionalizing racial discrimination into law long after slavery was abolished in the New World, and indeed such ideologies survive to the present day.

The international community gradually became opposed to slavery. By 1919 the Allies had signed conventions which contained, *inter alia*, a brief clause committing them to the suppression of slavery, and the covenant of the League of Nations had also determined that slavery and the slave trade should be suppressed. Nevertheless, slavery was not outlawed in Saudi Arabia until 1962 and in Oman until 1970. Furthermore, certain Christian sects still justify the institution of slavery, and Muslim religious fundamentalists still argue that enslavement of infidels is justified. Regardless of religious doctrine in Christianity and Islam, international mores and law did not, and do not, hold that "due recognition" requires that these religious sects be allowed to determine the issue of slavery for themselves or to practice slavery. Slavery, particularly slavery based on belonging to a particular racial group, constitutes gross systematic discrimination and fails to give "due recognition" to the rights and freedoms of the group suffering discrimination. It is in this fashion that international law has rendered the standard of "due recognition" for religious rights consistent with the standard of "due recognition" for the rights of a racial group.

Given the equal treatment of race and sex discrimination under the Charter and Universal Declaration, the international standard of "due recognition" of religious rights would thus not require that religious fundamentalist groups be allowed to determine the issue of the equality of women for themselves and to practice systematic sex discrimination. Comparison may be drawn between slavery on the basis of race as it has been justified under religious rhetoric and women's inferior position as it is currently justified under religious fundamentalist rhetoric.[386] Both rhetorics regard

---

[386] A comparison between the ideology of slavery and the ideology of women's subordination is not only apt, but is so complete that some sects themselves have compared slavery to the servile state of women in simultaneous justification of both systems of domination. For example, Muslim ideology has explicitly compared the condition of the slave to the servile status of a wife to her husband: "a comparison is drawn between the dominion imposed by the husband through which his wife is caused to surrender her sexual self, and the sovereignty established by the master whereby the slave is compelled to alienate his right to dispose of his services. . . . [T]he master buys his slave, whereas in marriage, the husband purchases his wife's productive

the roles of women and slaves as part of a divine plan, where spiritual equality may be neatly separated from earthly hierarchies. Contemporary religious fundamentalism (of all religions) promotes doctrine to women very similar to Christian doctrine preached to slaves: wives should accept their servile position as part of the divine plan; they are spiritually equal even if not equal in the world; their religious duty is one of obedience to their husband; they should feel happy and content with their position; and they should accept discipline and correction since it is for their sins, and in any event their reward for bearing their punishments patiently is in heaven or in rebirth.

The second example of international consensus demonstrating that due recognition for religion nevertheless allows suppression of a religious manifestation is in the case of systematic racial discrimination and apartheid in South Africa and territories under South Africa's control. The Dutch settlers (Boers or Afrikaners) of South Africa practiced slavery and justified it on similar religious grounds to those used in the New World. . . .

Despite the religious underpinnings of apartheid, international opinion had turned against it by the early 1970s. The international community did not consider manifestation of religious belief as taking precedence over freedom from systematic racial discrimination and thereby constituting a defense of apartheid. Indeed, the international community did not even take seriously the idea that a certain Christian sect's ideology could determine the standards for discrimination or practice. It was self-evident that systematic racial discrimination was a gross violation of the Charter and the Universal Declaration, and that "due recognition" of the right to religious freedom did not require the allowance of systematic discrimination as a manifestation of religious belief.

N O T E

"Due Recognition" for Religious Rights. Howland asserts that limits can be placed on religious rights in order to secure "due recognition" of a racial group's rights. Conversely, can limits be imposed on the rights of people to be free from slavery to secure "due recognition and respect" for a "religious right" to practice slavery? To answer that question, review UDHR Article 29(2) and (3), and apply each test (e.g., "by law," "solely") needed to justify limits on person's freedom from enslavement in order to secure recognition for religious rights. If "women's right to equality" is substituted for "freedom from slavery," should the answer be different?

C. Lessons from the UN Charter

The decision below by the International Court of Justice (ICJ) supports Howland's point about the relationship between religious rights and freedom from racial apart-

---

part. For the security of dower, the woman's sexual self is enslaved—for the protection of his lord, the slave's person is secured." [John R. Willis, *Introduction: The Ideology of Enslavement in Islam, in* SLAVES AND SLAVERY IN MUSLIM AFRICA: VOL. I, ISLAM AND THE IDEOLOGY OF ENSLAVEMENT 1 (John R. Willis ed., 1985).] . . . .

heid under international law. Note, however, that the decision does not discuss religion as such. The Court, established by the UN Charter,[B] has jurisdiction to give advisory opinions to the General Assembly, Security Council, or other UN organs, and to rule in contentious international law matters brought to it by States Parties.[C] In this decision, the Court renders an advisory opinion to the Security Council. It rules that the continued presence of South Africa in Namibia after the 1966 General Assembly resolution terminating the South African Mandate requires South Africa to withdraw and end its occupation of Namibia. It also finds that States Members must recognize that illegality and refrain from taking any action that would appear to recognize the legality of South Africa's presence. In the following excerpt, the Court addresses South Africa's request to submit additional evidence before the Court issues its decision.

Legal Consequences for States of the Continued Presence of South Africa in Namibia (South West Africa) Notwithstanding Security Resolution 276

(International Court of Justice)
1971 I.C.J. 16, 56–57 (1970), *available at* RossRights

127.   As to the general consequences resulting from the illegal presence of South Africa in Namibia, all States should bear in mind that the injured entity is a people which must look to the international community for assistance in its progress towards the goals for which the sacred trust was instituted. . . .

128.   In its oral statement and in written communications to the Court, the Government of South Africa expressed the desire to supply the Court with further factual information concerning the purposes and objectives of South Africa's policy of separate development or *apartheid,* contending that to establish a breach of South Africa's substantive international obligations under the Mandate it would be necessary to prove that a particular exercise of South Africa's legislative or administrative powers was not directed in good faith towards the purpose of promoting to the utmost the well-being and progress of the inhabitants. It is claimed by the Government of South Africa that no act or omission on its part would constitute a violation of its international obligations unless it is shown that such act or omission was actuated by a motive, or directed towards a purpose other than one to promote the interests of the inhabitants of the Territory.

129.   The Government of South Africa having made this request, the Court finds that no factual evidence is needed for the purpose of determining whether the policy of *apartheid* as applied by South Africa in Namibia is in conformity with the international obligations assumed by South Africa under the Charter of the United Nations.

[B] The Charter of the United Nations, articles 92–96, 59 Stat. 1031, *entered into force* Oct. 24, 1945, *available at* RossRights.

[C] Statute of the International Court of Justice, 59 Stat. 1055, Bevans 1179, articles 34–38, *available at* Ross Rights.

In order to determine whether the laws and decrees applied by South Africa in Namibia, which are a matter of public record, constitute a violation of the purposes and principles of the Charter of the United Nations, the question of intent or governmental discretion is not relevant; nor is it necessary to investigate or determine the effects of those measures upon the welfare of the inhabitants.

130.   It is undisputed, and is amply supported by documents annexed to South Africa's written statement in these proceedings, that the official governmental policy pursued by South Africa in Namibia is to achieve a complete physical separation of races and ethnic groups in separate areas within the Territory. The application of this policy has required, as has been conceded by South Africa, restrictive measures of control officially adopted and enforced in the Territory by the coercive power of the former Mandatory. These measures establish limitations, exclusions or restrictions for the members of the indigenous population groups in respect of their participation in certain types of activities, fields of study or of training, labour or employment and also submit them to restrictions or exclusions of residence and movement in large parts of the Territory.

131.   Under the Charter of the United Nations, the former Mandatory had pledged itself to observe and respect, in a territory having an international status, human rights and fundamental freedoms for all without distinction as to race. To establish instead, and to enforce, distinctions, exclusions, restrictions and limitations exclusively based on grounds of race, colour, descent or national or ethnic origin which constitute a denial of fundamental human rights is a flagrant violation of the purposes and principles of the Charter.

NOTES

The Court's Interpretation of the Charter. Review the Charter provisions excerpted above at II.A. What provisions does the Court rely on?

Intent. What does South Africa argue as to this issue? What does the ICJ decide? Should the intent of a State Party matter?

Apartheid Policy and Law. The ICJ notes the "limitations, exclusions or restrictions" concerning "certain types of activities, fields of study or of training, labour, or employment." It also mentions "restrictions or exclusions of residence and movement." How many parallels in the treatment of women can you find in Afghanistan law as described in Chapter One, Part IV, Case Study: Afghanistan? In Philippine law before the 1987 revision of the Family Code? *See* Chapter Three, Part III, Case Study: Philippine Family Law. Are there any areas for which there are no parallels? Is it accurate to describe Afghanistan law as imposing gender apartheid? Philippine law? Should the two countries' laws be treated the same under international law or differently? Why? Consider also the Japanese prewar Meiji Civil Code described in Part III.B.1.b of Howland's section on Buddhism and the effect of a repeal of the Hindu Marriage Act of 1955 and the Hindu Succession Law of 1956 described in Part III.B.3.b of her section on Hinduism.

The Howland article continues below. Here, she argues for a particular interpretation of the UN Charter concerning the conflict between religious rights and women's equality rights.

Courtney W. Howland, *The Challenge of Religious Fundamentalism*
35 Colum. J. Transnat'l L. 271, 327–32 (1997)

A. The United Nations Charter . . .

Almost all states are members of the United Nations and are thus bound by the minimum standards set by the Charter. The promotion of women's liberty and equality appears in the preamble of the Charter, alongside the promotion of peace, security and tolerance among nations. The preamble makes no reference to religion. Rather, the underlying premise is that the dignity of each human being and equal rights among humans (and specifically between men and women) are of paramount importance.

The Charter affirms the broader purposes of the United Nations in article 1(3), including "promoting and encouraging respect for human rights and for fundamental freedoms for all without distinction as to race, sex, language, or religion. . . ." Furthermore, in article 56, all members "pledge themselves to take joint and separate action in cooperation with the Organization for the achievement of the purposes set forth in article 55," specifically, the promotion of "universal respect for, and observance of, human rights and fundamental freedoms for all without distinction as to race, sex, language, or religion" as guaranteed by article 55(c).

1. Implications of the Language of the Charter

This language of articles 55(c) and 56 carries several important implications. First, under article 56 member states have a twofold legal duty with respect to article 55(c). The article 56 pledge constitutes an affirmative obligation to cooperate with the work of the United Nations in observing and promoting human rights. Moreover, "[a]n undertaking to cooperate in the promotion of human rights certainly does not leave a State free to suppress or even to remain indifferent to those rights."[254] Member states must not put themselves in the position of being incapable of cooperating as this would undermine the object and purpose of the Charter.[255] The language of these articles is at once binding and aspirational, and both qualities demand that member states take no action to prevent or undermine the development and understanding of human rights in accordance with the Charter. This two-fold duty—the duty of cooperation and the obligation not to undermine—exists for each U.N. member state, regardless of whether it is a party to any other human rights treaty.

I would also argue that the duty of each state to cooperate and not to undermine

---

[254] [F. Blaine Sloan, *Human Rights, The United Nations and International Law*, 20 Nordisk Tidsskrift for International Ret, Acta Scandinavica Juris Gentium 31 (1950)].

[255] Vienna Convention on the Law of Treaties, . . . art. 31(1). . . . [,] art. 18. . . .

now extends to a direct obligation of the state to promote and observe human rights, including with respect to the state's internal affairs. The United Nations has already acted extensively in the area of human rights by setting standards for promotion and observance of human rights and by establishing goals for the achievement of respect for human rights. This activity is of such breadth and depth that the affirmative obligations of states to cooperate and not to undermine may only be understood to mean that states have an individual affirmative duty to promote and observe human rights. Thus, the nature of a member state's affirmative obligation, as delineated under article 55(c), is to observe the rules of human rights and fundamental freedoms and to promote their observance.

Second, the language of the Charter makes clear that human rights under the Charter are not dependent upon religion, nor is any particular religion their source. The Charter contains provisions in favor of religion, but these are simply one manifestation of the principle of nondistinction. The Charter establishes the principle of nondistinction by explicitly listing those characteristics of human beings that may not be used as a basis for denying human rights and fundamental freedoms. These characteristics—race, sex, language and religion—are listed as separate and independent characteristics. Religion is not privileged in protection over any other characteristic, and moreover, the prohibition of distinction based on religion means that no religion is privileged over any other religion. By direct implication, the language of the nondistinction provision establishes that the entitlement to human rights and fundamental freedoms under the Charter is not to be determined or evaluated by any religious law.[259]

A third important implication of this Charter language is that it recognizes and anticipates the potential for denying human rights and fundamental freedoms on the basis of the specified characteristics. Moreover, it is clear that groups of the very types that article 55 protects may be the source of unlawful distinctions against other such groups. For example, the prohibited distinctions made on the basis of race will generally be made by another race, and the prohibited distinctions on the basis of religion will generally be those made by a different religion. The Charter language presupposes that restrictions may need to be imposed on the very groups that article 55 protects. Therefore, with the protections of human rights and fundamental freedoms based on a particular group identity come corollary duties of these same groups to respect the liberty and the equal protections afforded to the other protected groups.

---

[259] There is nothing to prevent religious laws providing inspiration for international legal standards, and various religions have influenced the formation of international law. Moreover, international law does not require that states be secular or that church and state be separated. A religious state, with its own municipal religious laws, merely needs to conform to international human rights standards. States and U.N. studies have acknowledged a danger in a state recognizing a single, particular religion in that the mere recognition discriminates against other religions. Nonetheless, the existence of a state religion is not *per se* a violation of international law as long as there is "no discrimination against persons practicing other religions." For this reason, it is particularly important at the international level that no one religion be preferred over any other and that no one religion is determinative of human rights. . . .

Fourth, the Charter's command that human rights and fundamental freedoms are to be enjoyed "without distinction" sets a minimum standard of conduct required of all members. . . . Provisions that on their face either impose unequal burdens, or grant unequal favors, are obvious barriers to equal enjoyment of human rights and fundamental freedoms.

Fifth, the "without distinction" language establishes the principle that the distinctions are themselves of equal importance. There is no notion of any hierarchy among these distinctions that might privilege one prohibited distinction over another. The explicit language of article 55 does not differentiate between distinctions on the basis of race, distinctions on the basis of sex, and distinctions on the basis of religion. Thus, not only are these distinctions equally prohibited, but the standard for evaluating whether there is a violation of the "without distinction" language must be the same.

Sixth, in addition to the right to be free from illegal distinctions, the Charter protects substantive "human rights and fundamental freedoms." Scholars differ as to the meaning of "human rights and fundamental freedoms." Nonetheless, merely because the international community is unable to agree exactly which human rights and fundamental freedoms are covered by article 55 does not transform it into a "procedural" statute such that if there are rights, then article 55 prohibits certain distinctions, but if there are no rights, then article 55 does not supply them. The preamble of the Charter particularly reaffirms a faith in fundamental rights and the dignity and worth of the person. The Charter thus presumes the existence of fundamental rights and freedoms and article 55 reaffirms this presumption along with the substantive prohibition of distinction.

N O T E

Religious Counter Arguments Under the UN Charter. Howland presents strong arguments for interpreting the UN Charter to preclude giving preference to religious rights over women's rights. How might fundamentalist religious proponents respond to her arguments?

D. A French Case Study: Veils and Polygamy

The French government is facing a difficult issue. Anger among African immigrants, especially the Algerian fundamentalist Islamic community, is on the rise. Some leaders of this fundamentalist community have protested two general French laws that they contend constitute discrimination against them on the basis of their religion and violate their right to religious freedom. They are particularly upset about the laws that prohibit all children attending French schools from wearing religious clothing or symbols such as Christian crosses, Jewish yarmulkes, or Islamic veils. They insist Muslim girls must be allowed to wear veils. They also oppose the French criminal law that prohibits polygamous marriage, arguing that their religion permits such marriages. They have met with representatives of the French government to demand separate laws for Muslims that would permit the schoolgirls to wear veils and would allow Muslim men to marry up to four wives.

What are the strongest arguments you can make in support of the Muslim community's demands under the UN Charter? Under the UDHR? What are the strongest arguments for rejecting the demands under the Charter and UDHR? If you were drafting new international law on the subject what would it say about the conflict between these two rights?

III. Religious Freedom and Women's Rights Under the ICCPR and CEDAW

In contrast to the UDHR, international human rights treaties are binding on states parties. They are also far more specific and detailed. In this part, we turn to the ICCPR and CEDAW to explore whether they address the conflict between women's rights and religious rights. After examining relevant provisions, we will return to the French case study.

A. The International Treaties

International Covenant on Civil and Political Rights
U.N. Doc. A/6316 (1966), 999 U.N.T.S. 171, *entered into force* Mar. 23, 1976, *available at* RossRights

Article 2

1. Each State Party to the present Covenant undertakes to respect and to ensure to all individuals within its territory and subject to its jurisdiction the rights recognized in the present Covenant, without distinction of any kind, such as race, colour, sex, language, religion, political or other opinion, national or social origin, property, birth or other status. . . .

Article 3

The States Parties to the present Covenant undertake to ensure the equal right of men and women to the enjoyment of all civil and political rights set forth in the present Covenant. . . .

Article 18

1. Everyone shall have the right to freedom of thought, conscience and religion. This right shall include freedom to have or to adopt a religion or belief of his choice, and freedom, either individually or in community with others and in public or private, to manifest his religion or belief in worship, observance, practice and teaching.

2. No one shall be subject to coercion which would impair his freedom to have or to adopt a religion or belief of his choice.

3. Freedom to manifest one's religion or beliefs may be subject only to such limitations as are prescribed by law and are necessary to protect public safety, order, health, or morals or the fundamental rights and freedoms of others.

4. The States Parties to the present Covenant undertake to have respect for the liberty of parents . . . to ensure the religious and moral education of their children in conformity with their own conviction. . . .

Article 23. . . .

4. States Parties to the present Covenant shall take appropriate steps to ensure equality of rights and responsibilities of spouses as to marriage, during marriage and at its dissolution. . . .

Article 26

All persons are equal before the law and are entitled without any discrimination to the equal protection of the law. In this respect, the law shall prohibit any discrimination and guarantee to all persons equal and effective protection against discrimination on any ground such as race, colour, sex, language, religion, political or other opinion, national or social origin, property, birth or other status.

Article 27

In those States in which ethnic, religious or linguistic minorities exist persons belonging to such minorities shall not be denied the right, in community with the other members of their group, to enjoy their own culture, to profess and practice their own religion, or to use their own language.

Vienna Convention on the Law of Treaties
1155 U.N.T.S. 331, *entered into force* Jan. 27, 1980, *available at* RossRights

Article 26: *Pacta sunt servanda*

Every treaty in force is binding upon the parties to it and must be performed by them in good faith.

Article 27: Internal law and observance of treaties

A party may not invoke the provisions of its internal law as justification for its failure to perform a treaty. . . .

B. The French Case Study—Applying the ICCPR

We renew our consideration of the fundamentalist Muslim community's demand that France enact laws to permit their men to practice polygamy and their girls to wear veils in school. Assume France has ratifed the ICCPR and the Vienna Convention without reservations. What arguments can you make under the ICCPR on behalf of the Muslim community? On behalf of the French Ministry of Women's Affairs, which opposes any changes in the law? The Human Rights Committee's General Comment 28 speaks to these issues. What are the Committee's views? *See* its paras. 5, 13, 21, 23–26, 28, 31–32, *available at* RossRights. Similarly, review the Human Rights Committee's General Comment 22, paras. 3, 4, and 8, *available at* RossRights. Does this change your conclusions?

C. CEDAW's Application to the French Case Study

Finally, reread CEDAW in Chapter One. Assume again that France has ratified CEDAW without reservations. How do you think the issues posed by the fundamentalist Muslim community should be resolved taking CEDAW into account? Which articles are relevant?

IV. A Comparative View of How the Conflict Between Religious Freedom and Women's Rights Is Resolved Under the U.S. Constitution

The following case illustrates how one U.S. court has resolved a similar conflict under U.S. law. Title VII of the 1964 Civil Rights Act prohibits sex-based discrimination in employment. Prohibited practices include, *inter alia*, discrimination in the "compensation, terms, conditions and privileges of employment." The Title VII enforcement agency, the Equal Employment Opportunity Commission, sued a Christian school for providing employment fringe benefits to married male—but not female—teachers. The school defended on the basis of the Constitution's First Amendment. It provides: "Congress shall make no law respecting an establishment of religion, or prohibiting the free exercise thereof. . . ."

Equal Employment Opportunity Comm'n v. Fremont Christian School
(United States Court of Appeals for the Ninth Circuit)
781 F.2d 1362 (1986), *available at* RossRights

J. BLAINE ANDERSON, CIRCUIT JUDGE:

Fremont Christian School (Fremont Christian), a church-owned and operated private school, appeals from the district order granting the Equal Employment Opportunity Commission's (EEOC) motion for partial summary judgment and an injunction prohibiting unequal compensation of married female and male employees. The district court granted summary judgment to EEOC on the issue of liability on the grounds that Fremont Christian had violated Title VII, 42 U.S.C. § 2000e *et seq.*, and the Equal Pay Act, 29 U.S.C. § 206(d), and is barred from raising the religion clauses of the First Amendment as a defense for its personnel policies. The employment policy involved here is a health insurance plan provided by Fremont Christian but only to "head of household" employees interpreted by the school to be single persons and married men. Because of the existence of a strong compelling state interest in eradicating discrimination, coupled with the fact that eliminating the employment policy involved here would not interfere with religious belief, and only minimally, if at all, with the practice of religion, we affirm the judgment of the district court.

I. Facts

Fremont Christian School is a private educational institution providing instruction from the pre-school years through twelfth grade. It is wholly owned and operated by the Assembly of God Church, located in Fremont, California.

While persons employed by Fremont Christian need not be members of the Fremont Assembly of God Church, they must be a member in good standing of an evangelical church and subscribe to specific tenets of faith. These tenets include the belief that the Bible is to be taken literally. Among the doctrinal beliefs held by the Church is the belief that, while the sexes are equal in dignity before God, they are differentiated in role. In light of this conviction the Church believes, based on, *inter alia*, Ephesians 5:23, that in any marriage the husband is the head of the household and is required to provide for that household.

In keeping with this belief until 1976, the Church and Fremont Christian compensated their married male employees at a rate higher than similarly situated female employees. After learning in January, 1976, that this practice may have been illegal, the school board determined at its September, 1976 meeting that "[s]ince it is possibly illegal to pay a head of household allowance to employees, it was moved . . . and seconded . . . to eliminate this provision from our contracts. Motion so carried."

Fremont Christian compensates its employees according to pay scales set for the teaching and administrative staff. For teachers, these take into account years of teaching experience, education, and post-degree continuing education efforts. The pay scales are now applied uniformly to both male and female teachers.

As part of its compensation package, Fremont Christian offers all full-time employees disability and life insurance regardless of sex or marital status, the premiums for which are paid by Fremont Christian.

Fremont Christian also provides health insurance as a fringe benefit. However, this benefit is available only to heads of households, interpreted by Fremont Christian to be single persons and married men. Fremont Christian believes that, in any marriage, only the man can be the head of the household, regardless of what his salary is in relation to that of his wife. As explained by Rev. Rankin, the superintendent of Fremont Christian, the test for routine eligibility for health insurance for women is whether they are married. If so, the husband is presumed to be the head of the household, rendering women ineligible for health benefits.

In certain situations, however, where the husband is incapable of providing for his family, by virtue of non-working student status, or illness, Fremont Christian undertakes, as an "act of Christian charity," to extend health benefits to a full-time married female employee for the limited period of her husband's incapacity. Nevertheless, the husband is still scripturally the head of the household.

On June 16, 1981, Ruth P. Frost, a married female employee of the School, filed with the EEOC a charge of sex discrimination against Fremont Christian on the ground that it gives health insurance coverage to its married male employees but not (with minor exceptions) to its married female employees. . . .

II. Discussion

Fremont Christian presents both statutory and constitutional arguments against application of Title VII to its employment policies. Before reaching Fremont Christian's constitutional arguments, this court must determine whether the dispute may be resolved on statutory grounds. The nature of our inquiry is established by *NLRB v. Catholic Bishop of Chicago*, 440 U.S. 490 (1979). We must first determine whether the proposed application of the statute 'would give rise to serious constitutional questions.' *Id.* If so, we cannot find the statute applicable unless there is an "affirmative intention of Congress clearly expressed" to apply it.

A. Application of Title VII

The application of Title VII to the employment practice before us would definitely give rise to serious constitutional questions. However, we conclude that Congress has clearly expressed the intention that Title VII apply to the present circumstances.

Fremont Christian argues that the exemption created by Section 702 of Title VII . . . for religious institutions extends beyond hiring practices and encompasses all other employment practices (e.g., the health insurance compensation program). Both the language and legislative history of Title VII, however, indicate that the statute exempts religious institutions only to a narrow extent. Section 702 provides:

This subchapter shall not apply . . . to a religious corporation, association, educational institution, or society with respect to the employment of individuals of a particular religion to perform work connected with the carrying on by such corporation, association. educational institution or society of its activities. . . .

While the language of § 702 makes clear that religious institutions may base relevant hiring decisions upon religious preferences, "religious employers are not immune from liability [under Title VII] for discrimination based on . . . sex. . . ." [*EEOC v. Pacific Press Publishing Ass'n*, 676 F.2d 1272 (9th Cir. 1982)]. Furthermore, Congress and this court have specifically "rejected proposals that provide[ ] religious employers a complete exemption from regulation under the [Civil Rights] Act [of 1964]." . . .

We now turn to the constitutional questions.

B. Free Exercise Clause

Fremont Christian alleges that Title VII and the Equal Pay Act do not apply to its employment policy of supplying health insurance to the head of the household because it is grounded in religious belief and is therefore shielded by the free exercise clause of the First Amendment. To determine whether a neutrally-based statute, such as Title VII or the Act, violates the free exercise clause, this court weighs three factors: (1) the magnitude of the statute's impact on the exercise of a religious belief; (2) the existence of a compelling state interest justifying the burden imposed upon the exercise of the religious belief; and (3) the extent to which recognition of an exemption from the statute would impede objectives sought to be advanced by the statute.

(1) Magnitude of Statute's Impact upon Exercise of Religious Beliefs

In [*Pacific Press*], the plaintiff, an employee of a religiously affiliated publishing house, had two complaints: (1) she was being denied monetary allowances paid to similarly situated male employees, and (2) her employment was terminated in retaliation for filing charges under Title VII.

Addressing the first complaint, this court held that requiring Pacific Press to refrain from discriminating against the plaintiff, as required by Title VII, does not violate Press's free exercise of its religious beliefs. This court reasoned that "[p]reventing discrimination can have no significant impact upon the exercise of Adventist beliefs because the Church proclaims that it does not believe in discriminating against women or minority groups, and that its policy is to pay wages without discrimination on the basis of . . . sex. . . . Thus, enforcement of Title VII's equal pay provision does not and could not conflict with Adventist religious doctrines, nor does it prohibit an activity 'rooted in religious belief.'"

Similarly in the present case, Pastor Goree, the head of the Fremont Assembly of God Church, stated: "[T]he Church, believing as it does in the God-given dignity and the special role of women, could not, without sin, treat women according to unfair distinctions." This would indicate, as it did in *Pacific Press*, that preventing the sex discrimination involved in this case should have no significant impact on Fremont Christian's religious beliefs or doctrines.

Furthermore, Fremont Christian has previously abandoned a policy of paying the "head of household" at a rate higher than similarly situated female employees (the very problem at issue in *Pacific Press*) because they felt it may have been illegal to continue to do so. We find this to be evidence that there would be no substantial impact upon religious beliefs by forcing Fremont Christian to drop a similar policy of giving heads of household health insurance to the exclusion of similarly situated women. Finally, the female employees at Fremont Christian are eligible for group life and disability insurance and the School's wages and other usual conditions of employment are comparable for all employees, regardless of sex. The district court held that "if those practices do not undermine the School's religious goals then it is inconceivable that providing health benefits to female employees will have the opposite effect." We agree.

(2) Compelling State Interest

Pacific Press speaks clearly to the importance of eliminating employment discrimination in relation to actions by the EEOC that would have a *substantial* impact on the exercise of religious beliefs. "By enacting Title VII, Congress clearly targeted the elimination of all forms of discrimination as a 'highest priority'. . . . Congress' purpose to end discrimination is equally if not more compelling than other interests that have been held to justify legislation that burdened the exercise of religious convictions."

Eliminating the employment policy involved here would not interfere with religious belief and only minimally, if at all, with the practice of religion. Because the impact on religious belief or practice is minimal and the interest in equal employment opportunities is high, the balance weighs heavily in favor of upholding Fremont Christian's liability under Title VII for its sexually discriminatory health insurance compensation program.

(3) Least Restrictive Means

It has been recognized that although EEOC jurisdiction over religious organizations may have far-reaching effects should the Commission seek injunctive relief, as in this case, or monetary damages against a religious employer, "the relevant inquiry is not the impact of the statute upon the institution, but the impact of the statute upon the institution's exercise of its sincerely held religious beliefs." Having found the impact on religious beliefs to be minimal at best, we find this third factor to be satisfied.

[In Part II.C. the court rejects the Fremont Christian School's establishment clause argument.]

N O T E S

Free Exercise Today. The compelling interest test the U.S. Court of Appeals applies in *EEOC v. Fremont Christian School* was first established in *Sherbert v. Verner,* 374 U.S. 398 (1963). In that case, the Supreme Court granted a constitutional free exercise exemption to a state law denying unemployment benefits to people who refused to work on Saturdays. The exemption permitted people whose religious convictions required not working on Saturday to receive the unemployment benefits.

After the 1986 *Fremont* decision, however, the Supreme Court rejected the *Sherbert* compelling interest standard and applied a more lenient First Amendment test. *Employment Division v. Smith,* 494 U.S. 872 (1990), concerned an Oregon criminal law prohibiting possession of "controlled substances." The long list of banned drugs included peyote, which is used in religious ceremonies in the Native American Church. When a drug rehabilitation organization fired employees Alfred Smith and Galen Black for using peyote in this way, the state unemployment compensation board found the dismissals to be based on work-related "misconduct" and denied the men's application for unemployment benefits. On appeal, the Supreme Court upheld the board's ruling, finding that it did not violate the men's free exercise rights. Justice Scalia's opinion for the Court explained that unless the "object of the law" is to burden religious activity, its "incidental effect" on religious conduct does not violate the First Amendment when certain conditions are met.

We have never held that an individual's religious beliefs excuse him from compliance with an otherwise valid law prohibiting conduct that the State is free to regulate. . . . We first had occasion to assert that principle in *Reynolds v. United States*, 98 U.S. 145 (1878), where we rejected the claim that criminal laws against polygamy could not be constitutionally applied to those whose religion commanded the practice.

Subsequent decisions have consistently held that the right of free exercise does not relieve an individual of the obligation to comply with a "valid and neutral law of general applicability on the ground that the law proscribes . . . conduct that his religion prescribes [commands]. . . ."

Reexamine the issue in *EEOC v. Fremont Christian School* using the *Smith* free exercise test. How does the analysis change? Does the result? Which approach do you prefer and why?

In 2008, it is unclear what constitutional test the Court would now apply. It has never overruled *Smith*. Yet it applied a statutory compelling interest test under the 1993 federal Religious Freedom Restoration Act (RFRA) in a case raising issues similar to those in Smith. In *Gonzales v. O Centro Espirita Beneficiente Uniao Do Vegetal*, 126 S.Ct. 1211, 1216–17 (2006), Justice Roberts described RFRA as adopting "a statutory rule comparable to the constitutional rule rejected in *Smith*."

The Federal Government may not . . . substantially burden a person's exercise of religion, "even if the burden results from a rule of general applicability." The only exception recognized by the statute requires the Government to satisfy the compelling interest test—to "demonstrat[e] that application of the burden to the person—(1) is in furtherance of a compelling government interest; and (2) is the least restrictive means of furthering that compelling governmental interest."

Applying that test, the Court unanimously upheld the right of a religious sect to a federal criminal drug ban exemption that permitted the sect to use a ceremonial tea containing banned drugs.

RFRA only applies to federal statutes. In *City of Boerne v. Flores*, 521 U.S. 507 (1997), the Court declared it unconstitutional as applied to state and local legislation because Congress lacked the necessary power under the 14th Amendment, Section 5. Thus, the *Smith* free exercise decision remains controlling federal constitutional law as to state laws. It also remains controlling constitutional law as to federal laws that might impede a person's free exercise rights. Free exercise litigants, however, would obviously choose to assert their statutory RFRA rights rather than their constitutional free exercise rights.

The French Case Study. Assume the facts are the same as in the French case, but this time it occurs in the United States. How would you resolve the issue under the First Amendment's free exercise clause interpreted in *Smith*? Under RFRA? Does the Fourteenth Amendment's equal protection clause, as interpreted in *VMI*, affect the resolution?

Comparing the U.S. Supreme Court to the UN Human Rights Committee. Would the result under the U.S. Supreme Court's interpretation of the Constitution be the same as or different from the UN Human Rights Committee's interpretation of the ICCPR?

Chapter 5
Enforcing Women's International Human Rights Under Regional Treaties: The American Convention on Human Rights and the African Charter on Human and Peoples' Rights

We have examined women's rights using both domestic and international law. In this chapter, we will look to regional human rights systems and their effects on women's rights. Both the American States and the African States have created regional human rights treaties. What rights do these treaties create for women in each region and how effective is each in enforcing such rights? Consider both the content of the substantive rights and the procedures for asserting the rights. How many steps must a victim take? Can she take the case all the way to the top? Can NGOs file suits on the behalf of many victims? What remedies can be ordered? Are they binding? How long would it take to establish a right?

I. Introduction to the American Convention on Human Rights

The American Convention on Human Rights, *available at* RossRights, developed along lines very similar to the Universal Bill of Rights. Just as the UN Charter established the UN, so too did the Organization of American States Charter establish the OAS. It opened for signature in 1948 and entered into force in 1951; it was ratified by all 34 American States. At about the same time, the American Declaration of the Rights and Duties of Man was proclaimed by the Ninth International Conference of American States. The Declaration, like its companion UDHR, was not binding. The binding treaty, the American Convention on Human Rights, was adopted in 1969 and entered into force in 1978. As of August 7, 2007, twenty-five American States had ratified the treaty; nine had not, including Antigua and Barbuda, Bahamas, Belize, Canada, Guyana, St. Kitts and Nevis, St. Lucia, St. Vincent and Grenadines, and the United States. It is similar to the international conventions but does not require regular reports from States Parties.

Under the Convention, there are two enforcement bodies: the Inter-American Commission on Human Rights; and the Inter-American Court of Human Rights. The Commission can receive and act on petitions from any person, group of persons, or

NGO claiming violations of Convention rights. There are the usual requirements to exhaust domestic remedies and submit in a timely fashion. The Commission seeks information, investigates, and may hold hearings. It tries to help the parties reach a friendly settlement and, if not, issues a report with its findings and recommendations. In most cases of non-compliance the Commission forwards the case to the Court. Petitioners cannot refer cases to the Court, and so lack direct access, but can submit requests to the Commission to do so. Once the Court takes a case, the petitioners can participate in the proceedings. The Court has both advisory and contentious jurisdiction. Its contentious decisions are binding. It can award money damages and issue declaratory judgments which tell the states what remedies they should provide. While the framework is powerful, women's rights advocates have rarely used it.

The Court's advisory jurisdiction is not binding, but the Court is well respected and its opinions carry great weight. The following case illustrates one possible use of the Convention to advance women's rights. But if the Convention is to have any effect on women's rights, women's rights proponents will have to use it much more.

II. A Challenge to Costa Rica's Gender-Based Nationality Law

Proposed Amendments to the Naturalization Provisions of the Constitution of Costa Rica

(Inter-American Court of Human Rights)
Advisory Opinion OC-4/84, Inter-Am. Ct. H.R. (Ser. A) No. 4 (1984),
available at RossRights

THE COURT . . . gives the following Advisory Opinion:
1.   In . . . 1983 . . . the [Costa Rican Legislative Assembly] Special Committee set up to study certain proposed amendments to Articles 14 and 15 of [the Costa Rican] Constitution . . . decided to seek an advisory opinion from the Court on the proposed constitutional amendments. . . .

I. Statement of the Issues . . .

7. The relevant parts of the Government's request for an advisory opinion read as follows:

II. PROVISIONS TO BE ANALYZED IN THE DETERMINATION OF COMPATIBILITY . . .

a) Domestic legislation:

1) Present text of Articles 14 and 15 of the Constitution of Costa Rica:

Article 14. The following are Costa Ricans by naturalization: . . .

2.   Nationals of the other countries of Central America . . . who have resided at least one year in the republic, and who declare . . . their intention to be Costa Ricans;
3.   Native-born Spaniards and Ibero-Americans . . . , provided they have been domiciled in the country during the two years prior to application;

4.   Central Americans, Spaniards and Ibero-Americans who are not native-born, and other foreigners who have been domiciled in Costa Rica for a minimum period of five years. . . .
5.   A foreign woman who by marriage to a Costa Rican loses her nationality or who indicates her desire to become a Costa Rican. . . .

Article 15. [Requirements for Naturalization]. Anyone who applies for naturalization must give evidence in advance of good conduct, must show that he has a known occupation or means of livelihood, and must promise to reside in the republic regularly. . . .

2) AMENDMENTS PROPOSED by the Special Committee of the Legislative Assembly in its Report of June 22, 1983.

Article 14. The following are Costa Ricans by naturalization: . . .

2) Native-born nationals of the other countries of Central America, Spaniards and Ibero-Americans with five years official residence in the country. . . .
3) Central Americans, Spaniards and Ibero-Americans, who are not native-born, and other foreigners who have held official residence for a minimum period of seven years. . . .
4) A foreign woman who, by marriage to a Costa Rican loses her nationality or who after two years of marriage to a Costa Rican and the same period of residence in the country, indicates her desire to take on our nationality; . . .

Article 15. Anyone who applies for naturalization must give evidence of good conduct, must show that he has a known occupation or means of livelihood, and must know how to speak, write and read the Spanish language. The applicant shall submit to a comprehensive examination on the history of the country and its values and shall, at the same time, promise to reside within the national territory regularly and swear to respect the constitutional order of the Republic. . . .

3) MOTION OF AMENDMENT to Article 14(4) of the Constitution presented by the Deputies of the Special Committee [the Deputies' amendment]:

A foreigner, who by marriage to a Costa Rican loses his or her nationality and who after two years of marriage to a Costa Rican and the same period of residence in the country, indicates his or her desire to take on the nationality of the spouse.

b) *Articles of the [American] Convention [on Human Rights]*

The above-mentioned legal texts should be compared to the following articles of the American Convention on Human Rights in order to determine their compatibility:

Article 17. Rights of the Family

Paragraph 4. The States Parties shall take appropriate steps to ensure the equality of rights and the adequate balancing of responsibilities of the spouses as to marriage, during marriage, and in the event of its dissolution. In case of dissolution, provision shall be made for the necessary protection of any children solely on the basis of their own best interests.

Article 20. Right to Nationality.

1.   Every person has the right to a nationality.
2.   Every person has the right to the nationality of the state in whose territory he was born if he does not have the right to any other nationality.
3.   No one shall be arbitrarily deprived of his nationality or of the right to change it.

Article 24. Right to Equal Protection

All persons are equal before the law. Consequently, they are entitled, without discrimination, to equal protection of the law.

III. SPECIFIC QUESTIONS ON WHICH THE OPINION OF THE COURT IS SOUGHT

In accordance with the request originally made by the Special Committee to study amendments to Articles 14 and 15 of the Constitution, the Government of Costa Rica requests that the Court determine:

a) Whether the proposed amendments are compatible with the aforementioned provisions of the American Convention on Human Rights.
Specifically, within the context of the preceding question, the following questions should be answered:
b) Is the right of every person to a nationality, stipulated in Article 20(1) of the Convention, affected in any way by the proposed amendments to Articles 14 and 15 of the Constitution?
c) Is the proposed amendment to Article 14(4) according to the text proposed in the Report of the Special Committee, compatible with Article 17(4) of the [American] Convention with respect to equality between spouses?
d) Is the text of the motion of the Deputies . . . to amend this same paragraph compatible with Article 20(1) of the [American] Convention?

III. Issues Relating to the Right to Nationality

31.   The questions posed by the Government involve two sets of general legal problems which the Court will examine separately. There is, first, an issue related to the right to nationality established by Article 20 of the Convention. [The Court finds no violation of Article 20 because although the changes make it more difficult to acquire nationality, they do not withdraw any Costa Rican citizen's nationality or deny any Costa Rican the right to change it.] A second set of questions involves issues of possible discrimination prohibited by the Convention. . . .

43.   Among the proposed amendments there is one that, although it does not violate Article 20 as such, does raise some issues bearing on the right to nationality. It involves the [Deputies'] amendment motion to Article 14, paragraph 4, of the proposal presented by the Members of the Special Legislative Committee. Under that provision, Costa Rican nationality would be acquired by

A foreigner who, by marriage to a Costa Rican loses his or her nationality and who after two years of marriage to a Costa Rican and the same period of residence in the country, indicates his or her desire to take on the nationality of the spouse.

44.   Without entering into an examination of all aspects of the present text that touch on the subject of discrimination—a topic which will be considered later on this opinion [—] . . . some related problems raised by the wording of the proposal need to be addressed. As a matter of fact, the above wording differs in more than one respect from the text of Article 14, paragraph 5, of the present Constitution and from

the text of Article 4, paragraph 4, of the proposed amendment as originally presented. The two latter texts read as follows:

Article 14. The following are Costa Ricans by naturalization:
    5. A foreign woman who by marriage to a Costa Rican loses her nationality or who indicates her desire to become a Costa Rican;

Article 14. The following are Costa Ricans by naturalization:
    4. A foreign woman who, by marriage to a Costa Rican loses her nationality or who after two years of marriage to a Costa Rican and the same period of residence in the country, indicates her desire to take on our nationality.

The above provisions indicate that a foreign woman who loses her nationality upon marrying a Costa Rican would automatically acquire Costa Rican nationality. They prescribe additional specific requirements only for cases where no automatic loss of the previous nationality occurs.

45. It is clear, on the other hand, that the [Deputies' amendment] text proposed by the Members of the Special Legislative Committee effects a substantial change in the here relevant provision, for it imposes additional conditions which must all be complied with in order for a person to become eligible for naturalization.

46. One consequence of the [Deputies'] amendment as drafted is that foreigners who lose their nationality upon marrying a Costa Rican would have to remain stateless for at least two years because they cannot comply with one of the obligatory requirements for naturalization unless they have been married for that period of time . . . .

47. Furthermore, whereas in the [Deputies' amendment] text here under consideration the automatic loss of nationality is one of the concurrent conditions for naturalization by reason of marriage, no special provisions are made to regulate the status of foreigners who do not lose their nationality upon marriage to Costa Ricans.

48. The [Deputies'] amendment proposed by the Members of the Special Legislative Committee would not as such create statelessness. This status would in fact be brought about by the laws of the country whose nationals, upon marrying a Costa Rican, lose their nationality. It follows that this amendment cannot therefore be deemed to be directly violative of Article 20 of the Convention.

49. The Court nevertheless considers it relevant, for the sole purpose of providing some guidance to the Costa Rican authorities in charge of this subject and without doing so in extenso and with lengthy citations, to call attention to the stipulations contained in two other treaties bearing on the subject. The Court refers to these treaties, without enquiring whether they have been ratified by Costa Rica, to the extent that they may reflect current trends in international law.

50. Thus, the Convention on the Nationality of Married Women provides in its Article 3:

1. Each Contracting State agrees that the alien wife of one of its nationals may, at her request, acquire the nationality of her husband through specially privileged naturalization proce-

dures; the grant of such nationality may be subject to such limitations as may be imposed in the interests of national security or public policy.
2. Each Contracting State agrees that the present Convention shall not be construed as affecting any legislation or judicial practice by which the alien wife of one of its nationals may, at her request, acquire her husband's nationality as a matter of right.

51.   The Convention on the Elimination of all Forms of Discrimination against Women provides in its Article 9:

States Parties shall grant women equal rights with men to acquire, change or retain their nationality. They shall ensure in particular that neither marriage to an alien nor change of nationality by the husband during the marriage shall automatically change the nationality of the wife, render her stateless or force upon her the nationality of the husband.

IV. Issues Relating to Discrimination

52.   The provisions of the proposed amendments that have been brought before the Court for interpretation as well as the text of the Constitution that is now in force establish different classifications as far as the conditions for the acquisition of Costa Rican nationality through naturalization are concerned. Thus, under paragraphs 2 and 3 of Article 14 of the proposed amendment, the periods of official residence in the country required as a condition for the acquisition of nationality differ, depending on whether the applicants qualify as native-born nationals of "other countries of Central America, Spaniards and Ibero-Americans" or whether they acquired the nationality of those countries by naturalization. Paragraph 4 of that same Article in turn lays down special conditions applicable to the naturalization of "a foreign woman" who marries a Costa Rican. Article 14 of the Constitution now in force makes similar distinctions which, even though they may not have the same purpose and meaning, suggest the question whether they do not constitute discriminatory classifications incompatible with the relevant texts of the Convention.

53.   Article 1(1) of the Convention, a rule general in scope which applies to all the provisions of the treaty, imposes on the States Parties the obligation to respect and guarantee the free and full exercise of the rights and freedoms recognized therein "without any discrimination." In other words, regardless of its origin or the form it may assume, any treatment that can be considered to be discriminatory with regard to the exercise of any of the rights guaranteed under the Convention is *per se* incompatible with that instrument.

54.   Article 24 of the Convention, in turn, reads as follows:

Article 24. Right to Equal Protection
All persons are equal before the law. Consequently, they are entitled, without discrimination, to equal protection of the law.

Although Articles 24 and 1(1) are conceptually not identical . . . Article 24 restates to a certain degree the principle established in Article 1(1). In recognizing equality before the law, it prohibits all discriminatory treatment originating in a legal prescription. The prohibition against discrimination so broadly proclaimed in Article 1(1) with regard to the rights and guarantees enumerated in the convention thus extends to the domestic law of the States Parties, permitting the conclusion that in these provisions the States Parties, by acceding to the convention, have undertaken to maintain their laws free of discriminatory regulations.

55.   The notion of equality springs directly from the oneness of the human family and is linked to the essential dignity of the individual. That principle cannot be reconciled with the notion that a given group has the right to privileged treatment because of its perceived superiority. It is equally irreconcilable with that notion to characterize a group as inferior and treat it with hostility or otherwise subject it to discrimination in the enjoyment of rights which are accorded to others not so classified. It is impermissible to subject human beings to differences in treatment that are inconsistent with their unique and congenerous character.

56.   Precisely because equality and nondiscrimination are inherent in the idea of the oneness in dignity and worth of all human beings, it follows that not all differences in legal treatment are discriminatory as such, for not all differences in treatment are in themselves offensive to human dignity. The European Court of Human Rights, "following the principles which may be extracted from the legal practice of a large number of democratic States," has held that a difference in treatment is only discriminatory when it "has no objective and reasonable justification." There may well exist certain factual inequalities that might legitimately give rise to inequalities in legal treatment that do not violate principles of justice. They may in fact be instrumental in achieving justice or in protecting those who find themselves in a weak legal position. For example, it cannot be deemed discrimination on the grounds of age or social status for the law to impose limits on the legal capacity of minors or mentally incompetent persons who lack the capacity to protect their interests.

57.   Accordingly, no discrimination exists if the difference in treatment has a legitimate purpose and if it does not lead to situations which are contrary to justice, to reason or to the nature of things. It follows that there would be no discrimination in differences in treatment of individuals by a state when the classifications selected are based on substantial factual differences and there exists a reasonable relationship of proportionality between these differences and the aims of the legal rule under review. These aims may not be unjust or unreasonable, that is, they may not be arbitrary, capricious, despotic or in conflict with the essential oneness and dignity of humankind.

58.   Although it cannot be denied that a given factual context may make it more or less difficult to determine whether or not one has encountered the situation described in the foregoing paragraph, it is equally true that, starting with the notion of the essential oneness and dignity of the human family, it is possible to identify circumstances in which considerations of public welfare may justify departures to a greater or lesser degree from the standards articulated above. One is here dealing with values which take on concrete dimensions in the face of those real situations in which they have to be applied and which permit in each case a certain margin of appreciation in giving expression to them.

59.   With this approach in mind, the Court repeats its prior observation that as far as the granting of naturalization is concerned, it is for the granting state to determine whether and to what extent applicants for naturalization have complied with the conditions deemed to ensure an effective link between them and the value system and interests of the society to which they wish to belong. To this extent there exists no doubt that it is within the sovereign power of Costa Rica to decide what standards should determine the granting or denial of nationality to aliens who seek it, and to establish certain reasonable differentiations based on factual differences which, viewed objectively, recognize that some applicants have a closer affinity than others to Costa Rica's value system and interests.

60.   Given the above considerations, one example of a non-discriminatory differentiation would be the establishment of less stringent residency requirements for Central Americans, Ibero-Americans and Spaniards than for other foreigners seeking to acquire Costa Rican nationality. It would not appear to be inconsistent with the nature and purpose of the grant of nationality to expedite the naturalization procedures for those who, viewed objectively, share much closer historical, cultural and spiritual bonds with the people of Costa Rica. The existence of these bonds permits the assumption that these individuals will be more easily and more rapidly assimilated within the national community and identify more readily with the traditional beliefs, values and institutions of Costa Rica, which the state has the right and duty to preserve.

61.   Less obvious is the basis for the distinction, made in paragraphs 2 and 3 of Article 14 of the proposed amendment, between those Central Americans, Ibero-Americans and Spaniards who acquired their nationality by birth and those who obtained it by naturalization. Since nationality is a bond that exists equally for the one group as for the other, the proposed classification appears to be based on the place of birth and not on the culture of the applicant for naturalization. The provisions in question may, however, have been prompted by certain doubts about the strictness of the conditions that were applied by those states which conferred their nationality on the individuals now seeking to obtain that of Costa Rica, the assumption being that the previously acquired nationality—be it Spanish, Ibero-American or that of some other Central American country—does not constitute an adequate guarantee of affinity with the value system and interests of the Costa Rican society. Although the distinctions being made are debatable on various grounds, the Court will not consider those issues now. Notwithstanding the fact that the classification resorted to is more difficult to understand given the additional requirements that an applicant would have to meet under Article 15 of the proposed amendment, the Court cannot conclude that the proposed amendment is clearly discriminatory in character.

62.   In reaching this conclusion, the Court is fully mindful of the margin of appreciation which is reserved to states when it comes to the establishment of requirements for the acquisition of nationality and the determination whether they have been complied with. But the Court's conclusion should not be viewed as approval of the practice which prevails in some areas to limit to an exaggerated and unjustified degree the political rights of naturalized individuals. Most of these situa-

tions involve cases not now before the Court that do, however, constitute clear instances of discrimination on the basis of origin or place of birth, unjustly creating two distinct hierarchies of nationals in one single country.

63.   Consistent with its clearly restrictive approach, the proposed amendment also provides for new conditions which must be complied with by those applying for naturalization. Draft Article 15 requires, among other things, proof of the ability to "speak, write and read" the Spanish language; it also prescribes a "comprehensive examination on the history of the country and its values." These conditions can be deemed, prima facie, to fall within the margin of appreciation reserved to the state as far as concerns the enactment and assessment of the requirements designed to ensure the existence of real and effective links upon which to base the acquisition of the new nationality. So viewed, it cannot be said to be unreasonable and unjustified to require proof of the ability to communicate in the language of the country or, although this is less clear, to require the applicant to "speak, write and read" the language. The same can be said of the requirement of a "comprehensive examination on the history of the country and its values." The Court feels compelled to emphasize, however, that in practice, and given the broad discretion with which tests such as those mandated by the draft amendment tend to be administered, there exists the risk that these requirements will become the vehicle for subjective and arbitrary judgments as well as instruments for the effectuation of discriminatory policies which, although not directly apparent on the face of the law, could well be the consequence of its application.

64.   The fourth paragraph of draft Article 14 accords "a foreign woman who [marries] a Costa Rican" special consideration for obtaining Costa Rican nationality. In doing so, it follows the formula adopted in the current Constitution, which gives women but not men who marry Costa Ricans a special status for purposes of naturalization. This approach or system was based on the so-called principle of family unity and is traceable to two assumptions. One has to do with the proposition that all members of a family should have the same nationality. The other derives from notions about paternal authority and the fact that authority over minor children was as a rule vested in the father and that it was the husband on whom the law conferred a privileged status of power, giving him authority, for example, to fix the marital domicile and to administer the marital property. Viewed in this light, the right accorded to women to acquire the nationality of their husbands was an outgrowth of conjugal inequality.

65.   In the early 1930's, there developed a movement opposing these traditional notions. It had its roots in the acquisition of legal capacity by women and the more widespread acceptance of equality among the sexes based on the principle of nondiscrimination. These developments, which can be documented by means of a comparative law analysis, received a decisive impulse on the international plane. In the Americas, the Contracting Parties to the Montevideo Convention on the Nationality of Women of December 26, 1933 declared in Article 1 of that treaty that "There shall be no distinction based on sex as regards nationality, in their legislation or in their practice." And the Convention on Nationality, signed also in Montevideo on that

same date, provided in Article 6 that "Neither matrimony nor its dissolution affects the nationality of the husband or wife or of their children." The American Declaration, in turn, declares in Article II that "All persons are equal before the law and have the rights and duties established in this declaration, without distinction as to race, sex, language, creed or any other factor." These same principles have been embodied in Article 1(3) of the United Nations Charter and in Article 3(j) of the OAS Charter.

66.   The same idea is reflected in Article 17(4) of the [American] Convention [on Human Rights], which reads as follows:

The States Parties shall take appropriate steps to ensure the equality of rights and the adequate balancing of responsibilities of the spouses as to marriage, during marriage, and in the event of its dissolution. In case of dissolution, provision shall be made for the necessary protection of any children solely on the basis of their own best interests.

Since this provision is consistent with the general rule enunciated in Article 24, which provides for equality before the law, and with the prohibition of discrimination based on sex contained in Article 1(1), Article 17(4) can be said to constitute the concrete application of these general principles to marriage.

67.   The Court consequently concludes that the different treatment envisaged for spouses by paragraph 4 of Article 14 of the proposed amendment, which applies to the acquisition of Costa Rican nationality in cases involving special circumstances brought about by marriage, cannot be justified and must be considered to be discriminatory. The Court notes in this connection and without prejudice to its other observations applicable to the [Deputies'] amendment proposed by the members of the Special Legislative Committee [cf. *supra*, paras. 45 *et seq.*] that their proposal is based on the principle of equality between the spouses and, therefore, is more consistent with the Convention. The requirements spelled out in that amendment would be applicable not only to "a foreign woman" but to any "foreigner" who marries a Costa Rican national.

68.   For the foregoing reasons, responding to the questions submitted by the Government of Costa Rica regarding the compatibility of the proposed amendments to Articles 14 and 15 of its Constitution with Articles 17(4), 20 and 24 of the Convention,

THE COURT IS OF THE OPINION . . . .

As regards Articles 24 and 17(4) of the Convention,

By unanimous vote . . . .

2. That the provision stipulating preferential treatment in the acquisition of Costa Rican nationality through naturalization, which favors Central Americans, Ibero-Americans and Spaniards over other aliens, does not constitute discrimination contrary to the Convention.

By five votes to one

3. That it does not constitute discrimination contrary to the Convention to grant such preferential treatment only to those who are Central Americans, Ibero-Americans and Spaniards by birth.

By five votes to one

4. That the further requirements added by Article 15 of the proposed amendment for the acquisition of Costa Rican nationality through naturalization do not as such constitute discrimination contrary to the Convention.

By unanimous vote

5. That the provision stipulating preferential treatment in cases of naturalization applicable to marriage contained in Article 14(4) of the proposed amendment, which favors only one of the spouses, does constitute discrimination incompatible with Articles 17(4) and 24 of the Convention.

Dissenting:

JUDGE BUERGENTHAL with regard to point 3.

JUDGE PIZA EXCALANTE with regard to . . . [point] 4.

NOTE

Judicial Standards for National Origin, Place of Birth, Language and History Tests, and Sex Classifications. What standard does the Court use when examining discrimination based on national origin, place of birth, and the language and history tests? What standard does the Court use when examining discrimination based on sex? What is the difference between these two standards and how will this affect the women of Costa Rica?

III. Case Study: Costa Rican Nationality Law Revisited in a Costa Rican Court

Rosa Martínez, a lifelong resident and citizen of Costa Rica, met her husband, Jorge Martínez, in graduate school in Costa Rica four years ago. The two were married in Costa Rica three years ago, and have spent their entire married life in Costa Rica. They wish to remain in Costa Rica permanently, and Jorge would like to become a Costa Rican citizen immediately in order to run for political office. Jorge is currently a citizen of Argentina.

Assume that Costa Rica changed its Constitution after the Inter-American Court decision to provide that:

Article 14. The following are Costa Ricans by naturalization: . . .

2) Native-born nationals of the other countries of Central America, Spaniards and Ibero-Americans with five years official residence in the country . . .

4) A foreigner who by marriage to a Costa Rican loses his or her nationality and who after two years of marriage . . . , indicates his or her desire to take on the nationality of the spouse is entitled to naturalization as a Costa Rican citizen.

The Constitution also contains an equality provision:

Article 33. All persons are equal before the law and there shall be no discrimination against human dignity.

Jorge applied for Costa Rican citizenship under both Article 14(2) and 14(4). The government official in charge denied immediate citizenship. He pointed out that Jorge did not have the necessary five years of official residence in Costa Rica. Nor did he meet the conditions of Article 4(4). Argentinean law provides that an Argentinean woman automatically acquires the nationality of her husband if she marries a foreigner, or if her husband changes his nationality to that of a foreign country. No comparable law automatically deprives an Argentinean man of his nationality upon marriage to a foreign woman or upon a change of nationality by his wife.

In the Costa Rican Advisory Opinion, the Inter-American Court considered the language concerning "a foreigner who by marriage to a Costa Rican loses his or her nationality . . ." and noted that the language "is based on the principle of equality between the spouses, and, therefore, is more consistent with the Convention." *See* paragraph 67. Do you agree with the Inter-American Court that the Constitution's new Article 14(4) is "based on the principle of equality between the spouses"? Why or why not?

If Rosa wants to file a case in a Costa Rican court to challenge the official denial of Jorge's citizenship application, what provisions of the Constitution or Convention, if any, should she cite? How could she argue that she should prevail under the Constitution? Is there any convincing argument that the Advisory Opinion notwithstanding, Costa Rica's law violates the American Convention's Equal Protection provision? What would be the government's defense as to both the Constitution and the Convention? Could it use Article 17(4) of the Convention to defend its decision? For its text, *see* paragraph 66 of the Advisory Opinion. How would you decide the case if you were the judge?

Who should file such a lawsuit: Rosa, Jorge, or both? Why?

Could either of them win claims under CEDAW Articles 9, 15, or 16? Under ICCPR Article 26? Take into account the CEDAW Committee's General Recommendation 21 and the Human Rights Committee's General Comment 28, *available at* RossRights. How do the Human Rights Committee's decisions affect your views?

IV. Other Women's Issues in the American System

Elizabeth A. H. Abi-Mershed, *The Inter-American Commission on Human Rights: Prospects for the Inter-American Human Rights System to Protect and Promote the Human Rights of Women*

in 2 WOMEN AND INTERNATIONAL HUMAN RIGHTS LAW 417, 430–33 (Kelly D. Askin and Dorean M. Koenig eds., 2000)

On January 12, 1995, the Inter-American Commission on Human Rights submitted the case of *María Elena Loayza-Tamayo v. Peru* to the Inter-American Court. The Commission, having found violations of Articles 5, 7, 8, 25, and 1.1 of the American Convention pursuant to its review of the case, presented claims concerning Loayza's arbitrary arrest on February 6, 1993, the arbitrary and illegal deprivation of her liberty, the torture and inhuman treatment to which she was subjected, and subsequent violations of her right to a fair hearing and trial. According to the pleadings, she was held incommunicado for the first ten days of her detention, and was subjected to torture and cruel and degrading treatment in order to coerce her to confess to having ties to *Sendero Luminoso* (the Shining Path). While held incommunicado, Ms. Loayza was raped by several state agents. This case remains pending on the merits. One aspect that is being closely watched is how specifically the Court will address rape as a human rights violation. [The Court later found that the rape could not be substantiated, but held that the other acts amounted to cruel, inhuman and degrading treatment.[A]]

In March of 1996, the Commission adopted its final decision on the case of *Raquel Martin de Mejía v. Peru*, which is notable for its treatment of rape as torture (Article 5).[52] The fact that the government contested the admissibility of the case, but never responded to the Commission's requests for information on the merits, raised certain questions with respect to the burden and standard of proof. Pursuant to Article 42 of its regulations and its longstanding practice, when a government fails to respond in a case, the Commission may presume the facts alleged to be true, as long as they are not contradicted by other evidence. On the basis of the petitioners' claims and other reports before it, measured against the criteria of "consistency, credibility and specificity," the Commission presumed the facts alleged to be true. In so doing, the Commission noted that the area in question, Oxapampa, had been under a state of emergency and military control at the time of the facts, which had placed the population at serious risk for human rights violations. The Commission further noted that the practice of rape by members of the security forces in such areas had been extensively documented and reported on by intergovernmental and nongovernmental groups, including the U.N. Special Rapporteur on Torture, Amnesty International, and Human Rights Watch.

In addressing the rape of Raquel Mejía, the Commission determined that each of the three elements set forth in the Inter-American Convention to Prevent and Punish Torture[54] had been met: 1) "an intentional act through which physical and mental pain and suffering is inflicted on a person;" 2) "committed with a purpose;" 3) "by a public official or by a private person acting at the instigation of the former." The

---

[A] *Loyazo-Tamalo v. Peru*, Inter-Am. Ct. H.R., Ser.C/33 (Sept. 17, 1997), *available at* http://www.corteidh.or.cr/index.cfm.

[52] The denunciation alleged that on June 15, 1989, members of the Peruvian military came to the home of Raquel Martin de Mejía and Fernando Mejía Egocheaga seeking the latter. They took Mr. Mejía, a lawyer and political activist, away with them. Within minutes, one of those agents returned to the house, told Raquel Martin de Mejía that she too was suspected of subversion, and raped her. That same agent returned a short time later and raped her again. She filed a complaint concerning her husband's disappearance with the authorities, but did not denounce the treatment to which she herself had been subjected. The body of Mr. Mejía was discovered several days later bearing signs of torture and a gunshot wound. Raquel Martin de Mejía continued to pursue legal claims concerning his death; however, having received threats and fearing for her safety, she eventually sought and received political asylum abroad. After she left the country, government authorities included her name in a list of Peruvians abroad suspected of subversion, and filed criminal charges against her. The claims concerning Fernando Mejía Egocheaga had been dealt with by the Commission in a separate case, and so were not revisited.

[54] It may be noted that Peru had signed, but had yet to ratify, the Convention.

analysis relative to the first element takes into account both the physical and psychological suffering caused by rape. The report notes the contemporaneous consequences for the victim, as well as the long-term sequelae, and addresses the reluctance of many victims to admit this violation. The analysis relative to the second element takes into account that "Raquel Mejía was raped with the aim of punishing her personally and intimidating her," and the fact that, under the circumstances, she was "terrorized not only for her own safety but also for that of her daughter who was sleeping in another room [at the time of the rapes] and for the life of her husband."

In addition to determining that the rapes were inflicted against Raquel Mejía as torture, the Commission found that they violated her right to have her honor respected (Article 11). Recalling the words of the U.N. Special Rapporteur against Torture, that rape affects women "in the most sensitive part of their personality" with the effects aggravated by the fact that "in the majority of cases the necessary psychological treatment and care will not . . . be provided," the Commission characterized sexual abuse generally as "a deliberate outrage" to the dignity of women.

Most recently, in October of 1996, the Commission adopted its final report on the case of *X and Y v. Argentina*, which concerned a practice of routinely requiring that female family members wishing to have contact visits with inmates undergo vaginal inspections.[57] A petition had been filed with the Commission in December of 1989, alleging that the victims, the wife of an inmate and their thirteen-year-old daughter, had been subjected to such inspections without regard for whether there were special circumstances to warrant extraordinary measures.[58] Ms. X had filed a writ of *amparo* demanding that the inspections cease. This writ was rejected at first instance, accepted on appeal, and then rejected by the Supreme Court of Argentina on the basis that the inspections were not flagrantly arbitrary under the terms of the law of *amparo.*

In balancing the interests of those subject to such searches against the state's interest in maintaining security within its prisons, the Commission characterized "a vaginal search [as] more than a restrictive measure as it involves the invasion of a woman's body." "Consequently, the balancing of interests involved" must hold the government "to a higher standard." In its report, the Commission set out a four-part test to determine the lawfulness of a vaginal inspection or search:

---

[57] The government's pleadings indicated that men were subject to inspections of the anal area, although this was never developed to indicate the frequency or conditions of such inspections.

[58] At one point, plastic explosives were found in the cell of Ms. X's husband, although it was never actually clarified how the substance was brought into the prison. Much was made in the pleadings of the need for special security measures in response to this situation. However, the inspections had been instituted by the authorities some time before, and had been practiced on Ms. X, her minor daughter, and other female visitors. The pleadings indicate that this measure had been imposed in response to general reports that relatives were transporting drugs into prison facilities.

(1) it must be absolutely necessary to achieve the security objective in the particular case;[60]
(2) there must not exist an alternative option;
(3) it should be determined by judicial order;[61] and
(4) it must be carried out by an appropriate health professional.[62]

The report suggests that this extraordinary measure would probably never be reasonable in the case of a child, finding with respect to Ms. Y (who was thirteen years old at the time in question) that "it is evident that the vaginal inspection was an absolutely inadequate and unreasonable method." The Commission found violations of Articles 5 and 11, 25 and 8, and 1.1.[64]

V. Introduction to the African Charter on Human and Peoples' Rights

The African Charter, *available at* RossRights, entered into force in 1986 and is the weakest regional instrument. It was adopted by the Organization of African Unity (OAU) and ratified by all 53 OAU member states. In 2001, the OAU was replaced by the African Union (AU), but the framework of the Charter mechanisms remains unchanged.

The African Commission on Human and Peoples' Rights oversees treaty enforcement. The Commission can consider individual or group complaints—"communications other than those of States parties"—and can act on them if a Commission majority so votes, and the complaining parties have exhausted domestic remedies. There is no specific provision for relief, however. The Commission can also investigate "a series of serious and massive violations" if it brings these to the attention of the African Union Assembly and the Assembly requests an "in-depth study." The Commission then issues a report, findings and recommendations. In either event, all measures taken by the Commission remain confidential unless the African Union Assembly decides otherwise. States parties submit periodic reports to the Commission on how they have complied with the Charter.

A Protocol to the African Charter on the Establishment of the African Court on Human and Peoples' Rights, *available at* RossRights, entered into force on January 25,

---

[60] "Absolutely necessary" means required in a specific instance by a real threat. Such measures cannot be imposed as a generalized response.

[61] The Commission analogized the extreme intrusion of a vaginal search to other official action "considered to be especially intrusive or potentially liable to abuse," such as the search of one's home. Accordingly, in principle, a judge should determine when such an inspection is justified for a contact visit.

[62] "[A]ny type of corporal probing . . . must be performed by a medical practitioner with the strictest observance of safety and hygiene, given the potential of physical and moral injury." Id. at para. 84.

[64] With respect to Article 11, concerning the right to privacy, the Commission underscored the fact that "the present case involves a particularly intimate aspect of a woman's private life" and that such an inspection, whether justifiable or not is likely to provoke intense feelings of shame and anguish in almost all persons who are submitted to it. In addition, subjecting a thirteen year old child to such a procedure could result in serious psychological damage. . . ."

2004, and should strengthen enforcement once it is fully in place. As of March 2007, only 23 of the 53 African states had ratified the protocol. The first 11 judges were sworn in on July 2, 2006, and the Court will be based in Arusha, Tanzania. In ratifying states that declare they will accept the Court's competence to receive individual complaints (only Benin as of June 2007), the Court "may entitle" women to file complaints against the state directly with the Court. It may also authorize NGO complaints if the NGO has observer status with the African Commission. The Court will have the power to order remedies, compensation, and reparation. States parties agree to comply with such judgments and to guarantee their execution.

Women filing with the Commission or Court must first exhaust domestic remedies and act within a "reasonable period" after doing so. They may not rely solely on news accounts or use "disparaging or insulting language" about the state or the African Union. The Court first decides whether a complaint is admissible and may either hear the case or transfer it to the Commission.

VI. The Relevance to Women of the African Charter on Human and Peoples' Rights

A basic question under the African Charter is the extent to which it can be used to advance women's rights to equality and freedom from violence. There are many factors that contribute to the question, but the most important is the role of traditional cultural values. Proponents of traditional ways unabashedly support giving men superior rights while human rights organizations and women's rights activists assert that their culture has changed and must grant women their fundamental human rights and freedoms.

The African Charter speaks to customary values in contradictory ways. The Preamble's fifth paragraph mentions "the virtues of [the African States Parties'] historical tradition and the value of African civilization which should inspire and characterize their reflection on the concept of human and peoples' rights. . . ." Article 17(3) gives States Parties the "duty" to promote and protect "morals and traditional values recognized by the community. . . ." Article 18(2) provides that the "State shall have the duty to assist the family which is the custodian of morals and traditional values recognized by the community." But Article 18(3) requires states to "insure the elimination of every discrimination against women and also ensure the protection of the rights of the woman and the child as stipulated in international declarations and conventions." If morals and traditional values require discrimination against women, how should this tension be resolved?

And what is the significance of Article 29? It provides that every "individual shall . . . have the duty: 1) to preserve the harmonious development of the family and to work for the cohesion and respect of the family; . . . 7) to preserve and strengthen positive African cultural values in his relations with other members of the society, in the spirit of tolerance, dialogue and consultation and, in general, to contribute to the promotion of the moral well being of society. . . ." If a husband believes a wife's obedience is necessary to family harmony, does she have a duty to obey?

Other factors that can undermine the African Charter include the use of meaning-less limits on state restriction of rights, often referred to as "clawbacks." For example, Article 8 guarantees "[f]reedom of conscience, the profession and free practice of religion" and then states "[n]o one may, subject to law and order, be submitted to measures restricting the exercise of these freedoms." Compare the broader scope of the ICCPR's Article 18(1) protection for religious freedom granting everyone: "freedom of thought, conscience and religion," including "the right to adopt a religion or belief of his choice, and freedom . . . to manifest his religion or belief in worship, observance, practice and teaching." Contrast the narrower scope of the ICCPR Article 18(3) exceptions that permit states to infringe the manifestation of "religion or belief" only if: "such limitations . . . are prescribed by law and are necessary to protect public safety, order, health, or morals or the fundamental rights and freedoms of others."

On the other hand, a Protocol to the African Charter on the Rights of Women in Africa entered into force on November 25, 2005, and may greatly enhance women's rights as against the weight of culture. For example, Article 5, on the "Elimination of Harmful Practices," specifically condemns "all forms of harmful practices which negatively affect the human rights of women."

In the rest of this Chapter, we present two state court decisions—from Tanzania and Zimbabwe—which illustrate the tensions between culture and human rights. Women do the vast majority of the agricultural work on the continent, but own virtually none of the land. The cases demonstrate the culture and traditions that create this result, their impact on specific women, and the differing approaches to international human rights of African judges from two countries in the same region. In the next part, Florence Butegwa describes other laws and practices that systematically deprive women of land and other economic resources. The last part considers the new African Protocol on Women's Rights and what its contribution to this issue might be.

A. Two State Courts: Opposing Views on Women's Land Rights

Ephrahim v. Pastory and Kaizilege
(Tanzania High Court)
[1990] LRC (Const) 757

MWALUSANYA J. This appeal is about women's rights under our Bill of Rights. Women's liberation is high on the agenda in this appeal. Women do not want to be discriminated against on account of their sex. What happened is that a woman, one Holaria Pastory, who is the first respondent in this appeal, inherited some clan land from her father by a valid will. Finding that she was getting old and senile and had no one to take care of her, she sold the clan land on 24 August 1988 to the second respondent, Gervazi Kaizilege, for Shs 300,000. This second respondent is a stranger and not a clan member. Then on 25 August 1988 the present appellant, Bernardo Ephrahim, filed a suit at Kashasha primary Court in Muleba District, Kagera Region, praying for a declaration that the sale of the clan land by his aunt, the first respondent, to the second respondent was void as females under Haya customary law have no power to sell clan land. The primary court agreed with the appellant and the sale was declared void and the first respondent was ordered to refund the Shs 300,000 to the purchaser.

Indeed the Haya customary law is clear on the point. It is contained in the Laws of Inheritance of the Declaration of Customary Law (GN No 436 of 1963) which in [Rule] 20 provides:

Women can inherit, except for clan land, which they may receive in usufruct but may not sell. However, if there is not male of that clan, women may inherit such land in full ownership.

In short that means that females can inherit clan land which they can use in usufruct, i.e., for their life time. But they have no power to sell it, otherwise the sale is null and void. As for male members of the clan the position is different. Cory and Hartnoll in . . . *Customary Law of the Haya Tribe,* tell us that a male member of the clan can sell clan land but, if he sells it without consent of the clan members, other clan members can redeem that clan land. The land returns to the clan and becomes the property of the man who repays the purchase price. It will be seen that the law discriminates against women. . . . [As one High Court judge noted in 1968]:

Now however much this court may sympathise with these very natural sentiments, it is in cases of this nature bound by the customary law applicable to these matters. It has frequently been said that it is not for courts to overrule customary law. Any variations in such law as takes place must be variations initiated by the altering customs of the community where they originate. Thus, if a customary law draws a distinction in a matter of this nature between males and females, it does not fall to this court to decide that such law is inappropriate to modern development and conditions. That must be done elsewhere than in the courts of law.

The Tanzania Court of Appeal [agreed in three opinions dated 1981, 1986, and 1988]. . . . It appeared then that the fate of women as far as sale of clan land was concerned was sealed. The position was as an English novelist Sir Thomas Browne (1605–1682) had pointed out in his book *Religio Medici* where he said:

The whole world was made for man; but the twelfth part of man for woman: man is the whole world, and the breath of God; woman the rib and crooked piece of man. I could be content that we might procreate like trees, without conjunction or that there were any way to perpetuate the world without the trivial and vulgar way of union.

However, the Senior District Magistrate of Muleba . . . did not think the courts were helpless or impotent to help women. He took a different stand in favour of women. He said in his judgment:

What I can say here is that the respondents' claim is to bar female clan members on clan holdings in respect of inheritance and sale. That female clan members are only to benefit or enjoy the fruits from the clan holdings only. I may say that this was the old proposition. With the Bill of Rights of 1987 (sic) female clan members have the same rights as male clan members.

And so he held that the first respondent had the right under the Constitution to sell clan land and that the appellant was at liberty to redeem that clan land on payment of the purchase price of Shs 300,000. That has spurred the appellant to appeal to this court, arguing that the decision of the district court was contrary to the law.

Is the Doctrine That Women Should Not Be Discriminated Against Because of Their Sex Part of Our Law?

Since this country adopted the doctrine "Ujamaa and Self-Reliance" discrimination against women was rejected as a crime. In his booklet *Socialism and Rural Development*, Mwalimu J. K. Nyerere[B] states:

Although every individual was joined to his fellow by human respect, there was in most parts of Tanzania an acceptance of one human inequality. Although we try to hide the fact and despite the exaggeration which our critics have frequently indulged in, it is true that the women in traditional society were regarded as having a place in the community which was not only different, but was also to some extent inferior. . . . This is certainly inconsistent with our socialist conception of the equality of all human beings and the right of all to live in such security and freedom as is consistent with equal security and freedom from all other. If we want our country to make full and quick progress now, it is essential that our women live in terms of full equality with their fellow citizens who are men.

And as long ago as in 1968, [High Court Judge] Saidij . . . pointed out the inherent wrong in this discriminatory customary law. . . . He said:

Now it is abundantly clear that this custom, which bars daughters from inheriting clan land and sometimes their own father's estate, has left a loophole for undeserving clansmen to flourish within the tribe. Lazy clan members anxiously await the death of their prosperous clansman who happens to have no male issue and as soon as death occurs they immediately grab the estate and mercilessly mess up things in the dead man's household, putting the widow and daughters into terrible confusion, fear, and misery. . . . It is quite clear that this traditional custom has outlived its usefulness. The age of discrimination based on sex is long gone and the world is now in the stage of full equality of all human beings irrespective of their sex, creed, race or colour.

But the customary law in question has not been changed up to this day. The women are still suffering at the hands of selfish clan members.

What is more is that since the Bill of Rights was incorporated in our 1977 Constitution (vide Act No 15 of 1984) by art 13(4)[c] discrimination against women has been

---

[B] Dr. Julius Nyerere was the first Tanzanian President, in 1964–1985. "Mwalimu" is the Kiswahili name for teacher.

[c] Article 13(4) of the Tanzanian Constitution provides: "No person shall be discriminated against by any person or any authority acting under any law or in the discharge of the functions or business of any state office." Judge Mwalusanya does not quote Article 13(5) which states: "For the purposes of this Article the expression 'discriminate' means to satisfy the needs, rights or other requirements of different persons on the basis of their nationality, tribe, place of origin, political opinion, colour, religion or station in life such that certain categories of people are regarded as weak or inferior and are subjected to restrictions or conditions whereas persons of other categories are treated differently or are accorded opportunities or advantage outside the specified conditions or the prescribed necessary qualifications."

prohibited. But some people say that that is a dead letter. And the Universal Declaration of Human Rights (1948), which is part of our Constitution by virtue of art 9(f)[D], prohibits discrimination based on sex as per art 7[E]. Moreover, Tanzania has ratified the Convention on the Elimination of All Forms of Discrimination against Women. This is not all. Tanzania has also ratified the African Charter on Human and Peoples' Rights which in art 18(3)[F] prohibits discrimination on account of sex. And finally, Tanzania has ratified the International Covenant on Civil and Political Rights which in art 26[G] prohibits discrimination based on sex. The principles enunciated in the above-named documents are a standard below which any civilised nation will be ashamed to fall. It is clear from what I have discussed that the customary law under discussion flies in the face of our Bill of Rights as well as the international conventions to which we are signatories.

Petitions Under Art 30(3) of the Constitution to Invalidate Discriminatory Laws

Courts are not impotent to invalidate laws which are discriminatory and unconstitutional. The Tanzania Court of Appeal . . . [in two cases] agreed that the discriminatory laws can be declared void for being unconstitutional by filing a petition in the High Court under art 30(3)[H] of the Constitution.

In . . . [one of these cases the Judge] pointed out that the constitutionality of a statute or any law could not be challenged in the course of an appeal by an appellate

---

[D] Article 9 of the Tanzanian Constitution provides: "The object of this Constitution is to facilitate the building of the United Republic as a nation of equal and free individuals enjoying freedom, justice, fraternity and concord, through the pursuit of the policy of Socialism and Self-Reliance which emphasizes the application of socialist principles while taking into account the conditions prevailing in the United Republic. Therefore, the state authority and all its agencies are obliged to direct their policies and programmes toward ensuring- . . . (f) that human dignity is preserved and upheld in accordance with the spirit of the Universal Declaration of Human Rights. . . ."

[E] Article 7 of the UDHR provides: "All are equal before the law and are entitled without any discrimination to equal protection of the law. All are entitled to equal protection against any discrimination in violation of this Declaration and against any incitement to such discrimination."

[F] Article 18(3) of the African Charter on Human and Peoples' Rights provides: "The State shall ensure the elimination of every discrimination against women and also ensure the protection of the rights of the woman and the child as stipulated in international declarations and conventions."

[G] Article 26 of the ICCPR provides: "All persons are equal before the law and are entitled without any discrimination to the equal protection of the law. In this respect, the law shall prohibit any discrimination and guarantee to all persons equal and effective protection against discrimination on any ground such as race, colour, sex, language, religion, political or other opinion, national or social origin, property, birth or other status."

[H] Article 30(3) provides: "Any person alleging that any provision in this Part [on Basic Rights and Duties] of this Chapter or in any law concerning his right or duty owed to him has been, is being or is likely to be violated by any person anywhere in the United Republic, may institute proceedings for redress in the High Court."

court. He said that the proper procedure was for the aggrieved party to file a petition in the High Court under art 30(3) of our Constitution. Equally here, as there is no petition under art 30(3) of the Constitution, and so the question of deciding any constitutionality of a statute or any law does not arise. When the issue of basic rights under the Constitution is raised or becomes apparent only after the commencement of proceedings in a subordinate court, it seems that the proper thing to do is for the subordinate court concerned to adjourn the proceedings and advise the party concerned to file a petition in the High Court under art 30(3) of the Constitution for the vindication of his or her right . . . .

The Reception Clause of Section 5(l) of Act No 16 of 1984

It has been provided by section 5(l) of the Constitution (Consequential, Transitional & Temporary Provisions) Act (No 16 of 1984) that with effect from March 1988 the courts will construe the existing law, including customary law:

with such modifications, adaptations, qualifications and exceptions as may be necessary to bring it into conformity with the provisions of the [Fifth Constitutional Amendment Act (No 15 of 1984) i.e. Bill of Rights].

All courts in Tanzania have been enjoined to interpret that section in the course of their duties. And I think it is the section which the Senior District Magistrate of Muleba had invoked in hearing this appeal. In the book *Law and its Administration in a One-Party State* . . . the former Chief Justice of Tanzania, Mr T. Georges, says:

Apart from judicial review, the courts can usually be depended upon to be astute in finding interpretations for enactments which will promote rather than destroy the rights of the individual and this is quite apart from declaring them bad or good.

The shape in which a statute is imposed on the community as a guide for conduct is that statute as interpreted by the courts. The courts put life into the dead words of the statute. By statutory interpretation courts make judge-made law affecting the fundamental rights of a citizen. . . .

Now how should s 5(l) of Act 16 of 1984 be interpreted by the courts? That is the big question.

Lord Denning MR in the case of *Seaford Court Estates Lid v. Asher* (1949) 2 KB 481 tells us what a judge should do whenever a statute comes up for construction. He says:

He must set to work on the constructive task of finding the intention of Parliament, and he must do this not only from the language of the statute, but also from a consideration of the social conditions which gave rise to it, and of the mischief which it was passed to remedy, and then he must supplement the written word so as to give "force and life" to the intention of the legislature. . . .

In two more cases Lord Denning MR had to repeat his warnings as regards the use for the courts to invoke a purposive approach of interpretation . . . :

The literal method is now completely out of date. It has been replaced by the approach which Lord Diplock described as the "purposive approach". In all cases now in the interpretation of statutes we adopt such a construction as will "promote the general legislative purpose" underlying the provision.

The Tanzania Court of Appeal has adopted the above purposive approach. . . . Now what was the intention of the Parliament of Tanzania in passing s 5(1) of Act 16 of 1984, and what was the mischief that it intended to remedy?

There can be no doubt that Parliament wanted to do away with all oppressive and unjust laws of the past. It wanted all existing laws (as they existed in 1984) which were inconsistent with the Bill of Rights to be inapplicable in the new era or be treated as modified so that they are in line with the Bill of Rights. It wanted the courts to modify by construction those existing laws which were inconsistent with the Bill of Rights such that they were in line with the new era. We had a new ground norm since 1984, and so Parliament wanted the country to start with a clean slate. That is clear from the express words of s 5(I) of Act 16 of 1984. The mischief it intended to remedy is all the unjust existing laws, such as the discriminatory customary law now under discussion. I think the message the Parliament wanted to impart to the courts under s 5(I) is loud and clear . . . .

If Parliament meant otherwise it could have said so in clear words. Many countries in the Commonwealth which had to incorporate Bills of Rights in their constitutions have expressly indicated what they wanted to be the position of the existing law after the introduction of the Bill of Rights in their constitutions. For example in Sri Lanka, art 18(3) of their 1972 Constitution clearly states that: "an existing law shall operate notwithstanding any inconsistency with the provisions of the Bill of Rights." [Judge Mwalusanya then cited similar Constitutional provisions in Trinidad and Tobago, Jamaica, and the Cook Islands.] . . .

But we in Tanzania did not want to adopt the above provisions which "saved" the existing law operating prior to the introduction of the Bill of Rights. We wanted to start with a clean slate, a new ground norm. That was nice for the people. The people of Zimbabwe did the same when their Constitution came into effect on 18 April 1980. And they had a similar provision like our s 5(I) of Act 16 of 1984. . . .

[Thus,] any existing law that is inconsistent with the Bill of Rights should be regarded as modified such that the offending part of that statute or law is void.

Parallel with the Reception Clause of the Common Law

The reception clause of s 5(1) of Act 16 of 1984 has its parallel in the reception clause of the English common law introduced by the Tanganyika Order in Council of 1920. Both clauses give the mandate to the courts to construe the received law with some modifications and qualifications. The reception clause of the English common law said: "the received law was subject to the qualification that it be applied so far as the circumstances of the territory and its inhabitants permit and subject to such qualifications as local circumstances may render necessary". Mfalila J very correctly lamented in his [1988] paper "The Challenges of Dispensing Justice in Africa According to Common Law":

If these colonial judges had wished they could have developed over the years a version of the common law relevant to Africa as the reception statutes themselves stated. They could have done this by construing the reception statutes strictly, for instance in East Africa where only "the substance" of the common law and equity was received the colonial judges had even greater scope of creativity. They could have proceeded to create a body of laws responsive to the emergent demands of each territory. As one writer put it, "the colonial judges never approached the problem as one calling essentially for the exercise of a policy-making legislative power." This was a pity because in West Africa they had the power to determine whether the limits of the local jurisdiction and local circumstances permitted the application of the received rules and to what extent. In East Africa they had the further power to decide whether a specific rule of English law was part of the "substance" of the common law and in all the territories they had the power to determine whether the statutes were of general application.

It is for this reason that for the colonial judges in criminal trials a customary law spouse was not regarded as a wife or husband for the purposes of the rules of evidence and as a result she or he could be compelled to testify against her or his spouse, whereas the common law counterpart could not be so compelled. . . .

But even under the reception clause of the English common law there were judges who liberally construed the provision under discussion. For example Sir Udo Udoma, then Chief Justice of Uganda, in *Alai v. Uganda* [1967] EA 596 interpreted the phrase "any married woman" from the reception clause to include a wife of common law marriage as well as a wife of a customary law marriage, contrary to the stand of the previous judges discussed above. But the hero of the construction of the reception clause of the English common law is Lord Denning MR who [wrote in a 1955 decision]:

This wise provision should, I think, be liberally construed. It is a recognition that the common law cannot be applied in a foreign land without considerable qualification. . . . It has many principles of manifest justice and good sense which can be applied with advantages to peoples of every race and colour all the world over: but it also has many refinements, subtleties and technicalities which are not suited to other folk. These offshoots must be cut away. In these far off lands the people must have a law which they understand and which they will respect. The common law cannot fulfil this role except with considerable qualifications. The task of making these qualifications is entrusted to the judges of these lands. It is a great task. I trust that they will not fail therein. . . .

I am inclined to think that if Lord Denning MR was confronted with the present problem now at hand he would have unhesitatingly said:

This wide provision should, I think, be liberally construed. It is a recognition that the law existing before the introduction of the Bill of Rights cannot be applied in the new era without considerable qualification. It has many principles of manifest justice and good sense which can be applied with advantages to the people of Tanzania. But it also has many provisions which are not suited to a country with a Bill of Rights. These offshoots must be cut away. The people must have a law which they understand and which they will respect. The law existing prior to the introduction of the Bill of Rights cannot fulfil this role except with considerable qualifications. The task of making these qualifications is entrusted to the judges of Tanzania. It is a great task. I trust that they will not fail therein.

Therefore Lord Denning MR will wriggle in his chair (not in the grave for he is still alive) to hear that some judges interpret the reception clause in s 5(I) of Act 16 of 1984 *as not to affect the content and the quality of the law* existing prior to the enactment of the Bill of Rights. But it should be noted that the reception clause in s 5(1) affects only statutes and customary law existing prior to 1984 but does not affect any later law. And the position is understandable because for three years from March 1985 to March 1988 the government was given a period of grace to put its house in order, i.e. to amend all laws that were inconsistent with the Bill of Rights. And so the statutory interpretation that we have adopted here need not raise any eye-brows.

Women's Liberation

I have found as a fact that [Rule] 20 of the Rules of Inheritance (GN No 436 of 1963) of the Declaration of Customary Law is discriminatory of females in that unlike their male counterparts they are barred from selling clan land. That is inconsistent with art 13(4) of the Bill of Rights of our Constitution which bars discrimination on account of sex. Therefore under s 5(1) of Act No 16 of 1984 I take [Rule] 20 of the Rules of Inheritance to be now modified and qualified such that males and females now have equal rights to inherit and sell clan land. Likewise the Rules Governing the Inheritance of Holdings by Female Heirs (1944) made by the Bukoba Native Authority which in [Rules] 4 to 8 entitle a female who inherits self-acquired land of her father to have usufructuary rights only (rights to use for their lifetime only) with no power to sell that land is equally void and of no effect. Females just like males can now and onwards inherit clan land or self-acquired land of their fathers and dispose of the same when and as they like. The disposal of the clan land to strangers without the consent of the clansmen is subject to the fiat that any other clan member can redeem that clan land on payment of the purchase price to the purchaser. That now applies to both males and females. Therefore the District Court of Muleba was right to take judicial notice of the provisions of s 5(1) of Act No 16 of 1984, and to have acted on them the way it did.

From now on, females all over Tanzania can at least hold their heads high and claim to be equal to men as far as inheritance of clan land and self-acquired land of their father's is concerned. It is part of the long road to women's liberation. But there is no cause for euphoria, as there is much more to do in other spheres. One thing which surprises me is that it has taken a simple, old rural woman to champion the cause of women in this field but not the elite women in town who chant jejune slogans years on end on women's lib but without delivering the goods. To the male chauvinists, they should remember what that English writer John Gay (1685–1732) had said in *The Beggar's Opera*:

Fill every glass, for wine inspires us, And fires us, with courage, love and joy, Women and wine should life employ. Is there aught else on earth desirous? If the heart of a man is depressed with cares, the mist is dispelled when a woman appears.

It is hoped that, from the time the woman has been elevated to the same plane as the man, at least in respect of inheritance of clan land, then the mist will be dispelled. . . .

Conclusion . . . .

Like the district court I hold that the clan land in question was sold for Shs 300,000. Like the district court I hold that the sale was valid. The appellant can redeem that clan land on payment of Shs 300,000. I give the appellant six months from today to redeem the clan land, otherwise if he fails the land becomes the property of the purchaser—the second respondent. The appeal is dismissed with costs . . . .

Venia Magaya v. Makayi Shonhiwa Magaya
(Supreme Court of Zimbabwe)
[1999] 3 LRC 37

MUCHECHETERE JA (GUBBAY CJ, EBRAHIM and SANDURA JJA concurring):

This is an appeal against the decision of the magistrate, the effect of which was to appoint the respondent [male] heir to the estate of the late Shonhiwa Lennon Magaya (the deceased).

The facts in the matter are that the deceased died intestate. He had two wives. The first wife was the mother of the [female] appellant (born in 1941) and the second wife is the mother of the [male] respondent (born in 1946). The first wife had only one child, the appellant, and it appears that the second wife had three children, the respondent and two other sons, namely Frank Shonhiwa Magaya (born 1942) and Amidio Shonhiwa Magaya (born in 1950). The property in the deceased's estate included house number 767 Old Mabyuku in Harare ("the said house") and some cattle at the communal home.

It is apparent from the above that the appellant is the eldest child of the deceased and is female. The respondent is not the eldest male child of the deceased. He, however, claimed the heirship because the eldest male child, Frank Shonhiwa Magaya, declined to claim the heirship on the ground that he was not able to look after the family.

Soon after the death of the deceased the appellant, with the support of her mother and three other relations, went to claim the heirship of the estate in the community court and it was granted to her. The respondent later discovered this and applied to the community court for the cancellation of the appointment on the ground that he and other persons interested in the deceased's estate were not summoned to the hearing at which the appellant was appointed heir—[a] failure to comply with the provisions of s 69 (2) of the Administration of Estates Act ("the Act").

The appointment was duly cancelled and all interested parties were summoned to and did attend a new hearing on the matter on 14 October 1992. After hearing from the claimants, . . . the learned presiding magistrate awarded the heirship to the respondent. The learned magistrate stated the following in arriving at his decision:

. . . There are only two contestants, that is, (the respondent) and Venia. *Venia is a lady (and) therefore cannot be appointed to (her) father's estate when there is a man.* (Muchechetere JA emphasis)[1] .

The provisions of the Act [state]:

68(1) *If any African who has contracted a marriage according to African law or custom or who, being unmarried, is the offspring of parents married according to African law or custom, dies intestate his estate shall be administered and distributed according to the customs and usages of the tribe or people to which he belonged.*

It was not in dispute that the deceased was an African who contracted his two marriages according to African law and custom. . . .

I therefore agree with what Bennett said [in] *Human Rights and African Customary Law Under the South African Constitution* [(1995)]:

In customary law succession is intestate, universal and onerous. Upon the death of a family head his oldest son (if the deceased had more than one wife it would normally be the oldest of his first wife) succeeds to the status of the deceased. *Emphasis on the term "status" implies that an heir inherits not only the deceased's property but also his responsibilities, in particular his duty to support surviving family dependants.* . . .

The said rule *which prefers males to females as heirs to the deceaseds' estates constitutes a prima facie discrimination against females* and could therefore be a prima facie breach of the Constitution of Zimbabwe ("the Constitution") . . . [,which provides in s 23]:

(1) Subject to the provisions of this section—

    (a) no law shall make any provision that is discriminatory either of itself or in its effect; and
    (b) no person shall be treated in a discriminatory manner by any person acting by virtue of any written law or in the performance of the functions of any public office or any public authority.

(2) For the purposes of subsection (1), a law shall be regarded as making a provision that is discriminatory and a person shall be regarded as having been treated in a discriminatory manner if, as a result of that law or treatment, persons of a particular description by race, tribe, place of origin, political opinions, colour or creed are prejudiced—

    (a) by being subjected to a condition, restriction or disability to which other persons of another such description are not made subject; or
    (b) by the according to persons of another such description of a privilege or advantage which is not accorded to persons of the first-mentioned description; and the imposition of that condition, restriction, or disability or the according of that privilege or advantage is wholly or mainly attributable to the description by race, tribe, place of origin, political opinion, colour or creed of the persons concerned.

---

[1] All emphases in this opinion are those of Muchechetere JA.

However it seems to me that these provisions do not forbid discrimination based on sex. But even if they did on account of Zimbabwe's adherence to gender equality enshrined in international human rights instruments, there are exceptions to the provisions. The relevant exceptions are . . . :

23(3) Nothing contained in any law shall be held to be in contravention of subsection (1) (a) to the extent that the law in question relates to any of the following matters—

> (a) adoption, marriage, divorce, burial, *devolution of property on death or other matters of personal law;*
> (b) *the application of African customary law in any case involving Africans or an African* and one or more persons who are not Africans where such persons have consented to the application of African customary law in that case. . . .

In my understanding of the above provisions, matters involving succession are exempted from the discrimination provisions, firstly because they relate to "devolution of property on death or other matters of personal law" and secondly in this case because they relate to customary law being applied between Africans. The application of customary law generally is sanctioned under s 89 of the Constitution. . . .

I would therefore dismiss the appeal on the ground that . . . the discriminatory aspects of the law applicable are saved by the exemptions in the Constitution.

There is, however, need to discuss the effect of the Legal Age of Majority Act 1982 ("the Majority Act") on customary law. . . . [It provides]:

15(1) On and after the 10th December, 1982, a person shall attain the legal age of majority on attaining eighteen years of age. . . .
(3) [Subsection] (1) . . . shall apply for the purpose of any law, including customary law and, in the absence of a definition or any indication of a contrary intention for the construction of "full age", "major", "majority", "minor", "minority", and similar expressions in—

> (a) any enactment whether passed or made before, on or after the 10 December; and
> (b) any deed, will or other instrument of whatever nature made on or after that date.

The first opportunity to interpret the above provisions was in the case of *Katekwe v. Muchabaiwa* 1984 (2) ZLR 112. This was a seduction damages case brought by the guardian of an unmarried female where sexual intercourse had taken place between the female and the seducer with consent. The purpose of an action of this nature, under customary law, is to compensate the guardian for the loss in the female's potential *lobola* price.[J]

. . . [T]he Court in that case laboured under what I consider was the wrong view

---

[J] *Lobola,* or brideprice, is the amount the groom pays to the father of the bride to insure a valid customary marriage. Often, the new husband believes he has purchased his wife and that she must therefore obey him. If the wife later wants a customary divorce because the husband beats her or sleeps around, her father must repay the brideprice. Most fathers refuse to, and have already spent it in any event. Thus her birth family may refuse to take her back and urge her to stay with her husband. If she has no financial resources, survival drives her back.

. . . that seduction damages under customary law belong to the seduced female. They belong to the guardian. He is the person who charges and receives *lobola*. The action belongs to him in all circumstances and the seduced female does not have the right of action in the matter. When a guardian sued under customary law, he did not sue as a representative of the seduced female, he sued in his own capacity because he was the person who had suffered loss—diminution of *lobola*. . . .

[T]he following sentiments expressed by Dumbushena CJ [in *Katekwe*] only apply, in my view, under common law:

The action for the seduction embraces in our general law two claims: one is for satisfaction for the defloration of the girl and the other for lessening her chances of a successful marriage. The girl seduced is entitled to be compensated for the loss of her virginity, and for her diminished chances of making a suitable marriage.

Indeed the case cited in support of the above sentiments was concerned with seduction under common law. In the circumstances, the new "age, status and capacity" of a woman would not bestow on her rights she never possessed. On that basis I would also say the case [*Katekwe*] was wrongly decided.

The Court in . . . *Katekwe* . . . also assumed, without . . . a full consideration of the matter, that the "disability" or "discrimination" suffered by women under customary law was due to "their perpetual minority." From that position it went on to hold that on the passing of the Majority Act, once they gained majority, all the "disabilities and discrimination" fell away. In this connection Dumbutshena CJ said [in his *Katekwe* opinion]:

It seems to me that an African woman with majority status can if she so desires, allow her father to ask for *roora/lobola* from the man who wants to marry her. She and she alone can make that choice. If she does agree to her father asking for *roora* from his future son-in-law before marriage the father can go through the contractual procedures required before an African marriage is effected. The position, as from 10 December 1982, when the Legal Age of Majority Act came into effect, is that an African woman of majority status can contract a marriage, whether that marriage be in terms of the African Marriages Act or the Marriage Act[K] without the consent of her guardian. . . .
In my view, the above was the intention of the Legislature, and the object the Legislature sought to achieve was the liberation of African women from the legal disadvantages of perpetual minority. . . .

The question to consider is whether the "disabilities" and "discrimination" suffered by women under customary law were based on "their perpetual minority." In [an earlier case] *Mwazozo's case supra* I came to the conclusion that they were not based on their perpetual minority but on the nature of African society, especially the patrilineal, matrilineal or bilateral nature of some of them. I reasoned that concepts of "minority" and "majority" status were not known to African customary law but that they were common law concepts which, in my view, should only be used in customary law situations with great care. And I attempted to explain why allowing female

---

K As is typical in Africa, Zimbabwe law separates citizens on the basis of religion and ethnicity, providing different marriage and divorce laws for each community.

children to inherit in a broadly patrilineal society, such as in the present case, would disrupt the African customary laws of that society. In an article by Ncube entitled "Voodoo Law Brewed In an African Pot: Judicial Reconstruction of the Customary Law of Inheritance," it was stated that the sentiments I expressed on the matter were not persuasive because they were not based on "a single legal sociological or anthropological authority". This view was repeated in the submissions made by Mr. Ncube [in this case as amicus curiae]. Although no "authorities" were cited, the sentiments were based on the Court's knowledge, experience, understanding and appreciation of African customary law (the Court's composition included two Africans). I observe that the submissions which were made by all counsel in this case were, apart from in most cases unnecessarily and unjustifiably partisan, intemperate and, as Mr. Ncube put it, "trenchant" articles written by academics criticizing various cases of this Court, also largely not backed by "authorities."

I agree with what Bennett says about the nature of African society. The learned author states that at the heart of the African socio-political order lay the family, a unit that was extended both vertically and horizontally to encompass a wide range of people who could be called "kin." The family was therefore the focus of social concern. [I]ndividual interests were submerged in the common weal and the system stressed individual duties instead of his or her rights. And the legal relationships of most consequence in customary law were those of a family's dealings with other families, not those flowing from one person's relations with another.

At the head of the family there was a patriarch, or a senior man, who exercised control over the property and lives of women and juniors. It is from this that the status of women is derived. The woman's status is therefore basically the same as that of any junior male in the family. Mr. Ncube conceded that males in a family are as subordinate to the patriarch as females until they are "liberated." The liberation generally comes with the death of the patriarch and the male "taking over" or with the male moving away from the family and founding his own family. An example of the male's status was demonstrated in a recent criminal case. . . . [A]ppellant, who was married and had a family of his own, was accused of having indecently assaulted one of his nieces. The father of the complainant, a relation, went and reported the matter to the father (patriarch) of the appellant so that the appellant could be disciplined. The father of the appellant and other relatives had to hold a meeting where the appellant was forced to answer the allegations and was thereafter reprimanded for his actions. Clearly the appellant, even at his stage in life was still not liberated. He was to use the inappropriate term, still "a minor."

In my understanding of African society, especially that of a patrilineal nature, the perpetual "discrimination" against women stems mainly from the fact that women were always regarded as persons who would eventually leave their original family on marriage, after the payment of *roora/lobola*, to join the family of their husbands. It was reasoned that in their new situation—a member of the husband's family—they could not be heads of their original families as they were more likely to subject the interests of the original family to those of their new family. It was therefore reasoned that in their new situation they would not be able to look after the original family. It was also reasoned that the appointment of female heirs would be tantamount to diverting the property of the original family to that of her new family. This would most likely occur on the death of a female heir. Then her property would be inherited by her children who would be members of her new family. This, is my view, would be a distortion of the principles underlying customary law of succession and inheritance. . . .

I am also of the view that the finding in *Katekwe* . . . is tantamount to bestowing on women rights which they never had under customary law. A woman had no rights under customary law to heirship, demanding payment of lobola (it never depended on her acceptance), or to contract a marriage under the Customary Marriages Act without the consent of her guardian and others. In this connection see Bennett . . . :

[Under *Katekwe*,] [if] women gained full contractual powers when they turned eighteen, they could contract marriages without the consent of their guardians. It followed that a father's consent was irrelevant to the marriage and that he could not insist on bridewealth, the seal of a valid union (under customary law). Arguably this case was wrongly decided. Majority status gives women powers (or competencies) that they formerly lacked. It does not necessarily give them additional rights. Women subject to customary law never had the right to sue for damages for their own seduction (the delict was conceived to be in the interest of their guardians) nor did they have a right to claim bridewealth for their own marriages. The fact that a woman's capacity is governed by common law does not mean that her substantive rights should be determined by the same system. . . .

On the intention of the Legislature in passing the Majority Act, my view is that although it wanted to emancipate women by giving them *locus standi* for "competencies" in all matters generally, especially under common law, it was never contemplated that the courts would interpret the Majority Act so widely that it would give women additional rights which interfered with and distorted some aspects of customary law. As already indicated above, matters such as "marriage, divorce, burial, devolution of property on death or other matters of personal law," and customary law in general, were specifically exempted from the provisions of the Constitution forbidding "discrimination"—s 23(3)(a) and (b) of the Constitution. It was therefore not expected that any interpretation of the Majority Act would interfere with these. That the Legislature considered the Court's interpretation of the Majority Act as being too wide and out of its contemplation was shown by the widespread calls in and out of Parliament for the Majority Act to be amended so as to reflect its true wishes. In this connection see Ncube's Critique on *Katekwe* . . . :

The Prime Minister (now President of Zimbabwe) replied that "if there has been a flaw in drafting the regulation (the Majority Act) that flaw will be amended." He added, apparently in a moment of jest, that if his sister were to get married, he would demand *lobola* and if the intended husband pointed to the *Katekwe* judgment, he would say to him: "OK that is the judgment. Do you want to marry my sister or not?"

The various Ministers involved in the drafting of the legislation promised to look at the Majority Act and make changes if necessary. However, the important words were that changes would be made "if there had been a flaw in drafting." My view is that there was no flaw in the drafting and that it was the Court which wrongly interpreted the Majority Act too widely. There was, therefore, in my view, no need to amend the Majority Act.

Mr. Ncube and Ms. Makarau [lawyers for appellant Venia] both urged this Court to, in any event, exercise its discretional lawmaking role to ensure that women are not excluded from being appointed heiresses at customary law. This, they submitted, would be achieved by supporting in full the [decision] in . . . *Katekwe*. . . . They argued that this was necessary because the system of appointing single male heirs had caused untold hardship to the deceased's widows and dependants in that the heirs have too often not lived up to their responsibilities and used all the deceased's property for their own personal benefit. They also argued that the change would be proper because culture and custom are dynamic and change with changes in society and in particular the fact that urbanization had made African society less and less patriarchal. It was further argued that the change would be in keeping with the principle of advancing gender equality enshrined in the international human rights instruments to which Zimbabe is a party.

Whilst I am in total agreement with the submission that there is a need to advance gender equality in all spheres of society . . . care must be taken when African customary law is under consideration. In the first instance, it must be recognized that customary law has long directed the way African people conducted their lives and the majority of Africans in Zimbabwe still live in rural areas and still conduct their lives in terms of customary law. In the circumstances, it will not readily be abandoned especially by those such as senior males who stand to lose their positions of privilege. . . .

Secondly, the application of customary law generally is sanctioned by the Constitution and some would elevate this to a right having been conferred by the Constitution.

Thirdly, the application of customary law, especially in inheritance and succession, is in a way voluntary, that is to Africans married under customary law or those who choose to be bound by it. It could therefore be argued that there should be no or little interference with a person's choice. [In one case] it was held that when an African contracts a marriage according to African law and custom s 69(1) (now s 68(1)) of the [Administration of Estates] Act lays down that customary law will apply to the administration of the estate of the African. And that, on the other hand, the general [statutory civil] law will apply to [the monogamous] marriages under the Marriages Act.

In view of the above, I consider it prudent to pursue a pragmatic and gradual change which would win long term acceptance rather than legal revolution initiated by the courts.

Further, I do not consider that the Court has the capacity to make new law in a complex matter such as inheritance and succession. In my view, all the courts can do is to uphold the actual and true intention and purport of African customary law of succession against abuse, as was done in the *Masango* case. [In *Masongo v. Masongo*, the heir—the eldest surviving son of the first or second marriage—refused to support his deceased father's third wife and children. The court ruled that he could not evict them from the house he inherited and owned because he had failed to provide another home for them.] See Bennett. . . .

The obligation to care for family members, which lies at the heart of the African social system, is a vital and fundamental value, which Africa's Charter on Human and People's Rights is careful to stress. Paragraph 4 of the Preamble to the Charter urges parties to pay heed to "the virtues of (the African) historical tradition and the values of African civilization", and Ch. 2 provides an inventory of the duties that individuals owe their families and society. Article 29(1), in particular, states that each person is obliged to preserve the harmonious development of the family and to work for the cohesion and respect of the family, to respect his parents at all times, to maintain them in case of need.

Matters of reform should be left to the Legislature. In this connection see Bennett . . . :

The customary rules governing parental rights to children are flexible and the courts have already decided that in custody orders the interests of the children must come first. The indeterminate nature of customary law, and the fact that reform has already begun, are reasons to continue the process by applying a norm of non-discrimination to mothers who claim rights to their children. To abolish the principle of agnatic succession[L] is a different matter. Customary rules of succession are firmly established. . . . *Even more to the point is the court's capacity to make new law. In the case of guardianship a court has only to declare that a mother has the same right with father. In the case of succession a court could not simply rule customary norms void; it would have to stipulate how much widows could inherit and in what circumstances. Details of this nature cannot be determined in judicial proceedings. The proper medium for reform would be legislation, which permits full investigation of the social context and consultation with interested groups.*

And indeed our Legislature, after what I understand was wide consultation with interested groups, has undertaken the reform of succession in estates of persons subject to customary law. In s 3 of the Administration of Estates Amendment Act 1997 ("the amendment") it repealed the said s 68 of the Act. [For the text of s 68, *see* the sixth paragraph of this opinion.] The amendment went into detailed provisions about all matters of concern in succession. Those details could never have been undertaken during judicial proceedings. The impression that these provisions are acceptable to most of the persons concerned is given by the fact that there was wide consultation before the promulgation of the amendment and there has so far been no outcry about the provisions.

In the circumstances, if the deceased in this case had died on or after 1 November 1997 his estate would have been administered in terms of the amended s 68 of the Act. So as far as succession under customary law is concerned the law has now been reformed.

Ms. Makarau made submissions to the Court about what she considered were the peculiar circumstances of this case. These were to the effect that the respondent, as the child of the deceased's second wife, was unlikely to look after the deceased's first wife and her child (the appellant). It was also submitted that because an heir under

---

[L] Agnatic succession means that property is inherited only by male blood relatives of the deceased.

customary law inherited "any immovable property or any rights attaching thereto forming part of the estate of such deceased person" in his individual capacity, the respondent would evict the deceased's first wife and the appellant from the said house to do with it as he pleased. This, she submitted, would work hardship on both the first wife and the appellant because the said house was acquired by the deceased and the first wife without the participation of the second wife and because when the deceased died he was living in the said house with the first wife and both were being looked after by the appellant. If this was the position . . . , it would be the same as that which obtained in the *Matambo* case [a case cited for the same holding as *Masongo v. Masongo*]. In my view, it would be resolved in the same way . . . if the matter were to be brought before the courts. . . .

MCNALLY JA: The central point made by Muchechetere JA, which compels me to accept the weight of his reasoning, is that the Legal Age of Majority Act . . . removed disabilities but was not intended (except for the reduction in age from twenty-one to eighteen) to create positive new rights. Thus a woman of eighteen years of age in the communal area who wished to marry without her father's consent might do so, under the Marriage Act. But she could not do so under the provisions of customary law. She could not, as it were, accept and reject customary law at the same time.

Similarly, where by statute it was provided that immovable property, in a deceased estate to which customary law applied, passed to the [male] heir in his individual capacity and not as a representative of his family [a statute later repealed by the 1997 Administration of Estates Act], the Courts did not treat that [pre-1997] enactment as a repeal of the heir's duty to maintain the dependants of the deceased. The statutory amendment had to co-exist with customary law. It did not replace it. So the majority status of women had to co-exist with customary law. It did not replace it. If no suitable male heir were available, a woman could lawfully be appointed heir. But the customary law preference for a male heir was not eliminated.

N O T E S

The Aftermath. Women's rights NGOs were indignant about the Court's decision and sent a letter of protest to the Court. In response, the Court sent a letter to the seven NGOs (which included, for example, the Zimbabwe Women Lawyers Association) refuting their points:

1. "A retrogressive precedent"
The judgment was careful to explain that it was interpreting the law as it existed before the passing of the Administration of Estates Amendment Act on 1 November 1997. Section 68 F(2) [of the amended Act] makes it clear that while (F)(2)(e) males are to remain ceremonial heirs, the deceased's estate is now to be one third to the surviving widow/s and two-thirds to the children, whether they be male or female. So to say that it sets a precedent (meaning a guideline for the future) is incorrect, misleading, and gratuitously insulting.

2. Greatly undermining women's rights
The judgment seeks to state what the rights of women married under customary law were before the amendment to the law in the Administration of Estates Amendment Act, 1997. The judges considered that those rights had previously been overstated, for reasons which were care-

fully argued in the judgment. If there is any carefully reasoned submission to the contrary, the judges would be glad to receive it but emotional and insulting generalisations do not fall into that category.

3. Challenging the authority of Parliament

This is a very serious allegation indeed. It suggests that the court is undermining the very constitutional foundation upon which the balance of powers is based. The court has been at pains to explain why it does not consider that it is going against the intention of Parliament. What the writer of the letter has done is to assume that the Parliament thinks as she does, and then to accuse the court of disagreeing with her. In the court's view this is a serious contempt of court.

4. Alleged misinterpretation of the Legal Age of Majority Act

This Act does two things. First it recognised the majority status of all persons who attained a certain age. Second it reduced the age of majority, for men and women, from 21 to 18. The court set out its reasons for concluding that the Act had previously been wrongly interpreted. The court is entitled to expect that if anyone has a different view, that view will be expressed thoughtfully and courteously. The question in this case was not whether Mrs. Magaya was a minor, but whether she was entitled to be appointed as the heir under customary law. The court accepts that she is not a minor. The criticism of the judgement therefore seems to the judges to be misconceived.

5. The criticism of the judgement's definition of "customary law"

The judgement did not state that the country has a single customary law in all respects. It is not fair or right to set up an allegation which your opponent is supposed to have made, and then knock it down triumphantly, when your opponent did not say that. See the conclusion that:

> What is common and clear from the above is that under the customary law of succession of the above tribes males are preferred to females as heirs.

No point was made by counsel on either side that the general Shona customary law of succession did not apply in this case. Note again that the question is not whether women over 18 are majors or minors. The question is whether in Shona Customary Law unamended by statute women could be heirs.

6. It is true that this judgment changed the law as previously enunciated

The court is slow to do this, but is empowered to do so where necessary. . . .

7. The court's carefully thought out conclusion was that the general Shona Customary Law of Succession was that men rather than women qualified as heirs

To alter this, in the face of an express provision in the Constitution to the contrary was considered to be well beyond the powers of the court.

8. To conclude from this that the court is unprogressive, ignorant of the people's needs, not people-oriented, ignorant of realities, and adjudicating in a vacuum, is gratuitously insulting to the judges of the Supreme Court

No action will be taken on this occasion, but a formal warning must be issued that registered legal practitioners especially, but others as well, who indulge in gratuitous and unfounded insults to the Judiciary, and in public demonstrations against the Judiciary, will be dealt with under the laws of contempt of court.

The 1997 Administration of Estates Amendment. The Court notes in its first point that children will inherit property in equal shares without regard to sex under the 1997 amendment. In the Magaya family, there are two wives and four children. The conflict concerns one house and some cattle. Under the new law, the two wives will share one-third of the property and the four children two-thirds. They will probably have to sell the property. If the property were worth $10,000, the wives would get $3,333 and the children $6,667. Thus, each wife's share would be $1,666 and each child's share also $1,666. Under the old law which the court applied, Venia's younger half-brother received $10,000 and everyone else nothing. What are the pros and cons of the two different systems? Notice that the male primogeniture system was also used under ancient British common law.

The Women's Organizations. How do you explain their intense emotions given the 1997 Amendments? The Court's intense emotions?

B. Different Methods for Obtaining Land in Africa: Marriage; Divorce; Inheritance; State Allocation; and Purchase

As you read the following article about the discrimination African women face in acquiring property, consider to what extent these same barriers have faced women in the developed world, both in the past and today.

Florence Butegwa, *Using the African Charter on Human and Peoples' Rights to Secure Women's Access to Land in Africa*
in HUMAN RIGHTS OF WOMEN: NATIONAL AND INTERNATIONAL PERSPECTIVES 495, 495–500 (Rebecca J. Cook ed., 1994)

Introduction

Insofar as there exists a de jure or de facto significant difference in opportunities for access to land in any country, and that difference is based purely on whether one is a man or a woman, there is discrimination. . . . In many African countries, there is both de jure and de facto discrimination against women in opportunities to acquire, hold, and deal in land. . . .

The chapter is divided into . . .[two] sections: an overview of the situation regarding women's access to land in Africa [and] the international principle of nondiscrimination and its relevance to women's access to land. . . .

Women and Access to Land in Africa

Access to land in many African countries is governed by a dual system of law. Customary law and statutory law apply alongside each other often raising situations of internal conflict of laws and general confusion in case law and in popular understanding of the law. The diversity of customary and legislative frameworks for land ownership in Africa do not render themselves to easy combined analysis. Therefore, for purposes of this chapter, the situation of women regarding access to land is presented here with special reference to Tanzania and Uganda.

In both countries, land is owned by the state and individuals can only acquire rights of occupancy and usufructuary. The technical difference between usufructuary rights and ownership as understood in western legal theory is not material in this chapter. Both confer rights of control and power to deal in the land and the interest of the holder may be transferred by will, under laws of intestacy or through commercial transactions. Tanzania has attempted to codify its customary law rules and provides some insights into land ownership among matrilineal societies in Africa. In both countries, access to land is mainly through "family transfers," direct allocation from a state agency or through a commercial transaction. The situation of women under each method is dealt with separately.

Family Transfers and Women's Access to Land

The term "family transfers" is used here to refer to three methods of acquiring land. The first is the case where a man transfers land to his son when he is ready to marry and is quite common in the rural areas, where land is not registered. The transfer is accomplished by simply showing the son that part of the land on which he can establish his new home. Daughters are never beneficiaries of this type of land acquisition.

The second covers the rare instances where a woman is given a share of her husband's landed property on divorce. In Uganda, legislation and courts do not regard a married woman's domestic duties as contributions toward the accumulation of property by her husband. A woman will only share in the distribution of matrimonial property if she can prove actual monetary contribution toward the purchase. In Tanzania, however, the Law of Marriage Act provides that property acquired during the subsistence of the marriage shall be presumed as belonging to both parties. Courts are given wide powers when called upon to divide matrimonial property between the parties on divorce. They may take into account, inter alia, "the contributions by either party in money, property or work towards the acquisition of the assets." Courts have differed in their interpretation of this provision. In *Hamid Amir v. Maryam Arris* [1977], a woman's claim to a share in the matrimonial property was rejected, and the judge stated:

With due respect I'm unable to agree because the wife runs a household, washes, cleans, cooks and saves money each month, this should be termed as her contribution and joint effort towards acquisition of property during subsistence of marriage.

In *Bi Hawa Mohamed Ally Sefu* [1983], however, the Tanzania Court of Appeal [the State's highest court] held a different view:

It is apparent that the Act seeks to liberate married women from such exploitation and oppression by reducing the traditional inequality between them and their husbands in so far as their respective rights and duties are concerned. Although certain features of traditional inequality [remain] under the Act . . . , these do not detract from the overall purpose of the Act as an instrument of liberation and equality between the sexes.

It is hoped that the Court of Appeal has set a precedent that is soundly based on considerations of women's human rights and will pave the way for further inroads into customary law-based sex discrimination.

The third method of family transfers is through the inheritance of a deceased relative's parcel of land. As virgin land available for state allocation decreases, succession to a relative's land may be the only viable avenue left for many people in Africa. This is especially so for those without the economic means to purchase land on the market or to qualify for land allocation by State agencies. Allocation is normally dependent on financial ability to develop the land within a specified period.[9]

Customary law governs succession to land held under customary tenure. In Uganda the Succession Act and the Succession Amendment Decree 1972 allow a surviving widow to inherit any property, including land, bequeathed to her under her deceased husband's will. In practice very few people make wills in Uganda. It is considered a bad omen for one to make a will.

In case of intestacy, the widow has no claim to her late husband's land. The land goes to the customary law heir, normally the deceased's eldest son. The widow was traditionally allowed to remain on the matrimonial land until her death or remarriage. The past decade, however, has seen a marked erosion of this custom. Heirs tend to sell off the land and use the proceeds for their own benefit. The Uganda Succession Act allows a widow a 15 percent share in the estate of a deceased husband [while the widower is given 100 percent of a deceased wife's estate], but this percentage is very rarely calculated to include any land.

In Tanzania's matrilineal societies, where property is inherited through a wife's lineage, women do not have effective control or ownership of the family land. Contrary to popular belief, land and other valuable property is controlled by the male members of the woman's family, normally her father, brothers, or uncles. They are responsible for showing her and her husband a piece of land to use as family land. In patrilineal societies, a wife is not regarded as a member of the family for land ownership and inheritance purposes. The widow's contribution toward the acquisition of the property is not taken into consideration either. Under [Rule 19 of] the Local Customary Law (Declaration) Order, the eldest son in the deceased's first marriage has the primary right to the family land. Failure of a male issue in this marriage passes the right to sons in subsequent marriages. As a Tanzania High Court ruling [of 1967] puts it aptly,

a widow does not acquire any proprietary rights in her husband's landed property simply because she contributed labour in developing them [sic] and therefore she gains no inheritance rights therein.

Daughters of the deceased cannot inherit land. They are allowed to live on and cultivate the family land as long as they are not married. Progressive judges have attempted to interpret Rule 19 more liberally. In *Ndewawosia d/o Ndeamtzo v. Imanuel s/o Malasi* [1968], for instance, the judge said:

this custom, which bars daughters from inheriting clan land and sometimes their own fathers' estate, has left a loophole for undeserving clansmen to flourish within the tribe. . . . These

---

[9] Land Regulations 1948, sec. 3, made under the Land Ordinance, Cap. 113, Laws of Tanzania.

men are not entitled to take property towards the acquisition of which they have contributed absolutely nothing. . . . In Tanzania . . . and elsewhere the idea of equality between men and women has gained much strength. . . . The time has come when the rights of daughters in inheritance should be recognized.

Unfortunately this decision does not appear to have been followed consistently by other high court judges. The inconsistencies in case law are indicative of the fact that the issue remains undecided. The judge in *Ephrahim v. Pastory* [1990] and like-minded judges are pioneers in safeguarding women's human rights while reminding the government that it is a signatory to international human rights instruments guaranteeing equality and freedom from discrimination on the basis of sex. The situation might be clearer when the issue has been considered and determined by the Court of Appeal.

Access to Land Through Direct Purchase

The acquisition of land through direct purchase is generally governed by the law of contract. Contractual capacity is based on age. Once one has attained the age of majority in Uganda and Tanzania, he/she is eligible to contract. Theoretically, therefore, women have access to land on an equal footing with men. In practice, however, women remain at a significant disadvantage. Financial credit to purchase land requires security in the form of a developed piece of land. The majority of women do not have it since they do not inherit land. An outright purchase is even rarer as the majority of women do not earn enough from petty trading, formal employment, or the informal sector to raise the purchase price.

Women's Access to Land and International Human Rights Law

The whole question of women's access to land and other economic resources is one that is rarely discussed in the context of international human rights law. Freedom from discrimination is a central theme in international human rights law. . . . [Ms. Butegwa then discusses the relevant law.] The state of the law in Tanzania and Uganda determines access to land on the basis of sex. This discrimination against women is not based on any objective and reasonable justification. Much as the customs of the people of Uganda and Tanzania may have barred women from inheriting clan land, the tenets underlying the custom are no longer valid. It was feared that clan land would fall into the hands of non-clan members through marriage. It could even be said that this fear and consequent prohibition applied equally to men. No man had a right to sell clan land to a non-clan member. Clan membership was customarily the effective criterion on which usufructuary rights and control over the land was based.

This is no longer the case. Men, increasingly appreciative of commercial credit, have applied for and obtained direct grants (long-term leaseholds) and title deeds from government. The title documents are issued in the name of the individual rather than the clan. The deeds are then used as security for loans from commercial banks.

Men are also increasingly selling land to non-clan members. Urbanization and ease of geographical mobility have allowed more and more people to settle in areas far from their original clan territory. The individualization of land through individual titles, coupled with the fact that families can settle anywhere in the country, is indicative of the erosion of clanism as a basis for access to land. These developments mean that the retention of the custom that discriminates against women is not justifiable. The discrimination in cases of land that is not held under customary tenure is even less justifiable. Consequently, it is clear that both law and practice in Tanzania and Uganda relating to access to land unlawfully discriminates against women contrary to international human rights law.

NOTES

Using the African Charter. Consider Articles 2, 3, 14, and 18(3) of the African Charter, *available at* RossRights. How do they apply to the *Magaya* customary law requiring that the estate be left to the eldest male son? What do Articles 27–29 add to the discussion? For further discussion of widows and inheritance issues, *see* Uche U. Ewelukwa, *Post-Colonialism, Gender, Customary Injustice: Widows in African Societies,* 24 Hum. Rts. Q. 424 (2002).

CEDAW, the ICCPR, the ICESCR, and Access to Land. Consider each of these treaties, *available at* RossRights. Which articles could be used to help women like Venia Magaya?

C. The African Commission, the African Special Rapporteur, and the African Protocol on the Rights of Women—Hope for the Future?

The African Charter has structural weaknesses, a weak enforcement method, and States Parties who often ignore it. Yet there are signs of progress as the system matures.

Julia Harrington, *The African Commission on Human and Peoples' Rights*
in 2 Women and International Human Rights Law 455, 465–70 (Kelly D. Askin and
   Dorean M. Koening eds., 2000)

Women's Rights in the State Reporting Procedure

The state reporting procedure under the African Charter resembles that which exists under the Women's Convention, the U.N. Human Rights Committee, and the Race Convention. Article 62 of the African Charter states:

Each state party shall undertake to submit every two years, from the date the present Charter comes into force, a report on the legislative or other measures taken with a view to giving effect to the rights and freedoms recognized and guaranteed by the present Charter.

This procedure suffers from the same difficulties as its U.N. counterparts: simple lack of compliance on the part of states, reports of a cursory nature, and lack of time and expertise to examine the reports properly.

Early on, the Commission elaborated a set of guidelines to assist states in preparing these reports. They are broken down into two parts under each subject to be reported on: information that should be included in the initial reports (basic legal texts and statistics on the present situation) and information to be included in the second, or "periodic" report, namely, updates on the progress in the implementation of the rights and duties. These guidelines have been criticized as being overly lengthy and confusing; they take up twenty-five pages in the Commission's Second Activity Report, the only place they are officially published.

These guidelines are, however, of value to scholars because they reflect in detail the early ideas of the Commission on the meaning of certain articles of the Charter. The Commission has, through these guidelines, made extensive statements not only on economic and social rights but on women's rights specifically. For example, with regard to Article 18, the Commission specifies that states should "take measures to abolish such customs, ancient laws and practices as may affect the freedom of choice of a spouse." The Commission's interpretation of articles has primacy, and its notion of "measures to strengthen the family" consists of housing subsidies, tax-exemptions, and child-care institutions," not more cumbersome divorce laws. If these guidelines were more widely known and studied, they would have long since laid to rest fears about the "family" articles being used to oppress women.

The guidelines also dwell on "maternity protection," requesting information on appropriate medical and health care and maternity and other benefits, irrespective of marital status "and special protections for working mothers." It is reassuring to women's rights activists that the guidelines do not give less weight to the more controversial economic and social provisions of the Charter, but ask for extensive information on the right to an adequate standard of living, including measures taken to ensure equitable food distribution and to educate the population on nutrition. Reduction of still-births and infant mortality is also noted as a part of the right to health.

Going still further, the Commission devotes an entirely separate section of its guidelines to "women's rights," in addition to those instances noted above where women's rights may be implicated by the provisions of the Charter. After describing article by article the information states should provide in their reports, the guidelines revisit women's human rights extensively. Only racial and gender discrimination receive such special treatment, a clear indication that they are high priorities, at least on paper. Indeed, the guidelines seem to imply that states may even submit separate reports on women's rights: the special section is entitled, "General guidelines regarding the form and contents of reports received from States Parties on the Elimination of All Forms of Discrimination Against Women," although this could be the simple result of extensive borrowing from the U.N. guidelines.

The guidelines mention the Women's Convention by name and describe its reporting requirement. In paragraph 2, the Commission states:

Discrimination against women in Africa is of such widespread occurrence that the Commission would also like to receive reports on measures to eliminate this anachronism.

The Commission repeatedly refers to the Women's Convention as "the Convention" and requests information on its implementation. In light of this treatment, plus Article 60 [directing the Commission to draw inspiration from international human rights law] of the Charter and the stipulation on international conventions in Article 18.3, the Commission appears to take very seriously the incorporation of the Women's Convention into the Charter.

From the foregoing analysis of the Commission's guidelines, one might have the impression that women's rights are dealt with extensively under the state reporting procedure. Unfortunately, this is not the case. Women's rights are not singled out for neglect in the reporting procedure, but the Commission's guidelines generally go unheeded when states prepare their reports. Some reports cover hardly any of the subjects requested by the Commission. Few state reports have discussed women's rights explicitly, although a few commissioners (not necessarily the women) consistently ask for information on, for example, discriminatory land ownership and inheritance laws. If the state representatives devote time to answering these questions verbally, women's rights at least make an appearance in the examination procedure.

Quite aside from the attention, or lack thereof, devoted to women's rights under the state reporting procedure, the procedure generally may be criticized as ineffective in protecting women's rights. It is, at best, an exercise to raise awareness of the rights guaranteed by the Charter, but the audience at these examinations consists of government representatives and observers from nongovernmental human rights organizations, not the general population. It is hoped that through the process of examination, states will be educated and inspired to do more for women's rights. But this is not the mechanism through which individual women can advocate for their own rights.

Women's Rights Under the Communications Procedure

The potentially most effective procedure for individual women to advocate their rights before the African Commission is the individual communications procedure, which is lesser known than the state reports and frequently dismissed by women's rights activists. Article 55 provides:

1. Before each Session, the Secretary of the Commission shall make a list of the communications other than those of States parties to the present Charter and transmit them to the members of the Commission, who shall indicate which communications should be considered by the Commission.
2. A communication shall be considered by the Commission if a simple majority of its members so decide.

A communication is simply an accusation of a violation of the Charter, brought by an NGO or an individual (not necessarily the victim/survivor) against the government responsible. The low profile of this procedure is largely due to Article 59 of the Charter, which specifies that "measures taken" by the Commission in respect of communications be kept confidential until the Heads of State and Government of the OAU decide otherwise. In practice, this means that the Commission's decisions on communications are confidential until they are approved as part of the Commission's Annual Activity Report, which is submitted to the Assembly of Heads of State and Government of the OAU each year.

The Commission accepts communications brought by any individual or non-governmental organization, in contrast to the other regional mechanisms, which accept cases only from the victims themselves or their families. The Commission has a special provision for cases of grave or massive violations. [*See* Article 58 of the Charter, *available at* RossRights.]

In none of the decisions on cases published so far does the Commission take up questions of women's rights. Naturally, the Commission, like any judicial body, can only take up issues that are brought before it in relation to a specific set of facts.

A look at the decisions already published in the Activity Reports gives the impression that most of the cases before the Commission concern civil and political rights. This is not surprising, as the first parties to take advantage of adversarial, judicial recourse are likely to be lawyers or legal nongovernmental organizations, who are oriented towards civil and political rights, sometimes referred to as first-generation rights. The decisions, while not elaborate, do show that the Commission is not hesitant to condemn harmful government practices and laws. Several decisions have declared Nigerian decrees incompatible with the African Charter.

While the communications procedure has not, as of June 1997, yielded any judgement on women's rights, there is reason to believe that if such a communication is brought before the Commission, it will receive serious consideration. In the priority it gave to a seminar on women's rights and in its guidelines for state reporting, the Commission has evidenced a sensitivity to women's rights issues. It has also shown a willingness to condemn certain state practices. If a well-documented communication were brought on a women's rights issue, it would test the Commission's commitment and might result in a binding judgement.

It would be misleading to give the impression that all decisions taken by the Commission are immediately complied with by the governments affected or even acknowledged at all. However, the publication of the Commission's decisions has resulted in a far higher level of direct participation of governments in the Commission's sessions. The Commission's first reports on its decisions appeared in an annex of its Seventh Annual Activity Report, which became public in summer 1994. Since that time, every session has witnessed the presence of several government representatives. This presence suggests the governments are taking the Commission more seriously than in the past. An increasing number of governments send delegations to testify in their own defense in respect of communications.

Future Possibilities: The Special Rapporteur and the Special Protocol for Women's Rights

There are two spheres of possible Commission action that may, in the future, positively affect women's rights in Africa. The first is a proposal for an additional Protocol to the African Charter, which was accepted in principle by the Commission at the nineteenth session. Such a protocol, while it would no doubt encounter resistance from the OAU member states and might suffer the same treatment as the Women's Convention with regard to reservations if these are permitted, would dramatically elevate the importance of women's rights in the African regional system, and could even, depending on its formulation, result in the establishment of a separate body, a counterpart to the African Commission, that would focus exclusively on women's rights. As of August 1999 work on the Protocol was still in progress.

The second potentially important step for women's rights in Africa is the appointment of a Special Rapporteur for women, which is implicitly if not explicitly provided for under Article 46 of the Charter. This measure was suggested by nongovernmental organizations; the International Commission of Jurists is a particularly strong supporter. At its nineteenth session, the Commission agreed in principle to appoint a Special Rapporteur on women. At the Twenty-First Session, Julienne Ondziel-Gnelenga, a member of the Commission from Congo-Brazzaville, was appointed as Special Rapporteur on Women.

Depending on the terms of reference adopted by the Commission, the Special Rapporteur could have a very broad mandate to take missions, including investigations of particular abuses, to organize further conferences and seminars, and to write reports.

The Commission's history of Special Rapporteurs has been mixed. The Commission's rapporteur on extrajudicial executions was appointed from among the commissioners in 1994 without prior arrangements for funding the additional activities or providing administrative support. This created difficulties for the Special Rapporteur in actively fulfilling his mandate. A Special Rapporteur for prison conditions was also appointed from within the Commission at the twentieth session in October 1996. With substantial support from NGOs and U.N. Special Rapporteurs, the Commission's rapporteurs on extrajudicial executions and prison conditions have recently made progress in implementing their mandates, but the Commission will be reluctant to place responsibility upon an individual without prior concrete provisions for the funds necessary to fulfill their mandate.

Conclusion

The African regional system is still relatively young, and its record as concerns women's rights is neither extensive nor impressive. However, the fears that have been voiced by many, based only on the texts of the Charter, are unfounded. Where it has made statements or taken action with regard to women's rights, the Commission has shown itself to be progressive, and it has the power to interpret the Charter progressively. Women's rights, along with other rights, suffer from the African Commission's overall lack of resources. Yet as the system gains prestige, experience, and confidence, there is reason to be hopeful. Existing procedures may be improved and new ones utilized to advocate for women in Africa. Women activists in Africa know all too well that this will not be easy yet, if fully developed, the possibilities of the African system can make a positive difference to women across the continent and contribute to the growth of new areas of international law.

N O T E

Protocol to the African Charter on Human and Peoples' Rights on the Rights of Women in Africa. On November 25, 2005, a decade-long campaign by experts and NGOs to address the plight of African women came to a successful conclusion with the entry into force of the Women's Rights Protocol. As of August 7, 2007, 21 countries had ratified the protocol and another 22 had signed it. As a document intended to enhance women's status and eliminate discrimination against women, the protocol supplements the provisions of the African Charter and recognizes the particular human rights violations suffered by women as well as necessary requirements for effective protection of women's rights. For example, in addition to the prohibitions on trafficking in women and protections against violence in times of conflict, Article 4 includes broad protection from violence "whether the violence takes place in private or public."

Other articles address certain cultural practices that discriminate against women. For example, Article 5 contains provisions designed to eradicate traditional and cultural practices, such as female genital mutilation, which are physically harmful to women and girls. Article 20 requires that states adopt measures to protect widows from "inhuman, humiliating or degrading treatment" such as that described in the article by Uche U. Ewelukwa, *Post-Colonialism, Gender, Customary Injustice: Widows in African Societies*, 24 HUM. RTS. Q. 424 (2002). Article 21 speaks to the issues addressed in the Tanzania and Zimbabwe cases but hedges by requiring "equitable," not "equal," treatment. Thus, women and men "have the right to inherit, in equitable shares, their parents' properties." Similarly, a widow gets "an equitable share" of her deceased husband's property.

Addressing women's rights in the context of marriage, Article 6 requires that states take measures toward ensuring equality in marriage, such as enacting laws that set the minimum age for marriage at eighteen and ensure that while married the wife has "the right to acquire her own property and to administer and manage it freely." But although earlier versions of the protocol required states to prohibit polygamy, the final version does not. Instead, Article 6(c) requires states to enact legislation "to guarantee that . . . monogamy is encouraged as the preferred form of marriage and that the rights of women in marriage and family, including in polygamous marital relationships, are promoted and protected. . . ." This was a significant setback but one required by the steady opposition of representatives from countries with strong Islamic traditions, including Mali, Senegal, Sudan, Egypt, Tunisia, and Libya.

The protocol also guarantees women equal rights to political participation (Article 9), education (Article 12), employment (Article 13), health and reproduction (Article 14), and a positive cultural context (Article 17), as well as several provisions guaranteeing various economic and social rights. Article 14 on health issues is the first international document to specifically "protect the reproductive rights of women by authorising medical abortion in cases of sexual assault, rape, incest, and where the continued pregnancy endangers the mental and physical health of the mother or the life of the mother or the foetus."

Of particular importance is Article 2, which requires states to take affirmative steps, such as amending their constitutions, enacting legislation, and integrating women's rights into all aspects of policymaking. Article 2 even contains a provision modeled on Article 5(a) of CEDAW, requiring states to work toward eliminating cultural and traditional practices based on stereotyped gender roles.

Chapter 6

Enforcing Women's International Human Rights Under Regional Treaties: The [European] Convention for the Protection of Human Rights and Fundamental Freedoms

I. Introduction to the European Convention

In 1949, ten European countries—Belgium, Denmark, France, Ireland, Italy, Luxembourg, the Netherlands, Norway, Sweden, and the United Kingdom—established the Council of Europe through a new treaty, the Statute of the Council of Europe. The new body had many purposes, among them the "further realisation of human rights and fundamental freedoms." This led the Council to adopt the Convention for the Protection of Human Rights and Fundamental Freedoms ("European Convention") in November 1950. It entered into force on September 3, 1953.

By May 11, 2007, the Council had expanded to 47 member states with a population of more than 800 million citizens. All 47 states had also ratified the European Convention.[A] Many had ratified most of the 14 Protocols to the Convention, of which 13 had entered into force. Protocol 14 will further streamline the Court procedures described below. Although ratified by 46 states as of August 7, 2007, this Protocol will not enter into force until ratified by Russia.

EUROPEAN COURT OF HUMAN RIGHTS, THE COURT
available at http://www.echr.coe.int/echr (last visited Aug. 7, 2007) and RossRights

[I.] Historical Background

A. The European Convention on Human Rights of 1950

1. . . . Taking as their starting point the 1948 Universal Declaration of Human Rights, the framers of the Convention sought to pursue the aims of the Council of Europe through the maintenance and further realisation of human rights and funda-

---

[A] Monaco was the 47th state to ratify on November 30, 2005, but the Convention did not apply in all 47 countries until Montenegro's earlier ratification entered into force on June 6, 2006.

mental freedoms. The Convention was to represent the first steps for the collective enforcement of certain of the rights set out in the Universal Declaration.

2. In addition to laying down a catalogue of civil and political rights and freedoms, . . . the Convention set up a mechanism for the enforcement of the obligations entered into by Contracting States. Three institutions were entrusted with this responsibility: the European Commission of Human Rights (set up in 1954), the European Court of Human Rights (set up in 1959) and the Committee of Ministers of the Council of Europe, the latter organ being composed of the Ministers of Foreign Affairs of the member States or their representatives.

3. Under the Convention in its original version, complaints could be brought against Contracting States either by other Contracting States or by individual applicants (individuals, groups of individuals or non-governmental organisations). Recognition of the right of individual application was, however, optional and it could therefore be exercised only against those States which had accepted it (Protocol No. 11 to the Convention was subsequently to make its acceptance compulsory, see paragraph 6 below).

The complaints were first the subject of a preliminary examination by the Commission, which determined their admissibility. Where an application was declared admissible, the Commission placed itself at the parties' disposal with a view to brokering a friendly settlement. If no settlement was forthcoming, it drew up a report establishing the facts and expressing an opinion on the merits of the case. The report was transmitted to the Committee of Ministers.

4. Where the respondent State had accepted the compulsory jurisdiction of the Court, the Commission and/or any Contracting State concerned had a period of three months following the transmission of the report to the Committee of Ministers within which to bring the case before the Court for a final, binding adjudication. Individuals were not entitled to bring their cases before the Court.

If a case was not referred to the Court, the Committee of Ministers decided whether there had been a violation of the Convention and, if appropriate, awarded "just satisfaction" to the victim. The Committee of Ministers also had responsibility for supervising the execution of the Court's judgments.

B. Subsequent developments

5. Since the Convention's entry into force thirteen Protocols have been adopted. Protocols Nos. 1, 4, 6, 7, 12 and 13 added further rights and liberties to those guaranteed by the Convention, while Protocol No. 2 conferred on the Court the power to give advisory opinions. Protocol No. 9 enabled individual applicants to bring their cases before the Court subject to ratification by the respondent State and acceptance by a screening panel. Protocol No. 11 restructured the enforcement machinery (see below). The remaining Protocols concerned the organisation of and procedure before the Convention institutions.

6. From 1980 onwards, the steady growth in the number of cases brought before the Convention institutions made it increasingly difficult to keep the length of pro-

ceedings within acceptable limits. The problem was aggravated by the accession of new Contracting States from 1990. The number of applications registered annually with the Commission increased from 404 in 1981 to 4,750 in 1997. By that year, the number of unregistered or provisional files opened each year in the Commission had risen to over 12,000. The Court's statistics reflected a similar story, with the number of cases referred annually rising from 7 in 1981 to 119 in 1997.

The increasing case-load prompted a lengthy debate on the necessity for a reform of the Convention supervisory machinery, resulting in the adoption of Protocol No. 11 to the Convention. The aim was to simplify the structure with a view to shortening the length of proceedings while strengthening the judicial character of the system by making it fully compulsory and abolishing the Committee of Ministers' adjudicative role.

Protocol No. 11, which came into force on 1 November 1998, replaced the existing, part-time Court and Commission by a single, full-time Court. For a transitional period of one year (until 31 October 1999) the Commission continued to deal with the cases which it had previously declared admissible. . . .

[II.] Organisation of the Court. . . .

2. The provisions governing the structure and procedure of the Court are to be found in Section II of the Convention (Articles 19–51). The Court is composed of a number of judges equal to that of the Contracting States (currently forty-[seven]). Judges are elected by the Parliamentary Assembly of the Council of Europe, which votes on a shortlist of three candidates put forward by Governments. The term of office is six years, and judges may be re-elected. Their terms of office expire when they reach the age of seventy, although they continue to deal with cases already under their consideration.

Judges sit on the Court in their individual capacity and do not represent any State. They cannot engage in any activity which is incompatible with their independence or impartiality or with the demands of full-time office. . . .

4. Under the Rules of Court, every judge is assigned to one of the five Sections, whose composition is geographically and gender balanced and takes account of the different legal systems of the Contracting States. . . .

5. The great majority of the judgments of the Court are given by Chambers. These comprise seven judges and are constituted within each Section. . . .

7. The Grand Chamber of the Court is composed of seventeen judges. . . .

[III.] Basic Information on Procedures

1. General

1. Any Contracting State . . . or individual claiming to be a victim of a violation of the Convention . . . may lodge directly with the Court in Strasbourg an application

alleging a breach by a Contracting State of one of the Convention rights. A notice for the guidance of applicants and forms for making applications may be obtained from the Registry.

2. The procedure before the European Court of Human Rights is adversarial and public. Hearings, which are held only in a minority of cases, are public, unless the Chamber/Grand Chamber decides otherwise on account of exceptional circumstances. . . .

3. Individual applicants may present their own case, but legal representation is recommended, and indeed usually required once an application has been communicated to the respondent Government. The Council of Europe has set up a legal aid scheme for applicants who do not have sufficient means. . . .

2. Admissibility procedure

5. Each individual application is assigned to a Section, whose President designates a rapporteur. After a preliminary examination of the case, the rapporteur decides whether it should be dealt with by a three-member [Chamber] Committee or by a Chamber.

6. A Committee may decide, by unanimous vote, to declare inadmissible or strike out an application where it can do so without further examination.

7. Individual applications which are not declared inadmissible by Committees, or which are referred directly to a Chamber by the rapporteur, and State applications are examined by a Chamber. Chambers determine both admissibility and merits, in separate decisions or where appropriate together.

8. Chambers may at any time relinquish jurisdiction in favour of the Grand Chamber where a case raises a serious question of interpretation of the Convention or where there is a risk of departing from existing case-law, unless one of the parties objects to such relinquishment. . . .

9. The first stage of the procedure is generally written, although the Chamber may decide to hold a public hearing, in which case issues arising in relation to the merits will normally also be addressed.

10. Decisions on admissibility, which are taken by majority vote, must contain reasons and be made public.

3. Procedure on the merits

11. Once the Chamber has decided to admit the application, it may invite the parties to submit further evidence and written observations, including any claims for "just satisfaction" by the applicant. If no hearing has taken place at the admissibility stage, it may decide to hold a hearing on the merits of the case.

12. The President of the Chamber may, in the interests of the proper administration of justice, invite or grant leave to any Contracting State which is not party to the proceedings, or any person concerned who is not the applicant, to submit written

comments, and, in exceptional circumstances, to make representations at the hearing. . . .

13. During the procedure on the merits, negotiations aimed at securing a friendly settlement may be conducted through the Registrar. The negotiations are confidential.

4. Judgments

14. Chambers decide by a majority vote. Any judge who has taken part in the consideration of the case is entitled to append to the judgment a separate opinion, either concurring or dissenting, or a bare statement of dissent.

15. Within three months of delivery of the judgment of a Chamber, any party may request that the case be referred to the Grand Chamber if it raises a serious question of interpretation or application or a serious issue of general importance. Such requests are examined by a Grand Chamber panel of five judges. . . .

16. A Chamber's judgment becomes final on expiry of the three-month period or earlier if the parties announce that they have no intention of requesting a referral or after a decision of the [Grand Chamber] panel rejecting a request for referral.

17. If the panel accepts the request, the Grand Chamber renders its decision on the case in the form of a judgment. The Grand Chamber decides by a majority vote and its judgments are final.

18. All final judgments of the Court are binding on the respondent States concerned.

19. Responsibility for supervising the execution of judgments lies with the Committee of Ministers of the Council of Europe. The Committee of Ministers verifies whether States in respect of which a violation of the Convention is found have taken adequate remedial measures to comply with the specific or general obligations arising out of the Court's judgments.

5. Advisory opinions

20. The Court may, at the request of the Committee of Ministers, give advisory opinions on legal questions concerning the interpretation of the Convention and Protocols.

Decisions of the Committee of Ministers to request an advisory opinion are taken by a majority vote.

21. Advisory opinions are given by the Grand Chamber and adopted by a majority vote. Any judge may attach to the advisory opinion, a separate opinion or a bare statement of dissent.

II. Using the European Convention

The European Court of Human Rights has significantly expanded women's rights. As you read its decisions below, compare the test it uses for deciding whether a statute violates women's equality rights to those used by the Human Rights Committee, the U.S. Supreme Court, and the Inter-American Court of Human Rights. Which test do you prefer and why?

A. A Challenge to Gender-Based Immigration Rights in the United Kingdom

Abdulaziz, Cabales and Balkandali v. United Kingdom
(European Court of Human Rights)
7 Eur. H.R. Rep. 471 (1985)

1. The present case was referred to the Court by the European Commission of Human Rights ("the Commission"). . . . The case originated in three applications against the United Kingdom of Great Britain and Northern Ireland lodged with the Commission in 1980 and 1981 by Mrs. Nargis Abdulaziz, Mrs. Arcely Cabales and Mrs. Sohair Balkandali. When she filed her application, Mrs. Abdulaziz was either stateless or a citizen of Malawi, Mrs. Cabales was a citizen of the Philippines and Mrs. Balkandali was a citizen of the United Kingdom and Colonies. . . .

10. The applicants are lawfully and permanently settled in the United Kingdom. In accordance with the immigration rules in force at the material time, Mr. Abdulaziz, Mr. Cabales, and Mr. Balkandali were refused permission to remain with or join them in that country as their husbands. The applicants maintained that, on this account, they had been victims of a practice of discrimination on the grounds of sex [and] race, . . . and that there had been violations of . . . Article 8 [granting the right to respect for private and family life], taken alone or in conjunction with Article 14 [prohibiting sex discrimination as to Convention rights]. They further alleged that, contrary to Article 13 [granting the right to an effective remedy], no effective domestic remedy existed for the aforesaid claims. . . .

13. The . . . Immigration Act 1971 ("the 1971 Act") . . . was [designed] to assimilate immigration controls over incoming Commonwealth citizens having no close links to Britain to the corresponding rules for aliens. The Act created two new categories of persons for immigration purposes, namely those having the right of abode in the United Kingdom ("patrials") and those not having that right ("non-patrials").

14. "Patrials" were to be free from immigration controls. The status of "patrial" was intended to designate Commonwealth citizens who "belonged" to the United Kingdom and . . . was conferred . . . on:

(a) citizens of the United Kingdom and Colonies who had acquired that citizenship by birth, adoption, naturalisation or registration in the British Islands . . . , or were the children or grandchildren of any such persons;

(b) citizens of the United Kingdom and Colonies who had at any time been settled in the British Islands for at least five years;

(c) other Commonwealth citizens who were the children of a person having citizenship of the United Kingdom and Colonies by virtue of birth in the British Islands;

(d) women, being Commonwealth citizens, who were or had been married to a man falling within any of the preceding categories.

15. Under . . . the 1971 Act, "non-patrials" (whether Commonwealth citizens or aliens) "may live, work and settle in the United Kingdom by permission and subject to such regulation and control of their entry into, stay in and departure from the United Kingdom as is imposed" by the Act. . . .

[A] "non-patrial" shall not enter the United Kingdom unless given leave to do so. He may be given such leave (or, if he is already in the country, leave to remain) either for a limited or for an indefinite period; in the former case, the leave may be subject to conditions restricting employment or requiring registration with the police or both. . . .

20. The rules in force at the time of the events giving rise to the present case were contained in the "Statement of Changes in Immigration Rules," laid down before Parliament on 20 February 1980 ("the 1980 Rules"). . . .

21. A particular feature of the changes introduced by the 1980 Rules was the inclusion of . . . provisions . . . [to protect] the domestic labour market at a time of high unemployment by curtailing "primary immigration", that is immigration by someone who could be expected to seek full-time work in order to support a family. In taking these measures, the Government [was] concerned also to advance public tranquility and, by exercising firm and fair immigration control, to assist in securing good community relations.

To these ends, among the changes effected was the introduction of stricter conditions for the grant of leave to a "non-patrial" husband or fiancé seeking to join or remain with his wife or fiancée settled in the United Kingdom. Previously, any such husband or fiancé would normally have been allowed to settle after a qualifying period, provided that the primary purpose of the marriage was not to obtain settlement in that country. These new measures were not extended to the wives and fiancées of settled men, a fact attributed by the Government to long-standing commitments (based allegedly on humanitarian, social and ethical reasons) to the reunification of the families of male immigrants. . . .

33. Under . . . the 1971 Act, a person not having the right of abode in the United Kingdom and having only limited leave to enter or remain in that country who overstays the period of leave or fails to observe a condition attached thereto:

(a) commits a criminal offence punishable with a fine of not more than £200 or imprisonment of not more than six months or both, to which penalties the court may, with certain exceptions, add a recommendation for deportation; and

(b) is . . . liable to deportation, although he cannot be compelled to leave unless the Home Secretary decides to make a deportation order against him. . . .

As to the Law

I. Alleged Violation of Article 8

58. The applicants claimed to be victims of a practice in violation of their right to respect for family life, guaranteed by Article 8 of the Convention . . . :

1. Everyone has the right to respect for his private and family life, his home and his correspondence.

2. There shall be no interference by a public authority with the exercise of this right except such as is in accordance with the law and is necessary in a democratic society in the interests of national security, public safety, or the economic well-being of the country, of the prevention of disorder or crime, for the protection of health or morals, or for the protection of the rights and freedoms of others. . . .

B. Compliance with Article 8

66. The applicants contended that respect for family life—which in their cases the United Kingdom had to secure within its own jurisdiction—encompassed the right to establish one's home in the State of one's nationality or lawful residence: subject only to the provisions of paragraph 2 of Article 8, the dilemma either of moving abroad or of being separated from one's spouse was inconsistent with this principle. Furthermore, hindrance in fact was just as relevant as hindrance in law: for the couples to live in, respectively, Portugal, the Philippines or Turkey [as the Government said they should do] would involve or would have involved them in serious difficulties,[B] although there was no legal impediment to their doing so.

67. The Court recalls that, although the essential object of Article 8 is to protect the individual against arbitrary interference by the public authorities, there may in addition be positive obligations inherent in an effective "respect" for family life. . . . However, especially as far as those positive obligations are concerned, the notion of "respect" is not clear-cut: having regard to the diversity of the practices followed and the situations obtaining in the Contracting States, the notion's requirements will vary considerably from case to case. Accordingly, this is an area in which the Contracting Parties enjoy a wide margin of appreciation in determining the steps to be taken to ensure compliance with the Convention with due regard to the needs and resources of the community and of individuals. . . .

In particular, in the area now under consideration, the extent of a State's obligation to admit to its territory relatives of settled immigrants will vary according to the particular circumstances of the persons involved. Moreover, the Court cannot ignore that the present case is concerned not only with family life but also with immigration and that, as a matter of well-established international law and subject to its treaty obligations, a State has the right to control the entry of non-nationals into its territory.

68. The Court observes that the present proceedings do not relate to immigrants who already had a family which they left behind in another country until they had achieved settled status in the United Kingdom. It was only after becoming settled in the United Kingdom, as single persons, that the applicants contracted marriage. . . . The duty imposed by Article 8 cannot be considered as extending to a general obliga-

---

[B] Mrs. Abdulaziz alleged that she could not live in Portugal because "she had always been close to her family and because her sick father—who in fact died in September 1980—needed her company, . . . [and] her health was under strain because of her husband's settlement problems and that humanitarian considerations prevented her going to Portugal, a country where she had no family and whose language she did not speak." Mrs. Cabales alleged that she could not live in the Philippines because "she was too old, her qualifications [as a nurse] were not recognised there and, by working in the United Kingdom, she was able to support financially her parents and other members of her family." Mrs. Balkandali alleged that she could not live in Turkey because "she [has] strong ties to the United Kingdom and . . . as an educated woman

tion on the part of a Contracting State to respect the choice by married couples of the country of their matrimonial residence and to accept the non-national spouses for settlement in that country.

In the present case, the applicants have not shown that there were obstacles to establishing family life in their own or their husbands' home countries or that there were special reasons why that could not be expected of them. . . .

69. There was accordingly no "lack of respect" for family life, and hence, no breach of Article 8 taken alone. . . .

II. Alleged Violation of Article 14 Taken Together with Article 8

A. Introduction

70. The applicants claimed that, as a result of unjustified differences of treatment in securing the right to respect for their family life, based on sex . . . they had been victims of a violation of Article 14 of the Convention, taken together with Article 8. The former Article reads as follows:

> The enjoyment of the rights and freedoms set forth in [the] Convention shall be secured without discrimination on any ground such as sex, race, colour, language, religion. political or other opinion, national or social origin, association with a national minority, property, birth or other status.

In the event that the Court should find Article 8 to be applicable in the present case, the Government . . . submitted that since the differences of treatment on the ground of sex . . . had objective and reasonable justifications and were proportionate to the aims pursued, they were compatible with Article 14.

71. According to the Court's established case-law, Article 14 complements the other substantive provisions of the Convention and the Protocols. It has no independent existence since it has effect solely in relation to "the enjoyment of the rights and freedoms" safeguarded by those provisions. Although the application of Article 14 does not necessarily presuppose a breach of those provisions—and to this extent it is autonomous—there can be no room for its application unless the facts at issue fall within the ambit of one or more of the latter. . . .

The Court has found Article 8 to be applicable. . . . Although the United Kingdom was not obliged to accept Mr. Abdulaziz, Mr Cabales and Mr. Balkandali for settlement and the Court therefore did not find a violation of Article 8 taken alone (see paragraphs 68–69 above), the facts at issue nevertheless fall within the ambit of that Article. . . .

Article 14 also is therefore applicable.

72. For the purposes of Article 14, a difference of treatment is discriminatory if it "has no objective and reasonable justification", that is, if it does not pursue a "legiti-

---

and the mother of an illegitimate child she would have been treated as a social outcast in Turkey."

mate aim" or if there is not a "reasonable relationship of proportionality between the mean employed and the aim sought to be realized. . . ."

The Contracting States enjoy a certain margin of appreciation in assessing whether and to what extent differences in otherwise similar situations justify a different treatment in law . . . but it is for the Court to give the final ruling in this respect.

B. Alleged discrimination on the ground of sex

74. As regards the alleged discrimination on the ground of sex, it was not disputed that under the 1980 Rules [it] was easier for a man settled in the United Kingdom than for a woman so settled to obtain permission for his or her non-national spouse to enter or remain in the country for settlement . . . Argument centred on the question whether this difference had an objective and reasonable justification.

75. According to the Government, the difference of treatment complained of had the aim of limiting "primary immigration" (see paragraph 21 above) and was justified by the need to protect the domestic labour market at a time of high unemployment. They placed strong reliance on the margin of appreciation enjoyed by the Contracting States in this area and laid particular stress on what they described as a statistical fact: men were more likely to seek work than women, with the result that male immigrants would have a greater impact than female immigrants on the said market. Furthermore, the reduction, attributed by the Government to the 1980 Rules, of approximately 5,700 per annum in the number of husbands accepted for settlement in the United Kingdom . . . was claimed to be significant. This was said to be so especially when the reduction was viewed in relation to its cumulative effect over the years and to the total number of acceptances for settlement.

This view was contested by the applicants. For them, the Government's plea ignored the modern role of women and the fact that men may be self-employed and also, as was exemplified by the case of Mr. Balkandali [who was planning to open a restaurant] . . . create rather than seek jobs. Furthermore, the Government's figure of 5,700 was said to be insignificant and, for a number of reasons, in any event unreliable. . . .

76. The Government further contended that the measures in question were justified by the need to maintain effective immigration control, which benefitted settled immigrants as well as the indigenous population. Immigration caused strains on society; the Government's aim was to advance public tranquility, and a firm and fair control secured good relations between the different communities living in the United Kingdom.

To this, the applicants replied that the racial prejudice of the United Kingdom population could not be advanced as a justification for the measures.

77. In its report, the Commission considered that, when seen in the context of the immigration of other groups, annual emigration and unemployment and economic activity rates, the impact on the domestic labour market of an annual reduction of 2,000 (as then estimated by the Government) in the number of husbands accepted for settlement in the United Kingdom . . . was not of a size or importance to justify a

difference of treatment on the ground of sex and the detrimental consequences thereof on the family life of the women concerned. Furthermore, the long-standing commitment to the reunification of the families of male immigrants, to which the Government had referred as a reason for accepting wives whilst excluding husbands, no longer corresponded to modern requirements as to the equal treatment of the sexes. Neither was it established that race relations or immigration controls were enhanced by the rules: they might create resentment in part of the immigrant population and it had not been shown that it was more difficult to limit abuses by non-national husbands than by other immigrant groups. The Commission unanimously concluded that there had been discrimination on the ground of sex, contrary to Article 14, in securing the applicants' right to respect for family life, the application of the relevant rules being disproportionate to the purported aims.

At the hearings before the Court, the Commission's Delegate stated that this conclusion was not affected by the Government's revised figure (about 5,700) for the annual reduction in the number of husbands accepted for settlement.

78. The Court accepts that the 1980 Rules had the aim of protecting the domestic labour market. . . .

Whilst the aforesaid aim was without doubt legitimate, this does not in itself establish the legitimacy of the difference made in the 1980 Rules as to the possibility for male and female immigrants settled in the United Kingdom to obtain permission for, on the one hand, their non-national wives or fiancées and, on the other hand, their non-national husbands or fiancés to enter or remain in the country.

Although the Contracting States enjoy a certain "margin of appreciation" in assessing whether and to what extent differences in otherwise similar situations justify a different treatment, the scope of this margin will vary according to the circumstances, the subject-matter and its background. . . .

As to the present matter, it can be said that the advancement of the equality of the sexes is today a major goal in the member States of the Council of Europe. This means that very weighty reasons would have to be advanced before a difference of treatment on the ground of sex could be regarded as compatible with the Convention.

79. In the Court's opinion, the Government's arguments summarized in paragraph 75 above are not convincing.

It may be correct that on average there is a greater percentage of men of working age than of women of working age who are "economically active" (for Great Britain 90 per cent of the men and 63 per cent of the women) and that comparable figures hold good for immigrants (according to the statistics, 86 per cent for men and 41 per cent for women for immigrants from the Indian sub-continent and 90 per cent for men and 70 per cent for women for immigrants from the West Indies and Guyana).

Nevertheless, this does not show that similar differences in fact exist—or would but for the effect of the 1980 Rules have existed—as regards the respective impact on the United Kingdom labour market of immigrant wives and of immigrant husbands. In this connection, other factors must also be taken into account. Being "economically active" does not always mean that one is seeking to be employed by someone else. Moreover, although a greater number of men than of women may be inclined to seek employment, immigrant husbands were already by far outnumbered before the introduction of the 1980 Rules, by immigrant wives . . . many of whom were also "economically active". Whilst a considerable proportion of those wives, in so far as they were "economically active", were engaged in part-time work, the impact on the domestic labour market of women immigrants as compared with men ought not to be underestimated.

In any event, the Court is not convinced that the difference that may nevertheless exist between the respective impact of men and of women on the domestic labour market is sufficiently important to justify the difference of treatment, complained of by the applicants, as to the possibility for a person settled in the United Kingdom to be joined by, as the case may be, his wife or her husband.

80. In this context the Government stressed the importance of the effect on this immigration of husbands of the restriction contained in the 1980 Rules, which had led, according to their estimate, to an annual reduction of 5,700 (rather than 2,000 as mentioned in the Commission's report) in the number of husbands accepted for settlement.

Without expressing a conclusion on the correctness of the figure of 5,700, the Court notes that in point of time the claimed reduction coincided with a significant increase in unemployment in the United Kingdom and that the Government accepted that some part of the reduction was due to economic conditions rather than to the 1980 Rules themselves. . .

In any event, for the reasons stated in paragraph 79 above, the reduction achieved does not justify the difference in treatment between men and women.

81. The Court accepts that the 1980 Rules also had, as the Government stated, the aim of advancing public tranquility. However, it is not persuaded that this aim was served by the distinction drawn in those rules between husbands and wives.

82. There remains a more general argument advanced by the Government, namely that the United Kingdom was not in violation of Article 14 by reason of the fact that it acted more generously in some respects—that is, as regards the admission of non-national wives and fiancées of men settled in the country—than the Convention required.

The Court cannot accept this argument. It would point out that Article 14 is concerned with the avoidance of discrimination in the enjoyment of the Convention rights in so far as the requirements of the Convention as to those rights can be complied with in different ways. The notion of discrimination within the meaning of Article 14 includes in general cases where a person or group is treated, without proper justification, less favourably than another, even though the more favourable treatment is not called for by the Convention.

83. The Court thus concludes that the applicants have been victims of discrimination on the ground of sex, in violation of Article 14 taken together with Article 8. . . .

92. The applicants alleged that they had no effective remedy for their complaints under Article . . . 8 and 14 and that there had accordingly been a breach of Article 13, which reads:

Everyone whose rights and freedoms as set forth in [the] Convention are violated shall have an effective remedy before a national authority notwithstanding that the violation has been committed by persons acting in an official capacity.

93. The Court has found that the discrimination on the ground of sex of which Mrs. Abdulaziz, Mrs. Cabales and Mrs. Balkandali were victims was the result of norms that were in this respect incompatible with the Convention. In this regard, since the United Kingdom has not incorporated the Convention into its domestic law, there could be no "effective remedy" as required by Article 13. . . . Recourse to the available channels of complaint (the immigration appeals system, representations to the Home Secretary, application for judicial review . . . could have been effective only if the complainant alleged that the discrimination resulted from a misapplication of the 1980 Rules. Yet here no such allegation was made nor was it suggested that the discrimination in any other way contravened domestic law.

The Court accordingly concludes that there has been a violation of Article 13.

N O T E

The Court Test. What does the government identify as its purposes for enacting its legislation? Do you think they were the government's actual purposes? Are they all legitimate or important? What process should a lawyer use to identify the government's purpose? Identify the ways in which the legislation was over or under-inclusive in reaching its goals. Notice that this is in essence a process of identifying all the exceptions to stereotypes about or average statistics concerning women's and men's behavior. Redraft the legislation so that it achieves the government's legitimate purposes without using any sex-based lines.

B. A Challenge to the Irish Court System: Family Law, Domestic Violence, and the Right of Access to Court; The State's Positive Obligation to Ensure Respect for Private or Family Life

Airey v. Ireland
(European Court of Human Rights)
2 Eur. H.R. Rep. 305 (1979)

Particular facts of the case

8. Mrs. Johanna Airey, an Irish national born in 1932, lives in Cork. She comes from a humble family background and went to work at a young age as a shop assistant. She married in 1953 and has four children, the youngest of whom is still dependent on her. At the time of the adoption of the Commission's report, Mrs. Airey was in receipt of unemployment benefit from the State but, since July 1978, she has been employed. Her net weekly wage in December 1978 was £39.99. In 1974, she obtained a court order against her husband for payment of maintenance of £20 per

week, which was increased in 1977 to £27 and in 1978 to £32. However, Mr. Airey, who had previously been working as a lorry driver but was subsequently unemployed, ceased paying such maintenance in May 1978.

Mrs. Airey alleges that her husband is an alcoholic and that, before 1972, he frequently threatened her with, and occasionally subjected her to, physical violence. In January 1972, in proceedings instituted by the applicant, Mr. Airey was convicted by the District Court of Cork City of assaulting her and fined. In the following June he left the matrimonial home; he has never returned there to live, although Mrs. Airey now fears that he may seek to do so.

9. For about eight years prior to 1972, Mrs. Airey tried in vain to conclude a separation agreement with her husband. In 1971, he declined to sign a deed prepared by her solicitor for the purpose and her later attempts to obtain his co-operation were also unsuccessful.

Since June 1972, she has been endeavouring to obtain a decree of judicial separation on the grounds of Mr. Airey's alleged physical and mental cruelty to her and their children, and has consulted several solicitors in this connection. However, she has been unable, in the absence of legal aid and not being in a financial position to meet herself the costs involved, to find a solicitor willing to act for her.

In 1976, Mrs. Airey applied to an ecclesiastical tribunal for annulment of her marriage. Her application is still under investigation; if successful, it will not affect her civil status.

Domestic law

10. In Ireland, although it is possible to obtain under certain conditions a decree of nullity—a declaration by the High Court that a marriage was null and void *ab initio*—, divorce in the sense of dissolution of a marriage does not exist. In fact, Article 41.3.2 of the Constitution provides: "No law shall be enacted providing for the grant of a dissolution of marriage."

However, spouses may be relieved from the duty of cohabiting either by a legally binding deed of separation concluded between them or by a court decree of judicial separation (also known as a divorce *a mensa et thoro* [a Latin phrase meaning "from bed and board"]). Such a decree has no effect on the existence of the marriage in law. It can be granted only if the petitioner furnishes evidence proving one of three specified matrimonial offences, namely, adultery, cruelty or unnatural practices. The parties will call and examine witnesses on this point. . . .

[A]n individual against whom a decree of judicial separation is granted forfeits certain succession rights over his or her spouse's estate.

11. Decrees of judicial separation are obtainable only in the High Court. The parties may conduct their case in person. However, the Government's replies to questions put by the Court . . . reveal that in each of the 255 separation proceedings initiated in Ireland in the period from January 1972 to December 1978, without exception, the petitioner was represented by a lawyer.

In its report of 9 March 1978, the Commission noted that the approximate range of the costs incurred by a legally represented petitioner was £500–£700 in an uncontested action and £800–£1,200 in a contested action, the exact amount depending on such factors as the number of witnesses and the complexity of the issues involved. In the case of a successful petition by a wife, the general rule is that the husband will be ordered to pay all costs reasonably and properly incurred by her, the precise figure being fixed by a Taxing Master.

Legal aid is not at present available in Ireland for the purpose of seeking a judicial separation, nor indeed for any civil matters. In 1974, a Committee on Civil Legal Aid and Advice was established under the chairmanship of Mr. Justice Pringle. It reported to the Government in December 1977, recommending the introduction of a comprehensive scheme of legal aid and advice in this area. At the hearings on 22 February 1979, counsel for the Government informed the Court that the Government had decided in principle to introduce legal aid in family-law matters and that it was hoped to have the necessary measures taken before the end of 1979.

12. Since Mrs. Airey's application to the Commission, the Family Law (Maintenance of Spouses and Children) Act 1976 has come into force. Section 22 (1) . . . provides:

On application to it by either spouse, the court may, if it is of the opinion that there are reasonable grounds for believing that the safety or welfare of that spouse or of any dependent child of the family requires it, order the other spouse, if he is residing at a place where the applicant spouse or that child resides, to leave that place, and whether the other spouse is or is not residing at that place, prohibit him from entering that place until further order by the court or until such other time as the court shall specify.

Such an order—commonly known as a barring order—is not permanent and application may be made at any time for its discharge. Furthermore, the maximum duration of an order given in the District Court—as opposed to the Circuit Court or the High Court—is three months although provision is made for renewal.

A wife who has been assaulted by her husband may also institute summary criminal proceedings.

Proceedings Before the Commission

13. In her application of 14 June 1973 to the Commission, Mrs. Airey made various complaints in connection with the 1972 proceedings against her husband. . . . Her main complaint was that the State had failed to protect her against physical and mental cruelty from her allegedly violent and alcoholic husband:
    —by not detaining him for treatment as an alcoholic;
    —by not ensuring that he paid maintenance to her regularly;
    —in that, because of the prohibitive cost of proceedings, she could not obtain a judicial separation.

As regards the last item, the applicant maintained that there had been violations of:

—Article 6 para. 1 [right to a fair trial] of the Convention, by reason of the fact that her right of access to a court was effectively denied;

—Article 8 [right to respect for private and family life], by reason of the failure of the State to ensure that there is an accessible legal procedure to determine rights and obligations which have been created by legislation regulating family matters. . .

14. On 7 July 1977, the Commission accepted the application in so far as Mrs. Airey complained of the inaccessibility of the remedy of a judicial separation and declared inadmissible the remainder of the application.

In its report of 9 March 1978, the Commission expresses the opinion:

—unanimously, that the failure of the State to ensure the applicant's effective access to court to enable her to obtain a judicial separation amounts to a breach of Article 6 para. 1;

—that, in view of the preceding conclusion, there is no need for it to examine the case under Articles 13 and 14 (unanimously) or under Article 8 (twelve votes to one, with one abstention).

Final Submissions and Observations Made to the Court

15. At the hearings on 22 February 1979, the Government maintained . . . :

The Court is asked to find that the Commission should not have declared this application admissible.

The Court is asked to find that even if the case was correctly admitted by the Commission, it should have been dismissed on the merits.

The respondent Government is not in breach of its obligations under the European Convention on Human Rights.

On the same occasion, counsel for Mrs. Airey resumed her client's position as follows:

The applicant claims that the total inaccessibility and exclusiveness of the remedy of a judicial separation in the High Court is a breach of her right of access to the civil courts which the Irish Government must secure under Article 6 para. 1; she submits that the absence of a modern, effective and accessible remedy for marriage breakdown under Irish law is a failure to respect her family life under Article 8; she submits that the exorbitantly high cost of obtaining a decree of judicial separation, which results in fewer than a dozen decrees in any year, constitutes a discrimination on the ground of property in violation of Article 14 ["prohibition of discrimination . . . on any grounds such as sex, . . . property. . . ."]; and she submits that she lacks an effective remedy under Irish law for her marriage breakdown and that this in itself is a breach of Article 13. . . .

As to the Law

I. Preliminary Issues . . .

19. The Government maintain that the applicant failed to exhaust domestic remedies in various respects.

(a) In the first place, they contend that she could have entered into a separation deed with her husband or could have applied for a barring order or for maintenance under the 1976 Act (see paragraphs 10 and 12 above).

The Court emphasises that the only remedies which Article 26 [now Article 35][c] of the Convention requires to be exercised are remedies in respect of the violation complained of. The violation alleged by Mrs. Airey is that in her case the State failed to secure access to court for the purpose of petitioning for judicial separation. However, neither the conclusion of a separation deed nor the grant of a barring or a maintenance order provide such access. Accordingly, the Court cannot accept the first limb of this plea.

(b) In the second place, the Government lay stress on the fact that the applicant could have appeared before the High Court without the assistance of a lawyer. They also contend that she has nothing to gain from a judicial separation.

The Court recalls that international law, to which Article 26 [now article 35] makes express reference, demands solely recourse to such remedies as are both "to the persons concerned and . . . sufficient, that is to say capable of providing redress for their complaints." However, the Court would not be able to decide whether the possibility open to Mrs. Airey of conducting her case herself amounts to a "domestic remedy", in the above sense, without at the same time ruling on the merits of her complaint under Article 6 para. 1, namely the alleged lack of effective access to the High Court. Similarly, the argument that a judicial separation would be of no benefit to the applicant appears intimately connected with another aspect of this complaint, namely whether any real prejudice was occasioned. The Court therefore joins to the merits the remainder of the plea.

II. On Article 6 Para. 1 Taken Alone

20. Article 6 para. 1 reads as follows:

In the determination of his civil rights and obligations or of any criminal charge against him, everyone is entitled to a fair and public hearing within a reasonable time by an independent and impartial tribunal established by law. . . .

Mrs. Airey cites the Golder judgment of 21 February 1975 where the Court held that this paragraph embodies the right of access to a court for the determination of civil rights and obligations; she maintains that, since the prohibitive cost of litigation prevented her from bringing proceedings before the High Court for the purpose of

---

[c] Protocol No. 11 reorganized the European Court's procedure and eliminated the Commission. As a result, many articles of the Convention were renumbered. The content of Article 26 (as it existed in 1979 when this case was decided) is now contained in the current Article 35. Article 35(1) of the Covenant provides: "The Court may only deal with the matter after all domestic remedies have been exhausted, according to the generally recognised rules of international law, and within a period of six months from the date on which the final decision was taken."

petitioning for judicial separation, there has been a violation of the above-mentioned provision.

This contention is unanimously accepted in substance by the Commission but disputed by the Government. . . .

23. It is convenient at this juncture to consider the Government's claim that the applicant has nothing to gain from a judicial separation.

The Court rejects this line of reasoning. Judicial separation is a remedy provided for by Irish law and, as such, it should be available to anyone who satisfies the conditions prescribed thereby. It is for the individual to select which legal remedy to pursue; consequently, even if it were correct that Mrs. Airey's choice has fallen on a remedy less suited than others to her particular circumstances, this would be of no moment.

24. The Government contend that the application does enjoy access to the High Court since she is free to go before that court without the assistance of a lawyer.

The Court does not regard this possibility, of itself, as conclusive of the matter. The Convention is intended to guarantee not rights that are theoretical or illusory but rights that are practical and effective. . . . It must therefore be ascertained whether Mrs. Airey's appearance before the High Court without the assistance of a lawyer would be effective, in the sense of whether she would be able to present her case properly and satisfactorily.

Contradictory views on this question were expressed by the Government and the Commission during the oral hearings. It seems certain to the Court that the applicant would be at a disadvantage if her husband were represented by a lawyer and she were not. Quite apart from this eventuality, it is not realistic, in the Court's opinion, to suppose that, in litigation of this nature, the applicant could effectively conduct her own case, despite the assistance which, as was stressed by the Government, the judge affords to parties acting in person.

In Ireland, a decree of judicial separation is not obtainable in a District Court, where the procedure is relatively simple, but only in the High Court. A specialist in Irish family law, Mr. Alan J. Shatter, regards the High Court as the least accessible court not only because "fees payable for representation before it are very high" but also by reason of the fact that "the procedure for instituting proceedings . . . is complex particularly in the case of those proceedings which must be commenced by a petition," such as those for separation.

Furthermore, litigation of this kind, in addition to involving complicated points of law, necessitates proof of adultery, unnatural practices or, as in the present case, cruelty; to establish the facts, expert evidence may have to be tendered and witnesses may have to be found, called and examined. What is more, marital disputes often entail an emotional involvement that is scarcely compatible with the degree of objectivity required by advocacy in court.

For these reasons, the Court considers it most improbable that a person in Mrs. Airey's position can effectively present his or her own case. This view is corroborated by the Government's replies to the questions put by the Court, replies which reveal that in each of the 255 judicial separation proceedings initiated in Ireland in the period from January 1972 to December 1978, without exception, the petitioner was represented by a lawyer.

The Court concludes from the foregoing that the possibility to appear in person before the High Court does not provide the applicant with an effective right of access and, hence, that it also does not constitute a domestic remedy whose use is demanded by Article 26 [now Article 35].

25. The Government seek to distinguish the Golder case on the ground that, there, the applicant had been prevented from having access to court by reason of the positive obstacle placed in his way by the State in the shape of the Home Secretary's prohibition on his consulting a solicitor. The Government maintain that, in contrast, in the present case there is no positive obstacle emanating from the State and no deliberate attempt by the State to impede access; the alleged lack of access to court stems not from any act on the part of the authorities but solely from Mrs. Airey's personal circumstances, a matter for which Ireland cannot be held responsible under the Convention.

Although this difference between the facts of the two cases is certainly correct, the Court does not agree with the conclusion which the Government draw therefrom. In the first place, hindrance in fact can contravene the Convention just like a legal impediment. Furthermore, fulfilment of a duty under the Convention on occasion necessitates some positive action on the part of the State; in such circumstances, the State cannot simply remain passive and "there is . . . no room to distinguish between acts and omissions" (see . . . Marckx judgment [of 13 June 1979]). The obligation to secure an effective right of access to the courts falls into this category of duty.

26. The Government's principal argument rests on what they see as the consequence of the Commission's opinion, namely that, in all cases concerning the determination of a "civil right", the State would have to provide free legal aid. In fact, the Convention's only express provision on free legal aid is Article 6 para. 3 (c)[D] which relates to criminal proceedings and is itself subject to limitations; what is more, according to the Commission's established case law, Article 6 para. 1 does not guarantee any right to free legal aid as such. The Government add that since Ireland, when ratifying the Convention, made a reservation to Article 6 para. 3 (c) with the intention of limiting its obligations in the realm of criminal legal aid, *a fortiori* it cannot be said to have implicitly agreed to provide unlimited civil legal aid. Finally, in their submission, the Convention should not be interpreted so as to achieve social and economic developments in a Contracting State; such developments can only be progressive.

The Court is aware that the further realisation of social and economic rights is largely dependent on the situation—notably financial—reigning in the State in question. On the other hand, the Convention must be interpreted in the light of present-

---

[D] Article 6 para. 3 (c) of the Convention provides: "Everyone charged with a criminal offence has the following minimum rights: . . . (c) to defend himself in person or through legal assistance of his own choosing or, if he has not sufficient means to pay for legal assistance, to be given it free when the interests of justice so require. . . ."

day conditions and it is designed to safeguard the individual in a real and practical way as regards those areas with which it deals. Whilst the Convention sets forth what are essentially civil and political rights, many of them have implications of a social or economic nature. The Court therefore considers, like the Commission, that the mere fact that an interpretation of the Convention may extend into the sphere of social and economic rights should not be a decisive factor against such an interpretation; there is no water-tight division separating that sphere from the field covered by the Convention.

The Court does not, moreover, share the Government's view as to the consequence of the Commission's opinion.

It would be erroneous to generalize the conclusion that the possibility to appear in person before the High Court does not provide Mrs. Airey with an effective right of access; that conclusion does not hold good for all cases concerning "civil rights and obligations" or for everyone involved therein. In certain eventualities, the possibility of appearing before a court in person, even without a lawyer's assistance, will meet the requirements of Article 6 para. 1; there may be occasions when such a possibility secures adequate access even to the High Court. Indeed, much must depend on the particular circumstances.

In addition, whilst Article 6 para. 1 guarantees to litigants an effective right of access to the courts for the determination of their "civil rights and obligations", it leaves to the State a free choice of the means to be used towards this end. The institution of a legal aid scheme—which Ireland now envisages in family law matters—constitutes one of those means but there are others such as, for example, a simplification of procedure. In any event, it is not the Court's function to indicate, let alone dictate, which measures should be taken; all that the Convention requires is that an individual should enjoy his effective right of access to the courts in conditions not at variance with Article 6 para. 1. . . .

The conclusion appearing at the end of paragraph 24 above does not therefore imply that the State must provide free legal aid for every dispute relating to a "civil right".

To hold that so far-reaching an obligation exists would, the Court agrees, sit ill with the fact that the Convention contains no provision on legal aid for those disputes, Article 6 para. 3 (c) dealing only with criminal proceedings. However, despite the absence of a similar clause for civil litigation, Article 6 para. 1 may sometimes compel the State to provide for the assistance of a lawyer when such assistance proves indispensable for an effective access to court either because legal representation is rendered compulsory, as is done by the domestic law of certain Contracting States for various types of litigation, or by reason of the complexity of the procedure or of the case.

As regards the Irish reservation to Article 6 para. 3 (c), it cannot be interpreted as affecting the obligations under Article 6 para. 1; accordingly, it is not relevant in the present context.

27. The applicant was unable to find a solicitor willing to act on her behalf in judicial separation proceedings. The Commission inferred that the reason why the solici-

tors she consulted were not prepared to act was that she would have been unable to meet the costs involved. The Government question this opinion but the Court finds it plausible and has been presented with no evidence which could invalidate it.

28. Having regard to all the circumstances of the case, the Court finds that Mrs. Airey did not enjoy an effective right of access to the High Court for the purpose of petitioning for a decree of judicial separation. There has accordingly been a breach of Article 6 para. 1. . . .

IV. On Article 8

31. Mrs. Airey argues that, by not ensuring that there is an accessible legal procedure in family-law matters, Ireland has failed to respect her family life, thereby violating Article 8, which provides:

1. Everyone has the right to respect for his private and family life, his home and his correspondence.
2. There shall be no interference by a public authority with the exercise of this right except such as is in accordance with the law and is necessary in a democratic society in the interests of national security, public safety or the economic well-being of the country, for the prevention of disorder or crime, for the protection of health or morals, or for the protection of the rights and freedoms of others.

In its report, the Commission expressed the opinion that, in view of its conclusion concerning Article 6 para. 1, there was no need for it to consider the application under Article 8. However, during the oral hearings the [Commission's] Principal Delegate submitted that there had also been a breach of this Article. This contention is disputed by the Government.

32. The Court does not consider that Ireland can be said to have "interfered" with Mrs. Airey's private or family life: the substance of her complaint is not that the State has acted but that it has failed to act. However, although the object of Article 8 is essentially that of protecting the individual against arbitrary interference by the public authorities, it does not merely compel the State to abstain from such interference: in addition to this primarily negative undertaking, there may be positive obligations inherent in an effective respect for private or family life.

33. In Ireland, many aspects of private or family life are regulated by law. As regards marriage, husband and wife are in principle under a duty to cohabit[E] but are entitled, in certain cases, to petition for a decree of judicial separation; this amounts to recognition of the fact that the protection of their private or family life may sometimes necessitate their being relieved from the duty to live together.

Effective respect for private or family life obliges Ireland to make this means of protection effectively accessible, when appropriate, to anyone who may wish to have recourse thereto. However, it was not effectively accessible to the applicant: not hav-

---

[E] A HANDBOOK OF FAMILY LAW TERMS 111 (Bryan A. Garner, ed., 2001), defines cohabitation as "[t]he fact or state of living together, esp[ecially] as partners in life, usu[ally] with the suggestion of sexual relations."

ing been put in a position in which she could apply to the High Court, she was unable to seek recognition in law of her *de facto* separation from her husband. She has therefore been the victim of a violation of Article 8.

NOTES

Questions. What are the origins of Ireland's law prohibiting divorce? What is the government's strongest argument against the result obtained? Consider the situation of a poor woman whose government files a civil suit to deny her the right to her children's custody because it alleges she has abused and neglected her children. Does the Court's decision require that the state give her any relief?

Ireland's Divorce Law. Today Irish women (and men) can divorce their spouse for any reason. On November 24, 1995, 16 years after the *Airey* decision, Irish voters passed a referendum lifting the ban on divorce. *See The People Say Yes—Barely*, THE IRISH TIMES, Nov. 27, 1995 at 19.

C. A Challenge to a German Province's Gender-Based Service-or-Tax Requirement

Schmidt v. Germany
(European Court of Human Rights)
18 Eur. H.R. Rep. 513 (1994)

6. Mr. Karlheinz Schmidt, a German national who was born in 1939, lives at Tettnang, in the *Land* [State] of Baden-Württemberg.

On 30 April 1982 the relevant municipal authorities required him to pay a fire service levy of 75 German marks (DM) for 1982. This decision was based on section 43 of the *Land* Fire Brigades Act and on the municipal decree of 5 December 1979; it stated that all male adults residing in Tettnang at the beginning of the budget year (1 January) were liable to pay the contribution in question.

7. The applicant regarded this decision as contrary, *inter alia*, to the constitutional principle of equality before the law and he appealed against it. The administrative authority of the district of Lake Constance rejected this appeal on 20 July. . . . [Mr. Schmidt lost further appeals to an Administrative Court (1983), the Administrative Appeals Court (March 1986), and the Federal Administrative Court (October 1986).] . . .

11. On 11 November 1986 Mr. Schmidt applied finally to the Federal Constitutional Court, which on 31 January 1987, sitting as a panel of three members, declined to accept the appeal for adjudication, on the ground that it did not have sufficient prospects of success. It noted, *inter alia*: . . .

The Federal Constitutional Court has already held, in its judgment of 17 October 1961 . . . , concerning the provision which corresponds to the present section 43 of the Baden-Württemberg Fire Brigades Act, that there had been no violation of the principle of equal treatment. In subsequent decisions delivered . . . [in 1978, 1979, 1983, and 1985], it stated that from the point of view of Article 3, section 2 of the Basic Law [enshrining the principle of equality] there had still been no general change in legal opinion; the fact that the obligation to serve in the fire brigade was limited to the male residents of a municipality still continued to be objectively justified on account of the risks inherent in service in the fire brigade, even though some fire brigade duties were performed by women and recently fire brigades for female volunteers had even been set up.

Nor does the fact that the *Länder* of Lower Saxony and the Rhineland-Palatinate make provision for an obligation to serve in the fire brigades regardless of sex constitute a reason for departing from this case law. The sole decisive factor is that there remain today objective reasons on the basis of which the legislature is entitled to treat men and women differently in this regard. That does not mean that there is an obligation to enact regulations differentiating between the sexes . . . .

II. Relevant Domestic Law

12. The Baden-Württemberg Fire Brigades Act dates from 1 April 1956. . . .

13. The Act requires municipalities to set up proficient fire brigades which may be composed of volunteers or professionals. Their role is to deal with, among other things, fires, natural disasters and collapsed buildings, but they may also be required to ensure safety in theatres, at meetings and exhibitions and also at markets. All the male residents of the municipality between the ages of 18 and 50 inclusive may be required to serve as firemen, unless they can show that they are unfit to do so on health grounds. If there are insufficient volunteers, the municipalities may call upon these residents to serve, but so far this has never occurred in Baden-Württemberg.

As the Act does not recognise a right to active service, the municipalities may refuse to accept a volunteer.

14. The municipalities may adopt decrees making provision for a fire service levy of up to 200 DM; the resulting funds may only be used to meet the needs of the fire brigade.

Anyone who is liable for fire service duty and who resides in the municipality at the beginning of the budget year, may be required to pay this levy. Certain persons are, however, exempted, such as the members of the municipal fire brigade.

15. The system operated in Baden-Württemberg was challenged upon the entry into force of the Act on 1 April 1956. On 17 October 1961 the Federal Constitutional Court ruled that the fire service levy was compatible with the Basic Law and in particular with the general principle of equality before the law in so far as it constituted a "compensatory charge" deriving directly from the obligation to serve.

16. In 13 of the 16 *Länder* of the Federal Republic of Germany—including Baden-Württemberg—, the residents of municipalities are required by law to perform active service in the fire brigade if there are insufficient volunteers. Nine *Länder* make provision for such service solely for male residents. In addition to Baden-Württemberg, residents are required to pay a contribution to the fire brigade or to the fire protection department in Bavaria, Saxony and Thuringen. Where service is compulsory for residents of both sexes, both men and women are liable to pay the contribution.

17. Moreover, according to information provided by the applicant and not contested, 68,612 women had served in fire brigades in Germany as at 31 December

1991 and in Baden-Württemberg women have been permitted to serve in fire brigades since 1978.

Proceedings Before the Commission

18. Mr. Karlheinz Schmidt applied to the Commission on 11 August 1987. Relying on Article 14 [prohibiting sex discrimination as to Convention rights] taken in conjunction with Article 4 [prohibiting slavery and forced labour], para. 3(d) of the Convention and Article 1 [protecting enjoyment of possessions] of Protocol No. 1, he complained of a breach of the principle of sexual equality in so far as in the *Land* of Baden-Württemberg only men were subject to the obligation to serve as firemen or pay a financial contribution.

19. The Commission declared the application admissible on 8 January 1992.

In its report of 14 January 1993, it expressed the opinion, by 14 votes to three, that there had been a violation of Article 14 of the Convention taken in conjunction with Article 1 of Protocol No. 1 and with Article 4, para. 3(d) of the Convention . . . . [The Commission then referred the case to the Court for a decision on whether the German law violated the Convention.]

As to the Law

I. Alleged Violation of Article 14 of the Convention taken in conjunction with Article 4 para. (3)(d)

21. Mr Karlheinz Schmidt complained that he was required to pay a fire service levy under an Act of the *Land* of Baden-Württemberg, which made it compulsory for men, but not women, to serve in the fire brigade or pay a financial contribution in lieu of such service. He claimed to be the victim of discrimination on the ground of sex in breach of Article 14 taken in conjunction with Article 4, para. 3(d) of the Convention, which provisions state as follows:

Article 14
The enjoyment of the rights and freedoms set forth in this Convention shall be secured without discrimination on any ground such as sex. . . .

Article 4. . . .
2. No one shall be required to perform forced or compulsory labour.
3. For the purpose of this Article the term "forced or compulsory labour" shall not include:
. . .
(d) any work or service which forms part of normal civic obligations.

A. Applicability

22. As the Court has consistently held, Article 14 complements the other substantive provisions of the Convention and the Protocols. It has no independent existence since it has effect solely in relation to "the enjoyment of the rights and freedoms" safe-

guarded by those provisions. Although the application of Article 14 does not presuppose a breach of those provisions—and to this extent it is autonomous—there can be no room for its application unless the facts at issue fall within the ambit of one or more of the latter.

The Court reiterates that paragraph 3 of Article 4 is not intended to "limit" the exercise of the right guaranteed by paragraph 2, but to "delimit" the very content of that right, for it forms a whole with paragraph 2 and indicates what "the term 'forced or compulsory labour' shall not include". This being so, paragraph 3 serves as an aid to the interpretation of paragraph 2. The four sub-paragraphs of paragraph 3, notwithstanding their diversity, are grounded on the governing ideas of the general interest, social solidarity and what is normal in the ordinary course of affairs.[F]

23. Like the participants in the proceedings, the Court considers that compulsory fire service such as exists in Baden-Württemberg is one of the "normal civic obligations" envisaged in Article 4, para. 3(d). It observes further that the financial contribution which is payable—in lieu of service—is, according to the Federal Constitutional Court, a "compensatory charge". The Court therefore concludes that, on account of its close links with the obligation to serve, the obligation to pay also falls within the scope of Article 4, para. 3(d). It follows that Article 14 read in conjunction with Article 4, para. 3(d) applies.

B. Compliance

24. For the purposes of Article 14 a difference of treatment is discriminatory if it "has no objective and reasonable justification", that is if it does not pursue a "legitimate aim" or if there is not a "reasonable relationship of proportionality between the means employed and the aim sought to be realised". Moreover the contracting states enjoy a certain margin of appreciation in assessing whether and to what extent differences in otherwise similar situations justify a different treatment. However, very weighty reasons would have to be put forward before the Court could regard a difference of treatment based exclusively on the ground of sex as compatible with the Convention.

25. According to the applicant, the contracting states do not enjoy any margin of

---

[F] The complete text of Article 4 on "[p]rohibition of slavery and forced labour" provides:

1. No one shall be held in slavery or servitude.
2. No one shall be required to perform forced or compulsory labour.
3. For the purpose of this article the term 'forced or compulsory labour' shall not include:
   a. any work required to be done in the ordinary course of [criminal] detention imposed according to the provisions of Article 5 [granting due process rights to criminal defendants in order to secure the "[r]ight of liberty and security"] of this Convention or during conditional release from such detention;
   b. any service of a military character or, in case of conscientious objectors in countries where they are recognised, service exacted instead of compulsory military service;
   c. any service exacted in case of an emergency or calamity threatening the life or well-being of the community;
   d. any work or service which forms part of normal civic obligations.

appreciation as regards equality of the sexes. He argued that service in the fire brigade was comparable for men and for women and that account could be taken of the biological differences between the two sexes by a sensible division of the various tasks. The concern to protect women could not in itself justify a difference of treatment in this context. As at 31 December 1991, 68,612 women had served in fire brigades in Germany and even in Baden-Württemberg the fire brigades had accepted women since 1978. The financial contribution was of a purely fiscal nature, as in Baden-Württemberg no man had ever been called upon to serve. There was in any case discrimination since women were just as capable as men of paying the levy in question.

26. The Commission in substance accepted the applicant's argument.

27. In the Government's view, on the other hand, the difference of treatment is based on objective and reasonable grounds. Fire brigade duty is a traditional civic obligation in Baden-Württemberg defined by the Federal Constitutional Court as a "genuine and potential obligation to perform a public duty". The Government maintained that, in making this duty compulsory solely for the male sex, the legislature had taken account of the specific requirements of service in the fire brigade and the physical and mental characteristics of women. The sole aim which it had pursued in this respect was the protection of women. The financial contribution was purely compensatory in nature.

28. The Court notes that some German *Länder* do not impose different obligations for the two sexes in this field and that even in Baden-Württemberg women are accepted for voluntary service in the fire brigade.

Irrespective of whether or not there can nowadays exist any justification for treating men and women differently as regards compulsory service in the fire brigade, what is finally decisive in the present case is that the obligation to perform such service is exclusively one of law and theory. In view of the continuing existence of a sufficient number of volunteers, no male person is in practice obliged to serve in a fire brigade. The financial contribution has—not in law but in fact—lost its compensatory character and has become the only effective duty. In the imposition of a financial burden such as this, a difference of treatment on the ground of sex can hardly be justified.

29. There has accordingly been a violation of Article 14 taken in conjunction with Article 4, para. 3(d) of the Convention.

II. Alleged violation of Article 14 of the Convention taken together with Article I of Protocol No. 1

30. In view of the finding in paragraphs 28 and 29 above, the Court does not consider it necessary also to examine the complaint that the applicant was the victim of discrimination contrary to Article 14 of the Convention as regards his right to the peaceful enjoyment of his possessions, guaranteed under Article I of Protocol No. 1.[G]

[G] Article 1 of Protocol No. 1 provides:

Every natural or legal person is entitled to the peaceful enjoyment of his possessions. No one shall be deprived of his possessions except in the public interest and subject to the conditions provided for by law and by the general principles of international law.

III. Article 50

31. Under Article 50 [now revised in current Article 41],

If the Court finds that a decision or a measure taken by a legal authority or any other authority of a High Contracting Party is completely or partially in conflict with the obligations arising from the . . . Convention, and if the internal law of the said Party allows only partial reparation to be made for the consequences of this decision or measure, the decision of the Court shall, if necessary afford just satisfaction to the injured party.

32. The applicant sought the reimbursement of the fire service levy in respect of the years 1982 to 1984 (225 DM) and of the costs and expenses incurred before the national courts (395 DM). . . .

The Government raised no objection to this claim. The Delegate of the Commission regarded it as reasonable.

33. On the basis of the evidence available to it, the Court allows the applicant's claims in their entirety. . . .

JOINT DISSENTING OPINION OF JUDGES SPIELMANN AND GOTCHEV

We voted with the minority, finding that there was no violation in this case, for the following reasons.

The question whether there was discrimination arose essentially in relation to the obligation to effect fire brigade duty. The obligation to pay the financial contribution derives directly from the fact of being passed fit for such duty, even though in practice, as there are sufficient numbers of volunteer firemen, the obligation to serve is converted into an obligation to pay.

We note that in this instance the obligation to perform fire brigade duty applies only to able-bodied men aged between 18 and 50 inclusive.

In our view this is not a difference of treatment founded exclusively on sex, but a difference based on fitness to carry out the difficult and dangerous tasks inherent in fire brigade duty. The legislature could legitimately consider that men are ordinarily better suited to such tasks than women, just as men aged from 18 to 50 are normally better suited than those younger or older.

We believe that such a difference of treatment has an objective and reasonable justification. It follows that there was no discrimination on this point.

We consider that the same conclusion applies in respect of the compensatory charge, as the obligation to pay it derives directly from the obligation to perform the duty in question.

It is therefore our opinion that there was no violation in the present case.

N O T E

The Court's Logic. In *Schmidt,* is there a "right and freedom set forth" in the European Convention that is being secured through sex discrimination? Do you agree with

---

The preceding provisions shall not, however, in any way impair the right of a State to enforce such laws as it deems necessary to control the use of property in accordance with the general interest or to secure the payment of taxes or other contributions or penalties.

the Court's conclusion? Under *Schmidt,* could Germany exclude women from a draft for military service? From combat?

D. What's in a Name?

1. A Challenge to a Gender-Based Swiss Law on Marital Names

Burghartz v. Switzerland
(European Court of Human Rights)
18 Eur. H.R. Rep. 101 (1994)

1. The case was referred to the Court by the European Commission of Human Rights ("the Commission") on 11 December 1992 and by the Government of the Swiss Confederation on 8 January 1993. . . . It originated in an application against Switzerland lodged with the Commission . . . by Mrs. Susanna Burghartz and Mr. Albert Burghartz. . . .

6. The applicants, who are Swiss nationals, have both lived in Basle since 1975. They were married in Germany in 1984 and Mrs. Burghartz has German citizenship also. In accordance with German law, they chose the wife's surname, "Burghartz", as their family name; the husband availed himself of his right to put his own surname in front of that and thus call himself "Schnyder Burghartz".

7. The Swiss registry office having recorded "Schnyder" as their joint surname, the couple applied to substitute "Burghartz" as the family surname and "Schnyder Burghartz" as the husband's surname. On 6 November 1984 the cantonal government of Basle Rural turned down the application.

8. On 26 October 1988 the applicants made a further application to the cantonal Department of Justice of Basle Urban, following an amendment to the Civil Code as regards the effects of marriage, which had been made on 5 October 1984 and had come into force on 1 January 1988.

On 12 December 1988 their application was again refused, on the ground that they had not pointed to any serious inconvenience arising from the use of the surname "Schnyder". Furthermore, in the absence of any transitional provisions the new Article 30 para. 2 of the Civil Code could not apply to couples married before 1 January 1988. Lastly, under the new Article 160 para. 2, only a wife could put her own surname before the family name.

9. The applicants then lodged an appeal with the Federal Court in which they complained of, among other things, a breach of the new Articles 30 and 160 para. 2 of the Civil Code and Article 4 para. 2 of the Federal Constitution (see paragraphs 11 and 12 below).

On 8 June 1989 the Federal Court allowed the appeal in part. While refusing to apply paragraph 2 of Article 30, which concerned only engaged couples and had no retrospective effect, it held that in the particular case there were important factors which justified applying paragraph 1 in order to allow the applicants to call themselves "Burghartz"; apart from the couple's age and profession, account had to be taken of the differences between the relevant Swiss and German systems, which were made more acute by the fact that Basle was a frontier city.

As to Mr. Burghartz's application to be allowed to bear the name "Schnyder Burghartz", no support for it could be found in Article 160 para. 2 of the Civil Code; the drafting history showed that the Swiss Parliament, out of a concern to preserve family unity and avoid a break with tradition, had never agreed to introduce absolute equality between spouses in the choice of name and had thus deliberately restricted to wives the right to add their own surnames to their husbands'. This rule therefore could not avail by analogy a husband in a family known by the wife's surname. There was, however, nothing to prevent Mr. Burghartz from using a double-barrelled name (see paragraph 13 below) or even, informally, putting his surname before his wife's.

10. According to the applicant, a large number of official documents, in particular the certificate of his doctorate in history, had not since then contained the "Burghartz" element of his surname.

II. Relevant domestic law

11. Article 4 para. 2 of the Swiss Federal Constitution provides:

Men and women shall have equal rights. Equality shall be provided for by law, in particular in relation to the family, education and work. . . .

12. The relevant new Civil Code provisions that came into force on 1 January 1988 read as follows:

Article 30
(1) The government of the canton of residence may, if there is good cause, authorise a person to change his or her name.
(2) Engaged couples shall be authorised, if they so request and if they prove a legitimate interest, to bear the wife's surname as the family name once the marriage has been solemnised. . . .

Article 160
(1) Married couples shall take the husband's surname as their family name.
(2) A bride may, however, make a declaration to the registrar that she wishes to keep the surname she has borne to date, followed by the family name. . . .

Article 270
(1) The children of married couples shall bear their family name. . . .

Article 8a of the final section
Within one year of the entry into force of the new Act, a woman who was married under the old law may make a declaration to the registrar that she wishes to put the surname she bore before her marriage in front of the family name.

13. By a custom recognised in case law, married couples may also put the wife's surname after the husband's surname, joining the two with a hyphen. This double-barrelled name, however, is not regarded as the legal family name.

Proceedings Before the Commission

14. Mr. and Mrs. Burghartz applied to the Commission . . . , relying on Articles 8 [granting the right to respect for private and family life] and 14 [prohibiting state sex discrimination in securing Convention rights] of the Convention.

15. The Commission declared the application admissible [and] . . . expressed the opinion . . . that there had been a breach of Article 14 taken together with Article 8, and . . . that there was no need to examine the case under Article 8 taken alone. . . .

As to the Law

I. The Government's preliminary objections

A. Whether or not the first applicant is a victim

16. As before the Commission, the Government contested in the first place that Mrs. Burghartz was a victim within the meaning of Article 25[H] of the Convention. No one but Mr. Burghartz had been aggrieved by the refusal of his request, the only one in issue in the case as his wife had obtained satisfaction from the Federal Court, which had allowed her to keep her maiden name.

17. The applicants pointed to Mrs. Burghartz's personal interest in the success of her husband's action. Since, together with him, she had chosen "Burghartz" as their joint family name, she considered herself directly responsible for her husband's loss of his surname "Schnyder", and their married life might suffer from this. The Commission too thought that the question concerned both spouses.

18. The Court points out that the case originated in a joint application by Mr. and Mrs. Burghartz to change their joint family name and the husband's surname simultaneously. Having regard to the concept of family which prevails in the Convention system, it considers that Mrs. Burghartz may claim to be a victim of the impugned decisions, at least indirectly.

The objection must therefore be dismissed.

B. Exhaustion of domestic remedies

19. The Government, who had already raised the issue before the Commission, submitted that the applicants had not exhausted domestic remedies as they had neither relied on Articles 8 and 14 of the Convention in their appeal, nor also lodged a public-law appeal.

20. The Court observes that the Federal Court is required by Article 113 para. 3 of the Swiss Constitution to apply the laws passed by the Federal Assembly. It is expressly forbidden to suspend the effects of any such laws which might prove to be

---

[H] The content of Article 25 is now contained in current Article 34. Article 34 of the Convention provides that: "The Court may receive applications from any person, non-governmental organisation or group of individuals claiming to be the victim of a violation by one of High Contracting Parties of the rights set forth in the Convention or the protocols thereto. The High Contracting Parties undertake not to hinder in any way the effective exercise of this right."

incompatible with the Constitution. This prohibition seems to have been extended by current case law to cases in which there is a conflict between such a law and a treaty. That being so, the applicants cannot be blamed for having founded their appeal solely on domestic law—Articles 30 and 160 of the Civil Code, 8a of the final section of that code and 4 para. 2 of the Constitution—seeing that their arguments were identical in substance with those they submitted to the Commission. As to a public-law appeal, its subsidiary nature prevents it from being considered in this instance an adequate remedy which Article 26 of the Convention would also have required the applicants to exhaust. Accordingly, this objection likewise must be dismissed.

II. Alleged violation of Article 14 taken together with Article 8

21. The applicants relied on Article 8, taken alone and together with Article 14. Article 8 provides:

(1) Everyone has the right to respect for his private and family life, his home and his correspondence.
(2) There shall be no interference by a public authority with the exercise of this right except such as is in accordance with the law and is necessary in a democratic society in the interests of national security, public safety or the economic well-being of the country, for the prevention of disorder or crime, for the protection of health or morals, or for the protection of the rights and freedoms of others.

Article 14 provides:

The enjoyment of the rights and freedoms set forth in this Convention shall be secured without discrimination on any ground such as sex, race, colour, language, religion, political or other opinion, national or social origin, association with a national minority, property, birth or other status.

Given the nature of the complaints, the Court, like the Commission, deems it appropriate to examine the case directly under Article 14 taken together with Article 8.

A. Applicability

22. The Government argued that these two provisions were not applicable. Since the entry into force of Protocol No. 7 on 1 November 1988, the equality of spouses in the choice of surname had been governed exclusively by Article 5 [equality between spouses][1] of that Protocol, covering equality of rights and responsibilities of a private-law character between spouses. . . . When ratifying that Protocol, Switzerland had

---

[1] Article 5 of Protocol No. 7 provides that: "Spouses shall enjoy equality of rights and responsibilities of a private law character between them, and in their relations with their children, as to marriage, during marriage and in the event of its dissolution. This Article shall not prevent States from taking such measures as are necessary in the interests of the children."

made a reservation providing . . . that "[f]ollowing the entry into force of the revised provisions of the Swiss Civil Code [CC] of 5 October 1984, the provisions of Article 5 of Protocol No. 7 shall apply subject to . . . the provisions of Federal Law concerning the family name (Articles 160 CC and 8a final section CC). . . ." Examining the case under Articles 14 and 8 taken together would thus be tantamount to ignoring a reservation that satisfied the requirements of Article 64 [now 57][J] of the Convention.

23. The Court points out that under Article 7 of Protocol No. 7, Article 5 is to be regarded as an addition to the Convention, including [Article] 8 [right to respect for private and family life]. . . . Consequently, it cannot replace Article 8 or reduce its scope.

It must nevertheless be determined whether Article 8 applies in the circumstances of the case.

24. Unlike some other international instruments, such as the [ICCPR, CRC, and ACHR], Article 8 of the Convention does not contain any explicit provisions on names. As a means of personal identification and of linking to a family, a person's name nonetheless concerns his or her private and family life. The fact that society and the State have an interest in regulating the use of names does not exclude this, since these public-law aspects are compatible with private life conceived of as including, to a certain degree, the right to establish and develop relationships with other human beings, in professional or business contexts as in others.

In the instant case, the applicant's retention of the surname by which, according to him, he has become known in academic circles, may significantly affect his career. Article 8 therefore applies.

B. Compliance

25. Mr. and Mrs. Burghartz complained that the authorities had withheld from Mr. Burghartz the right to put his own surname before their family name although Swiss law afforded that possibility to married women who had chosen their husbands' surname as their family name. They said that this resulted in discrimination on the ground of sex, contrary to Articles 14 and 8 taken together.

The Commission shared this view in substance.

26. The Government recognised that what was at issue was a difference of treatment on the ground of sex but argued that it was prompted by objective and reasonable considerations which prevented it from being in any way discriminatory.

By providing that, as a general rule, families should take the husband's surname [Art. 160(1) CC], the Swiss legislature had deliberately opted for a traditional arrangement whereby family unity was reflected in a joint name. It was only in order to mitigate the rigour of the principle that it had also provided for a married woman's right to put her own surname in front of her husband's [Art. 160(2) CC]. On the other

---

[J] Article 57 (former Article 64) provides that: "1. Any State may . . . make a reservation in respect of any particular provision of the Convention to the extent that any law then in force in its territory is not in conformity with the provision. Reservations of a general character shall not be permitted under this article."

hand, the reverse was not justified to the advantage of a married man who, like Mr. Burghartz, deliberately and in full knowledge of the consequences, invoked Article 30(1) of the Civil Code to change his surname to that of his wife. It was all the more unjustified as there was nothing to prevent a husband, even in those circumstances, from using his surname as part of a double-barrelled name or in any other way informally.

27. The Court reiterates that the advancement of the equality of the sexes is today a major goal in the Member States of the Council of Europe; this means that very weighty reasons would have to be put forward before a difference of treatment on the sole ground of sex could be regarded as compatible with the Convention.

28. In support of the system complained of, the Government relied, first, on the Swiss legislature's concern that family unity should be reflected in a single joint surname. The Court is not persuaded by this argument, since family unity would be no less reflected if the husband added his own surname to his wife's, adopted as the joint family name, than it is by the converse arrangement allowed by the Civil Code.

In the second place, it cannot be said that a genuine tradition is at issue here. Married women have enjoyed the right from which the applicant seeks to benefit only since 1984. In any event, the Convention must be interpreted in the light of present-day conditions, especially the importance of the principle of non-discrimination.

Nor is there any distinction to be derived from the spouses' choice of one of their surnames as the family name in preference to the other. Contrary to what the Government contended, it cannot be said to represent greater deliberateness on the part of the husband than on the part of the wife. It is therefore unjustified to provide for different consequences in each case.

As to the other types of surname, such as a double-barrelled name or any other informal manner of use, the Federal Court itself distinguished them from the legal family name, which is the only one that may appear in a person's official papers. They therefore cannot be regarded as equivalent to it.

29. In sum, the difference of treatment complained of lacks an objective and reasonable justification and accordingly contravenes Article 14 taken together with Article 8.

30. Having regard to this conclusion, the Court, like the Commission, deems it unnecessary to determine whether there has also been a breach of Article 8 taken alone.

III. Application of Article 50

31. Under Article 50 [now revised in current Art. 41],

If the Court finds that a decision or a measure taken by a legal authority or any other authority of a High Contracting Party is completely or partially in conflict with the obligations arising from the . . . Convention, and if the internal law of the said Party allows only partial reparation to be made for the consequences of this decision or measure, the decision of the Court shall, if necessary, afford just satisfaction to the injured party.

32. The applicants claimed only the costs of legal representation before the national authorities and the Strasbourg institutions [the Commission and Court] in the sum of 31,000 Sfr.

The Government found this amount exorbitant and suggested reducing it to 10,000 Sfr. The Delegate of the Commission also regarded it as inflated.

33. The Court has considered the matter in the light of observations by those appearing before it and of the criteria laid down in its case law. Making its assessment on an equitable basis, it awards the applicants 20,000 Sfr for costs and expenses. . . .

DISSENTING OPINION OF JUDGE THOR VILHJALMSSON

The rules of domestic law dealt with in this case had no prejudicial effect on the applicants of a sufficient severity to bring it within the proper scope of international protection of human rights. In my opinion Article 8 of the Convention is not . . . applicable and there was accordingly no violation.

DISSENTING OPINION OF JUDGES PETTITI AND VALTICOS

1. We consider that Article 8 of the Convention, on which the Court's reasoning mainly rests, is not applicable to the assignment of married couples' family names, *at least* in circumstances such as those in the instant case. Not only does this Article not expressly refer to this issue, or even to naming in general, but political, legal, social and religious conceptions still vary so much from one country to another in this field, which is still in the process of change, that to claim to impose in this instance this or that view concerning the rules that should be followed in the matter of married or divorced couples' family names would certainly to be to go beyond the scope of Article 8 and of the undertakings entered into by the States.

While, as the majority of the Court hold, the principle of the equality of the sexes admittedly is today "a major goal in the Member States of the Council of Europe" and while the Court cannot ignore changes of views in this field, it does not follow that an extension of the scope of Article 8 of the Convention is justified, as the Court considers.

2. As in the determination of nationality, the legislation on assigning names must remain within the State's domain and does not come within the ambit of the Convention. It is well known that views on the assignment and choice of surnames and first names vary within each national system, both as regards births and as regards marriages and divorces. In different countries it would be possible to find hundreds of variants. Creating a right to choose names freely on the basis of such a minimal case as Mr. and Mrs. Burghartz's would have undue consequences and might lead to numerous applications lacking any proper justification. The couple had already been authorised to substitute the name "Burghartz" for the name "Schnyder".

3. In the present case, having regard to the fact that the couple had been allowed to change their name, the Swiss authorities' refusal cannot, in our view, be regarded as amounting to a discriminatory infringement of the equality of the sexes.

Basically, we are emphasising that in this instance the Chamber's interpretation is an extreme one, especially as, while the case is admittedly not of major importance in itself, the principle could lead too far in a Europe that is becoming more and more varied and in a field in which legal provisions, like opinions, are still very varied.

N O T E S

A Changed Test? The Court decided the *Abdulaziz* case in 1985, and *Schmidt* and *Burghartz* in 1994. Has it changed its standard of review in any way?

The Different Conventions. What are the strengths and weaknesses of the European Convention as compared to the American Convention? The African Charter? The ICCPR? Consider the substantive scope of the conventions and the procedural rules that prevail under them in answering the following question: If you could amend the European Convention today to enhance its protections for women, what changes would you make?

Europe Slowly Advances Toward Equal Rights for All. While Europe took the lead in producing the European Human Rights Convention in 1953, it lagged behind the world on equal rights for women, both in marriage and in general. In 1948, the UDHR provided, in Article 16(1), for "equal rights as to marriage, during marriage and at its dissolution." Not until 1988 did the European Convention provide, through Protocol 7, article 5, that spouses should have equal rights. *See* footnote I, *supra.* Forty European countries had ratified this Protocol as of August 7, 2007. Note that while ICCPR Article 23(4) provided for equal marriage rights in 1976, and CEDAW Article 16 did so in 1981, Europe did so only in 1988.

Europe took even longer—almost 30 years—to provide the equivalent of the ICCPR Article 26 right to equality without sex-based discrimination. Protocol 12 to the European Convention provides:

1. The enjoyment of any right set forth by law shall be secured without discrimination on any ground such as sex, race, colour, language, religion, political or other opinion, national or social origin, association with a national minority, property, birth or other status.
2. No one shall be discriminated against by any public authority on any ground such as those mentioned in paragraph 1.

This Protocol entered into force only on April 1, 2005. Only 15 countries had ratified this Protocol as of August 7, 2007.

Switzerland. This country reserved as to Protocol 7, Article 5. Why? Do you agree with the Court about the significance of this reservation? Consider the government's description of its purposes in enacting the laws at issue. Why does the Court reject them?

Names. Consider the dissenters' views in evaluating whether discrimination as to names has any importance. Is it too insignificant for women's advocates to pursue? Something that will make them the targets of jokes? Something that should be dropped to pursue more important matters? Something like excluding women from a professional golfing tournament?

2. An American Father's Attempt to Require Gender-Based Naming Rules

Gubernat v. Deremer

(Supreme Court of New Jersey)
657 A.2d 856 (NJ 1995)

STEIN, J.

The question presented by this appeal concerns the right of a father, in cases involving disputes over a child's surname, to insist that the child bear his surname. The issue arises in the context of a child, born to unmarried parents, who was given his mother's surname at birth, the father having refused to acknowledge paternity. When his paternity was established by tests performed approximately seven months later, the father acknowledged paternity and commenced visitation. Shortly thereafter, the father instituted litigation seeking joint custody, increased visitation, and a change of the child's surname. The trial court awarded the father joint custody and increased visitation, but the child's mother retained primary physical custody. The trial court, recognizing "the father's interest in maintaining his relationship with his child for their mutual benefit," ordered that the child assume the father's surname. The Appellate Division affirmed in an unreported opinion.

The recognition by the courts below of a preference for paternal surnames is supported by Western custom and law spanning more than six centuries. The practice of children assuming the father's surname is traceable to the English medieval property system in which the husband controlled all marital property. That preference continued in America, reflecting not only the long-standing English tradition but also the societal distinctions in the status of men and women. Until the latter part of this century, the assumption that children would bear their father's surnames was a matter of common understanding and the preference for paternal surnames was rarely challenged. But the historical justifications that once supported a tradition in the law for children to bear paternal surnames have been overtaken by society's recognition of full legal equality for women, an equality that is incompatible with continued recognition of a presumption that children must bear their father's surname. That presumption shall no longer apply in this State. We hold instead that in contested cases the surname selected by the custodial parent—the parent primarily charged with making custodial decisions in the child's best interest—shall be presumed to be consistent with that child's best interests, a presumption rebuttable by evidence that a different surname would better serve those interests. We apply that rule of law to the facts at hand, and reverse the judgment of the Appellate Division. . . .

II

The term "surname" comes from the French word "surnom"—"sur" meaning above or beyond, "nom" from the Latin "nomen," meaning name. Yvonne M. Cherena Pacheco, *Latino Surnames: Formal and Informal Forces in the United States Affecting the Retention and Use of the Maternal Surname*, 18 T. Marshall L.Rev. 1, 5 (1992) [*Latino Surnames*]. The use of surnames is a relatively recent historical practice. "In the early life of all races surnames were unknown, while given names have been used from the most distant times to identify and distinguish a particular individual from his fellows." *Smith v. United States Casualty Co.*, 197 N.Y. 420 (1910).

The Anglo-Saxon tradition of surnames dates back to the Norman Conquest in 1066. The Normans introduced a number of non-English given names, such as "Richard," "Robert," and "William," of which William "became and remained the single most common recorded name in the twelfth century." M.T. CLANCHY, ENGLAND AND ITS RULERS: 1066–1272 (1983). However, although each village or town might have had only " 'ten Williams, [and] a similar number of [Roberts and Richards,]' . . . distinctions often needed to be made if two villagers were talking about [William], misunderstandings would arise if each had a different [William] in mind. So qualifications were added. . . ." [*Latino Surnames*]. "Beginning with the influence exerted by the Normans following their conquest of England in the eleventh century, the practice of adding second names became more common as the relative scarcity of Christian names led to a great number of people bearing the same name." Richard H. Thornton, Note, *The Controversy Over Children's Surnames: Familial Autonomy, Equal Protection and the Child's Best Interests*, 1979 UTAH L.REV. 303, 305 [*Controversy*]. Although the growth of population and the development of cities required a means of distinguishing between individuals with identical given names, the Normans also introduced a number of social practices—the imposition of a feudal land system and the use of primogeniture as a system of inheritance—that likewise spurred the development of surnames. *See* Beverly S. Seng, *Like Father, Like Child: The Rights of Parents in Their Children's Surnames*, 70 VA.L.REV. 1303, 1323 (1984) [*Children's Surnames*].

Surnames came from a number of sources, including "accident, caprice, taste, and a multitude of other causes." *Smith.* "It is to be noted, however, that the surname in its origin was not as a rule inherited from the father, but either adopted by the son, or bestowed upon him by the people of the community where he lived." *Ibid.* Surnames often were derived from the area in which a person lived. Men who owned property commonly took their surnames from their places of habitation. "In the rush of conversation some words would get passed over which caused surnames to flourish. Thus, one ordinarily described as 'John from the hill' might eventually [become] 'John Hill.'" [*Latino Surnames*]. Artisans and craftsmen derived surnames from their occupations. "Thus, John the carpenter, evolved into John Carpenter." *Ibid.* In addition, a particular attribute or characteristic of a person could become that person's surname:

So, as suggested, something in the appearance, character, or history of the individual gave rise to the surname such as his color, as black John, brown John, white John, afterwards transposed to John Brown, [etc.]; or it arose from his bulk, height, or strength, as Little, Long, Hardy, or Strong; or his mental or moral attributes, as Good, Wiley, Gay, Moody, or Wise; or his qualities were poetically personified by applying to him the name of some animal, plant, or bird, as Fox or Wolf, Rose or Thorn, Martin or Swan; and it was in this way that the bulk of our surnames . . . originated and became permanent.

[*In re Snook*, 2 Hilt. 566, 570 (N.Y.Ct.Common Pleas 1859)]

"To give their children unique names, parents combined thematic words such as 'courage' or 'peace' to create compound names such as Ecgbeorht, the modern Egbert, meaning 'bright sword,' or Wulfraed, meaning 'wolve's [sic] cunning'" [*Children's Surnames*].

Additionally, surnames expressive of kinship were chosen. "The Normans brought with them a custom of naming sons after their fathers (as in *Ray son of Hugh*) as a convenience to the feudal system: the feudal lord could thus more easily identify sons of the soldiers most loyal to him." *Id.* However, [using] patronymics, a name derived from that of the father, was neither compelled nor universal:

Inquiry into the naming practices of Western societies demonstrates that names ordinarily express kinship but not necessarily paternity. Matronymics, names derived from the maternal line, have been employed in several Western cultures, including modern Spain and medieval England. In England, at least as late as the fourteenth century, both sons and daughters adopted their mothers' surnames, often upon succeeding to their mothers' estates or in hopes of doing so. Men also adopted their wives' surnames if the couple inherited property from the woman's family. The children of such couples presumably also took their mothers' surnames. Even among the non-propertied classes children sometimes used the maternal surnames. Historian and linguist C. M. Matthews explained the custom:

> [A]n illegitimate boy might be called by his mother's name, but it was equally natural and useful to refer to the son of a highly respected widow in the same way, or even, when the father was alive but away for years on some distant expedition or married to a dominant wife, the lad might be spoken of . . . as belonging to Moll or Alison or Margery.

The paternal surname, even if initially bestowed, did not necessarily survive the father's absence. Many of these English matronymics are still in use. As many as one-tenth of contemporary English surnames of relationship (as contrasted to those derived from names of places or occupations) were originally matronymics. [*Id.*]

Eventually the medieval property structure, which invested all marital property in the husband, and the firm and exclusive establishment of primogeniture in the fourteenth century, resulted in the widespread use of hereditary paternal surnames. "Some time after the early fourteenth century, surnames began to serve as hereditary family names, partly because the inheritance of property was often contingent upon an heir's retention of the surname associated with that property." [*Controversy*]; *see also* Cynthia Blevins Doll, Note, *Harmonizing Filial and Parental Rights in Names: Progress, Pitfalls, and Constitutional Problems*, 35 How.L.J. 227, 229 (1992) ("The custom of patrilineal succession evolved from the medieval property system, in which the husband controlled all marital property. . . . In addition, a married woman in medieval times could not contract or maintain suit in her own name. The male was the legal representative of the family and, as such, enjoyed the unilateral right to name his family.") "The custom of patrilineal succession seems to have been a response to England's medieval social and legal system, which came to vest all rights of ownership and management of marital property in the husband." *In re Schiffman*, 28 Cal.3d 640 (1980). As one commentator noted, the mechanics of recording entitlement to land prompted the retention of the paternal surname:

"The land could be claimed and awarded only at the Manorial Court, being held 'by copy of the Court Roll,' which meant that the life tenant's name was inscribed there on permanent record. This system provided a direct incentive to men to keep the same surname that had been put down on the roll for their father or grandfather. And even younger sons—having in mind the uncertainty of life—might think it just as well to use the name too, even if it was Whalebelly or Chickenhead." [*Children's Surnames*]

"Allowing the husband to determine the surname of their offspring was part of that system, wherein he was the sole legal representative of the marriage, its property, and its children." *In re Schiffman.* "Given the secondary status afforded to women at those times, it is not surprising that the masculine lineage was chosen." *M.D. v. A.S.L.,* 275 N.J.Super. 530 (Ch.Div.1994).

The customary use of hereditary parental surnames was further institutionalized during the reign of Henry VIII of England (1509–1547) in the early sixteenth century. The King established the Parish Registry System governing the recording of births, marriages, and deaths. Each parish had to keep records of the births, marriages, and deaths of the parish inhabitants. "The effect was to encourage families to identify themselves under the father's name for recording purposes." Shirley Raissi Bysiewicz & Gloria Jeanne Stillson MacDonnell, *Married Women's Surnames*, 5 CONN.L.REV. 598 (1973) [*Married Women's Surnames*]. Certain benefits of that practice accrued to the Crown:

[E]asier identification of the citizen would permit the government to call upon the citizen for purposes of taxation and other ways of serving the government.
The government bestowed the patronymic name upon each child whose parents were married, thus further legitimizing the child through the naming process. The father was also legitimized for bringing forth a new heir and subject to the king. [*Latino Surnames*]

Inevitably, the institutionalized tradition of assuming the hereditary patronymic surname, and the secondary legal status of women in England, diminished the importance of the maternal surname. As one commentator observed:

The matronymic name, on the other hand, was not even considered in this naming or recording process, nor was it viewed with the same level of legitimacy as that of the paternal name. Although it was the mother who gave birth, and who gave to the child part of her identity, she could not give the child her name. The English Crown had no interest in the mother's surname, it was not deemed legitimate or worth perpetuating. [*Id.*]

However, a distinction in English common law arose in respect of a child born of unmarried parents. "At common law, an illegitimate child was *filius nullius*, the son of no one, or *filius populi*, the son of the people." *D.R.S. v. R.S.H.,* 412 N.E.2d 1257 (Ind. Ct. App. 1980). The child had no mother or father recognized by law, and therefore had no legal rights. Because the child could not inherit property, the impetus to bear the paternal surname was diminished. "[C]ustom did not dictate the name by which an illegitimate child would be known; the child bore the name gained by reputation in the community." *Id.*

The traditional use of the paternal surname was brought to this country by the colonists. Historical review clearly demonstrates that the continuation of the English custom of patronymic surnames in the colonies was intrinsically linked to greater social forces, particularity the inferior legal status of women. *See In re Rossell*, 196 N.J.Super 109 (Law Div.1984) ("Names . . . are intimately involved with the status of women."). A 1632 document entitled *The Lawes Resolutions of Womens Rights* provides an insightful glimpse into the societal and familial role of woman. The woman, after marriage, is described as a "poor rivulet [that] looseth her name" on merging with the "Rhodanus, Humber, or the Thames." HOWARD ZINN, A PEOPLE'S HISTORY OF THE UNITED STATES (1980) [PEOPLE'S HISTORY](quoting *The Lawes Resolutions of Womens Rights* (1632)). "'A woman as soon as she is married, is called *covert* . . . that is, "veiled"; as it were, clouded and overshadowed; she hath lost her streame. I may more truly, farre away, say to a married woman, Her new self is her superior, her companion, her master. . . .'" *Id.* Colonial women had no legal identity separate from their husbands and were thus subordinated to them:

> Living within a family meant a state of dependence for everyone but the patriarch. Women rarely had an independent existence, at least in law. In public records women were usually referred to simply as the "wife of," or the "daughter of," or the "sister of" some male. Before marriage they legally belonged to their fathers and after marriage to their husbands. . . . With their husbands alive women were considered legally to be like children: they could not sue or be sued, draft wills, make contracts, or deal in property.
> [GORDON S. WOOD, THE RADICALISM OF THE AMERICAN REVOLUTION 49 (1991).] [RADICALISM]

In contrast, the rule of a father of the household over his family has been described as a diminutive version of the reign of a king over his people. "The head of the household remained a kind of miniature king, a governor or protector to whom respect and subjection were due." *Ibid.* "It has been suggested that [the] bestowal of the paternal surname upon a child not only has its basis in custom, but also in the absolute role a father had as head of his family." [*Controversy*].

> The father's position in the family was expressed in THE SPECTATOR, an influential periodical in America and England: "Nothing is more gratifying to the mind of man than power or dominion; and . . . as I am the father of a family. . . . I am perpetually taken up in giving out orders, in prescribing duties, in hearing parties, in administering justice, and in distributing rewards and punishments . . . . In short sir I look upon my family as a patriarchal sovereignty in which I am myself both king and priest."
> [PEOPLE'S HISTORY].

The retention of the English law of primogeniture and the related practice of entail, which allowed the testator to keep the land intact by passing it through the "stem" line of the family, ensured that "[t]he land belonged to the male line" and continued the custom of children receiving the male surname. [RADICALISM].

Most New England farmers, and perhaps most others too, thought mainly of providing for their families and rarely justified their acquisitiveness in any other terms than the needs of their families. What they principally wanted out of life was sons to whom they could pass on their land and who would continue the family name. For

Virginians as well as New Englanders, "a man's patrimony . . . is a sacred depositum."
[*Id.*]

The struggle to survive and prosper and the subsequent Revolutionary War blurred gender roles. "Certainly by 1750 ancient patriarchal absolutism no longer had the same ideological significance it had once possessed," *Id.*, and women gained limited practical and legal autonomy. "Married women in the colonies continued in general to have greater legal rights than their counterparts in England (though after mid-century efforts to bring colonial law into line with English common law did at times legally restrict the rights of wives)." *Id.* The American Revolution witnessed working-class women actively participating at both the home-front and battle-front. Women formed patriotic groups, campaigned against British practices, produced propaganda, and cared for and fought alongside men in the last years of the war. [PEOPLE'S HISTORY]. Abigail Adams wrote to her husband, John Adams, in 1776:

[I]n the new code of laws which I suppose it will be necessary for you to make, I desire you would remember the ladies, and be more generous to them than your ancestors. Do not put such unlimited power in the hands of husbands. Remember, all men would be tyrants if they could. [*Id.*]

After the Revolutionary War none of the States, with the exception of New Jersey, granted women the right of suffrage. (New Jersey rescinded the right in 1807.) Although women actively campaigned in the 1830's and 1840's on behalf of slaves, prisoners, the insane, and themselves, they nevertheless remained a class denied the right to vote, to hold marital property, and to pursue educational opportunities. Reforms that did occur often were either limited or equally constraining. "The passage of the Married Women's Property Acts in most states and in England during the latter half of the 19th Century removed the common law disability but did not achieve equality for women." [*Married Women's Surnames*].

Nineteenth-century reformers did attempt to rectify the status of illegitimate children as a "son[/daughter] of nobody," [*Controversy*], by placing the mother and child in a legal family unit. That was accomplished by legislation awarding custody of the child to the mother, consistent with "her duty to support him, as his natural guardian." *Secretary of Commonwealth.* One effect of those statutes was to incorporate into law what had already developed as custom that a child born of unmarried parents would assume the mother's surname. The assumption of the maternal surname by the child born out of wedlock was not the result of a right or privilege extended to women, but instead was incidental to the societally imposed duty on her to care for the child:

Prior to the mid-nineteenth century, a child born to unwed parents had the status of filius nullius. . . . This meant, among other things, that nobody had the right to the custody of the child. Among the ameliorative steps taken in the nineteenth century was the enactment of statutes placing custody in the birth mother. According to legal historian Michael Grossberg, choosing the birth mother as custodian was neither a coincidence nor inevitable. While based in part on the fact that she could be identified easily, the decision also turned on a belief that a mother would be a better parent. As Grossberg says,

> [M]aternal preference found its origins in the "cult of domesticity" that pervaded nineteenth-century American culture. These sentiments put immense pressure on legal authorities to place children with their mothers whenever possible. . . .
> The proposition that the grant of custody rights to mothers was a placement of responsibility rather than an award of privilege is further demonstrated when one looks at the additional rights granted the child at the time the mother was accorded custody rights: the use of the mother's name and an entitlement to inherit from and through her. [Karen Czapanskiy, *Volunteers and Draftees: The Struggle for Parental Equality*, 38 UCLA L.Rev. 1415 (1991) (quoting 'Michael Grossberg, Governing the Hearth: Law and Family in Nineteenth Century America (1985)).]

The broader effect of the nineteenth-century statutes was to create divergent treatment of children based on their birth status. Children born of wedded parents received the paternal surname; children born of unwed parents received the maternal surname. "This assumption of matriarchal surnames paralleled the then traditional view that an unmarried woman possessed greater rights to the child as opposed to the putative father." *M.D. v. A.S.L.*.

Despite significant gains, twentieth-century American women continued to confront gender-based obstacles. The ability of women to achieve financial and legal independence suffered under the "common-law fiction that the husband and wife are one. This rule has worked out in reality to mean that though the husband and wife are one, the one is the husband." *United States v. Yazell*, 382 U.S. 341 (1966) (Black, J., dissenting). American law reflected the subordinate role of women by deferring to the superior status of the father in naming his legitimate child, noting that "[f]rom time immemorial it has been the custom for male children to bear the family name of their father throughout life." *Kay v. Kay*, 112 N.E.2d 562 (Ohio Ct.Common Pleas 1953). American courts have described that customary right as one of "inherent concern" to the father, *Robinson v. Hansel*, 302 Minn. 34 (1974), as "the [father's] right to expect his kin to bear his name," *Sobel v. Sobel*, 46 N.J.Super. 284 (Ch.Div.1957), as a "natural and commendable desire of the father to have his children bear and perpetuate his name," *Clinton v. Morrow*, 220 Ark. 377 (1952), and as a "natural right [of the father] to have his son bear his name," *De Vorkin v. Foster*, 66 N.Y.S.2d 54, 54 (Sup.Ct.1946). One early activist described the "natural right" of men to name their children as derived from the maxim that what a man owns, he may name; what he names, he owns:

> In 1922 Ruth Hale, advocate of women's right to determine their own names and co-founder of the Lucy Stone League, in discussing the basis for men's demand that women take their husbands' surnames, articulated the underlying basis of men's expectation that they have the absolute right to name their children:
> Custom said, too, that man owned what he paid for, and could put his name on for which he provided money. He wrote his name more often than a little boy with chalk signs his to a fence. He put it on his land, his house, his wife and children, his slaves when he had them and

on everything that was his. [Priscilla R. MacDougal, *The Right of Women to Name Their Children,* 3 Law & Ineq. J. 91 (1985)]

Only the father who "wilfully abandons and neglects his young and helpless progeny, and ignores his responsibility to them, may well be deemed to have no natural paternal desires—and therefore to have forfeited his normal rights—to the perpetuation of his name." *In re Sloan,* 118 N.Y.S.2d 594 (Sup.Ct.1953).

The twentieth century, however, has produced dynamic social change. Specifically, "[p]rogress toward marital and parental equality has accelerated in recent years," *In re Schiffman,* and women have overcome the vast majority of the traditional forms of legal subordination. "This court [has found] that the society in which we live today is purportedly neither maternal nor paternal. The principle of gender neutrality is evident in the laws as administered by the courts of New Jersey and throughout the legal system; great efforts have been generated to further this concept." *K.K. v. G.,* 219 N.J.Super. 334 (Ch.Div.1987). The New Jersey Legislature has, in various contexts, taken steps to remedy past gender-based differences in the rights and responsibilities of parents and spouses. . . .

The Legislature clearly has ended gender-based differences in marital and parental rights, whether rooted in law or custom, and instead determined that parental disputes about children should be resolved in accordance with each child's best interests. Sex-based presumptions, such as the "tender years" doctrine, that had survived as a matter of custom for decades, have been replaced by an inquiry focused on the happiness and welfare of the child. Courts are required to engage in meticulous fact-finding to determine the "best interests" of the child. *See* N.J.S.A. 9:2-4(c); *In re Baby M.* "The 'best interests' doctrine is applied in almost every legal disposition involving minors: custody, adoption, abuse and neglect, guardianship, termination of parental rights, and even disposition following juvenile court proceedings." [*Children's Surnames*]. Today, "the best interests of the child" is the applicable standard governing most decisions affecting the welfare of children. *See In re Baby M.*

That standard is also the one that we apply in determining the appropriate surname to be given to a child regardless of the child's birth status. . . .

However, despite the steps legislatures and courts have taken to eradicate gender-based differences, some courts nevertheless rely on traditional presumptions that obscure a clear evaluation of what constitutes the child's best interests. Those courts have continued to favor the retention and use of the paternal surname by treating the child's best interests as synonymous with the father's best interests. "In resolving disagreements between parents regarding their child's surnames, the 'best interest of the child' test has customarily been defined in terms of the father-child relationship." *In re Schiffman* (Mosk, J., concurring). For example, the Indiana Court of Appeals has stated that "all agree that the welfare of the child is the paramount consideration in deciding whether a child's name should be changed over the opposition of one parent," *D.R.S. v. R.S.H.,* but in determining what constituted the welfare of the child, the court concluded that "[f]irst, significant consideration is given to the father's interest in having his child bear the paternal surname in accordance with tradition."

We do not accept the preference that some courts accord to paternal surnames in the context of determining the best interests of the child. . . .

III

Courts applying the best-interests-of-the-child standard consider a number of criteria in determining the advantages and detriments to a child of assuming either the maternal or paternal surname. Those factors include the length of time that the child has used one surname, the identification of the child as a member or part of a family unit, the potential anxiety, embarrassment, or discomfort the child might experience if the child bears a surname different from the custodial parent, and any preferences the child might express, assuming the child possesses sufficient maturity to express a relevant preference. Courts have experienced difficulty, however, in applying the factors underlying the best-interests-of-the-child standard, possibly because of the speculative quality of the inquiry into the effect that the chosen surname would have on the future welfare and happiness of the child. One author commented that as a result of the vagueness of the standard, "judges have proposed different and frequently conflicting subjective factors for deciding whether a particular name is in a child's best interests—factors that lead to inconsistent resolutions of child-naming controversies." Laura Anne Foggan, Note, *Parents' Selection of Children's Surnames*, 51 GEO. WASH.L.REV. 583, 595–96 (1983).

To enhance the predictability of the best-interest standard, some commentators have suggested, and a few courts have adopted, a presumption in favor of the surname chosen by the custodial parent. . . .

To the extent that the subject has been addressed in New Jersey, regulations promulgated by the New Jersey State Department of Health provide that if either parent is unavailable, the choice of name is to be made by the custodial parent N.J.A.C. 8:2-1.3(a)1. If both parents have custody but disagree on the name, the child shall be given a hyphenated surname based on alphabetical order. N.J.A.C. 8:2-1.3(a)2.

The presumption that the parent who exercises physical custody or sole legal custody should determine the surname of the child is firmly grounded in the judicial and legislative recognition that the custodial parent will act in the best interest of the child. Accordingly, we adopt a strong presumption in favor of the surname chosen by the custodial parent. However, we readily envision circumstances in which the presumption could be rebutted. A young child who has used the non-custodial surname for a period of time, is known to all by that surname, expresses comfort with the continuation of that surname, and maintains frequent contact with the non-custodial parent might be ill-served by the presumption that the assumption of the custodial surname would be in his or her best interests. Although we accord the presumption substantial weight, it is not irrefutable.

The non-custodial parent bears the burden of demonstrating by a preponderance of the evidence that despite the presumption favoring the custodial parent's choice of name, the chosen surname is not in the best interests of the child. Courts should examine scrupulously all factors relevant to the best interests of the child and should avoid giving weight to any interests unsupported by evidence or rooted in impermissible gender preferences. The rebuttable character of the custodial-parent presumption serves two ends: it protects the right of the custodial parent to make decisions in the best interests of the child; and it permits judicial intervention, on a sufficient showing by the non-custodial parent, when that decision does not reflect the best interests of the child.

We acknowledge that as a result of the standard we now adopt numerous children, whose parents have disagreed about their surnames, will be authorized to bear surnames different from their fathers'. That result can be perceived as conflicting with society's longstanding, customary expectation that children of married parents bear the paternal surname, generating concerns over whether designation of a nontraditional surname might cause the child to experience unnecessary discomfort. Our assumption is that society has become accustomed to and tolerant of departures from the familiar preference for paternal surnames, that that tolerance and acceptance of nontraditional surnames will grow as the practice becomes less uncommon and as the reasons for authorizing deviation from the paternal surname become better understood. That process of enhanced understanding will be gradual and evolutionary. But we are firmly convinced that our authorization of a strong preference for the surname chosen by the custodial parent not only is consistent with the best interests of the affected children, but also reflects the significant societal changes in womens' rights that require a modification of the age-old preference for paternal surnames.

IV

We apply the best-interests-of-the-child standard, and the custodial parent presumption, to the present case. Scott is a very fortunate child, having two parents who dearly love and care for him. Our review of the record clearly demonstrates that both Alan and Karen have proven fully capable of discharging their responsibilities as parents. Their willingness to provide for Scott's needs as he grows and matures, rather than the surname Scott bears, is what defines them as parents. "Only a parent who provides for these needs will build a psychological relationship to the child on the basis of the biological one and will become his 'psychological parent' in whose care the child can feel valued and 'wanted.'" *Ali v. Ali*, 279 N.J.Super. 154 (Ch.Div.1994) (quoting JOSEPH GOLDSTEIN ET AL., BEYOND THE BEST INTERESTS OF THE CHILD 17 (1979)). We are confident, irrespective of whose surname the child bears, that both Alan and Karen will continue to be loving and supportive parents to Scott.

In resolving the issue of the surname, we note that Karen named Scott while she was exercising complete physical custody of him. As the custodial parent, that she was acting in Scott's best interests at that time is presumed. Accordingly, Alan bore the burden of demonstrating by a preponderance of the evidence that a change in surname is in the child's best interests. Such evidence has not been presented. The essence of the evidence introduced in support of the change in surname from Deremer to Gubernat was the need for Scott to know that he "will always have a father." In our view, Alan's devotion, support, and commitment to Scott will ensure that Scott will always know that he has a father. The love of the parent, and not the name of the parent, is the "adhesive that binds parent and child and, further, gives unique strength and durability to the natural loyalty that the parent holds for the child." *M.H.B. v. H.T.B*, 100 N.J. 567 (1985) (Handler J., concurring). We reiterate that no empirical or circumstantial evidence has been produced to suggest that the retention of the paternal surname is essential to maintenance of the father-child relationship, and we suggest that such an assumption is predicated on forsaken, gender-based notions of parenthood.

Evidence has not been presented demonstrating that the retention of the Deremer surname would be contrary to Scott's best interests, nor has evidence been adduced that the Gubernat surname would better serve Scott's interests. There has been no showing that the Gubernat surname better advances the psychological, emotional or developmental needs of the child. Because insufficient evidence exists to support the requested surname change, we hold that the trial court and Appellate Division erred in granting the requested change in surname.

V

The judgment of the Appellate Division is reversed, and the matter remanded to the trial court for further proceedings consistent with this opinion.

N O T E

The Sad Postscript to *Gubernat v. Deremer.* One week after the New Jersey Supreme Court ruled in Deremer's favor, Alan Gubernat shot his son to death and then killed himself.

According to an article in the local paper, Gubernat did not leave a suicide note to explain his actions, but police did find letters indicating that he was distraught over the outcome of the case. Joe Nixon, *Police Probe Murder-Suicide; Dad Lost Case over Boy's Name*, ALLENTOWN MORNING CALL, May 16, 1995. In an earlier story in the same paper, Gubernat had stated that he would feel like "an outcast or uncle" if the child had Deremer's last name, and that he felt it would be "demeaning the role of the father." *Id.* What does this incident suggest about the significance of names?

Chapter 7
Economic Empowerment and Employment Discrimination: Europe and the United States Compared

I. Women's Economic Empowerment

We have seen many laws that directly cause women's economic subordination. In Afghanistan, inheritance law decrees that a female relative receive only half of the comparable male relative's share. The Taliban prohibited women from working for pay. Peruvian law did not allow a married woman professor to manage and control her own property. Dutch law granted married men unemployment benefits it denied married women, and forced a widowed woman to forego higher disability benefits that a widowed man would have received. In the United States, both federal and state laws ordered that a married woman employee would receive less economic benefits than an identically situated man, whether a housing allowance or a survivor benefit for her spouse. A California evangelical private school insisted on denying married women family health insurance benefits. In Tanzania, Zimbabwe, and Uganda customary laws have denied women the right to inherit clan land or to sell it.

Another major factor leading to women's relative poverty compared to men is sex-based employment discrimination. As the opening Chapter revealed, women constitute a third of the world's waged labor force, but are "concentrated in the least skilled and the lowest paying jobs." They rarely reach top management jobs where they could earn high pay. They form a disproportionately large share of part-time workers and as a result receive lower pay rates and are ineligible for maternity, health, and other insurance benefits given only to full-time workers. They are last hired and first fired. CEDAW explicitly recognizes the importance of ending sex- discrimination in employment, as does the ICESCR. Yet human rights advocates rarely describe employment discrimination as a human rights issue. And even 25 years after CEDAW entered into force (1981), the Committee had failed to issue general recommendations on effective measures for ending employment discrimination.

Many countries give women no protection at all against employment discrimination. If they were to adopt effective anti-discrimination statutes and enforcement mechanisms, they would help lift women from poverty and expand their nations' economies as well. The examples of European and U.S. laws on the subject demonstrate the success of that approach. The U.S. first took action on the subject in 1964; Europe followed suit in 1976. Since then, women in these countries have substantially narrowed the wage gap with male workers. They have obtained new jobs and entered new professions in droves. All the while, their nations' economies grew ever stronger as women's brain power and skills enriched the labor pool.

This Chapter and the next examine these legal systems for the lessons that can be drawn from them. What are some of the most flagrant discrimination issues women face? How do the different laws and courts resolve them? What kind of enforcement structure is used? Some answers are similar; others different. By analyzing similarities and differences, advocates can decide what system would work best in countries currently lacking such protections. They can identify likely discriminatory practices that could affect workers in their countries. They can conclude that current systems ought to be changed in particular directions. By working for effective laws, they can make giant strides towards women's economic empowerment.

II. The European System

Europe established its employment anti-discrimination law through what we now know as the European Communities and the European Union. To understand the law, it is first necessary to have a broad overview of the treaties and the governing structures they established.

A. The European Communities and the European Union: An Introduction

1. History and Institutions

In 1951, shortly after the Council of Europe was established, six Member States (Belgium, France, Italy, Luxembourg, the Netherlands, and the Federal Republic of Germany) created a new institution for "economic and political union." By establishing the European Coal and Steel Community (1951) (ECSC) (expired July 23, 2002) through a treaty of that name, they laid the groundwork for a "Smaller Europe," one that grew by 2007 to 27 countries with a population of 490 million.[A] The most significant treaties that concern us here are the following.

- Treaty Establishing the European Economic Community (EEC) (1957) ("Treaty of Rome" for the place where it was signed);
- Treaty on European Union (EU) (1992) ("Maastricht Treaty") (also renaming the EEC the "European Community" (EC)), as amended by the

---

[A] The 27 European Union countries as of January 1, 2007, were Austria, Belgium, Bulgaria, Cyprus, Czech Republic, Denmark, Estonia, Finland, France, Germany, Greece, Hungary, Ireland, Italy, Latvia, Lithuania, Luxembourg, Malta, Poland, Portugal, Romania, Slovakia, Slovenia, Spain, Sweden, the Netherlands, and the United Kingdom. Croatia, Macedonia, and Turkey were candidates to become Member States.

- Amsterdam Treaty (1997) (renumbering the EC and EU Treaties); and the
- Treaty of Nice (2001) (providing for enlargement to 25 countries).

See RossRights for the treaties and for websites offering more complete information.

The EEC Treaty established an economic common market, while the Maastricht Treaty focused on political goals and created the European Union. It is commonly said that the EU has three pillars: the European Communities [the European Community (EC) and the European Atomic Energy Community (Euratom)]; a common foreign and security policy; and police and judicial cooperation on criminal matters.

The European Communities and the European Union have a common set of ruling bodies that have helped develop the law requiring all Member States to enact laws prohibiting sex-based employment discrimination. The institutions include the Council of the European Union (formerly, the Council of Ministers), the European Commission, the European Parliament, and the Court of Justice of the European Communities.

The Council is a small but powerful body. It has a government minister from each Member State and enacts new Community legislation, usually with the participation of the European Parliament. The Parliament is elected directly by States Parties citizens and had 785 members as of the five-year election in June 2004.

The European Commission has 27 members (one for each Member State), all of whom are chosen for their competence and operate independently of their nations' governments. It has several functions, one of which is to propose legislation to the Council and Parliament. Another important one is to enforce Community law jointly with the Court of Justice. The Commission staff includes 24,000 civil servants, most of whom work in Brussels.

In addition to the governing treaties, European Community and European Union law includes regulations, directives, and decisions. If a Member State fails to comply with the relevant law, the Commission can initiate infringement proceedings against the offending state. If unsuccessful in resolving the matter, the Commission may then bring an action before the Court of Justice.

The Court of Justice is in turn responsible for insuring compliance with Community law, and its judgments are binding on Member States. The Court has one judge from each Member State and is assisted by eight Advocates-General; it is located in Luxembourg. It can issue preliminary rulings in referrals from national courts seeking its interpretation of Community law, which the national court will then apply to the case before it. This referral procedure is designed to help the Member States achieve uniformity in their application of Community law. The Court can also issue final decisions in cases brought before it by the Commission or Member States.

A court case generally proceeds as follows. Each case is initially assigned to a specific judge and advocate-general. The parties file written observations with the Court. The judge-rapporteur writes a report for the court's public hearing summarizing the legal background and the parties' positions. The parties' lawyers then orally present their parties' position and both the judges and the advocate-general question them. The advocate-general's role is to give the court an independent and impartial opinion on how the matter should be resolved. After receiving the advocate-general's opinion, the court meets and decides the case by majority vote.

2. The Equal Treatment Directive

On February 9, 1976, the Council of the European Communities issued Directive 76/207/EEC, the "1976 Equal Treatment Directive," *available at* RossRights. Its central thrust, defined in Article 1, was to require Member States to "put into effect . . . the principle of equal treatment for men and women as regards access to employment, including promotion, and to vocational training and as regards working conditions. . . ." Article 2 defined equal treatment in general, and provided three exceptions permitting unequal treatment in defined circumstances. Article 3 gave further definition to equal "access to employment," Article 4 to equal access to "vocational training," and Article 5 to equal "working conditions." Articles 6 through 11 required Member States to enact the necessary laws, protect employees against retaliation, inform employees of their rights, implement these measures within certain time periods, and provide the Commission with necessary information.

On September 23, 2002, the European Parliament and Council issued Directive 2002/73/EC amending the 1976 Equal Treatment Directive. The new Directive increased the overall protections against discrimination. For example, it broadened the scope of the original Directive by adding specific coverage of sexual harassment, defining direct versus indirect discrimination, tightening one exception to the equal treatment requirement, and requiring expanded judicial remedies in Member States courts. *See* Directive 2002/73/EC and the consolidated text of the 1976 Equal Treatment Directive as amended by Directive 2002/73/EC, *available at* RossRights. Read both to understand the particular changes and consider how they help strengthen women's rights.

The cases that follow were issued prior to September 23, 2002, and interpret the 1976 Equal Treatment Directive. They all concern Member State laws that explicitly treat female workers differently from male workers. For each case, consider whether the 2002 amendments to the Equal Treatment Directive would make a difference in the reasoning and result.

B. Men and Childbirth—Banning Men from Midwifery Jobs

Commission of the European Communities v. United Kingdom
(Court of Justice of the European Communities)
Case 165/82, 1983 E.C.R. 3431 (1983)

1   By application lodged at the Court Registry on 3 June 1982 the Commission of the European Communities brought an action before the Court under Article 169[B] of

---

[B] Article 169 of the 1957 EEC Treaty provides:

"If the Commission considers that a Member State has failed to fulfil an obligation under this Treaty, it shall deliver a reasoned opinion on the matter after giving the State concerned

the EEC Treaty for a declaration that by failing to enact within the prescribed period the provisions needed in order to comply with Council Directive 76/207/EEC of 9 February 1976 on the implementation of the principle of equal treatment for men and women as regards access to employment, vocational training and promotion, and working conditions, the United Kingdom has failed to fulfil its obligations under the Treaty.

2   The Commission charges the United Kingdom with only partially implementing the directive in so far it has failed to amend and supplement the Sex Discrimination Act 1975 (hereinafter referred to as "the 1975 Act") which, although abolishing discrimination in certain areas of employment, allows it to continue in other areas in which by virtue of the directive discrimination must be abolished by 12 August 1978 at the latest.

3   The Commission's complaints relate to the following points: . . .

(b) Contrary to the provisions of the directive, section 6 (3) of the 1975 Act provides that the prohibition of discrimination does not apply to employment in a private household or where the number of persons employed by an employer does not exceed five (disregarding persons employed in a private household).

(c) Finally, by virtue of section 20 of the 1975 Act the prohibition of discrimination based on sex does not apply to the employment, promotion and training of midwives. . . .

The Second Complaint

12   According to the United Kingdom, the exclusions from the prohibition of discrimination provided for in section 6 (3) of the 1975 Act in the case of employment in a private household or in undertakings where the number of persons employed does not exceed five are justified by the exception provided for in Article 2 (2) of the directive itself, according to which:

This directive shall be without prejudice to the right of Member States to exclude from its field of application those occupational activities and, where appropriate, the training leading thereto, for which, by reason of their nature or the context in which they are carried out, the sex of the worker constitutes a determining factor.

13   It must be recognized that the provision of the 1975 Act in question is intended, in so far as it refers to employment in a private household, to reconcile the principle of equality of treatment with the principle of respect for private life, which is also fundamental. Reconciliation of that kind is one of the factors which must be taken into consideration in determining the scope of the exception provided for in Article 2 (2) of the directive.

14   Whilst it is undeniable that, for certain kinds of employment in private house-

---

the opportunity to submit its observations.

If the State concerned does not comply with the opinion within the period laid down by the Commission the latter may bring the matter before the Court of Justice. . . ."

holds, that consideration may be decisive, that is not the case for all the kinds of employment in question.

15   As regards small undertakings with not more than five employees, the United Kingdom has not put forward any argument to show that in any undertaking of that size the sex of the worker would be a determining factor by reason of the nature of his activities or the context in which they are carried out.

16   Consequently, by reason of its generality, the exclusion provided for in the contested provision of the 1975 Act goes beyond the objective which may be lawfully pursued within the framework of Article 2 (2) of the directive.

The Third Complaint

17   The Commission's third complaint relates to the fact that the 1975 Act ensures access to the occupation of midwife and to training for that occupation only within certain limits. This is said to entail discrimination based on sex.

18   The United Kingdom acknowledges the facts. By virtue of paragraph (3) of Schedule 4 to the 1975 Act, until a day to be specified by order of the Secretary of State, men are granted access to the occupation in question and may be trained for that purpose only in certain specific places. This situation is due to the fact that in the United Kingdom the occupation in question is not traditionally engaged in by men. In a sphere in which respect for the patient's sensitivities is of particular importance, it considers that at the present time that limitation is in conformity with Article 2 (2) of the directive. However, it adds that it intends to proceed by stages and keep the position under review, in accordance with the obligations imposed by Article 9 (2)[c] of the directive.

19   That provision requires Member States periodically to assess the occupational activities referred to in Article 2 (2) in order to decide, in the light of social developments, whether there is justification for maintaining the permitted exclusions. They are to notify the Commission of the results of that assessment.

20   It is undeniable that in the area in question, as the United Kingdom acknowledges, the Member States are under an obligation to implement the principle of equality of treatment. It must however be recognized that at the present time personal sensitivities may play an important role in relations between midwife and patient. In those circumstances, it may be stated that by failing fully to apply the principle laid down in the directive, the United Kingdom has not exceeded the limits of the power granted to the Member States by Articles 9 (2) and 2 (2) of the directive. The Commission's complaint in that regard cannot therefore be upheld.

21   It is apparent from all the foregoing considerations that by failing to adopt in accordance with Directive 76/207 of 9 February 1976 the measures needed to ensure

---

[c] Article 9(2) of the Equal Treatment Directive provides: "Member States shall periodically assess the occupational activities referred to in Article 2(2) in order to decide, in the light of social developments, whether there is justification for maintaining the exclusions concerned. They shall notify the Commission of the results of this assessment."

that any provisions contrary to the principle of equality of the treatment contained in the collective agreements or in the internal rules of undertakings or in the rules governing the independent professions or occupations are to be, or may be declared, void or be amended, by excluding from the application of that principle employment for the purposes of private household and any case where the number of persons employed does not exceed five, the United Kingdom has failed to fulfil its obligations under the Treaty.

22   In all other respects, the application is dismissed. . . .

Opinion of Mrs. Advocate General Rozès, *Commission of the European Communities v. United Kingdom*
Delivered on 7 June 1983, Case 165/82, 1983 E.C.R. 3451

[The Advocate-General's opinion was delivered in June, five months before the Court's decision in November 1983. Compare her opinion to that of the Court.]

The last complaint made by the Commission against the United Kingdom regarding the fulfilment of its obligations under Directive No 76/207 also involves the question of the interpretation to be given to Article 2(2) thereof. It concerns the exclusion of midwives from the field of application of the Act.

1. Section 20 of the Act provides that midwives are excluded from the provisions of subsections 6(1) and (2)(a) and that section 14 concerning vocational training bodies does not apply to the training of midwives. It should however be added that that provision has also amended the legislation relating to midwives (for England and Wales, the Midwives Act 1951) so as to allow persons of the male sex access to and the right to engage in that occupation. However, on a transitional basis, that access is limited, since men are entitled to follow midwifery training courses only in centres approved by the Minister. At the present time, two centres have been approved, one in London and the other in the Central Region of Scotland. Similarly, by virtue of paragraph 3(2) of Schedule 4 to the Act, a man may engage in the occupation of midwife only at the places designated by the Minister, namely four hospitals in London and Edinburgh.

I would add that, as the United Kingdom pointed out in response to a question put to it by the Court, those restrictions should soon to be lifted. Those changes, which are to be made by means of orders which are in course of preparation, should enter into force at the end of August of this year. However, needless to say, that legislative development does not affect the assessment to be made, from the legal point of view, of the United Kingdom rules—only the state of the legislation when these proceedings were commenced is relevant for that purpose.

2. In the United Kingdom's view, the discriminatory provisions in force are justified by Article 2(2) of the directive by reason of the specific nature of the occupation of midwife and the conditions in which midwives work. The United Kingdom adds that those provisions have been periodically reviewed in the light of social developments, pursuant to Article 9(2) of the directive. It was in fact as a result of wide-ranging consultations with the health authorities, the professional and occupational groups concerned and other organizations regarding the report on two studies on male

midwives carried out in London and in the Central Region of Scotland that the United Kingdom Government recently reached the conclusion that the present restrictions on vocational training and the employment of men as midwives should now be lifted. It should however be noted that the removal of those restrictions has been made subject to two conditions: women must have the possibility of being cared for by a female midwife if they so choose and, if a male midwife is provided, there must be appropriate supervision.

(a) The defendant justifies its position in the first place on the basis of the features of the duties of a midwife in the United Kingdom. It emphasizes the unique role played by midwives during the pre-natal period and particularly during the post-natal periods as regards care involving intimate personal contact with the woman. It also points out that midwives remain with patients for extended periods and at frequent intervals and that they may have to be on duty alone, particularly at night, in the midwifery ward of a hospital and above all at the patient's home. Disregarding a minority of women who give birth at home aided only by a midwife (8,156 births in 1980), regard must be had to the much more frequent situation where women who have given birth in hospital are cared for at home by midwives for 10 days after delivery (586,352 in 1980; in the same year, there were 615,708 births where the mothers remained in hospital for the 10 days following delivery).

In that respect, the work of a midwife is distinguished, according to the United Kingdom, from that of gynaecologists (or obstetricians) and from general practitioners who undertake obstetric work. The United Kingdom admits that at the actual moment of birth, the difference between the role of midwife, the obstetrician and the general practitioner is less great. Moreover, it observes that the urgent needs of the moment may cause women and their husbands to be less concerned about intimate procedures carried out by a man.

But, for the rest, it states that specialists and general medical practitioners are rarely alone with patients because a female attendant is almost invariably present. It also notes that the care provided by them is usually intermittent and of short duration.

This distinction does not seem to me to be convincing at the present time, when facilities for the provision of care of various kinds at the same place are becoming more and more widespread and no longer raise the same problems.

(b) The United Kingdom placed emphasis on the specific features of the occupation of midwife and expresses the fear that certain women (or their husbands) may refuse the services of male midwives. It fears that if such women were not permitted to choose a female midwife, they may put themselves and their newborn children at risk by refusing any care. It considers in particular that members of certain ethnic minorities living in the United Kingdom may react in that way. Accordingly, a degree of caution is required: immediate and unrestricted access for men to the occupation of midwife would entail the risk of substantial opposition among those ethnic minorities, and indeed among other groups. In other words, the gradual introduction of the concept of male midwives and of the principle of equal treatment in the occupation of midwife is necessary, in the opinion of the United Kingdom, in order to take into account, in particular, the sensitivities and beliefs of people who live in the United Kingdom but whose cultural background is not in the strict sense British.

3. The Commission, without contesting the truthfulness of those observations, replies that in practice the reactions apprehended by the United Kingdom should not raise difficulties in so far as, on the one hand, account will be taken of the preferences of women in confinement and, on the other hand, at least for some time to come, male midwives will no doubt remain the exception rather than the rule. This argument is considered by the United Kingdom as tending to permit discrimination "in practice" but not in law.

I do not consider that the alleged specific nature of the conditions in which the occupation of midwife practised in the United Kingdom is such as to justify, under Article 2(2) of the directive, the discriminatory rules against men. I think that the guarantee of a free choice for patients, which is maintained in the proposed British rules, is a condition which is necessary and sufficient to allay the fears expressed by the United Kingdom Government.

NOTES

Privacy and Class. The United Kingdom justifies preventing men from being midwives by pointing to the alleged delicate feelings of immigrant women and their husbands. Why not prevent men from becoming obstetricians and gynecologists for the same reason? Would male midwives be more suspect than male doctors? Is the government suggesting that male midwives would be more likely to rape vulnerable women during the ten days of intimate care in their homes? Or would male doctors be equally liable to do so but for their lack of extended access and the fact that a female attendant is usually present?

The Reverse-Sex Hypothetical. Under the government's reasoning, could the United Kingdom bar women from becoming doctors? Perhaps immigrant men with testicular cancer would resist having female doctors examine them. If seeing a woman were their only option might they not refuse treatment and risk their lives?

The Government's Purpose. Do you think the asserted purposes are the real purposes?

Should Privacy Justify Employment Discrimination? One could imagine many other scenarios that could raise privacy concerns. Should a woman prison guard lose her job if a male prisoner objects to being observed by a woman?

A Gender-Neutral Solution? Many theorists justify statutes that treat women and men differently because they suppose that only a sex-based policy can address the concern in question. If they considered the situation in more depth, however, they could usually find gender-neutral alternatives that would equally solve the problem. What gender-neutral solution can you propose for the United Kingdom's asserted concerns?

C. Women and Guns—Banning Women from Jobs Using Guns

Johnston v. Chief Constable
(Court of Justice of the European Communities)
Case 222/84, 1986 E.C.R. 1651, 1676–89 (1986)

1   By a decision dated 8 August 1984, which was received at the Court on 4 Sep-

tember 1984, the Industrial Tribunal of Northern Ireland, Belfast, referred to the Court for a preliminary ruling under Article 177[D] of the EEC Treaty several questions on the interpretation of Council Directive No 76/207/EEC of 9 February 1976 on the implementation of the principle of equal treatment for men and women and of Article 224[E] of the EEC Treaty.

2   Those questions were raised in a dispute between Mrs. Marguerite I. Johnston and the Chief Constable of the Royal Ulster Constabulary (the 'RUC'). The Chief Constable is the competent authority for appointing reserve constables to the RUC Reserve in Northern Ireland and to full-time posts in the RUC full-time Reserve under three-year renewable contracts. The dispute concerns the Chief Constable's refusal to renew Mrs. Johnston's contract as a member of the RUC full-time Reserve and to allow her to be given training in the handling and use of fire-arms.

3   According to the decision making the reference for a preliminary ruling, the provisions of the Royal Ulster Constabulary Reserve (Appointment and Conditions of Service) Regulations (Northern Ireland) 1973, which govern the appointment and conditions of service of members of the reserve police force, do not make any distinction between men and women which is of importance in this case. It is also clear from Articles 10 and 19 of the Sex Discrimination (Northern Ireland) Order 1976, which lays down rules to eliminate sex discrimination and implements the principle of equal treatment as regards access to employment, vocational training and promotion and working conditions, that the ban on discrimination applies to employment with the police and that men and women are not to be treated differently in this respect, except as regards requirements relating to height, uniform or equipment, or allowances in lieu of uniform or equipment. . . .

4   In the United Kingdom police officers do not as a general rule carry fire-arms in the performance of their duties except for special operations and no distinction is made in this regard between men and women. Because of the high number of police officers assassinated in Northern Ireland over a number of years, the Chief Constable

---

[D] Article 177 of the EEC Treaty provides:

"The Court of Justice shall have jurisdiction to give preliminary rulings concerning:

(a) the interpretation of this Treaty; . . .

(c) the interpretation of the statutes [regulations or directives] of bodies established by an act of the Council, where those statutes so provide.

Where such a question is raised before any court or tribunal of a Member State, that court or tribunal may, if it considers that a decision on the question is necessary to enable it to give judgment, request the Court of Justice to give a ruling thereon.

Where any such question is raised in a case pending before a court or tribunal of a Member State against whose decisions there is no judicial remedy under national law, that court or tribunal shall bring the matter before the Court of Justice."

[E] Article 224 of the 1957 EEC Treaty provides: "Member States shall consult each other with a view to taking together the steps needed to prevent the functioning of the common market being affected by measures which a Member State may be called upon to take in the event of serious internal disturbance affecting the maintenance of law and order, in the event of war or serious international tension constituting a threat of war, or in order to carry out obligations it has accepted for the purpose of maintaining peace and international security."

of the RUC considered that he could not maintain that practice. He decided that, in the RUC and the RUC Reserve, men should carry fire-arms in the regular course of their duties but that women would not be equipped with them and would not receive training in the handling and use of fire-arms.

5   In those circumstances, the Chief Constable decided in 1980 that the number of women in the RUC was sufficient for the particular tasks generally assigned to women officers. He took the view that general police duties, frequently involving operations requiring the carrying of fire-arms, should no longer be assigned to women and decided not to offer or renew any more contracts for women in the RUC full-time Reserve except where they had to perform duties assigned only to women officers. Since that decision, no woman in the RUC full-time Reserve has been offered a contract or had her contract renewed, save in one case.

6   According to the decision making the reference for a preliminary ruling, Mrs. Johnston had been a member of the RUC full-time Reserve from 1974 to 1980. She had efficiently performed the general duties of a uniformed police officer, such as acting as station-duty officer, taking part in mobile patrols, driving the patrol vehicle and assisting in searching persons brought to the police station. She was not armed when carrying out those duties and was ordinarily accompanied in duties outside the police station by an armed male officer of the RUC full-time Reserve. In 1980 the Chief Constable refused to renew her contract because of his new policy, mentioned above, with regard to female members of the RUC full-time Reserve.

7   Mrs. Johnston lodged an application with the Industrial Tribunal challenging the decision, taken pursuant to that new policy, to refuse to renew her contract and to give her training in the handling of fire-arms. She contended that she had suffered unlawful discrimination prohibited by the Sex Discrimination Order.

8   In the proceedings before the Industrial Tribunal the Chief Constable produced a certificate issued by the Secretary of State in which that Minister of the United Kingdom Government certified in accordance with Article 53 of the Sex Discrimination Order, that 'the act consisting of the refusal of the Royal Ulster Constabulary to offer further full-time employment to Mrs. Marguerite I. Johnston in the Royal Ulster Constabulary Reserve was done for the purpose of (a) safeguarding national security; and (b) protecting public safety and public order'.

9   Mrs. Johnston referred to Directive No. 76/207. The purpose of that directive, according to Article 1[F] thereof, is to put into effect the principle of equal treatment

---

[F] Article 1 of the 1976 Equal Treatment Directive provides:

"1. The purpose of this Directive is to put into effect in the Member States the principle of equal treatment for men and women as regards access to employment, including promotion, and to vocational training and as regards working conditions and, on the conditions referred to in paragraph 2, social security. This principle is hereinafter referred to as 'the principle of equal treatment.'

2. With a view to ensuring the progressive implementation of the principle of equal treatment in matter of social security, the Council, acting on a proposal from the Commission, will adopt provisions defining its substance, its scope and the arrangements for its application."

for men and women as regards access to employment, including promotion, and to vocational training and as regards working conditions. According to Article 2 (1), the principle of equal treatment means that there shall be no discrimination whatsoever on grounds of sex, subject, however, to the exceptions allowed by Article 2 (2) and (3)[G]. For the purposes of the application of that principle in different spheres, Articles 3 to 5 [requiring equal treatment for access to jobs (3), vocational training (4), and working conditions (5)] require the member-States in particular to abolish any laws, regulations or administrative provisions contrary to the principle of equal treatment and to revise laws, regulations and administrative provisions where the concern for protection which originally inspired them is no longer well founded. Article 6 provides that all persons who consider themselves wronged by discrimination must be able to pursue their claims by judicial process.

10 In order to be able to rule on that dispute, the Industrial Tribunal referred the following questions to the Court for a preliminary ruling:

(1) On the proper construction of Council Directive No 76/207 and in the circumstances of this case, can a member-State exclude from the directive's field of application acts of sex discrimination as regards access to employment done for the purpose of safeguarding national security or of protecting public safety or public order?

(2) On the proper construction of the directive and in the circumstances of this case, is full-time employment as an armed member of a police reserve force, or training in the handling and use of fire-arms for such employment, capable of constituting one of those occupational activities and, where appropriate, the training leading thereto for which, by reason of their nature or the context in which they are carried out, the sex of the worker constitutes a determining factor, within the meaning of Article 2 (2)?

(3) What are the principles and criteria by which member-States should determine whether 'the sex of a worker constitutes a determining factor' within the meaning of Article 2 (2) in relation to (a) 'the occupational activities' of an armed member of such a force and (b) 'the training leading thereto', whether by reason of their nature or by reason of the context in which they are carried out?

(4) Is a policy applied by a chief constable of police, charged with a statutory responsibility for the direction and control of a police force, that women members of that force should not carry fire-arms capable, in the circumstances of this case, of constituting a 'provision concerning the protection of women', within the meaning of Article 2 (3), or an 'administrative provi-

---

[G] Article 2 of the 1976 Equal Treatment Directive provides:

"1. For the purposes of the following provisions, the principle of equal treatment shall mean that there shall be no discrimination whatsoever on grounds of sex either directly or indirectly by reference in particular to marital or family status.

2. This Directive shall be without prejudice to the right of Member States to exclude from its field of application those occupational activities and, where appropriate, the training leading thereto, for which, by reason of their nature or of the context in which they are carried out, the sex of the worker constitutes a determining factor.

3. This Directive shall be without prejudice to provisions concerning the protection of women, particularly as regards pregnancy and maternity.

4. This Directive shall be without prejudice to measures to promote equal opportunity for men and women, in particular by removing existing inequalities which affect women's opportunities in the areas referred to in Article 1(1)."

sion' inspired by 'concern for protection' within the meaning of Article 3 (2)(c)[H] of the directive?

(5) If the answer to question 4 is affirmative, what are the principles and criteria by which member-States should determine whether the 'concern for protection' is 'well founded', within the meaning of Article 3 (2)(c)? . . .

The applicability of Directive No 76/207 to measures taken to protect public safety

22   It is necessary to examine next the Industrial Tribunal's first question by which it seeks to ascertain whether, having regard to the fact that Directive No 76/207 contains no express provision concerning measures taken for the purpose of safeguarding national security or of protecting public order, and more particularly public safety, the directive is applicable to such measures.

23   In *Mrs. Johnston's* view, no general derogation from the fundamental principle of equal treatment unrelated to particular occupational activities, their nature and the context in which they are carried out, exists for such purposes. By being based on the sole ground that a discriminatory act is done for purposes such as the protection of public safety, such a derogation would enable the member-States unilaterally to avoid the obligations which the directive imposes on them.

24   The *United Kingdom* takes the view that the safeguard clauses contained in Articles 36, 48, 56, . . . 223 and 224 of the EEC Treaty show that neither the Treaty nor, therefore, the law derived from it apply to the fields mentioned in the Industrial Tribunal's question and do not restrict the member-States' power to take measures which they can consider expedient or necessary for those purposes. The measures referred to in the first question do not therefore fall within the scope of the directive.

25   The *Commission* suggests that the directive should be interpreted with reference to Article 224 of the EEC Treaty so that considerations of public safety could, in the special conditions envisaged by that article and subject to judicial review, justify derogations from the principle of equal treatment even where the strict conditions laid down in Article 2 (2) and (3) of the directive are not fulfilled.

26   It must be observed in this regard that the only articles in which the Treaty provides for derogations applicable in situations which may involve public safety are Articles 36, 48, 56, 223 and 224[I] which deal with exceptional and clearly defined

---

[H] Article 3(2)(c) provides:

". . . Member States shall take the measures necessary to ensure that—

(c). Those laws, regulations and administrative provisions contrary to the principle of equal treatment when the concern for protection which originally inspired them is no longer well founded shall be revised. . . .

[I] For Article 224, *see* note E, *supra*. Article 36 allows restrictions on exports and imports for "public security" and the "protection of health and life of humans." Article 48 bans discrimination based on nationality against workers but permits it for "public security or public health." Article 56 permits "special treatment for foreign nationals" if based on "public security or public health." Article 223 permits Member States to take necessary measures for protecting "the essential interests of its security which are connected with the production of or trade in arms, munitions, and war material. . . ."

cases. Because of their limited character those articles do not lend themselves to a wide interpretation and it is not possible to infer from them that there is inherent in the Treaty a general proviso covering all measures taken for reasons of public safety. If every provision of Community law were held to be subject to a general proviso, regardless of the specific requirements laid down by the provisions of the Treaty, this might impair the binding nature of Community law and its uniform application.

27   It follows that the application of the principle of equal treatment for men and women is not subject to any general reservation as regards measures taken on grounds of the protection of public safety, apart from the possible application of Article 224 of the Treaty which concerns a wholly exceptional situation and is the subject-matter of the seventh question[J]. The facts which induced the competent authority to invoke the need to protect public safety must therefore if necessary be taken into consideration, in the first place, in the context of the application of the specific provisions of the directive.

28   The answer to the first question must therefore be that acts of sex discrimination done for reasons related to the protection of public safety must be examined in the light of the exceptions to the principle of equal treatment for men and women laid down in Directive No 76/207.

The derogations allowed on account of the context in which the occupational activity is carried out

29   The Industrial Tribunal's second and third questions are concerned with the interpretation of the derogation, provided for in Article 2 (2) of the directive, from the principle of equal treatment and are designed to enable the Tribunal to decide whether a difference in treatment, such as that in question, is covered by that derogation. It asks to be informed of the criteria and principles to be applied for determining whether an activity such as that in question in the present case is one of the activities for which 'by reason of their nature or the context in which they are carried out, the sex of the worker constitutes a determining factor'.

30   *Mrs. Johnston* takes the view that a reply to this question is not possible in terms so general. She states that she has always worked satisfactorily in performing her duties with the police and maintains that women are quite capable of being trained in the handling of fire-arms. It is for the Industrial Tribunal to determine whether a derogation is possible under Article 2 (2) of the directive, having regard to

---

[J] The seventh question referred to the Court by the Industrial Tribunal was:

"(a) Does article 224 of the EEC Treaty, on its proper construction, permit Member States when confronted with serious internal disturbances affecting the maintenance of law and order to derogate from any obligations which would otherwise be imposed on them or on employers within their jurisdiction by the directive?

(b) If so, is it open to an individual to rely upon the fact that a Member State did not consult with other Member States for the purpose of preventing the first Member State from relying on Article 224 of the EEC Treaty?"

For Article 224, *see* note E, *supra.*

the specific duties which she is required to carry out. That provision does not make it possible for her to be completely excluded from any employment in the RUC full-time Reserve.

31   The *United Kingdom* submits that the member-States have a discretion in deciding whether, owing to requirements of national security and public safety or public order, the context in which an occupational activity in the police is carried out prevents that activity from being carried out by an armed policewoman. In determining that question the member-States may take into consideration criteria such as the difference in physical strength between the sexes, the probable reaction of the public to the appearance of armed policewomen and the risk of their being assassinated. Since the decision taken by the Chief Constable was taken on the application of such criteria, it is covered by Article 2 (2) of the directive.

32   The *Commission* takes the view that, owing to the context in which it is carried out but not to its nature, the occupational activity of an armed police officer could be considered an activity for which the sex of the officer is a determining factor. A derogation must, however, be justified in relation to specific duties and not in relation to an *employment* considered in its entirety. In particular, the principle of proportionality must be observed. The national court must look at the discrimination in question from that point of view.

33   In this regard it must be stated first of all that, in so far as the competent police authorities in Northern Ireland have decided, because of the requirements of public safety, to depart from the principle, generally applied in other parts of the United Kingdom, of not arming the police in the ordinary course of their duties, that decision does not in itself involve any discrimination between men and women and is therefore outside the scope of the principle of equal treatment. It is only in so far as the Chief Constable decided that women wold not be armed or trained in the use of fire-arms, that general policing duties would in future be carried out only by armed male officers and that contracts of women in the RUC full-time Reserve who, like Mrs. Johnston, had previously been entrusted with general policing duties, would not be renewed, that an appraisal of those measures in the light of the provisions of the directive is relevant.

34   Since, as is clear from the Industrial Tribunal's decision, it is expressly provided that the Sex Discrimination Order is to apply to employment in the police and since in this regard no distinction is made between men and women in the specific provisions that are applicable, the nature of the occupational activity in the police force is not a relevant ground of justification for the discrimination in question. What must be examined, however, is the question whether, owing to the specific context in which the activity described in the Industrial Tribunal's decision is carried out, the sex of the person carrying out that activity constitutes a determining factor.

35   As is clear from the Tribunal's decision, the policy towards women in the RUC full-time Reserve was adopted by the Chief Constable because he considered that if women were armed they might become a more frequent target for assassination and that their fire-arms could fall into the hands of their assailants, that the public would not welcome the carrying of fire-arms by women, which would conflict too much

with the ideal of an unarmed police force, and that armed policewomen would be less effective in police work in the social field with families and children in which the services of policewomen are particularly appreciated. The reasons which the Chief Constable thus gave for his policy were related to the special conditions in which the police must work in the situation existing in Northern Ireland, having regard to the requirements of the protection of public safety in a context of serious internal disturbances.

36   As regards the question whether such reasons may be covered by Article 2(2)[K] of the directive, it should first be observed that the provision, being a derogation from an individual right laid down in the directive, must be interpreted strictly. However, it must be recognized that the context in which the occupational activity of members of an armed police force are [sic] carried out is determined by the environment in which that activity is carried out. In this regard, the possibility cannot be excluded that in a situation characterized by serious internal disturbances the carrying of fire-arms by policewomen might create additional risks of their being assassinated and might therefore be contrary to requirements of public safety.

37   In such circumstances, the context of certain policing activities may be such that the sex of police officers constitutes a determining factor for carrying them out. If that is so, a member-State may therefore restrict such tasks, and the training leading thereto, to men. In such a case, as is clear from Article 9(2)[L] of the directive, the member-States have a duty to assess periodically the activities concerned in order to decide whether, in the light of social developments, the derogation from the general scheme of the directive may still be maintained.

38   It must also be borne in mind that, in determining the scope of any derogation from an individual right such as the equal treatment of men and women provided for by the directive, the principle of proportionality, one of the general principles of law underlying the Community legal order, must be observed. That principle requires that derogations remain within the limits of what is appropriate and necessary for achieving the aim in view and requires the principle of equal treatment to be reconciled as far as possible with the requirements of public safety which constitute the decisive factor as regards the context of the activity in question.

39   By reason of the division of jurisdiction provided for in Article 177 of the EEC Treaty, it is for the national court to say whether the reasons on which the Chief Constable based his decision are in fact well founded and justify the specific measure taken in Mrs. Johnston's case. It is also for the national court to ensure that the princi-

---

[K] Article 2(2) of the 1976 Equal Treatment Directive provides: "This Directive is shall be without prejudice to the right of Member States to exclude from its field of application those occupational activities and, where appropriate, the training leading thereto, for which, by reason of their nature or of the context in which they are carried out, the sex of the worker constitutes a determining factor."

[L] Article 9(2) of the 1976 Equal Treatment Directive provides: "Member States shall periodically assess the occupational activities referred to in Article 2(2) in order to decide, in the light of social developments, whether there is justification for maintaining the exclusions concerned. They shall notify the Commission of the results of this assessment."

ple of proportionality is observed and to determine whether the refusal to renew Mrs. Johnston's contract would not be avoided by allocating to women duties which, without jeopardizing the aims pursued, can be performed without fire-arms.

40   The answer to the Industrial Tribunal's second and third questions should therefore be that Article 2(2) of Directive 76/207 must be interpreted as meaning that in deciding whether, by reason of the context in which the activities of a police officer are carried out, the sex of the officer constitutes a determining factor for that occupational activity, a member-State may take into consideration requirements of public safety in order to restrict general policing duties, in an internal situation characterized by frequent assassinations, to men equipped with fire-arms.

The derogations allowed on the ground of a concern to protect women

41   In its fourth and fifth question the Industrial Tribunal then asks the Court for an interpretation of the expressions 'protection of women' in Article 2(3)[M] of the directive and 'concern for protection' in Article 3(2)(c)[N], which inspired certain provisions of national law, so that it can decide whether the difference in treatment in question may fall within the scope of the derogations from the principle of equal treatment laid down for those purposes.

42   In *Mrs. Johnston's* view, those provisions must be interpreted strictly. Their sole purpose is to protect their health and safety in the case of pregnancy or maternity. That is not the case where women are completely excluded from service in an armed police force.

43   The *United Kingdom* states that the aim of the policy with regard to women in the RUC full-time Reserve is to protect women by preventing them from becoming targets for assassination. The expression 'protection of women' may cover such an aim in a period of serious disturbances. The *Commission* also takes the view that an exceptional situation such as exists in Northern Ireland and the resultant dangers for armed women police officers may be taken into consideration from the viewpoint of the protection of women.

44   It must be observed in this regard that, like Article 2(2) of the directive, Article 2(3), which also determines the scope of Article 3(2)(c), must be interpreted strictly. It is clear from the express reference to pregnancy and maternity that the directive is intended to protect a woman's biological condition and the special relationship which exists between a woman and her child. That provision of the directive does not therefore allow women to be excluded from certain type of employment on the

---

[M] Article 2(3) of the 1976 Equal Treatment Directive provides: "This Directive shall be without prejudice to provisions concerning the protection of women, particularly as regards pregnancy and maternity."

[N] Article 3(2)(c) of the 1976 Equal Treatment Directive provides: "Those laws, regulations, and administrative provisions contrary to the principle of equal treatment when the concern for protection which originally inspired them is no longer well founded shall be revised; and that where similar provisions are included in collective agreements labour and management shall be requested to undertake the desired revision."

ground that public opinion demands that women be given greater protection than men against risks which affect men and women in the same way and which are distinct from women's specific needs of protection, such as those expressly mentioned.

45   It does not appear that the risks and dangers to which women are exposed when performing their duties in the police force in a situation such as exists in Northern Ireland are different from those to which any man is also exposed when performing the same duties. A total exclusion of women from such an occupational activity which, owing to a general risk not specific to women, is imposed for reasons of public safety is not one of the differences in treatment that Articles 2(3) of the directive allows out of a concern to protect women.

46   The answer to the Industrial Tribunal's fourth and fifth questions must therefore be that the differences in treatment between men and women that Article 2(3) of Directive 76/207 allows out of a concern to protect women do not include risks and dangers, such as those to which any armed police officer is exposed when performing his duties in a given situation, that do not specifically affect women as such.

NOTES

Nature or Context in Article 2(2). Does the Court rely on the nature of the activities or the context in which they are carried out in reaching its decision under Article 2(2)? Do you agree with its reasoning? Why or why not?

The Article 2(3) Test. What test does the Court apply in determining whether Article 2(3) applies? Does a state which desires to protect women's lives, but not men's lives, have a legitimate purpose?

Women with Guns. What assumptions lie behind the Constable's fears that assailants will be able to seize women's fire-arms? Do you agree with his conclusion?

Proportionality. The Court hints at how the national court should apply the concept of proportionality. Can you think of other ways to achieve proportionality?

Sylvia Paisley, *Arms and the Man? Johnston v. Chief Constable of the Royal Ulster Constabulary*

38   Northern Ireland Legal Quarterly 352 (1987)

On 27 November 1980 Mrs. Johnston, a former member of the Royal Ulster Constabulary full-time Reserve, complained to the Industrial Tribunal in Belfast that she had suffered unlawful discrimination contrary to the Sex Discrimination (Northern Ireland) Order 1976. Yet it took over six years and various court proceedings, including a reference to the European Court of Justice in Luxembourg, to resolve her case; the Industrial Tribunal finally announced on 9 March 1987 that a settlement had been reached between the parties, a settlement which was described by a lawyer for the women involved as one that "would have implications for policing far beyond Northern Ireland. . . ."

[T]he Industrial Tribunal was left to decide if the Chief Constable's reasons for not arming women in the RUC Reserve were justified within the terms of Article 2(2) of the Directive and, moreover, to apply the overriding principle of proportionality to the facts of the case. The stage seemed set for an extremely interesting decision by the Tribunal. But, after some argument and an adjournment, the parties decided to agree to a settlement rather than continue the case. And so the Tribunal agreed to adjourn the case . . . without making a declaration. It did, however, award all costs against the Chief Constable of the RUC because it considered that he had acted "unreasonably in failing to appreciate his obligations under the sex discrimination laws". . . . Because it was resolved by way of negotiations between the parties, the local Equal Opportunities Commission, which had supported Mrs. Johnston throughout, was able to include in the settlement some agreement about other contentious issues including other women's claims of discrimination by the Chief Constable. This explains why compensation was paid not just to Mrs. Johnston but also to some 30 other women. It was agreed that the statutory limit of £8000 under the 1976 Order be paid as compensation to 26 former full-time female RUC Reservists, nine of whom also received an additional £1500 because they had been refused part-time contracts. The other five complainants received a total of £18,420. In all, therefore, almost £250,000 was paid out in compensation to the 31 women.

In addition to compensation, the Chief Constable agreed to reduce the height requirement for women applicants to the RUC from 5 foot 6 inches to 5 foot 4 inches. Moreover, the Chief Constable agreed to access for women to all training and also to the establishment of an Advisory Committee on Equal Employment Opportunities in the Police Service. This Committee will have representatives from the RUC, the Northern Ireland Police Authority, the Police Association, and from the Equal Opportunities Commission for Northern Ireland. Its remit is to examine and keep under review the principle of equal treatment of men and women in respect to matters such as recruitment, training, promotion, conditions of service and any other matters covered by the principle of equal treatment in the regular RUC and the RUC Reserve and to advise and make recommendations to the Chief Constable having regard to the exigencies of the unusual situation prevailing in Northern Ireland. The setting up of such a Committee is to be welcomed as it should help to promote a genuine feeling of equality of treatment within the police force. . . .

It is, however, important to note that the Court of Justice referred to "certain policing activities" being confined to men. This would, however, only be in accordance with Community law if the general principle of proportionality were observed. . . . [T]he refusal by the Chief Constable to renew the contracts of the full-time women RUC reservists could only be justified if that refusal was proportionate to the aim of ensuing public safety. If women police constables could be spared the risk of assassination and if public confidence in them could be maintained without arming them but instead by allocating them duties that could be performed without fire-arms, then the refusal to renew their contracts would not satisfy the proportionality test. Since the case was ultimately settled, one can only speculate as to whether the Chief Constable could have satisfied the proportionality test. In Mrs. Johnston's case, where what was at issue was described by the Advocate General as "a human right as fundamental as that of equal treatment",[37] it is probable that . . . the proportionality test would not have been met by the Chief Constable. *Johnston* is authority for the proposition that any Member State . . . may differentiate between male and female members of the police as regards "certain policing duties" as well as the training thereto. But it may do so only in very limited circumstances; only where the *nature* or the *context* of the policing means that the sex of the police officer is a determining factor "within the meaning of Article 2(2) of the Directive" and even then, only if the treatment of the sexes satisfies the overriding principle of proportionality. So those who thought the outcome of the case would give women "Equal rights to shoot" were off target![38]

The Court decided the following case in 2000, after the Amsterdam Treaty of October 2, 1997, entered into force. The Amsterdam Treaty amended the EC Treaty and renumbered its articles. Thus, the Court here gives both the old and new article numbers. *See,* for example, paragraph 1, where the Court refers to "Article 177 of the EC Treaty (now Article 234 EC)."

Federal Republic of Germany (Bundesrepublik Deutschland) v. Kreil
(Court of Justice of the European Communities)
Case 285/98, 2001 E.C.R. I-69 (2000)

1   By order of 13 July 1998, received at the Court on 24 July 1998, the (Administrative Court), Hannover, referred to the Court for a preliminary ruling under Article 177 of the EC Treaty (now Article 234 EC) a question on the interpretation of Council Directive 76/207/EEC of 9 February 1976 on the implementation of the principle of equal treatment for men and women as regards access to employment, vocational training and promotion, and working conditions, in particular Article 2 thereof.

2   The question has been raised in proceedings between Tanja Kreil and the Bundesrepublik Deutschland concerning the refusal to engage her in the maintenance (weapon electronics) branch of the Bundeswehr.

The Law Applicable

3   Article 2(1), (2) and (3) of the Directive provides:

1. For the purposes of the following provisions, the principle of equal treatment shall mean that there shall be no discrimination whatsoever on grounds of sex either directly or indirectly by reference in particular to marital or family status.
2. This Directive shall be without prejudice to the right of Member States to exclude from its field of application those occupational activities and, where appropriate, the training leading thereto, for which, by reason of their nature or the context in which they are carried out, the sex of the worker constitutes a determining factor.

---

[37] [1986] 3 All ER 135, 152.
[38] Chris Ryder, *The Sunday Times,* 17 February 1985.

3. This Directive shall be without prejudice to provisions concerning the protection of women, particularly as regards pregnancy and maternity.

4   Article 9(2) of the Directive provides:

Member States shall periodically assess the occupational activities referred to in Article 2(2) in order to decide, in the light of social developments, whether there is justification for maintaining the exclusions concerned. They shall notify the Commission of the results of this assessment.

5   Article 12a of the (Basic law for the Federal Republic of Germany) provides:

(1) Men who have attained the age of eighteen years may be required to serve in the Armed Forces, in the Federal Border Guard, or in a Civil Defence organisation. . . .
(4) If, while a state of defence exists, civilian service requirements in the civilian public health and medical system or in the stationary military hospital organisation cannot be met on a voluntary basis, women between eighteen and fifty-five years of age may be assigned to such services by or pursuant to a law. They may on no account render service involving the use of arms.

6   Access for women to military posts in the Bundeswehr are governed in particular by Article 1(2) of the (Law on Soldiers) and by Article 3a of the (Regulation on Soldiers' Careers), according to which women may enlist only as volunteers and only in the medical and military-music services.

The Main Proceedings

7   In 1996, Tanja Kreil, who has been trained in electronics, applied for voluntary service in the Bundeswehr, requesting duties in weapon electronics maintenance. Her application was rejected by the Bundeswehr's recruitment centre and then by its head staff office on the ground that women are barred by law from serving in military positions involving the use of arms.

8   Tanja Kreil then brought an action in the (Administrative Court) Hannover claiming in particular that the rejection of her application on grounds based solely on her sex was contrary to Community law.

9   Considering that the case required an interpretation of the Directive, the [Administrative Court] Hannover decided to stay the proceedings and to refer the following question to the Court for a preliminary ruling:

Is Council Directive 76/207/EEC of 9 February 1976, in particular Article 2(2) of that directive, infringed by the third sentence of Article 1(2) of the (Law on Soldiers) and Article 3a (Regulations on Soldiers' Careers), under which women who enlist as volunteers may be engaged only in the medical and military-music services and are excluded in any event from armed service?

The Question Referred for a Preliminary Ruling

10   By its question the national court is asking essentially whether the Directive precludes the application of national provisions, such as those of German law, which

bar women from military posts involving the use of arms and which allow them access only to the medical and military-music services.

11   The applicant argues that this bar constitutes direct discrimination contrary to the Directive. She considers that, under Community law, a law or a regulation may not prohibit a woman from access to the occupation which she wishes to pursue.

12   The German Government, on the other hand, considers that Community law does not preclude the provisions of the [Law on Soldiers] and [Regulation on Soldiers' Careers] in question, which are in accordance with the German constitutional rule prohibiting women from performing armed service. According to it, Community law does not in principle govern matters of defence, which form part of the field of common foreign and security policy and which remain within the Member States' sphere of sovereignty. Secondly, even if the Directive could apply to the armed forces, the national provisions in question, which limit access for women to certain posts in the Bundeswehr, are justifiable under Article 2(2) and (3) of the Directive.

13   The Italian and United Kingdom Governments, which presented oral argument, argue basically that decisions concerning the organisation and combat capacity of the armed forces do not fall within the scope of the Treaty. Alternatively, they submit that in certain circumstances Article 2(2) of the Directive allows women to be excluded from service in combat units.

14   The Commission considers that the Directive, which is applicable to employment in the public service, applies to employment in the armed forces. It considers that Article 2(3) of the Directive cannot justify greater protection for women against risks to which men and women are equally exposed. As regards the question whether the employment sought by Tanja Kreil forms part of activities whose nature or the context in which they are carried out require, as a determining factor within the meaning of Article 2(2) of the Directive, that they be carried out by men and not by women, it is for the referring court to answer that question having due regard for the principle of proportionality and taking account both of the discretion which each Member State retains according to its own particular circumstances and of the progressive nature of the implementation of the principle of equal treatment for men and women.

15   The Court observes first of all that, it is for the Member States, which have to adopt appropriate measures to ensure their internal and external security, to take decisions on the organisation of their armed forces. It does not follow, however, that such decisions are bound to fall entirely outside the scope of Community law.

16   As the Court has already held, the only articles in which the Treaty provides for derogations applicable in situations which may affect public security are Articles 36, 48, 56, 223 (now, after amendment, Articles 30 EC, 39 EC, 46 EC and 296 EC) and 224 (now Article 297 EC), which deal with exceptional and clearly defined cases. It is not possible to infer from those articles that there is inherent in the Treaty a general exception excluding from the scope of Community law all measures taken for reasons of public security. To recognise the existence of such an exception, regardless of the specific requirements laid down by the Treaty, might impair the binding nature

of Community law and its uniform application (*see Johnston v. Chief Constable of the Royal Ulster Constabulary*).

17   The concept of public security, within the meaning of the Treaty articles cited in the preceding paragraph, covers both a Member State's internal security, as in the *Johnston* case, and its external security, as in the *Sirdar* case.

18   Furthermore, some of the derogations provided for by the Treaty concern only the rules relating to the free movement of goods, persons and services, and not the social provisions of the Treaty, of which the principle of equal treatment for men and women relied on by Tanja Kreil forms part. In accordance with settled case-law, this principle is of general application and the Directive applies to employment in the public service.

19   It follows that the Directive is applicable in a situation such as that in question in the main proceedings.

20   Under Article 2(2) of the Directive, Member States may exclude from the scope of the Directive occupational activities for which, by reason of their nature or the context in which they are carried out, sex constitutes a determining factor; it must be noted, however, that, as a derogation from an individual right laid down in the Directive, that provision must be interpreted strictly (*Johnston* and *Sirdar*).

21   The Court has thus recognised, for example, that sex may be a determining factor for posts such as those of prison warders and head prison warders, for certain activities such as policing activities performed in situations where there are serious internal disturbances (*Johnston*) or for service in certain special combat units (*Sirdar*).

22   A Member State may restrict such activities and the relevant professional training to men or to women, as appropriate. In such a case, as is clear from Article 9(2) of the Directive, Member States have a duty to assess periodically the activities concerned in order to decide whether, in the light of social developments, the derogation from the general scheme of the Directive may still be maintained (*Johnston* and *Sirdar*).

23   In determining the scope of any derogation from an individual right such as the equal treatment of men and women, the principle of proportionality, one of the general principles of Community law, must also be observed, as the Court pointed out in *Johnston* and *Sirdar*. That principle requires that derogations remain within the limits of what is appropriate and necessary in order to achieve the aim in view and requires the principle of equal treatment to be reconciled as far as possible with the requirements of public security which determine the context in which the activities in question are to be performed.

24   However, depending on the circumstances, national authorities have a certain degree of discretion when adopting measures which they consider to be necessary in order to guarantee public security in a Member State.

25   As the Court emphasised in paragraph 28 of its judgment in *Sirdar*, the question is therefore whether, in the circumstances of the present case, the measures taken by the national authorities, in the exercise of the discretion which they are recognised to enjoy, do in fact have the purpose of guaranteeing public security and whether they are appropriate and necessary to achieve that aim.

26   As was explained in paragraphs 5, 6, and 7 above, the refusal to engage the applicant in the main proceedings in the service of the Bundeswehr in which she wished to be employed was based on provisions of German law which bar women outright from military posts involving the use of arms and which allow women access only to the medical and military-music services.

27   In view of its scope, such an exclusion, which applies to almost all military posts in the Bundeswehr, cannot be regarded as a derogating measure justified by the specific nature of the posts in question or by the particular context in which the activities in question are carried out. However, the derogations provided for in Article 2(2) of the Directive can apply only to specific activities.

28   Moreover, having regard to the very nature of armed forces, the fact that persons serving in those forces may be called on to use arms cannot in itself justify the exclusion of women from access to military posts. As the German Government explained, in the services of the Bundeswehr that are accessible to women, basic training in the use of arms, to enable personnel in those services to defend themselves and to assist others, is provided.

29   In those circumstances, even taking account of the discretion which they have as regards the possibility of maintaining the exclusion in question, the national authorities could not, without contravening the principle of proportionality, adopt the general position that the composition of all armed units in the Bundeswehr had to remain exclusively male.

30   Finally, as regards the possible application of Article 2(3) of the Directive, upon which the German Government also relies, this provision, as the Court held in *Johnston*, is intended to protect a woman's biological condition and the special relationship which exists between a woman and her child. It does not therefore allow women to be excluded from a certain type of employment on the ground that they should be given greater protection than men against risks which are distinct from women's specific needs of protection, such as those expressly mentioned.

31   It follows that the total exclusion of women from all military posts involving the use of arms is not one of the differences of treatment allowed by Article 2(3) of the Directive out of concern to protect women.

32   The answer to be given to the question must therefore be that the Directive precludes the application of national provisions, such as those of German law, which impose a general exclusion of women from military posts involving the use of arms and which allow them access only to the medical and military-music services.

NOTES

A Change in the Court's Position? Compare this decision to *Johnston*. Has the Court changed its position? In *Sirdar v. Ministry of Defense*, 1999 Case C-0273/97 (*see Kreil* paragraphs 17, 20–23, 25), the Court held that the United Kingdom could exclude a woman chef because of her sex from a position in the Royal Marines under article 2(2). The *Kreil* court applied the same standard used in the earlier *Sirdar* decision, but reached a different result on the facts. Mrs. Sirdar had served in the British Army since

1983 and as a chef in a "commando regiment of the Royal Artillery" from 1990 to 1994. When 500 chefs were laid off to save costs, she obtained a transfer order to the Royal Marines which had a shortage of chefs. Once the Marines realized she was a woman, they informed her that the Marines had a policy of excluding all women and withdrew the offer. The Court upheld this decision based on the Marine policy of "interoperability":

[T]he organisation of the Royal Marines differs fundamentally from that of other units in the British armed forces, of which they are the 'point of the arrow head'. They are a small force and are intended to be the first line of attack. It has been established that, within this corps, chefs are indeed also required to serve as front-line commandos, that all members of the corps are engaged and trained for that purpose, and that there are no exceptions to this rule at the time of recruitment.

Why is this exclusion permissible while the one in *Kriel* was not? Do you agree with the Court's decision?

Women in Combat. If a woman were to challenge her exclusion from combat duties, whether flying aircraft or driving tanks, would she succeed? Should she? Why do so many countries persist in barring women from combat? Is it because women cannot do the work? Chivalry? To prevent women from learning combat skills? To preserve the lives of child bearers? Do you have any other theory?

D. The French Crime of Employing Women for Paid Night Work

Public Ministry v. Stoeckel
(Court of Justice of the European Communities)
Case 345/89, 1991 E.C.R. I-4047 (1991)

1   By judgment of 4 October 1989, which was received at the Court on 9 November 1989, the Tribunal de Police, Illkirch, referred to the Court for a preliminary ruling under Article 177 of the EEC Treaty a question on the interpretation of Council Directive 76/207/EEC of 9 February 1976 on the implementation of the principle of equal treatment for men and women as regards access to employment, vocational training and promotion, and working conditions.

2   That question was raised in criminal proceedings against Mr. Stoeckel, an executive of Suma, SA ('Suma'), who was charged with employing 77 women to work at night on 28 October 1988 contrary to Article L 213–1 of the French Code du Travail (Labour Code).

3   Pursuant to Article 5 of Directive 76/207, application of the principle of equal treatment with regard to working conditions means that men and women are to be offered the same conditions without discrimination on grounds of sex. To that end, the Member States are to take the measures necessary to ensure that any provisions contrary to the principle of equal treatment are to be abolished (paragraph 2(a) and that any provisions contrary to that principle are to be revised when the concern for protection which originally inspired them is no longer well founded (paragraph

2(c)).[o] However, by virtue of Article 2(3), the Directive is to be without prejudice to provisions concerning the protection of women, particularly as regards pregnancy and maternity.

4   Pursuant to Article 9(1) of the Directive, the Member States were required to put into force the laws, regulations and administrative provisions necessary in order to comply with the Directive within a period of 30 months of its notification and, with respect to Article 5(2)(c), within a period of four years. The latter period expired on 14 February 1980.

5   Pursuant to Article L 213-1 of the French Code du Travail, women may not be employed for any nightwork, in particular in plants, factories or workshops of any kind whatsoever. However, the same article provides for a number of exceptions, relating for example to management posts or executive technical posts and to situations where, because of particularly serious circumstances, provision must be made for the prohibition of nightwork by women employees working in successive shifts to be suspended when the national interest so requires, under the conditions and in the circumstances envisaged in the Code du Travail.

6   It is apparent from the documents before the Court that, as a result of economic difficulties brought about by foreign competition, Suma found it necessary to consider laying off about 200 people in its Obenheim factory. However, having calculated that the number and the effects of the redundancies could be limited if a continuous shift-work system were adopted, involving nightwork for all the workforce, Suma undertook negotiations with the unions with a view to concluding an agreement between them and the company.

7   In an agreement concluded for that purpose on 30 June 1988, it was stipulated that recourse to nightwork was an exceptional measure and that Suma would revert to day-work only as soon as the economic constraints had ceased. In view of the fact that the female workers in the company had the necessary skills for the posts that had been retained, the parties, wishing to ensure that women were given the same opportunities as men, agreed to make all posts available to both men and women, subject to approval by a majority vote of the female workers. A majority voted in favor of the shift-work system and it was introduced with effect from 1 October 1988.

8   Before the Tribunal de Police, Mr. Stoeckel contended that Article L 213 of the Code du Travail was contrary to Article 5 of Directive 76/207 and to the judgment in Case 312/86 *Commission v. France* [1988] ECR 6315, in which the Court held that, by

---

[o] Article 5 provides:

"1. Application of the principle of equal treatment with regard to working conditions, including the conditions governing dismissal, means that men and women shall be guaranteed the same conditions without discrimination on grounds of sex.

2. To this end, Member States shall take the measures necessary to ensure that—

(a) Any laws, regulations and administrative provisions contrary to the principle of equal treatment shall be abolished; . . .

(c) those laws, regulations and administrative provisions contrary to the principle of equal treatment when the concern for protection which originally inspired them is no longer well founded shall be revised. . . ."

failing to take all the necessary measures to eliminate inequalities prohibited by the Directive, the French Republic had failed to fulfill its obligations.

9 In those circumstances, the Tribunal de Police, Illkirch, stayed the proceedings pending a ruling by the Court on the following question:

Is Article 5 of the Directive of 9 February 1976 sufficiently precise to impose on a Member State an obligation not to lay down in its legislation the principle that nightwork by women is prohibited, as in Article L 213-1 of the French Code du Travail?

10 Reference is made to the Report for the Hearing for a fuller account of the facts of the case, the procedure and the written observations submitted to the Court, which are mentioned or discussed hereinafter only in so far as is necessary for the reasoning of the Court.

11 The purpose of the Directive is to implement in the Member States the principle of equal treatment for men and women with regard, *inter alia*, to access to employment and working conditions. To that end, the Directive required the abolition or the revision of national provisions that are contrary to that principle where the concern for protection which originally inspired them is no longer well founded.

12 As the Court stated in its judgment in Case 152/84 *Marshall v. Southampton and South-West Hampshire Health Authority* [1986] ECR 723, Article 5 of Directive 76/207 does not confer on the Member States the right to limit the application of the principle of equal treatment in its field of operation or subject it to conditions and that provision is sufficiently precise and unconditional to be capable of being relied upon by an individual before a national court in order to avoid the application of any national provision not conforming to Article 5(1), which lays down the principle of equal treatment with regard to working conditions.

13 Moreover, pursuant to Article 2(3), the Directive is to be without prejudice to provisions concerning the protection of women, particularly as regards pregnancy and maternity. In its judgment in Case 222/84 *Johnson v. Chief Constable of the Royal Ulster Constabulary* [1986], the Court held that it was clear from the express reference to pregnancy and maternity that the Directive was intended to protect a woman's biological condition and the special relationship which exists between a woman and her child.

14 The French and Italian Governments submit that the prohibition of nightwork by women, which in any case is subject to numerous exceptions, is in conformity with the general aims of protecting female workers and with particular considerations of a social nature relating, for example, to the risks of attack and the heavier domestic workload borne by women.

15 As far as the aims of protecting female workers are concerned, they are valid only if, having regard to the principles mentioned above, there, is a justified need for a difference of treatment as between men and women. However, whatever the disadvantages of nightwork may be, it does not seem that, except in the case of pregnancy or maternity, the risks to which women are exposed when working at night are, in general, inherently different from those to which men are exposed.

16   As regards the risks of attack, if it is assumed that they are greater at night than during the day, appropriate measures can be adopted to deal with them without undermining the fundamental principle of equal treatment for men and women.

17   As far as family responsibilities are concerned, the Court has already held that the Directive is not designed to settle questions concerned with the organization of the family or to alter the division of responsibility between parents (*see* the judgment in Case 184/83 *Hoffman v. Barmer Ersatzkasse* [1984] ECR 3047 [excerpted in Chapter 8 of this book]).

18   Thus, the concern to provide protection, by which the general prohibition of nightwork by women was originally inspired, no longer appears to be well founded and the maintenance of that prohibition, by reason of risks that are not peculiar to women or preoccupations unconnected with the purpose of Directive 76/207, cannot be justified by the provisions of Article 2(3) of the Directive which are referred to in paragraph 3 of this judgment.

19   As regards the numerous exceptions provided for in the legislation of the Member States which retain a prohibition of nightwork by women, to which the French and Italian Government refer, they cannot adequately uphold the objectives of the Directive, since the latter prohibits the laying down of a general principle excluding women from undertaking nightwork, and, moreover, they may be a source of discrimination.

20   It follows from the foregoing that it must be stated in reply to the question submitted by the Tribunal de Police, Illkirch, that Article 5 of Directive 76/207 is sufficiently precise to impose on the Member States the obligation not to lay down by legislation the principle that nightwork by women is prohibited, even if that is subject to exceptions, where nightwork by men is not prohibited.

Opinion of the Advocate General, *Public Ministry v. Stoeckel*
Delivered on 24 January 1991, Case-345/89, 1991 E.C.R. I-4055

The French legislation was adopted in order to give effect to International Labour Organization ("ILO") Convention No 89 of 9 July 1948, which was ratified in France by Law No 53-603 of 7 July 1953, which, subject to exceptions, prohibits nightwork by women. . . .

4. I will describe, albeit briefly, the origins of legislation of this kind. The prohibition of nightwork by women in the past represented a victory for the working classes, forming part of legislation intended to protect in particular women and children, in other words those who were regarded as the weakest members of society, exposed to the most risks.

A prohibition of that kind was laid down by the British legislature half-way through last century (1844). Switzerland then adopted similar legislation in 1877, being emulated subsequently by other countries such as Austria (1885), the Netherlands (1889) and, as the century drew to a close, France (1892).

In view of the fact that at that time women were employed predominantly in factories, the legislation applied first to the industrial sector and was then gradually extended, in accordance with varying requirements, to other sectors.

The first International Congress on Worker Protection, held in Berlin in 1890, passed a resolution condemning nightwork by women in industry. In 1906, 13 States signed the Bern Convention, which reiterated the prohibition but only for industrial undertakings employing more than 10 workers. These provisions were the precursor of the prohibition laid down in 1919 by the ILO; in fact, one of the first ILO Conventions, No 4, prohibited the employment of women in industrial premises during the night, except in family businesses.

In order to avoid the problems of too wide ranging a prohibition, a second convention, No 41, was adopted by the ILO in 1934. It excluded from its scope, in particular, women holding management posts or executive technical posts.

The third instrument, adopted in 1948 in order to allow for further exceptions, is Convention No 89 on which, as indicated earlier, the present French legislation on this subject was based.

5. The main arguments supporting legislation of that kind, when it was adopted, were medical, social, political and economic. It was contended that since women were denied civil and political rights, such as the right to vote, they were exposed to greater risk in the absence of statutory protection. Female workers were then regarded as physically weaker and thus more vulnerable to certain consequences of nightwork, such as the possibility of physical or mental problems. In addition, concern was expressed about the risks to which women might be exposed when going to their place of work at night and it was also regarded as somewhat "inappropriate" that women should undertake nightwork in the company of workers of the opposite sex.

An additional factor in the aversion to nightwork by female workers derived from deeply held convictions as to the social role of the woman as a mother and focal point of the family unit: the woman should preferably be at home, looking after the family. Nightwork was thus regarded as particularly disruptive to family life and harmful to society. . . .

It appears from the 1989 International Labour Conference report on nightwork to which I referred earlier that, from the medical point of view, nightwork may cause, *inter alia*, disturbances affecting sleep and the digestive system, problems which may be aggravated by the tendency to consume an excess of stimulants such as coffee and tobacco during the night and sleeping pills to facilitate rest during the day. The effects of nightwork on the health may thus vary considerably according to the age and family and financial situation of the workers concerned.

Whilst there are no detailed pathological studies relating to female workers, the existing research appears to show that, apart from the need for special protection during pregnancy in view of the risks to which the unborn child might be exposed, there are no additional real and specific reasons for which women should not undertake nightwork.

In other words, whilst it is true that nightwork is liable to have harmful effects on the physical and mental well-being of workers and should therefore be limited to what is strictly necessary and in any case be subject to regulations, it is also true that there is no significant information such as to raise fears of substantial harm specifically affecting the female to a greater extent than the male population.

8. The objection relating to the increased risk of attack to which women are allegedly exposed at night likewise does not seem to me to provide justification for limiting the scope of an essential right such as that of equal treatment regarding working conditions.

That risk might . . . perhaps be eliminated by the taking of appropriate measures such as, for example, the provision of appropriate transport facilities; and in any case the principle imposed by the French legislature whereby nightwork by women is prohibited is subject to so many exceptions of various kinds that it is very difficult to believe that it is justified by objective considerations and is not in fact the historical survivor of what in the past was a measure for the protection of (what was regarded then as) the more vulnerable part of the working class.

A study carried out in 1984 by the Research Department of the French Ministry of Social Affairs and Employment shows that between 1978 and 1984 there was a considerable increase in the number of women working at night; in 1984 in particular, the more than one million people regularly undertaking nightwork included about 170 000 women.

Furthermore, if it is borne in mind on the one hand that, according to a circular dated 30 June 1987 from the French Ministry of Social Affairs and Employment, it is not unlawful to employ women at night in industrial premises to carry out work of a non-industrial nature, as in the case of data-processing operatives and supervisors, and, on the other, that certain collective agreements for particular industries provide for the possibility of nightwork for women working shifts, it becomes even more difficult to accept such an explanation, it not being apparent why someone employed in information technology or in the steel industry should be less likely to be assaulted than, say, someone working in the chemical industry.

Finally, the fact cannot be overlooked that the inclusion in the French legislation of a general prohibition of nightwork by women, which is subject to so many exceptions that it is even possible to apply different conditions to women engaged in similar tasks, is liable to create further unjustified discrimination between those women.

NOTES

The Women Workers' Majority Vote. As the Court notes, the majority of the employed women wanted to keep their jobs and work at night. What should the result be if the majority had voted against women's night work, but a quarter of the women wanted the option?

Pregnant Women's Night Work. Both the Court and the Advocate General accept the idea that pregnant women who work at night may harm their fetus. Is this intuitively obvious? What factors make you accept or reject this conclusion? One of the original motivations in the late 19th and early 20th centuries for enacting the laws was the belief that women were more vulnerable to "physical or mental problems" as a result of nightwork. Is a similar belief at work or might there be scientific evidence concerning effects on the fetus?

France Changes Its Law. The French government subsequently denounced the ILO Convention on Night Work for Women, and in May 2001 amended its night work legislation so that it applies equally to men and women and provides night work protection for all workers. One provision, Article L213-4-3, allows any worker to refuse night work for pressing family obligations concerning the care of infants or dependants and protects such a worker from being considered at fault.

III. The United States System

A. Introduction

In 1964, the U.S. Congress enacted Title VII of the 1964 Civil Rights Act, 42 U.S.C. § 2000e *et seq.* Unlike the European system, it applied directly to employers, rather than requiring each state to enact an anti-discrimination law. But many states already had, or subsequently enacted, their own anti-discrimination laws. So Title VII created a system where victims of discrimination could first use their state law system, and then use the federal system. After negotiations between the state and federal bodies, a system eventually evolved which allowed an employee to go either to the one or the other body, and then to file suit in federal court.

Introduction to Title VII of the 1964 Civil Rights Act
in Barbara Allen Babcock et al., Sex Discrimination and the Law: History, Practice, and Theory 426–29 (2d ed. 1996)

A. Administration and Procedure

Title VII is the most comprehensive and important of all federal and state laws prohibiting employment discrimination based on sex. The statute establishes a complex administrative and procedural structure and reaches discrimination based on race, color, religion, and national origin, as well as sex. Federal courts have been interpreting its many provisions and its relationship to other statutes and to the Constitution for over 30 years. We present here a brief summary of the procedural and administrative outlines of Title VII law. . . .

Title VII covers most employers, labor unions, employment agencies, and entities providing apprenticeship and training programs. §§ 703(a)–(d).[2] Small employers (those with fewer [than] 15 employees) and small unions and agencies are not cov-

---

[2] 42 U.S.C. § 2000e-2(a)–(d) (1988). . . . The Equal Employment Opportunity Commission has issued detailed guidelines interpreting both the procedural and substantive sections of the statute. . . . The relevant procedural regulations are found at 29 C.F.R. parts 1601 and 1613, those on sex discrimination at part 1604.

ered, along with certain other entities (e.g., religious institutions, which are in some circumstances allowed to discriminate on the basis of religion). §§ 701(b), 701(c), 701(e), 702, 703(e)(2), 703(i). The covered employers, unions, and agencies are subject to a comprehensive ban on all forms of discrimination in employment, found in sections 703(a)–703(d) and 717(a) of Title VII. Section 704 also prohibits two other practices—(1) retaliating against persons for opposing employment discrimination or for participating in Title VII proceedings and (2) publishing discriminatory advertisements. Although the U.S. Department of Justice also has a limited role with regard to state and local government employers, the statute is primarily administered by the Equal Employment Opportunity Commission (the EEOC or the Commission). *See* § 705.

The administrative process established by the statute is as follows. Anyone who believes she has been discriminated against in employment on the basis of sex must first file a form charging discrimination (a "charge") with a state agency, if the discrimination took place in a state that prohibits employment discrimination. *See* § 706(c). (If the state has no such law, the aggrieved employee can go directly to the EEOC. § 706(b).) After 60 days (or earlier, if the state agency administering the state law terminates its proceedings before the 60-day period ends), she must file a charge with the EEOC. § 706(c). As a practical matter, many people go directly to the EEOC, and the EEOC files on their behalf with the state agency, but the EEOC cannot act on the charge until the 60-day state deferral period has ended.

The "charge" is a simple form providing basic information to the Commission: who discriminated, on what basis, in what way, and when. The EEOC then sends a copy of the charge to the employer and investigates to determine whether there is "reasonable cause to believe that the charge is true." § 706(b). In the course of the investigation, the EEOC may send written questionnaires to the employer, may hold a fact-finding conference with the parties, or may subpoena the production of documents or the testimony of witnesses; none of these steps is the equivalent of an evidentiary hearing, however. If the EEOC issues a "reasonable cause" decision after this investigation, Commission employees attempt to eliminate the unlawful practice through negotiation and settlement with the employer. § 706(b). If that fails, either the EEOC or the aggrieved employee has the right to sue the employer in federal court, although the employee must ask for a "notice of right to sue" from the Commission before doing so. § 706(f)(1). In the case of state and local government employers, the EEOC transfers the case to the U.S. Justice Department after the negotiation stage, because only the Justice Department is authorized to sue these entities (state and local government employees, of course, retain their separate right to sue their employer). § 706(f)(1). If the federal court finds a violation of the statute, the judge has broad discretion to award various forms of relief, including enjoining the violation, ordering affirmative relief such as reinstatement or hiring, and ordering the payment of back wages, interest, attorneys' fees and costs, and damages. §§ 706(g), 706(k), amended by Civil Rights Act of 1991.

B. Theories of Violation

The core nondiscrimination provision of Title VII, § 703(a), 42 U.S.C. § 2000e–2(a), is directed at employers of 15 or more employees and provides:

> It shall be an unlawful employment practice for an employer—(1) to fail or refuse to hire or to discharge any individual, or otherwise to discriminate against any individual with respect to his compensation, terms, conditions, or privileges of employment, because of such individual's race, color, religion, sex, or national origin; or (2) to limit, segregate, or classify his employees or applicants for employment in any way which would deprive or tend to deprive any individual of employment opportunities or otherwise adversely affect his status as an employee, because of such individual's race, color, religion, sex, or national origin.

Subsequent subsections prohibit discrimination by employment agencies (§ 703(b)), labor organizations (§ 703(c)), and apprenticeship programs (§ 703(d)).

Three theories of violation, based on three different patterns of discrimination, have emerged in litigation under sections 703(a)–703(d) of Title VII. In shorthand, these patterns are (1) facial discrimination (policy or practice on its face is explicitly based on sex distinction); (2) disparate treatment (employer treats employees differently "because of their sex" but, unlike facial cases, employer does not acknowledge this fact); and (3) disparate impact (formally neutral policy or practice does not draw an explicit sex line and does not treat employees differently "because of their sex," but does have a disparate negative impact on one sex).

The BFOQ Defense: Banning One Sex as Justifiable Facial Discrimination?

in Barbara Allen Babcock et al., Sex Discrimination and the Law: History, Practice, and Theory 470 (2d ed. 1996)

Once it has been determined that an employer's policy discriminates on the basis of sex in violation of section 703(a), the employer may nonetheless prevail in a Title VII suit if it can establish that being male (or female) is a bona fide occupational qualification (BFOQ) for the job in question under section 703(e). Section 703(e) provides: "[I]t shall not be an unlawful employment practice for an employer to hire and employ employees . . . on the basis of his [or her] sex . . . in those certain instances where . . . sex . . . is a bona fide occupational qualification reasonably necessary to the normal operation of that particular business or enterprise."

In the first decade after Title VII's passage, litigation over the breadth of the BFOQ exception dominated sex discrimination cases brought under the Act as employers sought to defend long-standing policies of sex segregation. At stake was the breadth and effectiveness of Title VII's prohibition on gender-based discrimination. Not until 1977, in *Dothard v. Rawlinson*, did the Supreme Court directly address the interpretation of the BFOQ defense. (It would be another 14 years before the Court would again take up BFOQs in the sex discrimination context. *International Union, UAW v. Johnson Controls, Inc.,* 499 U.S. 187 (1991).

B. The BFOQ and California's Ban on Women Working More Than Ten Hours per Day for Pay or Lifting More Than 25 to 50 Pounds for Pay

Rosenfeld v. Southern Pacific Co.
(U.S. Court of Appeals for the 9th Circuit)
444 F.2d 1219 (9th Cir. 1971)

Leah Rosenfeld brought this action against Southern Pacific Company pursuant to section 706(f) of Title VII of the Civil Rights Act of 1964 (Act), 42 U.S.C. § 2000e–5(f). Plaintiff, an employee of the company, alleged that in filling the position of agent-telegrapher at Thermal, California, in March, 1966, Southern Pacific discriminated against her solely because of her sex, by assigning the position to a junior male employee. . . .

On the merits, Southern Pacific argues that it is the company's policy to exclude women, generically, from certain positions. The company restricts these job opportunities to men for two basic reasons: (1) the arduous nature of the work-related activity renders women physically unsuited for the jobs; (2) appointing a woman to the position would result in a violation of California labor laws and regulations which limit hours of work for women and restrict the weight they are permitted to lift. Positions such as that of agent-telegrapher at Thermal fall within the ambit of this policy. The company concludes that effectuation of this policy is not proscribed by Title VII of the Civil Rights Act due to the exception created by the Act for those situations where sex is a "bona fide occupational qualification."

While the agent-telegrapher position at Thermal is no longer in existence, the work requirements which that position entailed are illustrative of the kind of positions which are denied to female employees under the company's labor policy described above. During the harvesting season, the position may require work in excess of ten hours a day and eighty hours a week.[6] The position requires the heavy physical effort involved in climbing over and around boxcars to adjust their vents, collapse their bunkers and close and seal their doors. In addition, the employee must lift various objects weighing more than twenty-five pounds and, in some instances, more than fifty pounds.

The critical question presented by this argument is whether, consistent with Title VII of the Civil Rights Act of 1964, the company may apply such a labor policy. The pertinent provision of Title VII is section 703(a) of the Act. . . .

Southern Pacific's employment policy under which, for example, it has denied Mrs. Rosenfeld an employment assignment on the ground that women, considered generically, are not physically or biologically suited for such work, results in distinguishing employees, thus discriminating against some because of sex, within the meaning of subsection (1) of this provision. It also constitutes a limitation upon, segregation of, or classification of the company's employees in a way which would deprive or tend to deprive an individual of employment opportunities because of such individual's sex, within the meaning of subsection (2) of the quoted section.

------

[6] It was, indeed this opportunity to earn overtime pay that made this position attractive to plaintiff.

There is therefore no doubt that the type of discrimination against women broadly prohibited by Title VII occurs under Southern Pacific's personnel policy. However, appellants contend that section 703(e) of the Act, 42 U.S.C. §2000e–2(e), provides specific authority for Southern Pacific's described employment policy. . . .

We deal first with Southern Pacific's argument that the strenuous physical demands of the position, both as to the hours of work and the physical activity required, render sex "a bona fide occupational qualification [hereinafter BFOQ] reasonably necessary to the normal operation of that particular business or enterprise. . . ." The company contends that under the formulation put forward by the Fifth Circuit in *Weeks v. Southern Bell Tel. & Tel. Co.*, 408 F.2d 228 (5th Cir. 1969), if Southern Pacific could prove it "had reasonable cause to believe, that is, a factual basis for believing, that all or substantially all women would be unable to perform safely and effectively the duties of the job involved," *Id.* at 235, it could properly rely on the BFOQ exception as a legal basis for including women generically from position[s] such as that of agent-telegrapher at Thermal. Southern Pacific contends that it should not have been denied the opportunity to present such proof by the mechanism of summary judgment.

The *Weeks* case involved, among other issues, a challenge to a company-imposed weight-lifting restriction for female employees. The case had gone to trial below. The Fifth Circuit thus decided only that the company had not met the burden of proof for establishing a BFOQ below. There was no need for it to consider the basic issue of whether employment restrictions based upon characterizations of a sex group's physical capabilities are, by their nature, capable of fitting within the BFOQ category. Since this case reaches us after summary judgment, we must decide this question.

The crucial language of section 703(e), 42 U.S.C. § 2000e–2(e) . . . provides an exception to Title VII's prohibition of discrimination when "sex . . . is a bona fide occupational qualification." The Equal Employment Opportunity Commission (Commission) has interpreted the particular exception to some extent in its published Guidelines. In pertinent part, the Guidelines provide that:

(a) The Commission believes that the bona fide occupational qualification exception as to sex should be interpreted narrowly. . . .

(1) The Commission will find that the following situations do not warrant the application of the bona fide occupational qualification exception: . . .

(ii) The refusal to hire an individual based on stereotyped characterizations of the sexes. Such stereotypes include, for example, that men are less capable of assembling intricate equipment; that women are less capable of aggressive salesmanship. The principle of non-discrimination requires that individuals be considered on the basis of individual capacities and not on the basis of any characteristics generally attributed to the group. . . .

(2) Where it is necessary for the purpose of authenticity or genuineness, the Commission will consider sex to be a bona fide occupational qualification, e.g., an actor or actress. 29 C.F.R. § 1604.1.

In the case before us, there is no contention that the sexual characteristics of the employee are crucial to the successful performance of the job, as they would be for the position of a wet-nurse, nor is there a need for authenticity or genuineness, as in the case of an actor or actress. 29 C.F.R. § 1604.1(a)(2). Rather, on the basis of a general assumption regarding the physical capabilities of female employees, the company attempts to raise a commonly accepted characterization of women as the "weaker sex" to the level of a BFOQ. The personnel policy of Southern Pacific here in question is based on "characteristics generally attributed to the group" of exactly the same type that the Commission has announced should not be the basis of an employment decision. 29 C.F.R. § 1604.1(a)(1)(ii). Based on the legislative intent and on the Commission's interpretation, sexual characteristics, rather than characteristics that might, to one degree or another, correlate with a particular sex, must be the basis for the application of the BFOQ exception. *See Developments in the Law—Title VII*, 84 HARV. L. REV. 1109, 1178–1179 (1971). Southern Pacific has not, and could not allege such a basis here, and section 703(e) thus could not exempt its policy from the impact of Title VII. There was no error in the granting of summary judgment on this issue.

The premise of Title VII, the wisdom of which is not in question here, is that women are now to be on equal footing with men. The footing is not equal if a male employee may be appointed to a particular position on a showing that he is physically qualified, but a female employee is denied an opportunity to demonstrate personal physical qualification. Equality of footing is established only if employees otherwise entitled to the position, whether male or female, are excluded only upon a showing of individual incapacity. *See Bowe v. Colgate-Palmolive Co.*, 416 F.2d 711, 718 (7th Cir. 1969). This alone accords with the Congressional purpose to eliminate subjective assumptions and traditional stereotyped conceptions regarding the physical ability of women to do particular work. . . .

We have considered the meaning which appellants would ascribe to BFOQ as provided for in the Act. We conclude, however, that the Commission is correct in determining that BFOQ establishes a narrow exception inapplicable where, as here, employment opportunities are denied on the basis of characterizations of the physical capabilities and endurance of women, even when those characteristics are recognized in state legislation.

Under the principles set forth above, we conclude that Southern Pacific's employment policy is not excusable under the BFOQ concept. . . .

But the company points out that, apart from its intrinsic merit, its policy is compelled by California labor laws. One of the reasons Mrs. Rosenfeld was refused assignment to the Thermal position, and would presumably be refused assignment to like positions, is that she could not perform the tasks of such a position without placing the company in violation of California laws. Not only would the repeated lifting of weights in excess of twenty-five pounds violate the state's Industrial Welfare Order No. 9-63, but for her to lift more than fifty pounds as required by the job would violate section 1251 of the California Labor Code. Likewise, the peak-season days of over ten hours would violate section 1350 of the California Labor Code.

It would appear that these state law limitations upon female labor run contrary to the general objectives of Title VII of the Civil Rights Act of 1964, as reviewed above, and are therefore, by virtue of the Supremacy Clause, supplanted by Title VII. However, appellants again rely on section 703(e) and argue that since positions such as the Thermal agent-telegrapher required weight-lifting and maximum hours in excess of those permitted under the California statutes, being a man was indeed a bona fide occupational qualification. This argument assumes that Congress, having established by Title VII the policy that individuals must be judged as individuals and not on the basis of characteristics generally attributed to racial, religious, or sex groups, was willing for this policy to be thwarted by state legislation to the contrary.

We find no basis in the statute or its legislative history for such an assumption. Section 1104 of the Act, 42 U.S.C. § 2000h-4, provides that nothing contained in the Act should be construed as indicating an intent to occupy the field in which the Act operates, to the exclusion of State laws or the same subject matter, nor be construed as invalidating any provision of state law ". . . unless such provision is inconsistent with any of the purposes of this Act, or any provision thereof." This section was added to the Act to save state laws aimed at preventing or punishing discrimination, and as the quoted words indicate, not to save inconsistent state laws.

Still more to the point is section 708 of the Act, 42 U.S.C. § 2000e-7, which provides that nothing in Title VII shall be deemed to exempt or relieve any person from any liability, duty, penalty or punishment provided by any present or future state law ". . . other than any such law which purports to require or permit the doing of any act which would be an unlawful employment practice under this title." This section was designed to preserve the effectiveness of state anti-discrimination laws.

The Commission, created by the provisions of Title VII of the Act, through its published Guidelines and Policy Statements has, albeit after considerable hesitation, taken the position that state "protective" legislation, of the type in issue here, conflicts with the policy of non-discrimination manifested by Title VII of the Act. On August 19, 1969, the Commission revoked a portion of its Guidelines on Discrimination because of Sex, formerly appearing as 29 C.F.R. § 1604.1(a)(3), (b) and (c), and inserted a new subsection (b), quoted in the margin.[9] It is implicit in this Commission pronouncement that state labor laws inconsistent with the general objectives of the Act must be disregarded. The Supreme Court has recently observed that the adminis-

---

[9] "(b) (1) Many States have enacted laws or promulgated administrative regulations with respect to the employment of females. Among these laws are those which prohibit or limit the employment of females, e.g., the employment of females in certain occupations, in jobs requiring the lifting or carrying of weights exceeding certain prescribed limits, during certain hours of the night, or for more than a specified number of hours per day or per week.

(2) The Commission believes that such State laws and regulations, although originally promulgated for the purpose of protecting females, have ceased to be relevant to our technology or to the expanding role of the female worker in our economy. The Commission has found that such laws and regulations do not take into account capacities, preferences, and abilities of individual females and tend to discriminate rather than protect. Accordingly, the Commission has concluded that such laws and regulations conflict with Title VII of the Civil Rights Act of 1964 and will not be considered a defense to an otherwise established unlawful employment practice or as a basis for the application of the bona fide occupational qualification exception." 29 C.F.R. §1604.1(b).

trative interpretation of the Act by the enforcing agency "is entitled to great deference." *Griggs v. Duke Power Co.*, 401 U.S. 424 (1971). . . .

We have considered the meaning which appellants would ascribe to BFOQ, as provided for in the Act. We conclude, however, that the Commission is correct in determining that BFOQ establishes a narrow exception inapplicable where, as here, employment opportunities are denied on the basis of characterizations of the physical capabilities and endurance of women, even when those characteristics are recognized in state legislation.

Under the principles set forth above, we conclude that Southern Pacific's employment policy is not excusable under the BFOQ concept or the state statutes.

NOTES

The *Rosenfeld* Test and the *Weeks* Test. What test does the Ninth Circuit use in deciding whether the conditions for the BFOQ are met? What test did the Fifth Circuit use in the *Weeks* case? Which do you prefer and why?

The BFOQ Compared to Article 2(2) of the Equal Treatment Directive. Compare the two provisions. What is the same about the two? What different? On the face of the statutory language, which is better and why? Or are they the same?

Applying the *Rosenfeld* Test to the *Johnston* Case. If the European Court of Justice were to apply the *Rosenfeld* test in deciding Mrs. Johnston's case, what would the result be? Under the *Weeks* test?

Title VII and "Protective" Labor Legislation

in Barbara Allen Babcock et al., Sex Discrimination and the Law: History, Practice, and Theory 484–89 (2d ed. 1996)

The effect of Title VII on state labor laws governing women's hours, the amount of weight they can lift, and other conditions of their employment was a major issue in the early Title VII sex discrimination litigation. In both *Weeks* and *Rosenfeld*, "protective" labor legislation concerning the weights women could lift, and, in *Rosenfeld*, the hours they were permitted to work, undergirded the employers' exclusionary policies. . . .

[T]he social reformers who lobbied for protective laws believed that they would protect women's health (particularly reproductive health) and their ability to fulfill their family roles by easing the double burden of those who worked both inside and outside the home. A vocal group of feminists as well as some working women whose jobs were negatively affected by the legislation opposed labor legislation that applied to women only. William Chafe summarizes:

The reformers and feminists . . . held diametrically opposite conceptions of female equality. The Women's Party and its allies were convinced that protective legislation discriminated against females and that women could not be free until they achieved absolute identity with men in all areas of public policy regulated by law. The reformers, in turn, believed that differences of physical and psychological makeup prevented women from ever competing on a basis of total equality with men and that special labor laws were required if females were to be protected against exploitation and given just treatment in their economic activities.

William Chafe, The American Woman, Her Changing Social, Economic and Political Roles, 1920–1970 (1972).

The earliest and most enduring form of such "protective legislation" was a limit on women's paid work hours. By the late 1960s, 39 states had such laws (with an additional three states limiting the hours of all workers). Examples of hour limits set by day and by week include eight and 40 (two states), eight and 48 (16 states), nine and 54 (five states), and ten and 60 (four states).

Despite their "protective" label, these laws often operated to deny women higher-paid overtime work. Pursuant to federal or state law or union contract, overtime pay is often one and a half times greater than "straight time" pay—or better. Thus, Ms. Rosenfeld, barred by California's ten-hour per-day/58-hour per-week law from work that sometimes ran to 80 hours per week, sued for the explicit purpose of obtaining the valuable overtime pay. Although maximum-hours legislation was the most common type, other state labor laws barred women from night work (19 states); lifting greater than specified weights (11 states); and holding certain jobs at all, bartending and mining being the most common (26 states). Another seven states barred women from working for specified numbers of weeks before and after childbirth.

Once Title VII was passed many women workers challenged these laws, contending—as did Lorena Weeks and Leah Rosenfeld—that they were being used to deny desirable jobs solely on the basis of sex.[18] Initially, the EEOC supported the state legislation. An early EEOC guideline took the position that the employer's compliance with reasonable protective legislation would constitute grounds for a BFOQ defense, explaining that "The Commission does not believe that Congress intended to disturb such laws and regulations which are intended to, and have the effect of, protecting women against exploitation and hazard." § 1604.1(3).

The debate was still vigorous in 1967, when the EEOC held hearings on the issue. The United Auto Workers Union argued the anti-protective legislation position:

Because employers have used these laws to circumvent our collective bargaining contracts and to discriminate against the women who are members of our union, the UAW has taken the

---

[18] Women workers generally did not challenge another set of women-only state labor laws that operated in a less restrictive manner, such as women-only minimum wages and overtime pay. By the late 1960s, many states had extended such laws to men, leaving few states with female-only provisions. In this shrinking category were the minimum wage (only seven states' laws were limited to women by the late 1960s), overtime pay (four states), and a day of rest (20 states). A third category of state laws provided for rather minor benefits and, unlike minimum wage or overtime pay, had not been extended to male workers by the late 1960s. These state-mandated benefits for women included a meal period (22 states), rest periods (13 states), and seats (46 states). Male workers sometimes sought extension of these state-mandated benefits. *See, e.g., Burns v. Rohr Corp.*, 4 Fair Empl. Prac. Cas. (BNA) 939 (S.D. Cal. 1972) (paid rest periods), and *Bastardo v. Warren*, 332 F. Supp. 501 (W.D. Wis. 1971). In contrast, no men sought extension of restrictive laws like the maximum hours and night work limits.

position that so-called "protective" state laws—that is, those based on stereotypes as to sex rather than true biological factors—are undesirable relics of the past.

At the end of World War II and the Korean conflict we first encountered the management practice of invoking state laws in order to bypass women's job rights. During war periods, management had been more than happy to employ females in practically any capacity and to ignore these state laws. They were honored only in the breach. Yet, when men were again available, the employers resorted to the technique of combining two jobs into one so that it was beyond the state maximum weight law, or scheduling hours of work beyond the statutory limit for women in order to avoid hiring women employees. . . .

Now what has happened since Title VII became law? More and more employers have been able to discriminate against women because of anachronistic, so-called "protective" state laws regulating the employment of women. Because of state laws and regulations limiting the weights a woman may lift, or the hours a woman may work, employers have been able to deprive women of jobs, promotions and overtime. . . .

It has been our experience that women work because they need the money—to make a living or to supplement a too meager family income. They are entitled to the same breaks in employment as men—a chance—(1) to share equally in overtime; (2) to bid on the basis of seniority for any job they can perform and (3) to the same promotion opportunities as men.

It is axiomatic that *some* women can lift more than *some* men. So it is that *some* women can work longer hours than *some* men. In Japan, the pearl divers who dive six hours a day to depths of 40 feet or more in icy waters are almost all women because, in that culture, women are thought to be stronger than men.

International Union, UAW, Statement at the Public Hearing of the Equal Employment Opportunity Commission (Washington, D.C., May 2 and 3, 1967).

The AFL-CIO maintained its long-standing position in favor of such legislation, echoing arguments used by progressive reform women decades earlier:

Where an existing law serves a valid protective purpose but is in a form not readily appropriate for direct extension to men, our position is that such a law, benefiting significant portions of the female work force, should not be invalidated because of adverse effects on particular individuals or groups bringing charges of denial of "equal employment opportunity."

We have no evidence that women generally prefer extended opportunity for overtime work to a clear hours limitation, even though obviously there are a number who do. In particular, most working women with family responsibilities, whether unmarried or with husbands who help with the household work, still face a "double work" schedule—additional hours of work and responsibility in the home after the day's job is done. Except for the privileged few, this remains a current reality in American life.

Andrew J. Biemiller, Director, Dept. of Legislation, AFL-CIO, Statement Before the Equal Employment Opportunity Commission on Guidelines on Discrimination Because of Sex (June 2, 1967).

Within a year of the hearings, the EEOC began finding sex discrimination in cases involving state labor laws. The Commission also appeared as amicus curiae in *Rosenfeld* at the trial level, arguing that there was an irreconcilable conflict between Title VII and the state "protective" laws requiring invalidation of the state laws under the Supremacy Clause of the Constitution. *Rosenfeld v. Southern Pacific Co.*, 293 F. Supp. 1219 (C.D. Cal. 1968). In August 1969, the Commission issued new guidelines declaring that "protective" labor legislation conflicted with Title VII and would not be considered as a basis for application of the BFOQ exception.[19]

The *Rosenfeld* decision, affirmed on appeal, was a turning point; three years later, state hours, weight, and job prohibition laws had been ruled invalid under Title VII by the highest court considering each case. Federal courts had invalidated the hours laws of nine jurisdictions, as well as the weight laws of three jurisdictions, and two job prohibition laws. The issue seemed so well settled that the validity of these laws was no longer even raised on appeal in many cases. State laws, particularly hours laws, that were not invalidated by federal courts were changed by state legislatures or attorneys general. By 1976, 23 states had repealed their hours laws, the attorneys general of 24 jurisdictions had ruled that the laws did not apply to employers covered by Title VII, and two states had amended the laws to provide for voluntary overtime for women. Every state maximum-hours law for women underwent major modifications or changes in status after the enactment of Title VII in 1964.[23]

One decade after Title VII's effective date, it had become settled law that the BFOQ defense was not a vehicle for preserving state labor laws that prevented women workers from taking jobs they wanted. Although the Title VII controversy was thus resolved, the underlying difference in attitudes about how best to help women workers was not. In the 1980s, a new generation of feminists argued for women-only labor laws, while other feminists argued for gender neutrality. *See, e.g.*, Ann C. Scales, *The Emergence of Feminist Jurisprudence: An Essay*, 95 YALE L.J. 1373, 1394–96 (1986). The feminist split over how best to ensure that pregnant workers can retain their jobs provides yet another example.

Thus the question at the end of the 20th century, as it was in 1923 and again in 1965, remains whether justice and equality for women are best delivered through neutrally phrased legislation designed to take both their interests and those of male workers into account, or whether ideology or tactical choices sometimes require seeking or settling for women-only laws.

---

[19] [For the text of n]ew 29 C.F.R. § 1604.1 (b) . . . [, *see* note 9 of the *Rosenfeld v. Southern Pac. Co.* decision above.]

[23] The EEOC completed its invalidation of restrictive laws by adding laws prohibiting employment [for certain periods of time] before and after childbirth to this category in its March 1972 amendments to the sex discrimination guidelines. . . .

Chapter 8
The Special Treatment Versus Equal Treatment Debate

I. The International Labour Organization

A. Introduction

The International Labour Organization (ILO) was the first specialized agency associated with the United Nations. A universal organization devoted to the promotion of social justice and internationally recognized human and labor rights, the ILO has its roots in nineteenth-century labor and social movements demanding social justice and higher living standards for the world's working people. Originally created in 1919, by Part XIII of the Versailles Peace Treaty ending World War I, the organization lived through the Great Depression, the collapse of the League of Nations, and World War II. In the process it has grown from an original membership of 45 countries to 181 (as of July 19, 2007), established international labor standards, and provided an organization where representatives of governments, employers, and workers can discuss social and labor questions of importance to the entire world.

The ILO has three major tasks: setting international labor standards; giving technical assistance to Member States; and providing research, publications, and training and education programs. The ILO accomplishes its work through a tripartite structure: the International Labour Conference; the Governing Body; and the International Labour Office. The International Labour Conference is the ILO's deliberative body to which each Member State sends four people (two representing government, one labor, and another employers). The Conference meets annually, establishes labor standards by adopting conventions and recommendations, and elects the Governing Body (the executive body of 28 government members and 14 each from workers and employers). As of August 2007, the Conference had adopted 188 Conventions (binding treaties) and 199 Recommendations (non-binding policy guidelines with greater detail than the treaties) *(available at* RossRights). The Governing Body meets three times a year to make policy decisions, propose an ILO budget and program, and elect the Director-General of the International Labour Office. The Labour Office provides a staff of about 1,900 officials who work in Geneva, Switzerland, or in the 40 ILO field offices.

B. The ILO and Special Protection for Women Workers

Since its founding, the ILO has adopted 14 conventions specifically addressing women's work. The subjects include maternity protections and prohibitions on working for too many hours, at night, in mines, or in jobs requiring heavy lifting. Starting with an equal pay convention in 1951, the ILO shifted course and began requiring action to eliminate discrimination in pay, employment, and occupation. In the 1990s, the ILO began promoting protections for disproportionately female job situations. These conventions helped part-time workers, home-based workers, and workers with family responsibilities.

As we saw in Chapter Seven, the ILO conventions had an enormous impact on state labor laws in the United States. While the United States did not ratify any of these treaties, social reformers and labor unions persuaded state legislatures to adopt laws to the same effect despite serious opposition from some working women and feminists on the grounds they caused discrimination against women.

In Europe, many countries ratified the women-only conventions. *Stoeckel* was just one example. A 1987 report by the European Communities Commission shows how widespread such laws were.

COMMISSION OF THE EUROPEAN COMMUNITIES, PROTECTIVE LEGISLATION FOR WOMEN IN THE MEMBER STATES OF THE EUROPEAN COMMUNITY
COM(87) 105 final 3–5, 19–23 (1987)

2. Historical Background

The Commission's 1981 Report defined the "protective" legislation covered by [ETD] paragraph 2(c) of articles 3 and 5 as that which excludes women from certain occupations, ostensibly for their protection, or stipulates that they should be entitled to special working conditions. Since such provisions are prima facie contrary to the principle of equal treatment, paragraph 2(c) of articles 3 and 5 provides that they should be repealed when the concern for protection which originally inspired them is no longer well founded. The Report observed that:

. . . there are no common permanent requirements concerning the specific protection of women which have proved imperative in all countries in identical circumstances but, on the contrary, that a mosaic of extremely varied and highly specific regulations exists, the reasons for which are not clearly defined.

The Commission therefore undertook to examine the situation in the Member States to ensure that the application of the principle of equal treatment is not unjustifiably limited by the maintenance of outmoded protective measures.

In the first instance, it examined the question in a further Report of 1982, on the basis of the national provisions which had been reported to it by the Member States and on analysis by a consultant, assisted by experts from the then nine Member

States.[10] This Report contained a general survey of exemptions and efforts made to revise protective measures and showed that many national measures remained which were detrimental both to equality of opportunity and to protection policy itself (see conclusions below).

The Commission therefore went on to target the "Revision of national and Community protective legislation" as a specific Action (action 3) of its New Community Action Programme on the Promotion of Equal Opportunities for Women 1982–1985. The aim of this Action was:

To abolish in accordance with Directive 76/207/EEC unjustified protective legislation in the field of access to employment and working conditions and to promote equal standards of protection for men and women.

Member States were required to continue their efforts to revise protective legislation, and the Commission undertook to back up these efforts by determining which protective measures should be abolished on the grounds that the concern for protection which originally inspired them is no longer well founded. At the end of the Programme, the Commission reported on measures which had been taken or were being considered in the Member States over the period. It was clear from this report that there had been some revision of individual protective measures, but no concerted treatment of the question.

In 1986, the Community embarked on the current Medium Term Community Programme. Member States were again required to take the necessary measures to revise protective measures. The Commission undertook to ensure that the Directive was applied, and to:

. . . submit in this context (following the study carried out in 1982/83) a report on the revision of protective legislation for women, so as to achieve a more even mix in employment; the problems of night work in particular will be examined, because the ban on night work for women only often has a very negative impact on women's employment, for example in the new technologies.

Most recently, the Council has specifically committed Member States to increase the equality of access to, and opportunity within, the labour market for women by a "re-examination of the need for certain types of restrictive legislation affecting women's employment, as for example that relating to night work in industry. . . ."

4. Scope and Legal Implications

Parts Two and Three of this Report contain specific recommendations concerning national protective measures known to the Commission. These recommendations represent the view of the Commission and follow closely the advice given by the Advi-

---

[10] Monique Halpern, "Protective measures and the activities not falling within the field of application of the Directive on Equal Treatment—Analysis and Proposals" V/707/3/82—EN fin.

sory Committee on Equal Opportunities for Women and Men. Part Five, the annexes, sets out the relevant national and international provisions by Member State.

The Report does not consider the situation in the two new Member States, Spain and Portugal. This will be considered separately in the Report currently being prepared on the legal situation upon accession in those Member States.

This Report will deal with two types of protective measures, those which lay down bans on women's employment in certain areas and those which require specific working conditions for women.

Bans on employment counter women's right to work and must therefore be based on well-founded arguments if they are to be justified.

In contrast, protective working conditions are less directly dangerous and less serious in the sense that they embody more favourable conditions and can often be extended by collective agreement on the basis that extension of the scope of protection is an improvement to the regulations concerned. Indeed they often represented a major factor of progress when they were originally formulated, and it has been strongly argued that they should be maintained as essential to women's right to work, especially where women have to run a family at the same time.

However, the distinction between bans on employment and protective working conditions is not in practice as great as might seem. They may both have considerable negative effects on women's work. In times of high unemployment, women can lose out on good jobs if employers are dissuaded from recruiting women because they are, for example, less flexible, even though not actually barred as such from hiring women. As a result, such protective measures may contribute to the marginalisation of women into new "atypical" forms of employment.

In addition, they are daily reminders of different treatment, where women are placed into a separate category, and there is a danger that they may serve to reinforce the traditional underlying sexual division of social functions and the unequal treatment at work of men and women. . . .

III. Summary Table of Recommendations

1. Anomalous provisions

1. administrative controls	F, G, IRL, UK, LUX (bars)	repeal
2. obligatory notification	F, G, IRL	repeal
3. internal navigation on the Rhine	B, D, F, NL, UK	repeal
4. regulation on the employment of women on board ship	D, UK	repeal
5. women freed from working outside shops on presentation of a medical certificate:	F	
—after 10 p.m.		repeal
—when the temperature is below [zero degrees]		repeal
6. provision on hygiene at the place of work	B, D, F, IRL, NL, UK (also goes for special working clothes)	generalisation

2. Humanitarian provisions

a. family commitments

1. specific length of (daily or weekly) working time	D, G, NL, UK	generalisation or repeal
2. specific access to part-time work	F (collective bargaining)	generalisation
3. limitation of overtime	D, NL, UK	generalisation
4. ban on continuous working	F	repeal
5. extra annual leave	F, NL (collective bargaining)	generalisation to workers with family commitments
6. family leave	F, NL (collective bargaining)	generalisation to workers with family commitments
7. leave to do housework	D	generalisation to workers with family commitments
8. ban on Sunday work (or on derogation from a general ban in the case of women workers)	D, F, G, IRL, NL, UK	generalisation or repeal
9. same provision as for public holidays	D, G, IRL, UK	generalisation or repeal

b. night work

ban on night work for women in industry (or fewer possibilities of derogating from a general ban in the case of women workers)	all countries except DK	raising of ban alongside general improvement in working conditions, e.g., by general reduction in night work where possible

c. strenuous or arduous work

1. provision of seats in shops	F, IRL, NL	generalisation
2. right to a break	D, F, G, UK (local)	generalisation
3. early retirement in certain jobs	F, NL	generalisation to: —parents (F) —all workers of a given age (NL)
4. work on machines that are running	IRL, UK	repeal
5. work on compressed air caissons	B, F, UK	repeal
6. loader-artificer-blaster-driller	G	repeal
7. shifting of loads	F (assisted)[,] D, F, IRL[,] NL, UK (manual)	lowering of levels to generalise better working conditions, relevant vocational training to be extended to women
8. certain construction jobs, transport of raw material and other material in all kinds of construction	D	repeal

9. manual earth shifting, digging and excavation; preparation of quarry stone	B, D, UK	repeal of ban
10. dangerous or unhealthy work	B, IRL	repeal or generalisation
11. work in blast furnaces, steel works, metal factories, plants producing laminates and plate, iron and steel works and work with other metal which is heat processed (production)	D, IRL	repeal
12. dockwork	IRL, NL	repeal

d. mines

ban on work down mines	all countries except DK

Recommendation: as a first stage, repeal of the ban for certain workers (engineers, cleaning staff). Timetable to be drawn up leading to repeal of the ban in a wider sense, on condition that working conditions improved where necessary.

3. Health and safety provisions

1. mercury	F	—ban limited to pregnant women
	UK	—sexual neutralisation of the regulation
2. estersthiophosphorics	F	repeal of ban
3. aromatic hydrocarbons	F	repeal of ban
4. zinc	D, IRL	repeal
5. demolition work on industrial ovens containing refractory materials containing free silica	F, UK	repeal of ban
6. specific measures on exposures to lead for:		
—all women	IRL	narrower protection
—all women of child-bearing age	D	narrower protection

Recommendation: carry out research to back up the EOC's definition, plan to extend it to men who are able or intending to have children, or take over the European Parliament's recommendation on a timetable fixing the same (lower) level for all.

7. special conditions on exposure to ionizing radiation for women of reproductive capacity	all countries in time	

Recommendation: pending greater medical and scientific knowledge and subject to further research:

(i)   any exclusion must be made conditional on proof that it is impossible to adapt the job to the special conditions of exposure decided on (13 mSv per quarter);

(ii) so far as possible, provisions relating to the protection of women of reproductive capacity should be extended to men who are able or intending to have children.

IV. Conclusions

The natural and international protective measures discussed in this Report were originally conceived in a spirit of social progress, which sought in the main to take account of current perceptions of women's physical characteristics or family obligations.

However, with the passage of time it has become clear that many national protective measures may now be criticised because they have become anomalous or inadequate, that is, because:

- they have lost their original justification;
- they have become negative in their effect upon women or upon workers generally, both with regard to the internal adaptability of undertakings and to the global policy of prevention;
- they do not in practice systematically consider, assess or apply themselves to all the problems involved.

This Report has shown that, for example, arduous work or work involving heavy loads may be barred to all women because women overall tend to be physically weaker than men; women are barred from work with certain substances or processes which are dangerous to reproduction whilst no account is taken of particular cases or of dangers to the reproductive functions of both sexes; and some women, but not all, and in certain sectors only, are given special protections against night work.

It could be concluded that, overall, today, this legislation protects women less than it maintains their difference and that by passing over the need to protect men too, it has a negative affect when it comes to the global policy of prevention.[1]

The Commission therefore takes the view that protective legislation should in principle be consistent across sexes and across occupational areas. The Equal Treatment Directive has provided a narrow exception to this principle which authorises measures strictly necessary to protect the special biological condition of women. The Commission regards this physiological test as the touch-stone for legislation protecting women, a rigorous approach which has been confirmed by the Court of Justice. It may be concluded that many of the protective measures discussed in this Report will have to be extended to both sexes or repealed.

Member States are therefore requested to consider the recommendations contained in this Report with a view to revising the measures concerned and taking any action at international level which they deem necessary in this context.

In 2002, the European Council and Parliament adopted Directive 2002/73/EC amending the 1976 Equal Treatment Directive 76/207/EEC. They agreed with the Commission's stance on protective legislation. The amended Directive no longer shelters special protection for women workers. Compare ETD 76/207/EEC, articles

---

[1] [sic] Halpern Report, *supra* [note 10].

3(2)(c) and 5(2)(c) with the ETD as amended by 2002/73/EC, article 3(2), *available at* RossRights. With this step, Europe joins the U.S. system in abolishing women-only restrictions and women-only benefits.

But the ILO remains profoundly divided. Night work provides the best illustration. The ILO first approached the subject in 1919 when it adopted ILO C4. That Convention provided, in Article 3, that women working in industrial undertakings (mines, manufacturing, and construction) "shall not be employed during the night . . . , other than an undertaking in which only members of the same family are employed." It adopted a broad definition of night. Night is "a period of at least eleven consecutive hours." It is also the seven hours "between ten o'clock in the evening and five o'clock in the morning."

By 1931, the ILO was discussing whether to allow women in management to work at night. The Conference voted down a proposal to do so by failing to achieve a two-thirds majority. Some Member States thought they could nevertheless allow women managers to work and eventually the Council of the League of Nations requested the Permanent Court of International Justice to interpret Article 3. Did it allow women managers to work at night? Relying on the ordinary meaning of the Convention terms, the Court ruled in 1932 that it did not. The pressure mounted and by 1934, the ILO adopted ILO 41. New Article 8 provided that the Convention "does not apply to women holding responsible positions of management who are not ordinarily engaged in manual work."

In 1948, the ILO adopted yet another convention, ILO C89, allowing yet more women to work at night. Now Article 8 exempted "women holding responsible positions of a managerial or technical character[,] and . . . women employed in health and welfare services who are not ordinarily engaged in manual work." But even in 1990, despite changes in European and U.S. law, the ILO still clung to night work bans. By now, though, the ILO, like Janus, faces both backward and forward. Compare the different approaches below.

P89 Protocol of 1990 to the Night Work (Women) Convention (Revised), 1948

(International Labour Organisation)
1 International Labour Conventions and Recommendations 1919–1951,
 International Labour Office, Geneva, at 551 (1996)

Article 1

1. (1) National laws or regulations, adopted after consulting the most representative organisations of employers and workers, may provide that variations in the duration of the night period as defined in Article 2 of the Convention and exemptions from the prohibition of night work contained in Article 3 thereof may be introduced by decision of the competent authority . . . [provided that employers and unions agree, or that they have been consulted and a state agency determines that there is

adequate protection] as regards occupational safety and health, social services and equality of opportunity and treatment for women workers. . . .

Article 2

1. It shall be prohibited to apply the variations and exemptions permitted pursuant to Article 1 above to women workers during a period before and after childbirth of at least 16 weeks, of which at least eight weeks shall be before the expected date of childbirth. National laws or regulations may allow for the lifting of this prohibition at the express request of the woman worker concerned on condition that neither her health nor that of her child will be endangered.

2. The prohibition provided for in paragraph 1 of this Article shall also apply to additional periods in respect of which a medical certificate is produced stating that this is necessary for the health of the mother or child:

(a) during pregnancy;

(b) during a specified time prolonging the period after childbirth fixed pursuant to paragraph 1 above.

3. During the periods referred to in paragraphs 1 and 2 of this Article:

(a) a woman worker shall not be dismissed or given notice of dismissal, except for justifiable reasons not connected with pregnancy or childbirth;

(b) the income of a woman worker concerned shall be maintained at a level sufficient for the upkeep of herself and her child in accordance with a suitable standard of living. This income maintenance may be ensured through assignment to day work, extended maternity leave, social security benefits or any other appropriate measure, or through a combination of these measures.

4. The provisions of paragraphs 1, 2 and 3 of this Article shall not have the effect of reducing the protection and benefits connected with maternity leave.

The other 1990 revision to the prohibition on Night Work, Convention No. 171, applies to both sexes and requires employers to provide a range of protections for night workers. As of August 2007, the Convention has been ratified by nine countries (Albania, Belgium, Brazil, Cyprus, Czech Republic, Dominican Republic, Lithuania, Portugal, and Slovakia).

C171 Night Work Convention, 1990

International Labour Organisation, *International Labour Conventions and Recommendations 1977–1995*, International Labour Office, Geneva, at 356 (1996)

Article 1 . . .

(a) the term night work means all work which is performed during a period of not less than seven consecutive hours, including the interval from midnight to 5 a.m. . . .

Article 2

1. This Convention applies to all employed persons except those employed in agriculture, stock raising, fishing, maritime transport and inland navigation. . . .

Article 3

1. Specific measures required by the nature of night work, which shall include, as a minimum, those referred to in Articles 4 to 10, shall be taken for night workers in order to protect their health, assist them to meet their family and social responsibilities, provide opportunities for occupational advancement, and compensate them appropriately. Such measures shall also be taken in the fields of safety and maternity protection for all workers performing night work.

2. The measures referred to in paragraph 1 above may be applied progressively.

Article 4

1. At their request, workers shall have the right to undergo a health assessment without charge and to receive advice on how to reduce or avoid health problems associated with their work:
   (a) before taking up an assignment as a night worker;
   (b) at regular intervals during such an assignment;
   (c) if they experience health problems during such an assignment which are not caused by factors other than the performance of night work. . . .

Article 5

Suitable first-aid facilities shall be made available for workers performing night work, including arrangements whereby such workers, where necessary, can be taken quickly to a place where appropriate treatment can be provided.

Article 6

1. Night workers certified, for reasons of health, as unfit for night work shall be transferred, whenever practicable, to a similar job for which they are fit.

2. If transfer to such a job is not practicable, these workers shall be granted the same benefits as other workers who are unable to work or to secure employment.

3. A night worker certified as temporarily unfit for night work shall be given the same protection against dismissal or notice of dismissal as other workers who are prevented from working for reasons of health.

Article 7

1. Measures shall be taken to ensure that an alternative to night work is available to women workers who would otherwise be called upon to perform such work:

(a)   before and after childbirth, for a period of at least sixteen weeks of which at least eight weeks shall be before the expected date of childbirth. . . .

2. The measures referred to in paragraph 1 of this Article may include transfer to day work where this is possible, the provision of social security benefits or an extension of maternity leave.

3. During the periods referred to in paragraph 1 of this Article:

(a)   a woman worker shall not be dismissed or given notice of dismissal, except for justifiable reasons not connected with pregnancy or childbirth;

(b)   the income of the woman worker shall be maintained at a level sufficient for the upkeep of herself and her child in accordance with a suitable standard of living. This income maintenance may be ensured by any of the measures listed in paragraph 2 of this Article, by other appropriate measures or by a combination of these measures;

(c)   a woman worker shall not lose the benefits regarding status, seniority and access to promotion which may attach to her regular night work position.

4. The provisions of this Article shall not have the effect of reducing the protection and benefits connected with maternity leave.

Article 8

Compensation for night workers in the form of working time, pay or similar benefits shall recognise the nature of night work.

Article 9

Appropriate social services shall be provided for night workers and, where necessary, for workers performing night work.

Anne Trebilcock, *ILO Conventions and Women Workers*

in 2 Women and International Human Rights Law 301, 311–13 (Kelly D. Askin & Dorean M. Koenig eds., 2000)

Over the years, the debate on night work has shifted from that of protection/exclusion to a focus on night work's negative effects on both men and women as well as the contradiction between a ban on night work for women and national equal opportunity legislation and policy. To summarize, the issue has been dealt with most recently by adoption of the Night Work Convention, 1990 (No. 171) and its Recommendation (No. 178), which covers all workers irrespective of sex, as well as a 1990 Protocol to the Night Work (Women) Convention (Revised), 194[8] (No. 89). The result is a more flexible and/or gender-neutral approach to the subject than that found in earlier instruments. The Protocol allows the competent authority to vary the duration of the applicable night period and to exempt certain female workers from the prohibition after consulting with the most representative employers' and workers' organizations. However, no variation or derogation can be applied to women workers for at least sixteen weeks before and after childbirth, or when a medical certificate prescribes any deviation. This condition may be waived at the request of the woman concerned so long as neither her health nor that of her child will be endangered. Member states that have ratified Convention No. 89 are thereby able to ratify the Protocol to ease or eliminate, in certain cases, the prohibition contained in the convention. The Night Work Convention, 1990 (No. 171), which is supplemented by the Night Work Recommendation, 1990 (No. 178), applies to *all* those employed in night work, and calls for specific measures to protect the health of the workers concerned, to provide maternity protection, to help them meet family and social responsibilities, to provide opportunities for occupational advancement, and to compensate workers appropriately in terms of time, pay, or similar benefits. The original proposal to consider new standards on night work—which led eventually to the adoption of these three instruments in 1990—arose from the controversy over prohibiting night work for women.

The ILO is still much criticized for retaining Convention No. 89 on its books and for having kept it open to future ratifications. This situation, however, reflects the consensus of the Organization's tripartite constituents. According to the documents prepared for the 1989 and 1990 conference discussions on the new night work instruments, the majority of countries restrict the employment of women at night to some degree and many prohibit women from working at night in industry. Furthermore, the issue of night work itself, irrespective of the gender of the worker, attracts controversy. During the conference discussions, the workers' members stated that, in most cases, the push to enable women to undertake employment at night was not motivated by a desire to reduce discrimination, but by the search for low-wage labor and in order to profit from the fact that women continued to suffer discrimination. In some countries, women workers themselves consider the provisions of Convention No. 89 a necessary guard against exploitation. Women in other countries have taken the opposite line.

Fifteen member states [21 as of August 2007] have denounced Convention No. 89; further denunciations are expected during the next denunciation period, which runs from February 2001 to February 2002. . . . A total of forty-nine [45 as of August 2007] member states now remain bound by the provisions of Convention No. 89, including two that have ratified the Protocol. Of those countries that have denounced the Convention, a number did so following the judgement of the Court of Justice of the European Communities in the *Stoeckel Case* (No. 345/89 of 22 July 1991), although the Court softened this decision in the *Levy Case* (No. C158/91).

In summary, the present trend is to move away from a blanket ban on night work for women in industry and to give the social partners at the national level the responsibility for determining the extent of the permitted exemptions. It is also evident that, in the future, more attention will be placed on regulating night work for both men and women. A similar development applies to special protection measures in relation to work that can be harmful to either gender's reproductive/nurturing functions. Because the 1979 Convention on the Elimination of All Forms of Discrimination against Women stipulates that protective legislation should be reviewed periodically in the light of scientific and technical knowledge, it can be anticipated that future ILO conferences will consider proposals to revise instruments on certain aspects of occupational safety and health. The White Lead (Painting) Convention, 1921 (No. 13) is an example, because it was written before it was known that lead poses a serious reproductive hazard to both sexes. As an ILO training manual notes, "There is strong opposition to protecting only women of child-bearing age from risks without considering at the same time the damage that might be caused to the reproductive function of men." This indeed mirrors the approach taken in a resolution on equal opportunity and treatment for men and women in employment that was adopted by the International Labour Conference in 1985. . . .

N O T E

Countries Faithful to C 89. As of August 2007, countries which had not denounced C 89 included 20 in Africa (Algeria, Angola, Burundi, Cameroon, Comoros, Congo, Democratic Republic of the Congo, Djibouti, Egypt, Ghana, Guinea-Bissau, Guinea, Kenya, Malawi, Mauritania, Rwanda, Senegal, South Africa, Swaziland, and Tunisia (also ratified the 1990 Protocol to C 89)), 12 in Asia (Bahrain, Bangladesh, India (also ratified the 1990 Protocol to C89), Iraq, Kuwait, Lebanon, Libyan Arab Jamahiriya, Pakistan, Philippines, Saudi Arabia, Syrian Arab Republic, and the United Arab Emirates), 6 in Europe (Bosnia and Herzegovina, Macedonia, Montenegro, Romania, Serbia, and Slovenia), and 7 in Central and South America (Belize, Bolivia, Brazil, Costa Rica, Guatemala, Panama, and Paraguay).

C. Case Study: Night Work in Suribia

Assume that you are all senior advisors to the Minister of Labour of "Suribia," a third world country. The President of Suribia has asked the Labour Department to decide what Suribia's stance should be concerning the ILO agreements on Night Work (i.e., Conventions 89 and 171 and the 1990 Protocol to Convention 89). Suribia became a party to Convention 89 in the 1960s, and is now considering three options:

(1) Maintaining the status quo (i.e., remaining a party to Convention 89, but not joining either Convention 171 or the 1990 Protocol);
(2) Remaining a party to Convention 89, and joining the 1990 Protocol; or
(3) Denouncing Convention 89, and joining Convention 171 in its stead.

Your boss, the Minister of Labour, is committed to improving working women's status in Suribia, but unsure of the best means to that end. She has read the 1990 International Labour Organization's Record of Proceedings, at which delegates discussed the 1990 Protocol to Convention 89. She was particularly struck by the following excerpt:

C. Proposed Protocol to the Night Work (Women) Convention (Revised), 1948

158. Consideration of the Protocol to the Night Work (Women) Convention (Revised), 1948 (No. 89), began with a general discussion. The Government members of Canada and New Zealand said that they would not participate in the discussion of the Protocol and would abstain during the vote on it in the plenary session of the Conference. They reiterated that Convention No. 89 was discriminatory and that any change would not change its discriminatory nature. The government member of Norway said that she would not participate in the discussion in the Committee for the same reason. The Government member of Portugal informed the Committee that in his country consultations with the social partners had been initiated to prepare for the denunciation of Convention No. 89. This had been suspended in the hope that a new Convention would revise Convention No. 89. Since this was not the case, Portugal would return to consideration of denunciation of Convention No. 89 in view of the constitutional provisions of his country. He did not believe that his participation in the discussion would be appropriate under these circumstances.

159. The Government members of Senegal and Egypt announced that they would not participate in the discussion because their governments had ratified Convention No. 89 and saw no need for a Protocol. The Government member of Senegal said that in his country the prohibition of night work of women was not considered discriminatory. It helped to preserve the family structure and values of society. No economic arguments could justify its lifting. The Government member of Egypt considered it appropriate, not discriminatory, to protect women from the psychological, security and health problems connected with night work.

160. The Employer's Vice-Chairperson maintained that Convention No. 89 was discriminatory and in conflict with the Discrimination (Employment and Occupation) Convention, 1958 (No. 111). However, the employers' members were aware that there were strong views on principles which would make any compromise difficult. He appreciated the explanations of Government members concerning abstention but hoped that they would participate in the discussion since it could have implications for the whole forms of standard setting, which was a matter of international concern. . . .

161. The Workers' Vice-Chairperson also appealed to Government members to share their experiences even if they were not bound by Convention No. 89. In particular it would be interesting to learn about the national experiences of governments which had denounced or were considering denouncing the Convention. Concerning the apparent contradiction between Convention No. 89 and Convention No. 111, she drew attention to Article 5 of Convention No. 111 which stated that "special measures of protection or assistance" under other Conventions or Recommendations were not "deemed to be discrimination" and allowed members to consider circumstances which warrant special measures. The link between the two Conventions was important. The prohibition of night work might appear theoretically to be an obstacle to equality but in reality this was not the case. The prohibition helped to prevent the exploitation of women as cheap labour and to ease their double load due to work and family responsibilities, situations which arose because of real discrimination against them in society. Though it might be considered discriminatory in some countries where the principle of equality of opportunity and treatment was fully applied, this certainly was not the case in most countries.

162. As to the content of the Protocol, the Workers' Vice-Chairperson agreed that the present text was a good basis for discussion and said that the Workers' members were ready to negotiate. They felt that the adoption of a Protocol presented an additional option for those countries which had ratified Convention No. 89 and which had considered denouncing it. It could be a transitional measure. She warned, however, that the workers would not accept a Protocol which would empty the Convention of its meaning.

The Minister of Labour's concern, as she explains it to you, is that the industrialized countries advocating denunciation of Convention 89 fail to appreciate the reality of women's lives in poverty-stricken countries like Suribia. She questions whether this is an area in which it is possible to arrive at standards of general applicability; maybe each country must work out its own solutions. The Western feminists who have argued to her against any form of special legislative protection for women fail to grasp just how powerless women negotiating with employers can be in a country like hers.

What do you recommend to her concerning which ILO option Suribia should adopt, and why?

II. Special Treatment Versus Equal Treatment in the Context of Childbirth and Childcare

Much passion has been devoted to the following question. Is childbirth and infant care for women only? Or should fathers be encouraged to participate at all? The following materials from the U.S. and Europe should help you develop your own views.

A. The United States Debate

Susan Deller Ross, *Legal Aspects of Parental Leave: At the Crossroads*
in Parental Leave and Child Care: Setting a Research and Policy Agenda 93, 94–98, 109 (Janet Shibley Hyde and Marilyn J. Essex eds., 1991)

The History

As women entered the labor market in ever increasing numbers in the late 1960s and 1970s, they found themselves faced with a Catch-22 when they decided to have babies. On the one hand, employers frequently fired pregnant women or forced them to take long, unpaid leaves of absence, starting as early as the fourth month of pregnancy and continuing months past the birth of their children. While most women were fully capable of working up to childbirth and of resuming work 6 to 8 weeks after it, employers forced them off the job under the pretense that the pregnant woman or new mother was incapable of working during the entire pregnancy and for months afterward. On the other hand, when these women workers were actually incapacitated from working because they had to go to the hospital for childbirth or were recuperating from childbirth, employers had a contradictory theory. Women giving birth were not disabled from working after all, they declared; pregnancy and childbirth were just normal conditions. Therefore, women giving birth could be denied the disability and medical benefits to which other hospitalized workers were entitled under company fringe benefit plans.

Women caught in this double bind began suing on both issues under the Constitution and Title VII of the 1964 Civil Rights Act, seeking both the right to work when they were able to and the right to be paid fringe benefits other workers received when they were not capable of working. Soon the Equal Employment Opportunity Commission—the federal agency charged with enforcing Title VII's ban on sex discrimination in employment—leaped into the fray. In 1972 it issued regulations on the subject of pregnancy and childbirth. Its theory was simple and confronted the double bind head on. Insofar as pregnant workers and new mothers were actually disabled from working by pregnancy complications, childbirth, and the post-partum recovery, they were entitled to the same fringe benefits received by other workers needing medical attention—generally, payments under health insurance programs to cover doctor and hospital bills, and money under paid sick leave programs or temporary disability insurance (TDI) plans to cover wage loss when they were unable to work. Insofar as they were able to work during pregnancy and the post-partum period, they were to be allowed to continue in paid employment.

The EEOC regulations were based on classic antidiscrimination legal concepts. In particular, they rested on a comparison. Employer treatment of male workers provided the standard measurement. Insofar as male workers had generous fringe benefit programs, the EEOC approach resulted in upgrading the fringe benefits of pregnant workers. But where male workers had sparse benefits, the standard left pregnant women equally badly off.

The practical result of the EEOC approach was that in most medium to large firms, pregnant workers gained substantially. These employers tended to have generous fringe benefit plans, so pregnant women working for them ended up with comprehensive coverage for medical bills running easily into thousands of dollars per pregnancy. Women also gained paid sick leave for childbirth and the post-partum period, which typically continued a woman's salary for 6 to 8 weeks after childbirth and guaranteed a return to her job. But many employers—often smaller companies—did not provide such generous fringe benefits, and some claimed not to provide any sick leave at all, not even an unpaid sick leave. Under the EEOC's theory, a pregnant woman working for such an employer could be legally fired when she needed to take time off for childbirth, as long as the employer could prove that men with medical problems that prevented them from working were also fired in such circumstances.

Although the Supreme Court rejected the EEOC approach in 1976 in the famous *General Electric Company v. Gilbert* [429 U.S. 125 (1976)] decision, Congress quickly repudiated the Court. In 1978 it passed the Pregnancy Discrimination Act, which essentially reinstated the EEOC approach.[12] By this time, too, a number of states had copied the federal approach, requiring that women disabled by pregnancy and childbirth be treated the same as other disabled workers, and that women not so disabled be treated as other able workers. But a few states adopted a different approach. Rather than equal treatment, these states created a special leave for one category of disabled workers: those women disabled by pregnancy, childbirth, and related medi-

---

[12] . . . [The Pregnancy Discrimination Act amended Title VII of the 1964 Civil Rights Act by adding to the Section 1 definitions, 42 U.S.C. 2000e, the following new definition in subsection (k)]: "The terms 'because of sex' or 'on the basis of sex' include, but are not limited to, because of or on the basis of pregnancy, childbirth or related medical conditions; and women affected by pregnancy, childbirth, or related medical conditions shall be treated the same for all employment-related purposes, including receipt of benefits under fringe benefit programs, as other persons not so affected but *similar in their ability or inability to work*". . . .

cal conditions. Under these laws, employers could not fire such women, at least so long as their disability did not last more than a certain period of time (ranging from a "reasonable" time to 8 weeks to 4 months). The theory of those who fought for these laws was rather like that of the Supreme Court in the *Gilbert* case, though with a more favorable twist for the women involved. Both saw pregnancy as unique. This had led the Court to decide that pregnancy-related disabilities were not comparable to other disabilities and could therefore be excluded from disability insurance and paid sick leave programs without causing sex discrimination problems. The proponents of special leaves for pregnant workers agreed that pregnancy disabilities were not comparable to other disabilities, but concluded that disabled pregnant workers could therefore receive a special, unpaid leave of absence to protect their jobs without creating sex discrimination problems.

With the Pregnancy Discrimination Act (PDA) on the books, employers in two of the "special leave" states—Montana and California—saw a chance to get rid of the statutorily mandated unpaid leaves of absence for disabled pregnant women. In two different lawsuits, they asserted that the special leave discriminated against disabled male workers, and that the PDA required that the state laws be invalidated. Feminists split on how to resolve the controversy. One group (the "equal-treatment" feminists) fought for the core PDA principle of equal treatment for all disabled workers, and therefore agreed with the employers about the conflict with the PDA. Unlike the employers, however, these feminists would have extended the statutory leave to all disabled workers rather than getting rid of it for pregnant workers as the employers wanted to do. The other feminist group (the "special-treatment" feminists) focused for comparison purposes, not on the PDA disability principle but on the parenting role. Men did not have to lose their jobs on becoming a parent; women should not have to either, they argued. Therefore, they concluded, there was no conflict with the PDA, and the California law was permissible as drafted. In early 1987, the Supreme Court resolved the controversy in the California case (*California Federal Savings and Loan Association v. Guerra,* or *Cal Fed* [479 U.S. 272 (1987)]). It decided that the PDA was designed only to prevent discrimination against pregnant women, not to prevent discrimination in their favor. Ignoring the disability comparison, it chose the parenting comparison, ruling that California law allowed "women, as well as men, to have families without losing their jobs." But it also emphasized the limited nature of the California law—and, in particular, the fact that it was "narrowly drawn to cover only the period of *actual physical disability* on account of pregnancy, childbirth, or related medical conditions" (emphasis in original). The Court concluded:

Accordingly, unlike the protective labor legislation prevalent earlier in this century, [the California law] does not reflect archaic or stereotypical notions about pregnancy and the abilities of pregnant workers. A statute based on such stereotypical assumptions would, of course, be inconsistent with Title VII's goal of equal employment opportunity.

The Court was alluding here to an argument of the equal-treatment feminists. They had urged extension of the unpaid leave to all disabled workers rather than supporting a female-only statute because they feared the effects of female-only legislation. Earlier in the century, many states had enacted laws limiting women's hours on the theory that women workers needed special protection so they could get home to their families and fulfill their home duties. But the laws also protected women right out of desirable jobs that male workers got instead; so once Title VII was enacted, women workers had used Title VII to get the jobs and get rid of the state laws. The equal-treatment feminist group feared the same kind of impact from the new female-only pregnancy leave laws. If employers had to give a special leave only to women, they reasoned, employers might prefer to hire men instead. They worried also that if positive pregnancy-based laws were found legal, then a precedent would be set allowing negative pregnancy-based laws as well.

But the Court rejected these arguments, reasoning that as long as the special pregnancy leave laws were disability-based, they did not stereotype pregnant women. In theory, then, there was now nothing to prevent many more states from passing mandatory leave laws based on the California model of a special, women-only, pregnancy disability leave. After all, the Court had given the green light to narrowly drawn women-only statutes.

However, that did not happen. For while the *Cal Fed* case was working its way up through the courts, the equal-treatment feminist groups had begun working at the federal level on a new model for providing leaves—one that incorporated both the disability and the parenting perspectives, and did so on a gender-neutral basis. This model went through various incarnations but eventually became known as the Family and Medical Leave Act. The act's medical leave section was designed to give all disabled workers—including women disabled by pregnancy, childbirth, and related medical conditions—an unpaid leave of absence. Under this provision, employers could not fire any worker who was forced to stop work for medical reasons, as long as the leave lasted less than 26 weeks. The family leave section provided an unpaid leave to all workers—male or female—who wanted time off to care for newborns or newly adopted children, as well as time to care for seriously ill children. The leave could also be used for the care of seriously ill parents. The family leave would originally have been for 18 weeks in a two-year period, and by 1990 was for ten weeks. As with the medical leave, this provision effectively prevented employers from firing workers who decided to take time off for these purposes. In the case of women giving birth, the FMLA approach assumed that the typical woman would receive 6 to 8 weeks of medical leave for childbirth and the post-partum recovery period, and that this leave would be a *paid* leave under PDA principles whenever the employer had paid sick leave or TDI plans for other disabled employees. After using the medical leave, the new mother could then take an additional 18 weeks (10 weeks, in early 1990) of unpaid family leave. Thus, even under the versions of the FMLA pending in 1990, mothers giving birth could get a total of 16 to 18 weeks off, using both forms of leave to which they are entitled. Fathers and adoptive parents of both sexes could not take the medical leave, since they are not medically affected by childbirth, but they could take the 10-week family leave.

The Family and Medical Leave Act of 1993 and Its Effect

in BARBARA ALLEN BABCOCK ET AL., SEX DISCRIMINATION AND THE LAW: HISTORY, PRACTICE, AND
THEORY 554–59 (2d ed. 1996)

On February 5, 1993, President Bill Clinton signed into law the Family and Medical
Leave Act (FMLA). The Act, which applies to employers of 50 or more employees,
guarantees to employees an up-to-12-week unpaid leave of absence, with continuation of health benefits and a right to return to the same or similar job: (A) Because of
the birth of a son or daughter of the employee and in order to care for such son or
daughter; (B) Because of the placement of a son or daughter with the employee for
adoption or foster care; (C) In order to care for the spouse, or a son, daughter, or
parent, of the employee, if such spouse, son, daughter, or parent has a serious health
condition; or (D) Because of a serious health condition that makes the employee
unable to perform the functions of the position of such employee. 29 U.S.C. §§ 2601–
2654 (West Supp. 1995). Initially much more generous to employees in terms of
leave time and employer size, the bill survived eight years of congressional scrutiny,
debate, and trimming before emerging from Congress as a new president took office.

Susan Deller Ross, *The Legal Aspects of Parental Leave: At the Crossroads, in* PARENTAL LEAVE AND
CHILD CARE: SETTING A RESEARCH AND POLICY AGENDA 98, 100–107 (Janet Shibley Hyde & Marilyn J.
Essex eds., 1991). Because [the FMLA] was pending in Congress by the time the Court issued
its *Cal Fed* decision, states that were motivated by the Court's decision to pass new mandatory
leave legislation had two models to choose from: the California female-only model at issue in
Cal Fed and the federal gender-neutral model of a combined medical and family leave. The
new model made an enormous difference. Prior to the *Cal Fed* decision, 9 states had laws or
regulations providing for a female-only leave. Between the *Cal Fed* decision on January 13,
1987, and June 1989, 14 more states enacted legislation, but only 3 adopted the female-only
California approach (Iowa, Louisiana, and Tennessee). Of the remaining 11 states, 3 passed
pared-down versions of the FMLA (Connecticut, Maine, and Wisconsin), 3 passed parental
leave laws (Minnesota, Oregon, and Rhode Island), 2 passed laws allowing the use of accrued
sick leave for parental or family obligations (South Carolina and Washington), and 3 passed
laws providing leaves for adoptive parents (Colorado, Missouri, and New York). All 11 laws
were applicable to both men and women. . . .
Advantages and disadvantages of the different models. The female-only pregnancy disability
approach is still that of the largest number of state mandatory leave laws. The major advantage
to this approach is that it is the cheapest way to ensure that pregnant women will not lose
their jobs when they have a baby. However, it is the cheapest way because it helps no other
workers, not even women with other medical problems, and therein lies a major disadvantage.
Even more significant is the exclusion of fathers from the new parenting process. The California
leave is theoretically available to women only for childbirth and the post-partum disability
period—typically 6 to 8 weeks—with a 4-month cap for those women whose disability lasts
longer than the 6- to 8-week norm. However, the rumor is that, in practice, California employers typically give women the full 4 months. If so, California women get a combined medical
and child care leave lasting 4 months, while a California man who wants to spend even one
day caring for his newborn child can be fired for doing so. If we exclude men from the experience of caring for newborns, are we not reinforcing the norms that drive them ever more into
seeking fulfillment at work? And if men put their major emotional energies into work, does that
not increase the pressure on their wives to play the most significant role at home? One can see
the vicious cycle this creates. . . .

[Another problem with the California model is that it contains provisions that discriminate *against* pregnant workers. This was apparently the compromise wrung from the legislature by employers in exchange for the special leave. Small employers (those with 5 to 14 employees) are specifically authorized to exclude pregnancy coverage from medical insurance, to cap paid disability benefits at 6 weeks, and to exclude pregnant women from training programs if they cannot finish the training program at least 3 months prior to their due date. It was these provisions that led equal-treatment feminists to fear that preferential pregnancy laws could easily boomerang into negative pregnancy laws. And, indeed, Louisiana passed a law in 1987 that copied all these provisions directly from the California law and extended them to employers large enough to be covered by Title VII and the PDA. While the extension to Title VII employers is flatly illegal, Louisiana's law is still on the books, and one would not be surprised to find at least some Louisiana employers cheerfully complying with a law that allows them (albeit in violation of federal law) to exclude health insurance for pregnant workers from their insurance plans, among other discriminatory measures.]

Yet another concern about the female-only statutes is their narrow focus even for women. . . . It does this woman's children little good to preserve her job when she has a baby, only to let her employer fire her when she is hospitalized for some other serious medical condition. The same is true, of course, for fathers. Firing workers with serious medical conditions seems even worse when one realizes that, in contrast to parental leave, workers do not choose to take medical leave. If the condition is serious enough, such an employee simply cannot go to work.

Nor does the second form of state law being passed now—the pure parental leave legislation—address this problem. Minnesota, Oregon, and Rhode Island are all in this category, providing leaves of 6, 12, and 13 weeks respectively for the care of newborns or newly adopted children. . . . The major advantage of this approach is that leave is available to both fathers and mothers, thus avoiding the reinforcement of traditional sex roles fostered by the California-type statute. However, while parental leave is an important step forward, it entirely ignores the plight of seriously ill workers—male or female—forced off the job by employers with no medical leave policies. . . . [Pregnant women do, however, get a de facto disability leave by taking parental leave upon birth of a child.]

That suggests yet another problem with the pure parental leave legislation. To understand it, one must recall that a major advance under the PDA was that women gained 6 to 8 weeks of paid leave time for the childbirth recuperation period, wherever employers had general paid sick leave programs for other workers, whether through accrued sick leave or TDI plans. Parental leave passed by itself, without an accompanying medical leave, may lead some employers to give mothers the new *unpaid* parental leave instead of the old *paid* sick leave. This might especially be the case when the length of the parental leave is the same as the length of the typical paid sick leave, as in Minnesota. And while this practice would clearly violate Title VII and the PDA, how many women will realize that, or have the resources to bring a lawsuit to stop it? . . . [T]he best remedy would be to enact laws providing a medical leave as well as a parental leave, thus ensuring that employers and employees alike realize that women need the former for childbirth and the typical 6-week recuperation period, and the latter for the post-recuperation period when the only purpose of the leave is to care for the newborn.

Close analysis of the parental leave laws now on the books reveals other problems as well. The Oregon statute contains restrictions that foster traditional sex roles in the family and discriminate against two-earner couples. And each of the statutes contains restrictions that seriously hamper their usefulness to families in need.

A unique feature of the Oregon law makes the 12-week leave a combined maximum for both parents, not an individual parent entitlement. Moreover, an employer may deny leave to one parent while the other parent is taking the leave. In contrast, both Minnesota and Rhode Island give their respective 6-week and 13-week leaves to the individual parent. Thus, to maximize parental time with the newborn or newly adopted child in these states, both the mother and father will have to take the leave (yielding a total of up to 12 or 26 weeks of leave during which one parent or the other can care for the infant). Under Oregon's combined entitlement, a family seeking the maximum parenting time with the newborn can allow the mother alone to be the parent on leave and still get the entire 12 weeks. The provision thereby reinforces all the societal pressures that discourage fathers from taking an active role in caring for newborns.

Oregon's unique feature allowing employers to deny simultaneous father-mother leaves plays a similar, though narrower, role. Even a traditional father might be willing—indeed, eager—to spend a few days home caring for the baby when mother and baby both arrive home from the hospital, and the mother is most in need of recuperation time and help with the infant. A father's care in these early days might cement his bond with the baby and give him a powerful incentive to take parental leave later on when the mother has recovered physically and can go back to work. But his employer can deny even these few days of leave to the father on the ground that the mother is on parental leave. Since she will always be on leave in the early days after childbirth, the father's employer has an automatic out—and an easy way to pressure the father not to become too involved with his baby.

The Oregon statute also discriminates against fathers in two-earner families, since in situations where the mother does not work outside the home, the father is guaranteed the full 12 weeks of leave. Where both spouses are in the paid workforce, however, the father will in most cases be forced to sacrifice at least part of his parental leave in order to allow his wife to take time off for recuperation. . . .

Thus, on balance, while the parental leave model offers an improvement over the female-only pregnancy disability model by allowing both mothers and fathers to care for infants, it too has significant disadvantages. It fails to provide medical leave to workers who can . . . be fired for illness, and Oregon's version makes it easy to leave fathers out of the parenting process. Moreover, all versions now on the books reflect a narrow, timid, and rigid approach to the problems of working parents. Many families needing leave time for young or sick children will simply not qualify under these restrictive laws.

Finally, we come to the states following the FMLA model—namely, Connecticut, Maine, and Wisconsin. These states take a major step beyond the parental leave model, since they do provide medical leaves in addition to parenting leaves. They also provide a genuine family leave, extending the concept of a parenting leave beyond the care of newborns and newly adopted children (but not foster children) to the care of seriously ill children, parents, or spouses. . . . In other respects, however, they are sharply narrower. Wisconsin, for example, offers a medical leave of a mere 2 weeks and a family leave of the same amount of time for the purpose of caring for a seriously ill child, spouse, or parent. Only for the care of a newborn or newly adopted child does a parent get 6 weeks of family leave. Although 2 weeks of medical leave is better than none, this provision has the same potential as a no-medical-leave policy to lead to a cutback in paid medical leave; that is, employers may be tempted to give only 2 weeks of paid leave to new mothers, rather than the 6 to 8 weeks required under the PDA standard.

Maine is not much better. It provides a grand total of only 8 weeks of "family medical leave" for all these purposes. . . .

In comparison, Connecticut's law is generous and comprehensive, providing for 24 weeks of leave in a two-year period for medical leave, and another 24 weeks for family leave. Although it is limited to state employees, the actual operation of this plan should be closely studied as a possible model for other states. Such studies will be made somewhat easier by the fact that the law specifically requires periodic reporting by state agencies on their experience with these leaves of absence.

That brings us back to the federal FMLA model. The federal FMLA has some significant strengths . . . derived from its equal treatment approach to the problems of both medical disability and parenting. First, it goes farther than any other model in recognizing workers' dual roles in the family and in the workplace. It helps to set the stage for a more complete integration of fathers at home by allowing them substantial time off to care for seriously ill children and their own parents [and spouses], as well as for newborns. And by giving fathers the right to do so, it takes pressure off mothers to be Super Mom and do all these tasks, thus setting the stage for women to be more completely integrated into the workforce. It ensures that workers will not be fired because of their own medical condition, thus preventing the economic collapse of families when a sick wage earner also loses a job. And because the FMLA provides medical leave that equal numbers of men and women will take, and family leave that a significant number of men will take, it also eliminates the incentive that special-treatment, female-only, state laws give employers not to hire women. Similarly, it has no pregnancy-based provisions, and hence no potential for encouraging the use of negative pregnancy-based classifications like those in California's and Louisiana's laws; at the same time, it provides comprehensive leave for medically disabled women (either while pregnant or while recuperating from childbirth), and leave to care for newborns once the mothers have recuperated.

Another important provision of the FMLA that is ignored in most state statutes is the availability of family leave on a reduced-hours basis and medical leave on an intermittent basis. Both provisions are designed to help lower-income workers by giving them at least part-time pay while they take part-time leave. . . .

Of all these models, the FMLA represents the biggest improvement over early attempts to deal with problems at the intersection of work and family caused by the enormous influx of women into the paid labor market. It reflects substantial movement away from a women-only legislative position that reinforces traditional sex roles to a gender-neutral solution that lays the foundation for a more egalitarian relationship at home and at work. The effort to enact the FMLA shows that the country is beginning to grapple with the changed demographics of work and family life.

Some cautionary notes must be struck, however. . . . Many of the state laws reveal a real paucity of imagination and an unfortunate lack of concern for changing sex roles and the needs of families with two parents in the paid workforce. At the end of the twentieth century, many employers are vigorously opposing the FMLA model—in effect, fighting for the right to fire seriously ill workers and force parents back on the job within a few weeks after the birth of a child. And Congress eliminated a provision in the FMLA bill that would have required a study of the concept of paid leaves, even though there are available models (such as the state TDI programs) that could be used to provide universal paid medical and family leaves in ways that would cost employers little or nothing. Clearly, it will be many more years before we have a achieved a genuine accommodation between work and family life, one that actually encourages employees to attend to family needs by continuing their pay while they do so, in the belief that both the family and employment spheres will thereby be strengthened. But at least we have begun to work toward that goal.

[This excerpt has been revised to reflect the passage of the Family and Medical Leave Act after the 1991 publication of the Ross article.]

For data and a report on the FMLA's positive impact on employees and employers, *see* COMMISSION ON LEAVE, A WORKABLE BALANCE: REPORT TO CONGRESS ON FAMILY AND MEDICAL LEAVE POLICIES (Apr. 30, 1996).

The Philosophical Split [Between Equal Treatment and Special Treatment Theorists]

in BARBARA ALLEN BABCOCK ET AL., SEX DISCRIMINATION AND THE LAW: HISTORY, PRACTICE, AND THEORY 552–54 (2d ed. 1996)

[One] view is that the split was fueled by different views of the fundamental nature of women and men, and the consequent desirability of comparing something unique to other conditions. One side wanted recognition for women's "special" nature, quintessentially expressed in pregnancy and childbirth. The other side had a vision that stressed the common humanity of women and men, and feared a boomerang from emphasizing how women are different. They believed that employers, still so reluctant to let women in, would react to the legislative image of "difference" by finding new ways to keep women out. Compare the following views in developing your own:

Ann Scales writes:

ANN SCALES, TOWARD A FEMINIST JURISPRUDENCE, 56 IND. L.J. 375, 435 (1981): The only differences between the sexes which apparently cannot be ignored are *in utero* pregnancy, and breast-feeding, the one function in the childrearing process which only women can perform. In observing that these are the capabilities which *really* differentiate women from men, it is crucial that we overcome any aversion to describing these functions as "unique." Uniqueness is a "trap" only in terms of an analysis, such as that generated in *Geduldig v. Aiello* [417 U.S. 484 (1974)], which assumes that maleness is the norm. "Unique" does not mean uniquely handicapped.

Linda Krieger and Patricia Cooney add:

LINDA KRIEGER & PATRICIA COONEY, THE MILLER-WOHL CONTROVERSY: EQUAL TREATMENT, POSITIVE ACTION AND THE MAKING OF WOMEN'S EQUALITY, 13 GOLDEN GATE U.L. REV. 513, 541–542 (1983): It is likely that to both the Supreme Court and the American public, the distinctions between the condition of pregnancy, of a potential child developing within a woman's body, and any medical condition faced by a man, would leap out with much greater force and vigor than the similarities. The liberal [equal treatment] model, however, relies completely on the acceptance of the analogy. It fails to focus on the effect of the very *real* sex difference of pregnancy on the relative positions of men and women in society and on the goal of assuring equality of opportunity and effect within a heterogeneous "society of equals."

In contrast, Wendy Williams argues:

WENDY WILLIAMS, EQUALITY'S RIDDLE: PREGNANCY & THE EQUAL TREATMENT/SPECIAL TREATMENT DEBATE, 13 N.Y.U. REV. L. & SOC. CHANGE 325, 366–370 (1984–1985): Unlike Scales's vision of inclusion, which encompasses disability and health for all, Krieger and Cooney . . . support legislation that singles out pregnant women for special protection. . . . A law which requires the employer to give pregnant women [a] "reasonable leave" of absence, but requires no leaves for other employees, they contend, "places women on an *equal* footing with men and permits males and females to compete *equally* in the labor market." It does not "provide women with an additional benefit denied to men; it merely prevents women from having to suffer an additional burden which no male would ever have to bear. . . ."

Krieger and Cooney's view leads them to assert that pregnancy is a difference which must be "accommodated," in the manner that Title VII requires employer accommodation to religious practices, or federal regulations require accommodation to employee handicaps. However, the Supreme Court has interpreted accommodation requirements very narrowly. It has little sympathy for provisions which make employers go out of their way for the atypical worker. This result seems predictable. Special "favors" for such workers are viewed as an imposition unconnected to the employer's business needs and interests. In contrast, provisions for the "typical" worker are more easily seen as necessary or desirable responses to the nature of the workforce which may increase employee loyalty and productivity. Moreover, the special treatment approach for women will always embroil its proponents in a debate about whether they are getting more or not enough. Finally, such provisions are a double edged sword for their beneficiaries because they impose upon employers special costs and obligations in connection with pregnant workers, rendering them less desirable employees and creating an incentive to discriminate against them. By contrast, the equal treatment approach, premised squarely on an androgynous rather than a male prototype and reaching for an incorporationist rather than accommodationist vision, seeks to avoid these consequences by requiring a fundamental reorganization of the way the presence of pregnant working women in the workplace is understood. The vision is not, as is Krieger and Cooney's, a workplace based on a male definition of employee, with special accom[m]odations to women's differences from men, but rather a redefinition of what a typical employee is that encompasses both sexes. . . .

The equal treatment feminists reject the fundamental assumption that men should be treated as the prototype. An androgynous prototype requires sex neutral schemes that take into account the normal range of human characteristics—including pregnancy. . . . More than the provision of identical services may seem necessary when services are geared to the male norm. But inherent in such an approach is the continued definition of women as "other." Dual standards have always been the law's response to the sexes. The equal treatment feminists seek a more radical transformation.

Nevada Department of Human Resources v. Hibbs
(United States Supreme Court)
538 U.S. 721 (2003)

CHIEF JUSTICE REHNQUIST delivered the opinion of the Court [on behalf of himself and JUSTICES O'CONNOR, SOUTER, GINSBURG, and BREYER. JUSTICE STEVENS filed an opinion concurring in the judgment. JUSTICE SCALIA filed a dissenting opinion, as did JUSTICE KENNEDY, joined by JUSTICES SCALIA and THOMAS.]

The Family and Medical Leave Act of 1993 (FMLA or Act) entitles eligible employees to take up to 12 work weeks of unpaid leave annually for any of several reasons, including the onset of a "serious health condition" in an employee's spouse, child or parent. 29 U.S.C. § 2612(a)(1)(C). The Act creates a private right of action to seek both equitable relief and money damages "against any employer (including a public agency) in any Federal or State court of competent jurisdiction," § 2617(a)(2), should that employer "interfere with, restrain, or deny the exercise of" FMLA rights, § 2615(a)(1). We hold that employees of the State of Nevada may recover money damages in the event of the State's failure to comply with the family-care provision of the Act.

Petitioners include the Nevada Department of Human Resources (Department) and two of its officers. Respondent William Hibbs (hereinafter respondent) worked for the Department's Welfare Division. In April and May 1997, he sought leave under the FMLA to care for his ailing wife, who was recovering from a car accident and neck surgery. The Department granted his request for the full 12 weeks of FMLA leave and authorized him to use the leave intermittently as needed between May and December 1997. Respondent did so until August 5, 1997, after which he did not return to work. In October 1997, the Department informed respondent that he had exhausted his FMLA leave, that no further leave would be granted, and that he must report to work by November 12, 1997. Respondent failed to do so and was terminated.

Respondent sued petitioners in the United States District Court seeking damages and injunctive and declaratory relief for, inter alia, violations of 29 U.S.C. § 2612(a)(1)(C). The District Court awarded petitioners summary judgment. . . . The Ninth Court reversed.

We granted certiorari, to resolve a split among the Courts of Appeals on the question whether an individual may sue a State for money damages in federal court for violation of § 2612(a)(1)(C).

For over a century now, we have made clear that the Constitution does not provide for federal jurisdiction over suits against nonconsenting States. Congress may, however, abrogate such immunity in federal court if it makes its intention to abrogate clear in the language of the statute and acts pursuant to a valid exercise of its power under § 5 of the Fourteenth Amendment. . . . This case turns, then, on whether Congress acted within its constitutional authority when it sought to abrogate the States' immunity for purposes of the FMLA's family-leave provision.

In enacting the FMLA, Congress relied on two of the powers vested in it by the Constitution: its Article I commerce power and its power under § 5 of the Fourteenth Amendment to enforce that Amendment's guarantees.[1] Congress may not abrogate the States' sovereign immunity pursuant to its Article I power over commerce. Congress may, however, abrogate States' sovereign immunity through a valid exercise of its § 5 power, for "the Eleventh Amendment, and the principle of state sovereignty which it embodies are necessarily limited by the enforcement provisions of the § 5 of the Fourteenth Amendment." *Fitzpatrick v. Bitzer*, 427 U.S. 445 (1976).

Two provisions of the Fourteenth Amendment are relevant here: Section 5 grants Congress the power "to enforce" the substantive guarantees of § 1—among them, equal protection of the laws—by enacting "appropriate legislation." Congress may, in the exercise of its § 5 power, do more than simply proscribe conduct that we have held unconstitutional. "Congress' power "to enforce" the Amendment includes the authority both to remedy and to deter violation of rights guaranteed thereunder by prohibiting a somewhat broader swath of conduct, including that which is not itself forbidden by the Amendment's text." [*Board of Trustees of Univ. of Ala. v.*] *Garrett*, [531 U.S. 356 (2001)]. In other words, Congress may enact so-called prophylactic legislation that proscribes facially constitutional conduct, in order to prevent and deter unconstitutional conduct. . . .

Valid § 5 legislation must exhibit "congruence and proportionality between the

---

[1] *Compare* 29 U.S.C. § 2601(b)(1) ("It is the purpose of this Act . . . to balance the demands of the workplace with the needs of families to promote the stability and economic security of families, and to promote national interests in preserving family integrity") *with* § 2601(b)(5) ("to promote the goal of equal employment opportunity for women and men, pursuant to [the Equal Protection C]lause") *and* § 2601(b)(4) ("to accomplish [the Act's] other purposes in a manner that, consistent with the Equal Protection Clause . . . , minimizes the potential for employment discrimination on the basis of sex").

injury to be prevented or remedied and the means adopted to that end." [*City of Boerne v. Flores*], 521 U.S. [507 (1997)].

The FMLA aims to protect the right to be free from gender-based discrimination in the workplace.[2] We have held that statutory classifications that distinguish between males and females are subject to heightened scrutiny. For a gender-based classification to withstand such scrutiny, it must "serv[e] important governmental objectives," and "the discriminatory means employed [must be] substantially related to the achievement of those objectives." *United States v. Virginia*, 518 U.S. 515 (1996). The State's justification for such a classification "must not rely on overbroad generalizations about the different talents, capacities, or preferences of males and females." *Ibid.* We now inquire whether Congress had evidence of a pattern of constitutional violations on the part of the States in this area.

The history of the many state laws limiting women's employment opportunities is chronicled in—and, until relatively recently, was sanctioned by—this Court's own opinions. For example, in *Bradwell v. State*, 16 Wall. 130 (1873) (Illinois), and *Goesaert v. Cleary*, 335 U.S. 464 (1948) (Michigan), the Court upheld state laws prohibiting women from practicing law and tending bar, respectively. State laws frequently subjected women to distinctive restrictions, terms, conditions, and benefits for those jobs they could take. In *Muller v. Oregon*, 208 U.S. 412 (1908), for example, this Court approved a state law limiting the hours that women could work for wages, and observed that 19 States had such laws at the time. Such laws were based on the related beliefs that (1) woman is, and should remain, "the center of home and family life," *Hoyt v. Florida*, 368 U.S. 57 (1961), and (2) "a proper discharge of [a woman's] maternal functions—having in view not merely her own health, but the well-being of the race—justif[ies] legislation to protect her from the greed as well as the passion of man," *Muller.* Until our decision in *Reed v. Reed*, 404 U.S. 71 (1971), "it remained the prevailing doctrine that government, both federal and state, could withhold from women opportunities accorded men so long as any 'basis in reason'"—such as the above beliefs—"could be conceived for the discrimination." *Virginia.*

Congress responded to this history of discrimination by abrogating States' sovereign immunity in Title VII of the Civil Rights Act of 1964, 42 U.S.C. § 2000e2(a), and we sustained this abrogation. . . . But state gender discrimination did not cease. "[I]t can hardly be doubted that . . . women still face pervasive, although at times more subtle, discrimination . . . in the job market." *Frontiero v. Richardson*, 411 U.S. 677 (1973). According to evidence that was before Congress when it enacted the FMLA, States continue to rely on invalid gender stereotypes in the employment context, spe-

---

[2] The text of the Act makes this clear. Congress found that, "due to the nature of the role of men and women in our society, the primary responsibility for family caretaking often falls on women, and such responsibility affects the working lives of women more than it affects the working lives of men." 29 U.S.C. § 2601(a)(5). In response to this finding, Congress sought "to accomplish the [Act's other] purposes . . . in a manner that . . . minimizes the potential for employment discrimination *on the basis of sex* by ensuring generally that leave is available . . . *on a gender-neutral basis*[,] and to promote the goal of equal employment opportunity *for women and men*". . . . §§ 2601(b)(4) and (5) (emphasis added).

cifically in the administration of leave benefits. Reliance on such stereotypes cannot justify the States' gender discrimination in this area. The long and extensive history of sex discrimination prompted us to hold that measures that differentiate on the basis of gender warrant heightened scrutiny; here . . . the persistence of such unconstitutional discrimination by the States justifies Congress' passage of prophylactic § 5 legislation.

As the FMLA's legislative record reflects, a 1990 Bureau of Labor Statistics (BLS) survey stated that 37 percent of surveyed private-sector employees were covered by maternity leave policies, while only 18 percent were covered by paternity leave policies. The corresponding numbers from a similar BLS survey the previous year were 33 percent and 16 percent, respectively. While these data show an increase in the percentage of employees eligible for such leave, they also show a widening of the gender gap during the same period. Thus, stereotype-based beliefs about the allocation of family duties remained firmly rooted, and employers' reliance on them in establishing discriminatory leave policies remained widespread.

Congress also heard testimony that "parental leave for fathers . . . is rare. Even . . . [w]here child-care leave policies do exist, men, *both in the public and private sectors,* receive notoriously discriminatory treatment in their requests for such leave." Joint [1986] Hearing 147 (Washington Council of Lawyers) (emphasis added). Many States offered women extended "maternity" leave that far exceeded the typical 4- to 8-week period of . . . childbirth,[4] but very few States granted men a parallel benefit: Fifteen States provided women up to one year of extended maternity leave, while only four provided men with the same. This and other differential leave policies were not attributable to any differential physical needs of men and women but rather of the pervasive sex-role stereotype that caring for family members is women's work.[5]

---

[4] *See* [BLS survey] (six weeks is the medically recommended pregnancy disability leave period); H.R. REP. No. 101-28 (1989) (referring to Pregnancy Discrimination Act legislative history establishing four to eight weeks as the medical recovery period for a normal childbirth).

[5] For example, state employers' collective bargaining agreements often granted extended "maternity" leave of six months to a year to women only. Gerald McEntee, President of the American Federation of State, County and Municipal Employees, AFL-CIO, testified that "the vast majority of our contracts, even though we look upon them with great pride, really cover essentially maternity leave and not paternity leave." In addition, state leave laws often specified that catchall leave-without pay provisions could be used for extended maternity leave but did not authorize such leave for paternity purposes. *See,* e.g., Family and Medical Leave Act of 1987: Joint Hearing before the House Committee on Post Office and Civil Service. (Rep. Gary Ackerman recounted suffering expressly sex-based denial of unpaid leave of absence where the benefit was ostensibly available for "child care leave").

Evidence pertaining to parenting leave is relevant here because state discrimination in the provision of both types of benefits is based on the same gender stereotype: that women's family duties trump those of the workplace. Justice KENNEDY's dissent ignores this common foundation that, as Congress found, has historically produced discrimination in the hiring and promotion of women. Consideration of such evidence does not, as the dissent contends, expand our § 5 inquiry to include *general* gender-based stereotypes in employment." To the contrary, because parenting and family leave address very similar situations in which work and family responsibilities conflict, they implicate the same stereotypes.

Finally, Congress had evidence that, even where state laws and policies were not facially discriminatory, they were applied in discriminatory ways. It was aware of the "serious problems with the discretionary nature of family leave," because when "the authority to grant leave and to arrange the length of that leave rests with individual supervisors," it leaves "employees open to discretionary and possibly unequal treatment." H.R.REP. NO. 103-8, pt. 2, pp. 10–11 (1993). Testimony supported that conclusion, explaining that "[t]he lack of uniform parental and medical leave policies in the work place has created an environment where [sex] discrimination is rampant." 1987 Senate Labor Hearings, pt. 2 (testimony of Peggy Montes, Mayor's Commission on Women's Affairs, City of Chicago).

In spite of all of the above evidence, Justice KENNEDY argues in dissent that Congress' passage of the FMLA was unnecessary because "the States appear to have been ahead of Congress in providing gender-neutral family leave benefits," and points to Nevada's leave policies in particular. However, it was only "since Federal family leave legislation was first introduced" that the States had even "begun to consider family leave initiatives." S.REP. NO. 103-3, at 20; *see also* S.REP. No. 102-68 (1991) (minority views of Sen. Durenberger) ("So few states have elected to enact similar legislation at the state level").

Furthermore, the dissent's statement that some States "had adopted some form of family-care leave" before the FMLA's enactment glosses over important shortcomings of some state policies. First, seven States had childcare leave provisions that applied to women only. Indeed, Massachusetts required that notice of its leave provisions be posted only in "establishment[s] in which females are employed."[6] These laws reinforced the very stereotype that Congress sought to remedy through the FMLA. Second, 12 States provided their employees no family leave, beyond an initial childbirth or adoption, to care for a seriously ill child or family member. Third, many States provided no statutorily guaranteed right to family leave, offering instead only voluntary or discretionary leave programs. Three States left the amount of leave time primarily in employers' hands. Congress could reasonably conclude that such discretionary family-leave programs would do little to combat the stereotypes about the roles of male and female employees that Congress sought to eliminate. Finally, four States provided leave only through administrative regulations or personnel policies, which Congress could reasonably conclude offered significantly less firm protection

---

[6] [Massachussetts] (providing leave to "female employees" for childbirth or adoption); *see also,* [Colorado] (pregnancy disability leave only); Iowa (same); [Kansas] ("a reasonable period" of maternity leave for female employees only); [New Hampshire] (pregnancy disability leave only); [Louisiana] (repealed 1997) (4-month maternity leave for female employees only); [Tennessee] (same).

The dissent asserts that four of these schemes—those of Colorado, Iowa, Louisiana, and New Hampshire—concern "pregnancy disability leave only." But Louisiana provided women with four months of such leave, which far exceeds the medically recommended pregnancy disability leave period of six weeks. This gender-discriminatory policy is not attributable to any different physical needs of men and women, but rather to the invalid stereotypes that Congress sought to counter through the FMLA.

than a federal law. Against the above backdrop of limited state leave policies, . . . Congress was justified in enacting the FMLA as remedial legislation.

In sum, the States' record of unconstitutional participation in, and fostering of, gender-based discrimination in the administration of leave benefits is weighty enough to justify the enactment of prophylactic § 5 legislation.

We reached the opposite conclusion in *Garrett* and *Kimel* [528 U.S. 62 (2000)]. In those cases, the § 5 legislation under review responded to a purported tendency of state officials to make age- or disability-based distinctions. Under our equal protection case law, discrimination on the basis of such characteristics is not judged under a heightened review standard, and passes muster if there is "a rational basis for doing so at a class-based level, even if it 'is probably not true' that those reasons are valid in the majority of cases." *Kimel. See also Garrett* ("States are not required by the Fourteenth Amendment to make special accommodations for the disabled, so long as their actions toward such individuals are rational"). Thus, in order to impugn the constitutionality of state discrimination against the disabled or the elderly, Congress must identify, not just the existence of age- or disability-based stated decisions, but a "widespread pattern" of irrational reliance on such criteria. *Kimel.* We found no such showing with respect to the [Age Discrimination in Employment Act] and Title I of the Americans with Disabilities Act of 1990 (ADA).

Here, however, Congress directed its attention to state gender discrimination, which triggers a heightened level of scrutiny. Because the standard for demonstrating the constitutionality of a gender-based classification is more difficult to meet than our rational-basis test . . . it was easier for Congress to show a pattern of state constitutional violations . . . .

The impact of the discrimination targeted by the FMLA is significant. Congress determined:

"Historically, denial or curtailment of women's employment opportunities has been traceable directly to the pervasive presumption that women are mothers first, and workers second. This prevailing ideology about women's roles has in turn justified discrimination against women when they are mothers or mothers-to-be." Joint Hearing 100.

Stereotypes about women's domestic roles are reinforced by parallel stereotypes presuming a lack of domestic responsibilities for men. Because employers continued to regard the family as the women's domain, they often denied men similar accommodations or discouraged them from taking leave. These mutually reinforcing stereotypes created a self-fulfilling cycle of discrimination that forced women to continue to assume the role of primary family caregiver, and fostered employers' stereotypical views about women's commitment to work and their value as employees. Those perceptions, in turn, Congress reasoned, lead to subtle discrimination that may be difficult to detect on a case-by-case basis.

We believe that Congress' chosen remedy, the family-care leave provision of the FMLA, is "congruent and proportional to the targeted violation." *Garrett.* Congress had already tried unsuccessfully to address this problem through Title VII and the amendment of Title VII by the Pregnancy Discrimination Act, 42 U.S.C. § 2000e(k).

Here, . . . Congress again confronted a "difficult and intractable proble[m]," *Kimel*, where previous legislative attempts had failed. Such problems may justify added prophylactic measures in response.

By creating an across-the-board, routine employment benefit for all eligible employees, Congress sought to ensure that family-care leave would no longer be stigmatized as an inordinate drain on the workplace caused by female employees, and that employers could not evade leave obligations simply by hiring men. By setting a minimum standard of family leave for *all* eligible employees, irrespective of gender, the FMLA attacks the formerly state-sanctioned stereotype that only women are responsible for family caregiving, thereby reducing employers' incentives to engage in discrimination by basing hiring and promotion decisions on stereotypes. . . .

[W]e conclude that § 2612(a)(1)(C) is congruent and proportional to its remedial object, and can "be understood as responsive to, or designed to prevent, unconstitutional behavior." *City of Boerne*.

The judgment of the Court of Appeals is therefore AFFIRMED.

B. The European Court of Justice Analyzes the Problem of Pregnancy and Maternity: The 1976 Equal Treatment Directive and Its Loopholes Revisited

1. *Italy's Female-Only Paid Adoptive Leave*

Commission of the European Communities v. Italian Republic
(Court of Justice of the European Communities)
Case 163/82, 1983 E.C.R. 3273 (1983)

1   By application received at the Court Registry on 1 June 1982 the Commission of the European Communities brought an action under article 169 of the EEC Treaty for a declaration that the Italian Republic, by failing to adopt within the prescribed period the provisions necessary to comply with Council Directive 76/207 of 9 February 1976 on the implementation of the principle of equal treatment for men and women as regards . . . working conditions, had failed to fulfil its obligations under the Treaty.

2   Article[] 5 . . . of the directive . . . provide[s] as follows:

1. Application of the principle of equal treatment with regard to working conditions, including the conditions regarding dismissal, means that men and women shall be guaranteed the same conditions without discrimination on grounds of sex.
2. To this end, Member States shall take the measures necessary to ensure that:
(a) any laws, regulations and administrative provisions contrary to the principle of equal treatment shall be abolished. . . .

3   The Italian Republic adopted Law No. 903 of 9 December 1977 concerning equal treatment between men and women in relation to employment. Article 1 thereof provides that any discrimination on grounds of sex as regards access to employment, regardless of methods of selection and in any sector or branch of activity whatsoever, at all levels of occupational hierarchy, is prohibited. Such discrimina-

tion is likewise prohibited if it is applied on the basis of marital or family status or pregnancy, or indirectly through selection procedures or the press or through any other form of publicity indicating as a requirement of recruitment that a person shall be of a particular sex. The prohibition applies equally to activities undertaken in connection with vocational guidance, vocational training, advanced vocational training and retraining as regards both access to and the content of such activities.

4   Article 2 provides that women are to be entitled to the same remuneration as men for work which is the same or of the same value. Job classification systems for determining remuneration must apply the same criteria for men and women. . . .

5   Article 3 prohibits any discrimination between men and women as regards the assignment of grading, duties and career development. . . .

7   The Commission considers in the first place that the provisions of Law No. 903 do not transpose the provisions of Article 5 of the Directive into Italian law . . . in conformity with . . . the Directive. The law covers certain working conditions such as remuneration . . . and the right to take leave from work in the case of adoption, but it does not cover all working conditions in spite of the wider nature of the provision of Article 5 of the Directive.

8   The government of the Italian Republic replies that consideration of the provisions of the aforesaid Law No. 903 shows that discrimination based on sex is prohibited in relation to access to employment, vocational . . . [matters] (Article 1), remuneration . . . (Article 2), assignment of grading, duties and career development (Article 3), . . . and entitlement to leave in certain circumstances (Article 6).

9   It must be remembered that according to Article 189 of the [EEC] Treaty, a directive is binding as to the result to be achieved upon each Member State . . . but leaves to the national authorities the choice of form and methods. The Italian legislature cannot therefore be criticized for having adopted a number of specific provisions in relation to the most important working conditions and whilst confining itself in relation to other working conditions to a general provision . . . covering . . . all other working conditions not specifically mentioned, unless it is shown that the result sought by the Directive has not in fact been attained.

10   Since the Commission has not shown that those specific provisions combined with a general supplementing provision have left some areas of the scope of the Directive unprovided for, the Commission's first complaint cannot be upheld.

11   The Commission alleges in the second place that the Law of 1977 gives a mother who adopts a child of less than six years of age at the time of adoption the right to compulsory leave and the corresponding financial allowance during the first three months after the child enters the adoptive family and the right to leave for a certain period, without according the adoptive father similar rights. It is said that such different treatment amounts to discrimination in working conditions within the meaning of the directive.

12   Article 6 of Law No. 903 of 1977 provides that women who have adopted children or who have obtained custody thereof prior to adoption may claim the maternity leave referred to in Article 4 of [the 1971 Maternity Law] and the financial benefits relating thereto for the first three months after the child enters the adoptive family or the family which has been given custody of it, provided the child is not more

than six years of age at the time of the adoption or award of custody. The second paragraph of Article 6 adds that such women may also claim the leave provided for in the first paragraph of Article 7 of [the 1971 Maternity Law] for a period of one year from the actual entry of the child into the family provided that the child is not more than three years of age, and the right to the leave provided for in the second paragraph of Article 7.

13   Article 4 of [the 1971 Maternity Law] provides that women may not be employed:

(a) During the two months immediately preceding the expected date of confinement;

(b) If confinement takes place after that date, during the period between the expected date and the actual date of confinement;

(c) During the three months following confinement.

14   Article 7 of the same [1971 Maternity] law provides that during the child's first year the woman is entitled, after the above-mentioned maternity leave, to leave from work during a period of six months during which her job is to be kept for her (first paragraph). She is also entitled to leave when a child of less than three years of age is sick, upon submission of a medical certificate (second paragraph).

15   Article 7 of Law No. 903 of 1977 gives a working father the right to leave allowed by Article 7 of [the 1971 Maternity Law], even if he is a father by adoption or a guardian within the meaning of Article 314/20 of the Civil Code, in lieu of the working mother or where the care and custody of the children are given to the father.

16   However, the adoptive father does not have the right given the adoptive mother of maternity leave for the first three months following the actual entry of the child into the adoptive family. That distinction is justified, as the government of the Italian Republic rightly contends, by the legitimate concern to assimilate as far as possible the conditions of entry of the child into the adoptive family to those of the arrival of a newborn child in the family during the very delicate initial period. As regards leave from work after the initial period of three months the adoptive father has the same rights as the adoptive mother.

17   In those circumstances the difference in treatment criticized by the Commission cannot be regarded as discrimination within the meaning of the directive.

2. Germany's Female-Only Paid Parental Care Leave (for Infants Aged Three to Six Months)

Hofmann v. Barmer Ersatzkasse
(Court of Justice of the European Communities)
Case 184/83, 1984 E.C.R. 3047 (1984)

I—Facts and procedure

Paragraph 6(1) of the Gesetz zum Schutz der erwerbstätigen Mütter of 18 April 1968 (German Law for the Protection of Working Mothers, hereinafter referred to as the "[Working Mothers' Law]") provides that mothers are to enjoy a compulsory convalescence period of eight weeks' leave after childbirth. During that period they are relieved of all their duties at work and continue to receive their net remuneration, which is paid to them by the sickness fund and/or their employer.

By a Law of 25 June 1979, the German legislature inserted a new provision, Paragraph 8a, into the Mother's Law, under which a mother may, on the expiry of the period of convalescence provided for by Paragraph 6 (1) and until the day on which the child reaches the age of six months, take so-called "maternity leave". Throughout that leave the mother is relieved of her duties at work and the State, through the intermediary of the sickness fund, pays her a daily allowance not exceeding DM 25. On the expiry of her leave she enjoys a guaranteed right to resume her employment on the same conditions as before. . . .

Decision . . . .

2   . . . . Mr. Hoffman, the plaintiff . . . , is the father of an illegitimate child, of which he has acknowledged paternity. He obtained unpaid leave from his employer for the period between the expiry of the statutory protective period of eight weeks which was available to the mother and the day on which the child reached the age of six months; during that time he took care of the child while the mother continued her employment [as a teacher].

3   At the same time the plaintiff submitted to the Barmer Ersatzkasse [the sickness fund], the defendant . . . , a claim for payment, during the period of maternity leave provided for by paragraph 8a of the Mutterschutzgesetz [Working Mothers' Law], of an allowance pursuant to the combined provisions of paragraph 13 thereof and paragraph 200 (4) of the . . . (German Insurance Regulation).

4   The defendant refused the plaintiff's request, and his appeal against that refusal was also unsuccessful. . . .

5   The plaintiff appealed against that decision to the Landessozialgericht [Higher Social Court] Hamburg. . . .

6   . . . . The . . . [Higher Social Court] . . . referred . . . [a question] to the Court . . . :

1. Are Articles 1, 2 and 5 (1) of . . . [the Equal Treatment Directive] infringed if, on the expiry of the eight-week protective period for working mothers following childbirth, a period of leave which the state encourages by payment of the net remuneration of the person concerned, subject to a maximum of DM 25 per calendar day, and which lasts until the day on which the child reaches the age of six months can be claimed solely by working mothers and not, by way of alternative, if the parents so decide, by working fathers? . . . .

9   Under Paragraph 6 (1) of the [Working Mothers' Law], women may not be employed during the eight weeks which follow childbirth. According to Paragraph 8a of that Law, mothers are entitled to maternity leave from the end of the protective period provided for by Paragraph 6 (1) until the day on which the child attains the age of six months. The leave must be claimed by the mother at least four weeks prior

to the expiry of the protective period and is subject to the condition that the mother must have held employment for a period of, generally speaking, nine months before the birth. If the child dies during the period of leave, the leave is, as a general rule, terminated three weeks after the death. Under Paragraph 9a, the employer is forbidden to terminate the employment contract during the maternity leave and for a period of two months thereafter. Under Paragraph 13 of the Law, the mother receives an allowance from the State which is equal to her earnings, but subject to an upper limit of DM 25 per day, according to the provisions in force at the material time.

10   The plaintiff claims, essentially, that the main object of the disputed legislative provisions, in contrast with the protective period provided for by Paragraph 6, is not to give social protection to the mother on biological and medical grounds but rather to protect the child. The plaintiff draws that conclusion, on the one hand, from the *travaux préparatoires* relating to the Law introducing maternity leave and, on the other hand, from certain objective characteristics of the Law. He draws particular attention to three characteristics:

(i)   The fact that the leave is withdrawn in the event of the child's death, which demonstrates that the leave was created in the interests of the child and not the mother;

(ii)   The optional nature of the leave, which means that it cannot be said to have been introduced to meet imperative biological or medical needs;

(iii)   Lastly, the requirement that the woman should have been employed for a minimum period prior to childbirth; this indicates that it was not considered necessary to grant the leave in the interests of the mother, otherwise it ought to have been extended to all women in employment irrespective of the date on which their employment commenced.

11   According to the plaintiff, the protection of the mother against the multiplicity of burdens imposed by motherhood and her employment could be achieved by non-discriminatory measures such as enabling the father to enjoy the leave or creating a period of parental leave, so as to release the mother from the responsibility of caring for the child and thereby allow her to resume employment as soon as the statutory protective period had expired. The plaintiff further claims that the choice between the options thereby created should, in conformity with the principle of non-discrimination between the sexes, be left completely at the discretion of the parents of the child. . . .

14   The Government of the Federal Republic of Germany . . . argues that legal protection afforded to the mother by the disputed legislation aims to reduce the conflict between a woman's role as a mother and her role as a wage-earner, in order to preserve her health and that of the child. It admits that there are differing views on the length of time for which a woman should enjoy special treatment following pregnancy and childbirth, but it argues that the period in question, although varying from woman to woman, extends considerably beyond the end of the statutory eight-week period of protection laid down by the Law. Hence the creation of maternity leave is justified for reasons which are connected with a woman's biological characteristics, since its aim is to avoid placing the mother, on expiry of the statutory protective

period, under an obligation to decide whether or not to resume her employment. Indeed, experience and statistics demonstrate that a considerable number of working women were compelled, under earlier legislation, to give up their employment as a result of motherhood.

15   In reply to the arguments put forward in particular by the plaintiff . . . , the . . . [German Government] maintains that maternity leave under German legislation constitutes an uninterrupted continuation of the protection given to a mother beyond the end of the protective period provided for by Paragraph 6 (1) of the [Working Mothers' Law]. The withdrawal of the leave in the event of the child's death is justified by the fact that its death puts an end to the multiplicity of burdens borne by the woman as a result of motherhood and her employment. The fact that the leave is optional and may be claimed by the mother is consistent with its objective, namely to enable the woman to choose freely, in the light of her physical condition and of other family and social factors, the solution which is better suited to her personal circumstances; by virtue of that provision the purpose of the leave, namely, to protect the mother, may be better achieved than by the adoption of other solutions, such as the grant of leave to the father or the assumption by other members of the family of responsibility for looking after the child. Finally, the provision which makes the grant of leave subject to the prerequisite that the mother shall have been in employment for a minimum period prior to giving birth is explained by the concern to avoid abuses whereby expectant mothers take up employment during pregnancy for the purpose of enjoying leave and the pecuniary benefits attaching to it. . . .

18   The directive is designed to implement the principle of equal treatment for men and women as regards *inter alia* "working conditions," with a view to attaining the social policy aims of the EEC Treaty to which the third recital in the preamble to the directive refers.

19   To that end, Article 1 defines "the principle of equal treatment" as meaning that the directive seeks to put into effect in the Member States the principle of equal treatment for men and women as regards access to employment, promotion, vocational training, and working conditions. According to Article 2 (1), the principle of equal treatment means "that there shall be no discrimination whatsoever on grounds of sex either directly or indirectly by reference in particular to marital or family status." Under Article 5 (1), application of the principle of equal treatment with regard to working conditions "means that men and women shall be guaranteed the same conditions without discrimination on grounds of sex;" paragraph (2) of the Article requires Member States to abolish any laws, regulations, and administrative provisions contrary to the principle of equal treatment and to amend those which conflict with the principle "when the concern for protection which originally inspired them is no longer well founded."

20   Paragraphs (2), (3), and (4) of Article 2 indicate, in various respects, the limits of the principle of equal treatment laid down by the directive. . . .

22   Paragraph (3) makes the following provision: "This directive shall be without prejudice to provisions concerning the protection of women, particularly as regards pregnancy and maternity."

23   Reference should also be made in the present context to paragraph (4), according to which the directive is to be without prejudice to measures to promote equal opportunity for men and women, "by removing existing inequalities which affect women's opportunities in the areas referred to in Article 1 (1)", that is to say, as regards access to employment, promotion and other working conditions.

24   It is apparent from the above analysis that the directive is not designed to settle questions concerned with the organisation of the family, or to alter the division of responsibility between parents.

25   It should further be added, with particular reference to paragraph (3), that, by reserving to Member States the right to retain or introduce provisions which are intended to protect women in connection with "pregnancy and maternity", the directive recognises the legitimacy, in terms of the principle of equal treatment, of protecting a woman's needs in two respects. First, it is legitimate to ensure the protection of a woman's biological condition during pregnancy and thereafter until such time as her physiological and mental functions have returned to normal after childbirth; secondly, it is legitimate to protect the special relationship between a woman and her child over the period which follows pregnancy and childbirth, by preventing that relationship from being disturbed by the multiple burdens which would result from the simultaneous pursuit of employment.

26   In principle, therefore, a measure such as maternity leave granted to a woman on expiry of the statutory protective period falls within the scope of Article 2 (3) of Directive 76/207, inasmuch as it seeks to protect a woman in connection with the effects of pregnancy and motherhood. That being so, such leave may legitimately be reserved to the mother to the exclusion of any other person, in view of the fact that it is only the mother who may find herself subject to undesirable pressures to return to work prematurely.

27   Furthermore, it should be pointed out that the directive leaves Member States with a discretion as to the social measures which they adopt in order to guarantee, within the framework laid down by the directive, the protection of women in connection with pregnancy and maternity and to offset the disadvantages which women, by comparison with men, suffer with regard to the retention of employment. Such measures are . . . closely linked to the general system of social protection in the various Member States. It must therefore be concluded that the Member States enjoy a reasonable margin of discretion as regards both the nature of the protective measures and the detailed arrangements for their implementation.

28   It follows from the foregoing that the reply to be given to the question submitted by the [Higher Social Court] Hamburg is that Articles 1, 2, and 5 (1) of Council Directive 76/207 must be interpreted as meaning that a Member State may, after the statutory protective period has expired, grant to mothers a period of maternity leave which the State encourages them to take by the payment of an allowance. The directive does not impose on Member States a requirement that they shall, as an alternative, allow such leave to be granted to fathers, even where the parents so decide.

3. France's Special Breaks for Working Mothers

Commission of the European Communities v. France
(Court of Justice of the European Communities)
Case 312/86, 1988 E.C.R. 6315 (1988)

1   By an application lodged at the Court Registry on 12 December 1986, the Commission of the European Communities brought proceedings pursuant to Article 169 of the EEC Treaty for a declaration that by failing to adopt within the prescribed period all the measures necessary to secure the full and precise implementation of Council Directive 76/207 of 9 February 1976 on the implementation of the principle of equal treatment for men and women as regards access to employment, vocational training and promotion, and working conditions, the French Republic has failed to fulfil its obligations under the Treaty.

2   Article 5 (2) (b) of Directive 76/207 . . . provides that Member States are to take the measures necessary to ensure that "any provisions contrary to the principle of equal treatment which are included in collective agreements . . . shall be, or may be declared, null and void or may be amended." Article 9 of the directive provides that Member States are to put into force the laws, regulations and administrative provisions necessary in order to comply with the directive within 30 months of its notification. For France, that period came to an end on 12 August 1978.

3   With a view to ensuring the application of the directive in France, Law No 83-635 of 13 July 1983 amending the Labour Code and the Criminal Code as regards equality at work between women and men was brought into force. Article 1 of that law redrafted Article L 123-2 of the Labour Code to provide that any term reserving the benefit of any measure to employees on grounds of sex included in any collective labour agreement shall be void, except where such a clause is intended to implement the provisions relating to pregnancy, nursing or pre-natal and post-natal rest.

4   The first paragraph of Article 19 of that law provides, however, that the above-mentioned provision in the Labour Code does not prohibit the application of usages, terms of contracts of employment or collective agreements in force on the date on which the law was promulgated granting special rights to women. The second paragraph of that article provides that employers, groups of employers and groups of employed persons "shall proceed, by collective negotiation, to bring such terms into conformity" with the provisions of the Labour Code mentioned in the law.

5   The Commission considers that the derogation to the scheme of Law No 83-635 embodied in Article 19 of that law shows that the French authorities have failed to observe their obligations under the directive. The French Government, on the other hand, maintains that the derogation is compatible with the provisions of the directive. . . .

7   The French Government's defence is based essentially on two arguments. It maintains, first, that the special rights for women safeguarded by Article 19 of French Law No 83-635 derive from a concern to protect women and ensure their effective equality with men, and that they do not therefore give rise to discriminatory working

conditions. Secondly, it claims that the machinery prescribed for the revision of clauses relating to special rights for women complies with the directive and that it constitutes the only appropriate method in the context of French labour law. Those arguments must each be considered in turn.

Special Rights for Women

8   According to the Commission, which has not been contradicted on this point by the French Government, special rights for women included in collective agreements relate in particular to: the extension of maternity leave; the shortening of working hours, for example for women over 59 years of age; the advancement of the retirement age; the obtaining of leave when a child is ill; the granting of additional days of annual leave in respect of each child; the granting of one day's leave at the beginning of the school year; the granting of time off work on Mothers' Day; daily breaks for women working on keyboard equipment or employed as typists or switchboard operators; the granting of extra points for pension rights in respect of the second and subsequent children; and the payment of an allowance to mothers who have to meet the cost of nurseries or child-minders.

9   The Commission considers that some of those special rights may be covered by the exceptions to the application of the directive provided for in Article 2 (3) and (4) thereof which involve, respectively, provisions concerning the protection of women, particularly as regards pregnancy and maternity, and measures to promote equal opportunity for men and women. It is of the opinion, however, that the French legislation, by its generality, makes it possible to preserve for an indefinite period measures discriminating as between men and women contrary to the directive.

10   The French Government observes first that, under French constitutional law, the law must ensure that women have rights equal to those of men in every field. The existence of special rights favouring women is nevertheless considered compatible with the principle of equality when those special rights derive from a concern for protection. The French Government considers that the directive should be interpreted in the same manner, and that such an approach is supported by the provisions of Article 2 (3) and (4) of the directive.

11   The French Government further considers that neither the directive nor the principle of equal treatment for men and women is intended to modify the organization of the family or the responsibilities actually assumed by the marriage partners. It claims that the special rights for women provided for in collective agreements are designed to take account of the situation existing in the majority of French households. Member States, moreover, have a degree of discretion in that regard when implementing the directive.

12   It must be borne in mind that the principle of equal treatment which is to be implemented, under Article 5 (2) (b) of the directive, with regard to collective labour agreements means, in the words of Article 2 (1) of the directive, that "there shall be no discrimination whatsoever on grounds of sex." Article 2 (3) and (4) provides that the directive is to be without prejudice either to provisions concerning the protection

of women, particularly as regards pregnancy and maternity, or to measures to promote equal opportunity for men and women, in particular by removing existing inequalities which affect women's opportunities in the areas referred to in the directive.

13   The exception provided for in Article 2 (3) refers in particular to the situations of pregnancy and maternity. In its judgment of 12 July 1984 in Case 184/83 (*Hofmann v. Barmer Ersatzkasse* [1984] ECR 3047), the Court held that the protection of women in relation to maternity is designed to protect the special relationship between a woman and her child over the period which follows pregnancy and childbirth, by preventing that relationship from being disturbed by the multiple burdens which would result from the simultaneous pursuit of employment.

14   It must be concluded, both from the generality of the terms used in the French legislation, which allows any clause providing "special rights for women" to remain in force, and from the examples of such special rights which have been cited in the pleadings, that the contested provisions cannot find justification in Article 2 (3). As some of those examples show, some of the special rights preserved relate to the protection of women in their capacity as older workers or parents—categories to which both men and women may equally belong.

15   The exception provided for in Article 2 (4) is specifically and exclusively designed to allow measures which, although discriminatory in appearance, are in fact intended to eliminate or reduce actual instances of inequality which may exist in the reality of social life. Nothing in the papers of the case, however, makes it possible to conclude that a generalized preservation of special rights for women in collective agreements may correspond to the situation envisaged in that provision.

16   The French Government has therefore not succeeded in demonstrating that the unequal treatment which forms the subject-matter of this application, and which it acknowledges, falls within the limits laid down by the directive.

Collective Negotiation

17   The Commission alleges that the second paragraph of Article 19 of French Law No 83-635, cited above, authorizes the maintenance of discriminatory conditions for an indeterminate period and leaves their removal to the discretion of the two sides of industry. The law does not provide for any machinery capable of remedying any inadequacy of the results achieved by collective negotiation.

18   The French Government maintains, first of all, that it would be difficult in the circumstances of French society to provide for the immediate removal by legislative act of rights acquired during past negotiations between the two sides of industry. Collective negotiation is the most appropriate means of ensuring that the clauses concerned are made to conform with the principle of equal treatment, being more likely than a legislative measure to influence the behaviour in practice of those involved and thus bring any discrimination to an end.

19   Secondly, the French Government points out that under French labour law national collective agreements for particular occupations are subject to an approval procedure which enables the agreement to be extended to the whole of the field of

activity concerned. That procedure can be used to ensure that discriminatory measures do not survive.

20   At the Court's request, the French Government has provided information on the extent to which, in practice, collective agreements have been renegotiated in the light of the second paragraph of Article 19 of Law No 83-635. That information shows that 16 collective agreements, 11 of them national, were renegotiated on that basis between 1983 and 1987. Such figures are extremely modest when compared with the number of collective agreements entered into each year in France (in 1983 there were 1,050 agreements covering different occupations and 2,400 applying to individual undertakings). The requirement that collective agreements must be approved and the possibility that they may be extended by the public authorities have therefore not led to a rapid process of renegotiation.

21   The French Government's argument that collective negotiation is the only appropriate method of abolishing the special rights in question must be considered in the light of that conclusion.

22   In that regard, it is enough to observe that, even if that argument were to be accepted, it could not be used to justify national legislation which, several years after the expiry of the period prescribed for the implementation of the directive, makes the two sides of industry responsible for removing certain instances of inequality without laying down any time-limit for compliance with that obligation.

23   It follows from those considerations that the French Government's argument that the task of removing special rights for women should be left to the two sides of industry working through collective negotiation cannot be accepted.

24   It must be therefore be held that by failing to adopt within the prescribed period all the measures necessary to secure the full implementation of Directive 76/207 the French Republic has failed to fulfil its obligations under the Treaty.

NOTES

The Effect of the 2002 Amendment on the ECJ Decisions. Review the Consolidated Equal Treatment Directive—that is, the 1976 ETD as amended by the 2002 ETD—*available at* RossRights. Would any of the ECJ decisions concerning leave policies in Italy, Germany, and France be decided differently under the 2002 amendments?

A Side Glance at U.S. Law. How would each of the cases be decided under U.S. law? Consider the impact of the Equal Protection Clause in the Constitution's Fourteenth Amendment, Title VII, the Pregnancy Discrimination Act, and the FMLA.

4. Case Study: Poland's Special Protection for Mothers

Assume you are a member of the board of directors of Women's Rights for All in Poland (WRAP), a grass-roots advocacy group based in Cracow with several thousand members throughout Poland. Assume that the Chairman of the Labor Committee of the upper house of Parliament has released the following press release:

The economic dislocation that our country has faced since the fall of Communism in 1989 has fallen particularly heavily on women. The introduction of market reforms and the loss of state-subsidized day care has had a devastating effect on working women, whose unemployment rate is now twice that of men, and whose average real incomes have plummeted from 90% of men's to less than 50%.

Moreover, notwithstanding the reforms in abortion and birth control law initiated at the urging of the Catholic Church in the last five years, the birth rate has plummeted and will soon fall below replacement levels if nothing is done. We want to make it possible for young people to have families again.

Accordingly, in order to help working women, to compensate for the economic dislocation they have faced, and to accelerate the *de facto* equality of women, we are introducing today a bill that would:

(1) guarantee every working woman six weeks of paid leave, and up to one year's unpaid leave with reinstatement after the birth of a child or to care for a seriously ill child;
(2) ensure the grant of bonuses to women from the birth of a second child for calculating pensions, with the result of increasing their pension payments upon retirement;
(3) payment of allowances to compensate mothers who have to pay the costs of nursery or child minders.

A. What should your organization's policy stance be with regard to the bill?

B. Suppose the bill passes, and your organization decides to challenge it. Will you challenge the legislation in Poland's domestic courts? Why or why not? Assuming you decide to seek a domestic remedy, what international legal arguments will you assert in court?

C. Does the bill violate international law? Why or why not? Consider specific provisions and language of relevant treaties.

D. Consider the advantages and disadvantages of challenging the legislation before the European Court of Human Rights, the European Court of Justice, the Human Rights Committee and the CEDAW Committee. Will you file complaints with all four bodies? Assuming you decide to bring a case in only one forum, which one would you choose and why?

Chapter 9
CEDAW in Practice

I. Egypt as Case Study: CEDAW's Effectiveness in Addressing the Subordination of Women in Marriage

A. Women's Human Rights in Egypt: An Overview

U.S. DEPARTMENT OF STATE, BUREAU OF DEMOCRACY, HUMAN RIGHTS, AND LABOR, COUNTRY
    REPORTS ON HUMAN RIGHTS PRACTICES FOR 2006: EGYPT
(released March 6, 2007), *available at* RossRights

The constitution provides for equality of the sexes . . . ; however, aspects of the law and many traditional practices discriminated against women. . . .

Women

The law does not prohibit spousal abuse; however, provisions of law relating to assault in general are applied. Domestic violence against women was a significant problem and was reflected in press accounts of specific incidents. According to a 2003 survey by the Center for Egyptian Women's Legal Affairs, an estimated 67 percent of women in urban areas and 30 percent in rural areas had been involved in some form of domestic violence at least once between 2002 and 2003. Among those who had been beaten, less than half had ever sought help. The 2005 Egypt Demographic and Health Survey indicated that 47.4 percent of women above age 14 had experienced domestic violence. Due to the value attached to privacy in the country's traditional society, abuse within the family rarely was discussed publicly. Spousal abuse is grounds for a divorce. However, the law requires the plaintiff to produce several eyewitnesses, a difficult condition to meet. Several NGOs offered counseling, legal aid, and other services to women who were victims of domestic violence.

The Ministry of Social Solidarity operated more than 150 family counseling bureaus nationwide, which provided legal and medical services. . . .

The National Council for Women proposed and advocated policies that promoted women's empowerment and also designed development programs that benefit women. The Office of the National Ombudsman for Women provided assistance to women facing discrimination in employment and housing, domestic violence, sexual assault, and child custody disputes.

The law prohibits non-spousal rape and punishment ranges from three years to life imprisonment; however, spousal rape is not illegal. Although reliable statistics regarding rape were not available, activists believed that it was not uncommon, despite strong social disapproval. A rapist, if also convicted of abducting his victim, is subject to execution. . . .

The law does not specifically address "honor" crimes (violent assaults by a male against a female, usually a family member, with intent to kill because of perceived lack of chastity). In practice, the courts sentenced perpetrators of such crimes to lesser punishments than those convicted in other cases of murder. There were no reliable statistics regarding the extent of honor killings; however, there were no reports indicating that honor killings were a widespread problem.

Female genital mutilation (FGM) remained a serious, widespread problem, despite the government's attempts to eliminate the practice and NGO efforts to combat it. Traditional and family pressures continued to play a leading role in the persistence of FGM. In 2005 a leading NGO reported that the percentage of women who had undergone FGM had fallen to 94 percent of all women age 18–49. The same study estimated that 60 percent of girls age 10–13 were at risk for FGM. The Ministry of Health estimated that 50 percent of girls age 10 to 18 were subjected to FGM. The 2005 Egypt Demographic and Health Survey, however, indicated that 95.8 percent of ever-married women were subjected to FGM. The government supported efforts to educate the public about FGM; however, illiteracy impeded some women from distinguishing between the deep-rooted tradition of FGM and religious practices. Moreover, many citizens believed that FGM was an important part of maintaining female chastity. FGM was equally prevalent among Muslims and Christians. In late November [2006], the three leading government-appointed Muslim religious leaders, participating in a conference in Cairo aimed at eradicating FGM . . . said that FGM is not encouraged by Islam. The . . . [three leaders] expressed the view that FGM was not condoned by the Holy Quran or by the teachings and traditions of the Prophet Muhammad. . . .

Prostitution and sex tourism are illegal but continued to occur, particularly in Cairo and Alexandria.

Sexual harassment is not prohibited specifically by law. There were no statistics available regarding its prevalence. . . .

By law, unmarried women under the age of 21 must have permission from their fathers to obtain passports and to travel. Married women do not require such permission, but police did not apply the law consistently. A woman's testimony is equal to that of a man in court. Under the Penal Code, a married man is adulterous only if the sexual act is committed in the marital home (Article 277) while a woman is adulterous wherever the act is committed.

While no law prohibits a woman from serving as a judge, there was only one female judge . . . appointed to the Supreme Constitutional Court in 2003. In the case of two female attorneys . . . who had challenged the government's refusal to appoint them as public prosecutors, the administrative court ruled that it had no jurisdiction and referred the case to the Supreme Judicial Council for determination. By year's end [2006], the . . . Council had not ruled in the case.

Laws affecting marriage and personal status generally corresponded to an individual's religion. *Khul'* divorce allows a Muslim woman to obtain a divorce without her husband's consent, provided that she is willing to forego all of her financial rights, including alimony, dowry, and other benefits. However, in practice, some judges have not applied the law accurately or fairly, causing lengthy bureaucratic delays for the thousands of women who have filed for *khul'* divorce. Many women have also complained that after being granted *khul'* divorce, their ex-husbands have been able to avoid paying required child support.

The Coptic Orthodox Church permits divorce only in specific circumstances, such as adultery or conversion of one spouse to another religion.

Muslim female heirs receive half the amount of a male heir's inheritance, while Christian widows of Muslims have no inheritance rights. A sole female heir receives half her parents' estate; the balance goes to designated male relatives. A sole male heir inherits all of his parents' property. Male Muslim heirs face strong social pressure to provide for all family members who require assistance; however, in practice this assistance was not always provided. Labor laws provide for equal rates of pay for equal work for men and women in the public sector. According to government figures from 2003, women constituted 17 percent of private business owners and occupied 25 percent of the managerial positions in the four major national banks. Educated women had employment opportunities, but social pressure against women pursuing a career was strong. Women's rights advocates claimed that Islamist influence inhibited further gains. Women's rights advocates also pointed to other discriminatory traditional or cultural attitudes and practices, such as FGM and the traditional male relative's role in enforcing chastity.

A number of active women's rights groups worked to reform family law, educate women on their legal rights, promote literacy, and combat FGM.

Children. . . .

[I]n practice, the government made some progress in eliminating FGM and in according rights to children with foreign fathers. . . .

Although reliable data is missing, several NGOs . . . reported that child marriages, including temporary marriages intended to mask prostitution, are a significant problem.

NOTES

U.S. State Department Human Rights Reports. Every year, the Department issues a world-wide human rights report. Advocates can turn to it for a brief synopsis of leading issues in any country. While the Department's initial reporting on women's human rights was cursory, it now covers a broader range of issues including discriminatory family law provisions. Notice, however, that the report does not describe the content of Egypt's marriage law.

Progress Since 1993? Based on the 2006 Egypt State Department Report, how does Egypt violate CEDAW (quoted in Chapter One)? Compare Egypt's current law concerning women's status as legal professionals to that reported over a decade earlier:

Egypt's prosecutor general, Ragaa Arabi, whose post is akin to that of U.S. attorney general, wiped one hand against the other and replied, "None," when asked how many female prosecutors are on his staff.

Arabi noted that "the law forbids a woman from being a judge or a general prosecutor" and added that a prosecutor's work "is extremely difficult for a woman . . . since a prosecutor goes to many villages and does a lot of traveling."

The all-male staff also "could have something to do with our Eastern mentality," he said, "and our religion, [which makes] us look at women as someone who cannot face the physical difficulties of men—difficulties like fatigue and severe stress. We look at the woman as a rare object."

Does he think his job is so difficult that a woman could not do it, Arabi was asked during an interview at his office in downtown Cairo. "I'm convinced she could not!" he replied with a smile.[A]

B. Egypt's Personal Status Laws:[B] Marriage, Polygamy, and Divorce

In countries with different family law rules for different religions or ethnic groups, personal status laws govern marriage, divorce, and inheritance rights for each group. Recall, for example, that Afghanistan Islamic law permits a man, but not a woman, to be married to several spouses at the same time. It also allows a man to divorce his wife for no reason and without going to court, while permitting divorce for a woman only for very limited reasons, and only if she goes to court. Finally, it gave a woman one-half of a man's share of inheritance. Egypt has similar rules, although it has made some changes in recent years. The excerpts that follow describe the history and content of Egyptian personal status law.

Dawoud Sudqi El Alami & Doreen Hinchcliffe, Islamic Marriage and Divorce Laws of the Arab World
51–52 (1996)

Egypt started to codify its law of personal status in the early part of this century, when the Egyptian government commissioned the then Minister of Justice, Muham-

---

[A] Caryle Murphy, *Lowering the Veil: Muslim Women Struggle for Careers in a Society Ruled by Men and Religion*, Wash. Post, Feb. 17, 1993, at A1.

[B] According to the Egyptian Court of Cassation, personal status is defined as "the sum total of the physical or family descriptions of a known person which distinguish him from the others, and gives legal effects under the law in his social life, such as being male or female, married, widowed or divorced, a parent or a legitimate child, being of full legal capacity or defective capacity due to minority. . . ." Civil Cassation on 21/6/1934, Appeal No. 40J, *quoted in* Jamal J. Nasir, 23 Arab and Islamic Laws Series: The Islamic Law of Personal Status 34 (3d ed. 2002).

mad Qadri Pasha, to compile formal provisions concerning personal status, with a view to creating a codified personal status law. Qadri Pasha's *Shari'a Provisions on Personal Status*, essentially a codification of Hanafi opinion, was published as a book in 1917, but was never enacted, due to the government's hesitance to take such a radical step. It has remained, however, a most important reference work and is used in the Egyptian courts and in the courts of many other Arab states. . . .

The most important of the laws, which were issued at different times dealing with specific issues of personal status, are Law No. 25 of 1920 Concerning Provisions on Maintenance and Certain Matters of Personal Status, and Draft Law No. 25 of 1929 Concerning Certain Provisions on Personal Status.

The law of 1929 made certain amendments to the law of 1920, and both were amended much later by Law No. 100 of 1985. This was issued as a consequence of controversy over the issuing of an earlier law. In 1979 a Presidential decree had been issued promulgating Law No. 44 of 1979, amending certain provisions of the laws of personal status, without reference to the Popular Assembly (*majlis al-sha'b*). This law was widely contested on grounds of unconstitutionality, as no circumstance had occurred which fulfilled the condition of Article 147 of the Constitution which allows the President of the Republic to introduce exceptional legislation, and the matter was transferred as a whole to the High Constitutional Court (*Al-Mahkama al-Dusturiyya al-Ulya*).

At a session on 4 May 1985 the Court issued its ruling that Law No. 44 of 1979 was unconstitutional. There had for some time been a movement to amend the personal status laws, which had remained unaltered despite social changes. Some members of the Popular Assembly proposed a draft law amending the laws of personal status, which was examined and confirmed by the Assembly during June and July 1985. The resulting Law No. 100 of 1985 revised and replaced certain provisions of the laws of personal status, including provisions in the areas of *ta'a* (obedience), registration of divorce, *mut'a* (compensation to a divorced woman), maintenance for the wife and custody.

Egypt Law No. 100 amending certain clauses in the Law of personal status, 1 July 1985

12 ANNUAL REVIEW OF POPULATION LAW 66 (Reed Boland & Jan Stepan eds., 1985)

[The following excerpt is a summary of the text of the law written by the editors of the Annual Review. The full text of the law is at *id.* at 335–38.]

This [1985] Law on personal status was passed after the Constitutional Court ruled unconstitutional Decree Law No. 44 of 1979 on personal status. While the new Law returns to the teachings of the Sharia for its provisions relating to traditional grounds for divorce and to allocation of support, it nonetheless attempts to retain some of the provisions of the 1979 Decree-Law that strengthened the position of divorced women and their children. It requires that the official act of marriage contain a statement about the social condition of the husband including the names and addresses of all his spouses; such spouses are to be informed if the husband remarries. It also requires a husband who repudiates his wife to register the repudiation, notice of which is to be given to the wife by the official who is in charge of the registry. As under the 1979 Law, a wife under the new Law may demand within one year a divorce if her husband takes another wife. However, unlike the 1979 Law, the new Law allows a wife to obtain a divorce on this ground only if a judge is satisfied that as a result of her husband's remarriage she has endured financial or psychological harm. Previous to making such a ruling a judge must direct the parties to attempt a reconciliation. The new Law also retains the following provisions of the 1979 Law relating to custody and to support not controlled by rules of the Sharia: a) it grants a mother custody of her male children until age ten and female children until age twelve; in addition a judge may extend custody to age fifteen for males and the age of marriage for girls; b) it gives a mother a right to remain in the marital home until the end of her guardianship over her children and in fact strengthens the provisions of the 1979 Law by including all housing in the definition of marital home; c) it prohibits a husband from deducting from support payments any debts that his wife may owe him; d) it requires a father to support his male children until age fifteen and his female children until the age of marriage or the time at which they are capable of caring for themselves; and e) it prohibits any interruption in support payments due children.

Dawoud Sudqi El Alami, The Marriage Contract in Islamic Law in the Shari'ah and Personal Status Laws of Egypt and Morocco
129–35 (1992)

9.29: *Egyptian law with regard to polygamy—equity and harm due to polygamy*

Polygamy has passed through several stages under Egyptian law. . . .
   The position of the Egyptian judiciary in respect of harm necessitating divorce as a result of polygamy may be illustrated by the following cases.

9.30: *Case concerning divorce on grounds of harm due to polygamy*

Illustrating the position of the judiciary as regards cases which arose under Law 44 of 1979 [declared unconstitutional in 1985].
   The appellant [wife] had brought *Case No. 478/1984 Personal Status, Gizah/*seeking a ruling to obtain an irrevocable divorce from her husband on the grounds of harm, as the appellee (the husband) had married another woman without her knowledge, thus causing her excessive material and moral harm. The Court of the First Instance, however, ruled to reject the case and obliged the appellant [wife] to pay costs. The ruling prejudiced the rights of the appellant and as such she appealed for the following reasons:
   Insufficient grounds for the ruling, as it was based on the material and moral harm caused by her husband taking another wife since the other wife shared his limited income with her and she had seven of his children, all of whom were in school and

needed a great deal of money spent on them. In addition, the fact that he had taken another wife led to him being absent from the home of the appellant wife and her children for long periods of time. The moral harm suffered by the appellant wife was inestimable as she suffered psychological injury as the result of there being another wife in addition to herself.

Furthermore, the Court did not examine the appellant's witnesses. In the session held on 9th February 1986, the appellant asked the Court to hear her witnesses in order to establish the material and moral harm which she had suffered as a result of the appellee having married another woman without her knowledge. The Court, however, did not respond to her request and the appellee (the husband) claimed that the wife was unable to prove her allegations. The Court listened to him although the wife's witnesses, who were relatives and neighbours of the husband himself, knew perfectly well that he had maltreated, beaten and abused the appellant. The minutes of the police and the prosecution contained details of such fights which made it impossible for them to continue living together. The Court of the First Instance, however, did not allow this evidence.

[The wife appealed]. . . .

The Ruling

The [Appellate] Court ruled to accept the appeal in form and reject it in content. It supported the initial ruling and obliged the appellant [wife] to pay the costs of both litigants.

[The wife had filed for divorce under the 1979 law, which allowed for divorce if the husband took another wife. Since that law was declared unconstitutional on May 4, 1985, the Court of Appeal concluded that the law to be applied was the pre-1979 *Shari'ah* based law, which "included nothing in respect of a husband taking another wife." Accordingly, she could not get a divorce under the 1979 law. Nor, the Court held, could she get a divorce under the 1985 law, since that law went into effect on May 16, 1985, and the husband had taken his second wife in 1983].

9.31: *Case concerning divorce on grounds of harm due to polygamy*

Illustrating the position of the Egyptian judiciary as regards cases arising under Law 100 of 1985, particularly Article 11a appended to this Law.

The facts of the case

An appeal against the ruling issued in the session held on 29th December 1987 by the Court of the First Instance, Cairo South, regarding *Case No. 98/1985 Personal Status, Cairo South.* A summary of the facts of the case is that the appellee [wife] had brought Case No. 98/1985 seeking a ruling to obtain an irrevocable divorce on the grounds of harm. She stated in explanation of her case that she was his lawful wife under a *Shari'ah* contract and that the marriage had been consummated and they lived together as man and wife. She was still his wife when he had married another woman, and furthermore, he had not provided for her financially and had expelled her from the marital home, thus constituting harm which made it impossible for them to continue living together. She had the right to demand a separation in accordance with the provision of Article 6 of Law 25 of 1929. On 29th December 1987 the Court of the First Instance had ruled that the appellee [wife] could obtain an irrevocable divorce and had based its ruling on statements made by the appellee's witnesses to the [e]ffect that the appellant had taken another wife and that the appellee had suffered harm as a result. The Court was unable to effect a reconciliation, and the appellant had indicated his dissatisfaction with the ruling by lodging a writ with the Clerks' Office of this Court (Court of Appeal).

After discussion of this case before the Court and submission by the appellant of a memorandum in which he requested that the appeal to quash the ruling be accepted in form and content because the appellee was unable to prove her case, and after submission by the appellee of a memorandum dated 21st May 1988 which concluded by seeking a ruling to accept the appeal in form and [not in] content, the Court ruled to accept the appeal in form and reject it in content, thus supporting the initial ruling [for the wife], and obliged the appellant [husband] to pay costs. Its ruling was based on the following reasons[:]

Article 11a appended under Law 100 of 1985 to Law 25 of 1929 stipulated that if a husband took another wife, the first wife in the case of harm could request a divorce within a year of the date of her learning of the marriage. If the Court failed to reconcile them, the judge could then grant her an irrevocable divorce, and since the Court was reassured by the statements of the wife's witnesses that she had suffered harm as a result of this marriage it concluded by issuing the said ruling.

Law 25 of 1929, amended by Law 100 of 1985[,] took a great step forward in restricting polygamy and gave special precedence to the first wife, giving her the right to seek divorce where harm was caused to her by the second marriage and putting the burden of proof on the husband if he claimed that she had consented to the new marriage.

In a [different] case in the Court of Cassation a ruling of the Appeal Court was challenged by the contestant who claimed that the decision was based on inadequate reasons and irregularity of evidence in that the said decision was based on lack of consent by the wife to the second marriage and the contestant did not produce any evidence of the wife's consent. The Court of Cassation rejected the contestation of the ruling on the basis that the text of the Article relating to this subject sets down a legal principle for the benefit of the woman, establishing that the husband's taking of a second wife without her consent is considered harm, without any need on her part to prove harm. The challenged ruling had applied this principle and was thus legally correct.

NOTES

The First Wife's Concerns. Why did each first wife seek a divorce?

The Evolution of Egyptian Law Concerning Polygamy. What rights did the first wife have before 1979? In the interval between the new 1979 law and the High Constitutional Court decision in 1985? After the 1985 law was enacted? Under the 1985 law, how difficult is it for the wife to prove she suffered harm when her husband took a second wife? Who has the burden of proof considering whether she consented to the second marriage?

C. CEDAW Reporting Process and Issuance of General Recommendations

This section examines the CEDAW Committee's current reporting process and its process for issuing general recommendations. The Committee has steadily improved these steps to make them more productive and efficient. Sections D and E illustrate the reporting process and its progress over time by excerpting: the dialogue after the first report between the Committee and Egypt's representative (1984); Egypt's second report (1987); its fourth and fifth reports (2000); and the Committee's concluding comments after reviewing the third report and the combined fourth and fifth reports (2001). All Egypt's reports can be found at RossRights. The Committee began using concluding comments only in the mid-1990s.

The Committee on the Elimination of Discrimination Against Women, *Ways and Means of Expediting the Work of the Committee: Overview of the Working Methods of the Committee*
U.N. Doc. CEDAW/C/2007/I/4/Add.1 (2007), *available at* RossRights

II. Guidelines for Reporting by States Parties

4. The Committee has adopted reporting guidelines to assist States parties in the preparation of initial and subsequent periodic reports. The Committee strongly encourages all States parties to submit reports in accordance with those guidelines. The Committee keeps the guidelines under review and updates them as appropriate.

5. Reports should be as concise as possible. Initial reports should be no more than 100 pages long and should deal specifically with every article of the Convention. Periodic reports should be no more than 70 pages long and generally should focus on the period between the consideration of the previous report and the current report, using concluding comments on the previous report as their starting point and highlighting new developments. . . .

6. The Committee recommends that States parties involve national non-governmental organizations in the preparation of their reports. It requests that reports of States parties describe the situation of non-governmental organizations and women's associations and their participation in the implementation of the Convention and the preparation of the report.

III. Consideration of Reports of States Parties by the Committee

7. The Committee usually invites eight States parties to present their reports at each three-week session. . . .

8. In order to enhance the effectiveness of the consideration of reports of States parties and to continuously improve the quality of the constructive dialogue with reporting States, the Committee designates from among its members a country rapporteur for the report(s) of each State party. . . . The . . . rapporteur's responsibilities pertain to the following three phases of the consideration of reports: the preparation of a draft list of issues and questions for the pre-session working work; consideration of the report(s) of the State party, in particular the identification of issues and priorities to be raised during the constructive dialogue; and the preparation of draft concluding comments. . . .

C. Concluding Comments. . . .

23. Concluding comments usually follow a standard format. . . . The introduction usually indicates . . . whether the reports complied with the Committee's reporting guidelines; refers to any reservations to the Convention . . .; and notes the level of the delegation and the quality of the dialogue. A section on positive aspects is generally organized in accordance with the order of the articles of the Convention. The last section of the concluding comments, on principal areas of concern and recommendations, is presented in the order of importance of the particular issues . . . and provides concrete proposals . . . on the concern identified. In comparison with concluding comments on initial reports, the concluding comments on periodic reports highlight a limited number of priority areas of concern and recommendations . . . and include . . . a paragraph highlighting issues of concern identified in previous concluding comments as well as action, or lack of action, taken in that regard by the State party. . . .

VIII. General Recommendations

37. Article 21 of the Convention provides that the Committee may make . . . general recommendations based on the examination of reports and information received from States parties. General recommendations are normally directed at States parties and usually elaborate the Committee's view of the content of the obligations assumed by States as parties to the Convention. The Committee elaborates general recommendation on articles or themes/issues of the convention. Most of them outline matters which the Committee wishes to see addressed in the reports of States parties and seek to provide detailed guidance to States parties on their obligations under the Convention and the steps that are required for compliance.

38. The Committee has so far adopted 25 general recommendations. Those adopted during the Committee's first ten years were short, addressing such issues as the content of reports, reservations to the Convention and resources. At its tenth session in 1991, the Committee decided to adopt the practice of issuing general recommendations on specific provisions of the Convention and on the relationship between the Convention articles and themes/issues. Following that decision, the Committee issued more detailed and comprehensive general recommendations which offer

States parties clear guidance on the application of the Convention in particular situations. Comprehensive general recommendations have been adopted on violence against women (No. 19), equality in marriage and family relations (No. 21), women in public life (No. 23), access to health care (No. 24) and temporary special measures (No. 25).

39. In 1997, the Committee adopted a three-stage process for the formulation of general recommendations. The first stage consists of an open dialogue between the Committee, non-governmental organizations and others on the topic of the general recommendation. Specialized agencies and other bodies of the United Nations system as well as NGOs are encouraged to participate in this discussion and to submit information background papers. A Committee member is then asked to draft the general recommendation, which is discussed at the next or a subsequent session of the Committee. At the following session, the revised draft is adopted by the Committee.

D. Egypt's 1984 Dialogue with the CEDAW Committee Regarding Its Personal Status and Nationality Laws and Its 1987 Report

The following excerpt summarizes the dialogue between CEDAW Committee members and the Egyptian government representative after the Committee received Egypt's first state report, *available at* RossRights. Such summaries are now freely available on websites.

CEDAW [Committee, *Summary Record of the 34th and 39th meetings:*] Egypt (1984)[c]
U.N. Doc. ST/CSDHA/5 + Corr.1 (1989)

181. The Committee considered the initial report of Egypt at its 34th and 39th meetings, held on 30 March and 3 April 1984.

182. In her introduction [on 30 March, the first day of the dialogue], the representative of Egypt stated that there was no discrimination against women in her country. . . . She added that Egypt believed in equality between men and women, and considered that the discrimination against women was a violation of the principles of respect for human dignity and an obstacle to the full development of the potentialities of women in the service of their countries.

183. Islam, she stated, attached great importance to the protection of women and guaranteed their rights and responsibilities as daughters, sisters, mothers and wives. The Egyptian Constitution enshrined equality of citizens regardless of sex, race, or religion: article 11 assured proper co-ordination between the duties of women towards the family and their work in society, considering them equal with men in the

---

[c] CEDAW, THE WORK OF CEDAW: REPORTS OF THE COMMITTEE ON THE ELIMINATION OF DISCRIMINATION AGAINST WOMEN: VOLUME 1 (1982–1985) 254–61, 405–11 (1989). The numbered paragraphs are the summary record of the dialogue and the text without numbered paragraphs a more complete summary with names.

fields of political, social, cultural and economic life without prejudice to the prescriptions of Islamic law (*Shari'a*). . . .

185. The Government of Egypt had ratified the Convention while registering reservations on article 9, paragraph 2, concerning the granting to women of equal rights with men with respect to the nationality of their children; article 16, concerning the equality of women and men in all matters relating to marriage and family relations during marriage and at its dissolution "which shall be without prejudice to the rights guaranteed by Islamic Religious Law". . . .

187. The Egyptian woman enjoyed from birth exactly the same legal rights as a man; she kept her own patrimony and was free to administer her own finances and inheritances independently from her husband upon marriage. . . .

204. [Committee members stated] more details were needed on divorce procedures, guardianship or custody of children and property. More explicit details as to nationality laws affecting children upon the marriage of mother or father were requested, as well as the nationality of the woman upon marriage. . . .

211. She [the Egyptian representative] explained that the *Shari'a* preceded the Convention, and it embodied many precepts which protected women and guaranteed their equality with men. . . .

213. In her replies [on 3 April, the second day of the dialogue,] the representative of Egypt explained that the provisions of the Convention were in compliance with the Constitution and other legislation valid in her country and that any contravention of the Convention was treated like a contravention of Egyptian legislation and was equally punishable.

214. Referring to a question whether discrimination against women was forbidden in her country, she stated that under the Constitution all citizens were equal irrespective of their sex, origin, language, religion or belief.

215. With respect to the prescriptions of Islamic religious law (*Shari'a*) and its effects on a reservation made on article 16 of the Convention, she explained that Islamic law had given a prominent position to all women and liberated them from any form of discrimination.

216. Except for certain rights and responsibilities during marriage and at its dissolution, Islamic law had given to women all the necessary rights even before the ratification of the Convention. The equality between the sexes corresponded to the provisions of the Constitution as much as to the principles of Islamic law and that equality applied to all civil, political, economic, cultural and social rights and to rights connected with the financial independence of women. Article 16 of the Convention was fully compatible with Islamic law concerning the right to enter into marriage and the right to choose a spouse. With regard to rights and responsibilities during marriage and at its dissolution, a certain difference existed between the Convention and Islamic law. . . .

Many of the experts had asked for explanations of the provisions of Islamic law and the consequences of her Government's reservations with regard to article 16 of the Convention. In Islamic religion, women had a sublime position as mothers, sisters and wives and Islam recognized their human dignity, granted them rights in all areas and relieved them of the burden of discrimination. Aside from matters relating to equality between men and women in connection with marriage and with family relations during marriage and after divorce, it could be seen that Islamic law had guaranteed to women all the rights and all the kinds of equality provided for by the Convention. That had happened hundreds of years before other States had thought of drafting the Convention and before the enactment of positive law by any State in the world. Egypt, as an Islamic country, had adopted the principles of Islamic law as the main source of the country's positive law. With regard to Ms. Ilic's question on whether positive law or Islamic law had priority or precedence, she expressed the view that positive law prevailed. She reaffirmed that equality between men and women was provided for in the Constitution in conformity with Islamic law and was applicable to civil and political rights, which included, for example, equality of educational opportunities. The financial independence of women, whether married or single, was also provided for. Such independence was important because it allowed women to enjoy the same rights as men and dispose of goods and property.

Replying to the question concerning the force that Islamic religious law (*Shari'a*) and the Convention had in Egypt, she said that article 16 of the Convention was, except for paragraph 1 (c), compatible with the principles of the *Shari'a*. Concerning paragraph 1 (a), she said that the *Shari'a* granted women the same rights as men to enter into marriage. Concerning paragraph 1 (b), she explained that Islamic law, like the Convention, gave both men and women the same right to choose a spouse and contract marriage of their own volition and with their full consent. It should be made clear, regarding the aforementioned reservation to paragraph 1 (c), that under the *Shari'a*, marriage was a contract, and that [a] contract contained clauses which had been agreed to between the contracting parties before a marriage and were binding on both spouses. Those clauses stipulated that the husband had to provide for financial expenses and the wife did not have to do so if she did not wish to. Actually, such discrimination worked in favour of women rather than against them because under that arrangement the wife was financially independent and had the right to spend her money freely.

As concerned divorce, the *Shari'a* granted women the right to divorce, provided that [the] marriage contract so stipulated. The Personal [Status] Law [of 1979] stipulated various cases in which women had the right to sue for divorce: specifically, if the husband contracted a second marriage, if he had concealed the fact of a previous marriage or if he refused to comply with the obligation to provide for his wife's financial support. The other paragraphs of article 16 of the Convention were perfectly compatible with Egypt's Personal [Status] Law, which gave women rights they did not enjoy in other parts of the world. With regard to polygamy, Islam permitted a man to contract marriage with more than one wife but imposed certain conditions. Egyptian legislation also imposed certain restrictions on the practice of polygamy. There were fewer and fewer men in Egypt who contracted marriage with more than one wife. The next report of Egypt would provide more statistics on the question.

Some members of the Committee had asked whether the *Shari'a* was applicable to both Moslems and non-Moslems; she said that it was applicable only to Moslems.

The provisions applicable to Moslems were those taken by Egyptian legislation from the *Shari'a* which was one of its sources. The *Shari'a* was not applicable to non-Moslems; with regard to the Personal [Status] Law, there were special courts for non-Moslems in Egypt.

As for Ms. Mukayiranga's questions regarding the tradition of stoning women, she stated that stoning absolutely did not exist in Egypt. The punishment for adultery, applicable to both men and women, was imprisonment for two years.

With regard to children, the Personal [Status] Law of 1979 stipulated special treatment in the case of divorce. The Law gave the mother custody of her sons until the age of 10 and of her daughters until the age of 12. After that, boys could remain with their mothers until they were 15 years of age, and girls until they married. Although boys were in their mothers' custody, their fathers could visit them and had an obligation to be fully concerned with them. The Law stipulated that the parent who had custody of the children in case of divorce should occupy the family home. . . .

In answer to the questions asked by several members of the Committee about the transmission of nationality, she said that children's acquisition of their father's citizenship did not constitute discrimination against the mother. When a woman married a foreigner, she could agree to have her child assume the foreign nationality. However, if the child of an Egyptian mother and a foreign father so desired, he could acquire Egyptian nationality by making an application to the Ministry of the interior.

In connection with a number of questions on the role of women in the family and society, she cited certain articles of the Constitution: article 9 stipulated that the family was the foundation of society and was based on the religious and moral principles which sustained it. Article 10 stipulated that the State guaranteed the welfare of children and mothers and would assume responsibility for children in order to develop their potential. Under article 11, the State ensured that women could combine their work obligations within the family with their social, economic and cultural activities, without prejudice to the terms of the *Shari'a*. . . .

Ms. CARON expressed her appreciation for the clarifications which had been given concerning the relationship between Islamic law and positive law; however, she wondered why the Government had decided to formulate reservations with respect to article 16 of the Convention. She asked whether women could seek divorce only when that possibility had been specified in their marriage contract. She asked whether the fact that husbands must assume responsibility for all their wives implied that polygamy was a widespread custom, particularly among certain social classes.

Ms. SMITH asked, in connection with article 11 of the [Constitution], what was meant by the statement that the State guaranteed harmony between women's family duties and their activities in society. She wondered whether that measure really promoted equality between men and women or whether it gave women the sole responsibility for domestic tasks.

Ms. MUKAYIRANGA said that no answer had been provided to her question about a husband's unilateral renunciation of his wife. She asked why women were kept in such a state of dependency *vis-a-vis* their husbands, especially in view of the fact that household expenses were the husband's responsibility.

Ms. CORTES said that the custom of renunciation, widely acknowledged in literature, did not indicate equality between men and women in marriage. She asked what happened if a woman did not wish a divorce when her husband took a new wife [and whether she had to accept another wife of her husband]ᴰ. . . .

Miss EMARA (Egypt) . . .

With regard to article 11 of the [Constitution], she said that a form of co-ordination between spouses existed within the family and that not all responsibilities fell to the woman. What the State was trying to achieve was a balance between women's family and social obligations. For example, the Labour Code stipulated that kindergartens or nurseries must be established to care for the children of working women.

With regard to Ms. Caron's question about women's right to divorce, she said that there were different cases. In general, grounds for divorce were included in the marriage contract; however, there were some cases in which women might institute divorce proceedings even though the contract did not mention that specific situation—for example, [under the Personal Status Law of 1979,] when a husband contracted marriage with another woman, served a term of imprisonment or withdrew financial support from the family, or when the wife no longer wished to live in the family home.

In reply to Ms. Mukayiranga, she said that there had been a misunderstanding: she had thought she had referred to "stoning" rather than "renunciation", to which Ms. Cortes had also referred. While the *Shari'a* was the source of much of Egyptian law, the latter did not necessarily reproduce all the provisions of Islamic law. That was the case with renunciation, which, while provided for under the *Shari'a*, was not included in Egyptian law. Egyptian law accorded equal rights to women in the matter of divorce [under the Personal Status Law of 1979].

Some members of the Committee had asked questions about polygamy, a notion which must be viewed within a historical context. Centuries ago, as a result of unfortunate social circumstances, there had been a much higher number of women than men in the population; since at that time women had not been employed, marriage had been the sole institution capable of offering them an honourable and secure life. Consequently, the institution of polygamy had been established; it should be stressed, however, that while it was admitted under Islamic law, it was subject to significant restrictions, the most important one being that equality, justice and equity must be guaranteed to both spouses. Egyptian law also imposed severe limitations on men's right to marry more than once, so that many men refrained from taking new wives and the number of persons living in polygamy was continually declining. Specific data on that subject would be added in the next report.

With regard to the manner in which household expenses were paid, Egyptian wives were in a privileged position. They had the right to dispose freely of their own finances; on the other hand, the husband was required to bear household expenses. Many women did, of course, spend their money on their own families, but that was

---

ᴰ The bracketed question was taken from paragraph 217, which preceded this part of the report.

entirely voluntary, and they were under no obligation to do so. In that respect Egyptian women held an advantage, and one might wonder whether there was reason for Egyptian men to demand equal conditions.

NOTES

Challenges in Implementing Article 16's Equality in Marriage Provisions. Identify the specific Egyptian laws concerning marriage and divorce that discriminate against women. For each one, identify the relevant Article 16 provision and the reform in the law it would require. How does the Egyptian representative characterize the relevant Egyptian law? Does she agree that the provisions are discriminatory? Can CEDAW be an effective tool for guaranteeing women's equality in the traditionally "private" sphere of the family?

The Committee Process. This was an early stage in the CEDAW Committee's work, just three years after the Convention had entered into force. If you were a member of the CEDAW Committee concerned about women's status in the family and hoping to advance it, what would you say or do: before the reporting process; during it; and after it? How would you reform the Committee process to make it more effective?

Egypt, *Second Periodic Reports of States Parties to CEDAW Committee*
U.N. Doc. CEDAW/C/13/Add.2 (1987)

3. Equality in acquiring, retaining and changing citizenship. . . .

Article 12 stipulates that an Egyptian woman who marries a foreigner shall retain her Egyptian citizenship, unless she desires to acquire her husband's nationality, and expresses such desire at the time of her marriage or during her marriage, and is permitted by the law of her husband's country to acquire its nationality. Nevertheless, she retains her Egyptian citizenship if she declares her desire to do so within one year of acquiring her husband's nationality. . . .

The law grants a woman equal rights with men with respect to the nationality of her children in the following cases:

(a) A child born in Egypt of an Egyptian mother and a father of unknown nationality or a stateless father;

(b) A child born in Egypt of an Egyptian mother, whose father is not legally determined;

(c) A child born abroad of an Egyptian mother, whose father is unknown or stateless or whose nationality is unknown, if he chooses Egyptian citizenship within one year of reaching the age of reason.

4. Equality in work. . . .

For the protection of women, they are not employed in certain jobs, for reasons of health or morals or because the work is too hard. Examples are working in bars or gambling clubs, working with blast furnaces, manufacturing explosives and working underground in mines and quarries, etc. The law also stipulates that women may not be employed at night (between 8 p.m. and 7 a.m.) except in certain situations, for jobs and on occasions laid down in a directive from the Minister of State for Manpower. Such jobs include, for example, work in hospitals, san[i]toria and other medical centres; in hotels, restaurants, pensions and cafeterias which are under the supervision of the Ministry of Tourism; in theaters, cinemas and similar places, and work in airports and tourist agencies. . . .

As a result of the increased numbers of workers in all sectors, a series of laws have been enacted to assist working women in reconciling their family duties with those of their work. The laws concerning workers in government administration, in public authorities and in units of the public sector, have laid down that working women have the right to leave without pay for the purpose of looking after their children, up to a maximum of two years at one time, and on three occasions during their working lives; and either that the administrative authority shall bear both the social security contributions payable by itself and those payable by the woman worker, or that the woman worker shall be granted compensation equal to 25 per cent of the salary to which she is entitled on the starting date of her leave, at her own choice. It was also decided that the woman worker shall be entitled to maternity leave for three months after confinement, on three occasions during her working life. This is fully paid leave, and is not to be included in the ordinary leave entitlement. The administrative authority also recommended that rules be drawn up for work on the basis of half-time work for half-pay.

With regard to the private sector, Law No. 137 of 1981 provided women workers with the protection they needed to reconcile family and work without detriment to the employer's interests. Its provisions include:

A woman worker who has worked for the same employer for six months is granted the right to 50 days' maternity leave on full pay, including the pre-natal and the post-natal period, on submission of a medical certificate indicating the probable date of confinement. However, the woman worker shall not be entitled to such leave on more than three occasions during her working life. A woman shall not be required to work for 40 days after her confinement. This care was also extended to the child. Article 155 of this law provides that for 18 months after confinement, a woman who breast-feeds her child is entitled to two breaks of not less than half an hour each for that purpose, in addition to the established work breaks. In addition, she has the right to combine those two periods and they are then calculated as working hours with no consequent reduction in pay.
—A woman worker may take leave without pay for a period not exceeding one year in order to look after her child. Such leave shall be granted three times during her working life, provided that the organization in which she works has at least 50 employees.
—The law requires that an employer who has one or more women workers shall display a copy of the regulations applying to women workers in his place of business.
—Emphasis is placed on the right of women workers to protect and take care of their children and to provide the appropriate conditions for developing their capacities. The law requires an employer with 100 or more women workers in one place either to set up a nursery or to employ one to look after the children. It also stipulates that organizations employing fewer than 100 female workers in one area should implement this obligation as a joint undertaking.

These will be supplementary to the nurseries set up by the State to provide care for the children of working and non-working women.

N O T E

The Reporting Process Today: Backlog. The CEDAW material you have just read concerns Egypt's initial report and its second periodic report. Egypt's third periodic report was due on 18 October 1990. It was submitted in January 1996. Its fourth report was due in October 1994 and its fifth in October 1998; Egypt submitted the combined fourth and fifth reports in March 2000. Not until 2001 did the CEDAW Committee consider the last three reports. Egypt's situation is typical. In 2000, CEDAW reported that there were 242 overdue reports, several of them more than six years overdue.

There is no sanction for failing to file a report on time. CEDAW is years behind in considering the reports that have been turned in. In 1997, for the first time it began meeting twice a year to consider the reports. On a temporary basis in order to address its backlog, it met three times a year in 2006 and 2007, with each session lasting three weeks.

E. Egypt's 2000 Country Report to CEDAW and the Committee's Response

Egypt, *Fourth and Fifth Periodic Reports of States Parties to CEDAW Committee*
U.N. Doc. CEDAW/C/EGY/4–5 (2000), *available at* RossRights

Article 16[E]

In Egypt, marriage is a contract by mutual consent, and by law it must be concluded by the free, mutual consent of both parties. Since marriage in Egypt is governed by the law on personal status, it is also subject to Shariah law, which imposes obligations on both parties with regard to the validity, conclusion, dissolution and annulment of the marriage.

The law states that the age of consent for males is 18, while that for females is 16. The marriage contract must be concluded and documented in official records, official documents must be issue[d] indicating that the marriage has taken place, and the marital status must appear in the identity papers, in accordance with the rules for registrars and other officials authorized to perform civil marriages. . . .

According to Egyptian law, marriage does not affect a woman's financial independence of her husband. A woman retains her first name and surname, which does not change after marriage, and she has complete liberty to manage and dispose of her finances, to conclude contracts and obtain loans, and to perform any other legal transaction, unimpaired by the fact of her marriage.

Women have the right to act as guardians of minors, and, in the case of divorce [or] dissolution of the marriage contract, to obtain custody of their male children up to the age of 10 and their female children up to the age of 12. They may also seek legal redress if they consider it to be in the interest of minors to extend custody of

---

[E] For the full text of Article 16, see Chapter One.

male children up to the age of 15, and of female children until they marry. The father has the right of frequent access to his children during this period and must provide for them as long as custody lasts.

Women and men share full responsibility for all matters arising from their marriage, including the maintenance and support of the family unit and decisions about the number and spacing of their children; the extent and impact of this shared responsibility differ according to the educational and cultural background of each partner. The State's development plans focus on the eradication of female illiteracy, particularly in backward and rural areas. The State also supports the role of women in sharing with her husband in their commitment to the family and children.

State agencies are currently implementing the recommendations made at the first National Conference on Women (June 1994), by undertaking a detailed study of a standard marriage document with a view to precluding disputes over its validity and the need for legal recourse. The law concerning the procedures for litigation in personal-status cases is also being updated in an attempt to simplify those procedures and reduce the number of conditions attached to them.

In 2000, Law No. 1, regulating certain litigation procedures in matters of personal status law, was promulgated with the purpose of speeding up such procedures and reducing the conditions attached thereto. The Law makes it incumbent upon the Nasser Bank to comply with monetary awards which have been made to women, and raises the established rate of income tax in order to ensure the implementation of these provisions.

[T]here are no legal impediments to the enjoyment by men and women of the right to enter into marriage with their free and full consent.

With regard to the practical difficulties, although the State has endeavoured to promote all aspects of the economic, social and cultural development of women, who constitute half of society and, in their capacity as citizens, mothers and workers, play an importan[t] and effective role in all spheres of community life, women face a number of difficulties and problems, such as early marriage below the legal age, illiteracy and a low standard of living, which prevent them from freely expressing their frank opinion on their prospective spouse. However, such problems are largely confined to rural and remote areas of the country, and currently affect only a small percentage of women. The State is endeavouring, through its effective development plans and programmes, to eradicate illiteracy and promote greater awareness among women and young girls in remote areas with a view to overcoming and eliminating these difficulties.

CEDAW Committee, *Concluding Observations: Egypt (2001)*
U.N. Doc. A/56/38 (PARTI) (2001), *available at* RossRights

312. The Committee considered the third report and the combined fourth and fifth periodic report[s] of Egypt at its 492nd and 493rd meetings, on 19 January 2001.

(a) Introduction by the State party

313. In introducing the reports, the representative of Egypt emphasized the improvement in favour of women in the legal, institutional and practical domains. In the legal domain, many laws, such as family laws, had been amended in favour of women. . . .

315. The legislative committee of the National Council for Women had reviewed the current nationality law and recommended that it be amended to entitle Egyptian women married to foreigners the right to confer their nationality on their children. . . . In addition, the legislative committee was reviewing the draft law on passports, which had been formulated in response to the ruling of the Supreme Constitutional Court that a ministerial decree requiring the husband's consent to the issue of a wife's passport was unconstitutional. The legislative committee within the National Council for Women would initiate a campaign to raise awareness of the draft law, and had formed a committee to elaborate a new family code.

316. The representative informed the Committee of recent laws and regulations that sought to eliminate discrimination between women and men. These included . . . Law No. 1 of 2000, enacted after a 10-year period of consultation. Law No. 1, which entered into force on 1 March 2000, grants women the right to "khul" or unilateral divorce by repudiation without the need to prove damage. Executive decrees issued as a result of Law No. 1 of 2000 included a new marriage contract, which came into effect on 16 August 2000, elaborating protective provisions relating to finances and polygamy. In addition, article 291 of the Penal Code, which provided a defence in cases of kidnap and rape where the defendant marries the victim, was repealed.

317. The representative noted that, despite the progress that had been made in implementing the Convention, there were a number of areas that required attention. They included discrimination against women with regard to the nationality of their children. . . .

318. The representative said that the Government intended to enhance efforts towards the achievement of equality between women and men and the elimination of discrimination against women. She noted that cultural constraints and traditions sometimes impeded change and obstructed implementation of the law. In this context, she said that the Government, through the National Council for Women . . . would seek to use indigenous formulations, which were deeply rooted in Egyptian and Islamic culture and which asserted the equality between women and men. With the aid of all concerned, . . . the National Council for Women would participate in raising awareness campaigns and to ensure proper interpretations, to clarify misinterpretations of religious concepts and to demonstrate that the principles of sharia provide for the full equality of women with men, and respect for women's dignity.

319. In conclusion, the representative informed the Committee that efforts were under way to address the reservations entered by the Government of Egypt upon ratification of the Convention. It had recommended the withdrawal of the reservation

to article 2 of the Convention and as far as article 9, paragraph 2, and article 16 were concerned, they were actively under review.

N O T E S

A Simulated Committee Dialogue. Consider everything you have learned about Egyptian law in this Chapter. Imagine that you are a member of the CEDAW Committee and prepare a question to ask the Egyptian representative during the session that follows her initial presentation in 2001. It should reflect what you see as a major area of concern under CEDAW. Once you have the question, imagine that you are the Egyptian representative and respond to the question. Based on the answer, what concluding observation would you make?

Progress and Problems. The CEDAW Committee typically lists both progress from previous reports and remaining obstacles in its concluding observations. Can you identify progress since 1984? What problems do women still face?

CEDAW Committee, *Concluding Observations: Egypt (2001)*
U.N. Doc. A/56/38 (PART I) (2001), *available at* RossRights

(b) Concluding comments of the Committee

320. The Committee commends the Government of Egypt on its third and combined fourth and fifth periodic reports, which are in accordance with the Committee's guidelines for the preparation of periodic reports. It also commends the Government for the comprehensive written replies to the questions of the Committee's pre-session working group, and the oral presentation of the delegation. . . .

321. The Committee congratulates the Government for its high-level and large delegation, headed by the Secretary-General of the National Council for Women. . . .

Positive aspects

322. The Committee welcomes the establishment of the National Council for Women, which was created by Presidential decree, reports directly to the President and is mandated to monitor laws and policies affecting women's lives, raise awareness and monitor the implementation of the Convention. . . . The Committee commends the fact that non-governmental organizations are represented in the Council and that they participated in the preparation of the reports.

323. The Committee notes the introduction of legal reforms . . . , particularly Law No. 1 of 2000, which . . . gives women a right to terminate marriage unilaterally (khul). . . .

Factors and Difficulties Affecting the Implementation of the Convention

325. The Committee notes that, although the Constitution guarantees equality of men and women and the Convention prevails over national legislation, the persistence of patriarchal attitudes and stereotypical behaviour with respect to the role of

women and men in the family and society limit the full implementation of the Convention.

Principal Areas of Concern and Recommendations

326. While appreciating the efforts of the National Council for Women to encourage the Government to withdraw its reservations to articles 2 and 9, paragraph 2, and article 16 of the Convention, the Committee expresses its concern that these reservations entered by the State upon ratification have been retained.

327. The Committee urges the State party to expedite the steps necessary for the withdrawal of the reservations and in that regard draws its attention to the Committee's statement on reservation in its report on its nineteenth session and, in particular, its view that articles 2 and 16 are central to the object and purpose of the Convention and that . . . they should be withdrawn.

328. The Committee notes with concern that women who seek divorce by unilateral termination of their marriage contract under Law No. 1 of 2000 (khul) must in all cases forego their rights to financial provision, including the dower.

329. The Committee recommends that the Government consider a revision of Law No. 1 of 2000, in order to eliminate this financial discrimination against women.

330. The Committee expresses its concern that the Egyptian nationality law prevents an Egyptian woman from passing on her nationality to her children if her husband is not Egyptian, while Egyptian men married to non-Egyptians may do so. It is concerned by the hardship faced by the children of Egyptian women married to non-Egyptian men, including financial hardship with regard to education. The Committee considers this limitation on the rights of women to be inconsistent with the Convention.

331. The Committee calls upon the State party to revise the legislation governing nationality in order to make it consistent with the provisions of the Convention.

332. The Committee notes with concern that the persistence of cultural stereotypes and patriarchal attitudes impedes progress in the implementation of the Convention and the full enjoyment of . . . [women's] human rights. In this regard, the Committee is concerned that article 11 of the Egyptian Constitution, which states that "the State shall enable a woman to reconcile her duties towards her family with her work in society and guarantee her equality with men in the sphere of political, social, cultural and economic life," appears to entrench the woman's primary role as mother and homemaker.

333. The Committee urges the Government to increase awareness-raising programmes, including those specifically directed towards men, and to take measures to change stereotypical attitudes and perceptions about the roles and responsibilities of women and men. . . .

344. The Committee expresses its concern that, although efforts have been made, there is no holistic approach to the prevention and elimination of violence against women, including domestic violence, marital rape, . . . and crimes committed in the name of honour. . . .

346. The Committee expresses its concern that several provisions of the Penal Code discriminate against women. In particular, in case of murder following the crime of adultery, men and women are not treated equally. . . .

352. The Committee expresses its concern about the high number of early marriages of girls, especially in rural areas.

353. The Committee recommends that the Government amend the law on the legal age of marriage to prevent early marriage. . . .

354. The Committee expresses its concern regarding the continued legal authorization of polygamy.

355. The Committee urges the Government to take measures to prevent the practice of polygamy in accordance with the provisions of the Convention and the Committee's general recommendation 21.9.

356. The Committee urges the Government to sign and ratify the Optional Protocol to the Convention. . . .

357. The Committee requests the Government to respond to the concerns expressed in the present concluding comments in its next periodic report. . . .

358. The Committee requests the wide dissemination in Egypt of the present concluding comments in order to make the people of Egypt, in particular government administrators and politicians, aware of the steps that have been taken to ensure de jure and de facto equality for women and of the future steps that are required in this regard.

F. Developments in Egyptian Divorce Law

Hossam Hassan, *Rights-Egypt: New Law Lets Women Divorce if They Waive Support*
INTER PRESS SERVICE, March 28, 2000

New legislation entitled the Personal Status Law, which allows women easier access to divorce and the right to apply to the courts for permission to travel alone, has been applauded by women and human rights activists.

Under the new law, a woman can apply for khul'—the right to obtain a divorce without her husband's consent—but only by waiving her financial rights.

Women's groups say they would like to see that part of the law changed.

"When it comes to her own freedom, a woman can forego her financial rights in exchange for getting a divorce. Although it is a major sacrifice, many wives feel they have no other choice to regain their freedom and get rid of a mean, violent or maybe even impotent husband," says activist Nawal Al-Saadawy.

Under previous Egyptian law, which is a blend of Islamic and French laws, married women needed their husbands' permission to travel abroad alone, and divorces took up to 10 years to obtain.

Nagad Al-Bora'i, head of the organization of Democratic Development, a prominent human rights group, praises the new legislation. He says giving women more rights to decide their personal life was definitely a step forward.

The new law, intended to facilitate personal status litigation, took effect on March 1. There are over 1.5 million divorce cases filed in the Egyptian courts, and legal sources say that due to bureaucratic red tape, cases can take up to a decade to be heard.

Hanaa Eid, a woman in her early thirties with two children aged five and seven, has applied for khul' without the assistance of a lawyer. After eight years of marriage, Hanaa says she had "had enough."

"I felt like I had gone through every possible pain and degradation and enough was enough," she says.

The fact that she has to give up any financial claims, despite her modest resources, has not deterred Hanaa. "He does not contribute a single piastre (the smallest Egyptian currency) to the household. I pay for everything and we have no home but my father's. So what is the difference?" she sighed.

Hanaa is desperate to "get it over and done with" so that she can apply for welfare benefits as a female heading a household with no regular source of income.

She says she has been a regular at the courts for the past four years trying to get a divorce under the old system, but to no avail. "My husband would not turn up for hearings and the case would be postponed. I don't even know where he is anymore," she said.

The first week of the month saw a steady flow of applications for khul' across the nation. By mid-March, Cairo's Zananeiri Personal Status Court alone had received over 3,000 applications.

But not everyone is thrilled with the new legislation. One newspaper described it as "the beginning of the breakdown of the family."

"Conservative forces are backed by the power of religion and the constitution, which stipulates that Islam is the state religion and that the *Shari'a* (Islamic Law) its primary source of legislation," says activist Farida Al Naqqash.

She says specialists in Islamic jurisprudence have agreed "virtually unanimously" that the law conforms with the principles of *Shari'a*.

"The debates show that the *Shari'a* has never been the issue. The issue is the patriarchal or class desire for control exhibited by most men," she said.

"Even university professors and lawyers were enraged by the possibility that women could share men's right to divorce. The discourse of ownership overrode considerations of justice and equality that make up the ethical framework of the Qur'an (the Muslim Holy Book)," said Al-Naqqash.

Several lawyers have come out against giving women the power to get a divorce so easily. They have expressed hope that the executive statutes, which have not yet been released and which provide guidelines on law's implementation, will introduce some restrictions.

They say the fact that men cannot appeal the khul' is unconstitutional, because it gives women exclusive power and ignores the wishes of the husband.

Under Islam, a man can take up to four wives at a time, and he can get a divorce by uttering the phrase "I divorce you" three times. Custody of the children is usually granted to the woman unless she re-marries or her ex-husband can prove she is promiscuous.

Hassan El-Meleighi, a lawyer, says the problem with khul' is that "any woman can ask for a divorce with or without justification."

He said women involved in relationships with other men, or who no longer want their husbands "because they don't love them," can just go and apply for divorce.

Sayed Tantawi, Egypt's Grand Sheikh of Al Azhar, the highest Sunni Muslim authority, confirmed that the new law agrees with Islamic laws.

"Khul' was known and approved by our Prophet Mohammed when a woman wants to get her freedom because she cannot keep her marriage to a husband she hates," he said.

Mahmoud El-Baroudi, deputy secretary general of the Zananeiri Court, says the fact that the executive statutes have not yet been issued has not kept the applications from pouring in. He said the statutes would be issued by April 1.

"Lawyers keep on citing reasons for khul' such as harm inflicted by the husband or the non provision of essentials. These are not necessary. All that is required is for the lawyer to argue that the woman does not want to be married to her husband anymore—that is enough for her to get her freedom," he said.

Egyptian Court Grants First Divorce to Be Sought by a Woman
AGENCE FRANCE-PRESSE, Aug. 23, 2000

A family affairs court has granted the first divorce to be sought by a woman under Egypt's new personal rights code passed earlier this year, the Al-Gomhurya daily reported Wednesday.

The court in Giza granted the 46-year-old woman divorce from her Egyptian husband, 39, the paper said, but their identities were not revealed.

The couple married in Kuwait in 1987, and in line with the stipulations of the new law the woman repaid her husband the money he gave her at the time of the marriage—one Kuwaiti dinar (3.14 dollars).

She also renounced all her financial rights in line with the law, which give[s] the judge the right to grant a divorce to a woman who asks for it after a period of three months during which the couple must attempt reconciliation.

HUMAN RIGHTS WATCH, DIVORCED FROM JUSTICE: WOMEN'S UNEQUAL ACCESS TO DIVORCE IN EGYPT
Vol. 16, No. 8(E), December 2004, *available at* RossRights

I. Summary

The Egyptian government has created two widely disparate systems for divorce, one for men and one for women. Egyptian men have a unilateral and unconditional right to divorce. They never need to enter a courtroom to end their marriages. Egyptian women, on the other hand, must resort to Egypt's notoriously backlogged and inefficient courts to divorce their spouses.

In the courts, women face procedural and evidentiary hurdles to divorce that are inherently discriminatory. Men, who can divorce their spouses at will with an oral renunciation later registered by a religious notary, can simply sidestep these procedures. Obtaining a divorce can also take years as men manipulate the many defenses and tactics Egyptian law reserves only for them. As a result, many Egyptian women . . . avoid the courts and are left with two equally distressing options: either remain in an unwanted marriage and possibly endure physical and psychological abuse, or beg their husbands to divorce them, giving up everything they own and cherish in return. . . .

Egypt's discriminatory divorce system is among the starkest examples of Egypt's oppressive personal status laws. These personal status laws—common in the region— govern marriage, divorce, custody, and inheritance and advance a model of the family based on the superiority of men to women. Laws and practices as applied violate the rights of Egyptian women to . . . equality in marriage and divorce, as enshrined in international human rights law.

Egypt's divorce laws discriminate against women in the procedures they impose and in their substantive provisions. . . . In order to initiate a divorce providing full financial rights, an Egyptian woman must show evidence of harm inflicted by her spouse during the course of their marriage, often supported by eyewitness testimony. Alternatively, since 2000, Egyptian women can file for "no-fault" divorce (khula) if they agree to forfeit their financial rights and repay the dowry given to them by their husbands upon marriage. Khula, adopted as a way to afford women easier access to divorce, still requires women to petition the court to terminate their marriages. The option is most accessible to women with the financial means to renounce all financial claims, or those with limited means but who are desperate for a divorce. . . .

For many Egyptian women, a divorce is tantamount to destitution because of the government's failure to enforce court rulings for alimony and child support. The Egyptian government's attempt to remedy this problem through the establishment of a specialized alimony and child support fund is a step in the right direction. However, the fund should not be a substitute for more aggressive enforcement of court rulings.

Divorced women are also permanently at risk of becoming homeless because they have no stake in marital assets, and retain no ownership interest in the marital home or any other property upon divorce. Egyptian law automatically transfers the legal and physical custody of adolescent children to the father, and ties a woman's right to live in the marital home to the period during which she has physical custody of the children. These inequalities deter many women from initiating divorce. . . .

The introduction of no-fault divorce in 2000, while sparing women the need to specify grounds for divorce, has not fundamentally altered the unequal divorce equation in Egypt. The fact that the Egyptian government has not reformed the fault-based divorce system means that the new law has simply created another avenue whereby women may choose to give up critically important rights in exchange for a divorce. . . .

II. Strategies for Using CEDAW to Effect Change at Home

The United Nations Development Fund for Women (UNIFEM) was created in 1976, in response to a call from women's organizations attending the 1975 UN First World Conference on Women in Mexico City. Its provides financial and technical assistance to women's organizations and innovative programs and strategies that promote women's human rights, political participation, and economic security. Within the UN system, UNIFEM promotes gender equality and links women's issues and concerns to national, regional and global agendas by fostering collaboration and providing technical expertise on gender mainstreaming and women's empowerment strategies. For further information, visit the UNIFEM website, *available at* RossRights.

UNIFEM developed the material below which illustrates the many ways women activists have used CEDAW to achieve domestic legal change granting women equality with men. As you read it, consider how women's activists in Egypt might use CEDAW to achieve equal rights in family law. Which would you recommend?

Consider also the extent to which CEDAW has already been used concerning inequality in marriage. How can the Committee better address the conflicts that often arise between women's rights and traditional, customary, or religious beliefs?

UNITED NATIONS DEVELOPMENT FUND FOR WOMEN, BRINGING EQUALITY HOME:
  IMPLEMENTING THE CEDAW
6–10, 12–14, 17–18, 22–31, 35–41 (Ilana Landsberg-Lewis ed., 1998)

Foreword from Unifem's Executive Director. . . .

In promoting the realisation of women's human rights, UNIFEM has developed an array of initiatives around . . . CEDAW. . . . [Its] framework can be tremendously useful in working for legal and policy changes at local, national, and international levels. We have developed new programming aimed at: (a) achieving universal ratification of the Women's Convention and removal/narrowing of States' reservations, (b) strengthening awareness of CEDAW and of the capacity of women's organisations to use it in their advocacy work and, (c) collaborating with other partners to support the work of the CEDAW Committee and strengthening the Women's Convention. . . .

[CEDAW] gains made on paper at the international level simply set the stage for the real work: the implementation of CEDAW . . . at the national level. This is where CEDAW really has meaning for women and translates into the potential to improve women's lives and their societies.

If the stories brought together in this booklet have any single message, it is that women themselves must be and will be the authors of [change]. . . . What is apparent in each case is that CEDAW, as a document, did not in and of itself bring about these changes. Rather, it was the determined, cooperative, innovative, and strategic work of women's NGOs—and the stimulation of the political will of Governments—that changed the conditions of women's lives. CEDAW provided them with a powerful, internationally recognised lever. . . .

Introduction [by the Director of International Women's Rights Action Watch (IWRAW) Asia Pacific]. . . .

Major breakthroughs have been made in the nineties for women's advancement, largely because of women's advocacy worldwide. The declaration that came out of the 1993 UN World Conference on Human Rights in Vienna unequivocally established women's rights and equality as essential preconditions to women's participation in development as agents and beneficiaries.

As women gain conviction of the legitimacy of their rights, demands arise for international and national mechanisms through which they can claim these rights. In this context, the Convention takes on added significance, as it is the principal legal instrument addressing women's rights and equality. Its uniqueness lies in its mandate for the achievement of substantive equality for women, which requires not only formal legal equality but also equality of results in real terms. By recognizing that discrimination is socially constructed and that laws, policies, and practices can unintentionally have the effect of discriminating against women, the Convention sets the pace for a dynamic, proactive approach to women's advancement. It is no longer possible to say that there is no discrimination against women if laws and policies do not overtly discriminate against women. Under the regime of the Convention, neutrality has no legitimacy. Positive actions are required of the State to promote and protect the rights of women.

Furthermore, the strength of the Convention rests on an international consensus on its mandate of equality and its principles, given more than 161 ratifications/ accessions. . . . Such a mandate is a strong counter to the claim that equality between women and men should be made relative to culture and tradition. As Rebecca Cook has noted, non-discrimination is now a principle of international customary law.

The existence of a positive legal framework for women's rights does not automatically confer rights on women. However, it does legitimize women's claims for rights and makes possible women's transformation from passive beneficiaries to active claimants. It creates the space for women's agency.

The Convention is largely dependent on the political will of Governments. This political will can be created through the development of a highly conscious constituency, not only among women and women's groups, but within Government bureaucracies as well. There is an urgent need to raise awareness and develop skills at various levels in relation to the Convention: among women, Government functionaries, lawyers and members of the judicial system. Advocacy for the application of the norms of the Convention has to be linked to the international mandate of equality and non-discrimination at the ground level.

This linkage also requires the establishment of a relationship between women's groups and the CEDAW Committee which monitors States parties' compliance with their obligations under the Convention. Women's interaction with the CEDAW Committee can help integrate their perspectives into the interpretation of the Convention's articles. This in turn will increase the Convention's scope for domestic application and contribute to the development of women's rights jurisprudence within the United Nations system. . . .

The participation of women from all regions—and in all their diversity—in the setting of international norms is also critical because of the need for universal minimum standards of human rights. This is so especially in light of the rising fundamentalism in many countries around the world. We need to engage in the process of evolving a core set of universal norms and standards for women's rights. If we do not do this, rights for women will be subject to changing ideologies and shifting socioeconomic and political contexts. The women we are working with are ready to engage in such standard-setting. It is, in fact, vital that they do this, so that their experiences and needs form the basis of such standard-setting, thus linking the national to the global and the global to the national. . . .

Note: The IWRAW Asia Pacific is a collaborative programme to facilitate and monitor the implementation of . . .[CEDAW]. It has projects in 13 countries in Asia and is based in Kuala Lumpur, Malaysia.

I. Constitutions

When women's human rights are included in a national constitution, they become part of a country's baseline for rights protection and Government obligations.

The ways in which constitutions incorporate women's human rights vary a great deal from country to country. Some constitutions make ratified international treaties and covenants part of national law. Other constitutions include explicit guarantees of gender equality, and women's non-governmental organisations (NGOs) have done important work since CEDAW was opened for ratification in 1979 to make sure these provisions are included in their States' constitutions.

Some of the most significant constitutional gains have been won in countries where there has been a broader national move for constitutional renewal, a recent ratification of CEDAW, and an interest from women's NGOs in using CEDAW as an advocacy tool.

CEDAW principles have been integrated into new constitutions and added to more established constitutions through amendments. CEDAW principles can also gain 'constitutional' status in a less direct fashion, when the courts are convinced to use the Women's Convention to help give existing constitutional guarantees of women's equality more detailed and concrete meaning.

Colombia

The Colombian Government ratified CEDAW in 1981, and women's NGOs quickly began exploring ways to use it in their advocacy work. By the mid-1980s, CEDAW had become a central part of campaigns for women's human rights in Colombia.

At the same time, demands were building in Colombia for constitutional reform. It was hoped a new constitution would help move the nation past the period of violent instability it had been experiencing. The President of Colombia invited all sectors of Colombian society—including "feminists and women's organisations"—to bring their reform proposals to the working groups that were developing the new constitution. In response to this call, women's NGOs made a series of proposals about women's human rights, the main proposal being that CEDAW principles should be written into the constitution.

The legislative assembly began drafting the new constitution out of the collected reform proposals in 1991. Women's groups were determined that their concerns would not be overlooked. NGOs from across the country decided to unite in a single umbrella organisation, for the first time ever, to frame a strategy that would keep women's human rights high on the constitutional agenda. In April 1991, 34 women's groups issued a statement that appeared in one of the country's leading newspapers. It reminded the assembly that a truly democratic constitution must respect women's rights and needs. It also listed their demands, starting with the incorporation of CEDAW principles. The following month, the Women and the Constituent Assembly National Network (the Network) was officially formed; soon it grew to include more than 70 women's NGOs from across Colombia.

María Isabel Plata and Adriana de la Espriella, of PROFAMILIA, explain why CEDAW was so useful for women trying to influence the shape to be taken by the new constitution:

The strengths of the proposals advanced by the Women and Constitution Network lay not only in their recognised support by the women's organisations, but in the fact that they emphasised that the principles embraced in their proposals were mandates contained in international human rights instruments, such as CEDAW. They won legitimacy by being framed as internationally recognised human rights provisions. In this case, the use of international human rights language proved to be an effective strategy for introducing women's rights into the constitution, taking advantage of the fact that Colombia is a country that is constantly scrutinised by the international community for its compliance with human rights principles.

The Network's efforts were successful. Not everything they advocated appeared in the final draft, but the Colombian constitution includes some of the most detailed and substantive guarantees of women's human rights in the world. . . .

The Colombian constitution includes several provisions that reflect CEDAW'S substantive vision of equality. For example, article 13 of the Colombian constitution guarantees legal equality between women and men not merely by prohibiting discrimination, but also by obliging the Government to actively promote the conditions needed to make legal equality real and effective. The Government also has an obligation to adopt affirmative action-style measures favouring disadvantaged groups to remove the effects of past discrimination. The same approach is taken in article 40, which deals with political representation. It provides that the State must "guarantee the adequate and effective participation of women in the decision-making levels of Public Administration."

The constitution also incorporates further guarantees of women's equality that parallel the provisions of CEDAW. For example, article 42 states that "family relations are based in the equality of rights and duties of couples and in reciprocal respect among all its members" (CEDAW, article 16), and it provides that the State must punish "any form of violence within the family." Article 42 also guarantees the right of couples to "freely and responsibly decide the number of their children" and guarantees State assistance and support to women during pregnancy and after birth (CEDAW, articles 16 and 12).

Finally, the constitution created an enforcement mechanism that individual women can use. A Constitutional Court was set up to hear petitions brought by citizens about violations of their rights. It has the power to make an "order of protection" if the petitioner shows that her rights are jeopardised by Government action or inaction. This court made a ground-breaking decision in 1992 in response to a petition brought by a female victim of domestic violence. Her husband's actions were not criminal; according to the Colombian penal code, domestic violence was seen as a private matter that did not concern the State. The court found that the absence of legal recourse violated her rights to life, and to integrity and security of the person. Even more important, the court established the principle that the State has a positive obligation to secure protection for women and prevent husbands from continuing to subject them to violence. The police and the Institute of Family Welfare were ordered to take immediate steps to protect the petitioner. . . .

Uganda

The Ugandan constitution was rewritten in 1995. To prepare for the drafting of the new constitution, the Government held consultations across the country. Women's NGOs felt strongly that this process was not designed to include women in a significant way, and started their own parallel consultation process. They also mobilised to get women elected to the Constituent Assembly, which would be drafting the constitution. Once the Constituent Assembly had been established, its women members formed a women's caucus to develop a united position on the proposals that would come before the assembly.

The women working on proposals for the new constitution referred to CEDAW as establishing a minimum acceptable standard, and the Convention is reflected in a number of important provisions of the Ugandan constitution. Its first provision, which declares the constitution's guiding principles, states that the need for gender balance and fair representation is to inform the implementation of the constitution and all Government policies and programmes. The constitution's Bill of Rights states that the rights it sets out are to be enjoyed without discrimination on the basis of sex.

The Ugandan constitution also contains powerful guarantees about women's political participation which are the direct result of the NGO advocacy efforts. The NGOs had relied on CEDAW's conceptualisation of equality, which recognises the need for temporary special measures to speed the achievement of equality and provides that these measures are not discriminatory (CEDAW, article 4). They argued that because of the history of discrimination against women in Uganda, the only effective way to guarantee equality in political representation would be to reserve a certain portion of elected seats for women candidates. They were successful—the Constitution reserves a minimum number of parliamentary seats for women, it requires that each administrative district have at least one woman representative, and it provides that at least one-third of the seats in local Government (city, municipal, and rural district councils) must be filled by women.

[The Constitution also provides in Article 31(1) that "[m]en and women of the age of eighteen years and above, have the right to marry and to found a family and are entitled to equal rights in marriage, during marriage and at its dissolution." Article 33(6) states that the Constitution prohibits "[l]aws, cultures, customs or traditions which are against the dignity, welfare, or interest of women or which undermine their status. . . ."]

Brazil

The Brazilian constitution was redrafted in 1988 and now includes extensive guarantees of women's human rights. The move to rewrite the constitution began in 1985, with the restoration of democracy in Brazil and the resurgence of public political activism. Between 1985 and 1988 women's NGOs, the National Council of Women's Rights, jurists, State and municipal councils, and women's deputies in the constituent assembly contributed to a national campaign to ensure that women's rights were given proper constitutional recognition. As part of the drafting process, the National Council of Women's Rights presented over 200 amendments relating to women.

According to Jacqueline Pitanguy, past president of the National Council, CEDAW was a very useful tool for women's advocacy around the constitution. It provided a reference and a framework for articulating specific rights. The Brazilian constitution contains provisions on gender equality, gender-based violence, State responsibility for the prevention of domestic violence, the equality of rights within marriage, family planning, and equality in employment that parallel CEDAW provisions. For example, the constitution revoked the long-standing principle of the husband's leadership ("chefia") of the family unit and established that "the rights and duties relating to the conjugal unit are exercised equally by the man and the woman" (CEDAW article 16). . . .

Brazil ratified CEDAW in 1984, but with a reservation on laws relating to the family. It was only after the passage of the 1988 amendments to the constitution that it was removed—the reservation was now in violation of the Brazilian constitution's guarantees of gender equality . . .

II. The Courts

Judges are not always prepared to base their decisions on international treaties such as CEDAW. If their country has ratified the Convention, they usually have the authority to consider it, either as part of national law or as an aid to interpreting national law, but many judges are unfamiliar and uncomfortable with the idea of doing so. To convince the courts to make use of the Women's Convention, it is often useful to provide examples of other countries in which the courts have done so, as well as instances in which the courts have applied other international treaties and covenants.

Some of the most interesting and significant decisions are produced when a court decides to combine a vague or inadequate constitutional guarantee of women's equality with the principles of gender equality articulated in CEDAW. A two-dimensional constitutional vision is thereby transformed into a three-dimensional vision, and the protection afforded women's human rights becomes stronger and more meaningful than might even have been anticipated when the constitution was drafted.

Popular education has to be part of any litigation strategy. Good arguments can persuade a court to rule in favour of women's human rights, but decisions still have to be implemented. If not enough work has been done to inform and educate the Government and the general public, there is a real possibility that a court's decision will not be properly enforced or even that the decision might be overturned by new legislation. . . .

Nepal

[In 1993,] in *Dhungana v. Nepal,* the Forum for Women, Law and Development asked the Supreme Court to overturn a law that gave sons a share of ancestral property at birth but severely restricted daughters' entitlements. Section 16 of the Chapter on Partition of Nepal's *National Code* denied daughters a share of their parents' property until they reached the age of 35 without having married, and required that it be returned to the family if a daughter subsequently married. Because CEDAW has the status of national law in Nepal, the case was argued both as a violation of the Convention and as a violation of the constitution's equality guarantee. The Supreme Court found that the law did discriminate against women, but did not act immediately to invalidate it. Instead, the court directed the Nepalese Government to "introduce an appropriate Bill to parliament within one year—by making necessary consultations with recognised Women's Organisations, sociologists, the concerned social organisations and lawyers—and by studying and considering also the legal provisions made in other countries in this regard."

The Government did not take any real steps to begin drafting new legislation after this decision was released, and women's NGOs decided to take the initiative themselves. A meeting was held with the Minister of Law and Justice and the lawyers who had been involved in the case to demand action. NGOs began work drafting a private bill to revise the inheritance law, which would give daughters inheritance rights at birth and give spouses the right to half of each other's property. They also conducted a study of foreign laws on inheritance rights and of the existing Nepalese system. The various districts of the country were mobilised to rally for support and were consulted for feedback on the proposed bill. At the same time, the Ministry of Women came up with its own draft bill, similar to the private bill.

Unfortunately, the bill the Government introduced in the 11th session of parliament was not based on the principles the NGOs and the Ministry of Women had advocated. It recognises a daughter's right to inherit, but, as with the earlier law, entitlements would be lost upon marriage. Clause 16 of the bill specifies that when a daughter marries after partition, whatever remains of her share in her father's property reverts to the successors of her maternal home. Women's NGOs have made an application to have this aspect of the bill amended.

As of May 1998, parliament still had not discussed the inheritance bill. Women's NGOs organised a demonstration to demand that the bill be moved forward. Over 200 women from over 60 districts in Nepal took part, and more than 100 of them were arrested when they tried to enter the house of representatives (they were released the following day). Among the women who were arrested was member of parliament Sapana Pradhan Malla, who had been legal counsel in the *Dhungana* case.

It is uncertain at present just what changes can be expected to Nepal's inheritance law. But what is already clear is that the law reform campaign has had a real effect on the public discourse around women's human rights in Nepal. According to Sapana Pradhan Malla,

. . . the advocacy to challenge Nepal's inheritance law led by women and women's groups had a positive impact on the empowerment of women in the country. Because of the court decision, the entire society was challenged to start rethinking the patriarchal structure, male supremacy, and the status and individual freedom of women. Women have begun to be vigilant about the issue and link it to the broader issue of equality. Because of the intervention, such issues have been elevated to the level of public debate, forcing Government to reconsider its understanding of the equality clause in the constitution. And women have become part of the law reform process. Finally, the advocacy has united women and NGOs to continue working for the advancement of the human rights of women.

Australia

In 1988, in *Aldridge v. Booth*, the court was asked to declare the sexual harassment provisions of Australia's new *Sex Discrimination Act* unconstitutional. According to the Australian constitution, the federal Government's powers to legislate are limited, and restricted to certain areas. Before the Convention was ratified in 1984, it was clear that the federal Government was prohibited from passing national legislation in the area of sexual harassment in employment. However, after ratification, the Government did pass a law, and it relied on the new international obligations it had undertaken as giving it the necessary authority.

The court upheld the *Sex Discrimination Act*, agreeing with the Government that CEDAW ratification had effectively expanded its ability to pass national laws regarding women's human rights. The constitution gave the federal Government the power to legislate with respect to external affairs, and this power included the implementation of its treaty obligations. The court found that this power extended, specifically, to the Government's obligations regarding the prevention of sexual harassment under CEDAW: the CEDAW Committee has defined sexual harassment as discrimination in a General Recommendation, and CEDAW article [2] requires states to eliminate all forms of discrimination against women. The Government therefore had both the authority and the obligation to pass a national law prohibiting sexual harassment.

Costa Rica

In 1991, at the Costa Rican constitutional court, Alda Facio for Comité de América Latina y el Caribe para la Defensa de los Derechos de la Mujer (CLADEM) challenged the practice of requiring a husband's consent for medical sterilisation. She argued that this administrative practice violated the constitution's guarantee of equality. The difficulty she faced in making this argument was that the equality guarantee did not specifically mention gender, and it was unclear what the scope of a woman's right to equality under the constitution might be. She proposed that the court interpret the constitution in the light of CEDAW principles for this purpose.

The court did rely on the CEDAW in reaching its decision. It referred to CEDAW's definition of discrimination, and to article 16, which provides that States shall ensure equality in marriage and family relations, to find that the practice violated women's equality rights. The court also found that the Government had a positive obligation to take action to stop this practice. . . .

III. National Laws

The connection between CEDAW advocacy and changes to national legislation often cannot be established very clearly. Many important laws for women have now passed following CEDAW ratification; women's NGOs have frequently used the Women's Convention as a component of their campaigns to push for these laws; and Governments will rely on these laws at CEDAW Committee sessions as proof that they are fulfilling their obligations under the Convention. But there is really no way to show just what was determinative in the passage of any given law. Furthermore, as the Women's Convention increasingly becomes an integral part of a nation's human rights culture, its contribution becomes harder to isolate and identify.

There are, of course, some laws in relation to which the role played by CEDAW is quite clear. These are laws that actually cite CEDAW in their preambles or text, and some have been passed in connection with efforts to get CEDAW ratified—either as preparation for ratification or in response to the Government's failure to ratify.

It is important that public education accompany the effort to pass or amend legislation. Women must be informed about new legal entitlements that have been created, before they can be expected to claim them. Government bureaucracies, local administrators, and police departments must also recognise and respect these new entitlements in order for these claims to be enforced.

United States: San Francisco

In April 1998, by unanimous vote, the San Francisco Board of Supervisors passed an ordinance to implement the CEDAW principles within the city. The ordinance endorses the principles of the Convention, and creates the framework for integrating them into city governance. A San Francisco CEDAW task force is created to oversee implementation, and gender analyses are initiated in the areas of city employment, funding allocation, and service delivery. Action plans will respond to the discrimination identified in these studies. In addition, human rights training will be conducted in all city departments. The city Government has allocated $100,000 in its 1999 budget to fund the first stage of implementation.

Successful passage of the ordinance followed 18 months of intensive political organising, led by the Women's Institute for Leadership Development for Human Rights (WILD). . . .

According to WILD: "While criticising human rights abuses abroad, the United States has systematically fallen short of producing these same rights within its own borders. Although the U.S. Government has acknowledged that everyone must have civil and political rights, it has continued to deny that economic, social and cultural rights are fundamental human rights." . . .

The focal point for the campaign was a public hearing, which was held to convince both the city Government and the people of San Francisco that implementing the Convention would make a difference to women's lives. Members of the Board of Supervisors were invited to be panelists at the hearing. They listened to over 2 hours of testimony from women, in the form of personal accounts and policy arguments, about violence against women, economic injustice, and inadequate health care. The Members of the Board made a commitment at the end of that hearing to take action. The next day the Board passed a resolution calling for national ratification of CEDAW and stating that the city would begin the process of implementing the Convention locally.

A small working group, composed of representatives from WILD, the Commission on the Status of Women, and the Board of Supervisors, immediately began drafting an implementation ordinance. . . .

The CEDAW ordinance was taken to the Board of Supervisors for a first vote in March 1998. Support was now quite solid for the ordinance, with the supervisors sensing that failing to vote for it might be damaging to them politically. The ordinance was quickly and unanimously passed into law. By their campaign to pass the ordinance the women's NGOs intend to improve conditions for women in San Francisco, but they also hope to have a broader impact on the state of women's human rights in the United States, where the U.S. Government has failed to ratify CEDAW. According to Krishanthi Dharmaraj, of WILD, "This legislation sends a strong message. . . . San Francisco may be the first city, but it will not be the last. Several cities have already contacted WILD about passing similar laws in their own communities." Advocacy work is currently being done to prepare for the passage of a CEDAW implementation law at the State level in California. If passed, this law would set a standard for the rest of the country. . . .

Costa Rica

Costa Rica became a signatory to the Women's Convention in 1980, but it was not until 1984, following intensive advocacy by women's NGOs and prominent politicians, that CEDAW was ratified. . . .

The women who had supported [President] Arias's campaign [for the 1986–1990 term], and those who now held positions in Government moved quickly to make sure that the Government kept its election promises. They crafted legislation to implement Costa Rica's CEDAW commitments that initially focused on women's political participation and representation. . . .

A broad coalition of women's NGOs began work on a multidimensional strategy to ensure the bill's passage into law. . . . [Events included] [t]own hall meetings[,] . . . '[c]ulture-fairs' . . . using puppet shows, music, dance, theatre, and poetry . . . [, meetings of] politically prominent women with individual reporters and media personalities . . . [and demonstrations.] . . .

The bill was passed into law in 1990, as *The Law of Promotion of the Social Equality of Women.* Unfortunately, the provisions relating to women's political participation had been watered down, so that parties were now only encouraged to increase women's nominations and required to spend an unspecified 'percentage' of public funds on improving women's participation. However, most of the bill's other provisions remained intact in the final version. Costa Rica's *Law of Promotion of the Social Equality of Women* requires the following:

- The State must share the cost of child care with all working parents of children under seven years of age;
- Property titles must be registered under the names of both spouses, and single women's property must be registered in their own names;
- Working women are protected against dismissal due to pregnancy; reinstatement can be ordered and employers may be sanctioned;
- Women are entitled to three-months maternity leave following adoption;
- Mothers and fathers are given equal rights over their children;
- Women in common-law relationships are entitled to inherit property of the relationship . . . [and]
- The courts are authorised to order an abusive spouse to leave the home and to continue providing economic support. . . .

Japan

Japan ratified CEDAW in 1985, and several pieces of legislation were enacted at that time to bring Japanese law into conformity with the Convention. The most important of these were the 1984 amendment to the *Nationality Law,* which conferred Japanese nationality on the children of Japanese women, and the 1985 *Equal Employment Opportunity Law (EEOL)* which prohibited employment discrimination in the private sector. Women's NGOs consistently criticised the *EEOL* because of the weakness of its enforcement provisions, and the Japanese Government was finally convinced in 1997 to amend the law to strengthen these provisions.

China

China passed the *Law on the Protection of Women's Rights and Interests* in 1992. It was developed under the authority of the All China Women's Federation, and was drafted over a three-year period by Government officials and legal academics. The law states that it is intended to implement both the Chinese constitution's guarantee of gender equality and China's obligations under CEDAW.

The law's scope is very broad. Its six chapters set out political rights, educational and cultural rights, labour rights, property rights, rights in marriage and the family and 'personal' rights encompassing personal freedom, bodily integrity, dignity, honour, and reputation. The law provides that affirmative action measures should be taken to increase women's participation in the legislatures and Government administration. It also issues a general call for greater attention to the structural problems underlying gender inequality in China.

Many of the law's provisions repeat entitlements already established in other recent Chinese legislation, such as the 1980 *Marriage Law*, the 1985 *Inheritance Law*, and the 1986 *General Principles of Civil Law.* Some new protections have been added, however, most notably in relation to housing and agricultural land.

Although the substance of the law is quite progressive, the challenge is implementation. Women are entitled to bring legal claims over the violation of their rights under the law, and the State has control over the progress of these claims. The law's enforcement is actually at the State's discretion. While it is not unusual for a Chinese law to give the State this determinative role, the impact of the *Law on the Protection of Women's Rights and Interests* will depend on the Government's commitment. . . .

V. The CEDAW Reporting Process

When a State ratifies CEDAW, it undertakes the obligation to present reports at the United Nations on the progress it has made implementing women's human rights. The first report is due one year after ratification, and a further report is required every four years following that date. These reports are made to the CEDAW Committee. The Committee engages in a "constructive dialogue" with the Government delegation presenting the report regarding implementation of the Convention, and comments on whether the steps the Government has taken to implement CEDAW constitute adequate progress. The Committee also produces recommendations ("concluding comments") about the actions the Government should be taking under CEDAW, and about areas in which it might focus its efforts. Both the State reports and the summaries of the Committee's concluding comments are public documents. . . .

Women's NGOs are not formally included in the CEDAW Committee sessions at which Government reports are presented, but their communication with the Committee is a crucial part of the process. The Committee has welcomed independent information to help it assess Government claims and to determine where improvements are needed, and the Committee has called on NGOs to help provide that information. For this purpose, many NGOs have joined together in coalitions to prepare "shadow reports" for the Committee, which describe the state of women's human rights in their countries and comment on their Governments' reports.

Women's NGOs have used the reporting process to good effect: to hold their Governments accountable for the claims and commitments made at the CEDAW Committee sessions, to continue dialogue with their Governments on implementing the CEDAW Committee's concluding comments, and as a vehicle to raise public awareness within their own countries.

Zimbabwe

The Government of Zimbabwe presented its first report to the CEDAW Committee in January 1998. The report painted a glowing portrait of the state of women's human rights in Zimbabwe, and its centrepiece was the 1982 *Legal Age of Majority Act (LAMA)*. This Act is very important to women in Zimbabwe. It places men and women on an equal legal footing, giving both full legal capacity at the age of 18. Because of *LAMA* women can: enter into any contract, including a marriage contract; acquire and dispose of property; open bank accounts; own businesses; be guardians of their children even if separated or widowed; apply for passports on their own; and access credit facilities. Also, it is *LAMA* that gave Zimbabwean women the right to vote.

Just two weeks after presenting its CEDAW report, the Government brought *LAMA* to parliament for review and revision, and a move developed to have it completely repealed. The women's NGOs in Zimbabwe were outraged. A group of women's NGOs, including the Women's Action Group (WAG), had gone to the United Nations in New York, and conveyed a shadow report to the CEDAW Committee. They had listened while the Government used *LAMA* to congratulate itself on its women's human rights record before the CEDAW Committee. There seemed to be no relationship between the Government's statements to the international community and its actual legislative agenda for Zimbabwe. According to Rumbidzai Nhundu of WAG, it was clear the Government would feel free "to give with one hand and take with another if there were no people at home committed to keeping the Government accountable. As NGOs, we had to organise ourselves to make sure the Government's promises became a reality."

Women's NGOs immediately began a campaign to defend *LAMA*, and got their concerns into the Zimbabwean press. They publicised their concern about the need for Government adherence to its recently reiterated CEDAW commitments. They also had to counter the misinformation about the *LAMA* that was coming from some parliamentarians. Some MPs claimed that *LAMA*, and especially its provisions on marriage, had imported foreign values into Zimbabwe's culture and was responsible for social decay. The NGOs argued that this claim about cultural values was false and dishonest: "It appears that instead of discussing economic and other crucial issues, our policy-makers have chosen to make an innocent and well-meaning piece of legislation the scape-goat for all social ills. Unemployment is skyrocketing, and both young boys and girls are forced to loiter in the streets and indulge in unacceptable behaviours. These are the issues that deserve attention." The NGOs also convinced the MPs who were fighting for *LAMA's* repeal to meet with them, and obtained their promise to set up a parliamentary caucus where they could articulate the reasons the Act should be left intact.

By March 1998, they had managed to turn the political tide. The Minister of Justice made a public announcement that *LAMA* would *not* be changed or repealed.[F]

The NGOs see their successful defence of *LAMA* as the first step in an ongoing struggle to hold the Zimbabwean Government accountable for its obligations under the Convention. Responsibility for CEDAW monitoring will be divided among the various NGOs according to their expertise, and annual monitoring meetings will lead up to Zimbabwe's second CEDAW report. They are also working to ensure that CEDAW principles are reflected in the forthcoming land redistribution policy, constitutional review, and prevention of discrimination bill. The women's NGOs are determined, according to Nhundu, to "remind the Government of its commitments. We were there in New York, so the Government knows that we were listening to its promises." . . .

Mauritius

Mauritius presented its report to the CEDAW Committee in 1995. Women's NGOs were not in attendance to give a shadow report, but women in Mauritius had been consulted prior to the CEDAW session, and their concerns had been communicated to the CEDAW Committee. The Committee relied on this information when the Government representatives presented their account of the state of women's rights in Mauritius, and engaged the Mauritius delegation on the Government's failure to pass legislation prohibiting sex discrimination.

After the session was over, the Government held several press conferences, where it presented a selective report of the Committee's concluding comments. When Pramila Patten, of Women's Legal Rights Action Watch, informed the press that the CEDAW Committee's criticisms were being kept hidden, the Government publicly attacked her credibility. However, she was able to obtain a copy of the Committee's concluding comments, and once they had been circulated, the Government backed down. The Prime Minister was reprimanded for the misrepresentation. Soon after, in 1995, Article 16(3) of the Constitution was amended to insert the word "sex" in the definition of discrimination.

VI. Reservations

[M]any [States] ratified with reservations that limited their obligations to implement CEDAW principles in significant ways. The focus of these reservations varies. Frequently they concern potential conflicts between CEDAW and customary or religious law, or they reduce the State's obligations in the area of family relations.

States are entitled to enter reservations when they sign on to a convention or treaty, but according to the Vienna Convention on the Law of Treaties, reservations that are not compatible with the object and purpose of the Convention should not be permitted. Many of the reservations that States have entered on CEDAW seem to

---

[F] *See*, however, *Magaya v. Magaya*, [1999] 3 LRC 37 (Zimbabwe), in Chapter Five.

have crossed this line. States have reserved on whole areas of rights entitlement. In a few instances, they have made reservations that would seem to remove their obligation to implement the Convention as a whole. For example, Malaysia has reserved on CEDAW's implementation (article 2(f)), that requires the State "to take all appropriate measures" to end discrimination against women.

The high number of CEDAW reservations [that] do effectively withhold key Convention guarantees from women, or that undermine its core concepts of gender equality and non-discrimination, is deeply troubling. The CEDAW Committee has expressed its concern, and both the Vienna Declaration and the Beijing Programme of Action have urged countries to withdraw reservations "that are contrary to the Convention or which are otherwise incompatible with international law."

Because so many substantial reservations have been entered on the Women's Convention, women's NGOs frequently find themselves in the position of having to conduct two separate campaigns to bring CEDAW home. After ratification, their work has to begin a second time, to remove the constraints that reservations impose on CEDAW's application. Even if the State cannot be convinced to lift its reservations completely, real progress can be achieved if a blanket reservation to a CEDAW article can be narrowed down, so that all women are not deprived of this article's protection in all circumstances. Women's NGOs are engaged in important work on reservations, and there have been some successes—for example, Brazil has lifted its reservation, and Bangladesh has limited its reservation.

India

India ratified CEDAW in 1993 but effectively reserved on the articles relating to cultural and customary practices (5(a)) and to equality in marriage and family relations (16(1)). The Government made a declaration stating that it would follow a "policy of non-interference in the personal affairs of any Community without its initiative and consent," when implementing these provisions.

This declaration has been deeply troubling to women's NGOs, as it seriously undermines one of the most important contributions they felt CEDAW could make to the reform of Indian law. Women's equality rights are already recognised and respected in many of India's laws affecting public life. However, discrimination has not been challenged in the key laws that regulate and structure private life. The Indian personal laws, which control matters such as inheritance, property rights, and adoption, continue to follow patriarchal principles. For example, according to Hindu personal law, daughters are denied most of the important coparcenary property rights that are granted to sons; women's right to the family dwelling home is subordinate to men's rights; women's guardianship of their children is secondary to that of men's; and wives cannot initiate adoption. Women's NGOs . . . believe that so long as private life is thoroughly regulated according to patriarchal principles, it will not be possible for women to exercise their public rights in a meaningful way. As Ran Jethmalani, of Women's Action Research and Legal Action for Women (WARLAW), explains the problem:

The regime of personal laws which are gender discriminatory and violate article [16] of CEDAW have reduced women to second class citizens. Unless these laws are amended women cannot be empowered to combat violence and cultural practices that frustrate and deny them equality and dignity. It is futile to empower women by giving them decisive voices in decision making bodies where those voices are feeble and unequal without at the same time changing the laws—if each one's voice including the voices of women is to have significance and meaning then those voices must be the voices of free persons and not slaves.

What Indian women's NGOs find especially valuable about the way the Convention conceptualises equality is its recognition that equality in private life and equality in public are integrally connected. CEDAW requires the State to ensure conditions of equality in all aspects of women's lives, not just in their public legal and political interactions. In particular, article 5 of CEDAW obliges the Government to intervene in private life and eliminate "prejudices and other customary practices which are based on the idea of the inferiority or the superiority of either of the sexes or on stereotyped roles for men or women." In addition, CEDAW article 16 requires that the State guarantee relations of equality within marriage and family relations. With its reservations on articles 5 and 16, however, the Indian Government appears to have adopted a strategy of passive inaction on discrimination in women's private lives, under the rubric of respect for the wishes of minority communities.

WARLAW has developed an innovative and incisive legal challenge to force the Government to take action on its CEDAW commitments. In 1994, it brought a petition to the Indian Supreme Court. The petition asks the court to order the Government to state exactly how it intends to determine whether communities want the personal laws changed—and to state exactly how the Government intends to include the voices of women from these communities when making its assessment. In effect, WARLAW is challenging the monolithic and static model of community that is implicit in the Government's declaration. WARLAW is taking the position that the Government cannot simply assume that communities want discriminatory traditions to continue unchanged, or that male community leaders necessarily speak for the women in their communities.

NOTE

The Complaints Procedure. At the time the report above was written, there was no CEDAW Committee jurisprudence. By August 2007 the Committee had issued seven individual decisions and a report on an inquiry under Article 8 of the Optional Protocol. In several decisions, the Committee ruled that since the complainant had not exhausted domestic remedies or because the injuries occurred prior to the entry into force of the Protocol in that country, the Committee could not entertain her complaint. One decision was issued in favor of a Hungarian woman seeking protection from her severely abusive husband. The Committee found that the State had not fulfilled its obligations under CEDAW to protect women from domestic violence and ordered the State to take immediate action to counter domestic violence. *Ms. A.T. v. Hungary*, Communication No. 2/2003 (2005). Another decision, *Ms. A.S. v. Hungary*,

Communication No. 4/2004 (2006), found in favor of a Hungarian Roma woman who had been subjected to a coerced sterilization by hospital medical staff. In the Article 8 inquiry, the Committee's *Report on Mexico* describes the Committee findings concerning a pattern of abductions, rapes, and murders of women in the Ciudad Juarez area of Chihuahua, and the government's failure sufficiently to investigate and prosecute the cases. U.N. Doc. CEDAW/C/2005/Op.8/Mexico (2005). *See* RossRights for access to all CEDAW Committee decisions.

Chapter 10
Enforcing Women's International Rights at Home: International Law in Domestic Courts

I. The Relationship Between National and International Law: Theory

Since 1948, the world has developed a comprehensive regional and international human rights system. Many nations have begun to implement these norms at the domestic level by passing and enforcing new laws. But many more states comply in name only. They ratify human rights treaties and conventions without reservations yet leave grossly discriminatory laws on the books. In those countries, women's legal status remains deeply subordinate to that of men.

Human rights litigation in domestic courts could make a dent if courts strike down statutes that condemn women to a lesser position as a violation of their equality rights. But can domestic courts apply international human rights norms to cases before them? Litigators and judges are beginning to do so in countries as diverse as Botswana, Costa Rica, India, Tanzania, Papua New Guinea, South Africa, and the United States. Some are working within common-law jurisdictions; others are not. This chapter will introduce you to the relevant theory, demonstrate the different methods courts use in applying international law, and provide a case study of practices that might be attacked in court. As you read each of the cases, think about how the court uses international law.

Anne F. Bayefsky, *General Approaches to Domestic Application of Women's International Human Rights Law*
in Human Rights of Women: National and International Perspectives 351, 353–54, 359–60, 363–69 (Rebecca J. Cook ed., 1994)

Even where international human rights law has created . . . adequate enforcement machinery, it is often inaccessible to individual grievors. Correspondence with an international agency is beyond the reach of many potential clients. This can result from a lack of resources, ignorance of local counsel of international remedies, or a failure by national authorities to disseminate information about the international human rights obligations of the state.

For all these reasons, it is imperative to identify other means by which international standards, such as those affecting women, can be enforced. The concern of most states in refusing to participate in the creation of significant international machinery is the preservation of national sovereignty. Recourse to national enforcement agencies would therefore seem to offer a logical alternative.

International agencies readily concede their status as fora of last resort. The European Court of Human Rights, for example, reminds states that international machinery for protecting fundamental rights is subsidiary to national systems of safeguarding rights. The Court has stated that the national authorities are in a better position than the international judge to determine the appropriateness of limitations upon rights. International treaties that do permit a right of individual petition contain a standard clause requiring grievors to first exhaust domestic remedies before coming forward. In other words, there is an initial reliance on national agencies to protect human rights. It would be a natural extension of such reliance to encourage national judicial bodies to enforce international human rights standards.

Domestic courts can serve as a missing link between promulgation and realization of international human rights norms to the benefit of both international and domestic law. International bodies, whose work tends to be far more interstitial than that of national judicial organs, can benefit from more frequent interpretations of international standards by a variety of national courts. More enlightened interpretations of domestic human rights laws may also be fostered through reference to international law. . . .

Domestic Rules of the Relationship Between Municipal Law and International Law

Utilizing domestic courts to enforce women's international human rights law or enhancing domestic law by way of international human rights standards will be a function of domestic legal rules. The relevant domestic rules concern: . . .

2. the relationship between conventional international law and domestic law; in a federal state there will be the further issue of the relationship between conventional international law and each of state/provincial law and federal /national law.

These rules must be stated on a country-by-country basis. They do not differ, however, on the basis of the substance of international law. In other words, the domestic legal rules governing the relationship between international and municipal law will not be unique to international human rights law concerning women. . . .

The rules governing the relationship of international law to municipal law are attempts to reconcile a variety of policies: protection of national sovereignty, protection of the supremacy of domestic lawmaking institutions from the powers of the executive, satisfaction of the state's international obligations, and realization by individuals of the benefits of international norms. . . . The different ways of reconciling these policies are formulated in two general theories about the relationship between municipal law and international law: the adoption and the transformation theory.

The adoption theory states that international law is part of domestic law automatically, that is, without an act of incorporation, except where it conflicts with statutory law or well-established rules of the common law. Transformation theory states that international law is only part of domestic law when it has been incorporated into domestic law.

Again, whether a particular state and its legal system embraces the adoption theory or transformation theory must be stated on a country-by-country basis. A corollary of an adoption theory would be acknowledgment by domestic courts of the capacity for municipal law to change as international law changes. . . .

Conventional International Law and Municipal Law

(a) General. . . .

[T]here are an abundance of international treaties devoted to women and issues related to sexual discrimination. In states where such treaties have been ratified, they may serve as a useful tool in domestic litigation.

In states where treaty-making is an executive act, and the consent of domestic law-making institutions is not required, domestic courts will try to protect the authority of the law-making bodies from any attempt by the executive to change the law merely by way of ratification. . . . That protection is achieved by way of the transformation theory for the relationship between conventional international law and municipal law. In these states an important initial question for domestic courts will be whether the relevant treaty has been incorporated. This will likely require evidence that the lawmaking body intended to make the treaty part of the law of the land, either by passing a law that states simply that the treaty has the authority of domestic law, or by passing law(s) drawn from the treaty.

In common law countries the presumption that the law-making body(ies) do not intend to act in breach of the state's international obligations also applies to conventional international law. In the context of implementing legislation, this means that domestic courts should interpret domestic implementing legislation in conformity with a convention insofar as the domestic legislation permits. In other words, they should do so where there is no obvious inconsistency between the domestic law and the international law.

At the same time, if the domestic legislation cannot be given a possible meaning in conformity with the treaty, or if there is a conflict between the domestic legislation and international law, it is the domestic legislation which will prevail.

Even in the absence of implementing legislation, the presumption that the law-making institutions do not intend to legislate in violation of the state's treaty obligations still operates; wherever possible, statutes ought not to be interpreted as violating international conventional law. In this context, however, the transformation theory's rule that without implementing legislation the treaty is not part of domestic law suggests that a strong need for having recourse to international conventional law should first be established. This need could, for example, take the form of a requirement that an ambiguity in the domestic law must be established by considering the domestic law on its own, before recourse to the treaty as an interpretive aid becomes acceptable.

(b) A Canadian example

Many of these general rules are illustrated in the few Canadian court cases that mention the CEDAW Convention, which Canada has ratified. Canadian law takes a transformation theory approach to the relationship between domestic law and treaties.

Of the approximately 225 cases that both interpret Canadian human rights legislation and mention international human rights law, seven refer specifically to the CEDAW Convention. . . . In two cases the reference to the CEDAW Convention, although not directly determinative, supported the outcome of the case. In the first instance, the Convention supported the court's finding that "marital status" was a ground of discrimination under the constitutional Charter of Rights equality provision. In the second instance, the Convention was used to "reinforce the view that Canadian society is committed to equalizing the role of parents in the care of children as much as possible, . . . in particular for the achievement of greater equality in the work place for women." There is a third case in which a lower court used the Women's Convention, as well as the Racial Discrimination Convention and I.L.O. Convention No. 111 on Discrimination in Employment, to support its definition of the equality rights provision of the constitutional Charter of Rights. However, when the issue came before the Supreme Court of Canada it arrived at a different definition of discrimination in the context of interpreting the same provision without considering international law.

Overall, the Canadian experience with the use of the CEDAW Convention (and other international human rights instruments) to construe domestic law indicates that courts tend to be result-oriented. Where courts are inclined to come to a conclusion consistent with the CEDAW Convention, but on the basis of quite independent reasons, they may point to the Convention for support. Where courts are inclined to come to conclusions incompatible with the Convention, they will simply ignore it. Legal commentators are left to object that this result-oriented approach is inconsistent with the common law presumption that domestic law ought to be construed in conformity with Canadian international obligations in the absence of clearly inconsistent domestic provisions.

(c) Use of international material collateral to treaties

Encouraging domestic courts to use treaty obligations in interpreting and applying domestic law should go beyond consideration of the language of the treaty. In a number of contexts, international human rights law affecting women has been interpreted by international bodies. As the extent of this collateral material grows, it will be increasingly important to examine it along with the treaties themselves.

For example, domestic courts have difficulty distinguishing between positive laws designed to provide women with assistance that is not available to men, and discrimination. International human rights law is not so confused. The CEDAW Convention explicitly deems certain special measures not to be discrimination. The Convention makes obvious the link that is understood between providing special measures and preventing discrimination or implementing equality. Article 4(1) states:

Adoption by States Parties of temporary special measures *aimed at accelerating de facto equality* between men and women shall not be considered discrimination as defined in the present Convention, but shall in no way entail as a consequence the maintenance of unequal or separate standards; these measures shall be discontinued when the objectives of equality of opportunity and treatment have been achieved.

Special measures can thus be aimed at achieving equality, and while that objective remains unfulfilled, they are not discrimination.

The Human Rights Committee under the Civil and Political Covenant has made a General Comment [18] on nondiscrimination which helps to expand the point; it states that, "as long as such action is needed to correct discrimination in fact, it is a case of legitimate differentiation under the Covenant." CEDAW has affirmed the importance of this obligation in its General Recommendations contained in its annual report. General Recommendation No. 5 states:

Taking note that . . . there is still a need for action to be taken to implement fully the Convention by introducing measures to promote de facto equality between men and women, . . . Recommends that States parties make more use of temporary special measures such as positive action, preferential treatment or quota systems to advance women's integration into education, the economy, politics and employment.

The Human Rights Committee has similarly interpreted the Civil and Political Covenant to require affirmative action programs in certain circumstances. In its General Comment [18] on nondiscrimination the Committee states that:

the principle of equality sometimes requires States parties to take affirmative action in order to diminish or eliminate conditions which cause or help to perpetuate discrimination prohibited by the Covenant. For example, in a State where the general conditions of a certain part of the population prevent or impair their enjoyment of human rights, the State should take specific action to correct those conditions. Such action may involve granting for a time to the part of the population concerned certain preferential treatment in specific matters as compared with the rest of the population.

Thus discussion before domestic courts of the nature of certain treaty obligations concerning equality is usefully elaborated through the comments of the relevant treaty bodies . . .

Thus the recommendations of CEDAW give detailed guidance as to the content of particular articles and the types of steps that should be taken to give effect to those obligations. As the considered collective pronouncements of the body entrusted with monitoring the implementation of the Convention, general recommendations should have considerable authority, even if formally they do not constitute a binding interpretation of the Convention. They should therefore be an integral part of the domestic application of international law.

International Law That Does Not Bind the State

In some instances, domestic courts may still make use of international law as an aid to interpreting domestic law even where such international law does not bind the state concerned. In this context, regardless whether the domestic rules embrace the adoption or transformation theory, the international law in question is not part of the law of the land. Its relevance may result from other considerations. For instance,

(a) Courts often make some reference to non-binding sources of law from other jurisdictions, for the purpose of formulating informed responses to domestic legal questions.

(b) Sometimes domestic law suggests that the courts consider the requirements of a free and democratic society. In so doing, it invites comparison with the legal responses of other free and democratic societies.

(c) The drafting history and actual provisions of an international law that is not binding on the state may be closely related to an international law that is binding on the state (for example, the European Convention is closely related to the Covenant on Civil and Political Rights).

(d) Non-binding international conventional law may be associated with a sophisticated quasi-judicial and judicial system—like the European Convention on Human Rights—which makes its jurisprudence useful.

There is a danger, however, that the reasons domestic courts make use of such international law will not be articulated. And in the absence of explicit justification, reference to such sources will often be haphazard. In other words, such international law may simply be invoked where it supports a conclusion already determined. If it suggests any contrary result, it will often be ignored.

Expressions by Government Officials of the Relevance of International Human Rights Law in Applying Domestic Law

General

Government officials will be asked by members of international bodies about the relevance of international law in domestic courts. Those questions may be put in the context of consideration of government reports to the various human rights treaty bodies. The responses of government officials will be found in the summary records of those committees and (more briefly) in their annual reports.

These comments could be valuable in the context of domestic litigation—particularly in opposition to government counsel. An individual within a state wishing to convince a domestic court to use international law to interpret domestic law could usefully refer to an affirmation by government officials of the relevance of international law for this purpose. Furthermore, remarks by government officials—often heard in international fora—that domestic law provides rights protection at least as great as that provided by international law can also be helpful in encouraging domestic courts to take account of international law.

A Canadian Example. . . .

[Canada's Second Report to the CEDAW Committee] stated:

Another primary means of implementing the Convention in Canada is through human rights legislation which prohibits discrimination an various grounds, including sex and marital status.

The Report went on to refer specifically to

measures adopted by each government to implement the provisions of the Convention in areas within its jurisdiction. . . . Article 2: . . . In July 1983, the Act [Canadian Human Rights Act] was amended to specifically prohibit discrimination on the ground of pregnancy or childbirth. . . .

During the consideration of Canada's Second Report to CEDAW in February 1990, the Committee was told by the Canadian delegation that "the [constitutional Charter of Rights] was an important means of implementing the Convention in Canada."

Thus, in different international contexts, Canadian government officials have represented Canadian law as implementing international human rights obligations of Canada. Domestic courts could be encouraged to take such representations into account when interpreting domestic law.

This is at least one important reason why the comments of state officials before human rights treaty bodies should be closely monitored.

Mistakes

Judicial comprehension of public international law is frequently minimal. The rules of the relationship between international law and municipal law, which must be identified on a state-by-state basis, are often poorly understood. References to international law include many examples of errors concerning basic principles governing the relationship between domestic and international law, as well as the substance of international law.

Improvement of the familiarity of both bench and bar with international human rights law will require at least the following changes in domestic legal systems: increased judicial education, expansion of the number of law students reached by related law school courses, and significantly enriched library collections. Ultimately, these items turn on improving access to information and securing adequate financial resources, developments that in most states depend on a political will to recognize and enforce international human rights standards.

NOTES

Litigation Sources. Bayefsky identifies different sources and uses of international law. What are they? How do they differ?

Transformation and Adoption. Define the difference between transformation and adoption. Why would a lawyer need to know this before starting a lawsuit based on human rights law?

Educating Lawyers and Judges. In the late 1990s, the International Association of Women Judges (IAWJ) began organizing training sessions for judges on how to use international human rights norms in their courtrooms. They worked in different regions including Latin America and Africa. The Association developed materials on the subject and taught groups of highly-motivated judges from regional states in interactive one-week long sessions. The judges also learned how to become trainers themselves so that they could train judges within their countries once they returned home. For further information, *see* the IAWJ website, *available at* RossRights. The website includes decisions in cases relying on CEDAW.

Similarly, many law schools began developing international human rights courses that exposed students to these ideas. Law school clinical courses also allowed students to put theory into practice and to work with NGOs in litigating human rights cases. *See, e.g.*, the website for the International Women's Human Rights Clinic at Georgetown Law, *available at* RossRights.

P. N. Bhagwati, *Bangalore Principles*
14 COMMONWEALTH LAW BULLETIN 1196 (1988)[A]

Chairman's Concluding Statement

Between 24 and 26 February 1988 there was convened in Bangalore, India, a high level judicial colloquium on the Domestic Application of International Human Rights Norms. The Colloquium was administered by the Commonwealth Secretariat[B] on behalf of the Convenor, the Hon. Justice P. N. Bhagwati (former Chief Justice of India), with the approval of the Government of India, and with assistance from the Government of the State of Karnataka, India.

The participants were:
Justice P. N. Bhagwati (India) (Convenor)
Chief Justice E. Dumbutshena (Zimbabwe)
Judge Ruth Bader Ginsburg (USA)
Chief Justice Muhammad Haleem (Pakistan)
Deputy Chief Justice Sir Mari Kapi (Papua New Guinea)
Justice Michael D. Kirby, CMG (Australia)
Justice Rajsoomer Lallah (Mauritius)

[A] The Commonwealth is a voluntary organization composed of 53 sovereign member states, including Great Britain and many former colonies of the British empire. It was founded in 1965.

[B] The Commonwealth Secretariat staffs the Commonwealth. Its Legal and Constitutional Affairs Division works on issues related to human rights, the rule of law, and promotion of democratic values. The Bangalore conference is an example of attempts to create a cooperative legal environment in the member states, which share a common law legal tradition due to Great Britain's colonial influence.

Mr. Anthony Lester, QC (Britain)
Justice P. Ramanathan (Sri Lanka)
Tun Mohamed Salleh Bin Abas (Malaysia)
Justice M. P. Chandrakantaraj Urs (India)

There was a comprehensive exchange of views and full discussion of expert papers. The Convenor summarised the discussions in the following paragraphs:

1. Fundamental human rights and freedoms are inherent in all humankind and find expression in constitutions and legal systems throughout the world and in the international human rights instruments.

2. These international human rights instruments provide important guidance in cases concerning fundamental human rights and freedoms.

3. There is an impressive body of jurisprudence, both international and national, concerning the interpretation of particular human rights and freedoms and their application. This body of jurisprudence is of practical relevance and value to judges and lawyers generally.

4. In most countries whose legal systems are based upon the common law, international conventions are not directly enforceable in national courts unless their provisions have been incorporated by legislation into domestic law. However, there is a growing tendency for national courts to have regard to these international norms for the purpose of deciding cases where the domestic law—whether constitutional, statute or common law—is uncertain or incomplete.

5. This tendency is entirely welcome because it respects the universality of fundamental human rights and freedoms and the vital role of an independent judiciary in reconciling the competing claims of individuals and groups of persons with the general interests of the community.

6. While it is desirable for the norms contained in the international human rights instruments to be still more widely recognised and applied by national courts, this process must take fully into account local laws, traditions, circumstances and needs.

7. It is within the proper nature of the judicial process and well-established judicial functions for national courts to have regard to international obligations which a country undertakes—whether or not they have been incorporated into domestic law—for the purpose of removing ambiguity or uncertainty from national constitutions, legislation or common law.

8. However, where national law is clear and inconsistent with the international obligations of the State concerned, in common law countries the national court is obliged to give effect to national law. In such cases the court should draw such inconsistency to the attention of the appropriate authorities since the supremacy of national law in no way mitigates a breach of an international legal obligation which is undertaken by a country.

9. It is essential to redress a situation where, by reason of traditional legal training which has tended to ignore the international dimension, judges and practising lawyers are often unaware of the remarkable and comprehensive developments of statements of international human rights norms. For the practical implementation of these

views it is desirable to make provision for appropriate courses in universities and colleges, and for lawyers and law enforcement officials; provision in libraries of relevant materials; promotion of expert advisory bodies knowledgeable about developments in this field; better dissemination of information to judges, lawyers and law enforcement officials; and meetings for exchanges of relevant information and experience.

10. These views are expressed in recognition of the fact that judges and lawyers have a special contribution to make in the administration of justice in fostering universal respect for fundamental human rights and freedoms.

N O T E

Using the Bangalore Principles. Can international law be directly enforced in any common-law countries? In civil law countries? What do these judges see as the primary use of international law?

Vienna Convention on the Law of Treaties

1155 U.N.T.S. 331, *entered into force* Jan. 27, 1980, *available at* RossRights

Article 18. Obligation not to Defeat the Object and Purpose of a Treaty Prior to Its Entry Into Force

A state is obligated to refrain from acts which would defeat the object and purpose of a treaty when:

(a) it has signed the treaty or has exchanged instruments consituting the treaty subject to ratification, acceptance or approval, until it shall have made its intention clear not to become a party to the treaty. . . .

Article 26. "Pacta Sunt Servanda"

Every treaty in force is binding upon the parties to it and must be performed by them in good faith.

Article 27. Internal Law and Observance of Treaties

A party may not invoke the provisions of its internal law as justification for its failure to perform a treaty. . . .

N O T E S

Articles 18 and 26. What are the differences, if any, between the obligations imposed by Article 18 and Articles 26 and 27?

Status of the Vienna Convention. The United States signed the Vienna Convention on the Law of Treaties in 1970, but has not ratified it. As of August, 2007, 108 countries were parties to the treaty, which entered into force on January 27, 1980; forty-five other countries had signed but not yet ratified. The Vienna Convention was designed to codify customary international law—that is, customs treated by nations as general practices that are accepted as law. *Statute of the International Court of Justice*, art. 38 (1)(b), *available at* RossRights. Should the Convention be accorded the status of customary international law? If not, how should a country that has not ratified the Convention interpret its obligations with respect to other treaties? Consider the following analysis by the American Law Institute.

AMERICAN LAW INSTITUTE, RESTATEMENT (THIRD) OF THE FOREIGN RELATIONS LAW OF THE UNITED STATES
§§ 111, 114–15, Comments, and Reporters' Notes (1987)

§ 111. International Law and Agreements as Law of the United States

(1) International law and international agreements of the United States are law of the United States and supreme over the law of the several States.

(2) Cases arising under international law or international agreements of the United States are within the Judicial Power of the United States and . . . are within the jurisdiction of the federal courts.

(3) Courts in the United States are bound to give effect to international law and to international agreements of the United States, except that a "non-self-executing" agreement will not be given effect as law in the absence of necessary implementation.

(4) An international agreement of the United States is "non-self-executing"

(a)   if the agreement manifests an intention that it shall not become effective as domestic law without the enactment of implementing legislation.

(b)   if the Senate in giving consent to a treaty, or Congress by resolution, requires implementing legislation, or

(c)   if implementing legislation is constitutionally required.

Comment. . . .

b. . . . A rule of international law or a provision of an international agreement derives its status as law in the United States from its character as an international legal obligation of the United States. . . .

c. International law and agreements as law of the United States. The proposition that international law and agreements are law in the United States is addressed largely to the courts. In appropriate cases they apply international law or agreements without the need of enactment by Congress or proclamation by the President. . . . Some international agreements of the United States are non-self-executing and will not be applied as law by the courts until they are implemented by necessary legislation. . . .

d. International law and agreements as supreme federal law. Treaties made under the authority of the United States, like the Constitution itself and the laws of the United States, are expressly declared to be "supreme Law of the Land" by Article VI of the Constitution. . . . Interpretations of international agreements by the United States Supreme Court are binding on the States. . . . A determination of international law by the Supreme Court is binding on the States and on State courts. . . .

h. Self-executing and non-self-executing international agreements. In the absence of special agreement, it is ordinarily for the United States to decide how it will carry out its international obligations. Accordingly, the intention of the United States determines whether an agreement is to be self-executing in the United States or should await implementation by legislation or appropriate executive or administrative action. If the international agreement is silent as to its self-executing character and the intention of the United States is unclear, account must be taken of any statement by the President in concluding the agreement or in submitting it to the Senate for consent or to the Congress as a whole for approval, and of any expression by the Senate or by Congress in dealing with the agreement. . . . After the agreement is concluded, often the President must decide in the first instance whether the agreement is self-executing, i.e., whether existing law is adequate to enable the United States to carry out its obligations, or whether further legislation is required. Congress may also consider whether new legislation is necessary and, if so, what it should provide. Whether an agreement is to be given effect without further legislation is an issue that a court must decide when a party seeks to invoke the agreement as law. . . .

i. An international agreement cannot take effect as domestic law without implementation by Congress if the agreement would achieve what lies within the exclusive law-making power of Congress under the Constitution. Thus, an international agreement providing for the payment of money by the United States requires an appropriation of funds by Congress in order to effect the payment required by the agreement. . . .

Reporters' Notes. . . .

Since generally the United States is obligated to comply with a treaty as soon as it comes into force for the United States, compliance is facilitated and expedited if the treaty is self-executing. Moreover, when Congressional action is required but is delayed, the United States may be in default on its international obligation. Therefore, if the Executive Branch has not requested implementing legislation and Congress has not enacted such legislation, there is a strong presumption that the treaty has been considered self-executing by the political branches, and should be considered self-executing by the courts. (This is especially so if some time has elapsed since the treaty has come into force.) In that event, a finding that a treaty is not self-executing is a finding that the United States has been and continues to be in default, and should be avoided.

In general, agreements that can be readily given effect by executive or judicial bodies, federal or State, without further legislation, are deemed self-executing, unless a contrary intention is manifest. Obligations not to act, or to act only subject to limitations, are generally self-executing. In an opinion characterized by the Supreme Court as "very able" (see *United States v. Rauscher*, 119 U.S. 407 (1886)), the Court of Appeals of Kentucky said:

When it is provided by treaty that certain acts shall not be done, or that certain limitations or restrictions shall not be disregarded or exceeded by the contracting parties, the compact does not need to be supplemented by legislative or executive action, to authorize the courts of justice to decline to override those limitations or to exceed the prescribed restrictions, for the palpable and all-sufficient reason, that to do so would be not only to violate the public faith, but to transgress the "supreme law of the land."

Commonwealth v. Hawes, 76 Ky. (13 Bush) 697 (1878). . . .

[A]greements conferring rights on foreign nationals, especially in matters ordinarily governed by State law, have been given effect without any implementing legislation, their self-executing character assumed without discussion. This has been true from early in United States history. . . . See the numerous treaties assuring aliens the right to inherit property in the United States, . . . granting alien equal right to engage in trade[,] . . . assuring alien right to leave country and return. . . .

Treaties were held non-self-executing in *Cameron Septic Tank Co. v. Knoxville*, 227 U.S. 39 (1913) (giving effect to Congressional view that industrial property treaty was non-self-executing). . . . Treaties on subjects that Congress has regulated extensively are more likely to be interpreted as non-self-executing . . . [;] e.g., (peace treaty undertaking regarding patents on industrial property). The human rights provisions of the United Nations Charter were held to be non-self-executing in *Sei Fujii v. California*, 242 P.2d 617 (1952). . . .

§ 114. Interpretation of Federal Statute in Light of International Law or Agreement

Where fairly possible, a United States statute is to be construed so as not to conflict with international law or with an international agreement of the United States.

Comment:

a. Interpretation to avoid violation by the United States. The principle of interpretation in this section is influenced by the fact that the courts are obliged to give effect to a federal statute even if it is inconsistent with a pre-existing rule of international law or with a provision of an international agreement of the United States. See § 115.

Reporters' Notes

1. *Interpretation to avoid violation of international obligation.* Chief Justice Marshall stated that "an Act of Congress ought never to be construed to violate the law of nations if any other possible construction remains. . . ." *Murray v. Schooner Charming Betsy*, 6 U.S. (2 Cranch) 64, 118, 2 L.Ed. 208 (1804). On overall occasions the Supreme Court has interpreted acts of Congress so as to avoid conflict with earlier treaty provisions. . . .

§ 115. Inconsistency Between International Law or Agreement and Domestic Law: Law of the United States

(1)(a) An act of Congress supersedes an earlier rule of international law or a provision of an international agreement as law of the United States if the purpose of the act to supersede the earlier rule or provision is clear or if the act and the earlier rule or provision cannot be fairly reconciled.

(b) That a rule of international law or a provision of an international agreement is superseded as domestic law does not relieve the United States of its international obligation or of the consequences of a violation of that obligation.

(2) A provision of a treaty of the United States that becomes effective as law of the United States supersedes as domestic law any inconsistent preexisting provision of a law or treaty of the United States.

(3) A rule of international law or a provision of an international agreement of the United States will not be given effect as law in the United States if it is inconsistent with the United States Constitution.

Comment:

a. Federal statute inconsistent with earlier United States agreement or rule of international law. Acts of Congress, treaties and other international agreements of the United States, and principles of customary international law, are all federal law, § 111. An act of Congress and a self-executing treaty of the United States (§ 111(3)) are of equal status in United States law, and in case of inconsistency the later in time prevails. An act of Congress will also be given effect as domestic law in the face of an earlier international agreement of the United States other than a treaty, or a preexisting rule of customary international law. . . .

Reporters' Notes

1. *Equality of international agreements and statutes.* The principle that United States treaties and federal statutes are of equal authority, so that in case of inconsistency the later in time should prevail, was derived early from the Supremacy Clause, Article VI of the Constitution. That article declares the Constitution, the laws of the United States, and treaties to be "the supreme Law of the Land"; the courts inferred that treaties are law equal in authority to United States statutes. *Head Money Cases*, 112 U.S. 580 (1884); *Whitney v. Robertson*, 124 U.S. 190 (1888); *The Chinese Exclusion Case*, 130 U.S. 581 (1889). Some have questioned that inference as unwarranted. Moreover, the cases that declared that doctrine dealt with conflict between a statute and a bilateral agreement; it has been urged that the doctrine should not apply to inconsistency between a statute and general international law established by a general multilateral treaty. . . . The doctrine expressed in this section, however, is established, and a distinction between bilateral and multilateral agreements has not taken root. . . . The doctrine that laws and treaties are equal in authority and the later prevails in case of conflict has been applied in several cases giving effect to a later act of Congress [*Chinese Exclusion, Whitney, Head Money*]. . . .

2. Federal statute does not "repeal" international law or agreement. It is inexact to say that Congress has the power to "repeal a treaty." Congress has no authority to act on the treaty itself. But acting within its legislative authority under the Constitution, Congress may enact laws that are inconsistent with the law as previously represented by a self-executing international agreement. The courts, and the President, being unable to give effect to both the agreement and the statute as domestic law, will give effect to the later in time.

NOTES

Self-Executing Versus non-Self-Executing. What is the meaning of these terms? How do they compare with Bayefsky's "adoption" and "transformation" concepts? As a practical matter what difference do they make?

Last-in-time rule. U.S. courts have consistently held that self-executing treaties are equivalent in status to federal statutes. Under the last-in-time (or "later-in-time") rule, when any inconsistency arises between a federal statute and a self-executing treaty, the later in time will prevail. However, some countries follow a different practice. For example, the French and Dutch Constitutions give precedence to treaties over all inconsistent national laws. *See* Article 55 of the French Constitution (1958) and Article 94 of the Dutch Constitution (1999). What advantages or disadvantages might result from each approach? Should it matter whether the treaty in question is a multilateral or bilateral treaty?

Restatement of the Law of Foreign Relations of the United States. Compare the views of Bayefsky, the Bangalore Principles, the Vienna Convention, and the Restatement. Do they agree on all points? Disagree?

II. Applying the International Right to Equal Treatment Without Regard to Gender in Domestic Courts

This Part presents court decisions using the principles in Part I. As you read them, identify the specific principles applied by the courts.

Attorney General v. Unity Dow
(Appeal Court of Botswana)
[1992] LRC (Const) 628 (1992)

AMISSAH JP. . . . The facts of the case . . . were well summarized by the learned judge a quo [judge of the court below], and . . . I will repeat that summary. As he said ([1991] LRC (Const) 574 at 577:

The Applicant Unity Dow is a citizen of Botswana having been born in Botswana of parents who are members of one of the indigenous tribes of Botswana. She is married to Peter Nathan Dow who, although he has been in residence in Botswana for nearly 14 years, is not a citizen of Botswana but a citizen of the United States of America.

Prior to their marriage on the 7th of March 1984 a child was born to them on the 29th

October, 1979 named Cheshe Maitumelo Dow and after the marriage two more children were born Tumisang Ted Dow born 26th March 1985 and Natasha Selemo Dow born on 26th November 1987. She states further in her founding affadavit that "my family and I have established our home in Raserura Ward in Mochudi and all the children regard that place and no other as their home."

In terms of the laws in force prior to the Citizenship Act of 1984 the daughter born before the marriage is a Botswana citizen and therefore a Motswana, whereas in terms of the Citizenship Act of 1984 the children born during the marriage are not citizens of Botswana (although children of the same parents), and are therefore aliens in the land of their birth.

[Ms. Dow] claimed that the provisions of the Citizenship Act of 1984 which denied citizenship to her two younger children were 4 and 5. Those sections read as follows:

4. (1) A person born in Botswana shall be a citizen of Botswana by birth and descent if, at the time of his birth—
　(a) his father was a citizen of Botswana; or
　(b) in the case of a person brorn out of wedlock, his mother was a citizen of Botswana . . .

5. (1) A person born outside Botswana shall be a citizen of Botswana by descent if, at the time of his birth—
　(a) his father was a citizen of Botswana;
　(b) in the case of a person born out of wedlock, his mother was a citizen of Botswana. . . .

The case which [Ms. Dow] sought to establish and which was accepted by the court a quo was captured by paras 13 to 15, 18, 19, 21 and 22 of her founding affidavit. They read as follows:

13. I am prejudice[d] by the section 4(1) of the Citizenship Act by reason of my being female from passing citizenship to my two children Tumisang and Natasha.
14. I am precluded by the discriminatory effect of the said law in that my said children are aliens in the land of mine and their birth and thus enjoy limited rights and legal protection.
15. I verily believe that the discriminatory effect of the said sections, (4 and 5 supra) offend against section 3(a)[c] of the Constitution of the Republic of Botswana. . . .
18. I am desirous of being afforded the same protection of law as a male Botswana citizen and in this regard I am desirous that my children be accorded with Botswana citizenship. . . .
19. As set out above, I verily believe and state that the provisions of section 3 of the Constitution have been contravened in relation to myself. . . .

---

[c] The Botswana Constitution, Section 3, provides that:

"Whereas every person in Botswana is entitled to the fundamental rights and freedoms of the individual, that is to say, the right, whatever his race, place of origin, political opinions, colour, creed or sex, but subject to respect for the rights and freedoms of others and the public interest[,], to each and all the following freedoms, namely—
　(a) life, liberty, security of the person and the protection of the law;
　(b) freedom of conscience, of expression and of assembly and association; and
　(c) protection for the privacy of his home and other property and from deprivation of property without compensation, the provisions of this Chapter shall have effect for the purpose of affording protection to those rights and freedoms subject to such limitations of that protection as are contained in these provisions, as being limitations designed to ensure that the enjoyment of the said rights and freedoms by any individual does not prejudice the rights and freedoms of others or the public interest."

21. As a citizen of the Republic of Botswana, I am guaranteed under the Constitution, immunity from expulsion from Botswana and verily believe that such immunity is interfered with and limited by the practical implications of sections 4, 5 and 13 of the said Citizenship Act.
22. I verily believe that the provisions of the Constitution have been contravened in relation to myself. . . .

After hearing [Ms. Dow] . . . and the Attorney General in opposition, the learned judge a quo found in favour of the former. The relevant parts of his judgment are as follows ([1991] LRC (Const) 574 at 588–589):

I therefore find that s 4 [of the Citizenship Act] is discriminatory in its effect on women in that, as a matter of policy:
(i) It may compel them to live and bear children outside wedlock.
(ii) Since her children are only entitled to remain in Botswana if they are in possession of a residence permit and since they are not granted permits in their own right, their right to remain in Botswana is dependent upon their forming part of their father's residence permit.
(iii) The residence permits are granted for no more than two years at a time, and if the applicant's husband's permit were not renewed both he and applicant's minor children would be obliged to leave Botswana.
(iv) In addition the applicant is jointly responsible with her husband for the education of their children. Citizens of Botswana qualify for financial assistance in the form of bursaries to meet the costs of university education. This is a benefit which is not available to a non-citizen. In the result the applicant is financially prejudiced by the fact that her children are not Botswana citizens.
(v) Since the children would be obliged to travel on their father's passport the applicant will not be entitled to return to Botswana with her children in the absence of their father.
What I have set out at length may inhibit women in Botswana from marrying the man whom they love. It is no answer to say that there are laws against marrying close blood relations—that is a reasonable exclusion. . . .
It seems to me that the effect of s 4 is to punish a citizen female for marrying a non-citizen male. For this she is put in the unfavourable position in which she finds herself vis-a-vis her children and her country.
The fact that according to the Citizenship Act a child born to a marriage between a citizen female and a non-citizen male follows the citizenship of its father may not in fact have that result. It depends on the law of the foreign country. The result may be that the child may be rendered stateless unless its parents emigrate. If they are forced to emigrate then the unfortunate consequences which I have set out earlier in this judgment may ensue.
I have therefore come to the conclusion that the application [to invalidate Sections 4 and 5 of the Citizenship Act] succeeds. . . .

[The government appealed from this judgment, arguing principally that Section 3 of the Constitution was merely a nonbinding preamble, and that Section 15 of the Constitution should govern. Section 15 prohibited the government and its offices from treating "any person" in "a discriminatory manner," but defined "discriminatory" as:] . . . affording different treatment to different persons, attributable wholly or mainly to their respective descriptions by race, tribe, place of origin, political opinions, colour or creed whereby persons of one such description are subjected to disabilities or restrictions to which persons of another such description are not made subject or accorded privileges or advantages which are not accorded to persons of another such description.

[The government argued that the courts should afford significance to the exclusion of the word "sex" from Section 15, and that "the Citizenship Act was a law based on descent which was required to ensure that the male orientation imperative of Botswana society and the need to avoid dual citizenship be advanced." Pointing out that many other Botswana laws would have to be invalidated if the trial court's reasoning were upheld, the government urged that it was proper for Parliament to legislate "to preserve or advance . . . the patrilineal customs and traditions of the Botswana people."

[The appellate court described this case as one raising "difficult questions of constitutional interpretation," but after close textual analysis and an examination of its history, concluded that the Constitution's grant of rights without distinction on the basis of sex in Section 3 was substantive and not merely precatory, and that the exclusion of "sex" from Section 15's definition of "discriminatory" was therefore not dispositive.

[In reaching this result, the court relied in part on international law:[D]]

The learned judge a quo referred to the international obligations of Botswana in his judgement in support of his decision that sex-based discrimination was forbidden under the Constitution. That was objected to by the appellant. But by the law of Botswana, relevant international treaties and conventions . . . may be referred to as an aid to interpretation. We noticed this in our earlier citation of s 24 of the Interpretation Act which stated that, "as an aid to the construction of the enactment a court may have regard to . . . any relevant international treaty, agreement or convention. . . ." The appellant conceded that international treaties and conventions may be used as an aid to interpretation. His objection to the use by the learned judge a quo of the African Charter on Human and Peoples Rights, [the European] Convention for the Protection of Human Rights and Freedoms, and the Declaration on the Elimination of Discrimination against Women, was founded on two grounds. In the first place, he argued that none of them had been incorporated into the domestic law by legislation, although international treaties became part of the law only when so incorporated. According to this argument, of the treaties referred to by the learned judge a quo, Botswana had ratified only the African Charter on Human and Peoples Rights, but had not incorporated it into domestic law. That, the appellant admitted, however, did not deny that particular Charter the status of an aid to interpretation. The appellant's second objection was that treaties were only of assistance in interpretation when the language of the statute under consideration was unclear. But the meaning of both s 15(3) of the Constitution and ss 4 and 5 of the Citizenship Act was quite clear, and, therefore, no interpretative aids were required.

I agree that the meaning of the questioned provisions of the Citizenship Act is clear. But from the strenuous efforts that the appellant has made in justification of his inter-

---

[D] Note that the bracketed paragraphs, written by Anne Tierney Goldstein (*see* Acknowledgements), summarize the Court's opinion at [1992] LRC (Const) 628, 630–54 (1992).

pretation of s 15(3) of the Constitution his claim that the meaning of that subsection is clear seems more doubtful. The problem before us is one of discrimination on the basis of sex under the Constitution. Why, one may ask, do ss 3 and 15 of the Constitution apparently say contradictory things? It is the provisions of the Constitution itself which give rise to the difficulty of interpretation, if any; not the Citizenship Act. What we have to look at when trying to determine the intentions of the framers of the Constitution is the ethos, the environment, which the framers thought Botswana was entering into by its acquisition of statehood, and what, if anything, can be found likely to have contributed to the formulation of their intentions in the Constitution that they made. Botswana was, at the time the Constitution was promulgated, about to enter the comity of nations. What could have been the intentions and expectations of the framers of its Constitution? It is to be recalled that Maisels P. in the *Petrus Case* . . . said in this connection that:

. . . Botswana is a member of a comity of civilised nations and the rights and freedoms of its citizens are entrenched in its constitution which is binding on the legislature.

The comity of civilised nations was the international society into which Botswana was about to enter at the time its Constitution was drawn up. Lord Wilberforce in the case of *Minister of Home Affairs (Bermuda) and Another v. Fisher and Another* [1980] spoke of this international environment acting as one of the contributory influences which fashioned and informed the approach of the framers of the Constitution of Bermuda in words which could, with slight modification, have been written equally for Botswana. He said:

Here, however, we are concerned with a constitution, brought in force certainly by Act of Parliament, the Bermudian Constitution Art 1967 of the United Kingdom, but established by a self-contained document. . . . It can be seen that this instrument has certain special characteristics. 1. It is, particularly in Chapter 1, drafted in a broad and ample style which lays down principles of width and generality. 2. Chapter 1 is headed protection of fundamental rights and freedoms of the individual. It is known that this chapter, as similar portions of other constitutions instruments drafted in the post-colonial period, starting with the Constitution of Nigeria, and including the constitutions of most Caribbean territories, was greatly influenced by the European Convention for the Protection of Human Rights and Fundamental Freedoms (1953). . . . That convention was signed and ratified by the United Kingdom and applied to dependent territories including Bermuda. It was in turn influenced by the United Nations Universal Declaration of Human Rights of 1948. These antecedents, and the form of chapter 1 itself, call for a generous interpretation, avoiding what has been called 'the austerity of tabulated legalism,' suitable to give to individuals the full measure of the fundamental rights and freedoms referred to.

The antecedents of the Constitution of Botswana with regard to the imperatives of the international community could not have been any different from the antecedents found by Lord Wilberforce in the case of Bermuda. Article 2 the Universal Declaration of Human Rights of 1948 states that:

Everyone is entitled to all the rights and freedoms set forth in this Declaration, without distinction of any kind, such as race, colour, sex, language, religion, political or other opinion, national or social origin, property, birth or other status.

The British Government must have subscribed to this Declaration on behalf of itself and all dependent territories, including Bechuanaland, long before Botswana became a State. And it must have formed part of the backdrop of aspirations and desires against which the framers of the Constitution of Botswana formulated its provisions.

Article 2 of the African Charter on Human and Peoples' Rights provides that:

Every individual shall be entitled to the enjoyment of the rights and freedoms recognized and guaranteed in the present Charter without distinction of any kind such as race, ethnic group, colour, sex, language, religion, political or any other opinion, national and social origin, fortune, birth or other status.

Then paras 1 and 2 of art 12 state that:

1. Every individual shall have the right to freedom of movement and residence within the borders of a State, provided he abides by the law.
2. Every individual shall have the right to leave any country including his own, and return to his country. This right may only be subject to restriction, provided for by law for the protection of national security, law and order, public health and morality.

Botswana is a signatory to this Charter. Indeed it would appear that Botswana is one of the credible prime movers behind the promotion and supervision of the Charter. The learned judge a quo made reference to Botswana's obligations under such treaties and conventions. Even if it is accepted that those treaties and conventions do not confer enforceable rights on individuals within the State until Parliament has legislated its provisions into the law of the land, in so far as such relevant international treaties and conventions may be referred to as an aid to construction of enactments, including the Constitution, I find myself at a loss to understand the complaint made against their use in that manner in the interpretation of what no doubt are some difficult provisions of the Constitution. The reference made by the learned judge a quo to these materials amounted to nothing more than that. What he had said was:

I am strengthened in my view by the fact that Botswana is a signatory to the OAU Convention on Non-Discrimination. I bear in mind that signing the Convention does not give it power of law in Botswana but the effect of the adherence by Botswana to the Convention must show that a construction of the section which does not do violence to the language but is consistent with and in harmony with the Convention must be preferable to a narrow construction which results in a finding that s 15 of the Constitution permits unrestricted discrimination on the basis of sex.

That does not seem to me to be saying that the OAU Convention, or by its proper name the African Charter of Human and Peoples' Rights, is binding within Botswana as legislation passed by its Parliament. The learned judge said that we should so far as is possible so interpret domestic legislation so as not to conflict with Botswana's obligations under the Charter or other international obligations. Indeed, my brother Aguda J.A. referred in his judgment to the Charter and other international conventions in a similar light in the *Petrus Case*. I am in agreement that Botswana is a member of the community of civilised States which has undertaken to abide by certain standards of conduct, and, unless it is impossible to do otherwise, it would be wrong for its Courts to interpret its legislation in a manner which conflicts with the international obligations Botswana has undertaken. This principle, used as an aid to construction as is quite permissible under s 24 of the Interpretation Act, adds reinforcement to the view that the intention of the framers of the Constitution could not have been to permit discrimination purely on the basis of sex.

NOTES

The Court's Use of International Law. How did the Court use international law? What sources did it rely on? Was its decision based on the Botswana Constitution or on international law? Could you make an argument that Unity Dow should be able to rely directly on the African Charter in her lawsuit based on any articles in the African Charter? *See* RossRights. If Botswana had ratified CEDAW, should she be able to rely on CEDAW as a cause of action? *See* Article 2 in Chapter One.

Botswana's State Purpose. The government describes the purpose of the Botswana legislation. Is this an acceptable purpose?

DEDAW. In 1967, the General Assembly adopted the Declaration on Elimination of Discrimination against Women (DEDAW). The non-binding declaration laid the groundwork for the binding CEDAW.

Richard Fliman Wrgaft v. The Director and Chief of the Section of Options and Naturalizations

(Constitutional Chamber of the Supreme Court of Justice of Costa Rica)
Expediente 2965-S-91, Voto 3435-92, Ricardo Fliman Wrgaft v. Director y Jefe de la Seccion de Opciones y Naturalizationes, Sala Constitucional de la Corte Suprema de Justicia (Nov. 11, 1992) (unofficial translation on file with the author)

The Background

1. The appellant alleged that he had been married since the fourteenth of September, 1984 to a Costa Rican citizen, with whom he had two children, and that the 19th of July of 1991 he applied to the Civil Registry to have the option to become naturalized, without receiving any response.

2. The respondent declared in his statement that the application was received . . . and on November 6, 1991, they refused the petition presented because it did not apply to that particular case based on Article 14 (5) of the Constitution, criterion that in his report was held by the Chief of the Office of Options and Naturalization Section of the civil registry.

3. The application for naturalization filed by Sr. Fliman was denied in conformity with the constitutional norm, which establishes:

Art. 14. Costa Ricans by naturalization are:
. . . 5) A foreign women who has been married for two years to a Costa Rican, and who, having resided in the country during this same period, indicates her desire to acquire Costa Rican nationality.

Opinion by the MAGISTER DEL CASTILLO RIGGIONI. . . .

I. In the situation under examination, it is alleged that the right to equality on the basis of sex has been violated. Thus, it is imperative that we analyze the facts of the case in light of the constitutional provisions and the international norms that govern the material. The Political Constitution provides as follows, in articles 33 and 48:

Article 33. Every man is equal before the law, and no discrimination contrary to human dignity is allowed.
Article 48. Every person has the right of recourse to habeas corpus to guarantee his liberty and personal integrity, and of recourse to amparo to maintain or reestablish the enjoyment of the other rights consecrated in this Constitution, as well as those fundamental rights established in international human rights instruments applicable to the Republic.

The Universal Declaration of Human Rights establishes in relevant part that:

Article 2 . . .
Everyone is entitled to all the rights and freedoms set forth in this Declaration, without distinction of any kind, such as race, color, sex, language, religion. . . .
Article 7.
All are equal before the law and are entitled without any discrimination to equal protection of the law. All are entitled to equal protection against any discrimination in violation of this Declaration and against any incitement to such discrimination.

In the same respect, the American Declaration of the Rights of Man (1948) states:

Article II. Right to equality before law
All persons are equal before the law and have the rights and duties established in this Declaration, without distinction as to race, sex, language, creed or any other factor.

In the same spirit, the International Covenant on Civil and Political Rights (1966) points out that:

Article 3. The States Parties to the present Covenant undertake to ensure the equal right of men and women to the enjoyment of all civil and political rights set forth in the present Covenant.
Article 26. All persons are equal before the law and are entitled without any discrimination to the equal protection of the law. In this respect, the law shall prohibit any discrimination and guarantee to all persons equal and effective protection against discrimination on any ground such as race, color, sex, language, religion, political or other opinion, national or social origin, property, birth or other status.

Finally, the American Convention on Human Rights, "Pacto de San José" (1978) provides:

Article 1. Obligation to Respect Rights
1. The States Parties to this Convention undertake to respect the rights and freedoms recognized herein and to ensure to all persons subject to their jurisdiction the free and full exercise of those rights and freedoms, without any discrimination for reasons of race, color, sex, language, religion, political or other opinion, national or social origin, economic status, birth, or any other social condition.
2. For the purposes of this Convention, "person" means every human being. . . .
Article 24. Right to Equal Protection
All persons are equal before the law. Consequently, they have the right to equal protection under the law, without discrimination.

In conformity with the stated norms, it is unquestionable that section 5 of article 14 of the Political Constitution contains a provision that is inapplicable because it is contrary to the fundamental values of the Charter [the Political Constitution] concerning juridical equality and its complement, nondiscrimination, as well as for being contrary to the international norms, whose effect, *erga omnes* is to oblige enforcement and respect in the national sphere, both as required naturally and as mandated by Article 48 of the Constitution.

The simple comparison between the above norms and the provision in question demonstrates that the benefit given exclusively to a foreign woman married to a Costa Rican, constitutes a discrimination against the foreign man married to a Costa Rican citizen, against whom an artificial disadvantage is created, because it takes from him benefits on the basis of gender, in violation of the constitutional and universal spirit of equality and nondiscrimination.

This provision moreover, runs counter to matrimonial equality and unity, which also are values recognized by both the national and international norms, according to the Charter [Political Constitution] in its Articles 51 and 52, as follows:

Article 51. The family, as the natural and fundamental element of society, has the right to protection by the state.
Article 52. Marriage is the essential basis of the family and provides for equal rights for the spouses.

The International Covenant on Civil and Political Rights provides in the pertinent language of article 23:

Article 23.
1. The family is the natural and fundamental group unit of society and is entitled to protection by society and the State; . . .
4. States Parties to the present Covenant shall take appropriate steps to ensure equality of rights and responsibilities of spouses as to marriage, during marriage. . . .

Finally, the Pacto de San José [ACHR], in the relevant provision, states:

Article 17 . . . Protection of the family. . . .
4. The States Parties shall take appropriate steps to ensure the equality of rights and the adequate balancing of responsibilities of the spouses as to marriage, during marriage. . . .

We note that the kind of inequality that affects the interests of the appellant is not a simple differentiation "reasonable and objective," but rather an obviously unjustified, unfounded and disproportionate treatment, a product of social, cultural, economic and political conditions that fortunately have been transcended, a treatment that is currently demeaning to human dignity in particular. It is treatment that is subjective and specifically undermining of equality and family unity, which is an objective social right, from the moment when it establishes an odious restriction that through discrimination works against the juridical and spiritual equilibrium of the family, which is under the protection of the Constitution and international norms, and as a consequence, is the inherent birthright of the victim.

The challenged provision creates a form of marginalisation that affects the nuclear family and therefore the society in its entirety from the moment in which a member of this community is treated in a different manner concerning his rights to equality. The provision places appellant in a situation of social disadvantage with regard to his wife, children and other family members; this offends against the sense of justice.

In line with what has been said above, the challenged provision, which does not establish fundamental criteria for living together with others, lacks validity and applicability vis-à-vis the fundamental principles established by the Political Constitution and international agreements for which equality and non-discrimination are generic rights, and for that reason the cornerstone, the keystone, of our legal order; these are superior values that shape and permeate the spirit of democratic living together enjoyed by the Nation and the social status of law now in effect. The indicated discrimination recedes when faced with principles of superior status, given that the inequality in question does not tend to protect a superior concrete purpose meant to create, protect or promote superior common interests, but not discriminate against subjective rights.

II. For the purpose of avoiding future inequalities and discrimination that could arise by the application of the fundamental Charter [Political Constitution] and other juridical instruments in force, and in exercising the faculties that the Constitution grants to this Chamber, we order that when legislation uses the terms "man" or "woman", they must be understood as synonyms of the term "person," and in order to eliminate all possible "legal" discrimination by reason of gender, this correction must be applied by all public officials when they are presented with any question whose resolution requires the application of a norm that employs the vocabulary cited above.

For the foregoing reasons we proceed to grant the writ and give to the appellant the rights denied him by application of section 5 of article 14 of the Political Constitution, providing he meets the applicable legal and constitutional requirements. The authorities must respect the normative rules when similar situations occur in the future.

Conclusion

Appellant's petition is granted, in consequence of which appellant must be inscribed as a Costa Rican citizen if he satisfies the other constitutional and legal requirements for the privilege of naturalization of a foreigner who marries a Costa Rican, without distinction by gender. The State is ordered to pay costs and liquidated damages in this case.

NOTES

Comparing Equality in Marriage Provisions. Article 23(4) of ICCPR provides that, "States Parties to the present Covenant shall take appropriate steps to ensure equality of rights and responsibilities of spouses as to marriage, during marriage and at its dissolution. In the case of dissolution, provision shall be made for the necessary protection of any children." Similarly, Article 17(4) of the American Convention on Human Rights requires that, "The States Parties shall take appropriate steps to ensure the equality of rights and the adequate balancing of responsibilities of the spouses as to marriage, during marriage, and in the event of its dissolution. In case of dissolution, provision shall be made for the necessary protection of any children solely on the basis of their own best interests." What differences, if any, are there between ICCPR Article 23(4) and ACHR Article 17(4)?

A Civil Law State. How does the Costa Rica court use international law? Does it have the same significance as in Botswana? Is the decision based on the Constitution or on international law? What does the court strike down?

The Remedy. What does the court order public officials to do in Costa Rica? Is this a legitimate use of international law?

Vishaka v. Rajasthan
(Supreme Court of India)
[1997] 3 LRC 361 (1997)

VERMA CJ, MANOHAR and KIRPAL JJ. This writ petition has been filed for the enforcement of the fundamental rights of working women under arts 14, 19 and 21[E] of the Constitution of the Republic of India 1950 in view of the prevailing climate in which the violation of those rights is not uncommon. With the increasing awareness of and emphasis on gender justice, there is an increase in the effort to guard against such violations; and the resentment towards incidents of sexual harassment is also increasing. The present petition has been brought as a class action by certain social activists and NGOs with the aims of focusing attention towards this societal aberra-

---

[E] Article 14 provides:

"*Equality before law.*—The State shall not deny to any person equality before the law or the equal protection of the laws within the territory of India."

Article 19(1)(f) provides:

"*Protection of certain rights regarding freedom of speech, etc.*—

(1) All citizens shall have the right —

(f) to practise any profession, or to carry on any occupation, trade or business."

Article 21 provides:

"*Protection of life and personal liberty.*—No person shall be deprived of his life or personal liberty except according to procedure established by law."

tion, assisting in finding suitable methods for the realisation of the true concept of 'gender equality', to prevent sexual harassment of working women in all workplaces through judicial process, and to fill the vacuum in existing legislation.

The immediate cause for the filing of this writ petition is an incident of alleged brutal gang rape of a social worker in a village of Rajasthan. That incident is the subject matter of a separate criminal action and no further mention of it by us is necessary. The incident reveals the hazards to which a working woman may be exposed and the depravity to which sexual harassment can degenerate, and the urgency for safeguards by an alternative mechanism in the absence of legislative measures. In the absence of legislative measures, the need is to find an effective alternative mechanism to fulfil this felt and urgent social need.

Each such incident results in violation of the fundamental rights of 'gender equality' and the 'right to life and liberty'. It is a clear violation of the rights under arts 14, 15 and 21 of the Constitution. One of the logical consequences of such an incident is also the violation of the victim's fundamental right under art 19(1)(f) 'to practise any profession, or to carry out any occupation, trade or business'. Such violations therefore attract the remedy under art 32 for the enforcement of these fundamental rights of women. This class action under art 32 of the Constitution is for this reason. A writ of mandamus in such a situation, if it is to be effective, needs to be accompanied by directions for prevention, as the violation of fundamental rights of this kind is a recurring phenomenon. The fundamental right to carry on any occupation, trade or profession depends on the availability of a 'safe' working environment. Right to life means life with dignity. The primary responsibility for ensuring such safety and dignity is through suitable legislation, and the creation of a mechanism for its enforcement, is of the legislature and the executive. When, however, instances of sexual harassment resulting in violation of fundamental rights of women workers under arts 14, 19 and 21 are brought before us for redress under art 32, an effective redressal requires that some guidelines should be laid down for the protection of these rights to fill the legislative vacuum.

The notice of the petition was given to the state of Rajasthan and the Union of India. The learned Solicitor General appeared for the Union of India and rendered valuable assistance in the true spirit of a law officer to help us find a proper solution to this social problem of considerable magnitude. In addition to Ms. Meenakshi Arora and Ms. Naina Kapur who assisted the court with full commitment, Shri Fali S Nariman appeared as amicus curiae and rendered great assistance. We place on record our great appreciation for every counsel who appeared in the case and rendered the needed assistance to the court which enabled us to deal with this unusual matter in the manner considered appropriate for a cause of this nature.

Apart from art 32 of the Constitution, we may refer to some other provisions which envisage judicial intervention for eradication of this social evil. Some provisions in the Constitution in addition to arts 14, 19(1)(f) and 21 which have relevance are:

Prohibition of discrimination on grounds of religion, race, caste, sex or place of birth
   15. (1) The State shall not discriminate against any citizen on grounds only of religion, race, caste, sex, place of birth or any of them . . .

(3) Nothing in this article shall prevent the State from making any special provision for women and children. . . .

Provision for just and humane conditions of work and maternity relief
42. The State shall make provision for securing just and humane conditions of work and for maternity relief.

Fundamental duties
51A. It shall be the duty of every citizen of India (a) to abide by the Constitution and respect its ideals and institutions . . . (e) to promote harmony and the spirit of common brotherhood amongst all the people of India transcending religious, linguistic and regional or sectional diversities; to renounce practices derogatory to the dignity of women. . . .

Before we refer to the international Conventions and norms having relevance in this field and the manner in which they assume significance in application and judicial interpretation, we may advert to some other provisions in the Constitution which permit such use. These provisions are:

Promotion of international peace and security
51. The State shall endeavour to . . . (c) foster respect for international law and treaty obligations in the dealings of organised people with one another. . . .

Legislation for giving effect to international agreements
253. Notwithstanding anything in the foregoing provisions of this Chapter, Parliament has power to make any law for the whole or any part of the territory of India for implementing any treaty, agreement or convention with any other country or countries or any decision made at any international conference, association or other body.

Seventh Schedule: List 1—Union List:
14. Entering into treaties and agreements with foreign countries and implementing of treaties, agreements and conventions with foreign countries.

In the absence of domestic law occupying the field, to formulate effective measures to check the evil of sexual harassment of working women at all workplaces, the contents of international Conventions and norms are significant for the purpose of the interpretation of the guarantee of gender equality, the right to work with human dignity in arts 14, 15, 19(l)(f) and 21 of the Constitution, and the safeguards against sexual harassment implicit therein. Any international convention not inconsistent with the fundamental rights and in harmony with its spirit must be read into the provisions to enlarge the meaning and content thereof, to promote the object of the constitutional guarantee. This is implicit from art 51(c) and the enabling power of Parliament to enact laws for implementing the international Conventions and norms by virtue of art 253 read with Entry 14 of the Union List in Sch 7 to the Constitution. Article 73 also is relevant. It provides that the executive power of the Union shall extend to the matters with respect to which Parliament has power to make laws. The executive power of the Union is therefore available until Parliament enacts legislation expressly to provide measures needed to curb the evil.

Thus, the power of the court under art 32 for enforcement of the fundamental rights and the executive power of the Union have to meet the challenge to protect working women from sexual harassment and to make their fundamental rights meaningful. Governance of the society by the rule of law mandates this requirement as a logical concomitant of the constitutional scheme. The exercise performed by the court in this matter is with this common perception shared with the learned Solicitor General and other members of the Bar who rendered valuable assistance in the performance of this difficult task in the public interest.

The progress made at each hearing culminated in the formulation of guidelines to which the Union of India gave its consent through the learned Solicitor General, indicating that these should be the guidelines and norms declared by this court to govern the behaviour of the employers and all others at the workplaces to curb this social evil.

Gender equality includes protection from sexual harassment and the right to work with dignity, which is a universally recognised basic human right. The common minimum requirement of this right has received global acceptance. The international Conventions and norms are, therefore, of great significance in the formulation of the guidelines to achieve this purpose.

The obligation of this court under art 32 of the Constitution for the enforcement of these fundamental rights in the absence of legislation must be viewed along with the role of judiciary envisaged in the Beijing Statement of Principles of the Independence of the Judiciary in the LAWASIA region. These principles were accepted by the Chief Justices of Asia and the Pacific at Beijing in 1995 as those representing the minimum standards necessary to be observed in order to maintain the independence and effective functioning of the judiciary. The objectives of the judiciary mentioned in the Beijing Statement are:

Objectives of the Judiciary
   10. The objectives and functions of the Judiciary include the following:
   (a) to ensure that all persons are able to live securely under the Rule of Law; (b) to promote, within the proper limits of the judicial function, the observance and the attainment of human rights; and (c) to administer the law impartially among persons and between persons and the State.

Some provisions in the Convention on the Elimination of All Forms of Discrimination against Women of significance in the present context are:

   11. (1) States Parties shall take all appropriate measures to eliminate discrimination against women in the field of employment in order to ensure, on a basis of equality of men and women, the same rights, in particular: (a) The right to work as an inalienable right of all human beings . . . (f) The right to protection of health and to safety in working conditions, including the safeguarding of the function of reproduction . . .
   24. States Parties undertake to adopt all necessary measures at the national level aimed at achieving the full realization of the rights recognised in the present Convention.

The general recommendations [GR 19] of the UN Committee on the Elimination of Discrimination against Women in this context, in respect of art 11 are:

17. Equality in employment can be seriously impaired when women are subjected to gender-specific violence, such as sexual harassment in the workplace.

18. Sexual harassment includes such unwelcome sexually determined behaviour as physical contact and advances, sexually coloured remarks, showing pornography and sexual demands, whether by words or actions. Such conduct can be humiliating and may constitute a health and safety problem; it is discriminatory when the woman has reasonable ground to believe that her objection would disadvantage her in connection with her employment, including recruitment or promotion, or when it creates a hostile working environment.

24. . . . (i) Effective complaints procedures and remedies, including compensation, should be provided; (j) States parties should include in their reports information on sexual harassment, and on measures to protect women from sexual harassment and other forms of violence [or] coercion in the workplace.

The government of India ratified the above [Convention] on 25 June 1993 with some reservations which are not material in the present context. At the Fourth World Conference on Women in Beijing, the government of India also made an official commitment, inter alia, to formulate and operationalise a national policy on women which will continuously guide and inform action at every level and in every sector; to set up a commission for Women's Rights to act as a public defender of women's human rights; and to institutionalise a national level mechanism to monitor the implementation of the Platform for Action. We have therefore no hesitation in placing reliance on the above for the purpose of construing the nature and ambit of the constitutional guarantee of gender equality in our Constitution.

The meaning and content of the fundamental rights guaranteed in the Constitution are of sufficient amplitude to encompass all the facets of gender equality including prevention of sexual harassment or abuse. Independence of judiciary forms a part of our constitutional scheme. The international Conventions and norms are to be read into them in the absence of enacted domestic law occupying the field when there is no inconsistency between them. It is now an accepted rule of judicial construction that regard must be had to international Conventions and norms for construing domestic law when there is no inconsistency between them and there is a void in the domestic law. The High Court of Australia in *Minister for Immigration and Ethnic Affairs v. Teoh* [1995] 3 LRC 1 has recognised the concept of legitimate expectation of its observance in the absence of a contrary legislative provision, even in the absence of a Bill of Rights in the Constitution of Australia.

In *Nilibati Behera v. State of Orissa* [1994] 2 LRC 99 a provision in the International Covenant on Civil and Political Rights was referred to to support the view taken that 'an enforceable right to compensation is not alien to the concept of enforcement of a guaranteed right', as a public law remedy under art 32, distinct from the private law remedy in torts. There is no reason why these international Conventions and norms cannot therefore be used for construing the fundamental rights expressly guaranteed in the Constitution of India which embody the basic concept of gender equality in all spheres of human activity.

In view of the above, and the absence of enacted law to provide for the effective enforcement of the basic human right of gender equality and guarantee against sexual harassment and abuse, more particularly against sexual harassment at workplaces, we lay down the guidelines and norms specified hereinafter for due observance at all workplaces or other institutions, until legislation is enacted for the purpose. This is done in exercise of the power available under art 32 of the Constitution for enforcement of the fundamental rights and it is further emphasised that this would be treated as the law declared by this court under art 141 of the Constitution.

The GUIDELINES and NORMS prescribed herein are as below.

HAVING REGARD to the definition of 'human rights' in Section 2(d) of the Protection of Human Rights Act 1993;

TAKING NOTE of the fact that the present civil and penal laws in India do not *adequately* provide for specific protection of women from sexual harassment in workplaces and that enactment of such legislation will take considerable time

It is necessary and expedient for employers in workplaces as well as other responsible persons or institutions to observe certain guidelines to ensure the prevention of sexual harassment of women as follows.

1. *Duty of the employer or other responsible persons in workplaces and other institutions.* It shall be the duty of the employer or other responsible persons in workplaces or other institutions to prevent or deter the commission of acts of sexual harassment and to provide the procedures for the resolution, settlement or prosecution of acts of sexual harassment by taking all steps required.

2. *Definition.* For this purpose, sexual harassment includes such unwelcome sexually determined behaviour (whether directly or by implication), as: (a) physical contact and advances; (b) a demand or request for sexual favours; (c) sexually coloured remarks; (d) showing pornography; (e) any other unwelcome physical, verbal or non-verbal conduct of a sexual nature. Where any of these acts is committed in circumstances whereunder the victim of such conduct has a reasonable apprehension that in relation to the victim's employment or work, whether she is drawing salary, or honorarium or voluntary, whether in government, public or private enterprise, such conduct can be humiliating and may constitute a health and safety problem. It is discriminatory for instance when the woman has reasonable grounds to believe that her objection would disadvantage her in connection with her employment or work including recruiting or promotion or when it creates a hostile work environment. Adverse consequences might be visited if the victim does not consent to the conduct in question or raises any objection thereto.

3. *Preventative steps.* All employers or persons in charge of a workplace whether in the public or private sector should take appropriate steps to prevent sexual harassment. Without prejudice to the generality of this obligation they should take the following steps.

(a) Express prohibition of sexual harassment as defined above at the workplace should be notified, published and circulated in appropriate ways.

(b) The rules/regulations of government and public sector bodies relating to conduct and discipline should include rules/regulations prohibiting sexual harassment and provide for appropriate penalties in such rules against the offender.

(c) As regards private employers steps should be taken to include the aforesaid prohibitions in the standing orders under the Industrial Employment (Standing Orders) Act 1946.

(d) Appropriate work conditions should be provided in respect of work, leisure, health and hygiene to further ensure that there is no hostile environment towards women at workplaces and no employed woman should have reasonable grounds to believe that she is disadvantaged in connection with her employment.

4. *Criminal proceedings.* Where such conduct amounts to a specific offence under the Indian Penal Code or under any other law, the employer shall initiate appropriate action in accordance with law by making a complaint with the appropriate authority. In particular, it should ensure that victims or witnesses are not victimised or discriminated against while dealing with complaints of sexual harassment. The victims of sexual harassment should have the option to seek transfer of the perpetrator or their own transfer.

5. *Disciplinary action.* Where such conduct amounts to misconduct in employment as defined by the relevant service rules, appropriate disciplinary action should be initiated by the employer in accordance with those rules.

6. *Complaint mechanism.* Whether or not such conduct constitutes an offence under law or a breach of the service rules, an appropriate complaint mechanism should be created in the employer's organisation for redress of the complaint made by the victim. Such a complaint mechanism should ensure time-bound treatment of complaints.

7. *Complaints committee.* The complaint mechanism, referred to in (6) above, should be adequate to provide, where necessary, a complaints committee, a special counsellor, or other support service, including the maintenance of confidentiality. The complaints committee should be headed by a woman and not less than half of its members should be women. Further, to prevent the possibility of any undue pressure or influence from senior levels, such complaints committee should involve a third party, either an NGO or other body who is familiar with the issue of sexual harassment. The complaints committee must make an annual report to the government department concerned of the complaints and action taken by them. The employers and person in charge will also report on the compliance with the aforesaid guidelines including on the reports of the complaints committee to the government department.

8. *Workers' initiative.* Employees should be allowed to raise issues of sexual harassment at workers' meetings and other appropriate fora and it should be affirmatively discussed in employer-employee meetings.

9. *Awareness.* Awareness of the rights of female employees in this regard should be created in particular by prominently notifying the guidelines (and appropriate legislation when enacted on the subject) in a suitable manner.

10. *Third party harassment.* Where sexual harassment occurs as a result of an act or omission by any third party or outsider, the employer or person in charge will take all steps necessary and reasonable to assist the affected person in terms of support and preventative action.

11. The central/state governments are requested to consider adopting suitable measures including legislation to ensure that the guidelines laid down by this order are also observed by employers in the private sector.

12. These guidelines will not prejudice any rights available under the Protection of Human Rights Act 1993.

Accordingly, we direct that the above guidelines and norms would be strictly observed in all workplaces for the preservation and enforcement of the right to gender equality of the working woman. These directions would be binding and enforceable in law until suitable legislation is enacted to occupy the field. These writ petitions are disposed of, accordingly.

NOTES

A Commonwealth Country in the Common-Law Tradition. India is one of the 53 states which participate in the Commonwealth, a group of former British colonies. These countries share a common-law legal system and often cite to each other's court decisions. As you may recall, the Bangalore Principles were developed at a conference in India. How does the Court's use of international law compare with the rules developed at the Bangalore conference? Which is preferable? What is novel about the Court's approach? Is it relying on the Constitution or on international law?

Sexual Harassment. Would you add anything to the Court's order on sexual harassment? Would you delete anything?

Asakura v. City of Seattle
(United States Supreme Court)
265 U.S. 332 (1924)

Mr. JUSTICE BUTLER delivered the opinion of the Court.

Plaintiff in error is a subject of the Emperor of Japan, and, since 1904, has resided in Seattle, Washington. Since July, 1915, he has been engaged in business there as a pawnbroker. The city passed an ordinance, which took effect July 2, 1921, regulating the business of pawnbroker and repealing former ordinances on the same subject. It makes it unlawful for any person to engage in the business unless he shall have a license, and the ordinance provides "that no such license shall be granted unless the applicant be a citizen of the United States." Violations of the ordinance are punishable by fine or imprisonment or both. Plaintiff in error brought this suit in the Superior Court of King County, Washington, against the city, its Comptroller and its Chief of Police to restrain them from enforcing the ordinance against him. He attacked the ordinance on the ground that it violates the treaty between the United States and the Empire of Japan, proclaimed April 5, 1911, 37 Stat. 1504 [and that it] violates the due process and equal protection clauses of the Fourteenth Amendment of the Constitution of the United States. . . . It was shown that he had about $5,000 invested in his business, which would be broken up and destroyed by the enforcement of the ordinance. The Superior Court granted the relief prayed. On appeal, the Supreme Court of the State held the ordinance valid and reversed the decree. . . .

Does the ordinance violate the treaty? Plaintiff in error invokes and relies upon the following provisions: "The citizens or subjects of each of the High Contracting Parties shall have liberty to enter, travel and reside in the territories of the other to carry on trade, wholesale and retail, to own or lease and occupy houses, manufactories, warehouses and shops, to employ agents of their choice, to lease land for residential and commercial purposes, and generally to do anything incident to or necessary for trade upon the same terms as native citizens or subjects, submitting themselves to the laws and regulations there established. . . . The citizens or subjects of each . . . shall receive, in the territories of the other, the most constant protection and security for their persons and property. . . ."

A treaty made under the authority of the United States "shall be the supreme law of the land; and the judges in every State shall be bound thereby, any thing in the constitution or laws of any State to the contrary notwithstanding." Constitution, Art. VI, § 2.

The treaty-making power of the United States is not limited by any express provision of the Constitution, and, though it does not extend "so far as to authorize what the Constitution forbids," it does extend to all proper subjects of negotiation between our government and other nations . . . The treaty was made to strengthen friendly relations between the two nations. As to the things covered by it, the provision quoted establishes the rule of equality between Japanese subjects while in this country and native citizens. Treaties for the protection of citizens of one country residing in the territory of another are numerous, and make for good understanding between nations. The treaty is binding within the State of Washington. . . . The rule of equality established by it cannot be rendered nugatory in any part of the United States by municipal ordinances or state laws. It stands on the same footing of supremacy as do the provisions of the Constitution and laws of the United States. It operates of itself without the aid of any legislation, state or national; and it will be applied and given authoritative effect by the courts. . . .

The purpose of the ordinance complained of is to regulate, not to prohibit, the business of pawnbroker. But it makes it impossible for aliens to carry on the business. It need not be considered whether the State, if it sees fit, may forbid and destroy the business generally. Such a law would apply equally to aliens and citizens, and no question of conflict with the treaty would arise. The grievance here alleged is that plaintiff in error, in violation of the treaty, is denied equal opportunity.

It remains to be considered whether the business of pawnbroker is "trade" within the meaning of the treaty. Treaties are to be construed in a broad and liberal spirit, and, when two constructions are possible, one restrictive of rights that may be claimed under it and the other favorable to them, the latter is to be preferred. . . . The language of the treaty is comprehensive. The phrase "to carry on trade" is broad. That it is not to be given a restricted meaning is plain. The clauses "to own or lease . . . shops, . . . to lease land for . . . commercial purposes, and generally to do anything incident to or necessary for trade," and "shall receive the most constant protection and security for their . . . property . . ." all go to show the intention of the parties that the citizens or subjects to either shall have liberty in the territory of the other to engage in all kinds and classes of business that are or reasonably may be embraced within the meaning of the word "trade" as used in the treaty. . . . This ordinance violates the treaty . . .

We need not consider other grounds upon which the ordinance is attacked.

Decree reversed.

NOTES

Self-Executing or Non-Self-Executing. Mr. Asakura relied on both the Fourteenth Amendment and the U.S.-Japanese treaty. Does the Court use both in its ruling? What treaty provision does the Court rely on? Is this treaty self-executing or non self-executing? Why?

The U.S. Approach. The United States Constitution requires the Senate to ratify international treaties, but the House of Representatives has no say in the matter. Should U.S. courts ever apply international law where Congress has not enacted implementing legislation? Wouldn't it be anti-democratic and wrong to let the President and Senate bind the country to new law without the House of Representatives having a say? What does the Restatement say on the issue? What does the Supreme Court rule? Does the Supreme Court decision follow the guidelines described in Bayefsky's article? The Bangalore principles?

Ephrahim v. *Pastory* **Revisited.** In Chapter Five, you read the *Ephrahim* opinion. Reread the section "Discrimination Based on Sex." How does the Court's use of international law compare to that of the other courts we have seen?

III. Applying the International Right Against Slavery and Slave-like Practices in a Domestic Court

The Supplementary Convention on the Abolition of Slavery, the Slave Trade, and Institutions and Practices Similar to Slavery

226 U.N.T.S. 3, *entered into force* Apr. 30, 1957, *available at* RossRights

Article 1

Each of the States Parties to this Convention shall take all practicable and necessary legislative and other measures to bring about progressively and as soon as possible the complete abolition or abandonment of the following institutions and practices. . . .

(c) Any institution or practice whereby:

(i) A woman, without the right to refuse, is promised or given in marriage on payment of a consideration in money or in kind to her parents, guardian, family or any other person or group; or

(ii) The husband of a woman, his family or his clan, has the right to transfer her to another person for value received or otherwise; or

(iii) A woman on the death of her husband is liable to be inherited by another person;

(d) Any institution or practice whereby a child or young person under the age of 18 years is delivered by either or both of his natural parents or by his guardian to another person, whether for reward or not, with a view to the exploitation of the child or young person or of his labour.

Article 2

With a view to bringing to an end the institutions and practices mentioned in article 1 (c) of this Convention, the States Parties undertake to prescribe, where appropriate, suitable minimum ages of marriage, to encourage the use of facilities whereby the consent of both parties to a marriage may be freely expressed in the presence of a competent civil or religious authority, and to encourage the registration of marriages. . . .

Article 6

1. The act of enslaving another person or of inducing another person to give himself or a person dependent upon him into slavery, or of attempting these acts, or being accessory thereto, or being a party to a conspiracy to accomplish any such acts, shall be a criminal offence under the laws of the States Parties to this Convention and persons convicted thereof shall be liable to punishment.

2. Subject to the provisions of the introductory paragraph of article 1 of this Convention, the provisions of paragraph 1 of the present article shall also apply to the act of inducing another person to place himself or a person dependent upon him into the servile status resulting from any of the institutions or practices mentioned in article 1, to any attempt to perform such acts, to being accessory thereto, and to being a party to a conspiracy to accomplish any such acts.

The State v. Kule
(Papua New Guinea National Court of Justice)
[1991] PNGLR 404 (1991)

DOHERTY J. The defendant has been indicted and pleaded guilty to the unlawful killing of his cousin's sister. The facts presented by the State show that the deceased and some other women were sitting talking about the theft of peanuts from a garden. The defendant, [who] was in a house some distance away, thought that they were talking about him and came up to the deceased carrying a large piece of wood and struck her, she fell to the ground where he kicked her several times breaking three ribs which penetrated the spleen and caused death.

On arraignment, he explained that: "I felt they used bad language they swear at me and I hit the woman." There is no indication from the State witnesses that the defendant was being accused of the theft and all indications are that he only thought they were talking about him.

On allocutus, he explained that his two brothers had died and he, as the only remaining relative, had to care for their nine children, their two wives together with his own wife and three surviving children. He also said that the Sepik River is high for six months of the year when it is difficult to plant and find food. His counsel has stressed the provocative action on the part of the women and submitted, inter alia, that he has complied with certain customary rights and obligations but still has to comply with the customary obligation to give one of his daughters to the uncle apparently the father or other relative of the deceased.

I accept that he himself thought he was being accused although there is no evidence before me to show that he was in fact mentioned. He himself said "they only suspect me, she was talking bad language about me" and "they were suspecting me". . . . It is not clear if he was named.

It would seem from his allocutus that it is very difficult to survive in the area from which he comes so theft of food, such as peanuts, would be worse than in a more fertile area where food is more abundant.

It did occur to me that the care of nine children plus two women plus his own wife plus his own children plus two old parents is an incredible burden on any person living in a poor agricultural area and that this must have led to very great stress on the defendant. I would imagine that such stress could account for his reaction to a fairly petty matter in an irrational and disproportionate way.

I consider one of the worst elements in this case is the force used which I consider completely disproportionate to the actions of the deceased. If it was gossiping among several women why pick only her? It is clear from the medical reports that the force used was enough to break three ribs which in turn pierced the spleen. It is clear from the evidence that violence was directed at only one woman and not the other three and that he used wood as a weapon. Given an apparently poor diet in the area it may have been that her ribs were not too strong but there is no medical evidence to support this. He says she tried to get a bush knife—but that was after he hit her and he was kicking her.

Clearly he had a good record and lifestyle and I consider there was an excessive responsibility upon him in looking after so many children and in-laws and parents. However, I wish to refer to the aspect of compliance with customary obligation where he has paid compensation but in particular an obligation to hand over one of his daughters to the deceased's family.

There is no evidence before the Court about such a custom other than a statement in submissions by counsel for the defence that the defendant "must give one of his daughters to the uncle". Customary compliance is a matter that can be considered in mitigation, but it is not sufficient to say "this is a custom and we are going to comply with it". As stated in *Aisi v. Malaita Hoala* [1981]: "customs must be proved as a fact, that is by sworn evidence or affidavit evidence." The Court went on to say that the provisions of the *Customs Recognition Act* (Ch No 19) (as it now is) gave the court wide powers in hearing evidence to ascertain what a custom was. This included calling witnesses itself, hearing hearsay and opinion evidence, referring to books and asking questions of complainants and defendants and their witnesses and ruled that failure to hear such evidence before ascertaining and ruling on the custom is an error in law.

I am aware of this custom in that part of the Sepik from other cases but I consider in the case before me where a submission by counsel only is put forward it is insufficient evidence that a custom exists, what the custom exactly is and whether the defendant has complied with it.

Even if there was clear evidence that the defendant had complied with the custom I am not prepared to recognise it in accordance with s 2 of the *Customs Recognition Act* (Ch No 19) and enforce it under s 3 unless there is evidence to convince me that this is a custom which is not contrary to the welfare of a child under sixteen years and that it would not be contrary to the public interest to recognise and reduce a sentence where it was shown that a child or young person or even an adult was handed over by one group of people to another family or group in payment of obligations of some member of the child's clan or customary group.

I consider that not only does the *Customs Recognition Act* give power to this Court to refuse to recognise the custom but that it is contrary to the constitutional provisions relating to slavery. Section 253 of the *Constitution* states: "Slavery, and the slave trade in all its forms, and all similar institutions and practices, are strictly prohibited."

I am unable to trace any case law in our jurisdiction on the interpretation of this section and the word "Slavery" is not defined in our legislation, either in the *Constitution* itself or in case law. The International Convention on the abolition of Slavery and the Slave trade (Geneva 1926) article one refers to slavery as "the status or condition of a person over whom all or any other powers attaching to the right of ownership are exercised". The 1956 Supplementary Convention resolved to extend abolition to "institutions similar to slavery" and these were considered to include debt bondage, serfdom, bride price and exploitation of child labour.

Section 253 of the *Constitution* not only strictly forbids slavery and the slave trade but "all similar institutions and practices". It appears to me that the handing over of a child, or an adult, to another family or group in payment or recompense for the misdeeds of a third person where that child or adult had no say or ability to dispute the handing over is an institution or practice similar to slavery as the child concerned has no say in its transfer. The *Constitution*, Sch 1.5(2), provides that a constitutional law shall be given a fair and liberal meaning and in applying this to similar institutions and practices to "Slavery" I consider the handing over of a child in reparation for the misdeeds of another is similar and thereby prohibited by s 253 of the *Constitution*.

For the reasons:

1. I have no evidence under s 2 of the *Customs Recognition Act* No 19);

2. I consider it contrary to the welfare of a child and s 3(1)(b) of the *Customs Recognition Act* (Ch No 19); and

3. I consider the handing over of the child as an institution or practice similar to slavery and so prohibited by s 253 of the *Constitution*;

I refuse to recognise the custom of handing over one of the defendant's daughters to the relative of the deceased as a custom that may be considered in mitigation of punishment.

[After considering other case law and facts in mitigation the defendant was sentenced to four and a half years in hard labour less a period of three months in remand.]

N O T E

The Use of International Law in *Kule*. How does this court's approach compare with that of Botswana? Did the judge have to bring in international law? Why do you think she did? Does she use any principle from the Bangalore statement?

Fitnat Naa-Adjeley Adjetey, *Religious and Cultural Rights: Reclaiming the African Woman's Individuality: The Struggle Between Women's Reproductive Autonomy and African Society and Culture*
44 Am. U.L. Rev. 1351, 1359–61, 1364 (1994)

Brideprice

In the brideprice system, a prospective husband gives the parents of a prospective bride valuable property in exchange for the bride. This property is usually in the form of livestock, kola, or other gifts, and usually has to be returned by the parents if the bride decides to leave the marriage. In most cases, however, the wife would only want to leave the marriage after many years, by which time the brideprice would have been used for other purposes. Married women are thus trapped within restrictive marriages unless the brideprice can be returned. The brideprice system reinforces the notion that women are chattel that can be passed on from one male to another. Before marriage, women are under the control of their father or other male guardian, and after marriage this control passes on to her husband in return for the brideprice.

The payment of brideprice adversely affects a woman's ability to decide whether to use contraception and the type of contraception she will use. This is because after the payment of the brideprice all decisions in relation to a woman's reproductive life are determined by her husband, who has paid for this right. This in turn impacts on her ability to make decisions on how many children she will bear and the amount of spacing between each birth. She is also unable to demand safe sex to protect herself from sexually transmitted diseases and HIV infection. Thus, the effect of the brideprice system is to literally transform a woman's person and reproductive capabilities into part of her husband's property. . . .

Leviratic Marriage or Widow Inheritance

The leviratic marriage, or widow inheritance, is a custom in which a man is obliged to marry his brother's widow. This system perpetually restrains the widow from marrying any other person except the customary successor of her dead husband or a member of his family. The effect of this custom is to thrust many women into unwanted marriages and results in forced marriages and forced sex within marriage. Widow inheritance treats women as chattel, instead of human beings who have rights equal to those of a man. A widow who resists being inherited will most likely be evicted from her home by her in-laws, particularly if she is living on what is regarded as family land. Because most rural women are dependent on their husbands for their livelihood, the threat of eviction forces women to comply with the traditional practice. . . .

Child Marriage

During their infancy females in certain societies are betrothed to men of their parents' choice. Upon reaching the age of puberty, women are sent to live in their husband's homes and are forced into having sex at an early age. These girls get pregnant at tender ages and are particularly vulnerable to complications caused by childbirth such as vesicovaginal fistula, a disability resulting from a ruptured uterus and accompanied by tearing of the intestine or bladder, caused by obstructed labor. Without corrective surgery, the girls, sometimes as young as twelve, are rendered incontinent for life. An estimated 20,000 women in the predominantly Moslem Northern Nigeria suffer from vesicovaginal fistula. Another potential problem exists in Botswana, where twenty-eight percent of women who have ever been pregnant were pregnant before reaching the age of eighteen. Also, in Nigeria, one-quarter of all women are married by the age of fourteen, one-half by the age of sixteen, and three-quarters by the age of eighteen. . . .

Female Religious Bondage

Because women are viewed as mediums of exchange, and their reproductive labor is viewed as belonging to the family, young female virgins are given away as "gifts" to oracles and shrines to pacify gods for offenses allegedly committed by other members of their family. Such an example can be found in Ghana, where females, often as young as ten years old, are left completely at the mercy of the chief priest of the shrine, who becomes her husband/master. She and other females, who have been abandoned at the shrine by their families, serve their husband sexually with no access to healthcare.[51] In these instances, young girls are forced into marriage and forced to have sex. This practice is a form of discrimination against women, for it is interesting

---

[51] Once given to the shrine, the girls cannot go to clinics or health posts if they exist within the locality, cannot work except on the chief priest's farms, and cannot leave the shrine for fear of the wrath of the gods. No member of their families would take them back even if they contemplated running away. They are, in a manner of speaking, trapped. Their only mission from that point onward is to serve their husband and bear him children. Interview with Joan Atsu, Member: FIDA (Sept. 26, 1992). Ms. Atsu visited one of the shrines in Adidome, Ghana and wrote an internal report on the condition of these girls and women.

to note that these shrines, which are scattered all over the Volta Region of Ghana, have never required a male to pay for the iniquities of his family members.

NOTE

A Case Study in Human Rights Litigation for African Girls and Women. Assume that you are a lawyer with a human rights organization in Ghana, and that none of the practices discussed in the Adjetey article is prohibited by Ghana law. Plan to bring an NGO lawsuit on behalf of girls and women in these situations. Ghana has ratified without reservation CEDAW, the ICCPR, the African Charter, and the two Slavery Conventions. Ghana's Constitution provides that the President can execute treaties and that Parliament must ratify them. It does not describe the status of treaties in domestic law. The Constitution also provides:

Article 12. . . . (2) Every person in Ghana, whatever his . . . gender shall be entitled to the fundamental human rights and freedoms of the individual contained in this Chapter but subject to respect for the rights and freedoms of others and for the public interest. . . .

Article 15. (1) The dignity of all persons shall be inviolable. . . .

Article 16. (1) No person shall be held in slavery or servitude. . . .

Article 17. (1) All persons shall be equal before the law.

(2) A person shall not be discriminated against on grounds of gender. . . .

Article 26. (1) Every person is entitled to enjoy, practise, profess, maintain and promote any culture, language, tradition or religion subject to the provisions of this Constitution.

What claims would you assert in a Supreme Court lawsuit challenging Parliament's failure to act? The Supreme Court is the highest appellate court and has original jurisdiction of all matters involving enforcement or interpretation of its Constitution. How could plaintiffs use the court decisions in this chapter to brief and argue such a lawsuit? What are the conditions that must exist for plaintiffs to use that case law? How could the Attorney General of Ghana try to defeat such arguments?

Chapter 11
Strategies to Combat Domestic Violence

Women activists around the globe united to campaign against domestic violence starting in the late 1970s and early 1980s. They were successful in many ways. They forced the international community to acknowledge violence against women as a human rights issue. They persuaded international, regional, and state authorities to change the law. Yet women everywhere remain vulnerable to violence.

This Chapter addresses that reality. It provides an overview of the problem (Part I), the international law justifying holding states responsible for the actions of non-state actors (Part II), the international and regional human rights law on violence against women (Part III), and different state solutions (Part IV).

I. Domestic Violence and "Honor" Crimes

Barbara Burton, Nata Duvvury & Nisha Varia, Justice, Change, and Human Rights: International Research and Responses to Domestic Violence
(Washington, D.C.: International Center for Research and Women and The Centre for Development and Population Activities, 2002)

Introduction

Domestic violence[1] perpetrated by partners and close family members on women has long been a matter of silent suffering within the four walls of the home. Despite the awareness others may have of a woman's ongoing experience of abuse, the phenomenon of domestic violence against women has been identified primarily as a private concern. From this perspective, violence is seen to be a matter of individual responsibility, and the woman is perceived to be the one responsible for either adjusting more adequately to the situation as dictated by cultural norms or developing an acceptable method of suffering silently. This basic understanding of domestic violence as a personal issue has limited the extent to which legal resolution to the problem has been

---

[1] Any act of physical, sexual or psychological abuse, or the threat of such abuse, inflicted against a woman by a person intimately connected to her through marriage, family relation or acquaintanceship.

actively pursued. In most societies, domestic violence against women has typically not been perceived as a crime. However, as a result of feminist advocacy within the arenas of human rights and development, social responsibility for domestic violence is slowly being acknowledged in most parts of the world.

Domestic Violence and Human Rights. . . .

[A]ny effort to claim, protect or help realize a single right affects other outcomes as well. Violence against women in the form of physical assault, harassment, emotional abuse, sexual assault, deprivation of resources, destruction of property, torture or confinement clearly violate[s] women's rights to be free from violence. In addition, it prevents and inhibits women's ability to realize other human rights. For example, a woman cannot exercise her rights to livelihood, education, mobility, health or participation in governance, if she is prevented from leaving her home under the threat of violence or death. A woman cannot fulfill her right to choose whether, when or how often she will have children, if she is routinely denied the opportunity to consent to sexual relations, or to choose whether and whom she marries. For these reasons, concerted efforts are now being made to address violence against women as a fundamental human rights issue. Yet for most women throughout the world living with deeply embedded traditions that silence them and circumscribe their options, neither individuals nor institutions are enabled to fulfill or protect this most basic right. Many legal and community institutions simply have no capacity or political will to ensure the protection of women from violence. Further, in most cases, long-standing cultural beliefs and traditions as well as the social and economic arrangements that spring from them, habitually deny, sanction, and even promote violent practices against women. Thus, a framework that makes clear the links between rights and the institutional arrangements capable of promoting and protecting those rights is essential.

Human Rights Watch, Honoring the Killers: Justice Denied for "Honor" Crimes in Jordan

Vol. 16, No.1(E) (Apr. 2004), *available at* RossRights

I. Summary. . . .

In Jordan today, as in many other countries in the Mediterranean and Muslim worlds, "honor" killings of girls and women by their male relatives remain among the most prevalent physical threats to women. . . .

   In Jordan, a woman's life is at risk if she engages in "immoral or shameful" acts, such as talking with a man not her husband or a blood relative (even in a public place), or refusing to tell a close male relative where she has been and with whom, or marrying someone of whom her family does not approve: in short for doing or being imputed to have done anything that, in traditional terms, is perceived to bring sexual dishonor on herself and therefore on her family. Male relatives may beat, shoot, stab, or otherwise physically harm an accused woman, with the approval of both her family members and large sections of the general population. Police rarely investigate "honor" killings, seldom take any initiative to deter these crimes, and typically treat the killers as vindicated men. The police also routinely force threatened women to undergo painful and humiliating virginity examinations at the request of their families in order to determine whether their hymens are intact.

Many women who are threatened by family members end up imprisoned for their own safety. The perverse reality is that while many perpetrators of "honor" crimes walk free, many would-be victims end up incarcerated. . . .

"[H]onor" killings in Jordan rarely carry a sentence of more than one year of imprisonment. Under article 98 of the penal code, this can be reduced to six months if the victim's family waives charges against the perpetrator. Indeed, it is common for killers, having freely admitted their crime and served six or more months awaiting trial, to leave the courtroom as free men immediately after being found guilty. While there is some evidence of greater sensitivity in recent years, the courts still routinely accept a killer's excuse that he acted out of "fury" and diminished capacity—even when the murder occurs weeks after the alleged offensive act—and are willing to consider the slightest gestures of female autonomy as provocations tainting family honor.

Jordanian women's rights activists have tried to reform laws that protect family members who commit "honor" killings. However, the lower house of Parliament has blocked these efforts, along with other legislative proposals that would begin to equalize women's status under Jordanian law. . . .

II. Background. . . .

The persistent myth in Jordan surrounding domestic violence in general, and "honor" killing in particular . . . is that if a woman is sexually tainted—even if her sexual activity or rape is only suspected or rumored—this humiliation extends to the family and is grounds for her relatives to kill her without violating the Islamic prohibition against taking a life. . . .

"Honor" killing is the most extreme form of domestic violence. . . . A family's honor is seen as being dependent on the sexual conformity of its female family members. In part this means the virginity of its unmarried female members and the chastity of its married ones. . . . [I]t is the family as a whole, rather than an individual husband or partner, which perceives itself as injured. . . . In 2003, seventeen women were reportedly killed in Jordan in the name of "family honor." As of March 4, 2004 four more women had already been murdered in Jordan by male family members. . . . The third woman to die this year was seven-months pregnant. She was allegedly shot five times by her brother because of her "illegitimate pregnancy. . . ."

Jordan has one of the world's lowest rates of female homicide. However, a 1998 United Nations study of official figures from the mid-1990s showed that, at that time, murder was the most frequent crime against women and that "honor" crimes (including murder, attempted murder, and "accidental murder") accounted for the largest category—55 percent—of all homicides of women. The study found that violence against women was not restricted to any one social class, and that women were generally reluctant to report violence especially if perpetrated by a member of the family. . . .

As serious as this problem appears from the official statistics . . ., the actual situation is more acute. Exact, reliable numbers are not available because . . . crimes against women are under-counted in official statistics. Undoubtedly there are more "honor" killings than the average of fifteen per year that the government has recorded since 1999. . . .

The Jordan Times . . ., has consistently reported higher numbers than the government—for example, nineteen in 2001 and twenty-two in 2002. The difference is partially due to the newspaper including supposed accidents, suicides with suspicious features, and cases in which the perpetrators originally admit to "honor" killing but later change their stories at trial. Prosecutor General Sabr Yassin Rawashdeh . . . agrees that some "honor" killers camouflage their crimes as accidents or suicides. . . . [H]e added that police investigations into the killings may be too superficial to uncover the truth. . . .

Sophisticated police work and crime-solving expertise are rarely required to solve an "honor" crime. As a counselor at a women's center told Human Rights Watch, "[The murder] is not an individual decision. It's the decision of the whole family. [The killer] feels supported." The killing is meant to be a public statement, and in many cases, perpetrators freely confess. They may even act within earshot of the police. . . . [I]n December 2001, police in Amman found a thirty-six-year-old woman who had previously come to the JWU [the Jordanian Women's Union] for help; the officers took her home, after her father's promise not to harm her; he shot her while the police were still downstairs.

Occasionally, an "honor" killer attempts to deny responsibility. Relatives may contrive to place the murder weapon in the hands of a minor, sometimes a child as young as eleven or twelve, who is not subject to criminal punishment. . . .

Or, as Rawashdeh explained, the killer may attempt to make the killing appear to be an accident or suicide. He recounted the 2003 case of a girl from southern Jordan who had pre-marital sex, became pregnant, and . . . secretly had an abortion. At home afterward, she became ill, and her family took her to a doctor who, not knowing she was unmarried, told her family she had been pregnant. On the way home from the hospital, the family's car—with only the daughter inside it—went over a cliff into a valley. Her relatives reported her death as an accident, and the police and courts believed them. . . .

There is usually a period before the actual killing when the woman's male relatives threaten her life verbally. . . . According to Director General of Public Security Tahseen Shurdom, such threats are illegal. . . . "If the woman tells us [of the threats], we will do something," he told Human Rights Watch. Human Rights Watch was unable to confirm any instance in which a male relative had been prosecuted or even detained for threatening to kill a woman in his household over family honor. Rather, women's rights activists attest that police ask an angry family, at most, to promise not to harm the woman if she is left with them. . . .

There are no safe havens for women threatened by their relatives. Women's groups do not have the resources to offer adequate refuge outside the home for the number of women who face domestic violence. The government, despite years of promises, has yet to create a shelter. In short, most women under threat from their relatives cannot escape danger. Those who are removed from the home for their own protection are placed in prison, and may remain there for punitively long periods. Human Rights Watch is aware of one woman who has remained in prison for her own protection for ten years, and several whose detention has lasted five or six years. . . .

IV. Honor Crimes Under Jordanian Law. . . .

Multiple provisions of the Jordanian penal code can and have been applied by the judiciary to reduce penalties in "honor" crime cases. Article 340 has received the most attention in discussions focused upon legal justification or excuse for crimes of "honor." Under article 340, any man who kills or attacks his wife or any of his female relatives in the act of committing adultery or in an "unlawful bed" benefits from a reduction in penalty. Prior to its amendment in 2001, article 340 provided complete exemption from penalty in certain circumstances,[A] although it was seldom invoked. In an effort to make this law "gender-neutral," a second clause was added in 2001 granting female attackers the same reduction in penalty.[B] . . .

In mid-2001, while the lower house of Parliament was temporarily suspended, the Cabinet passed a number of "temporary" laws, subject to parliamentary ratification once the new legislature convened. Among the "temporary" laws were several granting equal rights to women. . . . In the case of article 340, the "temporary" law amended rather than repealed: husbands would no longer be exonerated for murdering unfaithful wives, but instead the circumstances would be considered as evi-

---

[A] Before amendment, Article 340 permitted murder in some cases, and sharply reduced sentences in others:

"1. He who surprises his wife, or one of his female relatives, committing adultery with somebody and kills, wounds, or injures one or both of them *shall be exempt from penalty* (emphasis added).

2. He who surprises his wife, or one of his female ascendants or descendants or sisters with another in an unlawful bed, and he kills, wounds or injures one or both of them, shall be subject to a reduction in penalty."

[B] Amended Article 340 now permits only a reduced sentence:

"1. There shall benefit from the mitigating excuse (*Uthur Mukhafif*) whosoever surprises his wife or one of his ascendants or descendants in the crime of adultery or in an unlawful bed, and kills her immediately or kills the person fornicating with her or kills both of them or attacks her or both of them in an assault that leads to death or wounding or injury or permanent disability.

2. Shall benefit from the same excuse the wife who surprises her husband in the crime of adultery or in an unlawful bed in the marital home and kills him immediately or kills the woman with whom he is fornicating or kills both of them or attacks him or both of them in an assault that leads to death or wounding or injury or permanent disability.

3. The right of lawful defence shall not be permitted in regard to the person who benefits from this excuse nor shall the provisions of "aggravated circumstances" (*Thuruf Mushaddida*) apply."

dence for mitigating punishment. . . . As of mid-April 2004, the changes in this law . . . remain pending.[c]

There is a common understanding that article 340, as it stands, does not conform to Islamic law. Jordanian officials and Islamists . . . told Human Rights Watch that Islam does not authorize a male family member to mete out punishment to an errant female relative. The provenance of the statute is said to be the Napoleonic Code, brought to Jordan via the Ottoman Empire. Nevertheless, the Islamic Action Front and other religious and cultural conservatives oppose repeal of article 340. They argue that the campaign is motivated by western values of which they do not approve. . . .

The section of the penal code most frequently invoked on behalf of perpetrators of "honor" killings is article 98. This statute mandates reduction of penalty for a perpe- trator (of either gender) who commits a crime in a "state of great fury [or "fit of fury"] resulting from an unlawful and dangerous act on the part of the victim." It does not require *in flagrante* discovery or any other standard of evidence of female indiscretion. If the extenuating excuse is established for a crime punishable by death, such as pre- meditated murder, article 98 provides that the penalty be reduced to a minimum of one year in prison. For other felonies, it is reducible to a minimum of six months and a maximum of two years. Moreover, courts may further halve the sentence if the vic- tim's family "waives" its right to file a complaint of the crime. In murders for "honor," given the family's complicity in the crime, the family nearly always "waives" the right to file a complaint. Thus, "honor" killers may receive sentences of six months—and often do. If a killer has served that much time awaiting trial, the sentence may be commuted to time served and he may walk away a free man.

Though gender-neutral in language, article 98 in practice is applied to benefit only men. "Honor" crimes which are plainly premeditated are commonly considered by the Jordanian courts to have been committed in a "fit of fury" as defined by the stat- ute, and the courts accept as "unlawful and dangerous" even trivial challenges to patriarchal authority. For example, a thirty-year-old man identified as Ziad H. who had murdered his divorced sister for being absent from the family home for one week told authorities, "people started talking about us, so I decided to kill her." A patholo- gist's report indicated that his sister, whom he stabbed thirty times, had not been involved in sexual activity. The father of the victim, who was also the father of the defendant, dropped charges. . . .

[I]t is not necessary that the murder be provoked by any actual proof of sexual indiscretion; . . . mere suspicion of a woman's "unlawful and dangerous" act . . . may be sufficient proof for the courts. . . .

News reports also indicate that reacting to perceived stains on family honor with

---

[c] Temporary laws remain in effect unless specifically rejected by Parliament under Article 94 of the Jordan Constitution; the Jordanian legal index available at the Library of Congress revealed no such rejection through 2005. Emails from Issam Michael Saliba, Foreign Law Spe- cialist, Middle Eastern and North African States, Law Library of Congress, to Susan Deller Ross, Professor of Law, Georgetown University Law Center (June 6 and 7, 2006) (on file with author).

violence will generally be found to have occurred in a "fit of fury" even where substantial time passes between knowledge of the alleged "bad act" and commission of the crime. . . .

In another reported case, a man heard his sister referred to as a "slut" and confronted her. She told him to "mind his own business." He went to bed, awoke the next morning and strangled her with a phone cord. The High Criminal Court ruled: "It does not matter that the defendant killed his sister hours after [learning of her supposed act]. He was still under the influence of extreme anger, which caused him to lose his ability to think clearly because of the unlawful act committed by his sister."

In a 2001 case, a brother visited his sister in a hospital—she was being treated for burns—and she admitted to him that she had had an affair and that she was pregnant. He left and bought a gun. Twenty-four hours later he returned and shot her seven times at close range. . . .

The reduction of sentence due to diminished capacity is a common feature of penal codes around the world. But in the case of article 98, the man's "fit of fury" and the woman's commission of a "bad act" are routinely assumed on the basis of the defendants' accounts and their families' waiving of charges. . . .

V. Betraying the Victim: The Official Response. . . .

Police frequently require threatened women to be examined by a forensic doctor to determine whether their hymens are intact. Virginity exams reflect the presumption that families, communities, and the state have a legitimate interest in a woman's sexual conduct. They involve pain, humiliation, and intimidation. . . . The practice was common in Jordan through the end of the 1990s when even a hint of suspicion had been aroused. Dr. Mu'men Hadidi, the nation's chief medical examiner, told Human Rights Watch that police routinely sent girls and women for virginity examinations upon their families' request without any evidence of sexual indiscretion. . . .

Now, according to Dr. Hadidi, the protocol has changed and there must be evidence of a crime before a virginity exam can be required. . . .

Not all officials believe that the practice has changed. Issa Ayoub, legal advisor to the Public Security Directorate, told Human Rights Watch that if a woman is found with a man who is not a close blood relative or her husband—not necessarily in a compromising circumstance, but simply in the man's company, even in a public place—the presumption continues to be that police "have to send" the woman for a virginity examination, and that "circumstances" would dictate whether such an examination was performed.

AMNESTY INTERNATIONAL, PAKISTAN: VIOLENCE AGAINST WOMEN IN THE NAME OF HONOUR (Sept. 21, 1999), *available at* RossRights

In Pakistan, hundreds of women, . . . for a variety of reasons connected with perceptions of honour are killed every year. The number of such killings appears to be steadily increasing as the perception of what constitutes honour—and what damages it—steadily widens. Often honour killings are carried out on the flimsiest of grounds, for instance when a wife does not serve a meal quickly enough or when a man dreams that his wife betrays him. . . . As state institutions . . . have dealt with such crimes against women with extraordinary leniency, and as the law provides many loopholes for murderers in the name of honour to get away, the tradition remains unbroken. . . .

Honour killings are no longer only reported from remote rural areas but also—though less frequently—from towns and cities. . . .

The fact that male relatives . . . are so frequently perpetrators . . . reflects the conviction that marriage and fidelity are not a matter between husband and wife but relate to the family and that a woman's assumed infidelity reflects on the honour of the entire family. While in the majority of cases, husbands, fathers or brothers commit the killings of girls and women in the name of honour alone or together with male relatives, in some cases, tribal councils or *jirgas* decide that they should be killed and send out men to carry out the deed. . . .

The frequency and randomness of . . . incidents contribute to an atmosphere of fear among young women in Pakistan. . . . [W]omen facing the danger of being branded *siahkari* [black women] by the merest chance contact with a man not belonging to their families, are driven into ever more profound seclusion. . . .

Honour killings are also reported from the Pakistani community living abroad. . . .

International support for women fleeing abroad when they fear for their lives from their families' death threats has been hesitant. The threat to the lives of women who refuse to accept their fathers' decisions relating to their marriages has only recently been recognized as a ground for granting asylum to such women. . . .

The perception of what defiles honour . . . is now very loose. . . . [M]ale control does not only extend to a woman's body and her sexual behaviour but all of her behaviour, including her movements, her language and her actions. In any of these areas, defiance by women translates into undermining male honour and ultimately family and community honour. Severe punishments are reported for bringing food late, for answering back, for undertaking forbidden visits. . . .

For women to choose their marriage partners, object to male violence, or seek divorce are outright acts of defiance and thereby shame the man. They require severe acts of violence to restore honour. . . .

While the media coverage of honour killings has no doubt increased, leading to more such cases being reported, the real incidence . . . appears to have gone up as well. The sense of righteousness manifest in the way killings are carried out in broad daylight, sometimes in public places in front of witnesses, appears to have grown, too.

Observers and analysts in Pakistan have pointed to a number of reasons for this increase. . . . Key among the contributing factors are the government's failure to take effective measures to end the practice . . . and the virtual impunity with which such killings are carried out. Others include the weakening of institutions of the state, a pervasive culture of violence, economic decline and a general disregard for women's issues. . . .

Many analysts in Pakistan have concluded that each of these crises . . . has turned urban populations to alternative models, such as that inspired by the Taleban movement of Afghanistan. . . . Some observers have also pointed out that the apparent 'tribalization of formal law' may have created the impression of official sanction for this orientation which plays into the popular perception that it is acceptable to take the law into one's own hands. . . .

The increased access to heavy weapons by rural populations in the wake of the Afghanistan conflict has made it easier to settle issues, including honour issues, violently. . . .

At the same time . . . economic decline has forced more and more women into the workforce but . . . men were not accustomed to seeing women move outside the traditional *char divari* [literally: the four walls]. They resent and fear the exposure of women to new people, ideas and influences as well as their increased self-confidence. . . .

[M]ore women are now aware of their rights, largely thanks to the awareness-raising work of women's rights groups but also to the media and greater mobility of women. Women's refusal to comply with decisions or traditions that violate their newly discovered rights has led to a backlash from men apprehending loss of control, involving violence, killings and threats of such violence. . . .

In its search for solutions to protracted tribal conflicts, the administration in upper Sindh has increasingly used the services of traditional tribal leaders and the institution of the tribal *jirga* to solve problems facing the administration. . . . In this process the official judicial system has been bypassed on the grounds that the tribal system provides faster, cheaper and more lasting solutions. However, this approach has also conveyed the impression that the rule of law as enshrined in the constitution and statutory law is dispensable, replaceable by alternate systems such as the tribal justice system built on tribal notions of honour and social organization.

AMNESTY INTERNATIONAL, PAKISTAN: INSUFFICIENT PROTECTION OF WOMEN
(Apr. 16, 2002), *available at* RossRights

Official Statements on 'Honour' Crimes

[O]n 21 April 2000 in Islamabad, General Musharraf said: ". . . The Government of Pakistan vigorously condemns the practice of so-called 'honour killings'. Such actions do not find any place in our religion or law." He also said that killing in the name of 'honour' "is murder and will be treated as such." . . .

According to a government hand-out of July 2000 . . . "The practice is carried over from ancient tribal customs which are anti-Islamic. . . . The government is committed to combatting this practice with all the resources at its disposal. . . ." In September 2000, Interior Minister General (retrd.) Moinuddin Haider said he had directed police to register First Information Reports (FIRs, complaints registered with police which start the inquiry process) in 'honour' crimes cases even if the killers tried to take shelter behind verdicts of *jirgas* [tribal councils] as these were not recognized by law. . . . Most media responses to the government announcement called it "a long overdue step. . . . At present such incidents are usually ignored by government officials, especially in rural or tribal areas, where some culprits are either powerful and well-connected or simply manage to bribe their way out of trouble. The real test of the government's intent to root out this savage practice would thus lie in elimination of all possible escape routes for the offenders.''

Other state bodies also denounced 'honour' killings but since they did not appear to make an effort to reach the grass roots, their pronouncements were not as effective as they might otherwise have been. Amnesty International in 1999 requested the Council of Islamic Ideology for its view on whether 'honour' killings are lawful according to Islam. It replied. . . . ''Although sexual immorality is one of the major sins according to Islam . . . , nobody is allowed to take the law in his hands. . . .''. . . .

'Honour' Crimes. . . .

Men in Pakistani society have virtually no other means of undoing a perceived infringement of 'honour' than to kill the women assumed to be guilty of it. Social pressures to eliminate the 'offending' woman are great and men who would rather ignore rumours of infringement of 'honour' are themselves considered dishonourable. Women, too, have to some extent internalized norms of 'honour' and are known to have approved of or assisted in killings of other women in the context of 'honour'. . . .

The exact number of honour killings is impossible to ascertain as many such killings go unrecorded and unreported. The HRCP [Human Rights Commission of Pakistan] noted hundreds of 'honour' killings in different parts of the country in the year 2000. . . .

While the condemnation of 'honour' crimes by the present Government of Pakistan in the Convention on Human Rights and Human Dignity in April 2000 was clear and unequivocal, no immediate action followed to prove its commitment. Even well-documented cases of 'honour' killings were not pursued. . . . Instead, public statements by some government officials sounded like excuses for inaction. . . .

In the recent past, new trends relating to 'honour' crimes have emerged. Increasingly, men kill not only the woman who they believe to have brought shame on them but also several other family members. In November 2000, Mohammad Umar Magsi, originally from southwestern Balochistan and living with his family in Karachi, killed his 11-year-old daughter Farzana with an axe as he suspected her of having an affair; when his wife and younger daughter, nine-year-old Sabra, tried to intervene, he killed them as well before turning himself in to police. . . .

The HRCP has observed that increasingly young boys are forced by their parents to attack or kill sisters who are opposed to a forced marriage. After committing the crime, the boys are formally pardoned by the fathers of the girls or women, which allows them to go free without charge or trial. . . .

In a few cases, women have begun to resist violence in the name of 'honour'. In November 2000, Parwatti, a young woman in Shahpur Chakar, near Nawabshah, Sindh, fought back when her husband tried to murder her despite her declaring her innocence. Her husband was injured in the struggle and the woman escaped. The local landlord subsequently held a *jirga* which established her innocence and asked the husband to apologize and take her back. . . .

Women who marry men of their own choice are frequently seen to damage their family's 'honour'; they are frequently detained by their parents, forcibly married to someone else, threatened, humiliated, assaulted or killed. If they chose to get married in court against the will of their parents, they may be charged, along with their husbands, with 'illicit' sexual relations under the country's Zina Ordinance if their parents do not recognize the legality of the marriage. . . .

In March 2000, 14-year-old Rahima Mugheri was killed by her 28-year-old husband Niazul Mugheri on their wedding night. He emerged from their bridal chamber to announce to family members and neighbours that his wife had confessed to pre-marital sex. The family then decided on the mode of her death: first Niazul's elder brother, then other male relatives, including the husband shot at her till she died. Rahima was buried within hours of her wedding. . . .

In October 2000, 15-year-old Asif Ali Hussain and his cousin used axes to kill Asif's sleeping sisters Firdous, 21, and Najma, 20, in their home in Sheikupra, Punjab province. Both young men were arrested; Asif Ali Hussain said in jail that the women had dishonoured their family when they spoke to men other than their relatives and therefore deserved to die. . . .

On 3 October 2000, Nathu, in Bangla Ichha in Rajanpur district, Punjab, killed his wife Gamil, who was eight months pregnant, pulled out the foetus and stabbed it as well; he had suspected his wife of infidelity. . . .

In December 2000, three brothers overpowered their sister-in-law, Anila, sprinkled kerosene on her clothes and set her on fire in a village near Sukkur when they suspected her of infidelity. Her father rescued her and took her to hospital where, with 85% burns, she died. . . .

In early 2001, Mir Afzal cut off the nose of his wife Amroz Khatoon in Karachi as he suspected her of infidelity. He then attempted to kill her.

Human Rights Watch, *Violence Against Women in Brazil*
in THE HUMAN RIGHTS WATCH GLOBAL REPORT ON WOMEN'S HUMAN RIGHTS 348–60 (1995)

A 1991 Human Rights Watch investigation in Brazil revealed that Brazilian women receive little or no justice when they reported physical abuse by their husbands or partners to the police. In spite of the approximately 125 specialized police stations (Delegacias De Defesa Da Mulher) established in Brazil to deal exclusively with violence against women, many women in rural and urban areas have found police to be unresponsive to their claims and have encountered open hostility or incredulity when they attempted to report domestic violence. Some delegacias are chronically underfunded and their staff poorly trained. The Brazilian Penal Code, in spite of indefatigable lobbying on the part of Brazilian women's rights activists, remains biased and discriminatory in its letter and in its implementation.

The continued application of the honor defense, which has no basis in law, is inherently biased, and is almost exclusively applied to wife-murder. The emphasis on "provocation" by the victim even in pre-meditated wife-murder crimes; the near total failure to prosecute battery and rape in the home; and the prejudicial treatment of rape victims both in law and in fact, represents a pattern of discriminatory treatment by the criminal justice system of female victims of domestic violence. This pattern demonstrates that Brazil does not meet its international obligations to guarantee to its female citizens the equal enjoyment of their civil and political rights and the equal protection of the law.

Brazil has taken limited steps toward meeting these obligations. . . . The 1988 constitution reflects a concern for familial violence and specifically calls for states to establish mechanism[s] to impede domestic violence. And, the creation of the women's police stations also indicates Brazil's recognition both of the wide-scale problem of violence against women and its obligations to take positive steps toward eradicating such abuse.

Nonetheless, . . . these changes have had very little impact. In 1991 the organization's Women's Rights Project issued its first report on domestic violence and state responsibility in Brazil. They responded to the severity of Brazil's domestic violence problem, made visible largely by the campaigning of the women's movement, and the degree to which such abuse continues to receive both the explicit and implicit sanction of the Brazilian government. The report concluded that impunity prevails for men who beat, rape and kill their wives and girlfriends, as epitomized in the use of the honor defense to exculpate men accused of killing their wives or partners. The Brazilian criminal justice system has failed generally to investigate and prosecute in a nondiscriminatory manner crimes of domestic violence against women, in contravention of Brazil's obligations under international law. . . .

While the government has created approximately six shelters for battered women throughout the country, the criminal justice system remains largely unresponsive to women's complaints of abuse, except where, as one women's rights activist and attorney told Human Rights Watch "[the battered woman] has lots of money to hire a very good lawyer to defend her case and push it through the Brazilian legal system. She went on to add that in many domestic violence cases, judges simply file away the complaints and they are rarely investigated."

The Role of the Women's Movement. . . .

Brazilian advocates of women's rights . . . [struggled for a decade] to force the state to prosecute wife-murder and other domestic violence crimes to the full extent of the law. . . .

Active women in both urban and rural areas and across racial and economic divides seized on domestic violence and used it successfully to propel gender concerns into the broader public policy debate. A series of local demonstrations led to several nationwide protests against domestic violence from which emerged the slogan that became the *crie* [sic] *de coeur* of the Brazilian women's movement: "Those who love don't kill. . . ."

By late 1985 eight women's police stations had opened in the state of São Paulo, and by 1990 there were seventy-four throughout the country. The women's delegacias represented an integrated approach to the problem of domestic violence. They were designed to investigate gender-specific crimes, and to provide psychological and legal counseling.

By the mid-1980s, the now active and institutionalized women's movement began to focus on legal reform to consolidate their hard-won gains. Women were granted the franchise in 1932, but until a 1962 civil code reform they were considered perpetual subordinates, legally equated with "minors, spendthrifts and back woodsmen" and could not, for example, work outside the home without their husband's permission. The constitution enacted in 1988 reflects many of the national women's movement's demands. In particular, Article 226, Paragraph 8 provides that "the state should assist the family, in the person of each of its members, and should create mechanisms so as to impede violence in the sphere of its relationships." Similar provisions have been adopted in state constitutions throughout Brazil.

Domestic Violence

Available statistics show that over 70 percent of all reported incidents of violence against women in Brazil take place in the home. In almost all of these cases the abuser was either the woman's husband or her lover. Over 40 percent involved serious bodily injury caused by, among other things, punching, slapping, kicking, tying up and spanking, burning of the breasts and genitals, and strangulation. Brazil's 1988 census . . . includes the first national statistics broken down by gender on crimes of physical abuse and the extent to which they are reported to the police and prosecuted in the courts. The . . . study found that from October 1987 to September 1988, 1,153,300 people declared . . . that they had been victims of physical abuse. A marked difference emerged in the nature of violence suffered by women as opposed to men. For Brazilian men, murder and physical abuse primarily involve acquaintances or strangers and occur outside the home. For Brazilian women, the opposite is true. The 1988 census showed that men were abused by relatives (including spouses) only 10 percent of the time, while women are related to their abuser in over half of the cases of reported physical violence. . . .

Wife-Murder. . . .

[E]xisting information indicates that wife-murder is a common crime. A 1991 study of more than 6,000 violent crimes against Brazilian women from 1987 to 1989 found that 400 incidents involved murders of women by their husbands or lovers.

The Legal Context

Under Brazilian law, homicide is defined as a crime against life . . . It is the only crime that requires a jury trial. . . .

A homicide is not considered a crime in Brazil if, among other things, it was committed in legitimate self-defense. . . . Under Article 25 of the Penal Code, self-defense is defined as "the case of one who using the necessary means with moderation reacts against unjust aggression present or imminent to his right or someone else's."

Charges in homicide cases are brought by the prosecutor. . . . Following receipt of the police report, the prosecutor conducts his own investigation and recommends to the judge whether and on what charge to try the suspect. . . .

During the pre-trial phase, which begins once the judge receives the prosecutor's recommendation, the judge hears the accused and witnesses on both sides and may subpoena additional witnesses or seek additional evidence. There is no grand jury. The judge alone determines whether there is sufficient evidence for a jury trial for homicide or attempted homicide—the only crimes in Brazil which merit a jury trial.

After hearing the arguments of both the prosecution and defense and reading the testimony of witnesses, the jury makes its final decision based on answers to a series of questions posed by the judge at the behest of the opposing sides. The questions follow a standard format, although their content reflects the specific facts of the case. The jurors only answer "yes" or "no." They do not consult with one another and convey their answers by secret ballot. Under Article 5 of the Brazilian Constitution, the sovereignty of the jury's decision is guaranteed. The judge determines the sentence based on the jury's verdict.

The Honor Defense

Prior to Brazil's independence in 1822, Portuguese colonial law allowed a man who caught his wife in the act of adultery to kill her and her lover, although the reverse was not true. Brazil's first post-independence penal code was enacted in 1830 and did away with this rule. Brazil's second penal code, enacted in 1890, included an exemption from criminal responsibility for those who committed a crime "under a state of total perturbation of the senses and intelligence." Wife-murder cases soon came to be defended as "crimes of passion" in which the wife's adulterous behavior occasioned such strong emotion in the accused that he experienced a kind of "momentary insanity" resulting in the crime. The emphasis in such cases was placed not on the nature of the crime itself, but on the degree to which the husband intended to commit it.

For the next fifty years, defense attorneys successfully used the "crime of passion" argument to obtain acquittal of husbands accused of murdering their wives and, on occasion, though far less frequently, of wives accused of murdering their husbands. It proved so effective in obtaining acquittal that Brazil's third penal code, which remains in force today, explicitly states that "emotion or passion does not exclude criminal responsibility."

As a result of this change in the penal code, acquittal in wife-murder cases became more difficult to obtain. Defense attorneys, unhappy with this development, devised the legitimate defense of honor as a new exculpatory strategy. Like the crime of passion argument, the honor defense shifts attention from the killing itself to the absence of intent on the part of the murderer. However, rather than focusing on the accused's "momentary insanity" as vitiating criminal intent, the honor defense characterizes the accused as having acted spontaneously in legitimate self-defense against an imminent aggression, though against his honor rather than his physical being.

The notion that a man's honor can be gravely threatened by his wife's adulterous action reflects proprietary attitudes towards women deeply rooted in Brazilian society. When Brazil's first civil code was passed in 1914, women were considered perpetual wards, like minors and the elderly. The 1988 constitution grants full equality to women, but the civil code has yet to be changed.

This subordinate status is the basis for the belief that the wife is the husband's property and any action by her that does not fall within the prescribed conjugal norm, especially adultery, constitutes an offense against his honor. In many cases, a successful honor defense depends less on showing the accused's passion or lack of intent to kill than on demonstrating the husband's honor and the wife's dishonorable behavior within a recognized conjugal relationship.[44] For example, in one 1972 case, the couple had been married for sixteen years. All was well in the marriage until she got a job, began coming home late and, according to testimony from the accused, refused to pay her "conjugal debt." The husband killed her and was acquitted, again on legitimate defense of honor. The decision was upheld on appeal.

As this case demonstrates, the honor defense has been successfully invoked in Brazil as if it were the equivalent of legitimate self-defense, with the defendant's resulting acquittal. Yet at no point does the law equate a threat to a man's honor with the danger posed by an imminent physical attack. The legitimate defense of honor accepts not only that a wife's adultery constitutes such an "imminent threat," but also, as in the case described above, that her merely alleged adultery or desire to separate or refusal to engage in sexual relations constitute such a threat as well.

A key aspect of the self-defense rule is proportionality of the means employed. The accused must "use the necessary means in moderation" in responding to an imminent threat. Even assuming that a wife's act of adultery tarnished her husband's honor, homicide, or in some cases double homicide, is obviously not a proportionate response. Yet, the Brazilian courts repeatedly legitimated such disproportionate responses.

As early as 1955, Brazil's high court began to overturn cases involving acquittal on the grounds of honor. In one 1968 decision, the court found that the "legitimate defense of honor does not exist in a homicide committed by a husband during a crisis of indignation, when the wife has threatened the conjugal honor." Although by

---

[44] As noted in a study prepared for the National Council on the Rights of Women, the jury "doesn't evaluate the crime in itself, but instead evaluates the victim and the accused's life, trying to show how adapted each one is to what they imagine should be the correct behavior for a husband and wife. . . . The man can always be acquitted if the defense manages to convince the jury that he was a good and honest worker, a dedicated father and husband, while the woman was unfaithful and did not fulfill her responsibilities as a housewife and mother. . . . This way the ones involved in the crime are judged distinctly. Men and women are attributed different roles, in a pattern that excludes citizenship and equality of rights."

Brazilian law the high court's decisions refer only to the specific case being judged and have no precedential value, its decisions in practice carry significant jurisprudential weight and are expected to establish precedent, particularly at the appellate court level. In honor defense cases, however, the high court's decisions have had no such unifying effect and, consequently, a history of contradictory jurisprudence has evolved.

For example, a review of appellate court records for the state of Rio de Janeiro from 1978 to 1987 reveals this long-standing contradictory trend. Of twenty cases involving the legitimate defense of honor, eight contained outright and principled rejections of the defense. In one 1979 case, the tribunal found that "the Penal Code doesn't allow a man to decree the death penalty to an unfaithful wife or lover." . . .

However, another five cases upheld the honor defense. In one 1984 case involving an attempted murder, the appellate court found:

[the victim,] who was in matrimonial litigation with the defendant, demanded he pay alimony. That should have made her adopt a more strict behavior to justify the onus she wanted to put on her ex-husband. However, she showed up in the company of an ex-employee said to be her lover, and caused a completely legitimate reaction on the part of the defendant under the point of view of the defense of his hurt honor.

The ongoing tension in Brazilian jurisprudence concerning the honor defense expressed itself in conflicting judicial decisions in the case of Joã Lopes, a bricklayer who stabbed to death his wife and her lover after catching them together in a hotel room in the city of Apucarana. On March 11, 1991, the Superior Tribunal of Justice, Brazil's highest court of appeal in criminal and civil cases, overturned lower and appellate court decisions acquitting Lopes of the double homicide on the grounds of legitimate defense of honor.

The court nullified the lower courts' decisions on the grounds that they were against all facts in the case. It found that "honor is a personal attribute which is the property of each spouse. There is no offense to the husband's honor by the wife's adultery. There is no such conjugal honor." In addition, the high court found that "homicide is not an appropriate response to adultery" and "given that there was no proof of revenge on the part of the wife, the adultery does not place the husband in a state of self-defense as contemplated by the penal code." Finally, the court proclaimed that what is defended in such cases "is not honor but the pride of the Lord who sees his wife as property."

However, when the *Lopes* case was re-tried on August 29, 1991, the lower court ignored the high court's ruling and again acquitted Lopes of the double homicide on the grounds of honor. The lower-court judge who presided over the second trial ruled that the honor defense was "essentially the heart" of the matter. The judge told reporters that "one decision of the Supreme Court does not necessarily form a national precedent." The lower court's ruling is particularly significant because the second jury's decision is definitive and cannot be appealed again, unless on other grounds.

The Response of the Courts

Several criminal justice officials interviewed by Human Rights Watch argued that, in the absence of precedential authority at the high court level, lower court judges cannot be held accountable for the honor defense's continued success. A prosecutor in Pernambuco stated that "the jury doesn't want to know about the law. She demeaned him. So to wash his honor, he killed her. The patriarchal concept is very strong." In his view, "the citizens don't judge correctly. In the interior [, juries] don't conform to the expectations of society. Justice is limited. A man kills his wife and goes back on the street." He estimates that in the country's interior the honor defense is still successful 80 percent of the time.

The defense attorney in *Lopes* told Human Rights Watch in April 1991 that "it's not the legal system, but macho society that acquits wife-killers. . . . Society talks louder than the courts." He was certain that the high court's decision would have no impact on the jury tribunal and, as it turned out, rightly expected that the honor defense would be upheld by the jury when the case was retried in the lower court in August 1991.

The argument that juries, not judges, are responsible for the continued success of the honor defense has some basis in Brazilian law. In all criminal and civil cases, except homicide, the judge is the sole adjudicator. In homicide cases, however, the popular jury assumes the responsibility for deciding cases, and the judge has remarkably little control over the legal or factual basis for its verdict. Judges can dismiss cases for lack of evidence or acquit defendants when convinced that there was no intention to commit a crime, but they have limited authority to impede the arguments of either party and almost no authority to exclude evidence. The lower court judge in the *Lopes* decision told reporters that "unless the defense's strategy is completely absurd or irrelevant, I can do nothing to impede it."

Several attorneys handling constitutional and criminal cases interviewed by Human Rights Watch stressed the limited authority of trial court judges. Under Article 483 of the Criminal Procedure Code, the judge cannot interfere in the jury's decision in any way and is largely restricted to posing the questions which the jury will answer in deciding the case. The jury's verdict is sovereign, and can only be appealed if it is against all material evidence in the case or if procedural irregularities occurred in the course of the trial or sentencing. . . .

In principle, Human Rights Watch does not dispute the desirability of the jury's sovereignty. Rather, we are concerned about the propensity of judges in honor defense cases to defer to that sovereignty even when the jury's verdict is not supported by the law or the facts. While the jury is sovereign, its sovereignty does not extend to deciding contrary to law or against all material evidence. The Superior Tribunal in *Lopes* reversed the verdict on both grounds. Although its decision is not binding, it does constitute an interpretation of the law that should guide lower court decisions in specific cases. The judge presiding at Lopes's second trial should have instructed the jury in the law consistent with the high court's decision. By permitting the jury to acquit Lopes on the grounds of honor a second time, the judge subordinated his role as guardian and explicator of the law to the whim of a jury ignorant of the law and motivated by social prejudice. To ignore a landmark ruling by the nation's highest court in the very same case makes a mockery of the appellate process and the administration of justice in Brazil.

N O T E

The Role of Law. In each of the countries featured in the human rights reports, identify the different ways state law has permitted or encouraged the murder of women. What legal changes would you recommend to improve the laws in each of these countries?

II. Holding the State Responsible for Private Violence

The following decisions, the first by the Inter-American Court of Human Rights, the second by the UN Human Rights Committee, developed a rationale for holding the state responsible when private parties commit crimes. Historically, international law regulated only state action. How then could states be held responsible for the actions of non-state actors? The first case develops that rationale. While the facts involve violence against men, consider how the rationale could be used to hold the state responsible for that most private of crimes—domestic violence.

Velásquez Rodríguez Case
(Inter-Am. Ct. H.R.), 28 I.L.M. 291 (1988), *available at* RossRights

1. The Inter-American Commission on Human Rights (hereinafter "the Commission") submitted the instant case to the Inter-American Court of Human Rights [on] April 24, 1986. It originated in a petition against the State of Honduras. . . .

2. . . . [T]he Commission . . . requested that the Court determine whether the State in question had violated Articles 4 (Right to Life), 5 (Right to Humane Treatment) and 7 (Right to Personal Liberty) of the Convention in the case of Angel Manfredo Velásquez Rodríguez (also known as Manfredo Velásquez). . . .

147. The Court now turns to the relevant facts that it finds to have been proven. They are as follows:. . . .

    e. On September 12, 1981, between 4:30 and 5:00 p.m. several heavily-armed men in civilian clothes driving a white Ford without license plates kidnapped Manfredo Velásquez from a parking lot in downtown Tegucigalpa. Today, nearly seven years later, he remains disappeared, which creates a reasonable presumption that he is dead. . . .

    f. Persons connected with the Armed Forces or under its direction carried out that kidnapping. . . .

    g. The kidnapping and disappearance of Manfredo Velásquez falls within the systematic practice of disappearances. . . . To wit:

i. Manfredo Velásquez was a student who was involved in activities the authorities considered "dangerous" to national security. . . .

ii. The kidnapping of Manfredo Velásquez was carried out in broad daylight by men in civilian clothes who used a vehicle without license plates.

iii. In the case of Manfredo Velásquez, there were the same type of denials by his captors and the Armed Forces, the same omissions of the latter and of the Government in investigating and revealing his whereabouts, and the same ineffectiveness of the courts where three writs of habeas corpus and two criminal complaints were brought. . . .

h. There is no evidence in the record that Manfredo Velásquez had disappeared in order to join subversive groups. . . . Nor is there any evidence that he was kidnapped by common criminals or other persons unrelated to the practice of disappearances existing at that time.

148. Based upon the above, the Court finds . . . (1) a practice of disappearances carried out or tolerated by Honduran officials existed between 1981 and 1984; (2) Manfredo Velásquez disappeared at the hands of or with the acquiescence of those officials within the framework of that practice; and (3) the Government of Honduras failed to guarantee the human rights affected by that practice.

149. Disappearances are not new in the history of human rights violations. However, their systematic and repeated nature and their use not only for causing certain individuals to disappear, either briefly or permanently, but also as a means of creating a general state of anguish, insecurity and fear, is a recent phenomenon. Although this practice exists virtually worldwide, it has occurred with exceptional intensity in Latin America in the last few years.

150. The phenomenon of disappearances is a complex form of human rights violation that must be understood and confronted in an integral fashion. . . .

154. Without question, the State has the right and duty to guarantee its security. It is also indisputable that all societies suffer some deficiencies in their legal orders. However, regardless of the seriousness of certain actions and the culpability of the perpetrators of certain crimes, the power of the State is not unlimited, nor may the State resort to any means to attain its ends. The State is subject to law and morality. Disrespect for human dignity cannot serve as the basis for any State action.

155. The forced disappearance of human beings is a multiple and continuous violation of many rights under the Convention that the States Parties are obligated to respect and guarantee. The kidnapping of a person is an arbitrary deprivation of liberty, an infringement of a detainee's right to be taken without delay before a judge and to invoke the appropriate procedures to review the legality of the arrest, all in violation of Article 7 of the Convention. . . .

156. Moreover, prolonged isolation and deprivation of communication are in themselves cruel and inhuman treatment, harmful to the psychological and moral integrity of the person and a violation of the right of any detainee to respect for his inherent dignity as a human being. Such treatment, therefore, violates Article 5 of

the Convention, which recognizes the right to the integrity of the person by providing that:

1. Every person has the right to have his physical, mental, and moral integrity respected.
2. No one shall be subjected to torture or to cruel, inhuman, or degrading punishment or treatment. All persons deprived of their liberty shall be treated with respect for the inherent dignity of the human person.

In addition, investigations into the practice of disappearances and the testimony of victims who have regained their liberty show that those who are disappeared are often subjected to merciless treatment, including all types of indignities, torture and other cruel, inhuman and degrading treatment, in violation of the right to physical integrity recognized in Article 5 of the Convention.

157. The practice of disappearances often involves secret execution without trial, followed by concealment of the body to eliminate any material evidence of the crime and to ensure the impunity of those responsible. This is a flagrant violation of the right to life, recognized in Article 4 of the Convention, the first clause of which reads as follows:

1. Every person has the right to have his life respected. This right shall be protected by law and, in general, from the moment of conception. No one shall be arbitrarily deprived of his life.

158. The practice of disappearances, in addition to directly violating many provisions of the Convention, . . . constitutes a radical breach of the treaty in that it shows a crass abandonment of the values which emanate from the concept of human dignity and of the most basic principles of the inter-American system and the Convention. The existence of this practice, moreover, evinces a disregard of the duty to organize the State in such a manner as to guarantee the rights recognized in the Convention. . . .

159. The Commission has asked the Court to find that Honduras has violated the rights guaranteed to Manfredo Velásquez by Articles 4, 5 and 7 of the Convention. The Government has denied the charges and seeks to be absolved.

160. This requires the Court to examine the conditions under which a particular act, which violates one of the rights recognized by the Convention, can be imputed to a State Party thereby establishing its international responsibility.

161. Article 1(1) of the Convention provides:

Article 1. Obligation to Respect Rights

1. The States Parties to this Convention undertake to respect the rights and freedoms recognized herein and to ensure to all persons subject to their jurisdiction the free and full exercise of those rights and freedoms, without any discrimination for reasons of race, color, sex, language, religion, political or other opinion, national or social origin, economic status, birth, or any other social condition.

162. This article specifies the obligation assumed by the States Parties in relation to each of the rights protected. Each claim alleging that one of those rights has been

infringed necessarily implies that Article 1(1) of the Convention has also been violated.

164. Article 1(1) is essential in determining whether a violation of the human rights recognized by the Convention can be imputed to a State Party. In effect, that article charges the States Parties with the fundamental duty to respect and guarantee the rights recognized in the Convention. Any impairment of those rights which can be attributed under the rules of international law to the action or omission of any public authority constitutes an act imputable to the State, which assumes responsibility in the terms provided by the Convention.

165. The first obligation assumed by the States Parties under Article 1(1) is "to respect the rights and freedoms" recognized by the Convention. The exercise of public authority has certain limits which derive from the fact that human rights are inherent attributes of human dignity and are, therefore, superior to the power of the State. On another occasion, this Court stated:

> The protection of human rights, particularly the civil and political rights set forth in the Convention, is in effect based on the affirmation of the existence of certain inviolable attributes of the individual that cannot be legitimately restricted through the exercise of governmental power. These are individual domains that are beyond the reach of the State or to which the State has but limited access. Thus, the protection of human rights must necessarily comprise the concept of the restriction of the exercise of state power.

166. The second obligation of the States Parties is to "ensure" the free and full exercise of the rights recognized by the Convention to every person subject to its jurisdiction. This obligation implies the duty of the States Parties to organize the governmental apparatus and, in general, all the structures through which public power is exercised, so that they are capable of juridically ensuring the free and full enjoyment of human rights. As a consequence of this obligation, the States must prevent, investigate and punish any violation of the rights recognized by the Convention and, moreover, if possible attempt to restore the right violated and provide compensation as warranted for damages resulting from the violation.

167. The obligation to ensure the free and full exercise of human rights is not fulfilled by the existence of a legal system designed to make it possible to comply with this obligation—it also requires the government to conduct itself so as to effectively ensure the free and full exercise of human rights. . . .

169. According to Article 1(1), any exercise of public power that violates the rights recognized by the Convention is illegal. Whenever a State organ, official or public entity violates one of those rights, this constitutes a failure of the duty to respect the rights and freedoms set forth in the Convention.

170. This conclusion is independent of whether the organ or official has contravened provisions of internal law or overstepped the limits of his authority: under international law a State is responsible for the acts of its agents undertaken in their official capacity and for their omissions, even when those agents act outside the sphere of their authority or violate internal law.

171. This principle suits perfectly the nature of the Convention, which is violated

whenever public power is used to infringe the rights recognized therein. If acts of public power that exceed the State's authority or are illegal under its own laws were not considered to compromise that State's obligation under the treaty, the system of protection provided for in the Convention would be illusory.

172. Thus, in principle, any violation of rights recognized by the Convention carried out by an act of public authority or by persons who use their position of authority is imputable to the State. However, this does not define all the circumstances in which a State is obligated to prevent, investigate and punish human rights violations, nor all the cases in which the State might be found responsible for an infringement of those rights. An illegal act which violates human rights and which is initially not directly imputable to a State (for example, because it is the act of a private person or because the person responsible has not been identified) can lead to international responsibility of the State, not because of the act itself, but because of the lack of due diligence to prevent the violation or to respond to it as required by the Convention.

173. . . . For the purposes of analysis, the intent or motivation of the agent who has violated the rights recognized by the Convention is irrelevant—the violation can be established even if the identity of the individual perpetrator is unknown. What is decisive is whether a violation of the rights recognized by the Convention has occurred with the support or the acquiescence of the government, or whether the State has allowed the act to take place without taking measures to prevent it or to punish those responsible. Thus, the Court's task is to determine whether the violation is the result of a State's failure to fulfill its duty to respect and guarantee those rights, as required by Article 1(1) of the Convention.

174. The State has a legal duty to take reasonable steps to prevent human rights violations and to use the means at its disposal to carry out a serious investigation of violations committed within its jurisdiction, to identify those responsible, to impose the appropriate punishment and to ensure the victim adequate compensation.

175. This duty to prevent includes all those means of a legal, political, administrative and cultural nature that promote the protection of human rights and ensure that any violations are considered and treated as illegal acts, which, as such, may lead to the punishment of those responsible and the obligation to indemnify the victims for damages. . . . Of course, while the State is obligated to prevent human rights abuses, the existence of a particular violation does not, in itself, prove the failure to take preventive measures. On the other hand, subjecting a person to official, repressive bodies that practice torture and assassination with impunity is itself a breach of the duty to prevent violations of the rights to life and physical integrity of the person, even if that particular person is not tortured or assassinated, or if those facts cannot be proven in a concrete case.

176. The State is obligated to investigate every situation involving a violation of the rights protected by the Convention. If the State apparatus acts in such a way that the violation goes unpunished and the victim's full enjoyment of such rights is not restored as soon as possible, the State has failed to comply with its duty to ensure the free and full exercise of those rights to the persons within its jurisdiction. The same is

true when the State allows private persons or groups to act freely and with impunity to the detriment of the rights recognized by the Convention.

177. In certain circumstances, it may be difficult to investigate acts that violate an individual's rights. The duty to investigate, like the duty to prevent, is not breached merely because the investigation does not produce a satisfactory result. Nevertheless, it must be undertaken in a serious manner and not as a mere formality preordained to be ineffective. An investigation must have an objective and be assumed by the State as its own legal duty, not as a step taken by private interests that depends upon the initiative of the victim or his family or upon their offer of proof, without an effective search for the truth by the government. This is true regardless of what agent is eventually found responsible for the violation. Where the acts of private parties that violate the Convention are not seriously investigated, those parties are aided in a sense by the government, thereby making the State responsible on the international plane.

178. In the instant case, the evidence shows a complete inability of the procedures of the State of Honduras, which were theoretically adequate, to carry out an investigation into the disappearance of Manfredo Velásquez, and of the fulfillment of its duties to pay compensation and punish those responsible, as set out in Article 1(1) of the Convention.

179. . . . [T]he failure of the judicial system to act upon the writs brought before various tribunals in the instant case has been proven. Not one writ of habeas corpus was processed. No judge had access to the places where Manfredo Velásquez might have been detained. The criminal complaint was dismissed.

180. Nor did the organs of the Executive Branch carry out a serious investigation to establish the fate of Manfredo Velásquez. There was no investigation of public allegations of a practice of disappearances nor a determination of whether Manfredo Velásquez had been a victim of that practice. . . . All of the above leads to the conclusion that the Honduran authorities did not take effective action to ensure respect for human rights within the jurisdiction of that State as required by Article 1 (1) of the Convention. . . .

182. The Court is convinced, and has so found, that the disappearance of Manfredo Velásquez was carried out by agents who acted under cover of public authority. However, even had that fact not been proven, the failure of the State apparatus to act, which is clearly proven, is a failure on the part of Honduras to fulfill the duties it assumed under Article 1(1) of the Convention, which obligated it to ensure Manfredo Velásquez the free and full exercise of his human rights.

183. The Court notes that the legal order of Honduras does not authorize such acts and that internal law defines them as crimes. The Court also recognizes that not all levels of the Government of Honduras were necessarily aware of those acts, nor is there any evidence that such acts were the result of official orders. Nevertheless, those circumstances are irrelevant for the purposes of establishing whether Honduras is responsible under international law for the violations of human rights perpetrated within the practice of disappearances. . . .

185. The Court, therefore, concludes that the facts found in this proceeding show that the State of Honduras is responsible for the involuntary disappearance of Angel

Manfredo Velásquez Rodríguez. Thus, Honduras has violated Articles 7, 5 and 4 of the Convention.

186. As a result of the disappearance, Manfredo Velásquez was the victim of an arbitrary detention, which deprived him of his physical liberty without legal cause and without a determination of the lawfulness of his detention by a judge or competent tribunal. Those acts directly violate the right to personal liberty recognized by Article 7 of the Convention and are a violation imputable to Honduras of the duties to respect and ensure that right under Article 1(1).

187. The disappearance of Manfredo Velásquez violates the [Article 5] right to personal integrity. . . . First, the mere subjection of an individual to prolonged isolation and deprivation of communication is in itself cruel and inhuman treatment which harms the psychological and moral integrity of the person, and violates the right of every detainee under Article 5(1) and 5(2) to treatment respectful of his dignity. Second, although it has not been directly shown that Manfredo Velásquez was physically tortured, his kidnapping and imprisonment by governmental authorities, who have been shown to subject detainees to indignities, cruelty and torture, constitute a failure of Honduras to fulfill the duty imposed by Article 1(1) to ensure the rights under Article 5(1) and 5(2) of the Convention. The guarantee of physical integrity and the right of detainees to treatment respectful of their human dignity require States Parties to take reasonable steps to prevent situations which are truly harmful to the rights protected.

188. The above reasoning is applicable to the right to life recognized by Article 4 of the Convention. The context in which the disappearance of Manfredo Velásquez occurred and the lack of knowledge seven years later about his fate create a reasonable presumption that he was killed. Even if there is a minimal margin of doubt in this respect, it must be presumed that his fate was decided by authorities who systematically executed detainees without trial and concealed their bodies in order to avoid punishment. This, together with the failure to investigate is a violation by Honduras of a legal duty under Article 1(1) of the Convention to ensure the rights recognized by Article 4(1).

Delgado-Paéz v. Colombia
(U.N. Human Rights Committee)
Case No. 195/1985 (1990), U.N. Doc. CCPR/C/39/D/195/1985, *available at* RossRights

1   The author of the communication is William Eduardo Delgado Paéz, a Colombian national who resided in Bogotá, Colombia, at the time of submission. In May 1986 he left the country and sought political asylum in France, where he was granted refugee status.

Background

2.1   In March 1983, the author was appointed by the Ministry of Education as a teacher of religion and ethics at a secondary school in Leticia, Colombia. He was elected vice-president of the teachers' union. As an advocate of "liberation theology", his social views differed from those of the then Apostolic Prefect of Leticia.

2.2   In October 1983, the Apostolic Prefect sent a letter to the Education Commission withdrawing the support that the Church had given to Mr. Delgado. On 10 December 1983, the Apostolic Prefect wrote to the Police Inspector accusing Mr. Delgado of having stolen money from a student.

2.3   On 25 August 1984, the Circuit Court dismissed all charges against the author, having established that the accusation of theft was unfounded.

2.4   On 5 February 1984, Mr. Delgado was informed that he would no longer teach religion. Instead, a course in manual labour and handicrafts, for which he had no training or experience, was assigned to him. In order not to lose employment altogether, he endeavoured to teach these subjects.

2.5   On 29 May 1984, the author requested from the Ministry of Education two weeks leave for the period from 26 June to 10 July 1984 to attend an advanced course at Bogotá to further his teaching qualifications. He and other teachers were admitted to the course on 5 July 1984, but Mr. Delgado was subsequently denied leave. He considered this to be unjustified discrimination and decided to attend the course, also taking into account that, as a result of a national strike, the teachers were, by decree of the Ministry of Education, on enforced vacation .

2.6   By administrative decisions of the Ministry of Education, dated 12 July, and 11 and 25 September 1984, he was suspended from his post for 60 days, and a six-months' salary freeze was imposed on him on grounds of having abandoned his post without permission from the Principal. On 27 November 1984, the author requested the annulment of these administrative decisions, arguing that he had not abandoned his post, but that the law allowed teachers to take such special courses and that he had been duly admitted to the course with the approval of the Ministry of Education. The action was dismissed. He then submitted an appeal, and on 3 December 1985, by decision of the Ministry of Education, the prior decisions of suspension and salary freeze were annulled.

2.7   Convinced that he was a victim of discrimination by the ecclesiastical and educational authorities of Leticia, the author took the following steps:

(a) On 17 May 1985, he submitted a complaint to the Office of the Regional Attorney on grounds of alleged irregularities committed by the Fondo Educative Regional (Regional Education Fund) in his case;

(b) On 18 May 1985, he submitted a complaint to the penal court of Leticia, accusing the Apostolic Prefect of slander and abuse;

(c) On 28 May, 4 June and 3 October 1985, he wrote to the Office of the Attorney General of the Republic, expressing concern about the denial of justice at the regional level, attributable to the alleged influence of the Apostolic Prefect;

(d) On 13 May 1986, he again wrote to the Attorney General describing the pressures he had been and was being subjected to in order to force him to resign. He indicated, *inter alia*, that on 23 November 1983 the Apostolic Prefect had written to the Secretary of Education asking the latter in specific and clear terms to bring pressure on me to resign from my post, and this in fact happened, for, on 2 December 1983, I was summoned to the office of the Secretary of Education and orally informed that the Monsignor was putting pressure on him and that I therefore had to resign from my post as a teacher, failing which criminal proceedings would be instituted against me. I promptly informed the president of the teachers' union and the teachers' representative on the Promotion Board of such an outrage and they immediately went to the office of the Secretary of Education, who repeated that it had nothing to do with him, but that he had been acting at the Monsignor's insistence. I of course refused to resign, but the threat was carried out and criminal proceedings were instituted against me.

2.8   While at his residence in Bogotá the author received anonymous phone calls threatening him with death if he returned to Leticia and did not withdraw his complaint against the Apostolic Prefect and the education authorities. He also received death threats at the teachers' residence at Leticia, which he reported to the military authorities at Leticia, the teachers'union, the Ministry of Education and the President of Colombia.

2.9   On 2 May 1986, a work colleague, Ms. Rubiela Valencia, was shot to death outside the teachers' residence in Leticia by unknown killers. On 7 May 1986, the author was himself attacked in the city of Bogotá and, fearing for his own life, left the country and obtained political asylum in France in June 1986.

The Complaint

3.1   The author claims to be a victim of violations by Colombia of articles 14, 18, 19, 25 and 26 in conjunction with article 2 of the International Covenant on Civil and Political Rights.[D]

3.2   He maintains that he was subjected to persecution—ideologically, politically and in his work—by the Colombian authorities, because of his "progressive ideas in theological and social matters", that his honour and reputation were attacked by the authorities who falsely accused him of theft, whereas the reason behind the charge was to intimidate him because of his religious and social opinions. Moreover, his professional qualifications were unjustly put into question, although he had studied and taken a degree at the University of Santo Tomá and had taught several years at a high school in Bogotá. . . .

3.6   He claims that he "found it absolutely essential to leave the country, as there are no guarantees for the protection of the most basic human rights, such as equality, justice and life, which the Colombian Government has a constitutional and moral obligation to protect". Allegedly, the threats on his life and on the lives of other teachers have not been duly investigated by the State party.

The State Party's Observations. . . .

4.2   [The State] . . . denies that Mr. Delgado's rights under the Covenant have been violated. In particular, it indicates that Mr. Delgado was cleared of all charges

---

[D] These articles protect the rights to equality before the courts (14), religious freedom (18), freedom of expression (19), access to public service (25), equal protection without discrimination (26), and a remedy for violations of these rights (2).

against him and contends that his complaints against various Colombian authorities were duly investigated: "William Eduardo Delgado Paéz has not been subjected to restrictions on his freedom of thought, conscience, religion, speech or expression, as is demonstrated by the steps he was able to take under the criminal law and in the administrative sphere throughout this investigation."

4.3   In the disciplinary action initiated by Mr. Delgado against various officials, the court of first instance of Leticia acquitted three persons and sanctioned two others with a suspension of 15 days without remuneration. Appeals are pending.

4.4   The criminal action against the Apostolic Prefect on grounds of slander and abuse was referred to the Apostolic Nuncius pursuant to the Concordat between the Republic of Colombia and the Vatican. The investigation was terminated upon the death of the Apostolic Prefect in 1990. . . .

4.7   The State party does not address the author's allegations concerning death threats against himself and other teachers, the alleged assault on his person on 7 May 1986, nor the general situation of persecution against named journalists and intellectuals, amounting to a violation of the right of security of the person.

The Issues and Proceedings Before the Committee. . . .

5.4   Although the author has not specifically invoked article 9 of the Covenant, the Committee notes that his submission of 14 September 1987, which was transmitted to the State party prior to the adoption of the Committee's decision on admissibility, raised important questions under this article. The Committee recalls that upon declaring the communication admissible, it requested the State party to address these issues. The State party has not done so.

5.5   The first sentence of article 9 does not stand as a separate paragraph.[E] Its location as a part of paragraph one could lead to the view that the right to security arises only in the context of arrest and detention. . . . Although in the Covenant the only reference to the right of security of person is to be found in article 9, there is no evidence that it was intended to narrow the concept of the right to security only to situations of formal deprivation of liberty. At the same time, States parties have undertaken to guarantee the rights enshrined in the Covenant. It cannot be the case that, as a matter of law, States can ignore known threats to the life of persons under their jurisdiction, just because . . . he or she is not arrested or otherwise detained. States parties are under an obligation to take reasonable and appropriate measures to protect them. An interpretation of article 9 which would allow a State party to ignore threats to the personal security of non-detained persons within its jurisdiction would render totally ineffective the guarantees of the Covenant.

5.6   There remains the question of the application of this finding to the facts of the case under consideration. There appears to have been an objective need for Mr.

[E] Article 9(1) of the ICCPR provides: "Everyone has the right to liberty and security of person. No one shall be subjected to arbitrary arrest or detention. No one shall be deprived of his liberty except on such grounds and in accordance with such procedure as are established by law."

Delgado to be provided by the State with protective measures to guarantee his security, given the threats made against him, including the attack on his person, and the murder of a close colleague. . . . [T]he Committee cannot but note that the author claims that there was no response to his request to have these threats investigated and to receive protection, and that the State party has not informed the Committee otherwise. . . . The Committee has . . . made clear that circumstances may cause it to assume facts in the author's favour if the State party fails to reply or to address them. The pertinent factors in this case are that Mr. Delgado had been engaged in a protracted confrontation with the authorities over his teaching and his employment. Criminal charges, later determined unfounded, had been brought against him and he had been suspended, with salary frozen. . . . Further, he was known to have instituted a variety of complaints against the ecclesiastical and scholastical authorities in Leticia. Coupled with these factors were threats to his life. If the State party neither denies the threats nor co-operates with the Committee to explain whether the relevant authorities were aware of them, and, if so, what was done about them, the Committee must necessarily treat as correct allegations that the threats were known and that nothing was done. Accordingly, while fully understanding the situation in Colombia, the Committee finds that the State party has not taken, or has been unable to take, appropriate measures to ensure Mr. Delgado's right to security of his person under article 9, paragraph 1. [The Committee did not discuss Mr. Delgado's claims under articles 14 and 2, found no violations of articles 18 and 19, but did find a violation of article 25 because he could not continue in public teaching.]

III. International and Regional Law Concerning Domestic Violence

As entered into force in 1981, CEDAW seeks to end discrimination against women; it does not, however, explicitly address the issue of violence against women—an issue as yet unnamed when CEDAW was drafted. In 1992, however, the CEDAW Committee adopted Recommendation No. 19 on Violence Against Women. This Recommendation declares that violence against women is a form of discrimination against women— thereby bringing domestic violence under the purview of CEDAW—and requires that States eliminate violence against women in every sphere of life. In 1993, the UN General Assembly adopted the Declaration on the Elimination of Violence against Women (DEVAW), which recognizes that violence against women serves to "impair or nullify" the ability of women to enjoy their "fundamental freedoms" and calls upon states to eradicate all forms of violence against women. In 1994, the UN Commission on Human Rights created the office of the Special Rapporteur on Violence Against Women. The initial report of Radhika Coomaraswamy, the first woman appointed to this position, is excerpted in Part IV below.

Change has also occurred at the regional level. The Organization of American States adopted the Inter-American Convention to Prevent, Punish and Eradicate Violence Against Women in 1994. This Convention makes significant advances over earlier efforts. It provides an individual cause of action against the state for failure to take required steps. It also names freedom from violence as a separate right, as does the

African Protocol on the Rights of Women which entered into force in November 2005. The Council of Europe has begun to explore the issue; its Committee on Crime Problems published, on June 5, 2007, a "Feasibility Study for a Convention Against Domestic Violence," *available at* RossRights.

A. Theoretical Issues

All the human rights documents discussed and presented below can be considered a form of special treatment, since they envision action only on behalf of women. But while women are disproportionately the victims of domestic violence, men also can be victims. Indeed, many women have been imprisoned for killing their husbands. Consider therefore whether civil or criminal remedies for domestic violence should be reserved for women only. Similarly, should the issue be addressed as a human rights issue or one of criminal enforcement? A prominent international law scholar addresses both issues.

Joan Fitzpatrick, *The Use of International Human Rights Norms to Combat Violence Against Women*
in HUMAN RIGHTS OF WOMEN 532, 534–40, 557–58 (Rebecca J. Cook ed., 1994)

[T]wo forms of gender-based violence seriously affect the quality of women's lives, rape (and the threat of rape) in the case of every woman, and domestic violence in the case of many. Yet no human rights treaty [as of 1994] explicitly requires governments to take specific action against either practice. . . .

The Committee on the Elimination of Discrimination Against Women (CEDAW) is attempting to remedy this flaw through creative interpretation of the Convention on the Elimination of All Forms of Discrimination Against Women. General recommendation No. 19, adopted at CEDAW's eleventh session in January 1992, defined gender-based violence as "a form of discrimination which seriously inhibits women's ability to enjoy rights and freedoms on a basis of equality with men." CEDAW noted that Article 1 of the Convention prohibits all gender-based discrimination that has the effect of impairing the enjoyment of fundamental rights and freedoms, and finds that gender-based violence (of all forms) has the effect of impairing enjoyment of the right to life, the prohibition on torture and cruel treatment, equal protection of humanitarian law, the right to liberty and security of the person, the equal protection of the law, the right to equality within the family, the right to physical and mental health, and the right to just and favorable conditions of work.

General Recommendation No. 19 also drew on Article 2 of the Convention, which requires states to take necessary action to eliminate discrimination against women by "any person." CEDAW read Article 2 as making states responsible for "private acts" if they fail "to act with due diligence to prevent violations of rights, or to investigate and punish acts of violence, and to provide compensation."

Having adopted the strategy of attacking the problem of violence within an equality paradigm (almost inescapable, given the framework of the Convention) and having surmounted the barrier of the public/private distinction, CEDAW then analyzed specific forms of violence in General Recommendation No. 19. With respect to domestic violence and rape, CEDAW asserted: (1) under Articles 2 and 3, laws on domestic violence and rape must give "adequate protection to all women" and "respect their integrity and dignity," and states must provide protective and support services to women and gender-sensitive training of judicial and law enforcement officers; . . . ; (3) under Articles 2.f, 5, and 10.c, states must seek to eradicate attitudes toward women as limited to stereotyped roles, attitudes that justify the use of gender-based violence to perpetuate structures of subordination; (4) under Article 12, states must establish support services for women whose health is damaged by domestic violence and rape; (5) under Article 14, states must provide services to rural women at risk of gender-based violence and monitor the employment conditions of domestic workers, many of whom migrate to cities from rural areas; and (6) under Article 16, states must impose criminal and civil penalties for domestic violence, remove the "defense of honor" in cases of assault or murder of female family members, create refuges and other services for victims of domestic violence, and provide rehabilitation to perpetrators and support services to victims of incest and intrafamily sexual abuse. . . .

CEDAW's attention to issues of violence against women occurs in the context of sustained, though inconclusive, examination of these issues by various bodies within the UN framework. This activity can be traced back at least to the World Conference of the International Women's Year in Mexico City in 1975, which touched on the questions of dignity, equality, and conflict within the family. These concerns were further addressed at the World Conference of the United Nations Decade for Women: Equality, Development and Peace in Copenhagen in 1980, which concluded that domestic violence had serious social consequences and perpetuated itself from one generation to the next, and that women must be protected from domestic violence and rape.

These initial, somewhat offhand, initiatives were followed by consideration of domestic violence and rape in two different types of UN fora: (1) within the Commission on the Status of Women and its parent body, the Economic and Social Council (ECOSOC); and (2) within the crime control bodies, in particular the quinquennial Congresses on the Prevention of Crime and the Treatment of Offenders and the Committee on Crime Prevention and Control. ECOSOC adopted resolution 1982/22, at the urging of the Commission, labeling domestic violence and rape as offenses against the dignity of the person and calling for steps to combat these evils. ECOSOC further addressed violence in the family in resolution 1984/14. Parallel with this discussion within human rights bodies, the Crime Committee in 1982 noted special difficulties in eradicating domestic violence, and a seminar was organized on the topic with non-governmental organizations (NGOs) and UN representatives involved in crime control issues. . . .

The simultaneous activity within the past two decades among these various UN bodies to address the issues of domestic violence and rape highlights a strategic concern: should international activity to combat domestic violence and rape primarily take the form of conceptualizing these practices in normative human rights terms, as CEDAW is seeking to do, and then to place pressure on governments to reduce their occurrence through the usual mechanisms of implementing human rights norms, or is the criminological perspective likely to be more effective? In the case of the latter, it is unnecessary to define domestic violence or rape, or government inactivity in the face of such practices, as violations of international human rights law. Rather, the UN bodies concerned with promoting good social policy or crime control can largely avoid the conceptual issues (though they cannot entirely finesse the cultural relativity questions), and focus on cooperation in research, education, and drafting of model penological standards, fostering interchange among governments to stimulate improvements in domestic institutions and policies. . . .

One inquiry in constructing a strategy should be whether domestic violence and rape would be more vigorously addressed as a matter of high priority by human rights or by criminological bodies. As Laura Reanda remarked with respect to prostitution, there is little prospect that the UN crime control bodies will devote the resources and energy to battling prostitution that they have directed to eradicating drug abuse. The same would certainly be true of domestic violence and rape, which have even fewer of the cross-boundary elements that help promote intergovernmental cooperation in matters of crime.

On the other hand, mainstream human rights bodies have shown a general lack of attention to domestic violence and rape. And CEDAW, for all its creativity in interpreting the Convention, has yet to overcome its paucity of resources and lack of effective implementation powers. . . .

If a human rights/normative approach to domestic violence is favored, use of an equality paradigm has a certain logic and force. In many respects, the problem of domestic violence results from a failure of the legal system to treat the battery, murder, and rape of women by husbands or lovers as crimes, in the same manner and to the same degree as if they had occurred between strangers. Selective tolerance for domestic violence frequently stems from cultural norms that encourage men to abuse their wives. Thus, victims of domestic violence are denied the equal protection of the criminal laws, contravening fundamental human rights principles of equality before the law. At a deeper level, an equality paradigm might also address the root problem of domestic violence, the structures of subordination that the violence reinforces. As Catharine MacKinnon notes, what women really need and are denied is "a chance at productive lives of reasonable physical security, self-expression, individuation, and minimal respect and dignity." These goods are, of course, what every human being deserves and what international human rights law supposedly aims to ensure.

The equality paradigm also appears to offer a solution to the problem of marital rape, which is often the subject of formal legal exemption from criminal liability. Under an equal treatment approach, all victims of forcible rape deserve to be treated alike, regardless of status. The same principle of equal treatment would bar invidious practices such as selective failure to punish rapists of prostitutes or members of vulnerable groups, such as disabled women.

Formal or customary legal rules that permit men to murder their wives on suspicion of infidelity or because they do not otherwise conform to the husband's demands, defenses not available to women who resort to violence against unfaithful husbands, would also logically be invalidated under an equality rationale mandating that spouses have equal rights in marriage. CEDAW's General Recommendation No. 19 explicitly calls for the abolition of the "defense of honor."

The acute problem of "bride burning" in India results from cultural practices that the state has prohibited but to which it shows selective indifference in practice. India has formally abolished the institution of dowry. However, the tradition not only continues but reportedly is being exacerbated by growing consumerism on the part of husbands and mothers-in-law who kill or maim brides whose families will not or cannot meet their escalating demands. The state undertakes few prosecutions, even though the law requires a special inquiry into suspicious deaths of women married fewer than seven years. The scope of the problem was highlighted by the recent report that bride burning claimed more victims in recent years than the armed conflict in the Punjab.

But a simple "equal treatment" approach to domestic violence leaves important issues unaddressed. As the UN studies on family violence note, victims of domestic violence operate under pressures not felt by other crime victims. Socialization to define oneself primarily through relationships with men and lack of economic opportunity leave many women economically, socially, and emotionally dependent on their batterers. An "equal treatment" approach (in the sense of equality of means) would provide victims of wife murder equality before the law, as it would serve the needs of women whose assault or rape had driven them to terminate their relationship to the attacker. But it does not so satisfactorily assist those victims of battery and marital rape who are not prepared to sever their ties to their assailants.

As the recommendations of CEDAW, the UN crime control bodies, the European Parliament and the draft Inter-American Convention all suggest, forms of "special treatment" may be necessary to ameliorate the problem of domestic violence. Institutions such as battered women's shelters and special police units to handle domestic violence complaints are constructive, if inadequate, steps to redress the economic vulnerability of battered women and the existing male-dominated police and prosecutorial apparatus which has historically been unresponsive to survivors of domestic violence. And even these forms of "special treatment" meet the needs only of those women who have decided to distance themselves from the batterers, sometimes temporarily.

Some women unable or afraid to sever their ties to the batterer might achieve a minimal level of safety and dignity only through "special treatment" of the batterer himself, in the form of rehabilitation programs that replace the imprisonment that would be meted out had he chosen a stranger as the target of his violence. CEDAW proposes such rehabilitation measures in General Recommendation No. 19, without any attempt to reconcile them with the equality principle that forms the textual basis for the recommendation. But such alternate dispositions are obviously at war with an equality paradigm, effectively decriminalizing the husband's conduct because of the identity and the dependency of his victim. . . .

The "needs" and "preferences" of battered women to remain with their batterers are . . . socially constructed. In fact, they raise the sensitive issue of "false consciousness," which also figures in the debate over genital mutilation and prostitution. Departing from the equal treatment paradigm to facilitate these "needs" appears humane and realistic, but carries the danger of reinforcing the same structures of subordination that promote the battering in the first place.

With respect to rape and other assault by non-family members, one could argue that all these acts are "political" in the broad sense because they manifest and reinforce patriarchal values. But sometimes the political element of this violence is especially strong. Beatings and acid attacks in order to force women to adopt Islamic dress are powerful examples of government-tolerated violence intended to deprive women of free opinion and expression, political, equal employment, and other rights. Recent "power rapes" of politically active women in Pakistan appear motivated by government officials' desire to suppress their expressive activity. Such acts violate not only equality norms but the basic civil and political rights guaranteed in instruments such as the ICCPR. . . .

The idea of a Special Rapporteur on Violence against Women has a great deal of merit. The advantages of such a "theme" mechanism, following the precedents of the Working Group on Enforced and Involuntary Disappearances and previous special rapporteurs, are multiple. Questions of state responsibility for the abuses need not be addressed in a judgmental way, as the role of the Special Rapporteur is to stop the abuses without necessarily casting blame. The Special Rapporteur can combine a humanitarian role of seeking redress for individual victims with an analytic exploration of the nature of the phenomenon and an examination of country situations through on-site visits. The appointment of a theme rapporteur or working group has come to signal an awareness of the need to deal vigorously with a particular human rights problem, and it would add welcome visibility to the previously neglected question of violence against women.

B. The Legal Documents

As you read the following key provisions of the four international and regional law documents speaking directly to violence against women, consider the following issues. How does each deal with the clash between women's rights and religious and cultural rights? Do you agree with that resolution? Should international NGOs such as Human Rights Watch and Amnesty that originated in the West criticize other cultures or religions that tolerate or support violence against women? Is that cultural imperialism?

To what extent do the documents use the *Velásquez Rodríguez* rationale for holding states responsible? Each document names specific rights that domestic violence violates. Consider Article 3 of the Inter-American VAW Convention. How is it different?

What is the legal status of each of the following documents? What countries does each affect and do they bind those countries? Finally, under which documents can complaints be filed? To what bodies?

See RossRights for the full text of the CEDAW Committee's General Recommendation 19, the UN Declaration on the Elimination of Violence Against Women, the Inter-American Convention on Violence Against Women, and the African Protocol on the Rights of Women.

Committee on the Elimination of Discrimination Against Women, *General Recommendation No. 19: Violence Against Women*
(11th Sess., 1992), U.N. Doc. A/47/38 at 1 (1993)

General Comments

6. The Convention in article 1 defines discrimination against women. The definition of discrimination includes gender-based violence, that is, violence that is directed against a woman because she is a woman or that affects women disproportionately. It includes acts that inflict physical, mental or sexual harm or suffering, threats of such acts, coercion and other deprivations of liberty. Gender-based violence may breach specific provisions of the Convention, regardless of whether those provisions expressly mention violence.

7. Gender-based violence, which impairs or nullifies the enjoyment by women of human rights and fundamental freedoms under general international law or under human rights conventions, is discrimination within the meaning of article 1 of the Convention.

These rights and freedoms include:
   (a) The right to life;
   (b) The right not to be subject to torture or to cruel, inhuman or degrading treatment or punishment;
   (c) The right to equal protection according to humanitarian norms in time of international or internal armed conflict;
   (d) The right to liberty and security of person;
   (e) The right to equal protection under the law;
   (f) The right to equality in the family;
   (g) The right to the highest standard attainable of physical and mental health;
   (h) The right to just and favourable conditions of work.

8. The Convention applies to violence perpetrated by public authorities. Such acts of violence may breach that State's obligations under general international human rights law and under other conventions, in addition to breaching this Convention.

9. It is emphasized, however, that discrimination under the Convention is not restricted to action by or on behalf of Governments (see articles 2 (e), 2 (f) and 5). For example, under article 2 (e) the Convention calls on States parties to take all appropriate measures to eliminate discrimination against women by any person, organization or enterprise. Under general international law and specific human rights covenants, States may also be responsible for private acts if they fail to act with due diligence to prevent violations of rights or to investigate and punish acts of violence, and for providing compensation. . . .

Comments on Specific Articles of the Convention. . . .

Articles 2(f), 5 and 10(c). . . .

11. Traditional attitudes by which women are regarded as subordinate to men or as having stereotyped roles perpetuate widespread practices involving violence or coercion, such as family violence and abuse, forced marriage, dowry deaths, acid attacks and female circumcision. Such prejudices and practices may justify gender-based violence as a form of protection or control of women. The effect of such violence on the physical and mental integrity of women is to deprive them of the equal enjoyment, exercise and knowledge of human rights and fundamental freedoms. While this comment addresses mainly actual or threatened violence the underlying consequences of these forms of gender-based violence help to maintain women in subordinate roles and contribute to their low level of political participation and to their lower level of education, skills, and work opportunities. . . .

Article 16 (and article 5)

23. Family violence is one of the most insidious forms of violence against women. It is prevalent in all societies. Within family relationships women of all ages are subjected to violence of all kinds, including battering, rape, other forms of sexual assault, mental and other forms of violence, which are perpetuated by traditional attitudes. Lack of economic independence forces many women to stay in violent relationships. The abrogation of their family responsibilities by men can be a form of violence, and coercion. These forms of violence put women's health at risk and impair their ability to participate in family life and public life on a basis of equality.

Specific Recommendations

24. In light of these comments, the Committee on the Elimination of Discrimination against Women recommends:. . . .
(r) Measures that are necessary to overcome family violence should include:
  (i) Criminal penalties where necessary and civil remedies in case of domestic violence;
  (ii) Legislation to remove the defence of honour in regard to the assault or murder of a female family member;
  (iii) Services to ensure the safety and security of victims of family violence, including refuges, counselling and rehabilitation programmes;
  (iv) Rehabilitation programmes for perpetrators of domestic violence;
  (v) Support services for families where incest or sexual abuse has occurred; . . .
(t) That States parties should take all legal and other measures that are necessary to provide effective protection of women against gender-based violence, including, inter alia:
  (i) Effective legal measures, including penal sanctions, civil remedies and compensatory provisions to protect women against all kinds of violence, includ-

     ing, inter alia, violence and abuse in the family, sexual assault and sexual harassment in the workplace;

(ii) Preventive measures, including public information and education programmes to change attitudes concerning the roles and status of men and women;

(iii) Protective measures, including refuges, counseling, rehabilitation and support services for women who are the victims of violence or who are at risk of violence.

NOTE

The Committee's First Optional Protocol Decision on Domestic Violence. In the case of a Hungarian woman who had been severely battered for many years and could obtain no effective relief against the violence under Hungarian law, the Committee in 2005 found violations of Articles 2(a), (b), and (e), 5(a), and 16, and ordered both interim and final relief. For a compelling description of the violence and the endless, pointless, Hungarian legal proceedings, *see* the Committee's Views in *Ms. A. T. v. Hungary*, U.N. Doc. CEDAW/C/32/D/2/2003 (2005), *available at* RossRights.

U.N. General Assembly, Declaration on the Elimination of Violence Against Women
G.A. Res. 48/104, U.N. Doc. A/48/104 (1993)

Article 1

For the purposes of this Declaration, the term "violence against women" means any act of gender-based violence that results in, or is likely to result in, physical, sexual or psychological harm or suffering to women, including threats of such acts, coercion or arbitrary deprivation of liberty, whether occurring in public or in private life.

Article 2

Violence against women shall be understood to encompass, but not be limited to, the following:

(a) Physical, sexual and psychological violence occurring in the family, including battering, sexual abuse of female children in the household, dowry-related violence, marital rape, female genital mutilation and other traditional practices harmful to women, non-spousal violence and violence related to exploitation;

(b) Physical, sexual and psychological violence occurring within the general community, including rape, sexual abuse, sexual harassment and intimidation at work, in educational institutions and elsewhere, trafficking in women and forced prostitution;

(c) Physical, sexual and psychological violence perpetrated or condoned by the State, wherever it occurs.

Article 3

Women are entitled to the equal enjoyment and protection of all human rights and fundamental freedoms in the political, economic, social, cultural, civil or any other field. These rights include, inter alia:
   (a)   The right to life;
   (b)   The right to equality;
   (c)   The right to liberty and security of person;
   (d)   The right to equal protection under the law;
   (e)   The right to be free from all forms of discrimination;
   (f)   The right to the highest standard attainable of physical and mental health;
   (g)   The right to just and favourable conditions of work;
   (h)   The right not to be subjected to torture, or other cruel, inhuman or degrading treatment or punishment.

Article 4

States should condemn violence against women and should not invoke any custom, tradition or religious consideration to avoid their obligations with respect to its elimination. States should pursue by all appropriate means and without delay a policy of eliminating violence against women and, to this end, should:. . .
   (b)   Refrain from engaging in violence against women;
   (c)   Exercise due diligence to prevent, investigate and, in accordance with national legislation, punish acts of violence against women, whether those acts are perpetrated by the State or by private persons;
   (d)   Develop penal, civil, labour and administrative sanctions in domestic legislation to punish and redress the wrongs caused to women who are subjected to violence; women who are subjected to violence should be provided with access to the mechanisms of justice and, as provided for by national legislation, to just and effective remedies for the harm that they have suffered; States should also inform women of their rights in seeking redress through such mechanisms.

Inter-American Convention on the Prevention, Punishment, and Eradication of Violence Against Women
33 I.L.M. 1534 (1994), *entered into force* Mar. 5, 1995

Article 1

For the purposes of this Convention, violence against women shall be understood as any act or conduct, based on gender, which causes death or physical, sexual or psychological harm or suffering to women, whether in the public or the private sphere.

Article 2

Violence against women shall be understood to include physical, sexual and psychological violence:

a. that occurs within the family or domestic unit or within any other interpersonal relationship, whether or not the perpetrator shares or has shared the same residence with the woman, including, among others, rape, battery and sexual abuse;

b. That occurs in the community and is perpetrated by any person, including, among others, rape, sexual abuse, torture, trafficking in persons, forced prostitution, kidnapping and sexual harassment in the workplace, as well as in educational institutions, health facilities or any other place; and

c. that is perpetrated or condoned by the state or its agents regardless of where it occurs. . . .

Article 3

Every woman has the right to be free from violence in both the public and private spheres.

Article 4

Every woman has the right to the recognition, enjoyment, exercise and protection of all human rights and freedoms embodied in regional and international human rights instruments. These rights include, among others:

a. The right to have her life respected;

b. The right to have her physical, mental and moral integrity respected;

c. The right to personal liberty and security;

d. The right not to be subjected to torture;

e. The rights to have the inherent dignity of her person respected and her family protected;

f. The right to equal protection before the law and of the law;

g. The right to simple and prompt recourse to a competent court for protection against acts that violate her rights;

h. The right to associate freely;

i. The right of freedom to profess her religion and beliefs within the law; and

j. The right to have equal access to the public service of her country and to take part in the conduct of public affairs, including decision-making.

Article 5

Every woman is entitled to the free and full exercise of her civil, political, economic, social and cultural rights, and may rely on the full protection of those rights as embodied in regional and international instruments on human rights. The States Parties recognize that violence against women prevents and nullifies the exercise of these rights.

Article 6

The right of every woman to be free from violence includes, among others:
a. The right of women to be free from all forms of discrimination; and
b. The right of women to be valued and educated free of stereotyped patterns of behavior and social and cultural practices based on concepts of inferiority or subordination. . . .

Article 7

The States Parties condemn all forms of violence against women and agree to pursue, by all appropriate means and without delay, policies to prevent, punish and eradicate such violence and undertake to:
a. refrain from engaging in any act or practice of violence against women and to ensure that their authorities, officials, personnel, agents, and institutions act in conformity with this obligation;
b. apply due diligence to prevent, investigate and impose penalties for violence against women;
c. include in their domestic legislation penal, civil, administrative and any other type of provisions that may be needed to prevent, punish and eradicate violence against women and to adopt appropriate administrative measures where necessary;
d. adopt legal measures to require the perpetrator to refrain from harassing, intimidating or threatening the woman or using any method that harms or endangers her life or integrity, or damages her property;
e. take all appropriate measures, including legislative measures, to amend or repeal existing laws and regulations or to modify legal or customary practices which sustain the persistence and tolerance of violence against women;
f. establish fair and effective legal procedures for women who have been subjected to violence which include, among others, protective measures, a timely hearing and effective access to such procedures;
g. establish the necessary legal and administrative mechanisms to ensure that women subjected to violence have effective access to restitution, reparations or other just and effective remedies; and
h. adopt such legislative or other measures as may be necessary to give effect to this Convention. . . .

Article 10

In order to protect the rights of every woman to be free from violence, the States Parties shall include in their national reports to the Inter-American Commission of Women information on measures adopted to prevent and prohibit violence against women, and to assist women affected by violence, as well as on any difficulties they observe in applying those measures, and the factors that contribute to violence against women.

Article 11

The States Parties to this Convention and the Inter-American Commission of Women may request of the Inter-American Court of Human Rights advisory opinions on the interpretation of this Convention.

Article 12

Any person or group of persons, or any nongovernmental entity legally recognized in one or more member states of the Organization, may lodge petitions with the Inter-American Commission on Human Rights containing denunciations or complaints of violations of Article 7 of this Convention by a State Party, and the Commission shall consider such claims in accordance with the norms and procedures established by the American Convention on Human Rights and the Statutes and Regulations of the Inter-American Commission on Human Rights for lodging and considering petitions.

Protocol to the African Charter on Human and Peoples' Rights on the Rights of Women in Africa

Adopted by the 2nd Ordinary Session of the Assembly of the Union, Maputo, CAB/ LEG/66.6 (Sept. 3, 2003), *entered into force* Nov. 25, 2005

Article 1
Definitions. . . .

j. "Violence against women" means all acts perpetrated against women which cause or could cause them physical, sexual, psychological, and economic harm, including the threat to take such acts; or to undertake the imposition of arbitrary restrictions on or deprivations of fundamental freedoms in private or public life in peace time and during situations of armed conflicts or of war. . . .

Article 2
Elimination of Discrimination Against Women. . . .

2. States Parties shall commit themselves to modify the social and cultural patterns of conduct of women and men through public education, information, education and communication strategies, with a view to achieving the elimination of harmful and traditional practices. . . .

Article 3
Right to Dignity. . . .

4. States Parties shall adopt and implement appropriate measures to ensure the protection of every woman's right to respect for her dignity and protection of women from all forms of violence, particularly sexual and verbal violence.

Article 4
The Rights to Life, Integrity and Security of the Person

1. Every woman shall be entitled to respect for her life and the integrity and security of her person. . . .
2. States Parties shall take appropriate and effective measures to:
a. enact and enforce laws to prohibit all forms of violence against women. . . ;
b. adopt such other legislative, administrative, social and economic measures as may be necessary to ensure the prevention, punishment and eradication of all forms of violence against women; . . .
c. identify the causes and consequences of violence against women and take appropriate measures to prevent and eliminate such violence; . . .
e. punish the perpetrators of violence against women and implement programmes for the rehabilitation of women victims;
f. establish mechanisms and accessible services for effective information, rehabilitation and reparations for victims of violence against women; . . .
i. provide adequate budgetary and other resources for the implementation and monitoring of actions aimed at preventing and eradicating violence against women.

IV. Examples of Different State Mechanisms in Action

A. A Global Report on State Problems and Solutions

Radhika Coomaraswamy, *Preliminary Report Submitted by the Special Rapporteur on Violence Against Women, Its Causes and Consequences*
U.N. Doc. E/CN.4/1995/42 (1994)

51. If the roots of female subordination lie in historical power relations within society, then the institutions of State and civil society must accept responsibility for female subordination, including violence against women. The State bears a primary responsibility not only to refrain from encouraging acts of violence against women but actively to intervene in preventing such acts from taking place. . . .

52. In fact, in modern times, the State has become an arena of conflict: on the one hand, it may act according to legislation and practices which are against women's interests; but on the other hand, the State may emerge as the major instrument in transforming certain legislative, administrative and judicial practices which empower women to vindicate their rights. The negligence of the State may be the cause of

increased violence against women, while the active intervention of the State may actually be the catalyst for reforming power relations within society. . . .

72. Perhaps the greatest cause of violence against women is government inaction with regard to crimes of violence against women. There appears to be a permissive attitude, a tolerance of perpetrators of violence against women, especially when this violence is expressed in the home. The seriousness of the crime is rarely acknowledged. There exists also a non-recognition of such crimes in the laws of many countries, especially in relation to domestic violence, marital rape, sexual harassment and violence associated with traditional practices. As a result, in most societies crimes of violence against women are invisible. In addition, even where crimes of violence against women are recognized in the law, they are rarely prosecuted with vigour. In the context of norms recently established by the international community, a State that does not act against crimes of violence against women is as guilty as the perpetrators. States are under a positive duty to prevent, investigate and punish crimes associated with violence against women. . . .

Domestic Violence

(a) Introduction

117. The family has been traditionally considered as a retreat, a place where individuals are able to find security and shelter. The family has been romanticized as the "private haven" where peace and harmony prevail. Recent research, however, points to the fact that the family may be a "cradle of violence" and that females within the home are often subjected to violence in the family.

118. There are many types of domestic violence. Young girls and children are often victims of sexual assault within the family. Elderly family members and the infirm may also be subject to ill-treatment. Female domestic servants are another category which is often at the receiving end of violence. In extended families, mothers-in-law are often violent towards their daughters-in-law. Though there are many incidents of assault directed against the husband, studies show that they are not so frequent and rarely result in serious injury. Despite all those different types of domestic violence, the most prevalent is the violence of the husband against the wife.

(b) Causes

119. The causes of violence against women in the home have been analysed in detail by a United Nations report on violence against women in the family. Among the causes discussed are:
  (i) Alcohol and drug abuse by the perpetrator: in one study of 60 battered women, drinking accompanied 93 per cent of the incidents. In other studies alcoholism was linked to violence in 40 per cent of the cases;
  (ii) A cycle of violence: the childhood of the abusive man may have been disrupted by violence in the family. Studies conclude that violence by parents begets vio-

lence in the next generation. Violence in this context is seen as learned behaviour;

(iii) "Provocation": it has been argued that in some cases the victim provokes the abuser. But research indicates that while such incidents may take place they are not the norm. The only real pattern with regard to "provocative" behaviour is the seeming failure on the part of the woman to comply with the husband's authority;

(iv) Economic and social factors: early studies on domestic violence point to, *inter alia*, economic and social factors such as unemployment, low wages and inadequate housing, as being causes of domestic violence. Research in developing countries seems to augment these findings. Poverty seems to aggravate violence, because of stress and frustration factors. However, violence against women also exists in wealthier circles;

(v) Culture: certain cultural factors may precipitate violence against women;

(vi) Structural inequality: the general structures of society and the family which accept male dominance and female submissiveness as the norm may help legitimate violence against women.

120. Violence against women within the family is a significant pattern in all countries of the globe. Of the 487 murders committed by men in England and Wales during the period from 1885 to 1905, 124 or more than a quarter, were murders of women by their husbands, while a further 115 were of mistresses or girlfriends by their men. Twentieth[-]century figures for the United Kingdom reveal that this pattern has not changed. Similar statistics have also been found when using samples from the United States of America. Official statistics on male violence against women, other than criminal homicide, similarly reveal that the victim is most likely to be the wife of the offender. The First Report of the British Crime Survey found that 10 per cent of all assault victims were women who had been assaulted by their present or previous husbands or lovers.

121. While statistics on domestic violence are more scarce in developing countries, it would appear that a similar situation exists there. For example, a retrospective study of 170 cases of murder of women in Bangladesh between 1983 and 1985 revealed that 50 per cent occurred within the family. In Papua New Guinea, of villagers interviewed, 55 per cent of females and 65 per cent of males felt that a man could use force to control his wife. In Thailand, statistics indicate that more than 50 per cent of married women studied in Bangkok's biggest slum are regularly beaten by their husbands. In Santiago, Chile, it has been found that 80 per cent of women acknowledged being victims of violence in their own homes. In Sri Lanka, 60 per cent of women interviewed in a sample survey responded that they had been subjected to domestic violence during their period of cohabitation. The recent case in the United States of the alleged murder by the athlete O.J. Simpson of his [ex-]wife and her friend has served to highlight the issue of domestic violence in the international media.

122. The traditional legal systems sanctioned violence in the family by recognizing the husband's "right to chastisement". W. Blackstone, *Commentaries on the Laws of England*. This right was recognized by courts (*Bradley v State*, 2 Miss. 156 1824) in

many jurisdictions. In addition many legal systems allowed men to use force to extract "conjugal duties" and the crime of marital rape was unrecognized. The legal systems were therefore relatively unconcerned with abused women unless there was serious injury or a public nuisance. In some countries the defence of "honour" allowed for the easy acquittal of husbands who killed their wives.

(c) Criminalization

123. In many jurisdictions this approach has changed. Today many States recognize the importance of protecting the victim of wife abuse and of punishing the perpetrator of the crime. One of the major questions facing law reformers is whether to "criminalize" wife battery. There is a sense that domestic violence is a crime between those who are linked by the bonds of intimacy. The question of intimacy, i.e. whether wife-battery should be treated as an ordinary crime or whether there should be an emphasis on counselling and mediation, poses a major dilemma for policy makers.

124. The question of whether the criminal justice system or a system of mediation and conciliation is most appropriate in dealing with domestic violence is one which arises constantly. Advocates of the criminal justice approach point to the symbolic power of the law and argue that arrest, prosecution and conviction, with punishment, is a process that carries the clear condemnation of society for the conduct of the abuser and acknowledges his personal responsibility for the activity. In addition, some research studies reveal that intervention by the criminal justice system is the most effective mechanism for stopping acts of violence both in the short term and in the long term. The Minneapolis Domestic Violence Experiment was designed to assess which of the three police responses—conducting informal mediations between the parties involved, ordering the suspect to leave the residence for eight hours or arresting the suspect—was the most effective in preventing subsequent assault. During a six-month period, research revealed that 19 per cent of those involved in mediation and 24 per cent of those ordered to leave, repeated the assault, but only 10 per cent of those who were arrested indulged in further violence towards their spouses.

125. Despite these advantages of the criminal justice model, it is critical that those involved in policy making in this area should take account of the cultural, economic and political realities of their countries. Whilst it is important to attach a criminal label to this type of activity it is impossible to ignore that it takes place within the family, between persons who are emotionally and financially involved with each other. Any policy which fails to acknowledge the singular nature of these crimes and which is unaccompanied by attempts to provide support for the victim and help for the abuser will be doomed to failure. Thus, for example, policy makers considering the domestic violence programme of London, Ontario, which is often cited as a model for domestic violence treatment where a charging policy exists, must take account of the fact that the police force, which receives intensive training in how to deal with wife battering, funds a family consultant service that provides a 24-hour crisis intervention service, whilst a community service exists which includes a battered women's advocacy clinic

to provide emotional and legal counseling for women, as well as a treatment group for men who batter.

(d) Police action

126. A criminal justice approach is fundamentally dependent on the role of the police. Since the police will be the body called upon for an initial response in a complex situation, it is important that there be clear standards with regard to police action in the context of domestic violence.

127. In most jurisdictions the power of the police to enter the private premises of the individual is limited, and this acts as an important guarantee which protects the lives of ordinary women and men from arbitrary state interference. In the context of domestic violence, however, too great an adherence to this guarantee can protect the violent man at the expense of the woman. In order to guard against this eventuality, a number of Australian states have introduced legislation to clarify and extend police powers of entry to investigate offences of domestic violence. Some legislations allow the police to enter if requested to do so by a person who apparently resides on the premises or where the officer has reason to believe that a person on those premises is under threat of attack or has recently been under threat of attack or an attack on such a person is imminent. This type of provision allows the police quicker and easier access to premises and thus an opportunity either to prevent or put a stop to the violence therein.

128. Although the power to arrest for domestic crime is usually the same as for any other crime, officers are often uncertain as to their legal powers and this is so even in cases of very serious violence. Many commentators argue that the police should be given special powers of arrest in situations of domestic violence and that they should be mandated to implement these powers. They believe that arrest not only provides the woman with immediate safety, but gives her a feeling of power, leaving the man with an immediate message that his behaviour is unacceptable, a message which is said to have long-term effects on his future behaviour. Australia, Canada and England have instituted policies for the management of domestic violence which generally advocate a presumption of arrest unless there are good, clear reasons for not arresting. Such policies make it clear to the officer on the ground what type of behaviour is expected of her/him.

129. In many cases of domestic violence, immediate release of the offender on bail may be dangerous for the victim and, certainly, release without prior warning to the victim may have serious consequences for her. A number of Australian jurisdictions attempt to strike a balance between the interests of the offender and the victim by specifying conditions designed to protect the victim to be attached to the release of the offender. Thus, the offender can be released on condition that he does not drink or approach his spouse, while bail may not be granted where the offender has previously broken protective bail conditions.

130. It is essential that police officers are made aware that domestic violence is a serious issue which is neither a normal part of family life nor a private problem that

will not profit from police intervention. The Musasa project in Zimbabwe introduced intensive education directed at police officers on the ground. As the programme progressed, the feedback indicated that women were receiving more sympathetic and prompt assistance at the police stations than was the case previously.

131. Some countries have introduced police units that have been specially and intensively trained for the purpose of dealing with spousal assault. Specific police stations for dealing with women's issues, including domestic violence, have been set up in Brazil. From the outset, the stations had two full-time police officers, eight investigators, three clerks and two prison warders, all of them women. These police stations have proved to be very successful and 41 such stations now exist in Sao Paulo. Special police desks, units and stations are increasingly becoming a means of refining police methods when it comes to the question of domestic violence.

(e) Legislation

132. Legislation with regard to domestic violence is a modern phenomenon. In the past, domestic violence was dealt with under the laws for general criminal assault. This has proved to be unsatisfactory. There is an increasing belief that special laws should be drafted, having special remedies and procedures which are most effective with regard to crime between "intimates". Though contained within the framework of criminal laws, these procedures would try to meet the special needs posed by domestic violence.

133. The first problem which arises with regard to legislation is to allow for prosecution of husbands who beat their wives even if the wives, under pressure, want to withdraw their claims. In response to this, some countries have instructed police and prosecutors to proceed with the cases even in situations where the woman indicated that she would rather not proceed. This mandatory prosecution has been one strategy employed. In addition since the wife will be the main witness, some jurisdictions have introduced legislation making the wife a "compellable witness" except in certain situations. Other jurisdictions move away from compulsory prosecution to advocacy support. In the United States of America many cities have been able dramatically to increase victim participation by providing advocates for battered women. In San Francisco, it was found that 70 per cent of women who initially wanted charges dropped agreed to cooperate once advocates addressed their concerns.

134. In addition to the criminal punishment attached to assault, even in a domestic violence context, most jurisdictions recognize quasi-criminal remedies. The most important of these are the "protection" or "bound over" orders. In most jurisdictions there is a procedure whereby someone can complain to a magistrate or a justice that violence has taken place and the violent party is then "bound over" to keep the peace or be of good behaviour. The standard of proof is lower than with strictly criminal proceedings and this may provide some women with appropriate relief. Law reformers in Australia, for example, recognized the potential of the "bind over" process in cases of domestic violence. In general terms, the legislation provides for a court order, obtained on the balance of probabilities, protecting the victim against further attacks

or harassment. Breach of the order is a criminal offence and the police may arrest, without a warrant, a person who has contravened a protection order. Orders that can be made include forbidding the offender to approach the woman and limiting his access to certain premises, even the matrimonial home that he legally owns.

135. In addition to quasi-criminal remedies, civil law remedies are also available to women victims of violence. The most useful civil law remedy in relation to cases of domestic violence is probably the remedy known as an injunction or an interdict, which is used to support a primary cause of action. Where domestic violence is concerned, an injunction can be granted as incidental or ancillary proceedings for divorce, nullity or judicial separation or other civil proceedings, such as assault or battery. Such incidental relief could, for example, take the form of an order directing that the husband refrain from making contact with his wife or that he vacate the shared matrimonial home. Some jurisdictions have enacted legislation removing the requirement of applying for [principal] relief and allow the woman to apply for injunctive relief independently of any other legal action. This is very useful as a battered woman is then able to apply for an order directing her husband not to molest or harass her without having to apply for primary or [principal] relief, such as divorce, at the same time. Another civil remedy which is available in the United States of America in certain states is an action in tort.

Part B below describes a typical civil remedy now provided in many countries around the world through the lens of a typical state statute in the United States. Part C focuses on typical criminal remedies seen through the lens of new Indian laws. The U.S. example provides an equal treatment approach, that of India a special treatment approach. Do you object to either approach? If so, why? What are the advantages of each and the disadvantages?

B. The Gender-Neutral Approach—Equal Treatment

Legal Mechanisms to Stop Women Abuse

in Barbara Allen Babcock et al., Sex Discrimination and the Law: History, Practice, and Theory 1334–37 (2d ed., 1996)

[U.S.] State Civil Protection Order Statutes

Legal tradition began by authorizing rather than prohibiting woman abuse. The process of change has been slow:

. . . [i]n the early 1900s, some American courts began to permit wives to sue their husbands for civil assault. But in many states, including California, Massachusetts, and New York, "spousal immunity" prohibited such suits until the late sixties or early seventies, when . . . [advocates for battered women pressed state legislatures to pass] laws giving women the right to obtain orders of protection.

Similarly, although by the 1960s and 1970s, most of the abusive acts that battered women's advocates wanted to deter and punish were already crimes, enforcement was virtually nonexistent. Rather than focus solely on reforming the unsympathetic criminal justice system, advocates for battered women chose to establish shelters and to craft new civil remedies that would be to the greatest extent possible under the control of the battered woman herself. Moreover, because these new remedies focus primarily on deterrence and protection rather than on punishment, the burden of proof is lower, and it was hoped that legal action would be quicker, simpler, and more effective.

As a result of the legislative successes of the battered women's movement, courts in all states can issue civil protection orders (CPOs) ordering the batterer to stop assaulting or threatening the victim, and to stay away from her. Under most of these statutes the injunctions can also settle child custody, visitation, and support issues between the parties, order the batterer out of his home, and require him to participate in a counseling program. If the batterer violates the order, in most jurisdictions, the victim can move to hold him in contempt of court and be sent to jail or fined.

The D.C. Intrafamily Offenses Act
D.C. Code Ann. §§16-1001 et seq. (1989 and 1995 Cum. Supp.)

The District of Columbia's statute, passed in 1970 and strengthened by amendments in 1982, 1991, 1994, and 1995, is representative of modem civil protection legislation. In the first Supreme Court case to consider such legislation, amici advocates for battered women highlighted four aspects of the D.C. law:

First, the scheme is civil and remedial . . . "[thus giving] the court 'a wider range of dispositional powers than criminal courts to effect rehabilitation rather than retribution. . . .'"

Second, the vast majority of individuals who proceed under the Act appear *pro se*, which was expressly intended when the legislature amended the statute in 1982 to authorize private rights of action. To facilitate *pro se* access to the system, simple forms exist for both Civil Protection Order Petitions and Motions for Contempt, and no filing fee is charged for either. . . .

Third, the Act provides for private enforcement of the civil injunctive orders by motion for contempt. . . . Witnesses before the [D.C. City] Council [had] testified that, "the same problems of administrative delay and dependence on prosecutorial discretion that limit a complainant's ability to petition for a CPO also limit the ability to have that CPO enforced."

Fourth, the legislature appreciated, and expressly stated, that contempt motions filed in civil actions in the Family Division must be in addition to criminal prosecution in the Criminal Division, by the U.S. Attorney for the criminal offense: "The institution of criminal charges by the United States Attorney shall be in addition to, and shall not affect the rights of the complainant to seek any other relief under this chapter."

. . . . Forty-one states provide for enforcement of [CPOs] through motions for contempt, an indispensable remedy if the underlying order is to have meaning.

The Court's subsequent decision [in *United States v. Dixon*, 509 U.S. 688 (1993)] largely preserved these complementary enforcement roles for victim and prosecutor.[72]

---

[72] Government prosecution (e.g., for crime of "assault with intent to kill") for the behavior giving rise to the victim's contempt motion (e.g., for violating CPO "assault" ban) is not barred by the Fifth Amendment's double jeopardy clause if each offense has a legal element not con-

The Act gives relief to victims of an "intrafamily offense," which is defined as:

... an act punishable as a criminal offense committed by an offender upon a person:
(A) to whom the offender is related by blood, legal custody, marriage, having a child in common, or with whom the offender shares or has shared a mutual residence; or
(B) with whom the offender maintains or maintained a romantic relationship not necessarily including a sexual relationship. ...

Either the victim or the D.C. Corporation Counsel can file a petition for civil protection in the Family Division of the D.C. Superior Court. The court can grant an ex parte temporary protection order valid for 14 days, on a finding that "the safety or welfare of a family member is immediately endangered by the respondent." After a trial, or on the batterer's consent, the court can grant a civil protection order valid for a period of up to one year, if the court "finds that there is good cause to believe the respondent has committed or is threatening an intrafamily offense. . . ." The relief provisions may include:

(1) directing the respondent to refrain from the conduct committed or threatened and to keep the peace toward the family member;
(2) requiring the respondent, alone or in conjunction with any other member of the family before the court, to participate in psychiatric or medical treatment or appropriate counseling programs;
(3) directing, where appropriate, that the respondent avoid the presence of the family member endangered;
(4) directing a respondent to refrain from entering or to vacate the dwelling unit of the complainant when the dwelling is (A) marital property of the parties; or (B) jointly owned, leased, or rented and occupied by both parties: Provided, that joint occupancy shall not be required if a party is forced by the respondent to relinquish occupancy; or (C) owned, leased, or rented by the complainant individually; or (D) jointly owned, leased, or rented by the complainant and a person other than the respondent;
(5) directing the respondent to relinquish possession or use of certain personal property owned jointly by the parties or by the complainant individually;
(6) awarding temporary custody of a minor child of the parties;
(7) providing for visitation rights with appropriate restrictions to protect the safety of the complainant;
(8) awarding costs and attorney fees;
(9) ordering the Metropolitan Police Department to take such action as the Family Division deem necessary to enforce its orders;
(10) directing the respondent to perform or refrain from other actions as may be appropriate to the effective resolution of the matter; or

-----

tained in the other (here, first requires proof of specific intent to kill, second does not; second requires proof of knowledge of the CPO, first does not).

(11) combining two or more of the directions or requirements prescribed by the preceding paragraphs.

Finally, the statute provides for both the contempt remedy with a maximum penalty of $300, six months' imprisonment, or both, per contempt, and, as of March 1995, a CPO violation misdemeanor with a maximum penalty of $1000 or 180 days.

C. The Women-Only Approach—Special Treatment

Susan Deller Ross, *Legal Framework Surrounding Domestic Violence in India*
in DOMESTIC VIOLENCE IN INDIA: RECOMMENDATIONS OF THE WOMEN'S RIGHTS TEAM, REPORT TO
   USAID/INDIA (1996) (on file with author)

Indian Laws and Strategies on Domestic Violence

As is the case in many other countries, Indian women's advocates, government entities, and NGOs have also been doing much to improve the law concerning battered women and domestic violence. As shown by the summary below of their efforts to date, their major success has been to achieve important reforms in the criminal justice system.

1. General Criminal Law

India has the same general criminal laws that could be used to prosecute husbands for battering and other forms of abuse that most countries have. This includes laws on murder, assault, abetment to suicide, incarceration, and the like. . . .

While all the general criminal laws except the prohibition on rape could normally be used to prosecute husbands for domestic violence, the recent enactment of special domestic-violence criminal laws indicates that India has the same problem of nonenforcement of general criminal law by police and prosecutors in the domestic violence setting that other countries have confronted.

2. Special Domestic-Violence Criminal Laws

India has two specific domestic-violence criminal laws, and has also enacted a wide variety of other criminal laws to stop violence against women in the public arena. . . .
The more general of the special domestic violence criminal laws is section 498-A of the Indian Penal Code, first enacted in 1983. It makes physical or mental cruelty to the wife by her husband or in-laws a new criminal offense, with imprisonment of up to 3 years or a fine as a sanction. It defines cruelty to include:

(a) any wilful conduct which is of such a nature as is likely to drive the woman to commit suicide or cause grave injury or danger to life, limb or health (whether mental or physical) of the woman; or

(b) harassment of the woman where such harassment is with a view to coercing her [or] any person related to her to meet any unlawful demand for any property or valuable security or is on account of failure by her or any person related to her to meet such demand.

The law does not allow courts to take such cases if someone other than the police or the wife and her family files a charge with a magistrate. Evidently the purpose behind this provision was to prevent harassment of the husband and his family by "a person who does not look kindly to them or is [inimical] to them", but its effect is to prevent neighbors who have witnessed the violence from going to a magistrate for help when the police have refused to take action.

The paragraph (a) language—specifically, "conduct which is of such a nature as is likely to . . . cause grave injury or danger to life, limb or health (whether mental or physical) of the woman"—is broad enough to cover beatings and other forms of physical and mental abuse that have no relationship to demands for dowry. It is not clear, however, that the criminal justice system uses this broad phrase to reach non-dowry-related beatings, threats, and other assaultive behavior against the wife. . . .

Moreover, the requirement that injury inflicted on the woman be grave clearly exempts some forms of husband abuse from punishment—that is, beatings which cause only mild injury. And if police, prosecutors, and judges interpret the law as requiring proof that "danger to life, limb or health" be grave danger, many forms of physical assault will also be treated as within the husband's normal range of authority, e.g., slaps. The statutory language, the literature about the subject, and interviews thus suggest that, in fact, the criminal justice system actors do not use the law to reach either non-dowry-related beatings or most forms of husband threats and other assaultive behavior against the wife.

The second new domestic-violence crime, added in 1986, focuses on deaths caused in a dowry context, i.e., "dowry deaths". The offender can be sentenced for any period from a minimum of 7 years in prison to a maximum of life imprisonment. The new section 304-B of the Indian Penal Code provides:

Where the death of a woman is caused by any burn or body injury or occurs otherwise than under normal circumstances within seven years of her marriage and it is shown that soon before her death she was subjected to cruelty or harassment by her husband or any relative of her husband for, or in connection with any demand for dowry, such death shall be called 'dowry death' and such husband or relative shall be deemed to have caused her death.

Since this presumption applies only where the wife was subject to "cruelty or harassment by her husband or any relative of her husband," it incorporates the IPC section 498-A definition of cruelty or harassment with all its limits. And as with the cruelty statute, the dowry death statute prohibits magistrates from taking action unless the wife's family or the police have filed a charge. Dowry death *has* been successfully prosecuted in India, though the intermediate courts have seemed rather hostile to the concept. Both the Diwans and Prof. Saxena discuss several dowry death cases in which the trial court convicted, but the intermediate court of appeals reversed. Years later, some of these convictions were reinstated by the highest court (the Supreme Court). . . .

Though there are strong new domestic-violence criminal laws on the books, Prof. Saxena asserted as late as 1995 [in her book, CRIMES AGAINST WOMEN AND PROTECTIVE LAWS,] that there was still a problem with enforcing such laws:

The experiences of women with the enforcement machinery are not very happy. Most of them, 94% of the 87 persons (both men and women questioned) were disappointed with the obstructive role of the police, the problems faced in hiring an efficient and knowledgeable lawyer and the tardy pace at which the case proceeded. Only 6% of the women, who belonged to the upper strata of society[,] were satisfied. . . .

6. Special All-Women Police Stations. . . .

[Special all-women police stations are] an area in which India has taken a lead. In 1986, the Crimes (Women) Cell was created, allowing special all-women cells associated with police stations. Yet Prof. Saxena is rather critical of this initiative, noting that it had "no specific guidelines," no "new powers," and no "observable autonomy." [*Id.*] She concludes:

There is a growth in the number of complaints registered in the Cell yet compromises, convictions and cases filed in courts by it [have] declined. Even the compromised cases are statistically unreliable. 60% of the 20 compromised cases examined during an investigation had never received any follow up call from the Cell, about 20% had broken up but the Cell was not even aware of them. The aggrieved women were so disgusted and disillusioned with the lack of concern of the officers of the Cell to find out about their welfare that they did not wish to go to the Cell again. [*Id.*]

Chapter 12
Strategies for Ending Female Genital Mutilation and Footbinding: Western Cultural Imperialism or Women's Human Rights?

I. Cultural Relativism

Cultural relativism is a doctrine holding that at least some cultural moral rules and social institutions are exempt from outsider criticism. It evolved as a reaction against cultural evolutionism, a Eurocentric view that human societies tend to progress from "primitive" or "savage" to modern. In essence, cultural relativists state that moral principles are not necessarily self-evident to or shared by all. It stresses the need for tolerance and respect for all customs.

Jack Donnelly, a Western political scientist, proposed that the theory of cultural relativism can be conceptualized as a series of points on a continuum, with radical relativism on one end and radical universalism on the other:

In its most extreme form, what we can call radical cultural relativism would hold that culture is the sole source of the validity of a moral right or rule. Radical universalism would hold that culture is irrelevant to the validity of human rights and rules, which are universally valid. The body of the continuum defined by these ideal typical end-points—that is, those positions involving varying mixes of relativism and universalism—can be roughly divided into what we can call strong cultural relativism and weak cultural relativism.

Strong cultural relativism would begin with the premise that culture is the principal source of the validity of a moral right or rule. Universal human rights standards, however, serve as a check on potential excesses of relativism. At its furthest extreme, just short of radical relativism, strong cultural relativism would accept a few basic rights with virtually universal application, but allow such a wide range of variation for most rights that two entirely justifiable sets might overlap only slightly.

Weak cultural relativism holds that culture may be an important source of the validity of a moral right or rule. Universality is initially presumed, but the relativity of human nature, communities, and rights serves as a check on potential excesses of universalism. At its furthest extreme, just short of radical universalism, weak cultural relativism would recognize a comprehensive set of prima facie universal human rights, but allow occasional and strictly limited local variations and exceptions.[A]

[A] Jack Donnelly, Universal Human Rights in Theory and Practice 109 (1989).

Where do you find yourself on this continuum? Are there some practices affecting women that should be exempt from criticism by people outside the culture? This chapter explores cultural relativism by asking you to examine the practices of African FGM, Chinese footbinding, and American breast implants. As you read the materials, consider whether your views change and if so, why.

II. FGM: The Practice; Its Consequences; and Its Prevalence

Lorna Martin, *Waris Dirie is the desert flower who rebelled against the might of Somalian ritual. And for this beautiful warrior, the fight is just beginning.*
THE HERALD (GLASGOW), June 29, 2002, at 22

The first vivid memory Waris Dirie has is of her own circumcision. She remembers the sense of breathless excitement in her family's camp in the Somalian desert the night before the ritual cutting. Her mother was making a special fuss of her, giving her extra food but warning her not to drink too much water or milk.

Dirie was about five and couldn't sleep because of the butterflies in her stomach. She knew something important was about to happen, but she had no idea what it was. All she knew was this thing was going to make her pure and it meant she was going to become a woman.

Before dawn and with the sky still black, Dirie was taken from her bed by her mother and into the bush to meet "the gypsy woman". After locating a suitably flat rock, Dirie's mother laid her daughter down on her back and sat behind her, pulling her head against her chest and gripping her body between her legs. Dirie circled her arms around her mother's thighs.

Just as her mother was urging her to be brave for her mama, Dirie peered between her legs and saw the old woman spit on to a blood-encrusted razor blade and wipe it on her dress. At this point, Dirie's world went dark as her mother blindfolded her. The next thing she felt was the flesh of her vagina being cut away. The wound was then sewn together using thorns from an acacia tree. The opening that was left for urine, and later menstrual blood and childbirth, was a hole the diameter of a matchstick.

"I remember it like it happened yesterday, I really do," says Dirie, sprawled on a sofa in her red-brick home in Cardiff some 30 years later. "Your life changes right that minute. Your pure, beautiful spirit suddenly crashes. Right from the day it happened I knew how wrong it was. I tried to rack my brain to find a reason. I was asking myself 'how could my mama put me through this?' I know God had made me perfect like all the other girls and if there had been anything very wrong with us he'd have changed it. But for our mamas to make that decision, to do such a horrific, vicious thing, is really beyond words." . . .

In 1997, Dirie was made a spokeswoman for the United Nations, working as a special ambassador against female genital mutilation (FGM). She also runs a charitable foundation, Desert Dawn, which aims to educate the women and children of Somalia, and provide them with better healthcare.

Before she was circumcised—she had the procedure reversed in London when she became a model—she remembers a harsh but idyllic life, looking after her father's camels and goats, sleeping under the stars and moving camp every couple of weeks in search of food and water. She is one of 12 children, several of whom died in infancy, one of her sisters after being circumcised.

At around 12, Dirie, which means desert flower, ran away after discovering her father was planning to sell her to a 60-year-old man in exchange for five camels. Trekking across the desert for six days and six nights, she encountered wild animals and two young tribesmen who tried to rape her, before she ended up in the war-ravaged capital of Mogadishu. There, she stayed with an aunt and got a job on a building site, after convincing the man in charge that she could carry sand and mix as well as the men.

A couple of months later, she met the Somalian ambassador to Britain, who was an uncle by marriage, and persuaded him to take her to London as a maid. . . .

When the family returned to Somalia, she stayed in London. . . . It was there, when she was about 19, that she was discovered by a fashion photographer. . . . [A]lmost overnight she became one of the few black supermodels. . . .

Despite her success in the distorted world of high fashion, it is not a subject she enjoys discussing. . . .

The real thing is her mission to bring to an end to female genital mutilation, which is practised in 28 African countries, on 6,000 girls every day. "No woman in this world should rest until we put a stop to it," says Dirie, banging her fists on her knees. "Some people do not want to talk about it or even think about it. But it is so brutal and wrong. And the saddest thing is everybody knows it is wrong: from the mother who is holding the child, to the father who makes the decision, to the one who is cutting the child."

Dirie feels no anger towards her mother who believed, like all of her people, that the practice was ordered in the Koran. "My Mama didn't think she was hurting me. She believed it would make me pure and clean. The mothers don't even question that it is the right thing to do for their daughters. My mother believed that by doing it she was ensuring my future because girls with intact genitals are considered unclean and sexually-driven sluts. No mother would consider such a girl a proper wife for her son.

"On their wedding night in my country, brides are cut open to allow their husband's entry. A woman takes a knife and slices through or the man just forces himself. Her mother-in-law inspects her the next morning to see if she is bleeding and has slept with her husband despite the pain. If the blood between her legs is fresh the women will dance through the village and announce it to everyone. That, my friend, is what we're up against."

Before Dirie returned to Somalia last year, she was warned that she risked being detained, kidnapped or worse because she speaks out against FGM. "Talking about it was a blessing and a curse," she explains. "I was glad people wanted to do something about it, but over and over I had to relive all the pain it caused in my life. Every time I spoke out about it, I spoke against something my mother, my father and my people believe. I denounced my family and a tradition that was important to them."

When she returned and spoke to her mother and other women in Somalia about the practice, though, she was pleasantly surprised by their reaction. "I said to my mama that she had been great and tried to hold everything together. But I said sometimes the things that happened in our lives weren't so great. My mama had her head down and she knew the truth of what I was saying. I told her she could do something about it. I spoke to some other women about it. We were surrounded by children playing outside huts and I said 'look at all those children running around. I would hate to come back one day and hear that they went through it.' Some of the women were crying because it is so very painful yet they have never been able to talk about it. . . ."

[At the end of the interview,] she turns to me and says: "The woman is a goddess, remember. We are stronger than men and should not be suffering to please them. There are so many myths about female genital mutilation. But it is done for one simple reason, to control and repress women by taking away their sexuality. We cannot rest, sister, until we have put a stop to it."

Her dedication has come too late for the 60 African girls who will have been cut in the time it has taken to read this article. But it is their younger sisters and the unborn who might just be transformed by her work. © Newsquest (Herald & Times) Ltd.

Ms. Dirie currently lives in Austria and is still very actively campaigning against FGM. Her Waris Dirie Foundation website is *available at* RossRights.

Halima Embarek Warzazi, *Final Report: Study on Traditional Practices Affecting The Health of Women and Children*
U.N. Comm'n on Human Rights, Sub-Comm'n on Prevention of Discrimination and Protection of Minorities, 43rd Sess., Agenda Item 4, U.N. Doc. E/CN.4/Sub.2/1991/6 (July 5, 1991)

A. FEMALE CIRCUMCISION AND ITS HEALTH IMPLICATIONS

7. According to the findings of the Working Group on Traditional Practices Affecting the Health of Women and Children, female circumcision can be defined as a practice which consists of the cutting away of all, or part, of the external female genital organs. The practice forms part of the initiation rite in some countries but the actual operation presents health risks.

8. The origin of female circumcision could not be established since it is an old custom which predates Christianity and Islam in the countries where it exists. In the older days, it is believed to have existed in pre-Islamic Arabia, ancient Rome and Tsarist Russia. In England, it was practised in the nineteenth and twentieth centuries to treat psychological disorders. . . .

10. Those who practise female circumcision are usually old women most of whom

serve as traditional birth attendants in their community. As instruments for the operation they use kitchen knives, razor blades, pieces of glass. To heal the wound they use herb mixtures, earth, cow dung, ashes, etc.

11. Female circumcision exists in at least 25 countries in Africa. In Somalia, Djibouti, the northern part of the Sudan, some parts of Ethiopia, Egypt and Mali, infibulation is practiced. Excision and circumcision exist in the Gambia, the northern part of Ghana, Nigeria, Liberia, Senegal, Sierra Leone, Guinea, Guinea Bissau, Burkina Faso, parts of Benin, Côte d' Ivoire, parts of Tanzania, Togo, Uganda, Kenya, Chad, Central African Republic, Cameroon and Mauritania.

12. Outside Africa, a certain form of female circumcision exists in Indonesia, Malaysia and Yemen. Recent information has revealed that the practice exists in some European countries and Australia among immigrant communities.

13. The age at which circumcision is performed varies from a few days old, as in parts of Ethiopia, to seven years old in Egypt and to adolescence in West Africa. . . .

15. The reasons presented for maintaining the practice are religion, custom, decreasing the sexual desire of women, hygiene, aesthetic, facility of sexual relations, fertility. . . . In general, it can be said that those who preserve the practice are largely women who live in traditional societies in the rural areas. . . . The educated women are in favor of eradicating it. A survey conducted in Alexandria in 1988 among informed urban women showed that the women disapproved the practice on ground of the violation of human rights, violation of the image of the women, marital problems and opposition to old customs.

16. In the countries where the practice exists, most women believe that as good Muslims they have to undergo the operation. In order to be clean and proper, fit for marriage, circumcision is a precondition. Among the Bambara in Mali, it is believed that if the clitoris touches the head of a baby being born the child will die. The clitoris is seen as the male characteristic of the woman. In order to enhance her femininity this male part of her has to be removed. Among the women in Sudan, Ethiopia, Djibouti and Somalia, circumcision is performed to reduce the sexual desire of the girl and also to maintain her virginity until marriage. A circumcised woman is considered to be clean.

17. Establishing identity and belongingness is another good reason advanced for the perpetuation of the practice. For example, in Sierra Leone and Liberia, girls of 12 and 13 years of the indigenous population undergo an initiation rite; accordingly, a group of girls are initiated by an older woman "Sowie": this involves education on how to be a good wife, a co-wife, the use of herbal medicine and the secrets of the women['s] society; this education also involves the ritual of circumcision. Once the initiation is over, the girls are accepted as full members of the society and are eligible for marriage. An uninitiated girl is not fit for marriage.

18. The underlying reasons for the persistence of the practice are lack of education and information on the part of women and their vulnerable social and economic status; marriage is the only social security for most women. It has been proved beyond any doubt that female circumcision does not ensure cleanliness or fertility; on the contrary, infection resulting from the operation can cause infertility. Prominent

religious leaders have stated that female circumcision is neither a Muslim nor a Christian obligation.

Mrs. Halima Embarek Warzazi, a Moroccan expert on FGM, wrote the report excerpted above. In 2003, she served as Chairperson of the Sub-Commission on the Promotion and Protection of Human Rights for the Commission on Human Rights, and continues as a member until 2008.[B]

NOTE

Human Rights and Culture. Mrs. Warzazi notes that Egyptian women surveyed in Alexandria thought female circumcision to be a violation of human rights. Yet it is deeply embedded in culture. What does human rights law say about this cultural conflict? What should it say?

Nahid Toubia, M.D., *Female Circumcision as a Public Health Issue*
331 New Eng. J. Med. 712–716 (Sept. 15, 1994)[C]

In many civilizations, certain surgical procedures have profound cultural and social meanings. Male circumcision, for example, has deep importance as a symbol of religious and ethnic identity and has played a major part in the political and social history of many peoples.[1] Female circumcision has particularly strong cultural meaning because it is closely linked to women's sexuality and their reproductive role in society.

Female circumcision is practiced today in 26 African countries, with prevalence rates ranging from 5 percent to 99 percent. It is rarely practiced in Asia. It is estimated that at least 100 million women are circumcised. The practice is known across socioeconomic classes and among different ethnic and cultural groups, including Christians, Muslims, Jews, and followers of indigenous African religions.[2] From the perspective of public health, female circumcision is much more damaging than male circumcision. The mildest form, clitoridectomy, is anatomically equivalent to amputation of the penis. Under the conditions in which most procedures take place, female circumcision constitutes a health hazard with short- and long-term physical complications and psychological effects. The influx of refugees and immigrants from different parts of Africa to North America, Europe, and Australia in the past decade requires

---

[B] The information about Ms. Warzazi is found at UN websites, *available at* RossRights. The UN Human Rights Commission conducted its final session on March 27, 2006, and was replaced by the Human Rights Council, which conducted its first session on June 19, 2006. *See* links to UN information at RossRights.

[C] Dr. Toubia's original article contains diagrams and photographs illustrating her points. Readers will find that the diagrams and photographs greatly enhance their understanding of FGM. The full text can be found at the website for the New England Journal of Medicine, *available at* RossRights.

[1] Remondino PC. History of circumcision from the earliest times to the present: moral and physical reasons for its performance. Philadelphia: F.A. Davis, 1891.

[2] Toubia N. Female genital mutilation: a call for global action. New York: Women, Ink, 1993.

that physicians and other health professionals familiarize themselves with the practice and its ramifications for their patients.

This article reviews the common types of circumcision, their complications, and the challenges in giving appropriate care to circumcised women. In counseling families who believe in the practice, it is important to understand the depth of cultural meaning it carries. Finally, a brief review of legal and ethical issues will include consideration of existing and expected pieces of legislation and what they mean to the medical profession.

The Procedures

Girls are commonly circumcised between the ages of 4 and 10 years, but in some communities the procedure may be performed on infants, or it may be postponed until just before marriage or even after the birth of the first child. The often quoted Shandall system of clinical classification adopted by Verzin in 1975[3] is not accurate and is of little clinical use. That system claims the existence of what is termed "circumcision proper," described as the circumferential excision of the clitoral prepuce in a manner analogous to male circumcision. In my extensive clinical experience as a physician in Sudan, and after a careful review of the literature of the past 15 years, I have not found a single case of female circumcision in which only the skin surrounding the clitoris is removed, without damage to the clitoris itself.

I have advanced a newer system of classification[2] that groups the most common forms of female circumcision into two broad categories: clitoridectomies (type I and II procedures) and infibulations (type III and IV procedures). [After publication of this article, the World Health Organization slightly revised this typology.]

Type I clitoridectomy involves the removal of a part of the clitoris or the whole organ. This is what is commonly referred to as "Sunna circumcision."[4]

Type II clitoridectomy, or excision, involves excision of the clitoris and part of the labia minora. Bleeding from the raw surfaces and from the clitoral artery may be halted with a few stitches of catgut or thorn or by the application of homemade poultices. After healing, the clitoris is absent, but the urethra and the vaginal introitus are not covered.

Type IV, or total infibulation, involves the removal of the clitoris and the labia minora, plus incision of the labia majora to create raw surfaces that are stitched together to cover the urethra and the entrance to the vagina with a hood of skin, leaving a very small posterior opening for passage of urine and menstrual blood.

Type III, or modified (sometimes called intermediate) infibulation, is a milder form of infibulation, which involves the same amount of cutting, but in which only the anterior two thirds of the labia majora are stitched, thus leaving a larger posterior opening.

---

[3] Verzin JA. Sequelae of female circumcision. Trop Doct 1975;5:163–169.

[4] Baasher T. Psychological aspects of female circumcision. In: WHO/EMRO technical publication no. 2. Traditional practices affecting the health of women and children. Geneva: World Health Organization, 1979:71–105.

This anatomically precise and simplified system of classification is only a guide to help clinicians and researchers standardize their descriptions of a multitude of operations. In reality, the extent of cutting and stitching varies considerably, since the operator is usually a layperson with limited knowledge of anatomy and surgical technique. With local or no anesthesia, the girl may move, and the extent of cutting cannot be accurately controlled.

Physical Complications

Because the specialized sensory tissue of the clitoris is concentrated in a rich neurovascular area of a few centimeters, the removal of a small amount of tissue is dangerous and has serious and irreversible effects. Common early complications of all types of circumcision are hemorrhage and severe pain, which can lead to shock and death. Prolonged lesser bleeding may lead to severe anemia and can affect the growth of a poorly nourished child. Local and systemic infections are also common. Infection of the wound, abscesses, ulcers, delayed healing, septicemia [blood poisoning],[D] tetanus and gangrene have all been reported.

Long-term complications are associated more often with infibulation than with clitoridectomy alone, because of interference with the drainage of urine and menstrual blood. Chronic pelvic infection causes pelvic and back pain, dysmenorrhea [painful menstruation], and possibly infertility. Chronic urinary tract infections can lead to urinary stones and kidney damage.

The most common long-term complication is the formation of dermoid cysts [cystic tumors containing hair, skin, or both] at the line of the scar. These result from the embedding of keratinized epithelial cells [cells which have been turned into a hornylike substance similar to hair or nails—i.e., keratinized—and which are covered by a tissue—i.e., epithelial] and sebaceous glands [which secrete oily or greasy material as around hair] in the stitched area. They can be as small as a pea or as large as a grapefruit. The formation of keloids [thick scars from excessive growth of fibrous tissue] is another disfiguring complication that, like dermoid cysts, causes anxiety, shame, and fear in women who think that their genitals are regrowing in monstrous shapes or who fear they have cancer. When painful stitch neuromas [tumors from nervous tissue] develop as a result of the entrapment of nerve endings in the scar, the result is severe dyspareunia [difficult or painful sexual intercourse] and interference with sexual intercourse. Recurrent stitch abscesses and the splitting of poorly healed scars, particularly when they occur over the clitoral artery, can plague women for many years.

Childbirth adds other risks for infibulated women, particularly where health services are limited. If deinfibulation is not performed, exit of the fetal head may be obstructed and strong contractions can lead to perineal tears. If contractions are weak and delivery of the head is delayed, fetal death can occur and necrosis [death of tissue

---

[D] This bracketed definition and the ones that follow are from the on-line Merriam-Webster Medical Dictionary, whose website is *available at* RossRights.

caused by a local injury such as loss of a blood supply] of the septum [dividing wall] between the vagina and bladder can cause vesicovaginal fistula [abnormal tunnels between the bladder and the vagina], a distressing condition of urinary incontinence for which women are often ostracized by their communities.[5]

Another problem related to labor and delivery is emerging among immigrants in Europe and North America, where physicians are not trained to deal with infibulated women. Unnecessary cesarean section can be avoided with a simple deinfibulation[6] performed with the woman under local anesthesia.

In summary, female circumcision is a major contributor to childhood and maternal mortality and morbidity [diseased state] in communities with poor health services.

Psychological and Sexual Effects

In contrast to numerous studies and case reports on the physical complications of genital mutilation, little scientific research is available on the sexual and psychological effects of the practice. This dearth of research has left the subject to a great deal of lay speculation.[7,8,9] Among girls who live in communities where female circumcision carries high social value, the desire to gain social status, please parents, and comply with peer pressure is in conflict with the fear, trauma, and after-effects of the operation.[4,10,11] Physical complications add to the psychological trauma.[12] In my clinical experience in Sudan, many infibulated women have a syndrome of chronic anxiety and depression arising from worry over the state of their genitals, intractable dysmenorrhea, and the fear of infertility.

One major study by two Egyptian psychologists suggests that a woman's sexuality is affected according to the extent of the operation and the degree to which other social messages inhibiting sexual expression are internalized.[13] However, the assump-

---

[5] Warsame M. Medical and social aspects of female circumcision in Somalia. In: Female circumcision: strategies to bring about change. Mogadishu, Somalia: Somali Women Democratic Organization, 1989:94–98.

[6] Baker CA, Gilson GJ, Vill MD, Curet LB. Female circumcision: obstetric issues. Albuquerque, N.M.: Mosby-Year Book, 1993.

[7] Lightfoot Klein H, Shaw E. Special needs of ritually circumcised women patients. J Obstet Gynecol Neonatal Nurs 1991;20:102–107.

[8] Walker A. Possessing the secret of joy. New York: Harcourt Brace Jovanovich, 1992.

[9] Walker A, Parmar P. Warrior marks: female genital mutilation and the sexual blinding of women. New York: Harcourt Brace, 1993.

[10] Taba AH. Female circumcision. In: WHO/EMRO technical publication no. 2. Traditional practices affecting the health of women and children. Geneva: World Health Organization, 1979:43–52.

[11] Warsame A. Social and cultural implications of infibulation in Somalia. In: Female circumcision: strategies to bring about change. Mogadishu, Somalia: Somali Women Democratic Organization, 1989:88–93.

[12] Singhateh SK. The incidence of female circumcision in Gambia and its effect on women and children. In: Female circumcision: strategies to bring about change. Mogadishu, Somalia: Somali Women Democratic Organization, 1989:77–84.

[13] Karim M, Ammar R. Female circumcision and sexual desire. Cairo, Egypt: Ain Shams University Press, 1965.

tion that all circumcised women have sexual problems or are unable to achieve orgasm is not substantiated by research or anecdotal evidence. The relation between the degree of anatomical damage and the ability of women to compensate for it through other sensory areas or emotions and fantasy is not well understood.

A few cases of psychopathologic disorders directly attributable to genital mutilation have been reported in Sudan.[4] Among the majority of girls and women, however, the psychological effects are often subtle and are buried in layers of denial and acceptance of social norms. Understanding the personal and community dynamics of accepting circumcision is important not only in uncovering psychopathologic disorders but also in comprehending why the practice continues. Such understanding is central to the design of efforts to stop the practice.

The psychological sequelae of female circumcision among immigrants differ from those where the practice is prevalent. Circumcised women living in societies where the procedure is not performed may have serious problems in developing their sexual identity. Sooner or later, health professionals will be called on to deal with these problems.

The Cultural Meaning of Female Circumcision

No ethical defense can be made for preserving a cultural practice that damages women's health and interferes with their sexuality. It is important, however, that those who are alien to the culture make themselves familiar with the causes and meanings of cultural practices and relate them to ideas of sex roles in their own societies.

Cultural identity is of paramount importance to everyone. Defending that identity becomes especially important when the group has faced colonialism (as in Africa), when immigrants are faced with a stronger majority culture, and when change does not favor those holding social power (that is, men). Female circumcision is part of the socialization of girls into acceptable womanhood.

In poorer societies, where the extended family is the principal source of social and economic security and has not been replaced by the modern state, women have very few options outside marriage. Female circumcision is the physical marking of the marriageability of women, because it symbolizes social control of their sexual pleasure (clitoridectomy) and their reproduction (infibulation). Cultural identity is often stronger than individual interest, and it may take some time and much new information for people to abandon traditional customs.

Clinical Management

Although clitoridectomies (type I and II procedures) have many short- and long-term complications, they usually do not create mechanical obstruction to first intercourse or to labor. Tightly infibulated women, on the other hand, may need deinfibulation before their first sexual intercourse or first vaginal examination can take place. Most women with infibulation (type III and IV procedures) are at serious risk, as are their unborn babies, if deinfibulation is not performed. Multiparous women usually have heavily scarred and deformed perineums from repeated deinfibulation and reinfibulation and routine (usually unnecessary) posterior episiotomy.

After deinfibulation, the raw, bleeding edges must be secured in some fashion. Two options are available. The first, a circular stitching around the edges of the labia majora, leaves the vulval area open, allowing the free flow of urine and menstrual blood. This also facilitates intercourse and may relieve dyspareunia. The second option is the one traditionally performed and is considered a reinfibulation. The raw edges are sewn back together to restructure the hood of skin covering the urethra and vaginal introitus.

This reinfibulation is medically harmful and raises ethical questions about the health professionals who perform it. Some women request reinfibulation and further tightening of the introitus to its virginal state because they feel "naked" if the area of infibulation is left open or because they believe that a tight vaginal entrance is more pleasurable for their husbands. Compassionate counseling for women and their partners is important to dissuade them from resorting to illegal community practitioners who may operate under inadequate and unhygienic conditions.

The management of gynecologic complications of female circumcision does not differ from the handling of other surgical complications. However, physicians should exercise extreme caution in deciding to operate on an already damaged and scarred area. The decision to incise an abscess or remove a dermoid cyst or keloidal scar must be made conservatively, and care must be taken to perform only the most minimal surgical dissection.

Legal and Ethical Considerations

The legal and ethical debate over female circumcision is not within the scope of this article. It is important, however, that medical practitioners be aware of the legislative and professional actions taken in various countries in recent years.

In Sweden, a law passed in 1982 makes all forms of female circumcision illegal;[14] a similar law was passed in the United Kingdom in 1985.[15] No specific law has been passed in France, but several cases have been brought against parents for circumcising or intending to circumcise their French-born daughters.[16] The cases were tried under child-abuse laws and established a precedent for illegality of female circumcision in France. The Netherlands and Belgium have also made it clear that the practice is illegal.[14,17] In the United States, a bill drafted by the Congressional Women's Caucus has been presented to Congress. It would make female circumcision illegal and recommend that the Department of Health and Human Services fund programs to assist

---

[14] Dorkenoo E, Elworthy S. Female genital mutilation: proposals for change. London: Minority Rights Group, 1992.

[15] Prohibition of Female Circumcision Act of the United Kingdom, 1985.

[16] Mutilation of girls' genitals: ethnic gulf in French court. New York Times International. November 23, 1992.

[17] Vrouwenbesnijdenis ontoelaatbaar. [Female circumcision inadmissible.] Nederlandse Staatscourant. February 1993;26:8.

immigrant communities in dealing with the practice.[18] Even without a specific law, circumcising a girl under the age of consent would most likely be considered illegal under child-abuse laws in the United States.[E]

It is only a matter of time before all forms of female circumcision in children will be made illegal in Western countries and, eventually, in Africa. The Vienna Declaration of the World Conference on Human Rights held that traditional practices such as female circumcision were violations of human rights.[19,20] This position has been adopted by various United Nations health and human-rights organizations.

Another medicolegal question, recently discussed by Baker et al.,[6] concerns the legality and ethics of reinfibulating a woman after vaginal delivery in the United States. Although physicians all have obligations to respond sensitively to a patient's request, reinfibulation is harmful and may be considered illegal. Citing the Prohibition of Female Circumcision Act of 1985, the Royal College of Obstetrics and Gynecology made it clear in a June 1993 press release that reinfibulation is illegal in the United Kingdom. It stated that

The agreed definition of the word infibulation is that it is a stitching together of the labia. By definition, therefore, when an obstetrician is faced with the repair of the vulva of a woman who has delivered a baby vaginally following a previous infibulation it is illegal then to repair the labia intentionally in such a way that intercourse is difficult or impossible.[21]

Although debate about the interpretation of various laws will continue, the medical profession must develop its own rules of ethical conduct concerning the clinical aspects of this practice. How regulations governing reinfibulation fit with the regulations governing other plastic and genital surgeries must be part of the discussion. As such regulations are being developed, it is important to ensure that women who request reinfibulation do not suffer ethnic or cultural bias.

In 1992 the International Federation of Gynaecology and Obstetrics published a joint statement on female circumcision with the World Health Organization,[22] and in 1993 the World Health Assembly, the highest authority of the World Health Organization, issued a similar statement.[23] Both statements condemn the practice of female circumcision as harmful and call for coalitions to abolish it. Greater efforts are needed by national and regional professional associations to promote the issue among their

---

[18] U.S. Congress. Women's Research Equity Act of 1993. Title II-M.

[E] *See* this Chapter's Part V.D., *infra*, for the U.S. law that was subsequently enacted.

[19] Sullivan D, Toubia NF. Female genital mutilation and human rights. Presented at the World Conference on Human Rights, Vienna, Austria, June 1993.

[20] World Conference on Human Rights: the Vienna Declaration and Programme of Action, June 1993. New York: United Nations Department of Public Information, 1993. (United Nations publication no. DPI/1394/39399.)

[21] Female circumcision (female genital mutilation). Press release of the Royal College of Obstetricians and Gynaecologists, London, 1993.

[22] Female circumcision: female genital mutilation. Int J Gynaecol Obstet 1992;37:149–149.

[23] Female genital mutilation—World Health Assembly calls for the elimination of harmful traditional practices. Press release of the 46th World Health Assembly, Geneva, World Health Organization, May 12, 1993.

members and to articulate their policy positions on the various aspects of the practice.

Conclusions

Female circumcision, or female genital mutilation, can no longer be seen as a traditional custom. It has become a problem of modern society in Africa as well as Western countries. In recent years, concern has grown over how to stop the practice, rather than whether it is appropriate to intervene.

There are two main areas of concern for health practitioners. The first is the danger that a trained and licensed practitioner could be expected to assist in circumcising a girl, particularly a young child. Legislation against the practice will resolve this question. The second area of concern is how to deliver the most appropriate clinical care and psychological support to girls and women who have already suffered from this practice.

More research is needed to examine the full range of physical, sexual, and psychological consequences of the various procedures. Guidelines and training materials must be developed to inform providers about how to manage the health needs of circumcised women and about appropriate ways to counsel patients when they request circumcision or reinfibulation. Professional associations should publish guidelines that outline their members' obligations and responsibilities to their patients.

Dr. Toubia, born in Khartoum, Sudan, wrote the article above and edited the book excerpt that follows. After completing medical school in Egypt, she became the first female surgeon in Sudan, and was the head of the pediatric surgery unit at a Khartoum hospital for many years. She is an Adjunct Assistant Professor at Columbia University School of Public Health, and the founder and Director of RAINB♀, based initially in New York and by 2007 in London, Kenya, and Sudan. The organization focuses primarily on Africa and African refugee and immigrant communities. Its Board of Trustees and staff are multi-cultural, with strong African leadership. She focuses on "issues of reproductive health, women's rights, and gender inequality particularly in Africa and the Middle East."[F]

FEMALE GENITAL MUTILATION: A GUIDE TO LAWS AND POLICIES WORLDWIDE
3–15 (Anika Rahman & Nahid Toubia eds., 2000)

Background and History

What Is FC/FGM? . . . .

Indigenous populations use a variety of terms in local dialects to describe the practice. These are often synonymous with purification or cleansing, such as the terms *tabara*

[F] The information about Dr. Toubia is found on several websites, *available at* RossRights.

in Egypt, *tabur* in Sudan and *bolokoli* in Mali. Local terminology for types of FC/FGM also varies widely among countries. In literature from Sudan, for example, clitoridectomy is referred to as *sunna*, and infibulation is referred to as *pharaonic*. In literature associated with French-speaking Africa, FC/FGM is commonly referred to as *excision*; while in English-speaking Africa, the term "circumcision" is predominant.

Within the international community, the term "female circumcision" was used for many years to describe the practice. Other expressions, such as "female genital cutting," "female genital surgery," "ritual genital surgery" and "sexual mutilation," have also been used. However, in the past decade, the term "female genital mutilation" has been adopted by a wide range of women's health and human rights activists because it clearly indicates the harm caused by the practice. The World Health Organization (WHO) also adopted the term "female genital mutilation." Similarly, in 1990, at a meeting in Addis Ababa, Ethiopia, the Inter-African Committee on Traditional Practices Affecting the Health of Women and Children (IAC) formally adopted this term. Subsequently, the international community has used this expression in several United Nations conference documents, including those relating to the 1994 International Conference on Population and Development in Cairo (Cairo Conference), the 1995 World Summit for Social Development in Copenhagen (Copenhagen Summit) and the 1995 Fourth World Conference on Women in Beijing (Beijing Conference).

Although the term "female genital mutilation" has been a very effective policy and advocacy tool, organizations working with communities that practice FGM have found that this term can be offensive or even shocking to women who have never considered the practice a mutilation. Out of respect and sensitivity, many organizations have opted to use local terminology or more neutral terms such as "female circumcision" or "female genital cutting" when working with these populations. In recognition of these two approaches, the dual term "FC/FGM" has been used for this book except when quoting materials from United Nations conference documents and national legislation. . . .

Women's sexuality

A fundamental reason advanced for female circumcision is the need to control women's sexuality. Because sexuality is socially constructed, it has different meanings depending on its context. For many communities that practice FC/FGM, a family or clan's honor depends on a girl's virginity or sexual restraint. This is the case in Egypt, Sudan and Somalia, where FC/FGM is perceived as a way to curtail premarital sex and preserve virginity. In other contexts, such as in Kenya and Uganda, where sexual "purity" is not a concern, FC/FGM is performed to reduce the woman's sexual demands on her husband, thus allowing him to have several wives. Notwithstanding the different reasons to control women's sexuality, FC/ FGM is intended to reduce women's sexual desire, thus promoting women's virginity and protecting marital fidelity, in the interest of male sexuality. FC/FGM also results in the reduction of women's sexual fulfillment, thus aiding in the construction of parameters around women's sexuality.

Religion

It is important to note that FC/FGM is a cultural, not a religious, practice. . . .

However, despite the fact that FC/FGM is not known in many Muslim countries, it is strongly identified with Islam in several African nations, and many members of the Muslim community advocate for the practice. While neither the Qu'ran, the primary source for Islamic law, nor the "hadith," collections of the sayings of the Prophet Mohammed, include a direct call for FC/FGM, debate over interpretations of statements from one hadith continues. Most recently, during the International Conference on Population and Reproductive Health in the Muslim World at Egypt's Al Azhar University, a traditional center of Islamic scholarship, it was agreed that certain harmful practices, including FC/FGM, were the result of misunderstandings of Islamic provisions. . . .

How Widespread Is FC/FGM?. . . .

Currently, FC/FGM is practiced in 28 African countries in the sub-Saharan and Northeastern regions. . . . Based on current estimates, 18 African countries have prevalence rates of 50 percent or higher. However, prevalence varies widely from country to country. It ranges from nearly 90 percent or higher in Egypt, Eritrea, Mali and Sudan, to less than 50 percent in the Central African Republic and Côte d'Ivoire, to 5 percent in the Democratic Republic of Congo and Uganda. There are also great disparities in prevalence within countries. For example, in Mali, prevalence in the regions of Timbuctou and Gao is less than 10 percent, while in Bamako and Koulikoro, the rates are 95 percent and 99 percent, respectively. In Asia, the practice has been documented among the Daudi Bohra Muslims in India and a few Muslim ethnic groups in Sri Lanka. In the Middle East, there are reports of the practice in Yemen and Oman.

As recently as the 1950s, physicians in the United Kingdom and the United States also performed FC/FGM to "treat" hysteria, lesbianism, masturbation and other so-called "female deviations." Women who have undergone FC/FGM are also found among African immigrant communities in Europe, Canada, Australia and the United States. However, there is little data about either the number of these immigrants or the prevalence of FC/FGM amongst them. The existing sporadic and incomplete data available are listed in the relevant country sections. Apart from judicial cases in France, there is no systematic documented evidence of the practice occurring in immigrant settings.

What Are the Health Consequences of FC/FGM?. . . .

While procedures differ greatly according to such factors as ethnic groups and geographic regions, they can be grouped broadly into four categories, as established by the WHO.

- *Type I* (commonly referred to as "clitoridectomy"): Excision of the prepuce with or without excision of part or all of the clitoris.

- *Type II* (commonly referred to as "excision"): Excision of the prepuce and clitoris together with partial or total excision of the labia minora.
- *Type III* (commonly referred to as "infibulation"): Excision of part or all of the external genitalia and stitching/narrowing of the vaginal opening.
- *Type IV* (unclassified): All other procedures that involve partial or total removal of the female external genitalia and/or injury to the female genital organs for cultural or any other non-therapeutic reasons. Type IV refers to numerous other procedures that have been documented, such as pricking, piercing, stretching or burning of the clitoris and/or surrounding tissues. . . .

Historical Account of Attempts to Bring Attention to or Stop FC/FGM

The first documented actions to bring attention to the practice of FC/ FGM date back to the turn of the twentieth century. However, it is possible that undocumented efforts and initiatives by local populations aimed at stopping the practice were carried out prior to this time. In the *early 1900s*, colonial administrations and missionaries in the countries of Burkina Faso, Kenya and Sudan attempted to stop the practice by enacting laws and church rules, but such actions only succeeded in provoking anger against foreign intervention. Later attempts by the governments of Sudan and Egypt to pass laws on FC/FGM in the *1940s and 1950s* were also ineffective, largely because of the lack of prior awareness campaigns against the practice. In the *1960s and 1970s*, indigenous African activism against FC/FGM further developed. In many countries, women's groups led intermittent campaigns to educate the population about the harmful effects of the practice. In addition, doctors—mostly in Sudan, Somalia and Nigeria—who observed patients suffering from complications of FC/ FGM began to document the procedure and write about its clinical complications in medical journals.

In *1979*, the WHO sponsored the first Seminar on Harmful Traditional Practices Affecting the Health of Women and Children, in Khartoum, Sudan. Fran Hosken, an American journalist who had traveled through Africa to collect information on FC/ FGM, presented her findings. A strong presence of women from several African countries led a vote to end all forms of the practice, against a suggestion from the medical participants for a milder form of the practice to be performed under hygienic conditions. The recommendations included the establishment of national commissions for the coordination of activities against FC/FGM. Despite this historical triumph of women's advocates to stop all forms of FC/FGM, their efforts are still repeatedly undermined by the attempts of the medical community in Africa and the West to medicalize the practice.

In the *1980s*, African women continued to organize to address the practice of FC/ FGM. In 1980 four African women activists attended the UN Mid-Decade Conference on Women and the NGO Forum Copenhagen to present a panel discussion on female circumcision. In that conference, the conflict between the approaches of indigenous African women to stop the practice and those of outsiders was apparent. A few Western women who spoke out against the practice were perceived by African women to be condescending and confrontational. Unfortunately that incident is still registered as the great schism between Western feminists and African cultural conservationists in a crude reading of the historical facts and a biased attempt to fuel the fire of cultural conflict. As a result of this conference, an informal African network was established to address the practice. In 1984, a group of African women organized a meeting of African NGOs in Dakar, Senegal, which resulted in the formation of the Inter-African Committee on Traditional Practices Affecting the Health of Women and Children (IAC). Over the 15 years subsequent to the Dakar seminar, IAC affiliates were founded in over 26 African countries. This regional network has since worked to educate national governments as well as the general public about the harmful effects of FC/FGM.

Another development during the 1980s was critical to later efforts to frame FC/FGM as a human rights violation. This decade marked a period of growing scholarship and thinking by international feminist legal scholars and advocates. They began increasingly to question the lack of a gender lens on the law and on human rights. One critical step in this questioning was the feminist critique of the manner in which most traditional law and human rights analysis focused attention on the "public" sphere—that is, the world of politics, government and the state. Little attention was paid to the "private" domain of the family and society despite the fact that the most frequent violations of women's rights occurred in this context. As a result of this false dichotomy between "public" and "private" spheres, many of the injuries inflicted upon women by private individuals—in the form of domestic violence, dowry deaths and FC/FGM—were not generally viewed as human rights abuses for which governments could be held accountable. In 1981, recognition of governments' responsibility to address violations of women's rights by both government actors and private parties was made explicit in the Convention on the Elimination of All Forms of Discrimination Against Women (Women's Convention). Also during the 1980s, Mrs. Halima Embarek Warzazi, a member of the Sub-Commission on the Promotion and Protection of Human Rights (formerly the Sub-Commission on Prevention of Discrimination and Protection of Minorities), was appointed by that body to serve as Special Rapporteur on Traditional Practices Affecting the Health of Women and Children. She has produced several reports documenting national- and international-level action to address FC/FGM.

In the *1990s*, strong African leadership on FC/FGM led to growing international awareness, which resulted in the recognition of FC/FGM as a fundamental violation of women's rights. In 1990, the Committee on the Elimination of Discrimination Against Women . . . released a general recommendation [14] pertaining specifically to FC/FGM. Moreover, the 1993 United Nations Declaration on the Elimination of Violence Against Women explicitly included FC/FGM within its definition of the phrase "violence against women." The international community again addressed the human rights implications of harmful practices such as FC/FGM at a series of international conferences. These included: the World Conference on Human Rights, Vienna 1993; the [Cairo Population and Development Conference, 1994]; and the [Beijing Conference on Women, 1995]. The Vienna and Cairo conferences were marked by the presence of a powerful women's lobby, which ensured that issues of women's rights remained critical on the world stage. It is thus not surprising that during these meetings and the subsequent women's conference in Beijing, the prevention of FC/FGM was given special attention and strategies for appropriate policies and actions were outlined in the final documents approved by the governments. One result of the increased pressure by the women's movement was the appointment, by the Commission on Human Rights, in 1994, of Rhadika Coomerswamy as Special Rapporteur on Violence against Women. Since her mandate includes FC/FGM, her reports have drawn attention to this subject.

There is currently an extensive network of African organizations working to stop FC/FGM, including women's NGOs, and health, human rights and legal organizations. They have been aided, in part, by a number of national and international donor and technical agencies. For example, several United Nations agencies have been active in promoting FC/FGM prevention worldwide. The WHO, the United Nations Children's Fund (UNICEF) and the United Nations Population Fund (UNFPA) have provided technical, administrative and financial support to a wide range of organizations in many spheres of activity. These agencies have also adopted formal policies and program plans to address the issue.

More recently, as migration from Africa to other parts of the world has increased, there are a growing number of immigrant and refugee service organizations that are working to address the practice among their African immigrant communities. Additional issues that result from dislocation and adapting to a new environment have created the need for new strategies and approaches to address FC/FGM in a broader setting.

Just as discussions about FC/FGM have undergone a transition in the past ten years, so have program interventions. Initially, much of the focus was on basic Information, Education and Communication (IEC) strategies. These centered on informing the population about the harmful health effects of FC/FGM. While provision of information was useful, this in itself was not sufficient to change people's thinking about the practice. In recent years, there has been increased use of innovative methods to reach the population, such as through music, theater and films. There have also been efforts to engage members of the community—such as opinion leaders, religious authorities and village elders—in local campaigns. In addition, there has been the development of more integrated activities on FC/FGM, involving incorporation of information and materials into programs in the health sector, schools and youth groups.

Along with these advances, there is an increased focus on addressing the practice as a violation of women's rights. Legal and human rights organizations are including information on FC/FGM in training programs on women's rights for lawyers, judges and society in general. Moreover, laws criminalizing the practice have been enacted or introduced in many countries. Efforts to make the law responsive to FC/FGM, either by drafting a specific law on the practice, or by pressing for use of existing laws to prosecute cases involving FC/FGM, are also underway in several other countries. While use of legal measures needs to be carefully considered and used in conjunction with other education efforts, laws can be a useful tool for change, giving NGOs and individuals greater leverage in persuading communities to abandon the practice.

More and more, the various actors involved in the fight against FC/FGM acknowledge the strategic importance of framing the issue as a matter of international human rights and obtaining governments' firm commitment to taking appropriate steps to stop the practice. Placing a particular traditional practice within a global paradigm is important for validating a universal reality—discrimination against women. Moreover, the use of an international framework is important in creating and maintaining international pressure for change. Although devising effective international campaigns is a complex task, there is little doubt that international pressure has played a role in efforts to stop FC/FGM.

Anika Rahman and Nahid Toubia edited this book, produced as a joint project of the Center for Reproductive Rights (CRR) and RAINB♀. Ms. Rahman was the Founding Director of the International Program at CRR, an NGO dedicated to promoting women's reproductive rights. In July 2004, she became President of Americans for UNFPA. She is a member of the New York bar, received her bachelor's degree from Princeton and her J.D. from Columbia, and is a native of Bangladesh.[G] Dr. Toubia founded and directed RAINB♀, as noted after the article she wrote.

Azizah al-Hibri, *Who Defines Women's Rights? A Third World Woman's Response*

in 2 No. 1 HUMAN RIGHTS BRIEF (Fall 1994)

The 1993 World Conference on Human Rights in Vienna revealed the wide gulf that separates "Third World" women from "First World" women. Arriving at the conference to discuss their human rights issues, Third World women were surprised to see that this task had been performed on their behalf by First World women, who used their organizational skills to take control of the conference and determine its agenda. The shock was so profound that, immediately upon leaving Vienna, Third World women began internal discussions to define a course of action that would avert a future repeat of this undemocratic/patriarchal situation.

In retrospect, the Vienna event did not usher in a new trend. Indeed, even during the 1980 United Nations Mid-Decade for Women conference in Copenhagen, the gulf was already apparent. At the Forum, the concurrent unofficial conference held in conjunction with the official UN conference, the gulf became so wide that a series of Third World women's meetings were held impromptu on site. As a result, at least one plenary session designed to express the views of Third World women was added.

In both instances, and many others, Third World women were frustrated by attempts on the part of First World women to speak for all the participants. They were also frustrated with the First World women's selection of Third World spokeswomen representing a First World point of view. The recent [1994] International Conference on Population and Development (ICPD) in Cairo unfortunately replicated these earlier

---

[G] The information about Ms. Rahman is on a website *available at* RossRights.

patterns. For this reason, as well as others, some Third World women carried placards during the last days of the ICPD criticizing it for not being responsive to their concerns.

The impact of American feminism on Third World women has been positive. Unfortunately, however, the positive effects have been diminished by some vocal First World women activists who appear to dominate international fora. The problem lies with the approach these activists take. They refuse to treat Third World women as equals, even as they claim to fight for their human rights. In a real sense, the approach reeks of the attitude of early colonialist women, in places such as Algeria, who appropriated and silenced the colonized woman's voice. In her . . . book, The Eloquence of Silence . . . , Marnia Lazreg, an Algerian-born feminist, provides an insightful analysis of this problem. She uses the issue of the veil as an example:

The veil made colonial women uncomfortable, as did every task that Algerian women performed, from rearing children to cooking and taking care of their homes. The veil, for the colonial woman, was the perfect alibi for rejecting the Algerian woman's culture and denigrating her. But it was also a constant reminder of her powerlessness in erasing the existence of a different way of being a woman. She often overcame her handicap by turning it into an advantage. She is superior to these veiled women. ... .

In Copenhagen, Third World women were told that their highest priorities related to the veil and clitoridectomy (female genital mutilation). In Cairo, they were told that their highest priorities related to contraception and abortion. In both cases, Third World women begged to differ. They repeatedly announced that their highest priorities were peace and development. They noted that they could not very well worry about other matters when their children were dying from thirst, hunger or war. Sometimes, First World women shook their heads and indicated that they understood. But nothing has changed. First World women still do not listen; they still do not hear.

Many Third World women went to Cairo with a sense of hope. Finally, a conference was prepared to address their issues. After all, it was clearly billed as a "development" conference. But, again, their hopes were left unrealized. The conference instead centered around reducing the number of Third World babies in order to preserve the earth's resources despite (or is it "because of") the fact that the First World consumes much of these resources.

What First World women succeeded in doing at Cairo, however, in fact damaged Third World women. They forced the issue of abortion on everyone, from a First World perspective. Many Third World governments allied to the United States acquiesced in the demands of the conference, thus making women's issues appear to their citizens (including women) as suspect, and the proposals as "foreign" and offensive. Other Third World countries were forced to evaluate their public policies on the matter from the First World's perspective. Because of the apparent racism motivating some of these First World reproductive concerns, the outcome in some cases has been disastrous to women.

In the case of abortion rights specifically, in certain Muslim countries the result was to produce a highly conservative official juristic analysis of the issue. This presents a retrenchment, since, for hundreds of years, Muslim jurists have had quite a liberal analysis of abortion, and, unlike the situation that used to exist in the United States, safe abortions were widely available in many Muslim countries.

The reason for this retrenchment derives to a great extent from the perception that the First World reproductive rights movements are part of a concentrated racist Western onslaught on Third World population. Had Muslim women been afforded the space to speak in their own voices, the results may have been remarkably different.

It is unfortunate that some First World women's discourse has poisoned the local well for Muslim and other Third World feminists. But Third World feminists will struggle on until they achieve all the rights their respective states and patriarchal cultures have thus far denied them. They will do this by developing feminist analyses of their own religious texts, much like Mary Daly and others did for Christianity, and then relying on these analyses to advance their cause. They will recruit supportive First World feminists to help them in their efforts, but they will specify the kind of support needed, and they will lead their own battles. They will not seek to achieve their liberation by denigrating their religion or culture or by forcing upon their communities inappropriate priorities and demands. They will do it their own way.

Azizah al-Hibri is a law professor at the University of Richmond and an expert in Islamic jurisprudence and feminist theory; she also teaches corporations and securities regulation. She received her bachelor's degree from the American University of Beirut in 1965, a master's degree from Wayne State in 1968, her Ph.D. in Philosophy from the University of Pennsylvania in 1975, and her J.D from that university in 1985. Originally from Lebanon, she has worked professionally in the United States since 1975. She is an American Muslim and President of Karamah: Muslim Women Lawyers for Human Rights, which she founded in 1993.[H]

NOTES

Who Speaks for Third-World Women? Many women have expressed their views in the excerpted materials. They come from Somalia (Waris Dirie), Morocco (Halima Embarek Warzazi), Sudan (Nahid Toubia), Bangladesh (Anika Rahman), and Lebanon (Azizah al-Hibri). They all have significant professional experience in the West. Does that make them First World or Third World women? What does each say about the perspectives of women who live in communities where FGM is practiced? Is there a "Third World" women's view? A "First World" women's view? What lessons about cultural relativism do you take away?

What Human Rights? Review all international and regional human rights treaties and documents that might apply to FGM. Consider the treaties and documents you have studied and any others that you think might be relevant. Which provisions apply

---

[H] The information about Azizah al-Hibri is from several websites, *available at* RossRights.

to FGM? Are there different provisions for children as opposed to adults? How does human rights law deal with cultural and religious difference?

What Strategies Work? As you consider the methods for addressing FGM discussed by these different authors, which are most effective? Would you suggest other steps?

III. Footbinding—Comparing Two Movements

As you read the following account of the movement to end footbinding in China, consider what lessons you might draw from experience there. Are those lessons applicable as to FGM? Why or why not?

Kathryn Sikkink, *Historical Precursors to Modern Campaigns for Women's Human Rights: Campaigns Against Footbinding and Female Circumcision*
in 3 Women and International Human Rights Law 797, 798–807 (Kelly D. Askin & Dorean M. Koenig eds., 2001)

Both female circumcision and footbinding represent early examples of practices we would now call violence against women, practices that resulted in bodily mutilation with long-lasting impact on the health and activity level of women. Both practices were ancient and deeply embedded culturally, involving highly ritualized rites of passage from girlhood to womanhood; indeed these characteristics defined womanhood. Both were prerequisites for marriage. . . .

Footbinding . . . has ancient roots. Although the Chinese had admired small feet since antiquity, there is little verifiable proof that women bound their feet before the tenth century. The practice became more widespread during the Sung dynasty, and was widely practiced by all classes during the Ming (1368–1644) and Ch'ing (1644–1911) dynasties. The origins of the practice are rooted in traditional folklore and aesthetic appeal. It has also been explained as a symbol of conspicuous leisure, and as a means to control women's movement, keep women at home, and protect chastity. It was widely believed that women without bound feet would not find husbands. . . .

The Campaign Against Footbinding in China . . .

[Y]oung girls, between four and eight years old, had their feet tightly wrapped to prevent growth. After years of intense pain, the toes were broken and flesh had fallen off to produce a narrow foot of three to five inches long. . . . [N]arratives of women who experienced footbinding testify to the physical pain of the practice, the pride women felt in their small feet, and the central role of the ritual of footbinding in female life. Some historians dispute the standard verdict that footbinding was "a men's conspiracy to keep women crippled and submissive;" indeed, "for all its erotic appeal to men, without the cooperation of women footbinding could not have been perpetuated." Instead they stress the functions that footbinding served in socialization, appropriation of female labor, defining nationhood and gender roles, and as a central event in domestic women's culture: "Footbinding prepared a girl physically and psychologically for her future role as wife and a dependent family member. . . . Through footbinding, the doctrine of separate spheres was engraved onto the bodies of female children."

For all the functions that footbinding may have served, it was ended after a focused campaign against it, initially spearheaded by Western missionary women. For hundreds of years some Chinese intellectuals and dynastic leaders had spoken out against footbinding, but their positions had no impact on changing practice. Although footbinding was widespread in China, it varied by class, ethnic group and region. Certain ethnic groups, such as the Manchu, Mongols, Tibetans, and the Hakka, did not practice footbinding; upper-class women were more likely than lower-class women to have their feet bound, and footbinding was less common in rural areas and in the rice-growing regions of China than it was elsewhere. . . .

The Manchu women had never bound their feet and, in the mid-1600s, the Manchu imperial court issued edicts to prohibit footbinding, but people evaded the edicts and the court was obliged to give tacit consent to the practice. . . . It is interesting that the Manchu were able to force every man to change his hairstyle and wear the queue, and yet they were not able to affect the practice of footbinding.

A vigorous movement to abolish footbinding originated in the late 1800s among foreigners in China's treaty ports, later spreading among those Chinese who had been most exposed to Western ideas. Later, and before it became truly widespread and effective, the campaign was embraced and taken over by Chinese intellectuals and politicians, until it culminated in the decree banning footbinding after the 1911 revolution. . . .

The campaign against footbinding had its most active phase and greatest impact at the turn of the century. . . . After the turn of the century, progressive literature by and about women moved on to other issues. In other words, changes in footbinding preceded rather than followed the main wave of reform [on other "issues of female emancipation"]. . . .

The defeat of China in the Opium War in 1842 led to the opening of treaty ports to foreign nationals and to the influx of missionaries and Western ideas. Chinese intellectuals began to argue that China needed reforms to avoid further humiliating defeat. At first, intellectuals argued for technological innovations and modern weapons, which were introduced between 1860 and 1894. Following China's defeat by the Japanese in 1895, intellectuals began to focus on the need to make social, cultural, and political reforms as well. A national reform movement emerged in the late 1890s and included the abolition of footbinding and the improvement of the status of women among its goals. The reform movement spread its message mainly through periodicals and study societies. Male reformers argued that improvements in women's status were a necessary part of their program for national self-strengthening. . . .

Three groups were involved in the initial campaigns against footbinding in China: 1) the Western missionary effort aimed at Chinese Christians; 2) a Western-led campaign focused on non-Christian Chinese elites; and 3) a Chinese-led campaign focused on non-Christian Chinese elites. The missionaries were the first to launch an organized campaign against footbinding when Reverend Jon Macgowan of the London Missionary Society founded the first anti-footbinding society in 1874. In 1895, ten women of different nationalities, led by Mrs. Archibald Little, the wife of a British merchant, founded the *T'ien tsu hui* (Natural Foot Society), a non-denominational umbrella organization. The first Chinese-initiated Anti-Footbinding Societies were set up in 1883 and again in 1895, but local opposition led to their collapse. In 1897, K'ang Kuang-jen and Liang Ch'i-ch'ao founded the *Pu'ch'an-tsu hui* (Anti-footbinding Society), China's largest non-Christian anti-footbinding organization, which later established branches in other cities and had a membership of 300,000.

Each of the three actors took a characteristic approach to the issue. The missionary approach was more aggressive and moralistic. Missionary schools promoted "natural feet" by first . . . offering scholarships only to girls with unbound feet, and later by refusing entry to girls with bound feet. The missionary schools focused their attention on Christian converts, usually non members of the Chinese elite. But perhaps the most innovative technique of the anti-footbinding society was to take on directly one social issue at the core of footbinding. Chinese families feared that daughters with unbound feet were unmarriageable. So the members of anti-footbinding societies pledged both not to bind the feet of their daughters, and to marry their sons only to women with unbound feet. Teachers in missionary schools also took responsibility for arranging marriages for their students with unbound feet. . . .

Mrs. Little's Natural Foot Society focused on influencing powerful officials and non-Christian Chinese women "of wealth and fashion," thus partially divorcing the issue from the Christian context. . . .

One of the first activities of the Natural Foot Society was to send a petition to the Dowager-Empress, inscribed in gold letters on white satin, enclosed in a silver casket, and signed by "pretty well every foreign lady in the Far East at that time." Although none of the original founders of the Natural Foot Society could read Chinese, they immediately began an outreach campaign, holding meetings and translating materials into Chinese. They even had long debates about which dialect of Chinese would be most appropriate. "We knew, of course . . . that feet are the most risque subject of the conversation in China. . . . In the end we took refuge in the dignified Wenli of the Chinese classics, confident that thus anti-footbinding would be brought with as great decorum as possible before the Chinese public." The Natural Foot Society also had a policy of getting their Chinese advisors to approve all their literature prior to publication to avoid any cultural or linguistic mistakes. . . .

Although most of the initial financial support, as well as labor power, came from foreigners, by 1908, the Natural Foot Society set up by Mrs. Little and her associates was operating entirely under the leadership of Chinese women, who continued the vigorous campaign. The foreign leaders of the Society argued in 1907 that it was "high time to trust the movement more to Chinese direction." This transfer from foreign to domestic leadership serves as a mark of the success of the campaign.

The Natural Foot Society attempted to turn the tide against footbinding among influential Chinese through lobbying, publications, speaking engagements, petitions, essay competitions, and submitting materials to local newspapers. A 1907 letter summarizing the work of the Natural Foot Society discusses 162 recorded meetings in thirty-three different cities, some with as many as 2,000 people present; over a million tracts, leaflets, and placards printed and circulated from the Shanghai office alone; as well as letters to the editor, and prize competitions for the best essays against binding. The Chinese anti-footbinding societies focused in particular on shifting ideas and on encouraging families opposed to footbinding to marry their sons to natural-footed girls. . . .

Only sixteen years passed between the formation of the first umbrella organization to the 1911 ban against footbinding; this is very rapid progress in the history of transnational campaigns. A corresponding behavioral change evolved slowly but surely. A source indicates that, in 1905, 70 percent of female children still had their feet bound. But by 1912, one of the missionaries described footbinding as "doomed" and "a social practice now on the wane and destined in course of time to disappear." The only systematic study of the practice, a 1929 study of a region to the south of Peking, shows very dramatic change over a short period of time: "99.2% of those born prior to 1890 had bound feet, only 59.7% of those born between 1905 and 1909, and 19.5% of those born from 1910 to 1914, had bound feet; no new cases at all were found among those born after 1919." . . .

The most in-depth treatment of the anti-footbinding movement concludes that it should be seen as part of a reform movement carried on "as a result of contact with the west." The campaign appeared to form a pattern characteristic of modern networks, where both foreign and domestic actors were crucial to the success of the campaign, with foreign actors instrumental in "first rolling the stone" and domestic actors leading the way for framing the issue in ways that resonated with the domestic audiences, and generating broad-based support necessary for the success of the movement. . . .

Although the anti-footbinding movement was initiated by foreign women, it was embraced by nationalist intellectuals and reformers. In China, footbinding became associated with nationalist reform sentiment that was both anti-feudal and anti-foreign. In the context of the military defeat by foreigners, improving the status of women and ending footbinding were seen as tools to modernize and strengthen China so it could resist foreign intervention. "Although missionaries and reformers differed in their ultimate goals—national salvation and religious conversion, they shared a common strategy—social reform, of which women's emancipation was an important part." Furthermore, "[n]ot until such efforts were perceived as Chinese phenomena in a nationalistic context did a majority of Chinese . . . espouse them. . . . [T]he Foreign and Christian roots of the anti-footbinding campaign had to be renounced in order for victory to be achieved. Yet Western women laid many of the foundations for the eradication of footbinding." . . .

Every campaign to change practices of this sort is a struggle about redefining the meaning of the practice. This is why foreign or international actors alone rarely succeed in changing embedded practices, because they do not understand how to frame debates in convincing and accessible way for the domestic audience. The Chinese reformers who were at the forefront of the anti-footbinding campaign used very different arguments than the ones used by the foreign missionaries, and yet their messages resonated better with the prevailing discourse of the time in China. The message was an unusual blend of appeals to modernity and tradition. For example, Chinese intellectuals stressed that footbinding was contrary to the ancient way of doing things, and that the Chinese classics offered no mention or words of praise for footbinding. Thus, to eradicate a traditional practice, intellectuals appealed to even more ancient tradition. They referred to issues of filial piety, stressing that footbinding damaged the body, a gift from one's parents, and that "natural footed woman could buy medicine for a sick parent in less time than it took a bound foot woman." Yet at the same time, reformers referred to international public opinion when they pointed out that the custom "became the laughing stock of foreigners."

In the context of military defeat, the connection that Chinese reformers made between footbinding and weakness, and between individual weakness and the collective weakness of the country, appears to have been a powerful rhetorical device in opposition to binding. Ironically, one of the more successful arguments against footbinding was a then popular, but scientifically erroneous one, based on the idea of acquired traits, leading to the claim that not only would women with bound feet be unable to resist foreign invaders, but that they would pass on weakness to their sons. The argument is factually incorrect, but it illustrates the broader point of the importance of the meaning that ideas take on within a particular political, cultural, and historical context.

IV. Breast Implants: Female Breast Mutilation?

Karen J. Carlson, M.D., Stephanie A. Eisenstat, M.D. & Terra Ziporyn, Ph.D., *Breast Implants and Enlargement*

in THE NEW HARVARD GUIDE TO WOMEN's HEALTH ISSUES 105–108 (2004)

Over a million women in the United States have silicone or saline breast implants, most of which were placed for the purpose of enlarging their breasts. Some women choose to have implants because they are unhappy with their breast size, while others want to enlarge breasts that have shrunk after childbearing or to enlarge one breast that is smaller than the other. It is important to recognize that this kind of surgery—as opposed to breast reconstruction . . . , which is sometimes performed in cancer patients after mastectomy—is designed to improve the appearance of otherwise healthy breasts.

The implant itself is a plastic pouch made of a combination of carbon, hydrogen, oxygen, and silicon and filled with either silicone gel or a saline (saltwater) solution. Although there has been considerable controversy surrounding the safety of silicone gel-filled breast implants, a number of recent studies suggest that earlier fears about health risks are mostly unwarranted. Nonetheless, only saline-filled implants are currently approved for cosmetic uses. . . .

How are these procedures performed?

During the surgery for breast enlargement, a pocket is created for the implant through a small incision. The incision can be located in the crease under the breast, around the areola, or in the armpit. The implant is inserted through this incision and placed behind the breast tissue to push it forward, thereby enlarging the breast. Usually the implant is placed behind the pectoral muscle in the chest wall. . . . Since the breast tissue itself is pushed forward, much of it remains accessible to physical examination and mammography. Additional incisions for a breast lift may be required if the breast is especially saggy. Implants alone will not correct significant sag.

What happens after the surgery?

Breast enlargement is often a day surgery procedure, even though general anesthesia may be required. A woman can expect her breasts to be sore and swollen for a week or so, and often black and blue, though excessive bruising, swelling, pain, redness, or firmness is abnormal. Some surgeons use drains to help decrease blood accumulation and discoloration. Vigorous physical activities will be restricted for several weeks while healing takes place. Some surgeons suggest using a special brassiere for a period of time after surgery.

The breasts should become softer during the first several months after surgery, although they may always be firmer than natural breasts. Sensory changes that occur with that surgery tend to be temporary but may become permanent. In some cases, these changes might affect sexual response to breast stimulation during the healing process or even thereafter. Massage may be recommended to enhance breast softness or to help sensory changes resolve more quickly. Enlargement surgery, after everything has healed, should not interfere with exercise or breastfeeding.

What are the risks and complications?

In qualified hands, breast enlargement surgery is a safe procedure with a low complication rate. It is essential, however, to seek a surgeon who is certified by the American Board of Plastic Surgeons.

Anyone considering breast enlargement needs to understand clearly what the surgery involves. There are certain potential complications connected with any type of surgery, while other complications are specific to surgery using implants.

All surgery requires some kind of anesthesia. A woman undergoing elective surgery should make sure that the anesthesia team and the operative facility are appropriately credentialed.

Bleeding is also a risk with almost any operation. During breast enlargement surgery a number of small blood vessels are exposed. If one of these vessels begins to bleed after the operation, it may cause a local accumulation of blood under the tissues. Such bleeding, called hematoma formation, is rare. It is also not life-threatening, though a second operation for drainage may be required.

All types of breast enlargement surgery require incisions, and all incisions leave scars, though some surgical techniques leave smaller or less conspicuous scars than others. Certain skin types, too, are more prone to developing particularly prominent scars. Scarring depends on an individual's genetic healing tendencies, not just on the skill of the surgeon. It is a good idea to discuss scarring in detail with the surgeon before making any final decisions. [The authors later refer to "keloid scarring" as a "related entry."]

The more complicated process of using natural tissues is not generally recommended for cosmetic breast enlargement; these operations rely solely on the use of artificial material. Infections, while uncommon during elective operations, can be a particular problem when artificial materials are involved. Once an infection settles around an implant, it is hard to get rid of. Usually an infected implant has to be removed in order for the infection to be controlled. The implant can be replaced at a later time after the infection has cleared up. Antibiotics are given around the time of surgery to minimize the chances of infection, and meticulous attention is paid to maintaining sterile conditions.

Also, no artificial material should be considered permanent: the human lifespan is longer than the useful life of most products made by human hands. If one lives long enough, sooner or later the implant shell will lose its strength and integrity. When this happens, the material inside the implant pouch will leak out. With saline implants, a hole or a tear in the pouch will allow all the saline inside to leak out (like water from a water balloon) and the implant will deflate. This is not dangerous, but it certainly could be inconvenient and embarrassing. If the implant deflates, it must be replaced, requiring additional surgery, though nothing as extensive as the original operation. In the past, saline implants had a significantly higher leakage rate than did silicone, but this problem seems to be less frequent with current versions.

Although silicone gel-filled implants are no longer used for cosmetic breast enlargement, they were quite common in the past, and many women still have them in place. A tear or rupture in a silicone gel implant causes the gel to escape from the shell. But since silicone gel is thick and does not migrate very rapidly, it is often not evident that a silicone gel implant is leaking. Small leaks can sometimes be felt as lumps in the breast as the body surrounds the gel with scar tissue. Any lump, however, needs to be taken seriously even if a woman has implants in place. A lump may be a silicone leak, but it could also be a breast cancer.

Concerns about whether leakage and breakdown of the implants containing silicone gel can lead to certain autoimmune or connective tissue diseases have largely been laid to rest by numerous scientific studies, although one large study did find a slight increase in self-reported connective tissue disease in women with silicone implants. Even so, because juries in several well-publicized cases awarded damages to women who claimed that breast implants led to autoimmune disorders—diseases that occur when the body produces antibodies that attack its own tissues—the Food and Drug Administration in 1992 banned further placement of silicone implants until their safety could be reviewed. The ban was subsequently modified to allow these implants to be used for breast reconstruction after mastectomy. The FDA ultimately judged silicone implants to be safe.

Because implants are foreign objects, the body reacts to them by walling them off with scar tissue. Scar tissue has a natural tendency to contract. If the scar tissue contracts excessively, the soft implant will become compressed into a firm ball that may shift in its pocket on the chest wall. This process is called capsule formation or capsular contracture. Implants are less likely to develop capsules if they are placed under the chest wall muscle, if they are saline filled, and if they have a textured surface. A new antibiotic solution that may help reduce or eliminate capsular contracture is under investigation.

Women who have the older silicone gel-filled implants in place experience capsule formation more frequently. Symptoms include firmness, tenderness, tightness, and even pain. Excessive capsule formation can also signal the leakage of silicone gel from the implant. A plastic surgeon experienced with implants can help identify specific problems. Often, a mammogram combined with an ultrasound or an MRI will be required to identify leaks or ruptures. Even if an implant is not leaking or ruptured, the firmness of a capsule may be bothersome. To treat the capsules, surgery is currently recommended to remove the capsule around the implant and replace the implant with a different kind. Squeezing the breast to rupture the capsule is not recommended, since this can actually damage the implant.

Although the capsules may make the breast feel firm or hard, they should not result in distinct masses or nodules. Any woman who feels a distinct mass in her breast should have a biopsy to eliminate the possibility of cancer. Having implants in place does not either increase or decrease a woman's chances of developing breast cancer, but it is important for a woman to undergo screening mammography and physical examination as appropriate for her age. Special mammogram views allow more of the breast tissue to be seen in cases where some of it is obscured by an implant. Investigations are under way to see if magnetic resonance imagining (MRI) may be a more sensitive screening method for women with implants.

Breast biopsies—either needle biopsies or surgical ones—are possible even with implants in place. There is a certain risk of damaging the implant with any biopsy technique, but the consequences of missing an early breast cancer are much more serious. It is desirable to have the biopsy done at a facility that is familiar with implants. If a cancer is detected, the treatment options include mastectomy or lumpectomy followed by radiation therapy. Implants do not react well to radiation, however, and there is a high incidence of complications (especially severe capsule formation and healing problems) when implants are exposed to radiation. A woman facing cancer treatment who wants to keep as much of her breast as possible should consider implant removal. Others might prefer a complete mastectomy with either immediate or delayed breast reconstruction. Breast cancer can be treated adequately in women with implants, but the pros and cons of the different types of treatment need to be weighed.

NOTE

Female Breast Mutilation? In what ways are breast implants similar to FGM? To footbinding? In what ways different? Should laws be passed to ban implants? If you were raised in the North, would you be offended by an African or Asian or Middle-Eastern critique of the practice? Does government permission for this practice mean that Western governments are violating women's human rights?

V. National Legal Approaches: What Works?

As you read the materials about the four countries here—Egypt, Sudan, Ghana, and the United States—what strategies strike you as most effective? Least effective? If you were an attorney advising an international human rights group that sought to ban this practice, what advice would you give them? Consider the type of FGM and the prevalence of the practice in each country.

A. Egypt

FEMALE GENITAL MUTILATION: A GUIDE TO LAWS AND POLICIES WORLDWIDE
140–43 (Anika Rahman & Nahid Toubia eds., 2000)

Egypt

Prevalence of FC/FGM: 97%
Type(s) of FC/FGM most commonly practiced: [WHO] Types II (72%), I (17%) and III (9%).

Criminal Law . . .

Enforcement of the law

Press reports in 1995 and 1996 covered the prosecution of at least 13 individuals—including physicians, midwives and barbers—accused of performing FC/FGM that resulted in complications such as hemorrhage, shock and death.[9] Similar cases were reported in December 1997 and July 1998.[10]

Other Measures: Laws, Regulations and Policies

In 1994, the then Minister of Health, Dr. Ali Abdel Fattah, issued a decree banning the practice of FC/FGM outside of public hospitals. The decree required physicians to discourage parents from having their daughters undergo FC/FGM. If the parents insisted, the procedure was to be carried out by physicians in hospitals. Feminists and human rights activists protested the decree and challenged the policy in administrative court. However, the case was never heard.

---

[9] Cairo Institute for Human Rights Studies, "The Health Minister's Decree Crowns NGOs Efforts," *Sawasiah*, No. 12 Sept. 1996, pp. 8–9.

[10] "Doctor Gets a Year in Jail for Causing Girl's Death," *Associated Press*, Dec. 15, 1997; "Two Doctors Charged with Performing Illegal Female Circumcision in Egypt," *Associated Press*, July 21, 1998.

In 1995, Dr. Abdel Fattah issued a decree reversing the 1994 policy on FC/FGM. On the rationale that Egyptian parents had been successfully convinced to eschew the practice of FC/FGM, the 1995 decree banned physicians from performing FC/FGM in public hospitals. The 1995 decree did not prevent physicians from performing FC/FGM in their private clinics. This was the policy until 1996, when the new Minister of Health, Dr. Ismael Sallam, issued a decree prohibiting FC/FGM for nonmedical purposes. The decree provided:

It is forbidden to perform circumcision on females either in hospitals or public or private clinics. The procedure can only be performed in cases of disease and when approved by the head of the obstetrics and gynecology department at the hospital, and upon the suggestion of the treating physician. Performance of this operation will be considered a violation of the laws governing the medical profession. Nor is this operation to be performed by non-physicians.

Shortly after the decree's issuance, it was challenged in administrative court by proponents of FC/FGM and by medical professionals concerned that the ban would lead to increased clandestine practice of FC/FGM with adverse effects on women's health. The court declared the health minister's decree unconstitutional for infringing upon parliamentary functions and for interfering with the right of physicians to perform surgery.

In December 1997, the highest administrative court overturned the lower court's ruling. In response to proponents of FC/FGM who asserted that Islam requires the practice, the court declared that Islam does not sanction FC/FGM and that the practice is punishable under the Penal Code. It concluded:

With this ruling everybody is banned from performing [female circumcision], even with the proven consent of the girl or her parents, except in cases of medical necessity, which must be determined by the director of the gynecology department in one of the hospitals. Otherwise, all those who do not comply will be subjected to criminal and administrative punishments.

B. Sudan

Female Genital Mutilation: A Guide to Laws and Policies Worldwide
215–17 (Anika Rahman & Nahid Toubia eds., 2000)

Sudan. . . .

Prevalence of FC/FGM: 89%
Type(s) of FC/FGM most commonly practiced: [WHO] Types III (82%), I (15%) and II (3%) [in the North]. . . .

Criminal Law . . .

Provisions

There are currently no Penal Code provisions that explicitly prohibit FC/FGM. The definition of "injury" in Article 138 of the Penal Code, however, is potentially applicable to FC/FGM. Article 138(1) provides:

One who causes the loss of a body part, or the loss of a mental function or sense or organ or limb of a person, or causes a cut or excess blood flow to a person's body has caused injury.

Penalties include fines and/or prison sentences ranging from a maximum of six months to a maximum of five years, depending upon the degree of premeditation on the part of the offender (Arts 139–41).

Enforcement of the law

Some FC/FGM practitioners have reportedly been placed under arrest.[6] Further information on the legal bases of these arrests and the penalties imposed, if any, is unavailable.

Other Measures: Laws, Regulations and Policies

Government health authorities have sanctioned traditional birth attendants and village midwives who participate in FC/FGM. Offenders have had their midwifery kits confiscated and been placed under close supervision.[7]

In 1984, the Minister of the Interior and Social Welfare established, by resolution, the Organization for Eradication of Traditional Harmful Practices Affecting the Health of Women and Children (ETHP). The ETHP succeeded the Sudanese National Committee for the Eradication of Female Circumcision, founded in 1981 by a decree of the same ministry. Concurrently with non-governmental organizations, the ETHP conducts workshops, seminars, courses and discussions on FC/FGM, targeting key groups, such as midwives.

Asma Mohammed A'Haleem (or Asma M. Abdel Haleem), author of the next excerpt, is described in the book as a member of the Sudan Bar Association concerned with women's issues, a practicing lawyer before Sudanese courts, a participant in the Arab Lawyers Union's Committee on the Status of Women, and a founder of Women in Law and Development in Africa (WiLDAF).

Asma Mohammed A'Haleem, *Claiming Our Bodies and Our Rights: Exploring Female Circumcision as an Act of Violence in Africa*

in FREEDOM FROM VIOLENCE: WOMEN'S STRATEGIES FROM AROUND THE WORLD 141–56 (Margaret Schuler ed., 1992)

Throughout the African continent women suffer the genital mutilation known as female circumcision. Although deplored as "brutal," "torture" and "mutilation," it has rarely been addressed as a crime or an act of violence. The phenomenon has

---

[6] Inter-African Committee on Traditional Practices Affecting the Health of Women and Children (IAC), "Sudan: Turning Point in the Sensitization Campaign," *Newsletter of the IAC*, No.19, June 1996, p.8.

[7] Ibid.

typically been studied either as a health hazard or as a problem of tradition. In conferences, seminars and workshops throughout Africa, women actively working against the practice have explored in detail the types of female circumcision, prevalence of each type in certain areas, the health hazards associated with it, and the means of eradication, including the use of law.

This paper looks at cultural, religious and legal aspects of female circumcision in Africa with special focus on the Sudan. It considers female circumcision in the context of violence against women and human rights, and identifies the religious and cultural underpinnings of female circumcision. It also addresses law reform and litigation strategies as approaches to eradication.

Female Circumcision: The "Loving" Act of Violence

The practice of female circumcision is shrouded in many cultures under the mystifying guise of "the loving act." Loving parents, they reason, could not commit an act of violence or a crime against their own daughters. It is difficult for many to see the contradiction involved in simultaneously viewing an act as a loving gesture and as brutal torture, infringing on human rights.

A brief description of the ritual may explain this conceptual incongruity. A little girl about six or seven years old is prepared for circumcision. She gets some fine, bright new clothes and shoes. A day or two before circumcision day her friends paint henna on her hands and feet. They have a little party in preparation for the event. On the circumcision day itself she is adorned with *jirtig*, a ritual widely practiced on wedding occasions. An older woman puts jewelry on the girl and winds red silk threads around her wrist. This custom is connected with an old belief that *jirtig* is necessary to drive away evil and keep angels by the side of the betrothed or the circumcised.

The child is then taken to a midwife's house, where most operations take place. In smaller towns a midwife may come to the family's home, especially when a group circumcision is to take place. The family may circumcise several girls from the same family on the same day. The scene on circumcision day, whether in the villages or in the city, is more like a funeral than a party. Despite the new clothes and the bridal appearance, complete with *firka*, a bright silk cloth covering the bride, little girls are not impressed or persuaded. Apparently they all know that some sort of amputation will take place.

Afterwards, a feast is given. It includes men if boys are circumcised on the same day. The size of the feast depends on the financial ability of the family. Amid the tears of the pain-ridden child, festivities go on, and children's tunes are played. The child is told that she will soon be better and should join the festivities. Women relatives and neighbors come to say congratulations, implying that what happened to that little girl calls for celebration; it is a happy event! Those offering felicitations usually give the girl a sum of money, which she is free to spend as she wishes.

Covering up the act of mutilation by creating the appearance of a happy occasion is clever cultural artifice. The cover up also extends to the immediate health consequences; the bleeding, high temperature and physical anguish resulting from difficulty in urinating are attributed to some metaphysical origin. . . .

Mushahara, the word used to explain accompanying complications, means that the *jirtig* was ineffective, or someone carrying bad luck entered the child's house. Rituals contrary to religious tenets are conducted; a girl may be taken on a trip to the Nile where she immerses her feet and washes her face and arms. Usually this trip is arranged as a protective measure. Other rituals include putting an axe under the bed, placing a gold coin such as a British sovereign under the pillow, or in extreme cases a cross, a Christian religious symbol, may be brought into the house. These traditions are so strong that they overcome, even override, religious beliefs.

Somalis, Ethiopians and Egyptians share the same traditions, with only a few subtle differences. In the Sudan the same rituals of *Mushahara* are repeated to treat complications resulting from de-circumcision [defibulation] during childbirth, or infertility after marriage. These rituals have begun to disappear in areas where education levels are higher and where better medical services are available. The ritual of the new clothes, gifts and festivities, that is still practiced, will eventually disappear as a result of economic pressure.

Stripping away the pretense of a happy occasion allows the act of mutilation to be seen for what it is—a crime. In the opinion of Sheikh Abdel Razig, President of Al Azhar Mission in Samal:

This practice is committed against an innocent victim and is a crime, and anyone who perpetrates it should be punished. How can anyone imagine in our present day civilization that a father or a mother would commit such an act against their beloved children. (International Seminar on Female Circumcision, 1988)

If an act of violence is defined as one which causes physical and/or psychological harm to a human being, then there is no doubt that female circumcision is such an act. However, defining it as an act of violence provokes strong reaction. Many hesitate to connect female circumcision with violence because of its deep rooted acceptance in culture and religion. However, justification of the practice on religious or cultural grounds is unacceptable since it causes health hazards which can often be fatal. The allegation that the law cannot help to eradicate female circumcision because of its tenacious cultural roots should also be challenged.

Health workers and others have worked to combat female circumcision and as a result, the tradition is being boldly challenged; it is finally coming "out of the closet." While some people will be shocked when accused of violence, it is necessary to confront them so that they clearly see the senselessness of a tradition that causes grievous damage to women. This makes it difficult for them to deny that female circumcision is harmful.

Cultural and Religious Dynamics

Throughout Africa, Muslim communities practice female circumcision, claiming that it is prescribed by Islam. In fact, female circumcision is a manifestation of the male's need to control women's sexuality, and contributes to the historical subordination of women. Rules and laws have always been made or interpreted by men and used to control women. Despite the fact that in the early days of Islam women, especially the prophet's wives, participated in disseminating Islamic teaching, this soon became a man's job. Women were barred from participating in social life under the guise of protecting them.

Islam is no exception when it comes to gender discrimination, which occurs through male interpretation and application of Islamic rules. Koranic verses and *hadith* or *Sunna* have for hundreds of years been used to dominate or belittle women. Widely accepted *hadiths* stipulating that women are subordinate to men are often used; for example, *hadiths* that affirm that women's religion and minds are diminished or are less developed than men's. "Diminished religion" was the rationale used by the prophet to absolve women from the practice of religious duties during certain times in their lives. They do not pray during menstruation, for example. No explanation is given for the claim of lesser intellectual capability, which almost all modern scholars dispute. . . .

In general, Islam has called for a gradual approach to changing the situation of women. However, some modern scholars think that the methodology of the prophet in correcting the cruel practices should be carried further with regard to women's status, as in the case of slavery. While slavery is sustained in Islam by clear Koranic verses, the prophet Mohamed treated it as a social evil that had to be abolished. This has been the indisputable understanding of Muslim scholars, such that no one would say that slavery is strategic to the Muslim world or that it is allowed. But for women it has been different. Control and subordination of women lie deep in the history of mankind. Holding women up as the symbol of the tribe's or the family's honor, validates the idea of complete control over women in Islam.

Women's Treatment in the Law

The traditional view that a woman is to blame for premarital sex is sustained by Islamic judicial standards. Fornication is regarded as a crime or social evil, and male-oriented social norms and legal rules ordain that prevention lies in controlling women's sexuality. She is not treated as a partner or a joint offender but as the cause of the evil. This happens even though Islamic statutes treat men and women involved in premarital sex as joint offenders. They receive the same punishment and are treated in the same way: an unmarried person is punished by flogging (80 lashes); the married or divorced person is stoned to death.

However equal the norms may appear, application of skewed justice is facilitated by the ease with which a crime may be proven against a woman, but not against a man. If a woman is pregnant and unmarried, her participation in sex will be unmistakable and she will be flogged even when she is the complainant. If she starts criminal proceedings against a man for rape and cannot establish a case against him, he is off the hook. But her pregnancy is irrefutable proof that she committed the crime, and if she is married or divorced she gets the death sentence!

In a recent case (*Sudan Government v. Elhgga El-Husien* 1988) in the Sudan, the accused was originally a complainant who was raped by two men while collecting wood. She was ashamed to mention it, but when she realized she was pregnant, she became afraid of her family and filed the complaint. She was a divorced woman and her pregnancy was found to be concrete evidence against her. The court of first instance found her guilty of fornication and so did the Court of Appeals. She was eventually acquitted by the Supreme Court because there was no evidence to rebut her claim of rape, and if she was raped she could not be guilty of fornication. However, since her acquittal came after three years of imprisonment and she had passed the four-month statute of limitations for establishing proof of rape, she could not pursue her complaint. She spent three years in prison and the men got away.

Convinced that they are a source of shame and that they should submit to male control, women blindly take on the burden of practicing control over their own sexuality. Linking the male interpretation of female sexuality to religion makes male control over females invulnerable to attack and acceptable to women. Female circumcision is one of those traditions tied to religion that takes on the appearance of self-inflicted injury, a pain accepted as God's will. Pious arguments subordinating women and giving full control of their lives to men serve to fortify religious regimes around the world. Some countries even pass legislation prohibiting women from driving cars!

In this religious frame of reference, women are viewed as part of the household responsibilities of the man. The woman's role is to be an obedient wife and satisfy her husband's sexual lusts. Her sexuality does not concern her as much as it concerns her husband. Circumcision is a sure way to keep a woman faithful. The religious guise fits nicely when the contract of marriage is interpreted in this primitive way; that is, the wife provides sexual pleasure in consideration of food, clothing and lodging.

Such a crude interpretation leaves out the bright side of the Islamic concept of marriage: a gentle, solemn and loving relationship between husband and wife. But if the marriage contract is interpreted in primitive terms, then the man has the right to avail himself of the woman on his terms. A woman must obey the rules before and after marriage; dependency drives her to secure a husband by proving her virginity.

The Strategy of Reinterpretation

The debate over a modern interpretation of Islamic rules is going on and may be at its peak. In the words of professor Gerda Lerner [in her book, THE HISTORY OF PATRIARCHY (n.d.)]:

When in that process of struggle, at certain historic moments, the contradictions in their relationship to society and to historical process are brought into the consciousness of women, they are then correctly perceived and named as deprivations that women share as a group. This coming into consciousness of women becomes the dialectical force moving them into action to change their condition and to enter a new relationship to male-dominated society.

Within the legal profession in Muslim countries a female point of view is blossoming. As a group, women are seeking a new interpretation. Disputed *hadiths* are targeted. Most of those disputed *hadiths* were invented to influence political or social life during different eras of Islamic rule and can be challenged on historical and scholarly grounds.

The problem (which also has a positive side) with Islamic interpretation is that not every idea is detailed in the seminal books; only general principles from which norms are extrapolated. Thus, if a principle seems to suggest that women are to be under the protection of men, men come up with practical ideas and rules to achieve that goal and strengthen the notion of control. The positive dimension of this approach to formulating regulations is that women may use the same method to secure just rules. Since the general tenets of Islam are just and tend toward equality, such a strategy seems plausible. The idea that women are intellectually inferior, for example, may be easily defeated on the grounds that Islam equated men and women in punishment in this world and on the last day. . . .

A reinterpretation of a *hadith* or principle suggesting that women are to be under the protection of men does not directly address female circumcision, but it does challenge the traditional view of male-female relationships, and attitudes toward women and their role in society. In Islam, the process of introducing new and creative ideas and thoughts for the reinterpretation of existing principles, or deriving new interpretations to address emerging issues within a society, is referred to as *Ijtihad*. An example of where *Ijtihad* could be applied with regard to female circumcision are to those principles pertaining to the contract of marriage and the sexual relations between husband and wife. Instead of placing importance only on a man's sexual desires and considering the role of a woman to be one of fulfilling them, equal importance should be given to a woman's sexual desires and needs. One interpretation of a principle defined a marriage contract as the husband having the right to his wife's sexual organs. By acknowledging that both partners have the right to derive pleasure out of a sexual relationship, the issue of a woman having domain over her own body would also be addressed.

Many reinterpretations come into existence gradually; an undesirable tradition is abolished step-by-step. An example of this is the change in the laws governing marriage. From the 1940s to the 1960s, Sudanese rules governing marriage stated that a woman was obliged to marry a partner chosen by her guardian. As a first step, women pushed to have this rule changed so that the guardian only had the right to marry off a minor without her consent. Later, women gained the right to void a marriage without consent. The contract of marriage nevertheless continues to be between two men, the guardian and the husband. In order to obtain a final reinterpretation of marriage laws, one that gives equal importance to both marriage partners, women will have to continue to push for their rights.

With regard to abolishing female circumcision, it is important that there be a final religious announcement clearly stating that it is a form of mutilation and therefore forbidden. It is not sufficient for religion to shun female circumcision, for that may be construed by those who promote its practice as tacit approval. Instead, religion should be used as a tool for condemning and preventing its occurrence. Here, the participation of women in the reinterpretation will be crucial.

The problem with correcting such practices and interpretations within the religious mainstream is the terrorism that accompanies reform. The rigid few who enjoy control over the public at large will soon depict reformers as heretics who want to change religion for the purpose of abolishing it. Islamic history is full of persecution of reformers. Rulers brandishing such terrorism usually subdue and punish reformers. . . .

Under the religious reign of terror people are afraid to dispute issues connected with religion. Control over any behavior in Muslim society is assured if religion provides the rationale. It not only gives men the right to control, but easily passes the burden of that control on to women themselves, who share the idea with men that they should be obedient if they are to attain paradise in the next world.

Reversing Traditional Attitudes

Tradition is another cornerstone sustaining female circumcision in African countries. In most communities it is a tradition that became entrenched because of its fusion to religion. The official religious stand in most African countries seems to be that infibulation is forbidden and religion is against it. Yet one type of female circumcision, excision, is condoned by religious leaders, again because someone cleverly tied it to Islam through a *hadith*. The tradition flourishes because its condemnation by Islam is weak and unenthusiastic.

It is doubtful that this tradition is accepted in most African countries as an affirmation of cultural identity, rendering the groups that practice it different from others. Other traditions kept for identification purposes are disappearing without great fuss; for example, face marks used by different tribes. . . . Curiously, male influence played an important role in effecting the change; as men's attitudes toward beauty changed, women quickly threw away the tradition. Songs that used to praise a woman with a marked face were countered with ones praising an unmarked face. Chances of marriage are far better now for a woman with unmarked face.

Men are not playing the same role in eradicating circumcision since they are also trapped in the tradition. It is not just a question of a woman's virginity, it is also a test of the man's virility. Masculinity, manhood and virility are proved by achieving the difficult act of penetrating the circumcised woman. Men who are not afraid of religious fanaticism may be afraid of social criticism; they don't want to be considered incompetent men.

The tradition also seems to be difficult to eradicate because it has the appearance of violence inflicted by women themselves.

They insist on it mostly to secure a husband and get the respect of the community, even if they do not get married. Again, it is a male-dominated society that prescribes the conditions of respectability for women. But the fallacy is being exposed mainly by women. The demands of development call for healthier women who can produce more food and participate effectively in enhancing the economic life of the community. Unfortunately, the psychological factor still remains; people want to keep their ancestral heritage.

Legal Strategies for Eradicating Female Circumcision

Law Reform

In spite of its known harmful effects, there is still reluctance in some circles to make a "direct" attack on female circumcision. But viewing it as an act of violence that inflicts bodily injury allows the law to be used as a recourse. The achievements of eradication advocates and women's active role in this effort have brought female circumcision to light as an unsafe and undesirable practice. Application of the law to punish and/or hold liable for compensation those who practice female circumcision is the next step.

Tony B.E. Ogiamen, a lecturer at the University of Benin, Nigeria, expressed the view that gradual eradication of female circumcision "[c]an be made possible if those who carry out the procedure are legally identified, officially recognized and given quasi-professional status." Legal sanction for any type of female circumcision would create more problems. Legal recognition provides the perfect medium for the practice to flourish. In the Sudan, midwives and even doctors who were expressly prohibited by law from practicing infibulation continued to do so secretly under the pretense that they performed the *Sunna* type. Naming it *Sunna* sanctioned it as religiously required. Legally recognized practitioners may give the impression that female circumcision is legal if practiced by them. If the law is to be used to prevent and eradicate . . . female circumcision, the practice must be clearly prohibited. Although female circumcision will not disappear immediately, even a gradual process of disappearance has to be framed within clear legal norms.

The experience of the Sudan and Kenya has often been cited to prove the ineffectiveness of law in the process of eradication. Such laws were rejected in both countries because they represented a colonialist attempt to control and oppress people's lives. When perceived in this way, such laws are doomed to failure.

In Kenya, the campaign against the law prohibiting female circumcision was tied to the struggle for independence. Any law imposed by the British was regarded as a tool for the British to control people's lives and tell them what was good for them. It was also regarded as an effort by the British to tarnish or weaken their traditional base. This strengthened the loyalty of the various tribes to their traditions, irrespective of whether or not the tradition was causing harm to members of their society.

In the Sudan, laws passed by the colonial government were viewed as a means of sending people to jail. In 1946, the British Administration added an amendment to Section 284(A) of the Sudanese Penal Code stating that anyone found guilty of committing female circumcision which was not of the *Sunna* type would be punished with up to five years imprisonment and/or fine. At that time, many Sudanese were not prepared for such a law and it was regarded by those leading the struggle for independence as a way of terrorizing the people. . . .

Section 284(A) of the Sudanese Penal Code remains a dead issue after more than 15 years of independence. It is clear that from the beginning, Section 284(A) never had a chance. The application of that section to punish female circumcision practitioners was made difficult, or for some people impossible, on procedural grounds. . . .

Linking Legal Awareness with Litigation

Laws cannot be effective if people are unaware of them. . . . Awareness of protective and preventive laws is increasing in Africa as a result of harsh government penalties for ignorance of the law. But complete awareness by the people of the existence of a law should never be presumed.

One effective way to create awareness is to educate people about laws that already exist. It is more practical to make people aware of an existing fact, than to make them aware of the hope that such a fact may soon take place. For example, in the case of female circumcision, prevention of the crime must be linked to knowledge of the prohibition. Practitioners need to be aware of the interdiction; since it affects them directly, they will pass the information on to all those who seek their skills to perform female circumcision. The sanction for noncompliance should be harsh, such as revoking the practitioner's license.

If existing laws do not directly address female circumcision, it may be possible to interpret them in a way that includes the concept. For example, Section 284(A) was abolished in 1983 when new laws, claimed to be based on Islamic law, were passed, eliminating explicit sanctions to female circumcision. Yet the sections included in the 1983 Penal Code regarding bodily injury may be interpreted to include female circumcision. Section 287 punished any intentional amputation with *Gisas*, amputation of the same part of the body of the convicted, or *Dia*, compensation for the victim. If the amputation caused inability to perform coitus (intercourse) it was punishable. Apparently the section was intended to address the ability of an injured male, but since it does not expressly state this, it can be applied to any person. While the strategy has not yet been pursued, perhaps provoking a dispute over the interpretation of this section may be enough to bring about an express section that deals with female circumcision as an offense. The same argument may be used with other penal codes that punish bodily injury.

A new penal code was introduced in the Sudan in March 1991. . . . Although there is no specific section addressing the issue of female circumcision, Section 138 of the new penal code defines injury as the amputation of an organ, rendering the mind or one of the senses dysfunctional, or causing cuts or wounds to the body. Female circumcision can be classified as a criminal act under this section. The lack of attention given to female circumcision by lawmakers may be due to declining pressure from groups and individuals who advocate its eradication.

Alternative Strategies

There appears to be a general belief among many activists that the law on its own is mostly ineffective when it deals with a practice that is tied to tradition. The Sudanese Paper in the October 1984 workshop on female circumcision held in Khartoum expressed the following view:

> First, it is extremely difficult if not impossible for legislation to wipe out such a deeply rooted tradition as female circumcision. Second and more important, laws and other similar measures do not give due consideration to such factors as the political climate and the socio-cultural way

of life of the communities concerned. Finally, if it is deemed necessary to introduce laws to combat a sensitive custom such as female circumcision, a genuine attempt must be made to grasp the full socio-psychological implications of these laws in order to avoid their undesirable results or unintended consequences.

When we discuss the role of the law in female circumcision most of the time it is done in the criminal context. However, the problem may also be dealt with by a civil action or even a constitutional action. The issue may be treated as one of human rights, the right to be protected from violation by others. Female circumcision is just one of the vehicles for the control of females, and should be treated as an infringement of a basic right.

Civil law preserves the right of a child to seek civil remedy, when she or he attains puberty, for harm done during childhood. If a woman has the right to sue when she is a grown up person, this may be a deterrent to the practitioner. A woman who would not execute a judgment against her parents still will have no problem executing it against a midwife. Knowing that may discourage midwives. Women successfully sued to enforce their right to refuse compulsory marriage. If supported by law women would more likely stand up for their rights. Although few resorted to court in the case of compulsory marriage, the majority benefitted from those who did: because families became afraid of having daughters go to court, the practice of compulsory marriage subsided. Similarly, knowing that their husbands have no right to beat them, women have resorted to police action in most African countries.

Calls for eradication of female circumcision voiced in conferences and publications seem to agree on the falsity of religious sanction of the tradition. They call for legal action against perpetuators. To move the struggle forward we cannot shy away from identifying female circumcision as an injury, a harmful bodily interference, and a violent act that should be punished just as any other crime. It should not be treated, as one woman said, the way we treat cigarette smoking, i.e., as a harmful act and health hazard. It should be treated as drug abuse, i.e., punishable despite the fact that it is self-inflicted. Moreover, religions should champion the attack on female circumcision, rather than remain silent or merely proclaim their guiltlessness. Religion should put its full weight to [the] cause of prevention.

C. Ghana

FEMALE GENITAL MUTILATION: A GUIDE TO LAWS AND POLICIES WORLDWIDE
164–66 (Anika Rahman & Nahid Toubia eds., 2000)

Ghana. . . .

Prevalence of FC/FGM: 30%
Type(s) of FC/FGM most commonly practiced: [WHO] Type II. . . .

Criminal Law

In 1994, the Parliament of Ghana amended the Criminal Code to make FC/FGM a criminal offense.

Provisions

The 1994 legislation created Article 69A of the Criminal Code, which provides:

(1) Whoever excises, infibulates or otherwise mutilates the whole or any part of the labia minora, labia majora and the clitoris of another person commits an offence and shall be guilty of a second degree felony and liable on conviction to imprisonment of not less than three years.
(2) For purposes of this section, "excise" means to remove the prepuce, the clitoris and all or part of the labia minora; "infibulate" includes excision and the additional removal of the labia majora.

Enforcement of the law

The law is reportedly being enforced. In March 1995, an eight-day-old girl was brought into a public hospital bleeding profusely after having undergone FC/FGM. After the incident was reported in the press, police arrested and charged the practitioner and the infant's parents. In another incident in June 1998, a practitioner of FC/FGM was sentenced to three years in prison for having performed the procedure upon three girls. While the girls—aged between 12 and 15 years—had given their consent to the procedure, it was performed without their parents' knowledge.

Other Measures: Laws, Regulations and Policies

The Ministry of Health has issued the National Reproductive Health Service Policy and Standards (RHSPS), which explicitly discourages FC/FGM. The RHSPS also advocates numerous strategies to stop FC/FGM, including: integration of FC/FGM-related services into all ongoing reproductive health services and activities, and into the school health education programs; encouragement of community involvement; training of service providers; and building a database on harmful traditional practices. In addition, the RHSPS calls for enforcement of the 1994 law prohibiting FC/FGM; the establishment of information, education and communication programs; and the provision of full medical services for those who have undergone FC/FGM. The RHSPS advocates cooperation among law enforcement officers, medical personnel, teachers, government officials, peer counselors, traditional rulers, religious bodies, opinion leaders and *wanzams* (circumcisors).

Fitnat Naa-Adjeley Adjetey, *Female Genital Mutilation: Tradition or Torture?*
57–59, 61–62 (May 2, 1994) (unpublished LL.M. thesis, Georgetown University Law
  Center) (on file with author)

The [Ghanaian] Constitution talks about the protection of right to life and protecting personal liberty. Article 15(2) proclaims that no person shall be subject to torture or cruel, inhuman or degrading treatment or punishment or any other condition that detracts from dignity and worth as a human being.

A prohibition is placed on discrimination on the grounds of gender and the Constitution gives Parliament the power to enact laws that are reasonably necessary for implementation of policies and programs aimed at redressing social, economic or educational imbalances in the Ghanaian society. FGM is discriminatory treatment of women on the basis of their gender and the Ghanaian parliament is thus under a duty to pass legislation banning FGM, so as to redress the social imbalance created by the practice of FGM.

Article 26(1) of the Constitution entitles every person to enjoy, practice, profess, maintain and promote any culture, language, tradition or religion subject to the provisions of the Constitution. Article 26(2) however, goes on to say that "all customary practices which dehumanize or are injurious to the physical and mental well-being of a person are prohibited." This article alone is sufficient to constitute a ban on FGM in Ghana. This means that the argument, that FGM is an important part of the culture of the tribes that practice it, will not hold. FGM is a dehumanizing customary practice and is injurious to the physical and mental well-being of the females that undergo it. Thus, the Constitution prohibits FGM.

The Constitution goes on to give a right of application to the High Court for redress, to any person who alleges that a provision of this Constitution, on the fundamental human rights and freedoms, has been, or is being or is likely to be contravened in relation to him. This is the mechanism for redress, provided under the Constitution, through which victims of FGM can process their claims, in that rights which they are entitled to under the Constitution have been, are being or are likely to be infringed upon. The High Court in such a case may issue such directions or orders as it may consider appropriate for the purposes of enforcing or securing the enforcement of any of the provisions on the fundamental human rights and freedoms to the protection of the applicant. An aggrieved person who is dissatisfied with the decision of the High Court may appeal to the Court of Appeal with a right of further appeal to the Supreme Court. Thus, a would-be victim of FGM can obtain a court order prohibiting anyone from performing the operation on her. A victim of FGM can also obtain a declaration from the courts, stating that the FGM operation is an infringement of the rights of women enshrined in the Constitution.

Thus, the Ghanaian constitution makes provisions for the protection of women and children from FGM. FGM is cruel and deprives a woman of her dignity as a person and is therefore contrary to article fifteen of the constitution. This form of mutilation deprives a woman of her sexuality, the enjoyment of which men are not deprived, and therefore constitutes discrimination against her on the basis of her gender. FGM goes on unabated because the women who practice it are unaware of the far reaching health risks involved. This is partly because traditional ideas of women have denied many women access to education and healthcare facilities that would make them aware of the detrimental effects of FGM. It is therefore the duty of the Ghanaian Parliament to pass laws necessary to redress the social, economic and educational imbalances that allow FGM to be practiced. . . .

FGM is a practice that treats women as chattel. This is because it is used ostensibly [to] ensure a woman's virginity at marriage and to ensure that she gets a brideprice upon marriage. It denies a woman her fundamental human rights and the dignity of the human person. The Ghanaian courts concluded that the custom in which men had a right to marry their dead brothers' wives [widow inheritance] was discriminatory against women and showed no respect for their fundamental human rights. As such, this practice could not under modern conditions be considered as part of the customary law. Without a doubt, the same Ghanaian courts will find the cruel, inhuman, and degrading treatment that victims of FGM have to endure even more abhorrent. Very clearly the custom or tradition of FGM cannot be upheld in view of the [Ghana Court of Appeals] decision in *Akorninga v. Akawagre* [(1987–1988) GLRD 101, the case refusing to uphold the custom of widow inheritance].

Dr. O. Y. Asamoah, *[Ghana] Criminal Code (Amendment) Bill: Memorandum*
(Feb. 9, 1994)

The object of this Bill is to amend the Criminal Code, 1960 (Act 29) to include in the Code the new offence of female circumcision.

The Ghana Law Reform Commission at the instance of the Ghanaian Association for Women's Welfare conducted extensive research into the traditional practice of female circumcision. The practice is carried out in certain parts of the country.

The health hazards affect every part of the victim's life. These may be immediate, intermediate or late. They may occur at consummation of marriage, at delivery of the first born child or may be post-natal.

A survey of public opinion was conducted through the district assemblies and religious bodies nationwide. The conclusion was unanimous that the abhorrent traditional practice should cease to exist.

Article 39 of the Constitution provides in part that "The State shall ensure that
. . . traditional practices which are injurious to the health and well-being of a person shall be abolished".

The amendment creates an offence and seeks to penalise any person who carries out female circumcision on another person.

It has been emphasized by the Law Reform Commission and elsewhere that the abolition of female circumcision by force of law though it may deter some practitioners may not eradicate it due to the deep traditional belief in the custom. In order to achieve any realistic impact on the problem other means in addition to legislation have to be found. It has to be acknowledged that it is only through education that the tradition, superstitions and general life style of the people can be changed, but nonetheless it is incumbent on government to proscribe the practice by legislation.

DR. O.Y. ASAMOAH
Acting Attorney-General and Minister for Justice

[Ghana] Law Reform Commission, *Abolishing Dehumanizing Customary Practices: Female Genital Mutilation*
(Report No. 2), October 1997

A number of Human Rights Instruments including the African Charter on the Rights and Welfare of the Child, CEDAW, the UN Convention on the Rights of the Child etc. prohibit harmful traditional practices which are detrimental to the health of a child. The 1992 Constitution of Ghana also prohibits such practice in Article 26 (2).

Ghana therefore took a bold step forward by introducing legislation to ban [FGM] in 1994. The Criminal Code (Amendment) Act, 1994, Act 484 includes in the Code, the offence of Female Circumcision, and a person convicted of the offence is liable on conviction to imprisonment to a term of not less than three years. There is no option of a fine.

Since the promulgation of the law, a number of successes have been achieved through nationwide education, review of professions of former circumcisers etc. These were achieved through the joint efforts of the NCWD [National Council on Women and Development], Ministries of Health, Education, Social Welfare, Ghana Association for Women's Welfare (GAWW—the national committee of IAC [Inter-African Committee]), UNFPA [United Nations Population Fund], The 31st December Women's Movement, The Ghana Red Cross Society, Muslim Family Counseling Services, etc.

However, there are still certain strategies which need to be taken in order to achieve full implementation of Act 484. . . .

It is important to note that Ghana's law is aimed primarily at the circumcisers who can be easily identifed and targeted. Even though the law has reduced the incidence among the practitioners, it was noted in the media that shortly after the promulgation of the law, some girls went to neighbouring countries to have themselves mutilated.

Due to the refusal of local circumcisers to perform the operation, reports from NGO's in the field revealed that some [parents contacted] circumcisers . . . from Togo or Burkina Faso to perform operations here in Ghana.

There have also been open calls of defiance by parents in the media that they would continue to subject their children to the practice. There is also a campaign by some practitioners in other countries advocating [f]or the medicalisation of the practice.

Law enforcement officers were therefore thwarted in their efforts since such people absconded after the operation and parents who connived in the act could not be arrested due to the narrow confines of the law. A number of people were therefore arrested by the police however short of putting them before the courts.

In Ghana, areas where FGM is practised have cultural roots which are far from the capital, Accra and rather close to neighbouring countries. However, the nation is mindful of the fact that harmful practices of any sector of the society impede the progress of the entire nation.

It is however pleasing to note that Burkina Faso currently has a law in operation which prohibits FGM.

In order for effective harmonisation of laws in the sub-region, it is interesting to note what is in operation in some of our neighbouring countries.

Burkina Faso

Under Article 380 of the Penal Code of Burkina Faso, anyone who performs any such operation is liable to imprisonment for a term ranging from 6 months to 3 [years] and a fine of 150,000 to 900,000 CFA or either of the two. The operations include infibulation, excision or partial removal of the labia majora and the labia minora.

In case of death the punishment is a term of imprisonment ranging from 2 years to 5 years.

Article 381

In cases of a doctor or para-medical performing the operation, such person is subject to a maximum term of imprisonment. His professional licence could also be suspended for a period not exceeding 5 years.

Article 382

Any person having knowledge of the operation is subject to a fine of 50,000–100,000 CFA.

Due to the widespread nature of the practice in Burkina Faso (70% as compared to Ghana's 20%), hot lines have been introduced to inform the police of anyone under the threat of FGM in any family.

Togo

Togo borders Ghana to the east and according to a study carried out in 1996 by the Université du Benin, every one out of eight women in rural Togo is excised.

Togo is still in the Information, Education and Communication stage. It does not have a specific law prohibiting the practice. However, the political will has been acknowledged and it is hoped that in the future, a law would be promulgated for the eradication of the practice.

Côte d'Ivoire

A National Demographic and Health survey carried out in 1994 showed that the practice is prevalent among 43% of the overall population. Even though there appeared to be a reduced rate of FGM amongst younger women, no significant variations occurred between urban and rural rates. Among the Muslim population, the practice was 80% as compared with 15% amongst Protestants and 17% of Catholics.

West African Sub-region

In the West African sub-region, Nigeria, Sierra Leone, Gambia, Mali, Guinea etc. still do not have specific laws banning the practice. However awareness programmes have been put into place for the eradication of the practice. Legislative measures are also being proposed. . . .

Addis Ababa Declaration

A recent symposium organised for legislators by the Inter-African Committee (IAC) in collaboration with the OAU [Organization of African Unity—now, the African Union

(AU)] and the United Nations Economic Commission for Africa, and the African Centre for Women (ACW/ECA) discussed harmful traditional practices in Africa and how to push for further legislative measures to completely abolish the practice.

A declaration adopted at the end of the conference advocated that Governments establish Concrete Mechanisms for the implementation of National Policy and Legislation for the Elimination of All Forms of Violence against women and children. These included strengthening existing structures and creating a conducive environment for the effective enforcement of laws so as to ensure that by the year 2005 the practice of Female Genital Mutilation has been completely eradicated.

African Governments are also being advised to prohibit the medicalisation or paramedicalisaton of all forms of female genital mutilation and other harmful traditional practices.

3.0   Recommendations for the Review of Act 484

3.1   Preventing Medicalisation

It is therefore recommended that in order for Ghana to carry out an effective programme for the eradication of the practice, and to prevent it being used as a ground for clandestine activities, there should be a provision in the law banning "medicalisation or paramedicalisation" of the practice.

3.2   Actions for Effective Elimination of FGM

The law should be also be amended so that families that subject their children to FGM be prosecuted. Thus anyone who aids, abets, counsels or procures the performance by another person of any of these acts on that person's own body or any other persons body, will be liable on summary conviction to a fine or to a term imprisonment.

Since a number of African countries are yet to initiate legislation banning the practice, the courts can also be empowered to initiate supervision orders as a last resort to prevent recalcitrant parents from carrying out a particular act in another country.

3.3   Community Action

Any person having knowledge of the operation should also be subject to a fine. This provision would encourage opinion leaders, chiefs, heads of families, etc. to co-operate for the full implementation of the Law.

4.0   Education

4.1   Establishment of a Co-ordinating Body

It is recommended that due to cultural factors influencing the practice, the support and educational aspect of FGM must be resourced and co-ordinated so as to make the operation of the law meaningful.

It is hoped that with the continued support of the National Population Council, the Ministries of Health, Education, Social Welfare, the Ghana Red Cross Society, NCWD etc., and donor agencies, the practice would be completely eliminated by a set target date.

4.2 Programmes for Intervention

Professionals should seek out responsible community leaders, work with them and assist them in securing the resources needed to initiate health education campaigns for their communities.

Community actions should also target young males and [show] films on the practice . . . to the community. This would help ease the societal pressure and the need for girls to perform the operation on their own.

Midwives should also be made aware of the law and resist any attempts at re-infibulation.

4.3 Legal literacy

Lawyers, social workers, NGOs, religious bodies, etc., should organise strong community outreach programmes that involve individuals, chiefs, etc. to make people aware of laws banning the practice. . . .

N O T E S

Ideal Solution? The proposed revisions in Ghanaian law were not enacted. What is your position on whether FGM should be medicalized? Should the law reach the families themselves in addition to those who perform the procedure? Should the law reach even beyond the families, and extend to the community at large? What are the pros and cons of each of these recommendations?

Changes in the Laws. This 1997 Law Reform Commission report mentions several countries that did not then have specific laws prohibiting FGM, including two of the three states bordering Ghana. Since then, Togo (1998), Côte d'Ivoire (1998), Kenya (2001), Benin (2003), Chad (2003), Niger (2003), and Ethiopia (2004) have adopted such laws.[1] Thus, all three states bordering Ghana—Togo, Burkina Faso, and Côte d'Ivoire—now prohibit the practice.

Ghana's Legislative Process. Ghana was the first independent African state to prohibit FGM. The Law Reform Commission recommended FGM legislation in April 1993, and the executive branch presented the bill to Parliament in February 1994. The Memorandum by Dr. Asamoah, Ghana's Acting Attorney-General and Minister for Justice, summarized the government's case for enacting the legislation. After Parliament acted, the President assented to the bill in August 1994; it entered into effect upon government publication in September 1994.

---

[1] Center for Reproductive Rights, *Female Genital Mutilation (FGM): Legal Prohibitions Worldwide,* Fact Sheet, Item: FO27, March 2007, website link *available at* RossRights.

Constitutional Litigation for Change? Ms. Adjetey, a Ghana lawyer, describes the possibility of suing the government to stop FGM. What rights does the 1992 Ghana Constitution provide that relate to this practice? How does the Ghana Constitution resolve the conflict between culture and rights?

D. United States

FEMALE GENITAL MUTILATION: A GUIDE TO LAWS AND POLICIES WORLDWIDE
237–39 (Anika Rahman & Nahid Toubia eds., 2000)

United States. . . .

Criminal Law

In 1996, Congress passed several legislative measures related to FC/FGM, one of which criminalized the practice. In addition to the federal law, fifteen states have also criminalized FC/FGM. . . .

Legislation on FC/FGM was first introduced in Congress in 1993 by Representative Patricia Schroeder, as part of the Women's Health Equity Act. It did not pass. However, legislation on FC/FGM was enacted as part of the Illegal Immigration Reform and Immigrant Responsibility Act of 1996.[6]

Provisions

Section 116 of the Illegal Immigration and Immigrant Responsibility Act of 1996 follows:

(a) Except as provided in subsection (b), whoever knowingly circumcises, excises, or infibulates the whole or any part of the labia majora or labia minora or clitoris of another person who has not attained the age of 18 years shall be fined under this title or imprisoned not more than 5 years, or both.
(b) A surgical operation is not a violation of this section if the operation is—
(l) necessary to the health of the person on whom it is performed, and is performed by a person licensed in the place of its performance as a medical practitioner; or
(2) performed on a person in labor or who has just given birth and is performed for medical purposes connected with that labor or birth by a person licensed in the place it is performed as a medical practitioner, midwife, or person in training to become such a practitioner or midwife.
(c) In applying subsection (b)(1), no account shall be taken of the effect on the person on whom the operation is to be performed of any belief on the part of that person, or any other person, that the operation is required as a matter of custom or ritual.[7]

At the state level, the following fifteen states have criminalized FC/FGM: California, Colorado, Delaware, Illinois, Maryland, Minnesota, Nevada, New York, North Dakota, Oregon, Rhode Island, Tennessee, Texas, West Virginia and Wisconsin.

---

[6] Illegal Immigration Reform and Immigrant Responsibility Act of 1995, Pub. L.104-208, sec. 645, 110 Stat. 3009-546 (1996).

[7] 18 USCA sect. 116.

Enforcement of the law

To date [2000], there have been no criminal prosecutions at federal or state level. . . .

Other Measures: Laws, Regulations and Policies

In addition to the criminalization of FC/FGM, Congress passed three other legislative measures relating to the practice.

The first law, adopted prior to the criminal law, required the Secretary of Health and Human Services to undertake a study on FC/FGM in the U.S. to determine the population that was at risk.[10] The Department of Health and Human Services (DHHS) commissioned the Centers for Disease Control (CDC) to carry out a study to determine the prevalence of the practice. Using data from the 1990 U.S. Census, the CDC estimated that, in 1990, there were approximately 168,000 girls and women in the country "with or at risk for FC/FGM." The Secretary of DHHS was also required to carry out educational outreach to affected communities and to develop and disseminate recommendations for students in medical and osteopathic schools. . . . DHHS also completed a survey of medical schools, medical osteopathy schools, nursing schools, midwifery schools and schools of social work and has formed a working group with representatives from these schools to work on incorporating FC/FGM into their curricula. DHHS commissioned RAINBO to produce a manual for use by health professionals.

The second legal measure, which was passed as part of the Illegal Immigration Reform and Immigrant Responsibility Act of 1996, requires the Immigration and Naturalization Service (INS), in cooperation with the Department of State, to provide information to immigrants and non-immigrants entering the U.S.A. from countries where FC/FGM is practiced about the harmful effects of FC/FGM and the potential legal consequences of its performance in the U.S.A. The legislation required that the information be compiled and presented in a culturally appropriate manner.[14]

Finally, as part of the fiscal year 1997, Congress enacted legislation requiring the U.S. executive directors of international financial institutions to oppose non-humanitarian loans to countries where FGM is practiced and whose governments have not implemented any educational programs to prevent the practice.[15]

The issue of FC/FGM has also arisen in the context of U.S. asylum law. In 1995 the Office of International Affairs issued the INS Gender Guidelines.[16] Elaborating on the relevant substantive and procedural law, Federal Judges have referred to the Guide-

---

[10] Pub. L. 104-134, Title I, sect. 101(d) [Title V sect. 520] Apr. 26, 1996, 110 Stat. 1321-250; renumbered Title I Pub.L. 104-140, sect. 1(a), May 2, 1996, 110 Stat. 1327 (see 42 USCA sect. 241, Historical and Summary notes (1998 Supp.)).

[14] Pub. L. 104-208, sect. 664, 110 Stat. 3009-546 (1996).

[15] 22 USCS sect. 262k-2 (1996).

[16] Memorandum from Phyllis Coven, INS Office of International Affairs, to All INS Asylum Officers and HQASM Coordinators, Considerations For Asylum Officers Adjudicating Asylum Claims From Women (May 26, 1995), reproduced in Deborah E. Anker, *Women Refugees: Forgotten No Longer?*, 32 San Diego L. Rev. 771, 794–817 (1995).

lines as statements of INS policy. The INS Gender Guidelines explicitly recognize FC/FGM as a form of persecution directed primarily at women and girls.

Following the promulgation of the INS Gender Guidelines, the Board of Immigration Appeals heard the case of Fauziya Kassindja,[19] a Togalese woman who sought asylum on the grounds that if she returned to her country she would be subjected to FC/FGM. In 1996, the Board granted asylum to Kassindja, finding that she had a well-founded fear of persecution. However, the Board declined to establish standards for granting asylum in future FC/FGM cases.[20]

NOTES

A Woman's Choice? Compare the U.S. law permitting women eighteen and above to elect to have an FGM procedure with Ghana's law, which applies to women of all ages. Which is the better policy? Why?

Due Diligence. Chapter Eleven's *Velásquez Rodríguez Case* determined the rationale for holding states responsible for violations of human rights by private persons. The Inter-American Court of Human Rights ruled that states must respect and ensure human rights. This state obligation extends to all branches of government—executive, legislative, and judicial. It requires that states "prevent, investigate, and punish" all human rights violations, and that they do so effectively. States are directly responsible for any actions by state actors, but they can also become responsible for an act by private persons, "not because of the act itself, but because of the lack of due diligence to prevent the violation or to respond to it as required by the Convention."[J]

You have now evaluated many different state strategies concerning FGM. How well do they meet the "due diligence" standard? Consider what additional actions could be taken by police, prosecutors, judges, and legislators to meet it.

---

[19] Her name was misspelled as Kasinga when she entered the country. Consequently, all legal documents referring to her case use the incorrect spelling of her name. See F. Kassindja and L. M. Bashir, *Do They Hear You When You Cry*, New York: Delacorte Press, 1998.

[20] See *in re* Fauziya Kasinga, Interim Dec. 3278, Bd of Immig. Appeals, File A73 476 695, 1996 BIA LEXIS 15 (June 13, 1996).

[J] *Velásquez Rodríguez*, para. 172; *see also* paras. 165–167, 173–177.

Chapter 13
Gender and Polygyny: Religion, Culture, and Equality in Marriage

Polygamy raises the most intractable of conflicts—that between women's right to equality in marriage and the rights to freedom of religion and culture. Polygyny means a marriage system under which a man may be simultaneously married to several women. Under state laws in many countries, men in specific religions or ethnic groups are permitted to practice polygyny. Polygyny is just one form of polygamy, the other being polyandry—multiple husbands for one woman. Although anthropologists sometimes list remote areas of the world where polyandry is practiced, no state law permits it.

Many different countries and points of view are presented here. After an historical overview of polygyny, readers will find women's voices from rural Tanzania. Courts from the United States, Bangladesh, and Mauritius and an Indian scholar grapple with the constitutional, Islamic, Hindu, and international human rights issues raised by polygyny. Perspectives from human rights law and then from law and economics follow. A case study from Uganda allows close examination of how women helped shape a new constitution against a customary law background permitting polygyny. Finally, a Uganda scholar proposes choices on how to resolve the conflict.

I. An Introduction to the Practice of Polygyny

Susan Deller Ross, *Polygyny as a Violation of Women's Right to Equality in Marriage: An Historical, Comparative and International Human Rights Overview*
24 Delhi L. Rev. 22, 22–27, 34–36 (2002).

I. Polygyny in History

While polygyny has been deeply rooted in human society, so too is the movement over time to eradicate it. The men interpreting religious doctrine or making secular law have gradually banned it for most people. The Jewish religion originally permitted it, but banned it over a thousand years ago. The ancient Romans criminalized bigamy. Christianity from the beginning seems to have condemned it and as it expanded its geographic reach over the first 1000 years succeeded in ending polygamy in regions where it was practiced as people there converted to Christianity. When various sects attempted to institute polygyny, these early Christians quickly moved to suppress it. And even the Muslim permission for polygyny represented Mohammed's effort to end the practice of a husband taking an unlimited number of wives; hence he permitted only four and cautioned further "but if you fear that you cannot be equitable, then only one."

In recent history, the United States successfully enforced its laws criminalizing polygyny against Mormon men in the Church of Jesus Christ of Latter-Day Saints, bringing a rapid halt to the Church's endorsement of the practice in less than forty years (1852–1890). The Russian Empire laws had allowed Muslims to practice polygyny, but it was successfully banned through decrees and laws issued in 1917, 1919, and 1926. Similarly, China outlawed both polygyny and concubinage in its 1950 and 1980 Marriage Laws and Vietnam did so in 1960. India banned polygyny for Hindus in 1955; Uganda and Kenya followed suit in their separate Hindu marriage laws.

Two majority Muslim countries have also outlawed polygyny—Turkey in 1923 and Tunisia in 1956, as have the Ismaili Khojas of East Africa.[A] . . . Finally, Australia and some African countries have also criminalized polygyny for all within the country, whether in customary, Muslim, or statutory marriages. Burundi, Côte d'Ivoire, and Madagascar are in this category.

II. Comparative Polygyny Law: Most Countries Ban; A Few Permit

Although polygyny is banned as the crime of bigamy for all in the Americas, Europe, the countries of the former Soviet Union, China, Vietnam and Nepal, and a few African countries, the national laws of a number of countries still permit it for the majority (or sometimes, the minority—e.g. India and the Philippines) of their male population. They typically do so by enacting marriage laws that vary depending on a person's religion or ethnic community as designated by birth. Women born into one religion or community may be subjected to polygyny. Women born into another may not.

Uganda, Iran, and India provide examples of such systems in Africa, the Middle East, and Asia. In Uganda, customary law permits a man who marries under traditional norms to take another wife whenever he wishes and without limit. He does not have to give existing wives any notice of a new marriage to another wife, nor does such a marriage entitle an existing wife to a divorce. Most wives have no access to the statutory monogamous marriage law, because that law gives men a veto over monogamy. Islamic law permits Muslim men to marry up to four wives with the same right of veto over monogamy. In contrast, men who marry under the civil law or who are Hindu, Buddhist, a Jain or a Sikh, are barred from marrying another wife while still married to the first under criminal penalty of bigamy with five years' imprisonment.

[A] The Khojas are one of the major branches of Ismaili Islam, a sect of Shi'ite Islam that recognizes only seven Imams. In East Africa, they trace their origins to traders from India.

At least fifteen other African countries permit men to marry several wives in systems that are often similar to Uganda's, with its separate codes for Muslim, Hindu, customary, and civil marriages. Only men who enter into a civil or Hindu marriage are subject to the bigamy criminal penalty in such countries.

In Iran, a man can have four permanent wives and if he is a Shi'a Muslim, as are most Iranians, as many temporary wives as he likes; Shi'a Muslims living in many other countries receive the same legal permission. A temporary marriage can be as short in duration as one hour or as long as ninety-nine years; it is a contract in which the woman agrees to have sex with the man in exchange for a predetermined sum to be paid to her. The children of temporary marriages are legally recognized as legitimate but the temporary husband is not financially obligated to them or his temporary wife except for the original fixed sum. At least nine other Middle Eastern countries permit polygyny, although Sunni Muslims (the majority of the world's Muslim population) may not marry temporary wives.

In India, the laws applying to Hindu, Christian, and Parsi men prohibit polygyny through a bigamy penalty of seven years imprisonment. The law permits Muslim men to marry up to four wives by exempting them from bigamy prosecutions. In the Indian state of Goa, however, the situation is paradoxically reversed, with Muslim men covered by the bigamy law and Hindu men exempted. At least nine other countries in Asia permit polygyny for Muslims, and in the case of Bangladesh and Pakistan, both Hindus and Muslims. Among these nine, Thailand (majority Buddhist; minority Muslim) does not recognize polygynous marriages as a matter of law, but polygyny is not a criminal offence either . . .

II. Women's Voices

Dominique Meekers & Nadra Franklin, *Women's Perceptions of Polygyny Among the Kaguru of Tanzania*
34 ETHNOLOGY 315, 315–27 (1995)

Much of the large body of research on polygyny in sub-Saharan Africa focuses on the sociocultural and demographic correlates of polygyny and on the demographic and economic implications of polygyny. In addition, there has been considerable emphasis on the future prospects of polygyny. Despite this widespread interest in African polygyny, relatively little research has been done to specifically address women's attitudes toward polygyny.

Many studies on polygyny in sub-Saharan Africa suggest that women's attitudes toward polygyny may vary both within and between societies. Polygyny can be advantageous for women. In some societies, they benefit from polygyny because polygynous husbands tend to be wealthy, the pool of laborers supplied by a larger domestic unit reduces the need for wage laborers, or because co-wives co-operate in trade and economic affairs. In such societies, women sometimes favor polygyny because it provides them with labor assistance. . . . But the benefits of polygyny are not necessarily restricted to economic advantages. In a study of women's attitudes toward polygyny among the Yoruba, Ware (1979) found that a majority of the women surveyed (60 per cent) indicated they would be pleased to be in a polygynous relationship because they could then share the burdens of work and also have another woman with whom they could gossip and play. In some African societies it is not uncommon for a woman to participate in the choice of her husband's next wife, or even to refuse to let her husband make that choice himself. In doing so, senior wives have the opportunity to maximize their economic benefits by selecting hard-working co-wives, and to limit intrafamily conflicts by choosing those junior co-wives they like, sometimes a sister.

However, in many instances women disapprove of polygynous unions. Yoruba respondents who would not be pleased to have a co-wife frequently indicated an aversion to having to share resources, both sexual and material. Such a situation may result in jealousy and this in turn reduces the potential for co-operation among co-wives. In several societies, the potential for jealousy or rivalry is reflected in the terminology used to refer to co-wives. For example, among the Luo (Kenya) a co-wife is called *nyieka* (my partner in jealousy), the Hausa (Nigeria) use the term *kishiya* (jealousy), and the Yoruba (Nigeria) word for co-wife is *orogun* (rival or competitor). Likewise, among the Bakgalagadi of Botswana the term for co-wives, *bagadikano*, means rivals, and the term for polygyny, *lefufa*, implies jealousy. . . .

The Kaguru have three distinct groups in opposition to polygyny: women (the wives), the Christian Church, and the state. Support for polygyny is voiced by some men and is reflected in the traditional views in favor of polygyny as perpetuated by the elders. Just as there are conflicting views of polygyny in cultures throughout Africa, we find them in Tanzania among the Kaguru.

This article analyzes interviews conducted among a sample of Kaguru women of the Morogoro region of Tanzania to illustrate women's attitudes toward polygyny and the options available to them when their husbands want to marry an additional wife. Precisely because our information is supplied by women only, we cannot comment upon others' views of polygyny. However, we do address women's perceptions of men's regard for polygyny, the elders' staunch support for polygyny, and the Church's opposition to it. . . .

The Kaguru

The Kaguru, who live in a hilly area near the Itumba Mountains in the Morogoro region of Tanzania, have matrilineal descent. The large majority of Kaguru live in the plateau surrounding the mountains, where the rivers form arable valleys that are cultivated year after year. In the higher and dryer regions, people practice slash-and-burn cultivation. The Kaguru cultivate millet, sorghum, and maize, and supplement their grain-based diet with a variety of vegetables. In addition to cultivating grains and vegetables, most Kaguru keep chickens, goats, and sheep. During the rainy season most of Ukaguru appears to consist of relatively fertile land, but recurrent droughts and related problems (such as floodings and rodent infestations) often destroy the harvest, resulting in food shortages.

While the Kaguru continue to have matrilineal descent, some patrilineal traits are apparent, particularly regarding marriage. Kaguru marriage is characterized by the transfer of bridewealth that gives the husband certain rights to the children born from the union. As in many societies, contracting polygynous unions can be beneficial. Although Kaguru women are responsible for household work, household food production, and for child rearing, it is not uncommon for women to assist their husbands in cash crop production, thereby making polygyny economically advantageous, particularly for males. Because cash crop production is controlled by males, and because males and females generally have separate budgets, women do not necessarily benefit equally from such co-operation.

For Kaguru men polygyny is also advantageous because it allows them to bypass the rules regarding postpartum sexual abstinence. The Kaguru believe that a woman should not have sexual intercourse during the period when she is nursing a child because a new pregnancy would dry up the breast milk. Polygyny provides men with normal sexual activity during the lengthy period (generally more than a year, and sometimes as long as two or three years) when one wife is nursing a child. Polygyny also enables a Kaguru man to have children even if his first wife is barren. While polygyny may provide a solution for a barren woman's husband and may prevent him from divorcing his wife, the barren woman herself will not regain her lost status through polygyny because her co-wife's children belong to a different lineage.

More important, the nature of social relations accords polygynously married Kaguru men with additional benefits. In Kaguru society, the main strategy for social advancement is to secure followers or dependents, rather than gaining access to land, ritual knowledge, or livestock. The latter are employed chiefly as a means to increase the number of dependents and do not constitute ends in themselves. Kaguru males employ polygyny as a strategy to increase the number of their dependents by adding a new wife, her children, and eventually perhaps daughters-in-law. Kaguru women, however, do not gain higher status from having co-wives because the latter belong to different matrilineages. Instead, in a polygynous union, each woman and her children will compete with co-wives over resources.

As in many societies, Kaguru family resources are controlled by the husband. Although polygyny may in some cases improve a family's economic situation (for example, because polygynous families are allocated more land), these benefits may have little effect on the situation of women and children. Indeed, a Kaguru man has a dual obligation to care not only for his own children, but also for his sisters' children, who belong to his own matrilineage. Consequently, it is not uncommon for a Kaguru woman to complain that her husband does not sufficiently support her and her children, particularly if support decreased after he married a subsequent wife.

While polygyny is socially approved in many African societies, some African countries have adopted legislation banning polygyny. Despite such legislation, the practice has persisted in most of these countries, albeit under a different form. While formal polygyny has decreased as a result of these measures, many men now have one legally married wife (i.e., a civil monogamous union), and one or more informal unions with other women.

The Tanzania Marriage Act of 1971 prohibits polygyny for Christian marriages, but still allows it for civil, Islamic, and traditional unions. Despite the Kaguru having adopted Christian values, Kaguru men are reluctant to marry Christian girls because Christianity condemns polygyny and divorce. This means that if a man's wife by a Christian marriage is barren he cannot divorce her nor marry a second wife to bear children for him. While men who contract a Christian marriage cannot legally become polygynous, they are able to initiate additional informal unions. According to data from the 1993 Tanzania Demographic and Health Survey, 28 per cent of all married women in Tanzania are currently in polygynous unions (including informal unions); for the Morogoro region, where the Kaguru live, the corresponding figure is 22.5 per cent.

Data

Our information on Kaguru women's perception of polygyny is drawn from a set of semi-structured interviews conducted under the supervision of Dr. Penina Mlama during the summer of 1992 as part of a demographic study on women's strategies and fertility. In these interviews, a small group of rural Kaguru women (43 cases) were asked to discuss their views of polygyny. Thirteen respondents indicated that they were or had previously been in a polygynous union. Of all respondents, five were under age 30, 22 were aged 30–49, and sixteen were aged 50 or older. While most respondents had attended primary school, only twelve had reached standard seven. All questions were open-ended: the standard interview questions served merely as a guideline for the interview, and respondents were allowed to raise additional topics for discussion.

Women who were or had been in polygynous unions were asked if they were happy when their husbands married another wife, and women who had never been in a polygynous union were asked how they would feel if their husbands were to marry another wife. Thus, the reports on women's views about polygyny presented here are based on actual experience as well as on women's perceptions of the effects of polygyny. Interestingly, women who had been in polygynous unions and those who had never been in a polygynous union have similar opinions regarding polygyny. Additional information about women's reactions to polygyny was not solicited specifically, but was volunteered by the respondents while discussing issues such as their marriage procedures, their role in spousal selection, the content of the teachings during their initiation ceremonies, and the position of women and the reasons for divorce in Kaguru society. While unsolicited information about polygyny may not be representative because it may reflect the opinion of respondents who hold strong views about polygyny, such information is retained here for illustrative purposes.

All interviews were conducted in Kikaguru by a female interviewer, trained and supervised by Dr. Penina Mlama. . . .

Social Support for Polygyny

If the advantages of polygyny outweigh the disadvantages, then we would expect the institution of polygyny to be supported through social mechanisms, and its acceptance as a way of life reflected in the socialization process of Kaguru adolescents. For Kaguru women, this socialization is institutionalized in the form of initiation ceremonies (*digubi*). During the digubi ceremonies, young girls are instructed by old women about the norms and values of Kaguru society, including proper behavior for married women. Several respondents indicated that during the digubi ceremonies they were instructed that polygyny is an aspect of life that may be hard to avoid.

> I was told to live peacefully with my husband. You should serve him as usual. If you won't care about him he can find other women outside. That will be the beginning of problems, that is what they told me. (R37, age 49).

After marriage, there is considerable social support (or even pressure) for males to marry additional wives. One respondent, who was the first wife of a headman, indicated that because of her husband's position, he had experienced a lot of social pressure to marry a second wife.

> People started talking that the headman is having only one wife, a headman should have two wives. . . . They tried very much to convince him, but I was refusing. . . . His bosses were against him having only one wife. One wife cannot cater for all the guests coming to the headman's house, a headman has many guests. . . . When they heard that I have got two babies, they said now it is a must that the headman should get another wife for himself. (R3O, age 92)

Despite his wife's opposition, this man was eventually pressured into marrying another wife. In addition to pressure from other males, a man may try to convince his wife that a co-wife is beneficial, arguing that it will reduce his wife's workload:

> [My husband] claims that there are many duties for one wife, he wants to give me assistance. (R42, age 33)

In addition to the social support for polygyny in Kaguru society, starting in early adolescence the socialization process is geared at informing women that it is common for a man to marry more than one wife. As Ware remarks, in some societies these social pressures to accept polygyny may be so strong that women may claim to be happy with a co-wife, even if such is not the case.

While polygyny endows Kaguru males with higher status because it increases their dependents, for females it implies competition between wives over scarce resources. With matrilineal descent, each Kaguru co-wife and her children belong to a different matrilineage, and each co-wife is ultimately responsible for providing for her own children. In other words, each co-wife and her children form a separate matrifocal unit within the polygynous family. Because a polygynous husband allocates a share of the limited family resources to each of his wives, it is likely that the share of a finite set of resources that are available for a woman and her children will reduce when her husband marries another wife. Consequently, polygyny does not accord the same status or economic benefits to Kaguru women as it does to men.

Women's Attitudes Toward Polygynous Unions

Despite strong social support for it, Kaguru women do not necessarily support polygyny. When asked how they would react if their husbands were to marry another wife, many indicated strong disapproval of polygynous unions.

R: I don't like it. If it happens I can't avoid it, but I hate to have a co-wife. (R12, age 45)

R: I don't want a co-wife. I don't want my children to be married to co-wives. I hated this even before I got married. Unfortunately, I was involved in one way or the other to have a co-wife, though not legally. It wasn't my will; I came to experience this, so I don't want my children to experience it. (R8, age 36)

A few of the respondents interviewed did indicate that they approved of polygyny. However, these respondents accepted polygynous unions not because polygyny itself appeared beneficial, but rather because it allowed them to share the burden of an unsatisfactory marriage with another woman.

R: I would like to have a co-wife because both of us would suffer the same. (R21, age 49)

I. Did you mind having a co-wife?

R: I was happy, how can one be unhappy for such thing? I thought maybe I treated my husband in an abnormal way. I was happy in the sense that I faced a lot of problems. So I wanted to see if the new wife could tolerate as I did. That was what made me happy.

I: That means that you were not happy to have a co-wife. You wanted her to experience the troubles you faced, but not really a thing you can be happy with.

R: To stay with a co-wife is not a bad thing, but there are many things. She can lie to you, even lie about things you haven't done. . . . To have a co-wife is not a good thing. You just let your husband marry another wife, since he has decided to do so. (R11, age 50)

This latter type of response provides support for the argument that polygyny may be considered either a deprivation or a gain, depending on whether the husband is valued positively or negatively. In the above examples, women are willing to share their husbands only because they have unsatisfactory relationships with them.

Women provided several explanations for their aversion to polygynous unions. Only one respondent noted that Christianity prohibits polygynous unions, and that people who do contract a polygynous union would be cast out by the Church. On the other hand, many respondents remarked that polygyny often causes problems in the household, either because the husband shows favoritism toward the youngest wife, or because it affects the relationship between the husband and the first wife.

R: Men have many problems: it depends. When a man marries a second wife, he starts troubles in the house. If a woman tries to comment on what her husband does, he will simply answer that it is due to jealousy. Every day there are a lot of problems. No more love between the two. In such a situation, a woman can demand for a divorce. (R25)

R: This is because if a man gets a co-wife, definitely one family will suffer. He won't manage to satisfy the needs of both women, as a result he will favor the junior wife. (R4)

R: Normally, couples divorce because of problems. If a man has a second wife, when he comes to you everything you prepare he feels like they are not well prepared. (R3)

R: I wouldn't be happy with a co-wife since life would change. You know, if a husband has two wives or more there will be no balance in love and in most cases the elder wife is the one disadvantaged. Normally, the junior wife is more favored than the senior wife, that is, the junior wife becomes number one, while the senior wife becomes number two. (R25)

R: When my husband married another wife I was not happy because it distorted my life, also you are not confident about your completeness as a woman. The thought erodes your love for him. (R14)

R: Marriage is for two people, if the third joins love will automatically fade away. (R16)

Evidently, at least some of these women disapprove of polygyny because they value romantic love as the basis for a successful marriage. Potential conflicts between co-wives is another reason why many Kaguru women oppose their husbands marrying another wife. . . .

R: I would not be happy [with a co-wife]. I do not want to quarrel with a co-wife. If [my husband] marries another wife, I will divorce him. (R26, age 42)

R: [Having a co-wife] would pain me, since I would think that he has degraded me and loves the other wife more. I think that I would quarrel very much with my co-wife. (R23, age 38)

I. Would you mind having a co-wife?

R: If my father was dead, okay. But because he is alive I could have gone back home.

I: Why?

R: It is not jealousness, but polygamy has a lot of problems.

I: Tell me one problem.

R: The first wife will be killed by the other wife.

I. So, the second wife is usually offensive?

R: Yes. (R29, age 35)

R: What causes [divorce] is mostly scorn. Sometimes the husband scorns you. The other wife scorns you, and the husband sides with her and sees you as nothing. You must get angry! (R43, age 60)

R: Having a co-wife is not good. It creates a lot of misunderstandings. You know if a junior wife comes in she can think that she is the most beloved and think that you are nothing. (R5, age 56)

Beidelman remarks that while Kaguru men have a tendency to think of all the women and children of a polygynous household as one large family, it is evident that with matrilineal descent each household with a different mother and her children has its own priorities. In other words, women in polygynous unions compete with co-wives over benefits and resources for themselves and/or their children. When a woman's husband marries another wife, or has an outside wife [a girlfriend to whom he is not married], the resources available to her will decline because the husband's resources are then divided between the two women. At least in some cases, the husband will only support his new wife.

R: When you become two it is not possible in fact to have an understanding. Also even the budget will be higher; how are you going to progress? . . . You don't progress. Do you think it is just paying bridewealth only! . . . The needs will increase. . . . You could buy one kilogram of meat and suffice, now you have to send for half a kilogram.
I: Here half, and there half?
R: I who came first have a family, the half kilogram what will it suffice? (R35)
R: When [my husband] married a second wife, I am now nothing, he no longer loves me. I don't lie about him. When I was sick he left me and went to another town with his junior wife. He did not mind about me being sick. He is now visiting me, but for one year when I was sick he was not visiting me. (R41)

The reduced support also affects a woman's children. In many cases, Kaguru women indicated that their husbands failed to provide for their children after the husbands married another wife.

I: When [your husband] married his second wife, did he continue to care for you?
R: He never did. I was living with my children facing troubles. He was only taking care of his new wife, he forgot about me and my children. (R22)
R: When I got my sixth child my husband tasted a better love from outside, this made him to concentrate with an outside woman, they had a child. They continued until they had three children. At this long period, I had a lot of problems of taking care of the family. If my children were sick I had to take care myself, for everything. I was mother and father. (R8)
I: When he married another wife, was he taking care of your children?
R: He wasn't caring. He could leave on Friday to Mamboya village—his woman was there—while a child is sick. He would only give me some tablets for the child. He wouldn't come back until Monday. (R14)

R: After he had other women, he never worked in our farms, he never brought food
    in the house and he never bought clothes for the children. He didn't even mind
    when the children were sick. (R25)

It is noteworthy that several women were upset about their husbands' lack of support, particularly when their children were sick. Clearly, the husband is expected to
contribute to the needs of his children, and failure to provide assistance when children are sick is unacceptable. This lack of material support is one of the main reasons
why Kaguru women oppose polygynous unions.

Until relatively recently, ethnographic studies tended to convey the general impression that most African women were passive victims of a male-dominated society.
Studies now emphasize that women are social actors in their own right who try to
achieve their own goals within certain constraints imposed upon them. This latter
perspective suggests that Kaguru women's aversion to polygynous unions should be
reflected in attempts to prevent their husbands from marrying additional wives or,
alternatively, in behavior geared at limiting the negative effects of such polygynous
unions.

Some Kaguru respondents expressed a fatalistic point of view, suggesting that
women have little bargaining power to stop their husbands from marrying another
wife.

I. If you tell [your husband] not to marry the second wife, would he listen to you?
R: Never, he will never listen to you. We women are considered as children, whatever
    the man says we have to tolerate. (R22)
I: Would you mind having a co-wife?
R: That depends on the man himself. If he decides to marry, he marries.
I: Yes, if he decides to marry he marries, but in your heart would you like that or you
    would not like it?
R: That is his own decision. A woman cannot decide for him not to marry. (R33)
I: If he married another woman and you don't like it, why can't you leave him and
    get married to another man?
R: You as the woman, you are married; you haven't married the man, how can you
    decide to quit?
I: So, you try to tolerate, even when you have problems you don't want to divorce.
    You bear and bring up your children in that situation?
R: Yes, there is no other way. (R24)

But other women are less passive. One option available to a Kaguru woman is to
threaten to divorce her husband should he become interested in marrying another
wife. Similarly, polygynously married women may use the threat of returning to their
brothers or parents when their husbands maltreat them or provide inadequate support. This is particularly important for women in polygynous unions, since they tend
to compete with reference to the interests of their children.

R: I wouldn't be happy [if my husband married another wife]. I would have told him to send me back home before getting another wife. (R15)

I: Would you mind having a co-wife?

R: I wouldn't be happy. I don't want to quarrel with a co-wife. If he marries another wife, I will divorce him. (R26)

R: [My husband] had another woman.

I: He had a woman in this same village?

R: He was mistreating me and therefore I told him to divorce me.

I: What did he say?

R: He didn't like to send me back home.

I: Did he care for you in all aspects as he did before he got the other woman?

R: Yes, then the elder people tried to warn him about his affair with the outside woman, so he decided to leave her. Then our life returned to normal.

I: Did he marry that woman or were they only friends?

R: He didn't marry her, they were friends. (R13)

Such threats of divorce are generally not actual divorce attempts, but rather attempts to avoid or resolve problems without dissolving the union. In his research on the Gusii of Kenya, Hakansson also notes that a Gusii wife may return to her parents in order to force her husband to abandon a new partner. Indeed, it is probably no coincidence that two of the Kaguru respondents quoted above indicate that they would not initiate a divorce, but rather would or did tell their husbands to divorce them. Chances are that a Kaguru husband will refuse to initiate a divorce because his bridewealth will not be returned if he initiates a divorce without valid reason. Threats of divorce are probably most effective when the woman has a strong support network. Such may be the case when the couple lives with the wife's kin because the husband was unable to pay a large bridewealth. From our interviews, it appears that although threats of divorce are not uncommon, only a few women actually left their husbands and returned to their parental home.

R: An evil spirit has entered [my husband], and he took another wife. That is why I am resting here at [my parents'] home. . . . What happened with my husband made me come back [to my parents], without a choice.

I: You yourself decided to come back?

R: I had to come back.

I: So, your life has been a nice life before that?

R: Yes, it was a happy life.

I: But when it came toward the end?

R: Difficult. But he has asked me to go back [to his house]; he has already divorced that other woman.

I: He has divorced her?

R: Yes, he has divorced her, but I haven't made up my mind to go back. (R28)

To some extent, this apparently low prevalence of women divorcing their husbands may be related to the fact that women may lack better marital alternatives, which implies that remarriage may not be an improvement. Furthermore, in Kaguru society divorce may be more difficult than in many other societies with matrilineal descent because a woman's family members often do not support her attempts to divorce her husband.

I: Did you ever consider leaving your husband?
R: It was not possible, my father objected. He said my husband having another wife is not good enough a reason for us to separate. Men are like elephants, they never eat from one tree! So, I tolerated it. (R14)

The lack of support for the divorce from a woman's kin members is not surprising, considering that a Kaguru marriage is based on bridewealth payments. Since a woman's kin members are her bridewealth recipients, they would be expected to return the bridewealth when the woman initiates the divorce.

Discussion. . . .

Despite institutionalized social support for polygyny through the initiation ceremonies, most Kaguru women do not support polygyny. Those women who have not experienced polygyny are wary of the institution and the effect it may have on their lives, and those who have had a co-wife express only negative remarks about polygyny. Our respondents did not provide much information about outside wives, but from the available information it is evident that opinions about such unofficial polygynous unions are at least equally stern. . . .

Although it appears that Kaguru women reject polygyny outright, their opinions about the effects of polygyny do vary. While some Kaguru women stated that polygyny was undesirable because it may negatively affect their own lives and happiness, others were much more concerned about the deleterious effects a co-wife may have on their children. Unlike other studies, Kaguru women failed to mention any benefits of having a co-wife, such as the reduction of one's workload or the friendship of a co-wife with whom one can bond and share gossip.

While it is not unusual to encounter such strong opposition to polygyny among educated and urban women in many African societies, in a more traditional setting, such as that of the Kaguru in Morogoro, a more tolerant attitude may be expected, at least for some of the women. The findings from this study support Beidelman's (1986) argument that Kaguru women in polygynous unions compete with co-wives over resources for themselves and for their children. Material support for a wife and her children frequently declines when the husband marries another wife. Considering that resources are scarce in Kaguru society, it is in a woman's best interest to oppose her husband marrying another wife. While a woman may have limited power to actually prevent her husband from marrying another wife, or to prevent him from taking an outside wife, it is not uncommon for a Kaguru woman to use the threat of divorce whenever the continued material support for herself and her children is at stake.

In part, this analysis of women's views toward polygyny underscores gender relations among the Kaguru. Polygyny as an institution is opposed by women, and yet institutionalized support for it, through the digubi instructions and the elders' demands on younger men, remains strong despite the Church and state prohibitions. Unlike women of other societies, Kaguru women have no active role in co-wife selection, nor do they appear to form any bonds of friendship or camaraderie with co-wives. This opposition remains, regardless of either the age of the woman or her years of experience with polygyny.

Given the reality that opposition to polygyny is not strong enough to prevent polygyny or its newer manifestation, girlfriends or outside wives, it appears that women have attempted to devise their own coping strategies. For example, several older respondents indicated that they were determined not to remarry if widowed or divorced, provided it were economically feasible. Others resort to accusations of witchcraft against other women, a culturally strong accusation among the Kaguru. Throughout it all, women appear to be resigned to the practice of polygyny and skeptical that a change will ever occur.

While Kaguru women oppose polygyny, societal props supporting the institution remain dominant. Whether men continue to marry more than one wife, or instead marry once but maintain girlfriends, wives are aware that either form of polygyny implies that they will be unable to lay full claim upon their husbands. Women's concerns for their own and their children's welfare will remain as they face economic competition from other women, either co-wives or girlfriends.

NOTES

Why Kaguru Women Dislike Polygyny. The women who were interviewed identified several reasons for being unhappy when a husband marries another woman. What are they? Do you have any theories about why none of these women approved of polygyny as compared to women in earlier studies?

Polygyny's Benefits. Who benefits, and how, from polygyny? Given the benefits, should African countries permit polygyny? In 2005, the Women's Legal Aid Centre in Tanzania and the International Women's Human Rights Clinic from Georgetown University Law Center conducted a joint fact-finding mission to investigate Tanzanian attitudes about polygyny. From a group of 92 interviewees, 13% identified benefits and 99% identified harms. The harms most frequently cited were, first, unequal division of economic assets between the different wives and children and, second, the fact that polygynous men were too poor to support more than one wife and their children. Among the 60 interviewees asked whether the law should permit polygyny only, both polygyny and monogamy, or monogamy alone, 65% chose monogamy; among the 17 Muslims in that group, 59% made the same choice.[B]

Who Is Married to Whom and What Are Their Legal Rights and Responsibilities?

[B] Tamar Ezer & Susan Deller Ross, *Fact-Finding as a Lawmaking Tool for Advancing Women's Human Rights*, 7 Geo. J. Gender & L. 331, 339 & n.23 (2006) (citing Anne Heavey Scheinfeldt & Ryan Keith Tindall, Marriage Matters: The Plight of Women in Polygamous Unions in Tanzania 2–3, 5 (May 17, 2005) (unpublished report) (on file with author)).

People from countries where polygyny is not legal sometimes assume that the term "co-wives" indicates that the wives are legally related to each other with attendant legal rights and responsibilities. That is not the case. A polygynous man has several simultaneous marriages, each with a different wife. CEDAW's Article 16 requires the elimination of discrimination in marriage and in particular that men and women have the "same rights and responsibilities during marriage" and "as parents." What are some of the common legal rights and responsibilities that marriage law creates? Among the most fundamental are those laws requiring the spouses to support each other and their children. Note that it is mathematically impossible for the husband to provide the same legally required support as that provided by his wife for their children. She can provide 100% of her emotional and financial assets for their children. He can only provide some fraction of his emotional and financial assets. If he has four wives, he provides only 25% of his resources to each wife and their children. In effect, polygamy marriage law requires that each wife bear a greater legal responsibility to their children than her husband. Conversely, the husband has a greater legal right to support from her for their children than does she from him. Notice how this correlates with the complaints voiced by Kaguru women.

III. Equal Protection Versus Religious Freedom

A. Four Courts' Views

Reynolds v. United States
(U.S. Supreme Court)
98 U.S. 145 (1878)

MR. CHIEF JUSTICE WAITE delivered the opinion of the court.

The assignments of error . . . present the following questions:. . . .

5. Should the accused have been acquitted if he married the second time, because he believed it to be his religious duty?[c]

6. Did the court err in that part of the charge which directed the attention of the jury to the consequences of polygamy?

These questions will be considered in their order. . . .

5. As to the defence of religious belief or duty

On the trial, the plaintiff in error, the accused, proved that at the time of his alleged second marriage he was, and for many years before had been, a member of the Church of Jesus Christ of Latter-Day Saints, commonly called the Mormon Church, and a believer in its doctrines; that it was an accepted doctrine of that church "that

---

[c] Reynolds was indicted under a federal statute that held that "[e]very person having a husband or wife living, who marries another, whether married or single, in a Territory, or other place over which the United States have exclusive jurisdiction, is guilty of bigamy, and shall be punished by a fine of not more than $500, and by imprisonment for a term of not more than five years."

it was the duty of male members of said church, circumstances permitting, to practise polygamy; . . . that this duty was enjoined by different books which the members of said church believed to be of divine origin, and among others the Holy Bible, and also that the members of the church believed that the practice of polygamy was directly enjoined upon the male members thereof by the Almighty God, in a revelation to Joseph Smith, the founder and prophet of said church; that the failing or refusing to practise polygamy by such male members of said church, when circumstances would admit, would be punished, and that the penalty for such failure and refusal would be damnation in the life to come." He also proved "that he had received permission from the recognized authorities in said church to enter into polygamous marriage; . . . that Daniel H. Wells, one having authority in said church to perform the marriage ceremony, married the said defendant on or about the time the crime is alleged to have been committed, to some woman by the name of Schofield, and that such marriage ceremony was performed under and pursuant to the doctrines of said church."

Upon this proof he asked the court to instruct the jury that if they found from the evidence that he "was married as charged . . . in pursuance of and in conformity with what he believed at the time to be a religious duty, that the verdict must be 'not guilty.'" This request was refused, and the court did charge "that there must have been a criminal intent, but that if the defendant, under the influence of a religious belief that it was right . . . deliberately married a second time, having a first wife living, . . . the want of understanding on his part that he was committing a crime . . . did not excuse him; but the law inexorably in such case implies the criminal intent."

Upon this charge and refusal to charge the question is raised, whether religious belief can be accepted as a justification of an overt act made criminal by the law of the land. The inquiry is not as to the power of Congress to prescribe criminal laws for the Territories, but as to the guilt of one who knowingly violates a law which has been properly enacted, if he entertains a religious belief that the law is wrong.

Congress cannot pass a law for the government of the Territories which shall prohibit the free exercise of religion. The first amendment to the Constitution expressly forbids such legislation. Religious freedom is guaranteed everywhere throughout the United States, so far as congressional interference is concerned. The question to be determined is, whether the law now under consideration comes within this prohibition.

The word "religion" is not defined in the Constitution. We must go elsewhere, therefore, to ascertain its meaning, and nowhere more appropriately, we think, than to the history of the times in the midst of which the provision was adopted. The precise point of the inquiry is, what is the religious freedom which has been guaranteed.

Before the adoption of the Constitution, attempts were made in some of the colonies and States to legislate not only in respect to the establishment of religion, but in respect to its doctrines and precepts as well. The people were taxed, against their will, for the support of religion, and sometimes for the support of particular sects to whose tenets they could not and did not subscribe. Punishments were prescribed for a failure to attend upon public worship, and sometimes for entertaining heretical opinions. The controversy upon this general subject was animated in many of the States, but seemed at last to culminate in Virginia. In 1784, the House of Delegates of that State having under consideration "a bill establishing provision for teachers of the Christian religion," postponed it until the next session, and directed that the bill should be published and distributed, and that the people be requested "to signify their opinion respecting the adoption of such a bill at the next session of assembly."

This brought out a determined opposition. Amongst others, Mr. Madison prepared a "Memorial and Remonstrance," which was widely circulated and signed, and in which he demonstrated "that religion, or the duty we owe the Creator," was not within the cognizance of civil government. At the next session the proposed bill was not only defeated, but another, "for establishing religious freedom," drafted by Mr. Jefferson, was passed. In the preamble of this act religious freedom is defined; and after a recital "that to suffer the civil magistrate to intrude his powers into the field of opinion, and to restrain the profession or propagation of principles on supposition of their ill tendency, is a dangerous fallacy which at once destroys all religious liberty," it is declared "that it is time enough for the rightful purposes of civil government for its officers to interfere when principles break out into overt acts against peace and good order." In these two sentences is found the true distinction between what properly belongs to the church and what to the State.

In a little more than a year after the passage of this statute the convention met which prepared the Constitution of the United States. Of this convention Mr. Jefferson was not a member, he being then absent as minister to France. As soon as he saw the draft of the Constitution proposed for adoption, he, in a letter to a friend, expressed his disappointment at the absence of an express declaration insuring the freedom of religion, but was willing to accept it as it was, trusting that the good sense and honest intentions of the people would bring about the necessary alterations. Five of the States, while adopting the Constitution, proposed amendments. Three—New Hampshire, New York, and Virginia—included in one form or another a declaration of religious freedom in the changes they desired to have made, as did also North Carolina, where the convention at first declined to ratify the Constitution until the proposed amendments were acted upon. Accordingly, at the first session of the first Congress the amendment now under consideration was proposed with others by Mr. Madison. It met the views of the advocates of religious freedom, and was adopted. Mr. Jefferson afterwards, in reply to an address to him by a committee of the Danbury Baptist Association, took occasion to say: "Believing with you that religion is a matter which lies solely between man and his god; that he owes account to none other for his faith or his worship; that the legislative powers of the government reach actions only, and not opinions, . . . I contemplate with sovereign reverence that act of the whole American people which declared that their legislature should 'make no law respecting an establishment of religion or prohibiting the free exercise thereof,' thus building a wall of separation between church and State. . . ." Coming as this does from an acknowledged leader of the advocates of the measure, it may be accepted almost as an authoritative declaration of the scope and effect of the amendment thus secured. Congress was deprived of all legislative power over mere opinion, but was left free to reach actions which were in violation of social duties or subversive of good order.

Polygamy has always been odious among the northern and western nations of Europe, and, until the establishment of the Mormon Church, was almost exclusively a feature of the life of Asiatic and of African people. At common law, the second marriage was always void, and from the earliest history of England polygamy has been treated as an offence against society. After the establishment of the ecclesiastical courts, and until the time of James I., it was punished through the instrumentality of those tribunals, not merely because ecclesiastical rights had been violated, but because upon the separation of the ecclesiastical courts from the civil the ecclesiastical were supposed to be the most appropriate for the trial of matrimonial causes and offences against the rights of marriage. . . .

By the statute of 1 James I., the offence, if committed in England or Wales, was made punishable in the civil courts, and the penalty was death. As this statute was limited in its operation to England and Wales, it was at a very early period re-enacted, generally with some modifications, in all the colonies. In connection with the case we are now considering, it is a significant fact that on the 8th of December, 1788, after the passage of the act establishing religious freedom, and after the convention of Virginia had recommended as an amendment to the Constitution of the United States the declaration in a bill of rights that "all men have an equal, natural, and unalienable right to the free exercise of religion, according to the dictates of conscience," the legislature of that State substantially enacted the statute of James I., death penalty included, because, as recited in the preamble, "it hath been doubted whether bigamy or poligamy be punishable by the laws of this Commonwealth." From that day to this we think it may safely be said there never has been a time in any State of the Union when polygamy has not been an offence against society, cognizable by the civil courts and punishable with more or less severity. In the face of all this evidence, it is impossible to believe that the constitutional guaranty of religious freedom was intended to prohibit legislation in respect to this most important feature of social life. Marriage, while from its very nature a sacred obligation, is nevertheless, in most civilized nations, a civil contract, and usually regulated by law. Upon it society may be said to be built, and out of its fruits spring social relations and social obligations and duties, with which government is necessarily required to deal. In fact, according as monogamous or polygamous marriages are allowed, do we find the principles on which the government of the people, to a greater or less extent, rests. Professor Lieber says, polygamy leads to the patriarchal principle, . . . which, when applied to large communities, fetters the people in stationary despotism, while that principle cannot long exist in connection with monogamy. . . . An exceptional colony of polygamists under an exceptional leadership may sometimes exist for a time without appearing to disturb the social condition of the people who surround it; but there cannot be a doubt that, unless restricted by some form of constitution, it is within the legitimate scope of the power of every civil government to determine whether polygamy or monogamy shall be the law of social life under its dominion.

In our opinion, the statute immediately under consideration is within the legislative power of Congress. It is constitutional and valid as prescribing a rule of action for all those residing in the Territories, and in places over which the United States have exclusive control. This being so, the only question which remains is, whether those who make polygamy a part of their religion are excepted from the operation of the statute. If they are, then those who do not make polygamy a part of their religious belief may be found guilty and punished, while those who do, must be acquitted and go free. This would be introducing a new element into criminal law. Laws are made for the government of actions, and while they cannot interfere with mere religious belief and opinions, they may with practices. Suppose one believed that human sacrifices were a necessary part of religious worship, would it be seriously contended that the civil government under which he lived could not interfere to prevent a sacrifice? Or if a wife religiously believed it was her duty to burn herself upon the funeral pile of her dead husband, would it be beyond the power of the civil government to prevent her carrying her belief into practice?

So here, as a law of the organization of society under the exclusive dominion of the United States, it is provided that plural messages shall not be allowed. Can a man excuse his practices to the contrary because of his religious belief? To permit this would be to make the professed doctrines of religious belief superior to the law of the land, and in effect to permit every citizen to become a law unto himself. Government could exist only in name under such circumstances.

A criminal intent is generally an element of crime, but every man is presumed to intend the necessary and legitimate consequences of what he knowingly does. Here the accused knew he had been once married, and that his first wife was living. He also knew that his second marriage was forbidden by law. When, therefore, he married the second time, he is presumed to have intended to break the law. And the breaking of the law is the crime. Every act necessary to constitute the crime was knowingly done, and the crime was therefore knowingly committed. Ignorance of a fact may sometimes be taken as evidence of a want of criminal intent, but not ignorance of the law. The only defence of the accused in this case is his belief that the law ought not to have been enacted. It matters not that his belief was a part of his professed religion: it was still belief, and belief only. . . .

6. As to that part of the charge which directed the attention of the jury to the consequences of polygamy.

The passage complained of is as follows: "I think it not improper, in the discharge of your duties in this case, that you should consider what are to be the consequences to the innocent victims of this delusion. As this contest goes on, they multiply, and there are pure-minded women and there are innocent children. . . . These are to be the sufferers; and as jurors fail to do their duty, and as these cases come up in the Territory of Utah, just so do these victims multiply and spread themselves over the land."

While every appeal by the court to the passions or the prejudices of a jury should be promptly rebuked, and while it is the imperative duty of a reviewing court to take care that wrong is not done in this way, we see no just cause for complaint in this case. Congress, in 1862, saw fit to make bigamy a crime in the Territories. This was done because of the evil consequences that were supposed to flow from plural marriages. All the court did was to call the attention of the jury to the peculiar character of the crime for which the accused was on trial, and to remind them of the duty they had to perform. There was no appeal to the passions, no instigation of prejudice. Upon the showing made by the accused himself, he was guilty of a violation of the law under which he had been indicted: and the effort of the court seems to have been not to withdraw the minds of the jury from the issue to be tried, but to bring them to it; not to make them partial, but to keep them impartial.

NOTES

Reynolds **Today: Still Good Law?** For the Court's new approaches to free exercise claims, review Chapter Four's Note on "Free Exercise Today," concerning the U.S. Court of Appeal's decision in *EEOC v. Fremont Christian School.* The *Reynolds* Court considered a federal criminal statute. Applying the law discussed in the Note, what result today as to a federal statute? What result as to a state law criminalizing polygamy? Consider how the Supreme Court's 1996 decision in *United States v. Virginia,* excerpted in Chapter Two, affects the analysis of a compelling state purpose.

The Supreme Court may have the occasion to revisit the *Reynolds* issue because Utah has recently begun prosecuting polygamists. The Mormons' Church of Jesus Christ of Latter-Day Saints abandoned polygamy in 1890, and excommunicates followers who practice it. But men in a small break-away sect, the Fundamentalist Church of Jesus Christ of Latter-Day Saints, with about 10,000 members living in rural Utah, Arizona, and Colorado, continue entering into plural marriages. The Utah Supreme Court has rejected the free exercise appeals of convicted polygamists in *Utah v. Green,* 2004 UT 76, 99 P.3d 820 (upholding bigamy convictions for man who, in 2000, had six wives and twenty-five children; defendant's conviction for criminal non-support not appealed), and in *Utah v. Holm,* 2006 UT 31, 137 P.3d 726 (upholding bigamy conviction for 32-year-old man who married the 16-year-old sister of his first wife against state and federal constitutional free exercise claims, and against federal due process liberty claims based on *Lawrence v. Texas,* 539 U.S. 558 (2003); also upholding conviction for unlawful sexual conduct with a minor on other grounds). The Utah Supreme Court also upheld Mr. Green's conviction for rape of a child in *Utah v. Green,* 2005 UT 9, 108 P.3d 710 (rejecting appeal based on jurisdictional and statute of limitations claims for conviction based on consummation of marriage between defendant and 13-year old bride). What similarities or differences do you see between women married to polygamous men in Utah and Tanzania?

The Significance of *Lawrence v. Texas.* *Lawrence* reversed the convictions of two gay men under a Texas statute criminalizing homosexual conduct. The Court found that the Texas statute violated their 14th Amendment due process rights:

Liberty protects the person from unwarranted government intrusions into a dwelling or other private places. . . . Liberty presumes an autonomy of self that includes freedom of thought, belief, expression, and certain intimate conduct. The instant case involves liberty of the person both in its spatial and in its more transcendent dimensions. . . .

The present case does not involve minors. It does not involve persons who might be injured or coerced or who are situated in relationships where consent might not easily be refused. It does not involve public conduct or prostitution. It does not involve whether the government must give formal recognition to any relationship that homosexual persons seek to enter. The case does involve two adults who, with full and mutual consent from each other, engaged in sexual practices common to a homosexual lifestyle. The petitioners are entitled to respect for their private lives. The State cannot demean their existence or control their destiny by making their private sexual conduct a crime. Their right to liberty under the Due Process Clause gives them the full right to engage in their conduct without intervention of the government. . . . The Texas statute furthers no legitimate state interest which can justify its intrusion into the personal and private life of the individual.

Should *Lawrence* lead the Supreme Court to overrule *Reynolds?* Consider *United States v. Virginia* in answering that question. What does the next decision by the Mauritius Supreme Court contribute to the analysis?

Bhewa v. Government of Mauritius
(Mauritius Supreme Court 1990)
[1991] LRC (Const) 298

GLOVER CJ and LALLAH J. . . .

The plaintiffs [in two consolidated cases raising the same issue] are followers of Islam and are still unmarried. They wish to be married only religiously and to be governed by the rules of their religion. They state that their right to observe and practise their religion is guaranteed under arts 3 and 11 of the Constitution. They contend that the observance and practice of their religion necessarily includes not only the right to marry solely in accordance with the rules of their religion but also to be governed by the rules of their faith in so far as marriage, divorce and devolution of property are concerned . . . .

[A]s Muslim religious marriages cannot now take place unless the parties also undergo a civil marriage, those marriages stand to be governed by the uniform provisions of the Civil Code [requiring monogamy].

It is the case for the plaintiffs that the Quran is the Holy Book of Muslims and that, together with the practices and traditions (Hadiths) of the last Prophet Mohammad, it forms the body of commandments or rules (Sharia) which govern all aspects of the life of a Muslim, including marriage, divorce and devolution of property. As Muslims, they are required by their religion to abide by those commandments and, since the legislative measures for the eventual introduction of Muslim personal law have been repealed by the Civil Status (Amendment) Act 1987, they no longer have an option to be governed by, and so to observe and practise, what their religion ordains. They therefore claim that this repealing Act should be pronounced to be unconstitutional.

The defendant joins issue with the plaintiffs on the constitutionality of the repealing Act and further contends, inter alia, that there is nothing preventing the plaintiffs from celebrating their marriage in accordance with their religious rites, that there would be grave risks of an unconstitutional and anarchical situation if every injunction of every religion were to be made into law in order to guarantee freedom of religion, that the rules of the Sharia in so far as they are understood to seal the position of women in society do not take away the competence of the state to legislate in that regard, and that the rules of religion do not override the lawful policies of the state as these evolve in the state's intercourse with the community of nations. . . .

Evidence has been led only by the plaintiffs. . . . It has been established that those plaintiffs are practising Muslims and that they would contemplate marriage only in accordance with their religion and only if they would be governed by the rules of their faith as regards marriage, divorce and devolution of property. They do not know in precise terms what those rules are but would be guided by those who are conversant with them. We do not think that their lack of knowledge is material for the purposes of the constitutional issue raised. Indeed most persons do not know the law regulating marriage, divorce or devolution of property until a problem arises and legal advice is then sought.

The Commission of Muslim Jurists which was in existence from 1981 to 1987 also had no expert knowledge of what a code of Muslim personal law should contain and sought assistance from an expert in Saudi Arabia. But, before the expert could produce a draft code and the Commission could consider it, the Commission was wound up. There was no evidence as to what, if anything definite, was understood within the Muslim community in this country to have been the religious rules applying to marriage, divorce or devolution of property. . . .

It is no doubt because of the absence of evidence as to any concrete and actual Mauritian experience of the content of the rules governing Muslim religious marriages that the plaintiffs led evidence from an Indian expert to indicate what a code of Muslim personal law, if it had been compiled and adopted, might or should have contained. A copy of the Quran, translated by Yusuf Ali (1989 Amana edn) was . . . used in evidence by the expert and he referred to a number of Suras (which we loosely translate as 'chapters' for want of a better term) and verses. The expert told us that the Quran and the practices and traditions (Hadiths) of the last Prophet together form the body of rules (Sharia) which govern the life of a Muslim.

Unfortunately, while we have been greatly assisted by having a copy of the Quran, we were not so fortunate with regard to the Hadiths. We were therefore unclear to whether there was one authoritative version or several versions which might be different and what precise aspects of the matters in issue they govern. So that we are left only with the Quran and such explanations as the expert gave about the verses that he relied upon to indicate what a code of Muslim personal law in Mauritius might or should have contained.

We were told that there are Sunni Muslims and Shia Muslims and that the Muslims in this country are Sunnis. We were also told that, among the Sunnis, there are four schools of thought on Muslim personal law with, so it was claimed, no marked differences among them and that the Muslims in this country belong to the Hanafi school.

We open a parenthesis here to say that it is common knowledge that there is in

Mauritius a section of the Muslim community consisting of the Ahmadis.[D] There was no evidence as to what the position would be in their case since, as is generally known, they do not accept Mohammad as the last Prophet so that it is unclear whether the Hadiths might be different in their case. We must also take judicial notice of the fact that there is another section, however small, made up of persons who are commonly known as Vohras or Ismailis.[E] We had no evidence as to whether the rules governing marriage, divorce and devolution of property are or are not the same in the case of those two sections when compared with the other section. Presumably, if Muslim personal law is found to be a constitutional necessity, provision would be necessary to accommodate their case.

We may now examine the evidence of the expert. He told us, in substance, that the 'true' Muslim must totally obey the teachings, injunctions and commandments of the Quran as it contains the revealed words of Allah which no one can alter. Among what has been revealed, there are certain rules governing marriage, divorce and devolution of property. These rules are in many respects detailed but, for the purposes of this case, we need not go into any detailed analysis. It will only be necessary to highlight some of the features that characterise these rules, the dominating overall feature being the superior position of men over women in terms of rights and duties.

First, there is polygamy, the number of wives that a man may legitimately have simultaneously being limited to four. Although the Quran uses the term 'orphans' in relation to women when dealing with the multiplicity of marriages as in ch 4, v 3 (4:3), the women, so the expert explained, need not be orphans. Secondly, the husband may unilaterally and, it would appear, with or without reason divorce his wife or wives whereas the woman can only divorce the husband for cause and as a result of judicial intervention and, additionally, subject to terms which, if the husband does not agree, require judicial intervention. Thirdly, in so far as devolution of property is concerned, the female child has half the share of the male child.

It is appropriate at this point to examine, if only summarily, the development of our law regarding marriage, divorce and devolution of property up to the reforms of 1981, with particular reference, first, to the treatment of religious marriage and, secondly, to the extent to which the provisions of our law differ from the three aspects of the Quranic rules we have highlighted above.

Our starting point regarding the civil law is the promulgation in Mauritus, during the French administration, of the French Civil Code in 1804. Well before that time, the Church had already lost its legislative and judicial powers in the regulation of marriage and its consequences. The state had taken over those functions. This new concept of the secular and civil character of marriage as a monogamous institution in the social order became entrenched in the Civil Code and was never open to question.

In order, however, to consolidate this changed concept of marriage as a matter affecting public order . . . , certain provisions had already been included in the Code Pénal in France in 1791 which was adopted in 1793 in Mauritius, then still under

---

[D] Ahmadi is a branch of Islam that believes the prophethood continues beyond Mohammed.

[E] The Vohras and Ismailis are branches of Shi'a Islam.

French administration. There were provisions to criminalise bigamy. There were also provisions to criminalise the celebration of religious marriages unless the officiating priest had proof that the parties had already been married by a Civil Status Officer [and were therefore bound by the Civil Code requiring monogamy]. . . .

[I]n 1914 new provisions were enacted to register religious marriages among Hindus and Muslims [following an increase in immigration from India] (the Indian Marriage Ordinance of May 1914) and among Christians (the Christian Marriage Ordinance of December 1914). The officiating priests had to be specially appointed and acted as unpaid civil status officers. Those marriages acquired civil effect on registration and became governed by the Civil Code. Nevertheless, a large number of religious marriages continued to take place and were never registered, with the result that the spouses were considered to be only concubines not having a right e.g. to maintenance or pensions or a right of action arising from the death of their partner. Another result was that the children were considered as natural [illegitimate] children.

There is no doubt that, since the sanctions were only social and not legal, religious unions were subject to some abuse with 'husbands' or even 'wives' abandoning their 'spouse' and progeny when they might not have done so if the union had been governed by the law. This situation created some measure of social instability and injustice. . . .

The Civil Status (Amendment) Act 1987 has had for effect the abandonment of [a proposal for a separate Muslim personal code requiring that Shariah law on marriage, divorce, and inheritance be imposed on all Muslims]. . . . The position is, therefore, that after 1987 one may marry only civilly or one may marry religiously with civil effect and the provisions of the Civil Code will apply uniformly whichever way one marries.

We may now address the complaint of the plaintiffs. Their claim to a constitutional right to be governed by Muslim personal law with regard to marriage, divorce and devolution of property is based on . . . [the assertion that] their freedom of religion, as guaranteed under arts 3 and 11 of the Constitution, entitles them to the benefit of Muslim personal law . . . .

It was . . . argued that, since art 16(4) removes personal laws from the incidence of the guarantee against discrimination and since, in the case of Muslims, Muslim personal law is an essential and inextricable element of religion, freedom of religion as guaranteed under arts 3 and 11 of the Constitution, supercedes all other fundamental rights to the extent to which that personal law may conflict with them. There is, as we read ch 2 of our Constitution [providing for fundamental rights], nothing in it that establishes any juridical hierarchy in the rights that it guarantees. Each right is subject only to the confines of its own inherent nature and the express limitations that are provided in the chapter. The relevant question is whether the right to freedom of religion compulsorily requires the enactment of personal laws and whether any law such as our Civil Code which conflicts with the provisions which are or might be contained in personal laws would be a violation of religious freedom.

Now arts 3 and 11 guarantee, inter alia, freedom of religion. The relevant part of the articles read as follows:

3. *Fundamental rights and freedoms of the individual*

It is hereby recognised and declared that in Mauritius there have existed and shall continue to exist without discrimination by reason of race, place of origin, political opinions, colour, creed or sex, but subject to respect for the rights and freedoms of others and for the public interest, each and all of the following human rights and fundamental freedoms— . . .

(b) freedom of conscience, of expression, of assembly and association and freedom to establish schools; . . .

and the provisions of this chapter shall have effect for the purpose of affording protection to those rights and freedoms subject to such limitations of that protection as are contained in those provisions, being limitations designed to ensure that the enjoyment of those rights and freedoms by any individual does not prejudice the rights and freedoms of others or the public interest.

11. *Protection of freedom of conscience*

(1) Except with his own consent, no person shall be hindered in the enjoyment of his freedom of conscience, and for the purposes of this section, that freedom includes freedom of thought and of religion, freedom to change his religion or belief, and freedom, either alone or in community with others and both in public and in private, to manifest and propagate his religion or belief in worship, teaching, practice and observance. . . .

(5) Nothing contained in or done under the authority of any law shall be held to be inconsistent with or in contravention of this section to the extent that the law in question makes provision—

(a) in the interests of defence, public safety, public order, public morality or public health; or

(b) for the purpose of protecting the rights and freedoms of other persons, including the right to observe and practise any religion or belief without the unsolicited intervention of persons professing any other religion or belief,

except so far as that provision or, as the case may be, the thing done under its authority is shown not to be reasonably justifiable in a democratic society.

Freedom of religion subject to the permissible derogations is a fundamental right which the European Convention for the Protection of Human Rights and Fundamental Freedoms recognises in art 9, and which the International Covenant on Civil and Political Rights also recognises in art 18. There is no case in point under those two international instruments which addresses the particular problem raised before this court.

The plaintiffs say that the nature of their religion is such that it requires total submission to the will of Allah, that it requires them to obey all that Allah has ordained as revealed in the Quran and that it is not possible for them to follow some of the injunctions of Allah and not others. Paragraph 8 of the plaint avers that the Sharia govern all aspects of the life of a Muslim and, in cross-examination, the expert witness agreed to the Solicitor General's suggestion that the Quran ordained the cutting off of the hands for the offence of theft (ch 5:38), the infliction of the severest of punishments for adultery (ch 4:15). Indeed flogging and stoning to death in public are prescribed in ch 24:2. It was argued that these were matters for the state to prescribe as part of criminal law or else would only avail in a state where Islam is the state religion.

We are, however, here dealing with arts 3 and 11 and not with art 16(4). If the reasoning of the plaintiff is correct when they say that in order to enjoy their freedom of religion guaranteed under arts 3 and 11, they must literally follow what the Quran ordains, that they cannot follow one part of the Quran and reject another part and that the enactment of appropriate laws is necessary to give effect to what the Quran ordains, then it stands to reason that the law should include matters that are relevant to the safeguard of marriage (eg the criminalisation of adultery with the appropriate punishment prescribed for that offence) and indeed matters that go beyond personal law in view of the averment in para 8 of the plaint and the evidence. Quite logically, one of the plaintiffs agreed that he would like the introduction of the punishment prescribed in the Quran for them. We do not think that it is a sufficient answer to say that the enactment of criminal law is a matter for the state. The enactment of personal laws is also a matter for the state. And if freedom of religion for Muslims, or for others for that matter, can be fully enjoyed only on the condition that all that is ordained in religion must be given effect to in the law, then the question of the violation of a number of fundamental rights would undoubtedly arise.

The reasoning of the plaintiffs is, in our judgment, based on an insufficient understanding of the duality of religion and state in a secular system. The secular state is not anti-religious but recognises freedom of religion in the sphere that belongs to it. As between the state and religion each has its own sphere, the former, that of law-making for the public good and the latter that of religious teaching, observance and practice. To the extent that it is sought to give to religious principles and commandments the force and character of law, religion steps out of its own sphere and encroaches on that of law-making in the sense that it is made to coerce the state into enacting religious principles and commandments into law. That would indeed be constitutionally possible where not only one particular religion is the state religion but also the holy book of that religion is the supreme law.

India was quoted to us as an example of a democracy where personal laws of several religions coexisted with a secular constitution which guarantees fundamental freedoms. India, however, had a heavy heritage. It had personal laws for a number of religious groups before it became a sovereign state. . . . Presumably, that is why it was found necessary to adopt art 44 in the chapter which deals with the directive principles of state policy in the Indian Constitution. That article reads: 'The State shall endeavour to secure for the citizens a uniform civil code throughout the territory of India'. And there have been some harsh comments from the Supreme Court of India on the lack of political will on the part of the state to give life to art 44 (. . . *Shah Bano Khan v Mohamed Ahmed Begum* AIR 1985 SC 945).

The position in our country is different. We have never had in our history, whether during French or British administration, any personal laws in spite of the fact that the major religions of the world have been present here for generations. Except for the attempt in 1981 to introduce Muslim personal law, a uniform Civil Code has always been in force.

To conclude we hold that neither art 3 nor art 11 can properly be relied upon as authority for the proposition that the enactment of personal laws is essential for the enjoyment of the rights that these provisions are designed to guarantee. The respondent must, therefore, succeed on this point.

Let us assume, however, that art 3 and 11 were to be or could be interpreted in the way suggested by the plaintiffs, to permit them to be governed, as a matter of guaranteed right, by the rules of their religion in respect of marriage, divorce and devolution of property. The question would then arise as to whether, in making provisions in those matters which are quite plainly inconsistent with the rules of the plaintiff's religion, the Civil Code and the Civil Status Act fail to meet the test of permissible inconsistencies under art 11(5), with regard particularly to public order and public morality, to the extent that those provisions are not reasonably justifiable in a democratic society. And the relevant question for that purpose would not be whether a code of Muslim personal law is consistent with public order or public morality (and not simply morality) or any of the other considerations covered under art 11(5), but whether the provisions of the Civil Code and of the Civil Status Act would be so consistent. In this context the plaintiffs have neither raised the question nor attempted to answer it as they should have done.

In our view and in the light of what evidence there was before us, we are not prepared to say that the provisions of the Civil Code and of the Civil Status Act governing marriage, divorce or devolution of property, to the extent that they are inconsistent with the essential features of what Muslim personal law might contain, and which we have earlier alluded to, violate the permissible derogations under art 11(5) or are not reasonably justifiable in a democratic society. Indeed, the maintenance of monogamy, including measures designed to safeguard the family and to ensure the largest measure of non-discrimination against women, whether as wives or daughters, are not only reasonably so justifiable but are also, as submitted by the respondent, in furtherance of the obligations undertaken by Mauritius under arts 2(l) and (2), 3, 23, 24 and 26 of the International Covenant on Civil and Political Rights . . . .

Both plaints are . . . dismissed with costs.

NOTES

The Constitutional and International Human Rights Rulings. Do the Mauritius Civil Code and Civil Status Act violate the Muslim plaintiffs' constitutional right to freedom of religion? Assuming they do, are there constitutional exceptions permitting the violation? Do the statutes violate plaintiffs' right to freedom of religion under the ICCPR? Chapter Four provides the text of the ICCPR articles considered by the Court, with the exception of article 24 (requiring family, society, and state to provide protection for children without sex discrimination). What does the Mauritius Supreme Court hold concerning the ICCPR? Given that the U.S. has ratified the ICCPR, consider how the *Bhewa* decision might affect the U.S. Supreme Court's ruling on the *Reynolds* issue.

Islamic Law. Note the factors that make it difficult to determine the content of Islamic law and lead to differences of opinion as to its requirements. The next two decisions from Bangladesh, a country that applies Islamic law in its courts, illustrate how different Muslim judges can arrive at opposing conclusions.

Sultana v. Elias

(High Court Division, Bangladesh)
17 BLD (HCD) 04 (1996)

MOHAMMAD GHOLAM RABBANI, J: In this Rule petitioner is Jesmin Sultana and the opposite party is her husband Mohammad Elias. They were married on 27.5.92, but they have been living separately since 2.8.92. She instituted a suit on 26.9.93 against him, for prompt dower and maintenance.

2. In Islamic glossary dower is called 'mahr' which means bridal-money given by the husband to the wife on marrying. In order to constitute a valid marriage under the Islamic law there should always be mahr as consideration from the bridegroom in favour of the bride. Though there is nothing in Qur-an or hadith to divide the mahr into two parts, but later jurisconsults ruled that only a portion of the mahr is to be fixed payable at once on demand known as 'mahr-i-muajjal' which means prompt dower and the remainder is to be paid in the event of divorce or death of the husband and is called 'mahr-i-muwajjal' which means deferred dower.

3. In the instant marriage dower was fixed at Tk. 1,50,000/00 and out of which prompt dower was fixed at Tk. 60,000/00. Trial Court decreed the suit awarding Tk. 60,000/00 prompt dower and Tk. 500/00 as monthly maintenance. On appeal preferred by the husband, lower appellate Court reduced the amount of prompt dower to Tk. 40,000/00. Hence this Rule obtained by the wife against the reduction of the prompt dower.

4. Lower appellate Court arbitrarily reduced the amount of the prompt dower upon one sentenced sweeping remark that the Qur-an does not support fixation of an amount of dower which the husband is not able to pay. This view is wrong. Qur-an says:—

And give the women (on marriage) their dower as a free gift; but if they, of their own good pleasure, remit any part of it to you, take it and enjoy it with right good cheer. (Fourth Sura Nisa, verse 4).
But if you decided to take one wife in place of another, even if you had given the latter a whole treasure for dower, take not the least bit of it back. (Sura Nisa, verse 20).

[5.] A Hadith in Sabih Al-Bukhari reads as follows:

Narrated Uqba: The Prophet (sm) said, 'The stipulations of the marriage contract most entitled to be abided are those with which you are given the right to enjoy the women's private parts.' (Hadith no. 81, Vol VII, translated by Dr. Mohammad Muhsin Khan).

6. We, therefore, hold that the lower appellate Court acted illegally in reducing the amount of the prompt dower.

7. In the case of *Mosammat Nur Akhtar Vs. Md. Abdul Mabud Chowdbury* reported in (1996) 16 BLD 396 this Division Bench held that a wife voluntarily leaving her husband and not interested in returning to him is not entitled to maintenance. In the

instant suit defendant-husband contested his wife's claims of maintenance alleging that she voluntarily left his house and is residing with her parents without any lawful cause, but both the Courts below overlooked this case of the defendant.

8. Petitioner has annexed with the supplementary affidavit a certified copy of an application dated 6.3.96 filed by her husband before the Chairman of the Local Union Council seeking permission under section 6 of the Muslim Family Laws Ordinance to take a second wife alleging that she is sickly and incapable to perform conjugal relation. For this attitude of her husband it is not difficult to hold that the petitioner was compelled to leave her husband and so she is entitled to get maintenance which both the Courts below have fixed at Tk. 500/00 per month. We affirm the decree of maintenance.

9. Section 6 of the Muslim Family Laws Ordinance states that no man during the subsistence of an existing marriage, shall, except with the previous permission of the Arbitration Council, contract another marriage. But this section does not declare the second marriage as illegal or invalid, but only prescribes simple imprisonment for one year and fine on conviction for violating the provision of section 6. We, therefore, find it necessary to examine the issue as to whether Islam truly approves polygamy or, more properly speaking, polygyny.

10. Since long, we find, there had been great difference of opinion regarding this issue and that arose while interpreting verse 3 of Sura Nisa as hereunder:—

If you fear that you shall not be able to deal justly with the orphans, marry women of your choice, two, or three, or four; but if you fear that you shall not be able to deal justly, then only one.

11. Abdullah Yousuf Ali in his book, "The Holy Qur-an: Text, Translation & Commentary," gives the following notes on the above-quoted verse:—

Notice the conditional clause about the orphans, introducing the rules about marriage. This reminds us of the immediate occasion of the promulgation of this verse. It was (battle of) Uhud, when the Muslim community was left with many orphans and widows. The occasion is past, but the principles remain. Marry the orphans if you are quite sure that you will in that way protect their interests and their property, with perfect justice to them.

The unrestricted number of wives of the 'Times of Ignorance' was now strictly limited to a maximum of four provided you could treat them with perfect equality, in material things as well as in affection and immaterial things. As this condition is most difficult to fulfil, I understand the recommendation to be towards monogamy.

12. Thus "to be able to deal justly" is the condition precedent to marry more than one woman. Some of the commentators held that the expression implies equality in love and affection and such equality being impossible in the weakness of human nature, the permission to take another wife amounts virtually to a prohibition. Others took the narrow view and held that equality means only equality in maintenance and lodgment.

13. We reject the narrow view of the meaning of the expression "to be able to deal justly" in view of the Hadith in Sahih Al-Bukhari as hereunder:

Narrated Al-Miswar bin Makhrama: I heard Allah's Apostle (sm) who was on pulpit saying, 'Banu Hashim bin Al-Mughira have requested me to allow them to marry their daughter to Ali bin Abi Talib, but I don't give permission, and will not give permission unless Ali bin Abi Talib divorces my daughter, because Fatima is a part of my body and I hate what she hates to see, and what hurts her, hurts me.' (Hadith no. 157 in Vol. VII translated by Dr. Mohammad Muhsin Khan).

14. So Prophet of Islam (sm) did not allow his son-in-law Ali to take another wife as that would hurt his daughter Fatima obviously on the understanding that Ali "shall not be able to deal justly" with two women. And who else is to be followed other than the Messenger of Allah (sm) about whom Allah certifies, "he commands them what is just and forbids them what is evil." (Seventh Sura Araf, verse 157).

15. It is to be remembered that after the battle for Uhud in A.H. 3, verse 52 of thirty-third Sura Ahzab was revealed in A.H.7 as hereunder:

It is not lawful for you to marry more women after this, nor to change them for other wives, even though their beauty attract you, except your right hand should possess (as handmaidens). And God doth watch over all things.

16. Prophet did not marry after this except a handmaiden named Mary. To Prophet she bore a son who died in infancy.

17. Polygamy is prohibited in Tunisia under the Law of Personal Status, 1957. According to Tunisian jurists, "to be able to deal justly" is the injunction legally enforceable and under the modern social and economic conditions this essential condition for polygamy is incapable of fulfilment. So we find that section 6 of the Muslim Family Laws Ordinance is against the principle of Islamic law. We recommend that this section be deleted and be substituted with a section prohibiting polygamy. Let a copy of this judgment be sent to The Ministry of Law.

This Rule is made absolute, Impugned Judgment and decree dated 27.9.95 of the 2nd Court of Subordinate Judge, Chittagong, in F.C. Appeal No. 52 of 1994 are set aside and those dated 28.6.94 of the Court of Assistant Judge and Family Court, Mirsarai, at Chittagong Sadar, in F.C. Case No. 35 of 1993, are restored.

Elias v. Sultana

(Bangladesh Appellate Division)
19 BLD (AD) 122 (1999)

A.T.M. AFZAK, C. J: This petition by the defendant-husband which arises out of a Family Suit No. 35 of 1993, of the Court of Assistant Judge and Family Court, Mirsarai, Chittagong for prompt dower and maintenance allowance filed by the respondent-wife is barred by 649 days and we are going to dismiss this petition as time-barred but not before we express ourselves against part of the impugned judgment dealing with polygamy in Islam and recommending amendment in the Muslim Family Laws

Ordinance, 1961 (Ordinance No. VII of 1961) prohibiting polygamy which was totally irrelevant for a decision in the matter.

2. The trial Court decreed Tk. 60,000/- as prompt dower, Tk. 4,500/- as maintenance allowance and further Tk. 500/- per month for same purpose. On appeal, however, the amount of prompt dower was reduced to Tk. 40,000/- whereupon the respondent [wife] took a revision, Civil Revision No. 4591 of 1995, against the appellate judgment and decree. A Division Bench, by the impugned judgment and order dated 26 November, 1996 disapproved the reduction of the amount of prompt dower and restored the decree as passed by the trial Court.

3. In course of the hearing of the matter the High Court Division noticed that the defendant-husband had filed an application to the Chairman of the Local Union Council seeking permission under section 6 of the aforesaid Ordinance to take a second wife alleging that the present wife, namely, the plaintiff, was sickly and incapable of performing conjugal relationship. The learned Judges observed that section 6 of the Ordinance prohibits contracting of a second marriage during the subsistence of an existing marriage without the previous permission of the Arbitration Council but it does not declare the second marriage as illegal or invalid but only prescribes for punishment for violation of the said section. Then the learned Judges observed: "We, therefore, find it necessary to examine the issue as to whether Islam truly approves polygamy or more properly speaking, polygyny". The learned Judges themselves noticed that there had been great difference of opinion regarding this issue since long and then embarked upon a legal monologue referring to the Holy Quran and the hadith and finally came out with a recommendation that section 6 of the aforesaid Ordinance be deleted and substituted a section prohibiting polygamy. A copy of the judgment was directed to be sent to the Ministry of Law.

4. It has been brought to our notice that the impugned judgment has also been published in a law journal (1997 BLD [Bangladesh Legal Decisions] 04).

5. From the facts of the case as noticed above briefly it is evident that it was totally unnecessary for the learned Judges to indulge in the discussion on polygamy in Islam which was neither an issue in the suit nor required to be decided in the context of the pleadings of the parties. The exercise taken by the learned Judge was not only gratuitous but wholly illegal being not within their jurisdiction under the Code of Civil Procedure. In a recent case relating to maintenance of a divorced Muslim wife we have noticed that the learned author Judge of the impugned judgment had indulged in the same kind of gratuitous exercise not required in the framework of that suit an[d] abruptly laid down a law which was contrary to the centuries old Muslim Personal Law. In the present case also the learned Judge quite unnecessarily expressed an opinion on a subject of Muslim Law without anybody asking for it and without hearing anybody whatsoever which the learned Judges themselves observed was a contentious subject since long. We must record our total disapproval to the learned Judge's practice of incorporating his personal opinion on a legal subject which is not at all required to be decided for the disposal of the matter before him, the parties not being in issue in the suit over such subject. We are sorry to say that this is a kind of aberration which seems to be pathological with the learned Judge which is not at all

desirable in a system of law and norms under which our Courts have been functioning in this country since long. In the circumstances of the case, we feel compelled to observe that the discussion on polygamy in Islam and recommendation thereon as recorded in the impugned judgment should be taken to be deleted lest it may create confusion in the mind of the subordinate Courts and the people at large.

With these observations, the petition is dismissed.

B. Personal Laws in India

Kirti Singh, *Obstacles to Women's Rights in India*
in HUMAN RIGHTS OF WOMEN (Rebecca J. Cook ed., 1994), 375, 377–81, 386–87

The Constitutional Position

The Indian Constitution has a "Fundamental Rights" chapter that guarantees various rights. The rights of special importance to women are the Right to Equality in Article 14 and the Express Prohibition Against Discrimination in Article 15. Article 14 mandates that "the state shall not deny to any person equality before the law or the equal protection of the laws within the territory of India." Article 15(1) prohibits discrimination against any citizen by the state "on grounds only of religion, race, caste, sex, place of birth, or any of them." Article 15(3) also allows for special provision for women and children by clarifying that "Nothing in this Article shall prevent the state from making any special provision for women and children." . . .

In addition, Article 16(1) mandates equality of opportunity for all citizens in matters relating to employment or appointment to any office under the state. Article 16(2) clarifies that "no citizen shall, on grounds only of religion, race, caste, sex, descent, place of birth, residence or any of them, be ineligible for, or discriminated against in respect of, any employment or office under the State." . . . These Fundamental Rights in Chapter III of the Constitution are obviously enforceable in a court of law.

Chapter IV of the Constitution of India contains principles of law known as the "Directive Principles of State Policy," which though not enforceable, are supposed to be fundamental in the governance of the country. . . .

[A] . . . very important article of the Directive Principles of State Policy aims at ending the regime of personal laws and states that "the State shall endeavour to secure for the citizens a uniform civil code throughout the territory of India.

Personal Laws

Personal laws in India deal with marriage and divorce, maintenance, guardianship, adoption, wills, intestacy and succession, joint family, and partition, and can broadly be characterized as "family laws." These laws are basically divided along religious lines, whether or not they are based on religion. Thus Hindus in India are governed by the Hindu Marriage Act of 1955, the Hindu Succession Act of 1956, the Hindu Guardianship and Minorities Act of 1956, and the Hindu Adoption and Maintenance

Act of 1956. Indian Muslims are governed by the Shari'a Act of 1937, the Muslim Women's Dissolution of Marriage Act of 1939, and the Muslim Women's (Protection of Rights on Divorce) Act of 1986, and uncodified Muslim personal laws. Christians are governed by their own Christian Marriage Act, the Indian Divorce Act, and the Indian Succession Act, while Parsis, too, have codified laws of marriage and divorce and of succession.

The main characteristic of all the personal laws is that they are anti-women, anti-liberal, and anti-human. It is ironic that while all Indian women suffer from the same or similar discrimination at home or within their families, the family or personal laws applicable to them are different and subject them to varying degrees of discrimination. We are thus confronted with a strange situation that while a Hindu, Christian, or Parsi woman can sue her husband for bigamy under the criminal law code for punishment of up to seven years imprisonment, Indian Muslim personal law allows a Muslim man to marry up to four times.

One of the main arguments advanced against reform of personal law has been that such reform violates the right of all Indian citizens to freedom of religion. If one examines Article 25 of the Constitution which gives all persons freedom of conscience and the right to profess, practice and propagate religion, it will be seen that this article is specifically subject to the following provisions:

(a) Public order, morality and health;

(b) The provisions of Part III of the Constitution including the right to equality and Article 15.

This article also makes it clear that

(a) The state can regulate any economic, financial, political or other secular activity that may be associated with religious practice;

(b) The state can make any law providing for social welfare and reform.

Article 25 therefore clearly states the parameters within which the right freely to practice, propagate, and profess religion is limited. It in fact defines the content of secularism by stating that the right to freely propagate and practice religion is not an unlimited right but is subject to the constitutional rights of equality and freedom from discrimination. It also enables the state to regulate any economic, financial, political, or other secular activity associated with religious practice. The state has also been empowered to make any laws for social welfare and reform which may interfere with the right to freedom of religion. A bare reading of this article shows clearly that the Constitution restricts the scope of the right to freedom of religion.

The question, however, of enacting a common civil code has never been on the agenda of the government, in spite of the fact that from time to time various committees, women's organizations, and others interested in women's rights have asked for a uniform secular family law based on equality. In fact, until the judgment of the Supreme Court in Shah Bano's case,[F] several women's groups and others were

---

[F] In *Mohammad Ahmed Khan v. Shah Bano*, A.I.R. (1985) S.C. 945, the Indian Supreme Court ruled that Muslim women were entitled to the same maintenance rights at divorce that non-Muslim women received, rather than the three-month maintenance allowed by Sharia divorce law. Muslim fundamentalists protested, while women's groups supported the decision. The

actively working toward a uniform civil code based on equality that would apply to all Indian women regardless of their community. After witnessing the opposition to a uniform civil code from sections of the Muslim population, however, women's groups and others have been demanding reforms in the personal laws of the different communities.

A look at the various reforms in Hindu personal laws shows that they have come about due to the separation of family laws from religion. In fact, the progressive changes that have been brought about in Hindu personal law have nothing to do with religion, but were instead based on the concept of equality and had nothing to do with *smritis* (old Hindu texts) and the laws of Manu (an ancient law-giver who prohibited divorce).

Prior to Independence, the British rulers also followed a policy of retaining and not reforming the family laws applicable to Hindus, Muslims, and Parsis. In fact, during this entire period the personal laws of various communities remained static, and the British system of courts relied heavily on religious pundits and the *ulama* for interpreting the personal laws applicable to Hindus and Muslims. In several instances, this resulted in further communalizing the law.

Family laws were therefore extremely backward at the time of Indian Independence and needed to be extensively amended. Changes, however, took place only in Hindu law. This law was codified and separate acts dealing with marriage and divorce, adoption and maintenance, succession and minority, and guardianship were passed. The concept of monogamy was introduced for the first time in the Hindu Marriage Act of 1955. Concomitantly, certain limited grounds of divorce were introduced into Hindu law for the first time. Prior to the change, while a man was free to marry an unlimited number of times without getting divorced, the woman could not do so and once married had to remain married until she died.

The passing of the Hindu Marriage Act with its provision for divorce was opposed by conservative members of Parliament who were members of Hindu communal organizations like the Jan Sangh and the Hindu Maha Sabha. These members claimed that the bill had been passed to "wound the religious feelings of the Hindus" and was "against the fundamental principles of Hinduism." It is interesting that one Hindu fundamentalist member of Parliament at that time, V. M. Trivedi, actually proposed an amendment to the effect that if the wife agreed that she did not object to her husband's having a second wife, this condition should not apply. Strangely enough, the fundamentalists demanded that a uniform civil code be introduced and stated that Hindus were being discriminated against since the bill did not apply to Muslims. It was only because the government of the day was in favor of reforming and codifying Hindu law that the Act was passed despite fierce opposition. In fact the Minister of Law in Parliament at the time, while introducing the bill, said it was a measure of great social importance to do good to women because men had been enjoying

---

Indian government caved to the Muslim fundamentalist pressure and enacted the Muslim Women's (Protection of Rights on Divorce) Act of 1986. Despite its name, it denied Muslim women the rights they had gained under *Shah Bano*.

disproportionate rights and privileges as compared with women and the government could not, in the name of preserving the sanctity of any ancient culture, try to treat women differently in the present time and conditions. The Minister also pointed out that ancient Hindu law had already been altered from time to time. . . .

Courts on Personal Law

As far as the courts are concerned, other than a few judgments like *Shah Bano,* they have been mainly concerned with preserving the status quo. It was only in the 1950s that the courts showed a determination to uphold the reforms passed in the Hindu Law. In the 1950s there were some challenges to certain laws prohibiting bigamy that had been passed in some states prior to the Hindu reforms referred to above. In *State of Bombay v. Narasu Appa Mali,* the Bombay High Court held that the "Bombay Prevention of Hindu Bigamous Marriage Act was a measure of social reform and the state was empowered to legislate with regard to Article 25(2)(b) [re social welfare and reform], notwithstanding the fact that it may interfere with the right of a citizen to freely profess, practice, and propagate religion." Similarly, in *Srinivasa v. Saraswati Ammal,* it was held that the freedom to practice religion was not an absolute right as Article 25 itself states, but that it is subject to the other provisions of Part III of the Constitution. It was further held that Article 25(2) empowered the legislature to enact a law providing for social welfare and reform and that religious practice, therefore, may be controlled by legislation if the states think that it is necessary to do so in the interest of social welfare and reform. Both cases also made a sharp distinction between religious belief and practice. In the former case it was held that what the state protects is religious faith and belief and quoted with approval an American case, *Davis v. Beason* [133 U.S. 333 (1890)], in which it had been held that "laws are made for the Governments of action and while they cannot interfere with mere religious beliefs and opinions, they may with practices." The court held that it was difficult to accept the proposition that polygamy is an integral part of the Hindu religion. In the latter case also the court quoted another American case, *Reynolds v. U.S.,* [98 U.S. 145 (1878),] in which religious belief and practice were distinguished, to show that the freedom to practice religion is not an absolute right, though it went on to justify the Madras Hindu (Bigamy and Divorce) Act of 1949, on the basis of Article 25(2). The two courts also held that there was no discrimination between Hindus and Muslims in spite of the fact that Muslims could marry more than once, because the classification between Muslim and Hindu was based on a reasonable and rational consideration and thus did not offend Article 15 of the Constitution. Thus in these cases the courts were mainly concerned with justifying the reforms in the laws.

NOTE

Women's Right to Equality in Marriage Versus Freedom of Religion. In Chapter Four we discussed whether French law should permit Muslims to practice polygyny as a matter of freedom of religion under international human rights law. What do the court decisions from the United States, Mauritius, and Bangladesh contribute to this discussion? How does Indian law handle this question? India is a State party to the ICCPR and CEDAW, but has declared as to CEDAW articles 5(a) and 16(1) that it shall "abide by and ensure these provisions in conformity with its policy of non-interference in the personal affairs of any Community without its initiative and consent." It has issued no such declaration or reservation as to ICCPR article 23(4). After reviewing these articles in CEDAW (Chapter One) and the ICCPR (Chapter Four, pages 145–46), consider whether India complies with its international human rights obligations.

IV. Perspectives on Polygyny

A. A Human Rights Approach

Susan Deller Ross, *Polygyny as a Violation of Women's Right to Equality in Marriage: An Historical, Comparative and International Human Rights Overview*
24 Delhi L. Rev. 22, 30–33, 35–36 (2002)

International law clearly establishes that polygyny violates women's most fundamental rights and freedoms. From the beginning of the international human rights system, international law required equality before the law and in marriage. Yet many countries have failed to take effective action against polygyny, citing freedom of religion and culture as reasons for inaction. . . .

The founding of the United Nations in 1945 and its subsequently enacted human rights system have brought ever-increasing attention to the need to eradicate all forms of discrimination against women. The opening clauses of the United Nations Charter show a "determina[tion] . . . to reaffirm faith in . . . the equal rights of men and women . . . ," and Article 55 declares that the UN will "promote . . . universal respect for, and observance of, human rights and fundamental freedoms for all without distinction as to . . . sex . . . or religion." Both reflect central awareness of the reality of women's lives, profoundly different from these aspirational goals, thus necessitating concrete action to change that reality. In Article 56, UN members pledge to take both "joint" action with the UN and "separate" action to achieve their Article 55 purposes.

From the beginning, women activists focused on the goal of ending polygyny and women's subjugation within marriage. The UN Commission on the Status of Women, meeting for the first time in 1947, agreed to work for "[f]reedom of choice, dignity of the wife, monogamy, [and] equal right to dissolution of marriage."[36] That goal was subsequently reflected in the [UDHR], adopted by the UN General Assembly on December 10, 1948. Article 16(1) proclaimed that "[m]en and women of full age . . . have the right to marry and . . . are entitled to equal rights as to marriage, during marriage and at its dissolution."

---

[36] . . . [U.N. Comm'n on the Status of Women, Legal Status of Women (Reports submitted by the Secretary-General), at 1, U.N. Doc. ST/SOA/35, U.N. Sales No. 1957.IV.8 (1958)].

An Indian woman lawyer, Hansa Mehta, and Eleanor Roosevelt worked together to insure that the UDHR would contain women's Article 16 right to equality in marriage. Roosevelt served as Chair of the newly formed United Nations Human Rights Commission while it drafted the UDHR. Each headed one of the three working groups; no other women served on the Commission. At the time, Mehta was also advising the Indian government (again, as one of only two women) on the rights and provisions of what became its 1949 Constitution.[38] There, she "battl[ed] purdah, child marriage, polygamy, [and] unequal inheritance laws, . . . striving to set these ancient customs on a course of extinction."[39] Eleanor Roosevelt also fought for women's right to equality in marriage. Indeed, she suggested adding to the right to marry, "the specification that men and women have equal rights when a marriage is dissolved."[40]

The UDHR focus on equal rights within marriage was further buttressed by the grand language of the Preamble and other articles. The Preamble spoke specifically of the United Nations' commitment to the "dignity and worth of the human person and in the equal rights of men and women." The very first article built on this core concept, and here again Hansa Mehta played a major role. Her efforts insured that Article 1 of the Declaration, which recognizes that all are born "free and equal in dignity and rights," be cast in inclusive terms. The first draft gave this right only to "men." At her insistence, the final version gave this right to "all human beings." Further commitments to women's rights to equality were reflected in Article 2 (all are entitled to the rights in the Declaration without "distinction" based on "sex"), and Article 7 ("[a]ll are equal before the law and are entitled without any discrimination to equal protection of the law; [a]ll are entitled to equal protection against any discrimination in violation of the Declaration and against any incitement to such discrimination").

The UDHR commitment to equality for women with particular reference to marriage was carried forth and amplified in two international human rights treaties. The [ICCPR] was forceful on this point. Article 23(4) required that ratifying states "shall take appropriate steps to ensure equality of rights and responsibilities of spouses as to marriage, during marriage and at its dissolution." The specific requirement that states "ensure" a particular right appears only in this article and in two other articles [2(1), 2(3), and 3] specifically dealing with women's rights. . . . The ICCPR also expanded on the Declaration's requirements about marriage. Now they covered "equal rights and responsibilities," rather than simply "equal rights."

[CEDAW] expanded yet again by listing the various areas of the law where married women commonly did not have equality with their husbands. It requires states, in Article 16(1), to "eliminate discrimination against women in all matters relating to marriage and family relations and in particular . . . [to] ensure on a basis of equality of men and women . . . [t]he *same* right[s]":

---

[38] Mary Ann Glendon, A World Made New: Eleanor Roosevelt and the Universal Declaration of Human Rights 90 (2001).

[39] *Id.*

[40] *Id.* at 93.

- to enter into marriage;
- choose a spouse freely;
- during and at dissolution of marriage;
- as parents vis-à-vis their children;
- as guardians or adoptive parents;
- in personal matters, including choice of family name, profession, and occupation; and
- with regard to owning, acquiring, managing, administering, enjoying or disposing of property.

Not only does CEDAW require that men and women have the same **rights**. It also requires that men and women have the same **responsibilities**:

- during marriage and at dissolution;
- as parents; and
- as guardians, trustees, or adoptive parents.

NOTE

The CEDAW Committee and the Human Rights Committee. Both Committees have taken a decisive stance on polygamy, religion, and culture. CEDAW *General Recommendation No. 21* (1994), Equality in Marriage and Family Relations, provides, with respect to Article 16:

13. The form and concept of the family can vary from State to State, and even between regions within a State. Whatever form it takes, and whatever the legal system, religion, custom or tradition within the country, the treatment of women in the family both at law and in private must accord with the principles of equality and justice for all people, as article 2 of the Convention requires. . . .

14. States parties' reports . . . disclose that polygamy is practised in a number of countries. Polygamous marriage contravenes a woman's right to equality with men, and can have such serious emotional and financial consequences for her and her dependents that such marriages ought to be discouraged and prohibited. The Committee notes with concern that some States parties, whose constitutions guarantee equal rights, permit polygamous marriage in accordance with personal or customary law. This violates the constitutional rights of women, and breaches the provisions of article 5 (a) of the Convention. . . .

17. An examination of States parties' reports discloses that many countries in their legal systems provide for the rights and responsibilities of married partners by relying on the application of common law principles, religious or customary law, rather than by complying with the principles contained in the Convention. These variations in law and practice relating to marriage have wide-ranging consequences for women, invariably restricting their rights to equal status and responsibility within marriage. . . .

Similarly, the Human Rights Committee's *General Comment No. 28* (2000), Equality of Rights Between Men and Women (article 3), states:

5. Inequality in the enjoyment of rights by women throughout the world is deeply embedded in tradition, history and culture, including religious attitudes. . . . States parties should ensure that traditional, historical, religious or cultural attitudes are not used to justify violations of women's right to equality before the law and to equal enjoyment of all Covenant rights. States

parties should furnish appropriate information on those aspects of tradition, history, cultural practices and religious attitudes which jeopardise, or may jeopardise, compliance with article 3, and indicate what measures they have taken or intend to take to overcome such factors. . . .

21. States parties must take measures to ensure that freedom of thought, conscience and religion, and the freedom to adopt the religion or belief of one's choice—including the freedom to change religion or belief and to express one's religion or belief—will be guaranteed and protected in law and in practice for both men and women, on the same terms and without discrimination. These freedoms protected by article 18, must not be subject to restrictions other than those authorized by the Covenant. . . . Article 18 may not be relied upon to justify discrimination against women by reference to freedom of thought, conscience and religion; States parties should therefore . . . indicate what steps they have taken or intend to take . . . to protect [women's] rights against any discrimination.

23. States are required to treat men and women equally in regard to marriage in accordance with article 23. . . .

24. . . . It should . . . be noted that equality of treatment with regard to the right to marry implies that polygamy is incompatible with this principle. Polygamy violates the dignity of women. It is an inadmissible discrimination against women. Consequently, it should be definitely abolished wherever it continues to exist.

25. To fulfill their obligations under article 23, paragraph 4, States must ensure that the matrimonial regime contains equal rights and obligations for both spouses, with regard to the custody and care of children, the children's religious and moral education, the capacity to transmit to children the parent's nationality, and the ownership or administration of property. . . . Equality during marriage implies that husband and wife should participate equally in responsibility and authority within the family. . . .

32. The rights which persons belonging to minorities enjoy under article 27 of the Covenant in respect of their language, culture and religion do not authorize any State, group or person to violate the right to equal enjoyment by women of any Covenant rights, including the right to equal protection of the law. . . .

In addition to condemning polygyny for violating women's right to equality in marriage, the CEDAW Committee, in its *General Recommendation No. 24* (1999), Women and Health, also noted a connection between this practice and the spread of HIV/AIDS:

18. The issues of HIV/AIDS and other sexually transmitted diseases are central to the rights of women and adolescent girls to sexual health. Adolescent girls and women in many countries lack adequate access to information and services necessary to ensure sexual health. As a consequence of unequal power relations based on gender, women and adolescent girls are often unable to refuse sex or insist on safe and responsible sex practices. Harmful traditional practices, such as female genital mutilation, polygamy, as well as marital rape, may also expose girls and women to the risk of contracting HIV/AIDS and other sexually transmitted diseases. . . .

Islam requires that a polygynous husband treat each of his wives equally with respect to each other. If he does so, does that fulfill the requirements of CEDAW article 16(1) and ICCPR article 23(4)?

B. A Law and Economics Approach

Richard A. Posner, Sex and Reason
253–60 (1992)

The Question of Polygamy

The importance of the ideal of companionate marriage in shaping marriage policy in

Christian culture may be the key to explaining the hard line which that culture has taken against polygamy (throughout this discussion I use *polygamy* as a synonym for *polygyny*). The prohibition of polygamous marriage may appear to make no sense from the standpoint of protecting women. Polygamy increases the effective demand for women, resulting in a lower average age of marriage for women and a higher percentage of women who are married. Of course, not all women want to marry young, or to be one of several wives of the same man, or indeed to marry at all. But rarely is a person made better off by having an option removed. Forbidding polygamy withdraws one option from a woman, namely that of being a nonexclusive wife. By doing so it reduces competition among men for women and thus reduces the explicit or implicit price that a woman can demand in exchange for becoming a wife—even a sole wife.

But this analysis is incomplete. In most polygamous cultures a woman cannot make an enforceable contract to be a man's only wife,[22] and this limitation on freedom of contract reduces the advantages of polygamy for women. The option of polygamy is given them, but the option of monogamy is withdrawn. Polygamous societies think polygamy a good thing just as monogamous societies think monogamy a good thing. We must consider why this is so and in particular why polygamy seems unnatural in a culture dedicated to companionate marriage.

The taboo against polygamy in Christian societies runs so deep that there is little felt need to justify it and therefore little sensitivity to the contradictions that such efforts to justify it as are made often involve. In *Hyde v. Hyde* [1 L.R. 130 (Matrimonial Ct. 1866)] the question for an English court was whether to recognize a Mormon marriage made in Utah at a time when polygamy was lawful there. The marriage was not itself polygamous. Both spouses had been single at the time of the marriage, and the husband had not taken any additional wives since; on the contrary, he had renounced the Mormon faith, and he and his wife were living in England. He wanted a divorce on the ground of her adultery. The court refused to give it to him. The ground was that persons united in a Mormon marriage could not be considered "husband" and "wife" within the meaning of English divorce law, since one of the "essential elements and invariable features" of marriage "as understood in Christendom" is monogamy. But Mormons are Christian, so the argument from the universality of Christian practice fails. The court added that England had "no law framed on the scale of polygamy, or adjusted to its requirements." A nice point—but inapplicable to the case at hand because the plaintiff had only one wife and he wanted to divorce her on a ground recognized in England as well as in Utah. He was not asking the court to create a law of polygamy to govern his conduct.

In the parallel American case, *Reynolds v. United States*, the issue was whether a federal law forbidding polygamy in the Territory of Utah infringed the right of Mormons, guaranteed by the First Amendment to the Constitution, to exercise their reli-

---

[22] There is a trend, however, in modern Muslim societies toward permitting such contracts. . . .

gion freely. The answer was no. "Congress was deprived [by the First Amendment] of all legislative power over mere opinion, but was left free to reach actions which were in violation of social duties or subversive of good order." . . . ". . . . Polygamy leads to the patriarchal principle . . . which, when applied to large communities, fetters the people in stationary despotism, while that principle cannot long exist in connection with monogamy." The opposite would be more accurate. Polygamy conduces to the creation of powerful families, offsetting the power of the center.

The question of polygamy returned to the Supreme Court in *Cleveland v. United States* [329 U.S. 14 (1946)], a prosecution for violation of the Mann Act, which at the time forbade transporting women across state lines for "immoral" purposes. The defendant—a Mormon who continued to believe in and practice polygamy despite the Mormon Church's abandonment of the practice—had taken one of his wives across a state line. The Court upheld his conviction, remarking without elaboration that "the establishment or maintenance of polygamous households is a notorious example of promiscuity." Yet one defense of polygamy—a defense prominent in Islamic thinking—is that it reduces promiscuity by providing additional lawful outlets for male sexuality.

We thus can get little help in our quest from the courts, but there is a rich literature, which goes back to Hume and indeed to Aquinas, on the relative merits of monogamy and polygamy, Mormon and otherwise. The pro side makes a number of points already touched on: polygamy ensures a husband for every woman and reduces the incidence of adultery, fornication, and prostitution; is accepted as normal in the Old Testament; is permitted already, in the form of remarriage; offsets a shortage of men; and increases the number of children. With regard to Mormon polygamy, the further point is made that by reducing the intensity of the emotional bond between husband and wife, polygamy frees the husband to devote more of his emotional energies to the Church. But this is also a point in the litany of criticisms of polygamy. Polygamy weakens the ties of affection between husband and wife; it is inconsistent, as Aquinas argued, with companionate marriage. The polygamist's wife is one of several, sometimes many, women among whom her husband must divide his time. She is sexually deprived, lonely, jealous, given to intrigue, and (particularly if she is his first wife) degraded. These consequences would be mitigated if a wife could make a contract with her husband that required her consent to his taking additional wives. But such contracts were forbidden in Mormon society, as they are in most polygamous societies.

Polygamy undermines companionate marriage in other ways. The literature harps on the insensitivity, brutality, and tyranny of the polygamous husband; he is the lord and master; he treats his wives like chattels, like slaves. These complaints may be exaggerated, but there are several reasons for believing that they contain a kernel of truth. The first is the frequent disparity in age between the husband and many of his wives (maybe all but the first). An older man is likelier to have the resources necessary to maintain multiple wives than a younger one, and the older he is relative to the wife, the more likely he is to strike her as tyrannous and she to strike him as naturally inferior.

Second and more interesting, the more wives a man has, the likelier he is to manage his household (or households) on a hierarchical rather than on an egalitarian basis. He may have little choice. The costs of coordination through negotiation are higher the greater the number of activities that have to be coordinated—indeed, those costs rise faster than the number of links necessary to connect all the parties. The higher the costs of transacting, the likelier is a substitution of hierarchical for transactional coordination and direction. And any hierarchical relationship bears a family resemblance to a master-servant relationship; thus we find the law continuing to use the terms "master and servant" to describe the legal relationship between an employer and his employee, just as prostitution, which . . . I called a form of polyandry (many husbands), itself a form of polygamy, tends to create a relationship that is commercial, impersonal—a transaction on the spot market—so polygyny (many wives, the usual form polygamy takes) creates a relationship tending more to the businesslike, the managerial, than to the affective.

A related point is that the lack of companionship implicit in a polygamous marriage gives the wives an incentive to engage in extramarital sex, at the same time that it gives them more opportunities to do so because they perforce spend most of their time away from their husband. Since the benefits of extramarital sex are greater for the polygamist's wife and the costs lower, the polygamous husband has an incentive to maintain intrusive surveillance over his wives, to restrict their activities, and to punish severely any flirtations or other infractions of strict fidelity; and the wives will perceive these measures as tyrannous.

It may not be an accident that the congeries of practices loosely referred to as "female circumcision"[35]—primarily, the removal of the clitoris and (until marriage) the sewing up of the entrance to the vagina (infibulation)—are found only, as far as I am able to determine, in polygamous societies, except that . . . Victorian doctors used clitoridectomy as a last resort to "cure" female masturbators. (Purdah, an alternative method of exerting close control over wives, also is found only in polygamous societies, for it is a Muslim institution, and Islam permits polygamy.) By reducing the woman's capacity to experience sexual pleasure, the removal of the clitoris reduces the risk of a wife's committing adultery, a more serious risk in a polygamous than in a monogamous culture because the satisfactions of marriage to the wife are fewer. Infibulation is a measure for ensuring virginity until marriage. . . .

[P]olygamy increases the agency costs of marriage, inciting cost-reducing efforts by the husband-principal that may be costly to the wives-agents and that therefore may make the freedom that wives in a polygamous marriage would otherwise have illusory. Female circumcision is analogous to the medieval chastity belt, a measure for preventing the wife from committing adultery when the husband, being away at war, would face insuperable costs of maintaining surveillance over her by normal methods.

---

[35] . . . Chinese foot-binding is analyzed as a method of sequestration of women in Mildred Dickemann, "Paternal Confidence and Dowry Competition: A Biocultural Analysis of Purdah." . . . [Her] essay is a veritable catalogue of the ways in which men in polygamous societies try to keep women from straying. . . .

One can see how, at a time when companionate marriage represented a step up the social ladder for most women, polygamy seemed retrograde and even misogynist, despite the fact that it reduced the number of spinsters. Whether this was a correct evaluation is difficult to say. Some women gain from polygamy—those who prefer being the nonexclusive wife of a wealthy man to either being the exclusive wife of a nonwealthy one or remaining unmarried. Other women lose, particularly those who would be the exclusive wife of a wealthy man in a monogamous society. If the costs stemming from the polygamous husband's efforts to police his wives weigh heavily on the wives, the balance may tip against the practice from the women's standpoint. In principle, polygamy with the consent of all of the husband's wives would be the unambiguously best regime for women because it would expand their choice set. But a premodern legal system might be incapable of determining whether consent had been freely given, which may explain, as we have seen, why divorce on grounds was preceded by a stage of no divorce. In these circumstances, the second best choice from the woman's perspective might be no polygamy.

One factor that strongly supports monogamy in a traditional Christian society (and that may explain the confidence with which the judges in *Hyde* and *Reynolds* denounced polygamy), but has no contemporary significance, is that polygamy undermines a system of marriage law in which divorce either is forbidden or is available only on specified grounds. If a man who does not like his wife but has no grounds for divorcing her is free to take another wife, the rule preventing divorce at will is set largely at naught (not entirely, because he may still be required to support the first wife), for we recall that the principal significance of divorce is as a license to remarry. As this point implies, systems of law such as the Islamic and the African tribal, in which polygamy is permitted, make it easy for men to divorce. A society that wants to make divorce difficult has perforce to forbid polygamy, unless the only reason that the society made divorce difficult was to protect the woman in a financial sense; for the taking of additional wives need not reduce a man's obligation to support his present wife or wives.

Other social concerns with polygamy are noted in the literature as well, or can readily be excogitated. It reduces the diversity of the gene pool, and by the same token increases the likelihood of incest. While at the same time it enables the exceptional man to spread his genes more widely, it reduces the opportunity for the exceptional woman to do so, because the average number of children per married woman is smaller under polygamy than under monogamy. Polygamy makes families into little states (this could of course be a good thing in a society that lacked an effective machinery of government). In a society that values marital chastity it promotes fraud: a man will offer marriage to overcome the woman's resistance to having intercourse with him but not tell her he is already married. It aggravates disparities of wealth and power between men; it is almost as if poorer men were emasculated. It reduces a father's per-child investment of time and other resources in the raising of his children, because more children are competing for those resources (a polygamous husband has a much greater reproductive capacity than a monogamous one), and also because men spend time competing with other men for women. Indeed, the male rivalry that polygamy incites can dissipate substantial resources. We can predict that as egalitarian sentiment rises in a society, as a society becomes more peaceable, and as the emphasis in the society shifts from quantity to quality of children—quality being a function in part of the father's investment in the child's upbringing—polygamy will come to seem ever more anomalous and benighted, whether or not it is good or bad for the typical woman in the society.

Finally, to persons acculturated to monogamy, a polygamous culture is bound to seem promiscuous, as it did to the Supreme Court in the *Cleveland* case. Recall the distinction—highly visible in the *Hyde* decision—between a nominalistic and a substantive notion of marriage. Anyone who adheres to a substantive notion, that is, a notion of marriage as a restriction on sexuality, is likely to think of polygamy as a matter of renaming concubines wives, and hence as a condonation of concubinage. Temporary marriage reinforces this impression. And note how it can make the Islamic limit of four wives illusory: since a temporary wife does not count against the limit, a man can, for example by specifying the duration of the temporary marriage at ninety-nine years, obtain a de facto permanent fifth wife. In addition, we have seen that wives in a polygamous system have more incentive to engage in extramarital sex than wives in a monogamous system. A related point is that the legion of young bachelors that a polygamous system creates increases the demand for extramarital sex on the part of men as well as of women and also foments opportunistic homosexuality. From a Christian perspective, then, the sexual practices of a polygamous society are bound to seem highly irregular.

The negative effects of polygamy are mitigated in a society in which women are highly productive of goods besides children, as they were in African tribal society (where polygamy flourished and brideprice was common), and as they are today. A society in which women did all the work, and men's only role was to inseminate them, might well be polygamous (provided the men held on to political power), since one man can inseminate many women. It is only when men provide affective and material support to women and children that companionate marriage—an institution inseparable, I have been arguing, from monogamy—is apt to emerge. It may well be that even when women are liberated from economic dependence on men, children still derive substantial benefits from the presence of a father in the household. But insofar as women are not completely altruistic toward their children, the cost to a child of being without a father will not be fully reflected in the woman's decision whether to become or remain married. . . .

NOTES

Does the Option of Polygyny Help Women? Posner notes that in most situations people benefit from having options. Do you agree that permitting the option of polygyny in addition to monogamy helps women? Does it help men? Note that an option suggests a woman has the power to choose. But in many countries the first wife in a customary or Islamic marriage has no choice. Her husband automatically has the right to marry other women in the future. If she wants a monogamous husband, she must find a man who will consent before they marry, because only monogamy requires both persons' consent. In effect, the man she wishes to marry can veto monogamy. Similarly, although the second wife can choose to marry a polygynous husband (assuming he tells her he is already married), she too has no choice if he chooses to marry a third wife. Should the default option be reversed? In such a system, all marriages would automatically be monogamous unless the wife agreed before the marriage took place that the husband was free to take additional wives during her marriage to him.

Does the Option Help Men? Posner notes that polygyny increases competition among men for women. He fails to note that with some men having more than one wife, other men are left with no wives.

V. A Case Study: Uganda

In 1995, Uganda adopted a new Constitution. Before doing so, it asked women what rights they wanted. Consider the extent to which the Constitution addresses their concerns.

THROUGH THE MINISTRY OF WOMEN IN DEVELOPMENT, RECOMMENDATIONS MADE BY THE
    WOMEN OF UGANDA TO THE CONSTITUTIONAL COMMISSION
2–3, 14–18 (1991)

1. Introduction

For the first time in the history of this Country the people [of] Uganda have been given an opportunity to discuss and freely participate in the framing of the National Constitution. . . .

In this regard, the Ministry of Women in Development (MIN/WID) in co-operation with other Governmental and Women's Non-Governmental Organizations . . . embarked on a Constitutional Program to ensure that as many Ugandan women as possible are mobilised, educated and consulted on the Constitution and its making.

Women's participation in this historical exercise is deemed necessary; not only do they make up the greater part of the population of Uganda (53%), but they also produce the greater percentage of the nation's wealth. Women are the main food producers and they perform 80% of all the agricultural work. Through the Constitutional Consultation Program the Ministry of Women in Development has tried to raise women's interest in political issues, to facilitate their effective and constructive contribution to the formulation of the new Constitution of Uganda and to guarantee that the needs, concern and rights of women are explicitly considered in the Constitution.

The Ministry of Women in Development Program was organised in order to supplement the exercise of the Constitutional Commission. The latter was set up in 1988 by The Uganda Constitutional Commission statute. . . . The functions of the Commission are:—

  (i) to study and review the Constitution with a view of making proposals for the enactment of a new Constitution; and

(ii) to formulate and structure a draft Constitution that will form the basis for the Country's new Constitution.

During the constitutional seminars women discussed a wide range of constitutional issues. However, women had more to say on issues that affected them directly, particularly on issues related to the fundamental rights and freedoms of the individual and the status of women. . . .

The participants at the constitutional seminars covered a wide cross-section of women in this country. They can be divided into two categories[:] the trainers and trainees. The first category of women were those trained to facilitate the program. These included, on the one hand, women leaders at higher levels like the NRC women representatives and the RCV Secretaries for women and, on the other hand, women chosen from diverse backgrounds. The second category of participants were those who were mobilised at the [county] level in the districts. This category included housewives, women leaders at the lower levels of the RC hierarchy, civil servants such as teachers, administrators, nurses and representatives of women's NGOs and National Council of Women Executive members at the district branches. However, in a few districts in the Northern region like Apac, Lira, Nebbi, Arua and Moyo a sizeable proportion of the participants were illiterate. The majority of the recommendations contained in this report were collected from the seminars organised for the women at county level. . . .

3.4.1 Discriminatory Legislation

The following recommendations were made:

  a) There should be no discrimination on the basis of sex. Therefore, Article 20(3) of the Uganda Constitution of 1967 should be amended. The expression 'discriminatory' described therein should also include among others mentioned ". . . on the grounds of . . . SEX". This they said, means that all provisions contained in Article 20(4)(a), (d), (e), (f) and (h) must not appear in the new Constitution. . . .[G]

  b) All discriminatory legislation in our law books should be repealed and replaced with more up-to-date legislations that are not discriminating against women.

The following areas of the Law were identified as the ones under which the majority of women have continued to suffer injustices because of the discriminatory provisions contained therein:

  (i)   Marriage Laws;
  (ii) Divorce Laws;
  (iii) Inheritance Laws and Property Rights. . . .

(i) Marriage Laws:

The following recommendations were made:

  a) There should not exist a multiplicity of types of marriages that are governed by different legislation.

   [G] The Article 20(4) provisions permitted sex discrimination concerning adoption, marriage, divorce, burial, devolution of property on death or other matters of personal law.

b) Government should put in place constitutional institutions that are accessible to an ordinary woman and man in Uganda to enable them [to] understand the rights and duties that arise from each particular type of marriage contract.

It was noted that the existence of numerous types of marriages and legislations that govern them is confusing.

c) A majority of the women who participated in the constitutional seminars recommended that a man should have one wife, and a woman one husband. Monogamous marriages should thus be promoted and the Government should create awareness among the women and men of Uganda about the evils of polygyny.

It was emphasized that a man should be made to understand that he does not have the right to get another wife without terminating the first marriage or obtaining the consent and approval of his wife or wives. Women noted that there is a lot of suffering in polygynous homes because the man cannot love his wives equally and usually he does not have enough to provide sufficient support to his wives and numerous children. This leaves a heavy burden on the women. This was the opinion of many women from Mbarara, Kapchorwa, Masaka, Arua and Nebbi, Bushenyi and Tororo Districts.

d) Women at various seminars throughout the country recommended that with the present scourge of AIDS polygynous unions should be outlawed by the new Constitution.
e) Customary marriages which confer unequal marital rights to the parties involved are unconstitutional and should be discouraged.

It was noted that customary marriages do not provide enough legal security for the female partner(s), but in fact undermine the legal status of women, because they are substantially polygynous.

f) The Kampala based Muslim women in their seminar recommended that if a man has more than one wife he should ensure that each wife has her own home.
g) The women of Mukono district recommended that a man who cohabit[s] with a woman for five years should be presumed married to that woman. However, in case such a man is married legally to another woman, all properties in the house where the two co-habit should belong to the woman. . . .

(iii) Divorce Laws

The following recommendations were made:

a) The practice of returning bridewealth to the man's family in the event of divorce or separation should be abolished by law.

It was noted that this practice is inhuman and unconstitutional because it forces many women, especially in the rural areas, to remain in marriages that are irretrievably broken down. It was also considered degrading to women in Lira, Apac, Kapchorwa, Arua, Mbale and Nebbi Districts to return bridewealth to the last penny irrespective of the time a woman has been married.

> b) The present position of the law should be amended in such a way that women are treated as equal partners with the men in divorce proceedings.

It was emphasized that just like in the case of man a woman should also be required to prove only one matrimonial wrong of adultery. Adultery as a matrimonial wrong should thus apply to both men and women in the same way.

> c) The properties of married people who are parties to divorce proceedings should be divided equally. This, they said should apply to those properties accumulated during the marriage in question.
> d) The welfare principle applied in cases of children's custody of divorced or separated parents should always be applied where the mother of a child is of sound mind and has reasonable means to support her child or children. She should always be granted custody of her children below 18 years as the first possible guardian. However, children who are 10 years old and above should have the right to choose the parent they prefer to stay with.

(iv) Inheritance And Property Rights

Article 13 (1) of the Constitution of 1967 provides that no person shall take away another person's property unless that person has been given the legal right to do so. Women were informed that there are no statutes that prevent women from acquiring and owning property. Having received this information they recommended the following:—

> a) All customary practices that deprive women of their constitutional right to own and acquire properties, for example cows, land and other fixed assets, should be outlawed.

The above recommendation was mostly made by women from Apac, Lira, Mbale and Kabale Districts.

> b) In the event of death of a husband who dies intestate the property of the deceased should be justly divided. The widow should be entitled to a bigger share of the property of the deceased than the 15% provided for in the present Decree amending the Succession Act (recommendations of the percentage ranged from 25% to 50%). . . .
> d) The women of Apac, Lira, Moyo, Mbale, Kapchorwa, Arua and Nebbi Districts strongly recommended that it should be the constitutional right of a widow to remain in the matrimonial home after the death of her husband. In other districts there was no comments on this issue.

It was noted that this should apply to all widows whether they have children or not. However, widows should not abuse this right by misusing the house for culturally unacceptable practices, for example staying in the house with another man.

e) The customary practice of inheriting a woman by a brother or any other near male relative upon the death of her husband (levirate) should be abolished. The widow should remain with the choice of taking on another husband/guardian from her late husband's clan.

Women bitterly complained that men fight to inherit a widow whose late husband left property which they can benefit from. However, several cases were also quoted where women were abandoned with their children by the clansmen of their late husbands because the man died poor. Women commented that the above mentioned cultural practice was meant to assist a widow by providing her with a guardian/adviser who would also take part in the upbringing of her children being a "father" to them. This aspect they lamented had been lost. They recommended that levirate should be discouraged because it encourages plunder and misuse of property leaving the widows and their children helpless.

f) The Sharia provisions concerning inheritance should be incorporated in the Uganda Laws of Succession.

Constitution of the Republic of Uganda (1995)

Chapter Four
Protection and Promotion of Fundamental and Other Human Rights and Freedoms. . . .

21. (1) All persons are equal before and under the law in all spheres of political, economic, social and cultural life and in every other respect and shall enjoy equal protection of the law.

(2) Without prejudice to clause (1) of this article, a person shall not be discriminated against on the ground of sex, race, colour, ethnic origin, tribe, birth, creed or religion, or social or economic standing, political opinion or disability.

(3) For the purposes of this article, "discriminate" means to give different treatment to different persons attributable only or mainly to their respective descriptions by sex, race, colour, ethnic origin, tribe, birth, creed or religion, or social or economic standing, political opinion or disability. . . .

29. (1) Every person shall have the right to—. . .

(c) freedom to practise any religion and manifest such practice which shall include the right to belong to and participate in the practices of any religious body or organisation in a manner consistent with this Constitution; . . .

31. (1) Men and women of the age of eighteen years and above, have the right to marry and to found a family and are entitled to equal rights in marriage, during marriage and at its dissolution.

[This provision was amended by the Constitution (Amendment) Act, 2005, to provide, as of September 30, 2005:

(1) A man and a woman are entitled to marry only if they are each of the age of eighteen years and above and are entitled at that age—

(a) to found a family; and

(b) to equal rights at and in marriage, during marriage, and at its dissolution.]

(2) Parliament shall make appropriate laws for the protection of the rights of widows and widowers to inherit the property of their deceased spouses and to enjoy parental rights over their children.

[The Constitution (Amendment) Act, 2005, also inserted a new article 31(2a):

(2a) Marriage between persons of the same sex is prohibited.]

(3) Marriage shall be entered into with the free consent of the man and woman intending to marry.

(4) It is the right and duty of parents to care for and bring up their children.

(5) Children may not be separated from their families or the persons entitled to bring them up against the will of their families or of those persons, except in accordance with the law. . . .

32. (1) Notwithstanding anything in this Constitution, the State shall take affirmative action in favour of groups marginalised on the basis of gender, age, disability or any other reason created by history, tradition or custom, for the purpose of redressing imbalances which exist against them . . . .

33. (1) Women shall be accorded full and equal dignity of the person with men.

(2) The State shall provide the facilities and opportunities necessary to enhance the welfare of women to enable them to realise their full potential and advancement.

(3) The State shall protect women and their rights, taking into account their unique status and natural maternal functions in society.

(4) Women shall have the right to equal treatment with men and that right shall include equal opportunities in political, economic and social activities.

(5) . . . . [W]omen shall have the right to affirmative action for the purpose of redressing the imbalances created by history, tradition or custom.

(6) Laws, cultures, customs or traditions which are against the dignity, welfare or interest of women or which undermine their status, are prohibited by this Constitution.

[The Constitution (Amendment) Act, 2005, transferred this provision to Article 32 to replace subsection (2) and broadened its reach to include minorities:

32. . . . (2) Laws, cultures, customs and traditions which are against the dignity, welfare or interest of women or any other marginalised group to which clause (1) relates or which undermine their status, are prohibited by this Constitution.]

NOTE

Successful Litigation Under the New Constitution. The women recommended and got a constitution prohibiting discrimination on the basis of sex. And, in a very significant development, once women began challenging the discriminatory laws in test cases before the Constitutional Court, they won some stunning victories. The first victory came in 2004 and concerned the divorce law criticized in RECOMMENDATIONS MADE BY THE WOMEN OF UGANDA TO THE CONSTITUTIONAL COMMISSION. Under the statute, the husband could divorce his wife for adultery with an unmarried man, but a wife could not divorce a husband who had sex with an unmarried woman. To make things even worse, the law authorized the court to award the divorcing husband title to his ex-wife's property. In *Uganda Ass'n of Women Lawyers v. Attorney General*, the Constitutional Court found violations of women's equality and dignity rights under Articles 21(1), 21(2), 31(1), 33(1) and 33(6) ; two of the five justices specifically noted that women and men would now have the same rights as to both divorce and relief, an issue not addressed by the others.[H]

In 2007, the Court again found women's human rights violations, this time in the double-standard crime of adultery under the Penal Code Act and in the Succession Act provisions giving men greater inheritance rights than women.[I] The Court declared all the provisions at issue null and void. The Penal Code violated the Constitution Articles 20(1), 20(2), 20(3), 24 (prohibiting torture and cruel, inhuman or degrading treatment or punishment), 31(1)(b) (as amended in 2005), and 33(6). Before the decision, married men could not be found guilty of adultery for having sex with a single woman, but married women who had sex with a single man could be and were convicted. Now, since the crime of adultery has been struck down, there will be no adultery crime at all unless Parliament chooses to reenact a gender-neutral version.

As to the Succession Act, the Court struck down many provisions giving preference to male heirs over female heirs, citing the same constitutional articles (except for 24). The Act had: granted a widower but not the widow the right to remain in the family home after remarriage; given widows a share of the estate so small (15%, divided by the number of wives) that it ignored their contributions; assumed married women had no estates to divide (leaving widowers, as a practical matter, owning 100% of their wives' estates); given husbands the power to write binding wills to deny their widows guardianship of their own children; denied female relatives the right to be appointed as statutory guardians; and required wives to take their husband's domicile. With these provisions gone, but the other sections in force, it will be up to Parliament to enact a new Succession Act to replace the discriminatory sections.

Consider whether the Court might strike down laws permitting polygyny under its existing precedents. What arguments could be made to support that result? What arguments in opposition?

VI. Resolving the Polygyny Question

Esther N. Mayambala [now Esther Kisaakye], *Changing the Terms of the Debate: Polygamy and the Rights of Women in Kenya and Uganda*

3 EAST AFRICAN JOURNAL OF PEACE & HUMAN RIGHTS 200, 229–36, 238–39 (1997)

Resolving the polygamy question should be considered a priority for both Uganda and Kenya, which like many other African countries, are still at the crossroads as to

---

[H] Const. Pet. No. 2/03 (Mar. 10, 2004), *available at* RossRights and *discussed in* Tamar Ezer & Susan Deller Ross, *Fact-Finding as a Lawmaking Tool for Advancing Women's Human Rights*, 7 GEO. J. GENDER & L. 331, 340–41 & nn. 28, 30–33 (2006).

[I] *Law and Advocacy for Women in Uganda [LAW-U] v. Attorney General*, Const. Pets. Nos. 13/05 & 05/06, [2007] UGCC 1 (Apr. 5, 2007), *available at* RossRights and *discussed in* Ezer & Ross, *supra* note H, at 342 & n. 35. The three successful cases were the result of a collaboration between

what should to be done. Reform is long overdue and in view of the AIDS epidemic, it is imperative that immediate action be taken. Different approaches have been taken by different countries in Africa and elsewhere to deal with this question. These approaches can be categorized in three different groups:

i)   allowing polygamy to co-exist with monogamy on the premise that the parties will make the choice for themselves;

ii) seeking to control polygamy by either giving the wife a right to divorce a polygamous husband if she can prove actual or potential injury to her health or the husband's inability to support two households, or by requiring the husband to seek permission from a specified judicial or quasi-judicial body before taking on another wife;

iii) completely outlawing polygamy.

A. Approach 1: Allowing Co-existence

Under this approach, polygamy is allowed to co-exist with monogamy and the parties are expected to choose the type of marriage they want. There is very little regulation by the government except to ensure that parties do not contract marriages under both systems. This is, by and large, the approach that was adopted by the colonial powers and has continued to the present day in Uganda and Kenya.

The proposals made by the Kenyan Commission[j] for an express declaration of the parties at the time of marriage would be but a slight improvement on the situation in view of the several problems that we highlight below. First, most people marry under customary law, where the marriage negotiations and the marriage contract that follows is between the father and the husband. It will always be questionable whether the woman's choice was obtained and if so, for which form of marriage. Additional problems arise since the underlying common assumption in both countries, if we are to go by the past debate, is that those who contract a customary mar-

---

the International Women's Human Rights Clinic at Georgetown Law and LAW-U. *See* Valerie Bennett, Ginger Faulk, Anna Kovina & Tatjana Eres, *Inheritance Law in Uganda: The Plight of Widows and Children*, 7 GEO. J. GENDER & L. 451, 495 (2006), for both the Clinic's Human Rights Report and proposed Succession (Amendment) Bill 2006.

[j] The author notes earlier that:

"The Kenyan Commission on the Law of Marriage and Divorce was specifically mandated 'to pay particular attention to the status of women in relation to marriage and divorce in a free democratic society.' The Commission made findings that the widespread belief in the country that women greatly outnumbered men was unfounded; that reduction in prostitution as a justification for polygamy was not valid; and that opinion on the subject of polygamy was sharply divided. In spite of these findings . . . , the Commission concluded that . . . there was a considerable body of opinion in favor of retaining the practice. The Commission therefore recommended the recognition of both monogamous and polygamous marriages, but that the character of the marriage should depend on express agreement between the parties."

riage which is by definition "potentially polygamous," have endorsed polygamy as their way of life and they should be left to live according to their choice.

This approach makes polygamous marriages unregulated, leaving the majority of women who marry under customary law with no legal right to seek redress for their husband's practice of polygamy. The other disadvantage with this approach is that it promotes confusion in practice as it is very difficult to ascertain who is governed by what system of marriage and what the status of the first marriage is.

B. Approach 2: Enhanced Rights for a Polygamous Wife

The first component of this second approach has been to allow polygamy to continue, but to give the wife a right to seek divorce from the courts. Egypt provides an example of a country which has taken this approach. Under Egyptian law, the divorce will only be granted to the wife upon showing that as a result of the second marriage, she has suffered a material or moral injury that renders continued marital life between her and her husband difficult. In Morocco, the law prohibits polygamy if injustice is feared.

While the introduction of the right to divorce in the case of the husband's taking on a second wife is a welcome reform and a necessary component of any polygamy reform, on its own it leaves the institution of polygamy largely intact. This is because it does not in any way curtail the right of a husband to take on any number of additional wives should he so wish. Second, the requirement placed on the wife to prove injury or suspected inequality, in effect places the burden of proof on the wife. This misses the point that the very act of the husband taking on another wife is by itself a wrong to the wife. Furthermore, this burden of proving injury is likely to prove onerous to many wives because it requires her to demonstrate injury by objective evidence at a stage when her injury will still be internalized. In view also of the financial constraints usually faced by wives in many parts of Africa, most would not be in a position to promptly exercise their right. This approach would, therefore, leave the husband's right to take additional wives unprohibited.

The other component of the second approach is to limit polygamy by requiring the husband to justify his need for a second wife, either before a court of law or a quasi-judicial body. This approach has been adopted by countries like Syria, Iraq, Somalia, Indonesia and Pakistan. In Syria, the judge has power to forbid a married man from taking another wife unless he proves that he has a legitimate reason and the financial capability to support both wives. In Pakistan, the husband has to prove his case before an Arbitration Council.

The most apparent benefit of this approach is the transfer of the burden of justifying the taking of an additional wife onto the husband, who is not only the most interested party in the new marriage but also has the financial ability to initiate the judicial process. The second advantage of this approach is that it allows both the wife and the State, which in this case is represented by the judiciary, to intervene in a timely manner before the second marriage takes place. At this stage, no third party rights of the new wife have been created. The third advantage of this approach is that the administrative barriers may act as a restraining factor to the husband for not taking on additional wives and it may in the long run reduce the incidence of polygamy. While the husband may be able to convince the court to take on a second wife, he will surely have an uphill task of doing so in the case of the third or fourth wife. These four advantages make this approach more appropriate than the two approaches already discussed.

C. Approach 3: Outlawing Polygamy

The third approach which many countries in Africa and the Arab world have shied away from, is to completely outlaw polygamy. However, Tunisia and Ivory Coast provide examples of African countries which opted for this approach. Tunisia abolished polygamy in 1957. Under Article 18 of the Tunisia Code of Personal Status, polygamy is prohibited and any man who marries another woman during the existence of a valid marriage is liable to imprisonment for one year or a fine of 240,000 francs, or both.

The greatest advantage of this approach is that it sends out a very clear and unequivocal message to anyone who may have intentions of practicing polygamy that the practice will not be tolerated under any circumstances. This is a message that many countries where polygamy is practiced have hitherto failed to send to their citizens, while hoping at the same time that the practice will simply gradually stop. The experience in many African countries where polygamy continues to thrive even to the present day, despite the harshness of economic conditions, proves that wishful thinking in this area is simply not going to work. Polygamy is not a dying institution; at least not in Africa. This message needs to be communicated in very clear terms to polygamists and potential polygamists, if there is any hope for any society to eradicate or reduce this practice to an insignificant level.

The sanctions in Tunisian law, which provide for a fine, imprisonment or both for breach of this law, send an additional promise of punishment which is not likely to be taken lightly by many law-abiding citizen in a given country.

There are two arguments that have frequently been made against the approach of abolition. First is that passing a law banning polygamy will not work in Africa, since the colonial powers tried it in their colonies and failed, and second that the ban will disadvantage the other wives and their children who will become illegitimate and will, therefore, not be entitled to inherit in the estate of the man.

The first argument, is in our opinion erroneous, in that no such effort was made to ban the practice, at least in former British colonies where the indirect rule system was by and large followed. In fact, to the contrary, the reason why polygamy has thrived in many countries, as in Uganda and Kenya, is largely because the laws recognize and encourage the practice.

The second argument, which advocates for the continuation of polygamy in order to protect children and the other wives, can easily be taken care of, with respect to the children, by allowing all children to partake in the inheritance of the estate, irrespective of their having been born outside the marriage. Indeed, the Uganda Succession Act already addresses this issue by not making any distinctions among the children of a deceased man if such children were accepted by him before his death. This entitlement to inherit is without prejudice to such children being specifically provided for by their father in his will.

The other component of the second argument is also not an insurmountable one. In the first place, it is my belief that this argument has always been made for the benefit of the men to protect the practice and to distract the debate, rather than to advance the case of the women who find themselves in this situation. In any case, this issue can be taken care of by a saving provision in the law which would allow courts to exercise equitable discretion in deserving cases, where a polygamous marriage was validly contracted before the ban on polygamy. In my opinion, a provision in the law to this effect would take care of this argument. Certainly, this approach would help to break the continuing vicious circle (which the continued recognition of polygamy gives rise to); a circle in which women's equality is denied by playing off the rights of the second or other wives against those of the first.

But despite the fact that banning polygamy is the most desirable approach a country should take, it may work to the disadvantage of women in two respects. The first one is a situation where the couple is childless and the second situation is where the wife's health is such that she cannot have sex and this condition is permanent. In view of the importance attached to having children, not only in the two countries under discussion but in African societies generally, it is very likely that a childless wife will be divorced by her husband if no option for taking a second wife is left open. The concept of adoption has not as yet taken root in many African societies. In both these cases, polygamy may turn out to be the lesser evil than divorce for a couple which does not desire to dissolve their marriage for reasons which are clearly beyond the control of either party. It is only realistic that we acknowledge these facts and try to accommodate them in the law.

In view of these concerns, we are inclined to recommend that the most appropriate approach in the prevailing conditions in both countries is to outlaw polygamy except in clearly deserving cases. These cases must be spelt out in the law in order to minimize the likelihood of unpredictable and probably subjective interpretation of the law by a judiciary dominated by male judges. The two situations we have already pointed out above, would in my opinion, qualify as exceptions to the rule. The list of exceptions could be extended through public debate of the issue, which unfortunately has not been carried out in the past. The permission, however, should only be granted for one additional wife and not during the existence of two valid marriages.

These exceptions should be without prejudice to the right of the wife to opt for divorce if she so desires. In such a case, she would be entitled to the same rights as any other wife seeking divorce. The husband should seek court's permission to take on a second wife as is the case in Syria. Such permission should only granted upon presentation of evidence that his claim qualifies under one of the specified exceptions.

Indonesia and Somalia provide examples of countries which have already adopted reforms similar to those recommended in this paper. Under the Indonesian legislation, a man may receive permission from a court to contract a second marriage if, and only if:

(i)   his wife cannot carry out her conjugal duties, or
(ii) his wife becomes crippled or terminally ill, or
(iii) his wife cannot bear him children, and
    (a) his present wife (or wives) give him permission to do so,
    (b) his ability to support all his wives and children is certain, and
    (c) his ability to be fair to all his wives and children is certain.

Article 13 of the Somali Family law requires prior permission of the court before a second polygamous marriage can be contracted. Such permission can be granted on the grounds of:

(i)   medically certified sterility of the wife,
(ii) her contagious or chronic ailment which is incurable,
(iii) her imprisonment for over two years, and
(iv) desertion by the first wife for more than a year.

The court, however, can in addition to these specific grounds, grant permission on the ground of "social necessity."

These provisions have been cited here as examples and should not in any way indicate that I am in total agreement with all the exceptions recognized under the two laws. In particular, I find the Somali exception of "social necessity" too broad and too subjective with the likelihood of encompassing many undeserving claims. These provisions, however, provide some insight into the kind of exceptions that would qualify for a man to justifiably take on another wife.

Three main reasons have influenced the position taken on polygamy in this article. First, it is an undisputed fact that practically all civil and even criminal laws of any given country provide for exceptions and defenses for any proscribed conduct. For example, even for acts like taking another person's life, the legal systems have allowed certain recognized defenses. Society has thus been forced from time to time to carve out some limited exceptions to conduct which it would otherwise never endorse under any circumstances. The recognition of certain exceptions to an undesirable social practice like polygamy therefore makes sense.

Secondly, this approach may reduce opposition to the reform as the advocates of polygamy will feel taken care of when those concerns of divorce on the basis of childlessness and poor health have been taken care of. Laws are and should be a compromise between competing interests of the members of a given society and I believe that this approach strikes a workable compromise. For example, after 10 years of debate, Algeria adopted a Family Code in 1984 that is a compromise between modernity and tradition. Although polygamy remains legal, a husband can take on a second wife only in such cases as a wife's infertility.

Thirdly, this reform coupled with the unfavorable economic conditions emerging in many African countries may reduce the incidence of the practice in the society, as it will be more difficult for the husband to obtain the court's consent to take additional wives. In order for such a ban to work, the inequalities in the rights of men and women should be removed and the same rights to divorce and to claim damages from the person who has sex with a married person should be available to both husband and wife. Under the Nigerian Matrimonial Causes Act, for example, both the husband and the wife have a statutory right to claim damages from the party who has committed adultery with the other spouse, either in a claim for dissolution of marriage or for judicial separation. Thus, in the [unreported] Nigerian case of *Alli v. Alli*, a wife was awarded damages against a co-respondent for adultery with her husband on the basis of being deprived of the enjoyment and association of her husband by the co-respondent.

It will also be necessary to build into the new law other factors, such as the husband's financial ability to maintain two homes and to discharge his existing family obligations, to provide separate residences for the wives, to determine the appropriate shares of the husband and the first wife in the family property and to inform the prospective wife to ensure that she has willingly entered into the polygamous marriage with her full knowledge and consent.

It is also necessary to point out here that the new law should permit the parties to contract a civil marriage, an Islamic marriage or a customary marriage. However, these marriages should be regulated by the same law and the rights of the spouses in each of these marriages should be the same. Customary marriages can continue to be recognized as legal without their being polygamous, as it is not polygamy that gives them legality but the various rites that have to be fulfilled. The same is true for the marriages contracted according to Islamic law.

Finally, I need to comment on the strategy of using a law to ban polygamy, as there has been considerable debate whether this is the right approach. In my view, such a debate is surprising when one considers the fact that every society today is regulated by laws which clearly spell out what a citizen can or cannot do. Every aspect of life has been regulated, even in the very societies where polygamy is practiced. One is therefore left to wonder what makes polygamy different. To a large extent, polygamy in Uganda and Kenya thrives on the confused state of affairs where it is very difficult to figure out who is married under the different systems of marriage. This is true of many other African countries which have plural legal systems. It therefore seems plausible to conclude that those who make this argument are the beneficiaries and not the victims of the practice of polygamy. For otherwise, everyone would wish to know what he or she can and cannot do and what their rights are, which is certainly one of the most important advantages of having a written law that clearly lays out the rights of men and women.

Second, I believe that a legal approach is not only appropriate but necessary if there is to be any hope of any society putting polygamy, and the injustice arising from it, behind its back. It is appropriate because the institution of polygamy has been given enough time to "die" a natural death which it has not.

Third, as pointed out earlier in the discussion of the advantages of the different approaches to polygamy reforms, the first step that should of necessity be taken by any country tackling the problem of polygamy, is to send out a clear and unequivocal message to the population that polygamy will not be tolerated. An effective communication of this message will require nothing less than a legislative enactment, clearly making the practice of polygamy unacceptable. Since polygamy has been legally recognized, it will have to be legally outlawed through specific legislation and not merely by implication . . . .

Conclusion

Resolving the polygamy question has been put off for too long despite the fact that there have been cries for reform in Uganda, Kenya and many African countries, at least since the end of the colonial era. Such cries for reform have been drowned out by the voices of the advocates of polygamy who have continued to justify the practice on the basis of claims of preservation of traditional values and cultural identity; religious sanction; benefits to women; and to society at large. It is no wonder, therefore, that the debate has not gone beyond these assertions, to focus on the injustice inflicted on women by the practice of polygamy and the inherent inequalities in the status of male and female members of a given society perpetuated by the practice.

There are additional issues that should influence a country to act from a progressive policy perspective. These issues comprise a multitude of the attendant social and economical problems that flow from polygamy for the wife, the children and society as a whole. They are related to child support, and the other educational and medical needs of children. In the long run, these seemingly private social issues have a direct bearing on the quality of the citizenry of any given country. Given the prevailing economic conditions, it is unlikely that polygamous men will have the financial capacity to attend to the needs of the children they father in the pursuit of unlimited sex.

With the exception of the limited situations, some of which have been highlighted in this article, the only identifiable interest that polygamy serves is to bestow on the husband the legal right to have unlimited sexual pleasure outside marriage at the expense of his wife's physical and mental well being. It is this individual interest that has over ages been "clothed" in unsubstantiated claims of preservation of traditional values and religious sanction. Polygamy has for centuries been a privilege of the male members of the societies where it is practiced. The fight against reform is not surprising therefore, for never in history has one group willingly surrendered its privileges. The enjoyment of men's privileges, however, should be relative and should not be achieved at the expense of women's rights.

This last word is for the prophets of doom who have continued to predict that a law outlawing polygamy would not be effective. For whatever the abolition of polygamy is worth, and despite the other numerous obstacles women would still have to overcome before they can achieve actual and meaningful equality with men, such a reform would be a step further in the eventual emancipation of women. In the final analysis it is always easier to assert a right that has be legally defined than to claim a right where none exists.

N O T E

The African Women's Rights Protocol on Monogamy and Polygamy. The African Women's Rights Protocol takes a more lenient stance toward polygamy than do the CEDAW and Human Rights Committees:

6. States Parties shall ensure that women and men enjoy equal rights and are regarded as equal partners in marriage. They shall enact appropriate national legislative measures to guarantee that: . . . c) monogamy is encouraged as the preferred form of marriage and that the rights of women in marriage and family, including in polygamous marital relationships are promoted and protected.

Can the regional and international approaches be reconciled? Consider whether Ms. Kisaakye's approach does so, and whether it is the best solution to the conflict between religion, culture, and women's rights that polygyny provokes.

Chapter 14
Women's Reproductive Rights

I. Introduction

Reproductive rights are the most controversial of all women's rights. Impassioned defenders of women's autonomy rights argue with equally impassioned defenders of fetal rights. The former contend that women can never be free to determine their own destiny in life if they cannot decide when and whether to bear children, a right ultimately guaranteed only by the right to choose abortion at any time. The latter contend that a fertilized cell (zygote), an embryo, or a fetus is an "unborn baby" whose innocent life must always take precedence over the rights of the pregnant woman, even if she must die as a consequence of giving birth. Between these two extremes lie many variations. For example, most abortion rights advocates accept some limits on the availability of abortion. They would concede that once the fetus is viable, the woman should have the right to choose abortion only where her life or health is at stake. Similarly, many fetal rights proponents would allow abortion where the woman might die during childbirth or the pregnancy is the result of rape or incest.

Starting in the late 1960s, many Western women's rights advocates, family planning organizations, and doctors began a campaign with domestic legislatures and courts to grant women expanded abortion rights and eliminate criminal penalties for abortion. As they achieved success, opponents began a counter-offensive to deny women those rights. Their efforts sometimes yielded new legislative barriers to abortion, which were then challenged in other lawsuits by women's rights advocates. This litigation raised many different issues over the years. Could states allow the male partner to veto the woman's choice to abort? Could a parent veto a teenager's abortion? For what reasons should abortion be available and up to what stage of pregnancy? In states with welfare systems, should the state pay the costs of an abortion? Should states require women to read certain information, receive counseling, or wait for a few days after the first visit before actually obtaining the abortion? Could abortions take place only in hospitals or in clinics as well? What free speech rights should anti-abortion advocates have, and when did their efforts cross the line into unacceptable coercion or violence? Could states criminalize all forms of abortion? If so, who should be jailed—the woman having the abortion, the medical personnel, or both? For how long? Should the penalty be the same as for murder? Did women have rights not to be coerced or forced to have an abortion? Should women have the right to use sex-selective abortion to insure the birth of a boy?

In a somewhat earlier era, women's access to sterilization and birth control measures were also controversial. Some laws denied women access to either or both, while other laws coerced or forced women to be sterilized or use birth control. Laws prohibiting birth control were successfully challenged and changed starting in the late 1950s. But family-planning issues continue to arise in the 21st century as well. While access to birth control is generally legal, millions of women cannot find contraceptives in the local market or afford them if they do. Millions of teenage students have no access to sex education. A few countries prohibit sterilization as a crime and others set minimum requirements for the procedure, such as being married, 35, and having a specified number of children.

The role of religion is one final element in making reproductive rights so controversial. Does each woman get to decide her own religious views, or should states allow the religious beliefs of the majority to decide what every woman should be permitted to do through the enactment of state laws conforming to majority religious beliefs? Chapter Four suggested ways to resolve the conflict between freedom of religion and women's rights. Do they apply to reproductive rights as well?

Given the controversies, it is not surprising that international and regional human rights law provides no clear resolution of some controversies. With one exception, such treaties and conventions do not use the "A" word—abortion, or the "C" word—conception. Human rights bodies must therefore reason from the explicit rights in these texts. Does the right to life mean that the rights of the fetus trump those of the pregnant woman? How about the woman's rights to privacy, physical integrity, health, life, and non-discrimination? Do they trump fetal rights? Should there be a balance in the middle? When a treaty explicitly grants women the right to control the number and spacing of their children does that refer only to birth control or to abortion as well? Are there measures that states must take to protect potential life?

Among these many issues, this chapter will introduce three topics. Part II concerns the first and most basic. Should women have the right to choose abortion? Or should their rights be limited because of the right to life of a zygote, embryo, or fetus? The Part examines these asserted rights through the lens of history and religion and the responses of international, regional and comparative human rights bodies and courts. Part III addresses the second topic: the perplexing issue of sex-selective abortions. Should they be banned as a form of sex discrimination against the female fetus? Or would such a ban deny women their equality-based reproductive rights? Finally, Part IV explores the impact of child marriage on girls' reproductive rights. When young girls give birth, they face increased risks of dying in childbirth, being severely injured, or having the baby die in childbirth. What should be done in the face of such risks? Are their reproductive rights being infringed?

These issues are deeply personal. Each person will arrive at his or her own conclusion as to the appropriate answers. Seeing how international, regional, and comparative human rights law has grappled with the issues may change your views as to either the substantive answers that the law should provide or the feasibility or desirability of doing so through regional or international human rights law.

II. Abortion: Women's Autonomy Versus Fetal Life

A. Abortion Law: History; Religion; and the Rights at Stake

International human rights law, as embodied in the ICCPR, ICESCR, and CEDAW, did not exist when the movement to change restrictive abortion rights first started in the 1960s. The ICCPR and ICESCR came into force only in 1976, and CEDAW only in 1981. Accordingly, the early legal changes to broaden women's right to abortion came about through changes in domestic law. Great Britain enacted new legislation permitting abortion in 1967, and the U.S. Supreme Court acted in 1973 to strike down Texas and Georgia criminal abortion statutes as a violation of women's right to privacy. The Court's landmark opinion outlined the history of changing attitudes to abortion over the centuries, differences in religious and philosophical views, and the two key interests—women's autonomy versus fetal life. The issue was the meaning of that part of the 14th Amendment to the U.S. Constitution which provides: "No State shall . . . deprive any person of life, liberty, or property, without due process of law. . . ."

Roe v. Wade
(United States Supreme Court)
410 U.S. 113 (1973)

MR. JUSTICE BLACKMUN delivered the opinion of the Court [in which BURGER, C. J., and DOUGLAS, BRENNAN, STEWART, MARSHALL, and POWELL, JJ., joined].

This Texas federal appeal and its Georgia companion, *Doe v. Bolton*, 410 U.S. 179, present constitutional challenges to state criminal abortion legislation. The Texas statutes under attack here are typical of those that have been in effect in many States for approximately a century. The Georgia statutes, in contrast, have a modern cast and are a legislative product that, to an extent at least, obviously reflects the influences of recent attitudinal change, of advancing medical knowledge and techniques, and of new thinking about an old issue.

We forthwith acknowledge our awareness of the sensitive and emotional nature of the abortion controversy, of the vigorous opposing views, even among physicians, and of the deep and seemingly absolute convictions that the subject inspires. One's philosophy, one's experiences, one's exposure to the raw edges of human existence, one's religious training, one's attitudes toward life and family and their values, and the moral standards one establishes and seeks to observe, are all likely to influence and to color one's thinking and conclusions about abortion. . . .

Our task, of course, is to resolve the issue by constitutional measurement, free of emotion and of predilection. We seek earnestly to do this, and, because we do, we have inquired into, and in this opinion place some emphasis upon, medical and medical-legal history and what that history reveals about man's attitudes toward the abortion procedure over the centuries. . . .

I

The Texas statutes . . . make it a crime to "procure an abortion," . . . or to attempt one, except with respect to "an abortion procured or attempted by medical advice for the purpose of saving the life of the mother." Similar statutes are in existence in a majority of the States.

Texas first enacted a criminal abortion statute in 1854. . . .

II

Jane Roe, a single woman who was residing in Dallas County, Texas, instituted this federal action in March 1970 against the District Attorney of the county. She sought a declaratory judgment that the Texas criminal abortion statutes were unconstitutional on their face, and an injunction restraining the defendant from enforcing the statutes.

Roe alleged that she was unmarried and pregnant; that she wished to terminate her pregnancy by an abortion "performed by a competent, licensed physician, under safe, clinical conditions"; that she was unable to get a "legal" abortion in Texas because her life did not appear to be threatened by the continuation of her pregnancy; and that she could not afford to travel to another jurisdiction in order to secure a legal abortion under safe conditions. She claimed that the Texas statutes . . . abridged her right of personal privacy, protected by the . . . Fourteenth Amendment. . . .

VI

It perhaps is not generally appreciated that the restrictive criminal abortion laws in effect in a majority of States today are of relatively recent vintage. Those laws, generally proscribing abortion or its attempt at any time during pregnancy except when necessary to preserve the pregnant woman's life, are not of ancient or even of common-law origin. Instead, they derive from statutory changes effected, for the most part, in the latter half of the 19th century.

1. Ancient attitudes. These are not capable of precise determination. We are told that at the time of the Persian Empire abortifacients were known and that criminal abortions were severely punished. We are also told, however, that abortion was practiced in Greek times as well as in the Roman Era, and that "it was resorted to without scruple." The Ephesian, Soranos, often described as the greatest of the ancient gynecologists, appears to have been generally opposed to Rome's prevailing free-abortion practices. He found it necessary to think first of the life of the mother, and he resorted to abortion when, upon this standard, he felt the procedure advisable. Greek and Roman law afforded little protection to the unborn. If abortion was prosecuted in some places, it seems to have been based on a concept of a violation of the father's right to his offspring. Ancient religion did not bar abortion.

2. The Hippocratic Oath. What then of the famous Oath that has stood so long as the ethical guide of the medical profession and that bears the name of the great Greek (460(?)–377(?) B. C.), who has been described as the Father of Medicine. . . . The Oath . . . is clear: "I will give no deadly medicine to anyone if asked, nor suggest any such counsel; and in like manner I will not give to a woman a pessary to produce abortion". . . .

Why did not the authority of Hippocrates dissuade abortion practice in his time and that of Rome? The late Dr. Edelstein provides us with a theory: The Oath was not uncontested even in Hippocrates' day; only the Pythagorean school of philosophers frowned upon the related act of suicide. Most Greek thinkers, on the other hand, commended abortion, at least prior to viability. For the Pythagoreans, however, it was a matter of dogma. For them the embryo was animate from the moment of conception, and abortion meant destruction of a living being. The abortion clause of the Oath, therefore, "echoes Pythagorean doctrines," and "in no other stratum of Greek opinion were such views held or proposed in the same spirit of uncompromising austerity."

Dr. Edelstein then concludes that the Oath originated in a group representing only a small segment of Greek opinion and that it certainly was not accepted by all ancient physicians. He points out that medical writings down to Galen (A. D. 130–200) "give evidence of the violation of almost every one of its injunctions." But with the end of antiquity a decided change took place. Resistance against suicide and against abortion became common. The Oath came to be popular. The emerging teachings of Christianity were in agreement with the Pythagorean ethic. The Oath "became the nucleus of all medical ethics" and "was applauded as the embodiment of truth." Thus, suggests Dr. Edelstein, it is "a Pythagorean manifesto and not the expression of an absolute standard of medical conduct."

This, it seems to us, is a satisfactory and acceptable explanation of the Hippocratic Oath's apparent rigidity. It enables us to understand, in historical context, a long-accepted and revered statement of medical ethics.

3. *The common law.* It is undisputed that at common law, abortion performed *before* "quickening"—the first recognizable movement of the fetus *in utero*, appearing usually from the 16th to the 18th week of pregnancy—was not an indictable offense. The absence of a common-law crime for pre-quickening abortion appears to have developed from a confluence of earlier philosophical, theological, and civil and canon law concepts of when life begins. These disciplines variously approached the question in terms of the point at which the embryo or fetus became "formed" or recognizably human, or in terms of when a "person" came into being, that is, infused with a "soul" or "animated." A loose consensus evolved in early English law that these events occurred at some point between conception and live birth. This was "mediate animation." Although Christian theology and the canon law came to fix the point of animation at 40 days for a male and 80 days for a female, a view that persisted until the 19th century, there was otherwise little agreement about the precise time of formation or animation. There was agreement, however, that prior to this point the fetus was to be regarded as part of the mother, and its destruction, therefore, was not homicide. Due to continued uncertainty about the precise time when

animation occurred, to the lack of any empirical basis for the 40–80-day view, and perhaps to Aquinas' definition of movement as one of the two first principles of life, Bracton focused upon quickening as the critical point. The significance of quickening was echoed by later common-law scholars and found its way into the received common law in this country.

Whether abortion of a quick fetus was a felony at common law, or even a lesser crime, is still disputed. Bracton, writing early in the 13th century, thought it homicide. But the later and predominant view, following the great common-law scholars, has been that it was, at most, a lesser offense. In a frequently cited passage, Coke took the position that abortion of a woman "quick with child" is "a great misprision, and no murder." Blackstone followed, saying that while abortion after quickening had once been considered manslaughter (though not murder), "modern law" took a less severe view. A recent review of the common-law precedents argues, however, that those precedents contradict Coke and that even post-quickening abortion was never established as a common-law crime. This is of some importance because while most American courts ruled, in holding or dictum, that abortion of an unquickened fetus was not criminal under their received common law, others followed Coke in stating that abortion of a quick fetus was a "misprision," a term they translated to mean "misdemeanor." That their reliance on Coke on this aspect of the law was uncritical and, apparently in all the reported cases, dictum (due probably to the paucity of common-law prosecutions for post-quickening abortion), makes it now appear doubtful that abortion was ever firmly established as a common-law crime even with respect to the destruction of a quick fetus.

4. *The English statutory law.* England's first criminal abortion statute, Lord Ellenborough's Act, came in 1803. It made abortion of a quick fetus a capital crime, but it provided lesser penalties for the felony of abortion before quickening, and thus preserved the "quickening" distinction. This contrast was continued in the general revision of 1828. It disappeared, however, together with the death penalty, and did not reappear in the Offenses Against the Person Act of 1861 that formed the core of English anti-abortion law until the liberalizing reforms of 1967. In 1929, the Infant Life (Preservation) Act came into being. Its emphasis was upon the destruction of "the life of a child capable of being born alive." It made a willful act performed with the necessary intent a felony. It contained a proviso that one was not to be found guilty of the offense "unless it is proved that the act which caused the death of the child was not done in good faith for the purpose only of preserving the life of the mother."

A seemingly notable development in the English law was the case of *Rex v. Bourne,* *[1939] 1 K. B. 687.* . . . [The judge interpreted the 1861 Act, which contained no exceptions to the criminal abortion ban, to incorporate the "life" exception to the 1929 Act, and then further interpreted "life"] broadly, that is, "in a reasonable sense," to include a serious and permanent threat to the mother's *health,* and instructed the jury to acquit Dr. Bourne if it found he had acted in a good-faith belief that the abortion was necessary for this purpose. The jury did acquit.

Recently, Parliament enacted a new abortion law. This is the Abortion Act of 1967. The Act permits a licensed physician to perform an abortion where two other licensed physicians agree (a) "that the continuance of the pregnancy would involve risk to the life of the pregnant woman, or of injury to the physical or mental health of the pregnant woman or any existing children of her family, greater than if the pregnancy were terminated," or (b) "that there is a substantial risk that if the child were born it would suffer from such physical or mental abnormalities as to be seriously handicapped." The Act also provides that, in making this determination, "account may be taken of the pregnant woman's actual or reasonably foreseeable environment." It also permits a physician, without the concurrence of others, to terminate a pregnancy where he is of the good-faith opinion that the abortion "is immediately necessary to save the life or to prevent grave permanent injury to the physical or mental health of the pregnant woman."

5. The American law. In this country, the law in effect in all but a few States until mid-19th century was the pre-existing English common law. . . . By 1840, when Texas had received the common law, only eight American States had statutes dealing with abortion. It was not until after the War Between the States [1861–1865] that legislation began generally to replace the common law. Most of these initial statutes dealt severely with abortion after quickening but were lenient with it before quickening. Most punished attempts equally with completed abortions. While many statutes included the exception for an abortion thought by one or more physicians to be necessary to save the mother's life, that provision soon disappeared and the typical law required that the procedure actually be necessary for that purpose.

Gradually, in the middle and late 19th century the quickening distinction disappeared from the statutory law of most States and the degree of the offense and the penalties were increased. By the end of the 1950's, a large majority of the jurisdictions banned abortion, however and whenever performed, unless done to save or preserve the life of the mother. The exceptions, Alabama and the District of Columbia, permitted abortion to preserve the mother's health. Three States permitted abortions that were not "unlawfully" performed or that were not "without lawful justification," leaving interpretation of those standards to the courts. In the past several years, however, a trend toward liberalization of abortion statutes has resulted in adoption, by about one-third of the States, of less stringent laws, most of them patterned after the ALI Model Penal Code.

It is thus apparent that at common law, at the time of the adoption of our Constitution, and throughout the major portion of the 19th century, abortion was viewed with less disfavor than under most American statutes currently in effect. Phrasing it another way, a woman enjoyed a substantially broader right to terminate a pregnancy than she does in most States today. At least with respect to the early stage of pregnancy, and very possibly without such a limitation, the opportunity to make this choice was present in this country well into the 19th century. Even later, the law continued for some time to treat less punitively an abortion procured in early pregnancy.

6. The position of the American Medical Association. The anti-abortion mood prevalent in this country in the late 19th century was shared by the medical profession. Indeed, the attitude of the profession may have played a significant role in the enactment of stringent criminal abortion legislation during that period.

An AMA Committee on Criminal Abortion was appointed in May 1857. It presented its report to the Twelfth Annual Meeting. That report observed that the Committee had been appointed to investigate criminal abortion "with a view to its general suppression." It deplored abortion and its frequency and it listed three causes of "this general demoralization":

"The first of these causes is a wide-spread popular ignorance of the true character of the crime—a belief, even among mothers themselves, that the foetus is not alive till after the period of quickening.

"The second of the agents alluded to is the fact that the profession themselves are frequently supposed careless of foetal life. . . .

"The third reason of the frightful extent of this crime is found in the grave defects of our laws, both common and statute, as regards the independent and actual existence of the child before birth, as a living being. These errors, which are sufficient in most instances to prevent conviction, are based, and only based, upon mistaken and exploded medical dogmas. With strange inconsistency, the law fully acknowledges the foetus in utero and its inherent rights, for civil purposes; while personally and as criminally affected, it fails to recognize it, and to its life as yet denies all protection." The Committee then offered, and the Association adopted, resolutions protesting "against such unwarrantable destruction of human life," calling upon state legislatures to revise their abortion laws, and requesting the cooperation of state medical societies "in pressing the subject."

In 1871 a long and vivid report was submitted by the Committee on Criminal Abortion. It ended with the observation, "We had to deal with human life. In a matter of less importance we could entertain no compromise. An honest judge on the bench would call things by their proper names. We could do no less." It proffered resolutions, adopted by the Association, recommending, among other things, that it "be unlawful and unprofessional for any physician to induce abortion or premature labor, without the concurrent opinion of at least one respectable consulting physician, and then always with a view to the safety of the child—if that be possible," and calling "the attention of the clergy of all denominations to the perverted views of morality entertained by a large class of females—aye, and men also, on this important question."

Except for periodic condemnation of the criminal abortionist, no further formal AMA action took place until 1967. In that year, the Committee on Human Reproduction urged the adoption of a stated policy of opposition to induced abortion, except when there is "documented medical evidence" of a threat to the health or life of the mother, or that the child "may be born with incapacitating physical deformity or mental deficiency," or that a pregnancy "resulting from legally established statutory or forcible rape or incest may constitute a threat to the mental or physical health of the patient," two other physicians "chosen because of their recognized professional competence have examined the patient and have concurred in writing," and the procedure "is performed in a hospital accredited by the Joint Commission on Accreditation of Hospitals." This recommendation was adopted by the House of Delegates. . . .

VIII

The Constitution does not explicitly mention any right of privacy. In a line of decisions, however . . . the Court has recognized that a right of personal privacy . . . does exist under the Constitution. . . .

This right of privacy . . . founded in the Fourteenth Amendment's concept of personal liberty and restrictions upon state action . . . is broad enough to encompass a woman's decision whether or not to terminate her pregnancy. The detriment that the State would impose upon the pregnant woman by denying this choice altogether is apparent. Specific and direct harm medically diagnosable even in early pregnancy may be involved. Maternity, or additional offspring, may force upon the woman a distressful life and future. Psychological harm may be imminent. Mental and physical health may be taxed by child care. There is also the distress, for all concerned, associated with the unwanted child, and there is the problem of bringing a child into a family already unable, psychologically and otherwise, to care for it. In other cases, as in this one, the additional difficulties and continuing stigma of unwed motherhood may be involved. All these are factors the woman and her responsible physician necessarily will consider in consultation.

On the basis of elements such as these, appellant and some *amici* argue that the woman's right is absolute and that she is entitled to terminate her pregnancy at whatever time, in whatever way, and for whatever reason she alone chooses. With this we do not agree. Appellant's arguments that Texas either has no valid interest at all in regulating the abortion decision, or no interest strong enough to support any limitation upon the woman's sole determination, are unpersuasive. The Court's decisions recognizing a right of privacy also acknowledge that some state regulation in areas protected by that right is appropriate. As noted above, a State may properly assert important interests in safeguarding health, in maintaining medical standards, and in protecting potential life. At some point in pregnancy, these respective interests become sufficiently compelling to sustain regulation of the factors that govern the abortion decision. The privacy right involved, therefore, cannot be said to be absolute. . . .

We, therefore, conclude that the right of personal privacy includes the abortion decision, but that this right is not unqualified and must be considered against important state interests in regulation. . . .

Where certain "fundamental rights" are involved, the Court has held that regulation limiting these rights may be justified only by a "compelling state interest". . . .

IX. . . .

A.

The appellee and certain *amici* argue that the fetus is a "person" within the language and meaning of the Fourteenth Amendment. In support of this, they outline at length and in detail the well-known facts of fetal development. If this suggestion of personhood is established, the appellant's case, of course, collapses, for the fetus' right to life would then be guaranteed specifically by the Amendment. The appellant conceded as much on reargument. On the other hand, the appellee conceded on reargument that no case could be cited that holds that a fetus is a person within the meaning of the Fourteenth Amendment.

The Constitution does not define "person" in so many words. Section 1 of the Fourteenth Amendment contains three references to "person." The first, in defining "citizens," speaks of "persons born or naturalized in the United States." The word also appears both in the Due Process Clause and in the Equal Protection Clause. "Person" is used in other places in the Constitution. . . . But in nearly all these instances, the use of the word is such that it has application only postnatally. None indicates, with any assurance, that it has any possible pre-natal application.[54]

All this, together with our observation that throughout the major portion of the 19th century prevailing legal abortion practices were far freer than they are today, persuades us that the word "person," as used in the Fourteenth Amendment [adopted in 1868], does not include the unborn. . . .

This conclusion, however, does not of itself fully answer the contentions raised by Texas, and we pass on to other considerations.

B.

The pregnant woman cannot be isolated in her privacy. She carries an embryo and, later, a fetus, if one accepts the medical definitions of the developing young in the human uterus. . . . [I]t is reasonable and appropriate for a State to decide that at some point in time another interest, that of health of the mother or that of potential human life, becomes significantly involved. The woman's privacy is no longer sole and any right of privacy she possesses must be measured accordingly.

Texas urges that . . . life begins at conception and is present throughout pregnancy, and that, therefore, the State has a compelling interest in protecting that life from and after conception. We need not resolve the difficult question of when life begins. When those trained in the respective disciplines of medicine, philosophy, and theology are unable to arrive at any consensus, the judiciary, at this point in the development of man's knowledge, is not in a position to speculate as to the answer.

It should be sufficient to note briefly the wide divergence of thinking on this most

---

[54] When Texas urges that a fetus is entitled to Fourteenth Amendment protection as a person, it faces a dilemma. Neither in Texas nor in any other State are all abortions prohibited. Despite broad proscription, an exception always exists. The exception for an abortion . . . for the purpose of saving the life of the mother, is typical. But if the fetus is a person who is not to be deprived of life without due process of law, and if the mother's condition is the sole determinant, does not the Texas exception appear to be out of line with the Amendment's command?

There are other inconsistencies between Fourteenth Amendment status and the typical abortion statute. It has already been pointed out that in Texas the woman is not a principal or an accomplice with respect to an abortion upon her. If the fetus is a person, why is the woman not a principal or an accomplice? Further, the penalty for criminal abortion is significantly less than the maximum penalty for murder. If the fetus is a person, may the penalties be different?

sensitive and difficult question. There has always been strong support for the view that life does not begin until live birth. This was the belief of the Stoics. It appears to be the predominant, though not the unanimous, attitude of the Jewish faith. It may be taken to represent also the position of a large segment of the Protestant community, insofar as that can be ascertained; organized groups that have taken a formal position on the abortion issue have generally regarded abortion as a matter for the conscience of the individual and her family. As we have noted, the common law found greater significance in quickening. Physicians and their scientific colleagues have regarded that event with less interest and have tended to focus either upon conception, upon live birth, or upon the interim point at which the fetus becomes "viable," that is, potentially able to live outside the mother's womb, albeit with artificial aid. Viability is usually placed at about seven months (28 weeks) but may occur earlier, even at 24 weeks. The Aristotelian theory of "mediate animation" . . . continued to be official Roman Catholic dogma until the 19th century, despite opposition to this "ensoulment" theory from those in the Church who would recognize the existence of life from the moment of conception. The latter is now, of course, the official belief of the Catholic Church. As one brief *amicus* discloses, this is a view strongly held by many non-Catholics as well, and by many physicians. Substantial problems for precise definition of this view are posed, however, by new embryological data that purport to indicate that conception is a "process" over time, rather than an event, and by new medical techniques such as menstrual extraction, the "morning-after" pill, implantation of embryos, artificial insemination, and even artificial wombs.

In areas other than criminal abortion, the law has been reluctant to endorse any theory that life, as we recognize it, begins before live birth or to accord legal rights to the unborn except in narrowly defined situations and except when the rights are contingent upon live birth. For example, the traditional rule of tort law denied recovery for prenatal injuries even though the child was born alive. That rule has been changed in almost every jurisdiction. In most States, recovery is said to be permitted only if the fetus was viable, or at least quick, when the injuries were sustained. . . . In a recent development, . . . some States permit the parents of a stillborn child to maintain an action for wrongful death because of prenatal injuries. Such an action, however, would appear to be one to vindicate the parents' interest and is thus consistent with the view that the fetus, at most, represents only the potentiality of life. Similarly, unborn children have been recognized as acquiring rights or interests by way of inheritance or other devolution of property, and have been represented by guardians *ad litem*. Perfection of the interests involved, again, has generally been contingent upon live birth. In short, the unborn have never been recognized in the law as persons in the whole sense.

X

In view of all this, we do not agree that, by adopting one theory of life, Texas may override the rights of the pregnant woman that are at stake. We repeat, however, that the State does have an important and legitimate interest in preserving and protecting the health of the pregnant woman . . . and that it has still *another* important and legitimate interest in protecting the potentiality of human life. These interests are separate and distinct. Each grows in substantiality as the woman approaches term and, at a point during pregnancy, each becomes "compelling."

With respect to the State's important and legitimate interest in the health of the mother, the "compelling" point, in the light of present medical knowledge, is at approximately the end of the first trimester. This is so because of the now-established medical fact that until the end of the first trimester mortality in abortion may be less than mortality in normal childbirth. It follows that, from and after this point, a State may regulate the abortion procedure to the extent that the regulation reasonably relates to the preservation and protection of maternal health. Examples of permissible state regulation in this area are requirements as to the qualifications of the person who is to perform the abortion; as to the licensure of that person; as to the facility in which the procedure is to be performed, that is, whether it must be a hospital or may be a clinic or some other place of less-than-hospital status; as to the licensing of the facility; and the like.

This means, on the other hand, that, for the period of pregnancy prior to this "compelling" point, the attending physician, in consultation with his patient, is free to determine, without regulation by the State, that, in his medical judgment, the patient's pregnancy should be terminated. If that decision is reached, the judgment may be effectuated by an abortion free of interference by the State.

With respect to the State's important and legitimate interest in potential life, the "compelling" point is at viability. This is so because the fetus then presumably has the capability of meaningful life outside the mother's womb. State regulation protective of fetal life after viability thus has both logical and biological justifications. If the State is interested in protecting fetal life after viability, it may go so far as to proscribe abortion during that period, except when it is necessary to preserve the life or health of the mother.

Measured against these standards, the Texas Penal Code, in restricting legal abortions to those "procured or attempted by medical advice for the purpose of saving the life of the mother," sweeps too broadly. The statute makes no distinction between abortions performed early in pregnancy and those performed later, and it limits to a single reason, "saving" the mother's life, the legal justification for the procedure. The statute, therefore, cannot survive the constitutional attack made upon it here. . . .

MR. JUSTICE STEWART, concurring.

[I]n *Griswold v. Connecticut, 381 U.S. 47 (1965),* the Court held a Connecticut birth control law [prohibiting its use by married couples] unconstitutional. . . . [T]he *Griswold* decision can be rationally understood only as a holding that the Connecticut statute substantively invaded the "liberty" that is protected by the Due Process Clause of the Fourteenth Amendment. . . .

Several decisions of this Court make clear that freedom of personal choice in matters of marriage and family life is one of the liberties protected by the Due Process

Clause of the Fourteenth Amendment. As recently as last Term, in *Eisenstadt v. Baird, 405 U.S. 438* [finding unconstitutional a law prohibiting single persons from using birth control], we recognized "the right of the *individual,* married or single, to be free from unwarranted governmental intrusion into matters so fundamentally affecting a person as the decision whether to bear or beget a child." That right necessarily includes the right of a woman to decide whether or not to terminate her pregnancy. "Certainly the interests of a woman in giving of her physical and emotional self during pregnancy and the interests that will be affected throughout her life by the birth and raising of a child are of a far greater degree of significance and personal intimacy than the right to send a child to private school protected in Pierce v. Society of Sisters, 268 U.S. 510 (1925). . . .

Clearly, therefore, the Court today is correct in holding that the right asserted by Jane Roe is embraced within the personal liberty protected by the Due Process Clause of the Fourteenth Amendment.

It is evident that the Texas abortion statute infringes that right directly. Indeed, it is difficult to imagine a more complete abridgment of a constitutional freedom than that worked by the inflexible criminal statute now in force in Texas. . . .

MR. JUSTICE REHNQUIST, dissenting.

If the Court means by the term "privacy" no more than that the claim of a person to be free from unwanted state regulation of consensual transactions may be a form of "liberty" protected by the Fourteenth Amendment, there is no doubt that similar claims have been upheld in our earlier decisions on the basis of that liberty. I agree with the statement of MR. JUSTICE STEWART in his concurring opinion that the "liberty," against deprivation of which without due process the Fourteenth Amendment protects, embraces more than the rights found in the Bill of Rights. But that liberty is not guaranteed absolutely against deprivation, only against deprivation without due process of law. The test traditionally applied in the area of social and economic legislation is whether or not a law such as that challenged has a rational relation to a valid state objective. The Due Process Clause of the Fourteenth Amendment undoubtedly does place a limit, albeit a broad one, on legislative power to enact laws such as this. If the Texas statute were to prohibit an abortion even where the mother's life is in jeopardy, I have little doubt that such a statute would lack a rational relation to a valid state objective. . . . But the Court's sweeping invalidation of any restrictions on abortion during the first trimester is impossible to justify under that standard.

MR. JUSTICE WHITE, with whom MR. JUSTICE REHNQUIST joins, dissenting [in both *Roe* and in the companion abortion case from Georgia, *Doe v. Bolton, 410 U.S. 179 (1973)*].

At the heart of the controversy in these cases are those recurring pregnancies that pose no danger whatsoever to the life or health of the mother but are, nevertheless, unwanted for any one or more of a variety of reasons—convenience, family planning, economics, dislike of children, the embarrassment of illegitimacy, etc. The common claim before us is that for any one of such reasons, or for no reason at all, and without asserting or claiming any threat to life or health, any woman is entitled to an abortion at her request if she is able to find a medical advisor willing to undertake the procedure.

The Court for the most part sustains this position: During the period prior to the time the fetus becomes viable, the Constitution of the United States values the convenience, whim, or caprice of the putative mother more than the life or potential life of the fetus; the Constitution, therefore, guarantees the right to an abortion as against any state law or policy seeking to protect the fetus from an abortion not prompted by more compelling reasons of the mother. . . .

The upshot is that the people and the legislatures of the 50 States are constitutionally disentitled to weigh the relative importance of the continued existence and development of the fetus, on the one hand, against a spectrum of possible impacts on the mother, on the other hand. . . . The Court apparently values the convenience of the pregnant mother more than the continued existence and development of the life or potential life that she carries. . . . In a sensitive area such as this, involving as it does issues over which reasonable men may easily and heatedly differ, I cannot accept the Court's exercise of its clear power . . . by interposing a constitutional barrier to state efforts to protect human life and by investing mothers and doctors with the constitutionally protected right to exterminate it.

MR. JUSTICE DOUGLAS, concurring [in *Doe v. Bolton*, 410 U.S. 179 (1973), the *Roe v. Wade* companion case which invalidated a Georgia statute permitting abortion only for specified reasons and requiring a 6-doctor review process to authorize an abortion].

The present statute has struck the balance between the woman's and the State's interests wholly in favor of the latter. I am not prepared to hold that a State may equate, as Georgia has done, all phases of maturation preceding birth. We held in [the] *Griswold* [birth control case] that the States may not preclude spouses from attempting to avoid the joinder of sperm and egg. If this is true, it is difficult to perceive any overriding public necessity which might attach precisely at the moment of conception. As Mr. Justice Clark has said:

To say that life is present at conception is to give recognition to the potential, rather than the actual. The unfertilized egg has life, and if fertilized, it takes on human proportions. But the law deals in reality, not obscurity—the known rather than the unknown. When sperm meets egg life may eventually form, but quite often it does not. The law does not deal in speculation. The phenomenon of life takes time to develop, and until it is actually present, it cannot be destroyed. Its interruption prior to formation would hardly be homicide, and as we have seen, society does not regard it as such. The rites of Baptism are not performed and death certificates are not required when a miscarriage occurs. No prosecutor has ever returned a murder indictment charging the taking of the life of a fetus. This would not be the case if the fetus constituted human life.

In summary, the enactment is overbroad. It is not closely correlated to the aim of preserving prenatal life. In fact, it permits its destruction in several cases, including pregnancies resulting from sex acts in which unmarried females are below the statutory age of consent. At the same time, however, the measure broadly proscribes aborting other pregnancies which may cause severe mental disorders. Additionally, the statute is overbroad because it equates the value of embryonic life immediately after conception with the worth of life immediately before birth.

NOTES

The Court's Conception of the Rights at Stake. The Court says women have the right to privacy and that it is derived from their right to liberty under the 14th Amendment. Which concept more accurately captures the nature of the woman's interest? Are there other rights that you think might be more relevant? The Court finds that a woman's privacy right is not absolute. Why not? Should it be?

Texas asserted that it had a compelling interest in protecting fetal life from the moment of conception and that its statute should therefore survive a 14th Amendment challenge. The Court accepts some, but not all, of this argument. How does the Court draw this line? If one followed the Texas logic to its endpoint, what other laws should Texas enact? *See* the Court's footnote 54. In the companion *Doe v. Bolton* case, concurring Justice Douglas rejected conception as the logical starting point. Why?

Supreme Court Decisions Since *Roe v. Wade*. The Court's abortion decisions have proved highly controversial. Indeed, the Court had decided more than 25 abortion cases by August 2007. In *Planned Parenthood v. Casey*, 505 U.S. 833 (1992), Justices O'Connor, Kennedy, and Souter affirmed *Roe*'s central holdings:

Roe's essential holding . . . has three central parts. First is a recognition of the right of the woman to choose to have an abortion before viability and to obtain it without undue interference from the State. Before viability, the State's interests are not strong enough to support a prohibition of abortion or the imposition of a substantial obstacle to the woman's effective right to elect the procedure. Second is a confirmation of the State's power to restrict abortions after fetal viability, if the law contains exceptions for pregnancies which endanger a woman's life or health. And third is the principle that the State has legitimate interests from the outset of the pregnancy in protecting the health of the woman and the life of the fetus that may become a child. These principles do not contradict one another; and we adhere to each.

The Court did, however, reject the trimester framework and lower the *Roe* strict scrutiny standard of review (*see*, in *Roe*, the last sentence of Part VIII and all of Part X):

The very notion that the State has a substantial interest in potential life leads to the conclusion that not . . . all burdens on the right to decide whether to terminate a pregnancy will be undue. In our view, the undue burden standard is the appropriate means of reconciling the State's interest with the woman's constitutionally protected liberty. . . .

A finding of an undue burden is a shorthand for the conclusion that a state regulation has the purpose or effect of placing a substantial obstacle in the path of a woman seeking an abortion of a nonviable fetus. A statute with this purpose is invalid because the means chosen by the State to further the interest in potential life must be calculated to inform the woman's free choice, not hinder it. . . . In our considered judgment, an undue burden is an unconstitutional burden.

In practical effect, this new test led the Court to strike down the Pennsylvania requirement that a wife notify her husband before obtaining an abortion. It noted that "millions of women" are "victims of regular physical and psychological abuse at the hands of their husbands," and that these women might have "very good reasons" for not notifying their abusers. For domestic violence victims, the notice requirement would "operate as a substantial obstacle to a woman's choice to undergo an abortion," thus imposing an invalid "undue burden."

On the other hand, the Court applied the test to uphold Pennsylvania legal provisions requiring that before a woman could undergo the abortion procedure she must wait 24 hours after receipt of required abortion information from a doctor. In reaching this decision, the Court overruled *Thornburgh v. American College of Obstetricians & Gynecologists*, 476 U.S. 947 (1986) and *Akron v. Akron Ctr. For Reproductive Health*, 462 U.S. 416 (1983).

Casey is also noteworthy for its new conception of a woman's liberty:

Our law affords constitutional protection to personal decisions relating to marriage, procreation, contraception, family relationships, child rearing and education. . . . These matters, involving the most intimate and personal choices a person may make in a lifetime, choices central to personal dignity and autonomy, are central to the liberty protected by the Fourteenth Amendment. At the heart of liberty is the right to define one's own concept of existence, of meaning, of the universe, and of the mystery of human life. Beliefs about these matters could not define the attributes of personhood were they formed under compulsion of the State. . . .

[T]he liberty of the woman is at stake in a sense unique to the human condition and so unique to the law. The mother who carries a child to full term is subject to anxieties, to physical constraints, to pain that only she must bear. That these sacrifices have from the beginning of the human race been endured by woman with a pride that ennobles her in the eyes of others and gives to the infant a bond of love cannot alone be grounds for the State to insist she make the sacrifice. Her suffering is too intimate and personal for the State to insist, without more, upon its own vision of the woman's role, however dominant that vision has been in the course of our history and our culture. The destiny of the woman must be shaped to a large extent on her own conception of her spiritual imperatives and her place in society. . . .

Finally, *Casey* also recognized the impact of abortion on women's equality rights: "The ability of women to participate equally in the economic and social life of the Nation has been facilitated by their ability to control their reproductive lives." Compare *Casey*'s articulation of the rights at stake with those set forth in *Roe*. Which do you prefer?

The Court took another step back in *Gonzales v. Carhart*, 550 U.S. ___ (2007). Not only did it lessen the protection for women's health in later-term abortions, it also extended this exception to the previability stage. The ruling upheld a federal law banning abortions performed by a certain method—intact dilation and evacuation (intact D&E)—while providing no exception when this method was necessary to preserve the woman's health, even though the Court had struck down a nearly identical state ban seven years earlier.

Justice Breyer wrote the Court's earlier opinion for five justices in *Stenberg v. Carhart*, 530 U.S. 914 (2000). Nebraska's prohibition was unconstitutional because it failed to provide a health exception and used such vague language that it could lead to prosecutions of doctors for previability abortions. Justice Kennedy dissented in *Stenberg* and then wrote the majority opinion in *Gonzales*, joined by new Justices Roberts (replacing Chief Justice Rehnquist) and Alito (replacing Justice O'Connor, a member of the *Stenberg* majority), and by Justices Scalia and Thomas, who had long opposed abortion rights. The Court upheld the federal ban despite the same health exception and vagueness challenges and despite the fact that it would not prevent a single abortion but would instead require some women to undergo a different abortion method subjecting them to significant health risks. It also rejected a *Casey* "undue burden" argument.

In some of the most controversial language in the opinion, Justice Kennedy wrote that the federal act furthered an important governmental interest:

While we find no reliable data to measure the phenomenon, it seems unexceptionable to conclude some women come to regret their choice to abort the infant life they once created and sustained. Severe depression and loss of esteem can follow.

In a decision so fraught with emotional consequence some doctors may prefer not to disclose precise details of the means that will be used, confining themselves to the required statement of risks the procedure entails. . . .

It is, however, precisely this lack of information concerning the way in which the fetus will be killed that is of legitimate concern to the State. . . . The State has an interest in ensuring so grave a choice is well informed. It is self-evident that a mother who comes to regret her choice to abort must struggle with grief more anguished and sorrow more profound when she learns, only after the event, what she once did not know: that she allowed a doctor to pierce the skull and vacuum the fast-developing brain of her unborn child, a child assuming the human form. . . .

Justice Ginsburg wrote an impassioned *Gonzales* dissent, backed by Justices Breyer, Souter, and Stevens:

Today's decision is alarming. It refuses to take *Casey* and *Stenburg* seriously. It tolerates, indeed applauds, federal intervention to ban nationwide a procedure found necessary and proper in certain cases by the American College of Obstretricians and Gynecologists. . . . It blurs the line, firmly drawn in *Casey*, between previability and postviability abortions. And, for the first time since *Roe*, the Court blesses a prohibition with no exception guarding a woman's health.

I dissent from the Court's disposition. Retreating from prior rulings that abortion restrictions cannot be imposed absent an exception safeguarding a woman's health, the Court upholds an Act that surely would not survive under the close scrutiny that previously attended state-decreed limitations on a woman's reproductive choices. . . .

As *Casey* comprehended, at stake in cases challenging abortion restrictions is a woman's "control over her [own] destiny." . . .

The Court offers flimsy and transparent justifications for upholding a nationwide ban on intact D&E [without] any exception to safeguard a woman's health. Today's ruling, the Court declares, advances "a premise central to [*Casey*'s] conclusion"—*i.e.*, the Government's "legitimate and substantial interest in preserving and promoting fetal life." . . . But the Act scarcely furthers that interest: The law saves not a single fetus from destruction for it targets only a *method* of performing abortion. And surely the statute was not designed to protect the lives or health of pregnant women. . . . In short, the Court upholds a law that, while doing nothing to "preserv[e] fetal life," bars a woman from choosing intact D&E although her doctor "reasonably believes [that procedure] will best protect [her]." *Stenberg* (STEVENS, J., concurring). . . .

[T]he Court invokes an antiabortion shibboleth for which it concededly has no reliable evidence: Women who have abortions come to regret their choice, and consequently suffer from "[s]evere depression and loss of esteem." Because of women's fragile emotional state and because of the "bond of love the mother has for her child," the Court worries, doctors may withhold information about the nature of the intact D&E procedure. The solution the Court approves, then, is *not* to require doctors to inform women, accurately and adequately, of the different procedures and their attendant risks. . . . Instead, the Court deprives women of the right to make an autonomous choice, even at the expense of their safety.

This way of thinking reflects ancient notions about women's place in the family and under the Constitution—ideas that have long been discredited. . . .

Though today's majority may regard women's feelings on the matter as "self-evident," this Court has repeatedly confirmed that "[t]he destiny of the woman must be shaped . . . on her own conception of her spiritual imperatives and her place in society." *Casey.*

If there is anything at all redemptive to be said of today's opinion, it is that the Court is not willing to foreclose entirely a constitutional challenge to the Act. "The Act is open," the Court states, "to a proper as-applied challenge in a discreet case." . . .

In candor, the Act, and the Court's defense of it, cannot be understood as anything other than an effort to chip away at a right declared again and again by this Court—and with increasing comprehension of its centrality to women's lives.

British and U.S. Law. Compare the grounds on which women can seek an abortion under the 1967 Abortion Act and *Roe v. Wade* and *Casey.* Which do you prefer and why?

Comparative Abortion Law. The Center for Reproductive Rights' map, *The World's Abortion Laws* (May 2007), website link *available at* RossRights, lists the grounds for which abortion is available in all nations. It notes that countries representing about 61 per cent of the world's population make abortion available either without restriction as to grounds (56 countries, 39.3 percent) or for a broad range of socioeconomic reasons (14 countries, 21.3 percent). Conversely, in 69 countries representing 26 per cent of the world's population, the laws generally prohibit women from having any abortions (35 countries) or permit them only to save the woman's life (34 countries). Other countries (34, or 9.4 percent) extend the grounds from life to add a physical health exception, and a few others include a mental health exception (23 countries, 4.2 percent). Among all groups, some countries permit abortions for rape, incest, or fetal impairment. Similarly, many countries require either spousal or parental consent.

Religion and Abortion. The *Roe* Court briefly mentions some Jewish and Protestant religious views on abortion and the shifting positions of the Catholic religion over the centuries. SACRED RIGHTS: THE CASE FOR CONTRACEPTION AND ABORTION IN WORLD RELIGIONS (Daniel C. Maguire ed., 2003), discusses the diversity of views among and within many world religions, including Buddhism and Hinduism, as well as Catholicism, Judaism and Protestantism.

Do you think the religious views of the Justices affected their decisions? The Justices in the *Roe* majority included a Catholic (Brennan), two Episcopalians (Marshall and Stewart), a Methodist (Blackmun), and three Presbyterians (Burger, Douglas, and

Powell). The dissenters included an Episcopalian (White) and a Lutheran (Rehnquist). In *Casey*, the four Justices whose different opinions confirmed the central *Roe* holding and struck down the spousal notification requirement included a Catholic (Kennedy), two Episcopalians (O'Connor and Souter), and a Protestant (Stevens); Justice Blackmun (Methodist) applied the *Roe* strict scrutiny review test to invalidate the spousal notification and other requirements. The four dissenters on these points included two Catholics (Scalia and Thomas), an Episcopalian (White), and a Lutheran (Rehnquist). The five Justices in the *Gonzalez v. Carhart* majority were Catholic (Alito, Kennedy, Roberts, Scalia, and Thomas); the dissenters' religions included the Episcopalian (Souter), Jewish (Breyer and Ginsburg), and Protestant (Stevens) faiths. *See* http://www.adherents.com/adh_sc.html (last visited Aug. 28, 2007).

B. International Human Rights Law and Abortion

No international human rights treaty specifically mentions abortion. But treaties grant many rights that could be construed either to grant women the right to choose abortion or to grant states the power to deny women that right in order to protect potential life. In 2005, the Human Rights Committee decided its first case under the ICCPR addressing abortion rights.

1. Treaty Jurisprudence: The Human Rights Committee

Huamán v. Peru
(U.N. Human Rights Committee)
U.N. Doc. CCPR/C/85/D/1153/2003 (2005), *available at* RossRights

1.   The author of the communication is Karen Noelia Llantoy Huamán, born in 1984, who claims to be a victim of a violation by Peru of articles 2, 3, 6, 7, 17, 24 and 26[A] of the [ICCPR]. . . .

2.1   The author became pregnant in March 2001, when she was aged 17. On 27 June 2001 she was given a scan at the Archbishop Loayza National Hospital in Lima, part of the Ministry of Health. The scan showed that she was carrying an anencephalic foetus [—one which has no brain or lacks a major part of its brain].

2.2   On 3 July 2001, Dr. Ygor Pérez Solf, a gynaecologist and obstetrician in the . . . Hospital . . . , informed the author of the foetal abnormality and the risks to her life if the pregnancy continued. Dr. Pérez said that she had two options: to continue the pregnancy or to terminate it. He advised termination by means of uterine curettage. The author decided to terminate the pregnancy, and the necessary clinical studies were carried out, confirming the foetal abnormality.

2.3   On 19 July 2001, when the author reported to the hospital together with her mother for admission preparatory to the operation, Dr. Pérez informed her that she

---

[A] These articles guarantee the rights to: a remedy (2); equality between women and men (3); life (6); freedom from cruel treatment (7); privacy (17); child protection without sex discrimination (24); and equal protection without sex discrimination (26).

needed to obtain written authorization from the hospital director. Since she was under age, her mother, Ms. Elena Huamán Lara, requested the authorization. On 24 July 2001, Dr. Maximiliano Cárdenas Díaz, the hospital director, replied in writing that the termination could not be carried out as to do so would be unlawful, since under article 120 of the Criminal Code, abortion was punishable by a prison term of no more than three months when it was likely that at birth the child would suffer serious physical or mental defects, while under article 119, therapeutic abortion was permitted only when termination of the pregnancy was the only way of saving the life of the pregnant woman or avoiding serious and permanent damage to her health.

2.4   On 16 August 2001, Ms. Amanda Gayoso, a [Peruvian] social worker . . . , carried out an assessment of the case and concluded that medical intervention to terminate the pregnancy was advisable "since its continuation would only prolong the distress and emotional instability of Karen and her family". However, no intervention took place owing to the refusal of the Health Ministry medical personnel.

2.5   On 20 August 2001, Dr. Marta B. Rondón, a [Peruvian] psychiatrist . . . , drew up a psychiatric report on the author, concluding that "the so-called principle of the welfare of the unborn child has caused serious harm to the mother, since she has unnecessarily been made to carry to term a pregnancy whose fatal outcome was known in advance, and this has substantially contributed to triggering the symptoms of depression, with its severe impact on the development of an adolescent and the patient's future mental health".

2.6   On 13 January 2002 . . . the author gave birth to an anencephalic baby girl, who survived for four days, during which the mother had to breastfeed her. Following her daughter's death, the author fell into a state of deep depression. This was diagnosed by the psychiatrist Marta B. Rondón. . . .

2.7   The author has submitted to the Committee a statement made by Dr. Annibal Faúdes and Dr. Luis Tavara, who . . . studied the author's clinical dossier and stated that anencephaly is a condition which is fatal to the foetus in all cases. Death immediately follows birth in most cases. It also endangers the mother's life. In their opinion, in refusing to terminate the pregnancy, the medical personnel took a decision which was prejudicial to the author. . . .

3.1   The author claims a violation of article 2 of the Covenant, since the State party failed to comply with its obligation to guarantee the exercise of a right. The State should have taken steps to respond to the systematic reluctance of the medical community to comply with the legal provision authorizing therapeutic abortion, and its restrictive interpretation thereof. This restrictive interpretation was clear in the author's case, in which a pregnancy involving an anencephalic foetus was considered not to endanger her life and health. The State should have taken steps to ensure that an exception could be made to the rule criminalizing abortion, so that, in cases where the physical and mental health of the mother was at risk, she could undergo an abortion in safety.

3.2   The author claims to have suffered discrimination in breach of article 3 of the Covenant, in the following forms:

(a) In access to the health services, since her different and special needs were ignored because of her sex. . . .

(b) Discrimination in the exercise of her rights, since although the author was entitled to a therapeutic abortion, none was carried out because of social attitudes and prejudices, thus preventing her from enjoying her right to life, to health, to privacy and to freedom from cruel, inhuman and degrading treatment on an equal footing with men. . . .

3.3   The author claims a violation of article 6 of the Covenant. She states that her experience had a serious impact on her mental health from which she has still not recovered. She points out that the Committee has stated that the right to life cannot be interpreted in a restrictive manner, but requires States to take positive steps to protect it, including the measures necessary to ensure that women do not resort to clandestine abortions which endanger their life and health, especially in the case of poor women. She adds that the Committee has viewed lack of access for women to reproductive health services, including abortion, as a violation of women's right to life, and that this has been reiterated by other committees such as the [CEDAW] Committee . . . and the Committee on Economic, Social and Cultural Rights. The author claims that in the present case, the violation of the right to life lay in the fact that Peru did not take steps to ensure that the author secured a safe termination of pregnancy on the grounds that the foetus was not viable. She states that the refusal to provide a legal abortion service left her with two options which posed an equal risk to her health and safety: to seek clandestine (and hence highly risky) abortion services, or to continue a dangerous and traumatic pregnancy which put her life at risk. . . .

3.5   The author points out . . . that, after considering Peru's report in 1996, the Committee expressed the view that restrictive provisions on abortion subjected women to inhumane treatment, in violation of article 7 of the Covenant, and that in 2000, the Committee reminded the State party that the criminalization of abortion was incompatible with articles 3, 6 and 7 of the Covenant.[2] . . . [The Committee's description of her other claims is omitted.] . . .

4. On 23 July 2003, 15 March 2004 and 25 October 2004, reminders were sent to the State party inviting it to submit information to the Committee concerning the admissibility and the merits of the complaint. The Committee notes that no such information has been received. . . . In the absence of a reply from the State party, due weight must be given to the author's allegations, to the extent that these have been properly substantiated. . . .

[The Committee ruled most of the author's claims admissible, but rejected those based on articles 3 and 26 because they had "not been properly substantiated" by "evidence."] . . .

6.2   The Committee notes that the author attached a doctor's statement confirming that her pregnancy exposed her to a life-threatening risk. She also suffered severe psychological consequences exacerbated by her status as a minor, as the psychiatric

---

[2] Concluding observations of the Human Rights Committee: Peru, 15 November 2000 (CCPR/CO/70/PER), para. 20.

report . . . confirmed. . . . It notes that the authorities were aware of the risk to the author's life, since a gynaecologist and obstetrician in the same hospital had advised her to terminate the pregnancy, with the operation to be carried out in the same hospital. The subsequent refusal of the competent medical authorities to provide the service may have endangered the author's life. The author states that no effective remedy was available to her to oppose that decision. . . . [D]ue weight must be given to the author's claims.

6.3   The author also claims that, owing to the refusal of the medical authorities to carry out the therapeutic abortion, she had to endure the distress of seeing her daughter's marked deformities and knowing that she would die very soon. This was an experience which added further pain and distress to that which she had already borne during the period when she was obliged to continue with the pregnancy. The author attaches a psychiatric certificate . . . , which confirms the state of deep depression into which she fell and the severe consequences this caused, taking her age into account. The Committee notes that this situation could have been foreseen, since a hospital doctor had diagnosed anencephaly in the foetus, yet the hospital director refused termination. The omission on the part of the State in not enabling the author to benefit from a therapeutic abortion was, in the Committee's view, the cause of the suffering she experienced. The Committee has pointed out in its General Comment No. 20 that the right set out in article 7 of the Covenant relates not only to physical pain but also to mental suffering, and that the protection is particularly important in the case of minors. . . . Consequently, the Committee considers that the facts before it reveal a violation of article 7 of the Covenant. In the light of this finding the Committee does not consider it necessary in the circumstances to make a finding on article 6 of the Covenant.

6.4   The author states that the State party, in denying her the opportunity to secure medical intervention to terminate the pregnancy, interfered arbitrarily in her private life. The Committee notes that a public-sector doctor told the author that she could either continue with the pregnancy or terminate it in accordance with domestic legislation allowing abortions in cases of risk to the life of the mother. . . . [D]ue weight must be given to the author's claim that at the time of this information, the conditions for a lawful abortion as set out in the law were present. In the circumstances of the case, the refusal to act in accordance with the author's decision to terminate her pregnancy was not justified and amounted to a violation of article 17 of the Covenant.

6.5   The author claims a violation of article 24 of the Covenant, since she did not receive from the State party the special care she needed as a minor. The Committee notes the special vulnerability of the author as a minor girl. . . . [D]ue weight must be given to the author's claim that she did not receive, during and after her pregnancy, the medical and psychological support necessary in the specific circumstances of her case. Consequently, the Committee considers that the facts before it reveal a violation of article 24 of the Covenant.

6.6   The author claims to have been a victim of violation of [article] 2 of the Covenant on the grounds that she lacked an adequate legal remedy. . . . [T]he Committee considers that due weight must be given to the author's claims as regards lack of an adequate legal remedy and consequently concludes that the facts before it also reveal a violation of article 2 in conjunction with articles 7, 17 and 24. . . .

8. In accordance with article 2, paragraph 3 (a), of the Covenant, the State party is required to furnish the author with an effective remedy, including compensation. The State party has an obligation to take steps to ensure that similar violations do not occur in the future. . . .

Dissenting Opinion by COMMITTEE MEMBER HIPÓLITO SOLARI-YRIGOYEN

My dissenting opinion . . .—the majority not considering that article 6 of the Covenant was violated—is based on the following grounds: . . . .

The Committee notes that when the author was a minor, she and her mother were informed by the obstetric gynaecologist at Lima National Hospital, whom they had consulted because of the author's pregnancy, that the foetus suffered from anencephaly which would inevitably cause its death at birth. The doctor told the author that she had two options: (1) continue the pregnancy, which would endanger her own life; or (2) terminate the pregnancy by a therapeutic abortion. He recommended the second option. Given this conclusive advice from the specialist who had told her of the risks to her life if the pregnancy continued, the author decided to follow his professional advice and accepted the second option. As a result, all the clinical tests needed to confirm the doctor's statements about the risks to the mother's life of continuing the pregnancy and the inevitable death of the foetus at birth were performed.

The author substantiated with medical and psychological certificates all her claims about the fatal risk she ran if the pregnancy continued. In spite of the risk, the director of the public hospital would not authorize the therapeutic abortion which the law of the State party allowed, arguing that it would not be a therapeutic abortion but rather a voluntary and unfounded abortion punishable under the Criminal Code. The hospital director did not supply any legal ruling in support of his pronouncements outside his professional field or challenging the medical attestations to the serious risk to the mother's life. . . . Refusing a therapeutic abortion not only endangered the author's life but had grave consequences which the author has also substantiated to the Committee by means of valid supporting documents.

It is not only taking a person's life that violates article 6 of the Covenant but also placing a person's life in grave danger, as in this case. Consequently, I consider that the facts in the present case reveal a violation of article 6 of the Covenant.

NOTES

The Woman's Right to Life. Unlike the dissenting member, the Committee does not reach Ms. Huamán's right to life claim. Why? Note its concluding observations to Peru (*see* para. 3.5). Similarly, the Committee's General Comment 28, para. 10, asks States parties how they "help women prevent unwanted pregnancies, and . . . ensure that they do not have to undertake life-threatening clandestine abortions. . . ." Is that relevant in this case?

One could argue that Ms. Huamán did not face certain death if the pregnancy continued and that only guaranteed death should permit an exception. How should the Committee determine such abortion-related issues? For abortion opponents willing to protect the woman's right to life, how should they redraft Peru's laws to permit such abortions? What provisions would be necessary to give doctors, hospitals, and public health officials sufficiently clear guidance?

Concluding Observations. Human rights bodies issue concluding observations after States parties provide their periodic State report and then meet with the committee. The purpose of these observations is to help the States parties comply with the Convention by noting progress made and recommending future action. The reports and concluding observations are now readily available on many websites, *available at* Ross-Rights. They provide a wealth of information about human rights legal developments in all States parties. Activists can use this information in domestic advocacy work, as can lawyers in litigation, both as to their own country and as to how other countries are progressing.

Which Rights? Compare the Human Rights Committee and the U.S. Supreme Court's positions as to which specific rights are violated by the abortion laws at issue. What formulation do you prefer and why? Could any of the rights at issue be asserted in the other forum? Note that the Committee finds inadmissible the asserted article 3 violations of women's right to be treated equally with men because Ms. Huamán did not submit any substantiating evidence. What evidence could she have presented, if any?

Significance of the Decision. One could argue that the decision does little to advance women's right to choose abortion, since it merely finds Peru's failure to enforce its own law the source of the violation. What benefits, if any, do you find in the Committee's decision?

The Prohibition on Executing Pregnant Women. ICCPR article 6(2) permits the death penalty but "only for the most serious crimes." Article 6(5), however, spares pregnant women: "Sentence of death . . . shall not be carried out on pregnant women." Consider the implications for a fetal right to life.

2. Treaty Language: CEDAW

CEDAW grants the most explicit family planning rights:

Article 16

1. States Parties shall take all appropriate measures to eliminate discrimination against women in all matters relating to marriage and family relations and in particular shall ensure, on a basis of equality of men and women: . . .

(e) The same rights to decide freely and responsibly on the number and spacing of their children and to have access to the information, education and means to enable them to exercise these rights. . . .

On the other hand, while CEDAW does not mention the word fetus, it does permit "special measures . . . aimed at protecting maternity" (art. 4(2)) and "special protection to women during pregnancy in types of work proved to be harmful to them" (art. 11(2)(d)).

Consider the best CEDAW arguments one could make to support a woman's right to choose. Undertake the same exercise for a fetal right to life. Which seems more persuasive and why?

NOTE

The Committee's First Reproductive Rights Decision. The right to bear children was at stake in *A. S. v. Hungary*, U.N. Doc. CEDAW/C/36/D/4/2004 (2006), *available at* RossRights. The Committee found violations of Articles 10(h), 12, and 16(1)(e), where a Hungarian Roma woman had been subjected to a coerced sterilization during an emergency caesarean section to remove a dead fetus, despite her clear desire to have more children.

3. CEDAW's General Recommendations

In its General Recommendation 24, Women and Health (20th sess., 1999), U.N. Doc. A/54/38 at 5 (1999), the CEDAW Committee seems to suggest that women have the right to choose:

11. Measures to eliminate discrimination against women are considered to be inappropriate if a health care system lacks services to prevent, detect and treat illnesses specific to women. It is discriminatory for a State party to refuse to legally provide for the performance of certain reproductive health services for women. . . .

14. The obligation to respect rights requires States parties to refrain from obstructing action taken by women in pursuit of their health goals. . . . For example, States parties should not restrict women's access to health services . . . on the ground that women do not have the authorization of husbands, partners, parents or health authorities, because they are unmarried or because they are women. Other barriers to women's access to appropriate health care include laws that criminalize medical procedures only needed by women and that punish women who undergo those procedures. . . .

31. States parties should also . . . reduce maternal mortality rates through safe motherhood services and prenatal assistance. When possible, legislation criminalizing abortion should be amended to remove punitive provisions imposed on women who undergo abortion. . . .

What conclusions do you draw?

C. The Regional Human Rights Conventions

Each regional human rights system has confronted the issue of the woman's autonomy rights versus a fetal right to life. The relevant convention language varies in each system. Do the results?

1. The American System and the Right to Life

White v. United States
(Inter-American Commission on Human Rights)
Case 2141, Inter-Am. C.H.R., Resolution 23/81, OEA/Ser.L/V/II.54, Doc. 9 rev. 1
   (1981),
available at RossRights

Summary of the Case

1. On January 19, 1977, Christian B. White and Gary K. Potter, filed with the Inter-American Commission on Human Rights a petition against the United States of America and the Commonwealth of Massachusetts. . . . The petition is accompanied by a cover letter of the Catholics for Christian Political Action. . . . [The Bishop of Arlington, Virginia, and Lawyers for Life also joined the petition.]
2. The pertinent parts of the petition are the following:

Name of the person whose human rights have been violated: "Baby Boy". . . . *Victim was killed by abortion process . . . by Dr. Kenneth Edelin, M.D., in violation of the right to life granted by the American Declaration of the Rights and Duties of Man* [American Declaration], *as clarified by the definition and description of the American Convention on Human Rights* [American Convention]. . . .[B]
Final decision of the authority . . . that acted in the matter: *The Supreme Judicial Court of Massachusetts, Boston, Massachusetts, acquitted Edelin on appeal, on December 17, 1976. . . .*

3. . . . [T]he petitioners add . . . the following information and arguments . . .

b) This violation . . . began on January 22, 1973, when the [U.S.] Supreme Court . . . handed down its decisions in the cases of *Roe vs. Wade* and *Doe vs. Bolton.*
c) The effect of the *Wade* and *Bolton* decisions . . . in ending the legal protection of unborn children set the stage for the deprivation of "Baby Boy's" right to life. These decisions in and of themselves constitute a violation of his right to life, and the United States . . . therefore stands accused of a violation of . . . Article I of the American Declaration. . . .
The United States Government, through its Supreme Court, is guilty of that violation.
d) At trial, the jury found Dr. Edelin guilty of manslaughter, necessarily finding as fact that the child was such as to fit within a "protectable exception" (over six months past conception and/or alive outside the womb) . . . in the *Wade* and *Bolton* cases. On appeal, the Supreme Judicial Court of Massachusetts reversed. . . .
e) This decision came down on December 17, 1976, and, by preventing Dr. Edelin from being punished for his acts, put the State of Massachusetts in the posture of violating "Baby Boy's" right to life under the Declaration. . . .

14. The U.S. Government [State Department] response . . . is developed in a three part argument that the right-to-life provision[] of the American Declaration . . . was not violated, even in the hypothesis that the American Convention . . . could be used as a means of interpretation in this case. . . .

[B] The Declaration's Article I provides: "Every human being has the right to life, liberty and the security of his person." The Convention's Article 4(1) provides a more expansive definition: "Every person has the right to have his life respected. This right shall be protected by law and, in general, from the moment of conception. No one shall be arbitrarily deprived of his life."

15. The State Department . . . [also] responded. . . .

In *Commonwealth v. Edelin*, the abortion was performed in the interim between the announcement of the *Wade* decision, which rendered inoperative the Massachusetts criminal abortion statute, and the enactment of new state legislation on abortions. From January 1973 until August 1974, there were no legal restrictions on the performance of abortions per se in Massachusetts, and Dr. Edelin was prosecuted under a manslaughter statute. He was acquitted; the record amply demonstrates the difficulty of bringing the facts of a legal abortion within the terms of a manslaughter statute. It does not establish, however, that the abortion was performed "arbitrarily." Complainants note that the *Edelin* opinion does not explain the factors which went into the decision to perform the abortion; the court makes only passing reference to the [unmarried] pregnant girl's and her mother's "having requested an abortion." Had the case been tried under the 1974 Massachusetts legislation on abortions . . . , this aspect would have been fully explored. However, it was not a central issue under the theory of manslaughter advanced by the Commonwealth. Thus, the record is silent as to the pregnant girl's motivation or medical need in seeking an abortion, and the *Edelin* case cannot legitimately be seen as sanctioning a "mother's desire to kill (unborn children) for improper reasons or no reason at all." It seems worth noting, however, that, at the time of the abortion, Dr. Edelin estimated the gestational period as twenty to twenty-two weeks—under the time generally believed required to produce a viable fetus and he did not believe the fetus was viable. The Court found nothing to impeach his good faith judgment in this regard. . . .

Whereas. . . .

15. The international obligation of the United States . . . , as a member of the Organization of American States (OAS), under the jurisdiction of the Inter-American Commission on Human Rights (IACHR) is governed by the Charter of OAS (Bogotá, 1948) . . . , ratified by [the] United States on April 23, 1968.

16. As a consequence . . . of this Treaty, the provisions of other instruments and resolutions of the OAS on human rights, acquired binding force. Those instruments and resolutions approved with the vote of [the] U.S. Government [include] . . . the . . . American Declaration . . . (Bogotá, 1948). . . .

17. . . . [T]he IACHR is the organ of the OAS entrusted with the competence to promote the observance and respect of human rights. . . . [which] are understood to be the rights set forth in the American Declaration in relation to States not parties to the American Convention on Human Rights (San José, 1969) [such as the U.S., which has not ratified the Convention].

18. The first violation denounced in the petition concerns article I of the American Declaration . . . : "Every human being has the right to life. . . ." The petitioners admitted that the Declaration does not respond "when life begins," "when a pregnancy product becomes a human being" or other such questions. However, they try to answer these fundamental questions with two different arguments:

a) The *travaux préparatoires*, the discussion of the draft Declaration during the IX International Conference of American States at Bogotá in 1948 and the final vote, demonstrate that the intention of the Conference was to protect the right to life "from the moment of conception."

b) The [1969] American Convention on Human Rights, promulgated to advance the Declaration's high purposes and to be read as a corollary document, gives a definition of the right to life in article 4.1: "This right shall be protected by law from the moment of conception."

[19.] A brief legislative history of the Declaration does not support the petitioner's argument . . . : . . . .

b) [The first draft of] Article I . . . reads: "Every person has the right to life. This right extends to the right to life from the moment of conception; to the right to life of incurables, imbeciles and the insane. Capital punishment may only be applied in cases in which it has been prescribed by pre-existing law for crimes of exceptional gravity."

c) A Working Group [prepared a new draft]. . . . : "Every human being has the right to life, liberty, security and integrity of . . . [the] person."

d) This completely new [draft was] . . . a compromise to resolve the problems raised by the Delegations of Argentina, Brazil, Cuba, United States of America, Mexico, Peru, Uruguay and Venezuela, mainly as consequence of the conflict existing between the laws of those States and the [first] draft. . . .

e) In connection with the right to life, the [first draft] definition . . . was incompatible with the laws governing the death penalty and abortion in the majority of the American States. In effect, the acceptance of this absolute concept—the right to life from the moment of conception—would imply the obligation to derogate the articles of the Penal Codes in force in 1948 in many countries because such articles excluded the penal sanction for the crime of abortion if performed in one or more of the following cases: A—when necessary to save the life of the mother; B—to interrupt the pregnancy of the victim of a rape; C—to protect the honor of an honest woman; D—to prevent the transmission to the fetus of a hereditary or contagious disease; E—for economic reasons.

f) In 1948, the American States that permitted abortion in one of such cases . . . were[:] Argentina—(cases A and B); Bra[z]il—(A and B); Costa Rica—(A); Cuba—(A, B and D); Ecuador—(A and B); Mexico [federal district and territories] . . . —(A and B); Nicaragua (frustrated attempt)—(C); Paraguay—(A); Peru—(A—to save the life or health of the mother); Uruguay—(A, B, C, and E—the abortion must be performed in the three first months from conception); Venezuela—(A); United States . . . —see the State laws and precedents; Puerto Rico—(A).

g) . . . . Finally, the definitive text of the Declaration [including the second draft of the right to life] . . . was approved . . . on April 30, 1948. . . . The only difference in the final text is the elimination of the word "integrity."

h) Consequently, the defendant is correct in challenging the petitioners' assumption that Article I of the Declaration has incorporated the notion that the right of life exists from the moment of conception. Indeed, the conference faced this question but chose not to adopt language which would clearly have stated that principle.

20. The second argument of the petitioners, related to the possible use of the Convention as an element for the interpretation of the Declaration requires also a study of the motives that prevailed at the [1969] San José Diplomatic Conference with the adoption of the definition of the right to life. . . .

22. . . . [The first draft of the Convention's right to life (article 2)] . . . reintroduced the concept that "This right shall be protected by law from the moment of conception." . . .

25. To accommodate the views that insisted on the concept "from the moment of conception," with the objection raised, since the Bogot[á] Conference, based on the legislation of American States that permitted abortion, *inter alia*, to save the mother's life, and in case of rape, the IACHR, redrafting article 2 (Right to life), decided, by majority vote, to introduce the words "in general." This compromise was the origin of the new [second draft] text of article 2 "1. Every person has the right to have his life respected. This right shall be protected by law, in general, from the moment of conception."

26. The rapporteur . . . proposed, at this second opportunity for discussion of the definition of the right of life, to delete [in a third draft] the entire final phrase " . . . in general, from the moment of conception." . . . [B]ased on the abortion laws in force in the majority of the American States, [he reasoned that the] . . . addition [was needed]: "to avoid any possibility of conflict with [ICCPR article 6(1)] . . . which states this right in a general way only."

27. However, the majority of the Commission believed that, for reasons of principle, it was fundamental to state the provision on the protection of the right to life in the [second draft] form. . . .

28. In the Diplomatic Conference that approved the American Convention, the Delegations of Brazil and the Dominican Republic introduced separate amendments to delete the final phrase of paragraph 1 of article 3 (Right to life) "in general, from the moment of conception". The United States delegation supported the Brazilian position.

29. Conversely, the Delegation of Ecuador supported the deletion of the words "and in general". Finally, by majority vote, the Conference adopted the text of the [second] draft . . . , which became the present text of article 4, paragraph 1, of the American Convention.

30. In the light of this history, it is clear that the petitioners' interpretation of the definition given by the American Convention on the right of life is incorrect. The addition of the phrase "in general, from the moment of conception" does not mean that the drafters of the Convention intended to modify the concept of the right to life that prevailed in Bogot[á], when they approved the American Declaration. The legal implications of the clause "in general, from the moment of conception" are substantially different from the shorter clause "from the moment of conception" as appears repeatedly in the petitioners' briefs.

31. However, accepting [for the sake of argument] . . . , that the American Convention had established the absolute concept of the right to life from the moment of conception—it would be impossible to impose upon the United States Government or that of any other State Member of the OAS, by means of "interpretation," an international obligation based upon a treaty that such State has not duly accepted or ratified. . . .

The Inter-American Commission on Human Rights Resolves:

1. The decision of the U.S. Supreme Court and the Supreme Judicial Court of Massachusetts and other facts stated in the petition do not constitute a violation of article[] I . . . of the American Declaration of Rights and Duties of Man. . . .

CHAIRMAN TOM J. FARER, SECOND VICE CHAIRMAN FRANCISCO BERTRAND GALINDO, and DOCTORS CARLOS A. DUNSHEE DE ABRANCHES, ANDRÉS AGUILAR, and CÉSAR SEPÚLVEDA concurred in approving this resolution. DR. AGUILAR presented a concurring explanation of his vote [omitted here; *available at* RossRights]. DOCTORS MARCO GERARD MONROY CABRA and LUIS DEMETRIO TINOCO CASTRO presented separate, dissenting, explanation of their votes.

Dissent of DR. MARCO GERARDO MONROY CABRA. . . .

3. In its resolution, the Commission states that Article I of the [first] . . . draft [of the American Declaration] was incompatible with the laws of some of the American States, which in certain cases permitted abortion, and this is true. This incompatibility, however, does not lead to the conclusion that the IX International Conference of American States in Bogotá intended to take the position that life should be protected only from birth and not from conception, since this conclusion is not evident from the Minutes of the Sixth Committee. The Commission's position implies that a conflict between domestic and international law is possible, which in each case would be resolved according to the principles of international doctrine, international jurisprudence, and the constitutional laws of each State. Needless to say, the now-prevalent concept is the monist position held by Kelsen, that in case of conflict international law takes procedence over domestic law, a principle adopted as a general rule in Articles 27 and 46 of the Vienna Convention on the Law of Treaties. This would imply that if the Declaration ran counter to the laws of some American States, international law would prevail.

4. In its opinion, the Commission argues that the sentence "This right extends to the right to life from the moment of conception" was eliminated from the . . . [first] draft and such is the case. However, one cannot thereby conclude that life should not be protected from conception, inasmuch as the statement "to the right to life of incurables, imbeciles, and the insane" was also eliminated, and no one could reasonably say that the life of incurables, imbeciles, or the insane should not be protected.

5. Since Article I does not define when life begins, one can resort to medical science which has concluded that life has its beginning in the union of two series of chromosomes. Most scientists agree that the fetus is a human being and is genetically complete. . . .

8. The intentional and illegal interruption of the physiological process of pregnancy, resulting in the destruction of the embryo or death of the fetus, is unquestionably an offense against life and, consequently, a violation of Article I of the American Declaration. . . . The maternal womb in which the flame of life is lighted is sacred and may not be profaned to extinguish what God has created in his image and in his likeness. It has been said repeatedly, that, from the biological standpoint, human life

exists from the moment that the ovum is fertilized by the sperm and, more specifically, from the time the egg travels to the uterus. The scientific process is the following: when in a fertile state, the sex cells (ova and spermatozoids) undergo a special process of chromosome division called myosis, in which the 46 chromosomes of each cell are reduced to 23, in such a way as to distinguish the sperm and the ovum, with each containing only one half the number of chromosomes present in the nucleus of the majority of human cells. After a process of search and rejection on the part of these fertile cells, comes what is known as activation, which occurs when a sperm cell succeeds in penetrating the interior of the ovum. This produces fertilization, the process whereby two sex cells (ovum and sperm) unite to form the first cell of an individual. This first stage, called activation, is followed by another, when the genetic messages carried by the sperm and those already possessed by the egg are attracted to each other and unite. Added together, the 23 chromosomes of the mother and the 23 of the father total the 46 chromosomes of the sister cell.

This union of male and female elements produces the zygote, which is simply the fertilized egg. We now have fertilization in the true sense of the word. It can then be said that conception has taken place and that a human being exists, since through the union that has occurred, we have a human cell containing its intrinsic 46 chromosomes. This new being, which scientists call a zygote, differs from the father and the mother, in that it has only one half of him and one half of her. What we have is a fertilized egg, representing a life—a life that contains the genes to make way for the appearance of new cells that will form the different parts of the human body. Thus fertilized, the egg begins its journey toward the uterus, which it will reach in a few days, and the embryo will then continue developing in stages. These stages have now been distinguished from each other by scientists, who are able to tell us the precise age of any of them. . . .

9. Life is the primary right of every individual. It is the fundamental right and the condition for the existence of all other rights. If human existence is not recognized, there is no subject upon which to predicate the other rights. It is a right that antecedes other rights and exists by the mere fact of being, with no need for the state to recognize it as such. It is not up to the state to decide whether that right shall be recognized in one case and not in another, since that would mean discrimination. The life of the unborn child, the infant, the young, the old, the mentally ill, the handicapped, and that of all human beings in general, must be recognized.

The foregoing means that if conception produces a human life, and this right is the primary and fundamental one, abortion is an attack on the right to life and, therefore, runs counter to Article I of the American Declaration.

Dissent of DR. LUIS DEMETRIO TINOCO CASTRO. . . .

[I]t is necessary first to answer the transcendental question of the nature of the unborn, the topic of most significant legal and moral consequences of stipulating whether what has been formed in the womb of a woman and is still therein is a "human being" with the right to life. Or whether it should be understood that the "right to life" that every human being has [is] in accordance with the [right of those] already living their own lives, outside the womb. In other words: at what moment in his long process of formation, development, decadence, and death is it considered that there exists a "human being" with the "right to life". . . ?. . . .

The question was put barely three years ago to the eminent Dean of the Teaching and Research Unit of the University of Paris, holder of the Chair of Fundamental Genetics, there, Professor Jerome Lejeune. . . . "Professor," he was asked, "may the first cell formed at the moment of conception be considered already to be a human being, with his own personality, independent of that of his mother?" "Of course," he replied, adding, "It has been shown that all the genetic qualities of the individual are already present in that first cell, that the embryo, seven days after fertilization . . . emits a chemical message that stops the menstruation of his mother . . . that at twenty days after fertilization . . . his heart (as large as a grain of wheat) begins to beat . . . at two months . . . he already has human form completely; he has a head, he has arms, he has his fingers and toes . . . and even the lines on his hands drawn . . . and between the second and third months . . . the finger-prints are already indicated . . . and will not change to the end of his life . . . at three months he is already able to close his eyes, to clench his fists, and if at that moment his upper lip were caressed with a thread, he would made a face. . . . A human being exists . . . there is no doubt about that." And the same Professor, in a magazine article, stated: "The fetus is a human being. Genetically he is complete. This is not an appearance; it is a fact". . . .

[T]he International Code of Medical Morality declared that the doctor should always bear in mind the importance of preserving human life from the time of conception; and the so-called Declaration of Geneva [The World Medical Association's Physician's Oath] makes the physician promise to maintain the greatest respect for human life from the time of conception.

Those scientific principles and principles of professional ethics have also found implicit welcome, as was to be expected, in the legislation of the immense majority of the countries of the western world, in which, almost without exception, the rule is in force that a woman sentenced to death may not be executed if she is pregnant, a benefit that is not limited to women who have reached the state of "advanced pregnancy" but extends also to those at any other stage of the process of gestation of the child. Now such an exceptional provision, which is also found in the International Covenant on Civil and Political Rights . . . can only be explained if one starts from the legal assumption that a human being is living in the womb of the woman who would have to be executed, and since this small and unseen human being had not been covered by the sentence, neither morally nor legally could it be made to suffer the death penalty that would fatally be derived from the execution of the mother. This is an evident recognition by the United Nations and by the law in force in many countries that a human being has existence, life, during the entire period of pregnancy of the wom[a]n.

The reasons stated leave no doubt in my mind that the American Declaration of the Rights and Duties of Man refers to the complete period of human life—from conception to death—when it states that "every human being has the right to life".

N O T E

Uruguay: Comparing the Convention to the Declaration. Note that the decision concerns the American Declaration because the United States had not ratified the American Convention. *See* paras. 15–17 for why the originally non-binding Declaration became binding. The Commission decision notes that Uruguay permitted abortion for economic reasons in 1948. It ratified the American Convention in 1985. Assuming a suit were brought against Uruguay to strike down this 1948 abortion right, develop arguments advocates for fetal rights might use. Consider the arguments Uruguay could use to support its law. What decision would the Inter-American Commission be likely to issue? What decision should it issue?

2. The European Convention: Respect for Private Life versus the Right to Life

This section presents two decisions from the European system. In the first case, decided by the now-defunct European Commission of Human Rights, women brought suit to claim a privacy abortion right against Germany, which had recently enacted a law narrowing access to abortion. In the second case, decided 27 years later by the European Court of Human Rights, a woman sued France for refusing to impose criminal penalties on a doctor whose negligence led to the loss of a desired pregnancy. She asserted a fetal right to life.

Bruggemann v. Federal Republic of Germany
(European Commission of Human Rights)
Application No. 6959/75, 3 Eur. H.R. Rep. 244 (1977)

I. Introduction. . . .

2. The applicants are German citizens living in Hamburg. The first applicant, Rose Marie Bruggemann, born in 1936 and single, is a clerk. The second applicant, Adelheid Scheuten, born in 1939, divorced and mother of two children, is a telephone operator and housewife.

3. The application concerns the criminal law on the termination of pregnancy in the Federal Republic of Germany. . . .

4. [T]he Fifteenth Criminal Law Reform Act entered into force in the Federal Republic of Germany on 21 June 1976. It maintains the principle that abortion is a criminal offense [for both the doctor and pregnant woman] but provides that, in specific situations of distress of the woman concerned, an abortion performed by a doctor with her consent after consultation is not punishable. [This 1976 Abortion Act was enacted because the German Federal Constitutional Court in 1975 struck down the 1974 Abortion Act allowing unlimited access to abortion during the first 12 weeks of a pregnancy. The German Court found the 1974 law violated the rights to life and dignity of "the child developing in the mother's womb . . . even as against the mother." In contrast, the 1976 Abortion Act permitted abortion during the initial 12

weeks "in order to avert the danger of a distress which (a) is so serious that the pregnant woman cannot be required to continue the pregnancy, and (b) cannot be averted in any other way she can reasonably be expected to bear. . . ." Both the 1974 and 1976 laws permitted abortion to protect the pregnant woman's life or health, as well as for rape or for fetal injury; those provisions were not at issue in the case before the German court.]

5. The applicants submit that . . . the Fifteenth Criminal Law Reform Act interfered in particular with their right to respect for their private life under Article 8 (1) of the European Convention on Human Rights and they consider that this interference was not justified on any of the grounds enumerated in paragraph (2) of that Article. . . .

IV. Opinion of the Commission

1. The point at issue

50. The applicants mainly allege a violation of Article 8 of the Convention by the Federal Republic of Germany in that they are not free to have an abortion carried out in case of an unwanted pregnancy. They state that, as a result, they either have to renounce sexual intercourse or to apply methods of contraception or to carry out a pregnancy against their will.

Article 8 of the Convention provides:

(1) Everyone has the right to respect for his private and family life, his home and his correspondence.
(2) There shall be no interference by a public authority with the exercise of this right except such as is in accordance with the law and is necessary in a democratic society in the interests of national security, public safety or the economic well-being of the country, for the prevention of disorder or crime, for the protection of health or morals, or for the protection of the rights and freedoms of others. . . .

2. The interference with the right to respect for one's private life

54. According to Article 8 of the Convention, 'Everyone has the right to respect for his private . . . life. . . .' [T]he Commission has already found that legislation regulating the interruption of pregnancy touches upon the sphere of private life. The first question which must be answered is whether the legal rules governing abortion . . . constitute an *interference* with the right to respect for private life of the applicants.

55. The right to respect for private life is of such scope as to secure to the individual a sphere within which he can freely pursue the development and fulfilment of his personality. To this effect, he must also have the possibility of establishing relationships of various kinds, including sexual, with other persons. In principle, therefore, within this sphere, it interferes with the respect for private life and such interference must be justified in light of Article 8 (2).

56. However, there are limits to the personal sphere. While a large proportion of the law existing in a given State has some immediate or remote effect on the individual's possibility of developing his personality by doing what he wants to do, not all of

these can be considered to constitute an interference with private life in the sense of Article 8 of the Convention. In fact, as the earlier jurisprudence of the Commission has already shown, the claim to respect for private life is automatically reduced to the extent that the individual himself brings his private life into contact with public life or into close connection with other protected interests. . . .

57. Thus, the Commission has held that the concept of private life in Article 8 was broader than the definition given by numerous Anglo-Saxon and French authors, namely, the 'right to live as far as one wishes, protected from publicity', in that it also comprises, '*to a certain degree*, the right to establish and to develop relationships with other human beings, especially in the emotional field for the development and fulfilment of one's own personality'. But it denied 'that the protection afforded by Article 8 of the Convention extends to relationships of the individual with his entire immediate surroundings'. It thus found that the right to keep a dog did not pertain to the sphere of private life of the owner because 'the keeping of dogs is by the very nature of that animal necessarily associated with certain interferences with the life of others and even with public life'. . . .

59. The termination of an unwanted pregnancy is not comparable with the situation . . . above. . . . However, pregnancy cannot be said to pertain uniquely to the sphere of private life. Whenever a woman is pregnant, her private life becomes closely connected with the developing foetus.

60. The Commission does not find it necessary to decide, in this context, whether the unborn child is to be considered as 'life' in the sense of Article 2 [protecting the right to life] of the Convention, or whether it could be regarded as an entity which under Article 8 (2) could justify an interference 'for the protection of others'. There can be no doubt that certain interests relating to pregnancy are legally protected, *e.g.* as shown by a survey of the legal order in 13 High Contracting Parties. This survey reveals that, without exception, certain rights are attributed to the conceived but unborn child, in particular the right to inherit. The Commission also notes that Article 6 (5) of the United Nations Covenant on Civil and Political Rights prohibits the execution of death sentences on pregnant women.

61. The Commission therefore finds that not every regulation of the termination of unwanted pregnancies constitutes an interference with *the right to respect* for the private life of the mother. Article 8 (1) cannot be interpreted as meaning that pregnancy and its termination are, as a principle, solely a matter of the private life of the mother. In this respect the Commission notes that there is not one member State of the Convention which does not, in one way or another, set up legal rules in this matter. The applicants complain about the fact that [in 1975] the Constitutional Court declared null and void the [1974 abortion law], but even this [1974] Act was not based on the assumption that abortion is entirely a matter of the private life of the pregnant woman. It only provided that an abortion performed by a physician with the pregnant woman's consent should not be punishable if no more that 12 weeks had elapsed after conception. . . .

62. According to [the 1976 abortion law], an abortion performed by a physician is not punishable if the termination of pregnancy is advisable for any reason in order

to avert from the pregnant woman the danger of a distress which is so serious that the pregnant woman cannot be required to continue the pregnancy and which cannot be averted in any other way the pregnant woman might reasonably be expected to bear. [The European Commission does not mention the 12-week limit for this "serious distress" reason.] In particular, the abortion is admitted if the continuation of the pregnancy would create a danger to the life or health of the woman [no time limit], if it has to be feared that the child might suffer from an incurable injury to its health [22-week limit] or if the pregnancy is the result of a crime [12-week limit]. The woman is required also to seek advice on medically significant aspects of abortion as well as on the public and private assistance available for pregnant women, mothers and children. In the absence of any of the above indications, the pregnant woman herself is nevertheless exempt from any punishment if the abortion was performed by a doctor within the first 22 weeks of pregnancy and if she made use of the medical and social counselling.

63. In view of this situation, the Commission does not find that the legal rules complained about by the applicants interfere with their right to respect for their private life.

64. Furthermore, the Commission has had regard to the fact that, when the European Convention of Human Rights entered into force, the law on abortion in all member States was at least as restrictive as the one now complained of by the applicants. In many European countries the problem of abortion is or has been the subject of heated debates on legal reform since. There is no evidence that it was the intention of the Parties to the Convention to bind themselves in favour of any particular solution under discussion. . . .

Conclusion

66. The Commission . . . concludes that the present case does not disclose a breach of Article 8 of the Convention.

Dissenting Opinion of MR. J. E. S. FAWCETT

I do not agree with the reasoning or conclusion of the Commission on Article 8. . . .

1. 'Private life' in Article 8 (1) must in my view cover pregnancy, its commencement and its termination: indeed, it would be hard to envisage more essentially private elements in life. But pregnancy has also responsibilities for the mother towards the unborn child, at least when it is capable of independent life. . . . But pregnancy, its commencement and its termination, as so viewed is still part of private and family life, calling for respect under Article 8 (1). I am not then able to follow the Commission in holding . . . that there are certain inherent limits to treating pregnancy and its termination as part of private life. Such limits . . . must be found and justified in Article 8 (2): in the absence of such limits, the decision to terminate a pregnancy remains a free part of private life.

2. I find it necessary to distinguish here between intervention and interference. By intervention in the present context I mean regulation of the termination of pregnancy by law, ranging from prohibition to requirements that various conditions be met; by

interference I mean forms of regulation which fail to respect private and family life in the sense of Article 8. Intervention may be justified under Article 8 (2); only if it is not justified does it become interference. But it must be added that regulation of termination of pregnancy by law constitutes intervention in private and family life even before pregnancy has begun because it will influence or govern decisions about commencement and termination of pregnancy.

3. The provisions of [the 1974 abortion law] themselves imposed limiting conditions on the termination of pregnancy, which could be justified under Article 8 (2) as necessary for the protection of health. However, it is not clear to me upon what grounds in Article 8 (2) the elimination of [the 12-week period for unlimited access to abortion under the 1974 Act], and the introduction of additional limiting conditions in the [1976] Act which replaces it [allowing abortions only to avoid the woman's "distress" during this 12-week period], are in fact based. The only possible grounds appear to be 'the economic well-being of the country'; 'the prevention of crime'; 'the protection of health and morals'; 'the protection of the rights and freedoms of others'.

4. No facts have been produced to the Commission to show that the new legislation is aimed in part at maintaining or increasing the birth-rate for the economic well-being of the country: indeed, its well-being might call for an opposite policy. Again, there is evidence in a number of countries that over-restrictive legislation not only fails to prevent 'back-street abortions', incompetently and even criminally performed, but may even encourage recourse to them.

5. The new legislation, like [the 1974 law] which it replaces, certainly secures the protection of health; but there is the further limitation that unacceptable distress to the mother from continuance of the pregnancy must be shown before it can be terminated simply at her wish. It may of course be said that this limitation will be generously interpreted, that in practice there will be little difference between the new provision and the original [1974 abortion law's 12-week unlimited access provision], and that that additional limitation is a compromise gesture to the anti-abortionists. But even if this were correct—and practice might well vary over the country in applying the limitation—I do not think it renders the new legislative provisions 'necessary' under Article 8 (2).

6. The intervention of the legislator in sexual morality may here have the purpose of preventing abortion being often reduced simply to a form of contraception, or of inducing a sense of moral responsibility in the commencement of pregnancy, but it is not shown how the new legislation, as distinct from what it replaces, will achieve these purposes. On the contrary, the statistics and other evidence quoted in the minority judgement in the Federal Constitutional Court demonstrate the ineffectiveness of the earlier [pre-1974] restrictive law in achieving these purposes or, for that matter, those considered in paragraph 4 above. . . . [I]t has not in my view been shown [that the 1976 12-week "distress" provision], in relation to the earlier [1974 12-week unlimited access provision] is 'necessary' under Article 8 (2) for the protection of morals.

7. There remains 'the protection of the rights and freedoms of others' and the

question how far this can cover the unborn child. The Convention does not expressly extend the right to life, protected by Article 2, to an unborn child; but that is not I think conclusive. . . . I can only say that I am unable to attribute rights and freedoms under the Convention to an unborn child not yet capable of independent life, that [the 1974 abortion law] did not extend the permitted termination of pregnancy beyond 12 weeks from conception, and that the elimination of that section of the Act was therefore not 'necessary' for the protection of the rights and freedoms of others.

I can only conclude that the changes in the law on termination of pregnancy that have taken place in consequence of the decision of the Federal Constitutional Court are interventions in private and family life, which are not justified under Article 8 (2), and are therefore an interference with it contrary to the Convention.

Separate Opinion of MR. T. OPSAHL. . . . (MR. C. NORGAARD and MR. L. KELLBERG concurring)

2. Although we have reached the same conclusion as the majority of the Commission . . . we take the view, personally, that laws regulating abortion ought to leave the decision to have it performed in the early stages of pregnancy to the woman concerned. . . . [W]e say this because we consider that among the various possible solutions, this one— . . . based on self-determination—is the one most consistent with what we think a right to respect for private life in this context ought to mean in our time.

3. Nevertheless, we must admit that such a view cannot easily be read into the terms of Article 8. The problem is not a new one and traditional views of the interpretation and application of this Article have to be taken into account, notwithstanding the rapid development of views on abortion in many countries. We are aware that the reality behind these traditional views is that the scope of protection of private life has depended on the outlook which has been formed mainly by men, although it may have been shared by women as well.

NOTES

The Practical Impact of the German Law. Does the change in law make any real difference to German women? Compare how easily women can obtain an abortion in Germany and the United States under the relevant law. In ABORTION AND DIVORCE IN WESTERN LAW: AMERICAN FAILURES, EUROPEAN CHALLENGES (1987), Mary Ann Glendon acknowledges that criminal abortion "distress" exceptions can be read as permitting abortion on demand but nevertheless defends their social value in contexts where the relevant law acknowledges the importance of fetal life. Criminalizing abortion as the taking of human life, she argues, permits the country to register disapproval of abortion, and granting abortion rights only when the woman's distress makes it necessary facilitates political compromise. In ABORTION: THE CLASH OF ABSOLUTES (1992), Laurence H. Tribe finds this approach capricious, permitting abortion in some regions but denying it in others because doctors who strongly oppose abortion on religious or moral grounds will interpret "distress" restrictively.

The Woman's Right to Privacy; the Fetal Right to Life. Identify the Commission's reasons for finding no violation of German women's privacy rights. How would the Commission rule if the German law had another requirement—for example, that the woman's male partner agree? The Commission states that there is no need to address whether there is a fetal right to life under Articles 2 or 8(2). Does the European Convention protect the fetus?

The next case, before the European Court of Human Rights, considers fetal rights more closely. The first excerpt below is from the amicus brief submitted by the Center for Reproductive Rights. The second excerpt is the Court's decision. Consider to what extent the Court adopts the Center's arguments.

Center for Reproductive Rights, *Written Comments, Vo v. France*
(European Court of Human Rights)
Vo v. France, 40 Eur. H.R. Rep. 259 (2004), *available at* RossRights

II. Interest of the Center for Reproductive Rights. . . .

5. The case of *Vo v. France* has significant implications for women's reproductive rights. The Court is being asked to grant for the first time an unborn foetus the status of a person with rights under the European Convention. While this case relates to a medical doctor's liability under a criminal statute, the precedent set by a ruling in favor of the applicant would have consequences for pregnant women throughout the Court's jurisdiction. It would lay the theoretical foundation for a claim that the rights of an unborn foetus may take priority over those of a pregnant woman. . . .

III. The Legal Issue

6. This case raises the question of whether Article 2 of the European Convention requires states to treat unborn foetuses as persons under the law. These written comments assert that such a reading of Article 2 is unwarranted and potentially threatening to women's human rights. Holding that unborn foetuses are persons protected by Article 2 would be inconsistent with the jurisprudence of the European Human Rights system, the laws and jurisprudence of member states, international and regional standards, and the jurisprudence of national-level courts around the world. In addition, finding for the applicant in this case would have serious implications for the human rights of women to privacy, life and security of the person, and non-discrimination. The Court should refrain from expanding the rights of the foetus and, rather, recognize the loss of a wanted foetus as an injury to the expectant mother. Recourse may be sought on behalf of the injured woman, but not the foetus.

IV. Discussion

A. There is no legal support for holding that states have an obligation to treat unborn foetuses as persons under the law.

1. Jurisprudence of the European Human Rights System

7. Recognition of a foetus's status as a person under the law would contradict the jurisprudence of the European Human Rights System, including that of its Commission and its Court of Human Rights. The Commission recognized no fewer than three times that the foetus is not a person under Article 2. . . .

8. In *Paton v. U.K.*, a husband who had been denied an injunction to prevent his pregnant wife from terminating her pregnancy claimed violations of the foetus's Article 2 right to life. The Commission held that the foetus's right to life did not outweigh the interests of the pregnant woman because usage of the word "everyone" in Article 2, and elsewhere in the Convention, did not include foetuses. . . . [The discussion of two other cases reaching the same result with respect to Norwegian and Italian laws is omitted.]

11. If the foetus were a person under Article 2, all three of these cases would have been wrongly decided. Recognizing foetal personhood in the case currently before the Court would open the door to eliminating the statutory rights to abortion in all Council of Europe member states.

2. The Laws of Member States of the Council of Europe. . . .

[The discussion of German and French law is omitted.]

18. National level courts have also addressed the legal status of the person in the context of abortion. In 1974, Austria's Constitutional Court considered a challenge to national legislation that removed restrictions on abortion during the first trimester of pregnancy. The petitioner claimed that the legislation violated Article 2 of the Convention as well as national constitutional protections of the right to life. The Constitutional Court held, inter alia, that Article 2 should not be interpreted to protect the unborn. The Constitutional Court of the Netherlands had a similar interpretation of Article 2 in upholding Dutch legislation liberalizing access to abortion. In its Judgment of January 15, 1975, the French Conseil Constitutionnel found no conflict between France's abortion law and the French Constitution's protection of the child's right to health, implicitly adopting the view that an unborn foetus is not a child entitled to protection under the French Constitution.

19. This reading of Article 2 and constitutional protections of the right to life and health is consistent with member states' statutory approach to abortion throughout Europe. The laws on abortion adopted by most European states reflect the primacy of women's choice during the first trimester of pregnancy, and protect women's rights to life and health throughout the pregnancy. This statutory approach implicitly weighs the rights of the pregnant woman more heavily than those of the foetus. Of the 45 state members of the Council of Europe, 39 permit a woman to terminate a pregnancy without restriction as to reason during the first trimester or on broad

therapeutic grounds. Only a handful—Andorra, Ireland, Liechtenstein, Malta, Poland and San Marino—have maintained severe restrictions on abortion, with only narrow therapeutic exceptions. . . .

4. National-Level Jurisprudence from Selected Non-European States

25. National-level courts around the world have declined to treat unborn foetuses as persons under the law. The Supreme Court of Canada ruled against recognition of foetal personhood in the case of . . . *R v. Morganthaler*. Declining to rule that a foetus is entitled to the protections of persons under the Canadian Charter of Rights and Freedoms, it struck down Canada's restrictive abortion law on the grounds that it unduly interfered with Canadian women's basic right to security of the person. . . .

28. In South Africa, in *Christian Lawyers Association of South Africa . . . v. Minister of Health . . .* , the High Court of South Africa, Transvaal Provincial Division[,] considered a constitutional challenge to the recently enacted Choice on Termination of Pregnancy Act, which permits abortion without restriction as to reason during the first trimester and on broad grounds at later stages of pregnancy. Plaintiffs argued that the law was in conflict with Section 11 of the Constitution, which guarantees that "everyone has the right to life." In considering whether the constitution's reference to "everyone" was intended to include the foetus, the court held that such an interpretation was untenable. It continued:

Moreover, if [Section] 11 were to be interpreted as affording constitutional protection to the life of a foetus far-reaching and anomalous consequences would ensue. The life of the foetus would enjoy the same protection as that of the mother. Abortion would be constitutionally prohibited even though the pregnancy constitutes a serious threat to the life of the mother. The prohibition would apply even if the pregnancy resulted from rape or incest, or if there were a likelihood that the child to be born would suffer from severe physical or mental abnormality. . . . If the plaintiff's contentions are correct then the termination of a woman's pregnancy would no longer constitute the crime of abortion, but that of murder. In my view, the drafters of the Constitution could not have contemplated such far-reaching results without expressing themselves in no uncertain terms. For the above reasons . . . I consider that under the Constitution the foetus is not a legal person.

Vo v. France
(European Court of Human Rights)
40 Eur. H.R. Rep. 259 (2005), *available at* RossRights

Procedure

1. The case originated in an application against the French Republic lodged with the Court under Article 34 of the Convention for the Protection of Human Rights and Fundamental Freedoms ("the Convention") by a French national, Mrs. Thi-Nho Vo ("the applicant"), on 20 December 1999. . . .

3. The applicant alleged, in particular, a violation of Article 2 of the Convention on

the ground that the conduct of a doctor who was responsible for the death of her child *in utero* was not classified as unintentional homicide. . . .

I. The Circumstances of the Case. . . .

10. On 27 November 1991 the applicant, Mrs. Thi-Nho Vo, who is of Vietnamese origin, attended the Lyons General Hospital for a medical examination scheduled during the sixth month of pregnancy.

11. On the same day another woman, Mrs. Thi Thanh Van Vo, was due to have a coil removed at the same hospital. When the doctor who was to remove the coil called out the name "Mrs. Vo" in the waiting room, it was the applicant who answered.

After a brief interview, the doctor noted that the applicant had difficulty in understanding French. Having consulted the medical file he sought to remove the coil without examining her beforehand. In so doing, he pierced the amniotic sac causing the loss of a substantial amount of amniotic fluid.

After finding on clinical examination that the uterus was enlarged, the doctor ordered a scan. He then discovered that one had just been performed and realised that there had been a mistake of identity. The applicant was immediately admitted to hospital. . . .

12. The applicant left the hospital on 29 November 1991. She returned on 4 December 1991 for further tests. The doctors found that the amniotic fluid had not been replaced and that the pregnancy could not continue further. The pregnancy was terminated on health grounds on 5 December 1991.

13. On 11 December 1991 the applicant and her partner lodged a criminal complaint. . . .

IV. Comparative Law

41. In the majority of the member States of the Council of Europe, the offence of unintentional homicide does not apply to the foetus. However, three countries have chosen to create specific offences. In Italy a person negligently causing a pregnancy to terminate is liable to a prison sentence of between three months and two years under section 17 of the Abortion Act of 22 May 1978. In Spain Article 157 of the Criminal Code makes it a criminal offence to cause damage to the foetus and Article 146 an offence to cause an abortion through gross negligence. In Turkey Article 456 of the Criminal Code lays down that a person who causes damage to another shall be liable to a prison sentence of between six months and one year; if the victim is a pregnant woman and the damage results in premature birth, the Criminal Code prescribes a sentence of between two and five years' imprisonment. . . .

C. The Court's assessment

74. The applicant complained that she had been unable to secure the conviction of the doctor whose medical negligence had caused her to have to undergo a therapeu-

tic abortion. It has not been disputed that she intended to carry her pregnancy to full term and that her child was in good health. Following the material events, the applicant and her partner lodged a criminal complaint . . . alleging . . . unintentional homicide of the child she was carrying. . . . [T]he Court of Cassation held that, regard being had to the principle that the criminal law was to be strictly construed, a foetus could not be the victim of unintentional homicide. The central question raised by the application is whether the absence of a criminal remedy within the French legal system to punish the unintentional destruction of a foetus constituted a failure on the part of the State to protect by law the right to life within the meaning of Article 2 of the Convention.[c] . . .

80. [I]n the circumstances examined to date by the Convention institutions—that is, in the various laws on abortion—the unborn child is not regarded as a "person" directly protected by Article 2 of the Convention and . . . if the unborn do have a "right" to "life", it is implicitly limited by the mother's rights and interests. The Convention institutions have not, however, ruled out the possibility that in certain circumstances safeguards may be extended to the unborn child. That is what appears to have been contemplated by the Commission in considering that "Article 8 § 1 cannot be interpreted as meaning that pregnancy and its termination are, as a principle, solely a matter of the private life of the mother" (see Brüggeman and Scheuten . . .). . . . It is also clear from an examination of . . . cases that the issue has always been determined by weighing up various, and sometimes conflicting, rights or freedoms claimed by a woman, a mother or a father in relation to one another or vis-à-vis an unborn child.

2. Approach in the instant case

81. The special nature of the instant case raises a new issue. The Court is faced with a woman who intended to carry her pregnancy to term and whose unborn child was expected to be viable, at the very least in good health. Her pregnancy had to be terminated as a result of an error by a doctor and she therefore had to have a therapeutic abortion on account of negligence by a third party. The issue is consequently whether, apart from cases where the mother has requested an abortion, harming a foetus should be treated as a criminal offence in the light of Article 2 of the Convention, with a view to protecting the foetus under that Article. This requires a preliminary examination of whether it is advisable for the Court to intervene in the debate

---

[c] Article 2 provides:

"1. Everyone's right to life shall be protected by law. No one shall be deprived of his life intentionally save in the execution of a sentence of a court following his conviction of a crime for which this penalty is provided by law.

2. Deprivation of life shall not be regarded as inflicted in contravention of this article when it results from the use of force which is no more than absolutely necessary:

a. in defence of any person from unlawful violence;

b. in order to effect a lawful arrest or to prevent the escape of a person lawfully detained;

c. in action lawfully taken for the purpose of quelling a riot or insurrection."

as to who is a person and when life begins, in so far as Article 2 provides that the law must protect "everyone's right to life".

82. As is apparent from the above recapitulation of the case-law, the interpretation of Article 2 in this connection has been informed by a clear desire to strike a balance, and the Convention institutions' position in relation to the legal, medical, philosophical, ethical or religious dimensions of defining the human being has taken into account the various approaches to the matter at national level. This has been reflected in the consideration given to the diversity of views on the point at which life begins, of legal cultures and of national standards of protection, and the State has been left with considerable discretion in the matter, as the opinion of the European Group on Ethics at Community level appositely puts it: "the . . . Community authorities have to address these ethical questions taking into account the moral and philosophical differences, reflected by the extreme diversity of legal rules applicable to human embryo research. . . . It is not only legally difficult to seek harmonisation of national laws at Community level, but because of lack of consensus, it would be inappropriate to impose one exclusive moral code".

It follows that the issue of when the right to life begins comes within the margin of appreciation which the Court generally considers that States should enjoy in this sphere, notwithstanding an evolutive interpretation of the Convention, a "living instrument which must be interpreted in the light of present-day conditions". The reasons for that conclusion are, firstly, that the issue of such protection has not been resolved within the majority of the Contracting States themselves, in France in particular, where it is the subject of debate and, secondly, that there is no European consensus on the scientific and legal definition of the beginning of life.

83. The Court observes that the French Court of Cassation, in three successive judgments delivered in 1999, 2001 and 2002, considered that the rule that offences and punishment must be defined by law, which required criminal statutes to be construed strictly, excluded acts causing a fatal injury to a foetus from the scope of Article 221-6 of the Criminal Code, under which unintentional homicide of "another" is an offence. However, if, as a result of unintentional negligence, the mother gives birth to a live child who dies shortly after being born, the person responsible may be convicted of the unintentional homicide of the child. The first-mentioned approach . . . was interpreted as an invitation to the legislature to fill a legal vacuum. That was also the position of the Criminal Court in the instant case. . . . The French parliament attempted such a definition in proposing to create the offence of involuntary termination of pregnancy, but the Bill containing that proposal was lost, on account of the fears and uncertainties that the creation of the offence might arouse as to the determination of when life began, and the disadvantages of the proposal, which were thought to outweigh its advantages. . . . [I]n France, the nature and legal status of the embryo and/or the foetus are currently not defined and . . . the manner in which it is to be protected will be determined by very varied forces within French society.

84. At the European level, the Court observes that there is no consensus on the nature and status of the embryo and/or foetus, although they are beginning to receive some protection in the light of scientific progress and the potential conse-

quences of research into genetic engineering, medically assisted procreation or embryo experimentation. At best, it may be regarded as common ground between States that the embryo/foetus belongs to the human race. The potentiality of that being and its capacity to become a person—enjoying protection under the civil law, moreover, in many States, such as France, in the context of inheritance and gifts, and also in the United Kingdom—require protection in the name of human dignity, without making it a "person" with the "right to life" for the purposes of Article 2. . . .

85. . . . [T]he Court is convinced that it is neither desirable, nor even possible as matters stand, to answer in the abstract the question whether the unborn child is a person for the purposes of Article 2 of the Convention. . . . As to the instant case, it considers it unnecessary to examine whether the abrupt end to the applicant's pregnancy falls within the scope of Article 2, seeing that, even assuming that that provision was applicable, there was no failure on the part of the respondent State to comply with the requirements relating to the preservation of life in the public-health sphere. With regard to that issue, the Court has considered whether the legal protection afforded the applicant by France in respect of the loss of the unborn child she was carrying satisfied the procedural requirements inherent in Article 2 of the Convention.

86. In that connection, it observes that the unborn child's lack of a clear legal status does not necessarily deprive it of all protection under French law. However, in the circumstances of the present case, the life of the foetus was intimately connected with that of the mother and could be protected through her, especially as there was no conflict between the rights of the mother and the father or of the unborn child and the parents, the loss of the foetus having been caused by the unintentional negligence of a third party. . . .

87. The applicant argued that only a criminal remedy would have been capable of satisfying the requirements of Article 2 of the Convention. The Court does not share that view, for the following reasons.

88. The Court reiterates that the first sentence of Article 2 . . . requires the State not only to refrain from the "intentional" taking of life, but also to take appropriate steps to safeguard the lives of those within its jurisdiction.

89. Those principles apply in the public-health sphere too. The positive obligations require States to make regulations compelling hospitals, whether private or public, to adopt appropriate measures for the protection of patients' lives. They also require an effective independent judicial system to be set up so that the cause of death of patients in the care of the medical profession, whether in the public or the private sector, can be determined and those responsible made accountable.

90. Although the right to have third parties prosecuted or sentenced for a criminal offence cannot be asserted independently, the Court has stated on a number of occasions that an effective judicial system, as required by Article 2, may, and under certain circumstances must, include recourse to the criminal law. However, if the infringement of the right to life or to physical integrity is not caused intentionally, the positive obligation imposed by Article 2 to set up an effective judicial system does not necessarily require the provision of a criminal-law remedy in every case. . . .

94. . . . [T]he Court considers that in the circumstances of the case, an action for

damages in the administrative courts could be regarded as an effective remedy that was available to the applicant. Such an action, which she failed to use, would have enabled her to prove the medical negligence she alleged and to obtain full redress for the damage resulting from the doctor's negligence, and there was therefore no need to institute criminal proceedings in the instant case.

95. The Court accordingly concludes [by a vote of 14 to 3] that, even assuming that Article 2 was applicable in the instant case (see paragraph 85 above), there has been no violation of Article 2 of the Convention. . . .

Separate Opinion of JUDGE ROZAKIS, joined by JUDGES CAFLISCH, FISCHBACH, LORENZEN and THOMASSEN

I have voted, together with the majority of the Grand Chamber, in favour of finding that there has been no violation of Article 2 in the instant case. Yet, my approach differs in certain respects from that of the majority. . . .

[T]he Court refuses to draw the relevant conclusions, namely that in the present state of development of science, law and morals, both in France and across Europe, the right to life of the unborn child has yet to be secured. Even if one accepts that life begins before birth, that does not automatically and unconditionally confer on this form of human life a right to life equivalent to the corresponding right of a child after its birth. This does not mean that the unborn child does not enjoy any protection by human society, since—as the relevant legislation of European States, and European agreements and relevant documents show—the unborn life is already considered to be worthy of protection. But as I read the relevant legal instruments, this protection, though afforded to a being considered worthy of it, is, as stated above, distinct from that given to a child after birth, and far narrower in scope. It consequently transpires from the present stage of development of the law and morals in Europe that the life of the unborn child, although protected in some of its attributes, cannot be equated to post-natal life, and, therefore, does not enjoy a right in the sense of "a right to life", as protected by Article 2 of the Convention. Hence, there is a problem of applicability of Article 2 in the circumstances of the case. . . .

[T]he majority of the Grand Chamber opted for a neutral stance, declaring: "the Court is convinced that it is neither desirable, nor even possible as matters stand, to answer in the abstract the question whether the unborn child is a person for the purposes of Article 2 of the Convention" (paragraph 85).

What also seems problematic with the majority's reasoning is that, despite their obvious doubts or, at any rate, their reluctance to accept that Article 2 was applicable in this case, the majority ended up abandoning their neutral stance and based their finding of no violation on the argument that the procedural guarantees inherent in the protection of Article 2 had been satisfied in the circumstances of the case. By using the "even assuming" formula as to the applicability of Article 2, and by linking the life of the foetus to the life of the mother ("the life of the foetus was intimately connected with that of the mother and could be protected through her . . ."—see paragraph 86), the majority has surreptitiously brought Article 2 of the Convention to the fore of the case. Yet, it is obvious from the case-law that reliance on the procedural guarantees of Article 2 to determine whether or not there has been a violation presupposes the prima facie applicability of that Article . . . ; and in the circumstances of the case there was not even the remotest threat to the mother's right of life such as would justify bringing the procedural guarantees of Article 2 of the Convention into play. . . .

Dissenting opinion of JUDGE RESS

1. France's positive obligation to protect the unborn children against unintentional homicide, that is to say against negligent acts that could cause a child's death, can only be discharged if French law has effective procedures in place to prevent the recurrence of such acts. On this point, I am unable to agree with the opinion expressed by the majority that an action in damages in the administrative courts (on account of the hospital doctor's alleged negligence) afforded the unborn child adequate and effective protection against medical negligence. . . .

It is not retribution that makes protection by the criminal law desirable, but deterrence. In general, it is through the criminal law that society most clearly and strictly conveys messages to its members and identifies values that are most in need of protection. Life, which is one of the values, if not the main value, protected by the Convention, will in principle require the protection of the criminal law if it is to be adequately safeguarded and defended. Financial liability to pay compensation is only a secondary form of protection. In addition, hospitals and doctors are usually insured against such risks, so that the "pressure" on them is reduced.

2. One might consider that imposing a disciplinary penalty on a doctor could be regarded as equivalent to imposing a criminal penalty in certain circumstances. . . . Here, though, is where the problem lies, as the authorities at no stage brought disciplinary proceedings against the doctor. For an error as serious as that committed by Dr G., such disciplinary proceedings accompanied by an adequate measure could at least have sent an appropriate signal to the medical profession to prevent the recurrence of such tragic events. I do not think it necessary to say that France requires criminal legislation. However, it does need to take strict disciplinary action in order to meet its obligation to afford effective protection of the life of the unborn child. In my opinion, therefore, there was no effective protection.

3. In order to reach that conclusion, it seems necessary to find out whether Article 2 applies to the unborn child. I am prepared to accept that there may be differences in the level of protection afforded to an embryo and to a child after birth. Nevertheless, that does not justify the conclusion (at paragraph 85 of the judgment) that it is not possible to answer in the abstract the question whether the unborn child is a person for the purposes of Article 2 of the Convention. All the Court's case-law and the Commission's decisions (see paragraphs 75–80 of judgments) are based on the "assuming that" argument. . . . Yet the failure to give a clear answer can no longer be justified by reasons of procedural economy. Nor can the problem of protecting the embryo through the Convention be solved solely through the protection of the mother's life. As this case illustrates, the embryo and the mother, as two separate "human beings", need separate protection. . . .

4. The structure of Article 2 and, above all the exceptions set out in paragraph 2 thereof, appear to indicate that persons are only entitled to protection thereunder

once they have been born and that it is only after birth that they are regarded as having rights under the Convention. In view of the "aim" of the Convention to provide extended protection, this does not appear to be a conclusive argument. . . . In all the cases in which that issue has been considered, the Commission and the Court have developed a concept of an implied limitation or of a fair balance between the interests of society and the interests of the individual, that is to say the mother or the unborn child. Admittedly, these concepts were developed in connection with legislation on the voluntary, but not the involuntary, termination of pregnancy. However, it is clear that they would not have been necessary if the Commission and the Court had considered at the outset that Article 2 could not apply to the unborn child. Even though the Commission and the Court have left the question open formally, such a legal structure proves that both institutions were inclined to adopt the ordinary meaning of "human life" and "everyone" rather than the other meaning.

Similarly, the practice of the Contracting States, virtually all of which had constitutional problems with their laws on abortion (voluntary termination of pregnancy), clearly shows that the protection of life also extends in principle to the foetus. Specific laws on voluntary abortion would not have been necessary if the foetus did not have a life to protect and was fully dependent till birth on the unrestricted wishes of the pregnant mother. . . .

9. Since I consider that Article 2 applies to human beings even before they are born, an interpretation which seems to me to be consistent with the approach of the Charter of Fundamental Rights of the European Union, and since France does not afford sufficient protection to the foetus against the negligent acts of third parties, I find that there has been a violation of Article 2 of the Convention. As regards the specific measures necessary to discharge that positive obligation, that is a matter for the respondent State, which should either take strict disciplinary measures or afford the protection of the criminal law (against unintentional homicide).

NOTES

The Role of Amicus Briefs. To what extent did the Court opinion reflect the views of the Center for Reproductive Rights? The Center has an international litigation strategy for advancing women's right to abortion before international and regional human rights bodies and national courts. Its website provides information about these cases and help for groups that want to bring lawsuits or file amicus briefs on this issue.

A Fetal Right to Life Under the European Convention? The European Court, like the European Commission, finds it unnecessary to decide whether Article 2 protects a fetal right to life. On what grounds, then, does the Court find that French law does not violate Article 2? Compare Judge Rozakis's separate opinion as to the reach of Article 2. Which opinion is preferable and why? Note dissenting Judge Ress's reasons for finding that Article 2 protection extends to the fetus. After comparing the reasoning of the three opinions, which is most persuasive?

3. *The African Women's Rights Protocol: Health and Reproductive Rights*

The Protocol to the African Charter on Human and Peoples' Rights on the Rights of Women in Africa speaks directly to women's reproductive rights:

14. 1. States Parties shall ensure that the right to health of women, including sexual and reproductive health[,] is respected and promoted. This includes:
   a) the right to control their fertility;
   b) the right to decide whether to have children, the number of children and the spacing of children;
   c) the right to choose any method of contraception; . . .
   g) the right to have family planning education.
2. States Parties shall take all appropriate measures to: . . .
   c) protect the reproductive rights of women by authorising medical abortion in cases of sexual assault, rape, incest, and where the continued pregnancy endangers the mental and physical health of the mother or the life of the mother or the foetus. . . .

NOTES

The Right to Abortion—How Much Progress? The African Protocol goes further than any other international or regional human rights treaty in specifically mentioning medical abortion for specified reasons. Does the use of the word give African women a stronger right to choose than women have in Europe, Latin America, Canada, the U.S., and South Africa? Compare the reasons for which an abortion is legal and the relevant time frames under the Protocol with those in the other treaties and state law you have studied. What are the advantages and disadvantages of listing specified reasons? Of providing time frames? What do you make of the fact that the rights listed in subparagraph 14(1) do not mention abortion, and that States Parties commit to taking "all appropriate measures" in subparagraph 14(2)?

Enforcement—The Key Issue. Will the Women's Rights Protocol be enforceable in the African Court on Human and Peoples' Rights? The Women's Rights Protocol requires states to provide domestic remedies for violations of rights (art. 25) and submit periodic reports to the African Commission (art. 26). It grants the African Court the power to be "seized with matters of interpretation arising from the application or implementation of [the Women's Rights] Protocol" (art. 27), and for the African Commission to have that same power in the interim before the Court is established (art. 32). Under the Court Protocol, the Court can decide whether to allow an individual or NGO to file a complaint (art. 5(3)) in states that accept the Courts' jurisdiction (art. 34(6)) and can also refer the case to the Commission (art. 6). None of the relevant documents specify a right of appeal from a Commission decision to the Court.

Human Rights Law and the Abortion Question. In Part II, you have examined different responses to the questions of whether women have a right to abortion and a fetus the right to life. The answers came from constitutional court decisions, national statutes, and international human rights laws as reflected in treaties, jurisprudence, general comments or recommendations, and concluding observations. The three regional human rights systems as reflected in treaty language and jurisprudence also yielded distinct approaches. Is there a way to synthesize the answers from these different bodies? What conclusions do you draw about the relevance of human rights law to abortion?

III. Sex-Selective Abortion: A Conflict of Interests?

A. Chinese Poetry

Anonymous, *Number 189, Si Gan (These Banks)*
in SHI JING [THE BOOK OF ODES],[D]

When a son is born
Let him sleep on the bed,
Clothe him with fine clothes
And give him jade to play with
How lovely his cry is!
May he grow up to wear crimson
And be the lord of the clan and the tribe.

When a girl is born,
Let her sleep on the ground.
Wrap her in common wrappings,
And give her broken tiles for playthings.
May she have no faults, no merit of her own
May she well attend to food and wine
And bring no discredit to her parents.

B. The CEDAW Committee's Concluding Observations About Sex-Selective Abortions and Female Infanticide

CEDAW Committee, *Concluding Observations: China*
U.N. Doc. A/54/38(PARTI) (1999), *available at* RossRights

299. The Committee recognizes that population growth is a genuine and severe problem and that considerable progress has been made in providing family planning

---

[D] SHI JING, translated as BOOK OF ODES, is a compilation of ancient writings by anonymous Chinese authors. *Si Gan*, translated as *These Banks*, is taken from the opening line of the poem, "Graceful these banks, distant South Hill," with reference to the banks of a river. E-mail from James V. Feinerman, James M. Morita Professor of Asian Legal Studies, Georgetown Law (Aug. 28, 2007) (on file with author). The book contains over 300 numbered poems written over hundreds of years, starting about 1027 B.C.E. and continuing to 476 B.C.E. *See* the University of Virginia Library's Chinese Text Information website for additional information, at http://etext .lib.virginia.edu/chinese/shijing (last visited Aug. 28, 2007). This translation of these two verses is that found in ELISABETH CROLL, ENDANGERED DAUGHTERS: DISCRIMINATION AND DEVELOPMENT IN ASIA 75–76 (2000).

services, but expresses concern about various aspects of the implementation of China's population policy, including the following: . . .

(c) The Committee is concerned about the growing disparity in the male/female sex ratio at birth as an unintended consequence of the population policy, owing to the discriminatory tradition of son preference. The shortage of females may also have long-term implications regarding trafficking in women;

(d) The Committee is concerned about illegal practices of sex-selective abortion, female infanticide and the non-registration and abandonment of female children. The Committee expresses particular concern about the status of "out-of-plan" and unregistered children, many of them girls, who may be officially non-existent and thus not entitled to education, health care or other social benefits. . . .

301. Recognizing that male children, especially in rural and remote areas, remain responsible for supporting people in old age, the Government should explicitly address the linkages between economic security in old age and its family planning policies. It should take all appropriate measures to modify and eliminate son preference, inter alia, by expanding educational and employment opportunities for women in rural areas. The Government should enforce laws against sex-selective abortion, female infanticide and abandonment of children and remove all legal disabilities from "out-of-plan" and unregistered children.

CEDAW Committee, *Concluding Observations: India*
U.N. Doc. A/55/38(PARTI) (2000), *available at* RossRights

38. Significant improvements in women's health had been achieved in the last decade, although the high maternal mortality ratio remained a concern. . . . [L]egislative and other strategies to confront female infanticide and sex-selective abortion had . . . been adopted. . . .

50. The Committee commends the Government for introducing legislation that has banned sex-selective abortions. . . .

78. The Committee notes . . . the adverse sex ratio and the incidence of sex-selective abortions despite the law banning that practice. . . .

79. . . . The Committee calls upon the Government to elicit the support of medical associations in enforcing professional ethics and preventing sex-selective abortions. The Committee also recommends that the Government obtain the support of the medical profession in creating awareness of the urgent need to eliminate practices associated with son preference.

C. Diverging Views on Prenatal Sex-Selection

Daniel Goodkind, *Should Prenatal Sex Selection Be Restricted? Ethical Questions and Their Implications for Research and Policy*
53 POPULATION STUDIES 49, 49–59 (1999)

Introduction

Major advances in prenatal sex testing technologies since the 1970s have given parents the option of aborting a foetus of an unwanted sex. . . . Because family sizes have declined rapidly in many less developed areas without a corresponding elimination of son preferences, many parents still want to have at least one son in their smaller families. The predominance of female foetuses among sex-selected abortions has contributed to rising sex ratios at birth throughout much of Confucian Asia. These ratios ordinarily total about 105–106 males per 100 females, but they have recently breached 113 in Korea and China, 110 in Taiwan, and 107 among Chinese in Singapore and Peninsular Malaysia.

The use of sex-selective abortion following prenatal sex testing has been almost universally condemned by international observers. . . . They . . . noted that governments in Korea, China, and in parts of India have attempted to restrict such procedures and have called for penalties against doctors who perform them. In response to the increasing use of prenatal sex selection, the Programme of Action resulting from the 1994 United Nations Conference on Population and Development in Cairo stated the following policy objectives:

To eliminate all forms of discrimination against the girl child and the root causes of son preference, which results in harmful and unethical practices regarding female infanticide and prenatal sex selection. (UN Programme for Action 1994; Article 4.15)

This call to end all forms of discrimination against daughters is heartening and easy to applaud. In the case of prenatal sex selection, however, the very blatancy of such discrimination has masked greater ethical complexities with respect to reproductive freedoms and human suffering. . . .

[U]nder what specific presumptions can we condemn prenatal sex selection and justify legislative interventions? This . . . constitutes a challenge for the aforementioned agenda articulated at the Cairo population conference, which shifted developmental priorities away from control over population growth, per se, and in favour of maternal empowerment, gender equality, and reproductive rights. However, a variety of concerns may counterbalance, to some extent, moral objections to prenatal sex selection.

First, the most liberal interpretation of reproductive rights might be taken to include not only the number and timing of children, but also their sex. Second, to the extent that policy restrictions of prenatal sex selection were effective, there might thereafter be more human suffering if discrimination against female foetuses were shifted from the prenatal to the postnatal period. Third, government restrictions on prenatal sex selection, in addition to being difficult to enforce, might have consequences that would be unwelcome to pro-choice advocates if these controls helped justify further restriction on prenatal testing or abortion based on other foetal characteristics. . . .

(1) How do culture and policy motivate prenatal sex selection? . . .

Intertwined with debates over the relative influence of culture and policy is the issue of whether prenatal sex selection is more a cause of discriminatory attitudes than simply a reflection of them. If parental preferences were sensitive to governmental exhortations, and if the prevention of sex-selective abortion did not lead to discrimination later on in the life course, a ban on prenatal sex testing (or on the act of sex-selective abortion itself) might be appropriate. However, to the extent that son preferences are rooted in a bedrock of cultural preferences independent of government decrees, these bans might be difficult to enforce. On the other hand, to the extent that the bans were effective, parents might seek out 'back-alley' sex tests or sex-selective abortions on the black market, which, in an ironic twist for those most concerned with reproductive rights, might prove to be more detrimental to women's health than if the test remained legal. A second-best policy option might be to try to alter the social or legal institutions which underpin sex preferences, such as laws related to inheritance. Indirect measures of this kind might not have an immediate impact on sex-selective abortion, but they might reduce it in the long run without incurring adverse short-run consequences. . . .

(3) Would objections to prenatal sex selection diminish if, as a result, postnatal sex discrimination declined?

The statement from the United Nations Programme of Action quoted earlier identified prenatal sex selection and excess female infanticide as two forms of discrimination against daughters. . . . [Son] preferences are manifested through an array of discriminatory practices which are often affected by the sex distribution of previous children. Such practices occurring prior to conception include the use of contraception or other measures to reduce the likelihood of having another child. Between conception and birth, parents may practice prenatal sex selection. . . . Between birth and early childhood, parents may express sex biases through infanticide, abandonment, or postnatal neglect. . . .

Observers who string together these indicators of sex discrimination and condemn them en masse assume that they rise or fall with some degree of similarity. However, although some of these indicators may be positively correlated, others may interact in such a way that more discrimination as measured by one indicator may lead to less discrimination as measured by others. For example, Lee et al. (1994) demonstrated that Qing dynasty Chinese nobility commonly killed unwanted infant daughters during the first few days of life, but thereafter the survival chances of daughters were quite good. More recently, Goodkind (1996) suggested that the contemporary use of sex-selective abortion might substitute for (rather than simply add to) postnatal discrimination. Since parents now have the option of sex-selective abortion, daughters (as well as sons) carried to term are more likely to be wanted, and, hence, increases in the sex ratio at birth may be followed by a decline of postnatal discrimination. . . . Why, for instance, should we be alarmed by rising sex ratios in country X? . . . [O]ther studies of country X might show improvements in the relative survival probabilities of daughters, a finding which presumably would be cause for relief. . . .

Moreover, to determine whether the availability and employment of sex-selective abortion represents a net social 'bad' rather than a new social 'good' requires us to consider the prevalence and relative evils of both prenatal and postnatal discrimination—we must no longer leave unstated our moral presumptions concerning the potential for suffering across the stages of the early life course. Where discriminatory substitutions occur, prenatal sex testing could be defended on utilitarian grounds if it was deemed to prevent even worse suffering during the postnatal period.

Put another way, if a ban were enacted against prenatal sex testing (or the use of abortion for sex-selective purposes), how many excess postnatal deaths would a society be willing to tolerate in lieu of whatever sex-selective abortions were avoided? Some observers might reject out of hand such a cold calculus. On the other hand, if we are unwilling to consider the relative value of foetal and infant lives, the assertion in the Cairo document that prenatal sex selection is, in toto, 'harmful and unethical' becomes contentious. . . .

(4) Would legislative action against prenatal sex selection have adverse consequences for pro-life or pro-choice advocates? . . .

Pro-lifers . . . find unexpected allies among pro-choice proponents in condemning sex-selective abortion. For instance, less than 20 per cent of American women ever having had an abortion support the right to choose abortion for sex selection, even though these women favour the use of abortion in the cases of rape, incest, congenital birth defects, or the mother's health. Thus, a veritable watershed in the history of the abortion rights movement has gone largely unrecognized—a solid majority of pro-choice advocates agree that a particular characteristic of a first trimester foetus renders abortion unacceptable.

Yet pro-choice advocates face formidable dangers in advocating legislation against, or perhaps even strongly condemning, prenatal sex selection. The basic reason is that many of these advocates call for government legislation to promote the twin goals of reproductive rights and gender equality. For some observers, the issue of prenatal sex selection renders these goals in awkward opposition. . . . [T]o enact legislation against prenatal sex selection seems destined to create tensions within whichever discourse abortion rights are typically discussed. Three of these discourses are identified below.

The first concerns the presumption that abortion should remain an individual choice to be undertaken without government interference. Put another way, viewed as a political struggle for control over women's bodies, foetal rights should defer to maternal rights. The slippery slope upon which pro-choice advocates navigate is thus obvious—under what ethical presumptions should maternal rights suddenly become trumped by foetal rights the moment the foetus's sex is discovered? . . .

The second challenge to the pro-choice position concerns the aforementioned substitution of prenatal for postnatal discrimination. Although that substitution has yet to be confirmed . . . , pro-choice supporters have always presumed that it does exist. The presumption is apparent from the oft-quoted slogan, 'every child should be a wanted child'. Why should all children be wanted? The basic logic is that unwanted children (or perhaps their potential parents or both children and parents) are presumed to suffer in one way or another and that the imposition of unnecessary suffering is morally repugnant. . . . [A]ccess to abortion is desirable in part because it will circumvent postnatal suffering. . . .

A third challenge for the pro-choice movement grows out of its own presumptions about when life begins. If a foetus becomes viable only at some point after the first trimester, it follows that some (unidentified) number of such foetuses are considered more expendable to society than a single infant. But what if discriminatory strategies can indeed be substituted for each other, the dynamic presumed to exist by pro-choice advocates? If so, and if one wishes to minimize human suffering during the early life course, the more staunchly one supports the pro-choice position regarding foetal viability, the more willing one should be to accept numerous sex-selective abortions in lieu of even a single excess infant or child death that might occur in the wake of a ban on prenatal sex selection. Yet pro-choice advocates often lead the charge against sex-selective abortion. Even more problematic [is] the increasing temptation to invoke metaphors equating it with 'violence' against the 'littlest girls' (e.g. Greenhalgh and Li 1995). Such powerful metaphors attempt to extend the locus of potential violence against women to include female foetuses, even though pro-choice advocates otherwise decry personification of the foetus or the notion that abortion itself represents violence in any physical sense. . . .

Concluding Summary: Implications for Future Research and Policy

Given that sex-selective abortion is so blatantly discriminatory and demeaning to women, moral objections to it are readily understood. Legislative restrictions and other public condemnations could potentially reduce the adoption of this practice now and gradually dilute in the future the underlying preferences that lead to all forms of sex discrimination. Yet, a variety of considerations discussed above counterbalance, to some extent, moral objections to sex-selective abortion and militate against government restrictions and perhaps even vociferous condemnations. . . .

Governments can, should, and it is to be hoped, will find ways to address social inequalities based on gender and other characteristics, and one cannot underestimate the symbolic comfort that vocal condemnations of inequality may have for those whose protection is sought. Nevertheless, in regard to sex-selective abortion, governments with otherwise liberal abortion laws might be best advised to maintain, quietly yet steadfastly, that it is wrong, while attempting to dilute the son preferences that underly it through more general legislation (e.g. regarding marital rights and inheritance). Given that public and political resources to combat inequality are limited, they should be used wisely and applied in ways that do not harm the broader agendas we espouse.

Barbara D. Miller, *Female-Selective Abortion in Asia: Patterns, Policies, and Debates*

103 AMERICAN ANTHROPOLOGIST 1083, 1090–92 (2001)

Many, but not all, social scientists and other experts view FSA [Female-Selective Abortion] as a serious problem that deserves high priority from international and national policy makers. Those who consider it a serious problem disagree about how policy should seek to address it. . . .

FSA Will Increase the Value of Women

Some commentators suggest that the practice of FSA is not urgently important because the future scarcity of women will eventually lead to their increased value and enhanced status. This crude "supply and demand" model is apparently very attractive, perhaps especially to people swayed by simpleminded "economic" formulae. For example, a simplistically optimistic editorial published in a prestigious international medical journal, The Lancet, comments: "If the use of sex selection were to increase the proportion of boys significantly, women would benefit from the wider choice of marriage partners and would acquire greater social value. The long-term outcome would be an increase in the birth of girls and restoration of balance". Those who argue for this model should consider the patriarchal context in which sheer scarcity is not likely to raise women's status. During the eighteenth century in some villages of northern India, people raised very few or no daughters. Brides were therefore scarce in the northwest, but women's status was not high. In China, the scarcity of females has led to an increase in the kidnapping of girls. Along this line, demographers Tuljapurkar, Li, and Feldman discuss the probability of continued high sex ratios in China's future and comment that over the long term, masculinization of births will "complicate efforts to increase the social and economic status of women and their control over reproductive decisions".

FSA as Preferable to Female Infanticide

Still others evaluate FSA as preferable to female infanticide or to girls being born who are unwanted and mistreated. Current levels of FSA, however, mean that far more females are being aborted than would ever have been born unwanted and treated less favorably than their brothers. With FSA, unwanted daughters who—if allowed to be born—would survive disfavored treatment are being "more efficiently" excluded from the population. FSA, in other words, is not a "replacement" for infanticide or discrimination—it outdoes these forms. Additionally, this position all too easily slides into being one that "accepts" a certain amount of son preference and daughter disfavor and simply compares techniques on the basis of whether they are more or less "humane" toward the unwanted females.

FSA Reduces Population Growth

Another supposedly positive aspect of FSA, though rarely directly stated, is its effect on reducing rates of population growth. "Population bomb" theorists and lay thinkers are so terrified of population growth—especially in the Asian giants of India and China—that they would avoid criticizing the use of FSA because it serves as a quiet way to deal with "overpopulation".

FSA Represents Free Choice

The discussion of FSA is further complicated by the divergent views of certain ethicists, feminists, and other commentators concerning the question of "choice" about abortion in general and FSA in particular. Many, if not most, Western feminists regard a woman's free reproductive choice as a right that has been fought hard for in the West and is worth protecting from legal encroachments as to grounds. Other views of some feminists and ethicists say that abortion on gender grounds alone is morally wrong. The question of women's reproductive "freedom" in highly son-preferential cultures bears close attention. Strong son preference and other structural facts of patriarchy limit women's "freedom" to exercise choice even when it appears that they are doing so. This notion of "illusory choice" is important in relation to FSA in Asia. Is a woman who uses FSA in fact exercising free "choice"? Interviews with the woman might show that she was extremely anxious to have a son, that she voluntarily pursued FSA, and that she was pleased with its positive results. Some argue, then, that she exercised freedom of choice and that to state otherwise is to be "reckless" with the concept of choice itself. But if we avoid considering the structural limitations that patriarchy places on women's choices, we deny the fact that a woman in such a context is not "free" to choose to have a daughter instead of a son. She is "free" only to comply with the masculinist reproductive mandate, but she is not free to resist that mandate. Pure reproductive freedom is the complete absence of constraints and structured choice and should, therefore, logically result in equal sex ratios at birth. . . .

Balanced Sex Ratios, Public Goods, and Human Rights

At the time of this writing, I know of no country in the world that places FSA high on its policy agenda, though the United Nations included prenatal sex selection as a form of discrimination in its 1994 Programme of Action following the Cairo Conference on Population and Development. If policy experts were to take FSA seriously and place it high on their agendas, what kinds of directions are indicated or counterindicated? Clearly, no single policy will bring an end to FSA, as is the case with any form of massive and blatant discrimination. Legal reforms are an important step, but they must be implemented. Economic reform is required that equalizes female entitlements. . . .

In terms of economic reforms, most scholars of Indian demography agree that the

only clear finding of all studies thus far is that high levels of female labor force participation are correlated with more equal sex ratios. Thus, any economic policies that
reduce female labor force participation should be subject to critical scrutiny. Education is the most controversial factor because research in several contexts in India and
Bangladesh reveals that higher levels of parental education are often correlated with
more son preference and heightened survival levels of sons compared with that of
daughters, though this correlation is less apparent in less patriarchal contexts such as
southern India and the Himalayan region of the far north of India, which typically
deviates from patterns in the northern plains region. These findings mean that a simple policy of investing in education in patriarchal contexts could actually reduce girls'
birth and survival relative to boys'.

A Balanced Sex Ratio as a Public Good

In general, however, the massive use of FSA in Asia requires massive amounts of
research and informed policy thinking. Perhaps one way to help place the issue of
unbalanced sex ratios in a more prominent place in academic research and policy is
to see a balanced sex ratio as both a local and a global public good. The concept of
a public good refers to something that is widely considered to be of value and should
be made available to everyone in order to sustain and improve their quality of life.
Economists tend to list things like clean water and air, streetlights, and sewage
removal as local public goods. Global public goods include health, peace and security, and environmental and cultural heritage.

A balanced sex ratio might be considered as both a local and a global public good
that should be promoted and supported by national governments, multinational
organizations including businesses, private institutions concerned with human development and welfare, and individual citizens. Why should such large-scale organizations be concerned about FSA? Intriguing studies, one several decades old and some
others more recent, point to the need to draw the topic of violence into analyses
of unbalanced sex ratios. A cross-cultural analysis of many "tribal" (nonagricultural)
societies of the mid-twentieth century shows that male-biased sex ratios are correlated with high levels of intersocietal warfare. More recently, a comparison of district-
level sex ratios and violence in one state in northern India has revealed the same correlation: where sex ratios are high, violence is more frequent. . . . Localized male violence toward women in India is another correlate of unbalanced sex ratios.

These studies, while few in number and not detailed in terms of what actually
occurs at an everyday level in high-violence contexts, suggest the need for further
attention to the possibility that patriarchal and territorially aggressive cultures
(including contemporary global capitalism) promote the reproduction of many males
as boundary protectors and boundary expanders and, therefore, disvalue females and
limit their numbers in the population through sex-selective infanticide, fetal neglect,
or FSA. Such a distorted demography takes its toll first and most directly on females
but also on males, whose survival may be impaired in their adult years through vio-

lence. Unbalanced sex ratios can be seen, therefore, as both local and global "public bads," closely related to violence in the home and the public domain.

Unbalanced Sex Ratios as Indicators of Human Rights Violations

Another important future direction is to consider FSA and male-biased sex ratios as human rights issues because of their links to violence. If assurance of personal and public security (freedom from violence) is accepted as a human right, then societies in which FSA is practiced and in which male-biased sex ratios exist are more likely to be societies in which security as a right is not assured. Seeing female-selective abortion in these new ways will challenge cultural anthropologists to refocus future research to take into account global connections and local contexts in reproduction, gender, and violence and to bring their findings to the world of policy makers and activists working for gender equality and greater assurances of personal and public security.

NOTES

CEDAW, Female-Specific Abortion, and Female Infanticide. In responding to China's and India's CEDAW Reports, the CEDAW Committee equates killing an infant girl with aborting a female fetus and recommends governmental action against both. What is similar about the two acts? What dissimilar? Does the treaty speak to either or both issues? The ICCPR? Compare the CEDAW Committee's Concluding Observations to India and China with its General Recommendation 24, excerpted above in Part II.B.3. Are they consistent?

The Policy Arguments. Daniel Goodkind suggests there may be reasons not to ban sex-specific abortions. Consider some of the moral and ethical problems he discusses in developing your own position. Is he right that banning such abortions would lead to banning abortions for other reasons and thus undermine women's reproductive rights? Barbara Miller views FSA as a serious problem and sees no reasons for taking a hands-off approach. Where do you stand on this issue? For further discussion of these complex issues, *see* REBECCA J. COOK, BERNARD M. DICKENS & MAHMOUD F. FATHALLA, REPRODUCTIVE HEALTH AND HUMAN RIGHTS: INTEGRATING MEDICINE, ETHICS, AND LAW 363–71 (2003).

Should Women Have to Justify Their Reasons for Seeking an Abortion? In deciding whether women should have the right to choose, some states demand that women have acceptable reasons before permitting them the choice. The most restrictive states permit it only to save the woman's life, while others add being the victim of rape or incest, carrying a fetus with a severe abnormality, or having physical or mental health problems. In this kind of view, some reasons will always be unacceptable—convenience, avoiding the results of a one-night stand, being unmarried or poor, having too many children already, wanting only boys. Another approach altogether is to permit abortions for any and all reasons, as long as the woman acts within the early stages of pregnancy. Which approach do you prefer and why?

IV. Child Marriage and Reproductive Rights

UNICEF Innocenti Research Center, *Early Marriage: Child Spouses*

INNOCENTI DIGEST NO. 7, 2–3, 9–11, 4, 6–7, 12–15 (2001).

Overview. . . .

Social reformers in the first part of the 20th century were concerned about early marriage, especially in India, and influenced the UDHR and other human rights conventions in the 1950s and 1960s. . . . Despite [these] efforts . . . , early marriage has received scant attention from the modern women's rights and children's rights movements. There has been virtually no attempt to examine the practice as a human rights violation *in itself.* Children and teenagers married at ages well below the legal minimum become statistically invisible as 'children.' Thus, in the eyes of the law, an adult male who has sex with a girl of 12 or 13 outside marriage may be regarded as a criminal, while the same act within marriage is condoned. . . .

The Impact of Early Marriage on Children. . . .

Adolescent health and reproduction

The notion of good reproductive health covers all aspects of the reproductive process—including a satisfying and safe experience of sexual relations, the capability to reproduce, and the freedom to decide if and when to bear a child. The right not to engage in sexual relations and the right to exercise control over reproduction may both be violated by early marriage.

Sexual relations

In the case of girls married before puberty, the normal understanding between families is that there will be no sexual intercourse until first menstruation. . . . However, this protection may fail, especially where the husband is much older than the girl. Cases of forced intercourse by much older and physically fully developed husbands with wives as young as eight have been reported.

For the vast majority of under-educated rural adolescent girls in the developing world, marriage remains the likely context for sexual intercourse. And while an unmarried teenage girl may find it difficult to resist unwanted sexual advances, her married sister may find it impossible. . . .

Access to contraception and reproductive health advice

Very few girls in early marriages in developing countries have access to contraception; nor would delayed pregnancy necessarily be acceptable to many husbands and in-laws. Indeed, in many societies, childbearing soon after marriage is integral to a woman's social status. . . .

Teenage girls are . . . more susceptible than more mature women to sexually-transmitted infections (STIs), including HIV. This is the result of both biological factors, such as hormonal fluctuations and the permeability of vaginal tissue, and social factors, such as skewed power relations between women and men that make it difficult for girls and young women to negotiate safe sex. STIs can lead to infertility, and in the case of HIV, the outcome is premature mortality and risks of transmission to the foetus. In a recent study in Rwanda, 25 per cent of girls who became pregnant at 17 or younger were infected with HIV, although many reported having sex only with their husbands. According to the study, the younger the age at sexual intercourse and first pregnancy, the higher the incidence of HIV infection. . . .

There are still a number of countries where reproductive health services are barred to adolescents, or require them to have reached a certain age. This excludes many married adolescents in countries such as Zambia or Bangladesh where age limits are in force—another of the anomalies surrounding early marriage.

Pregnancy and childbirth

The risks of early pregnancy and childbirth are well documented: increased risk of dying, increased risk of premature labour, complications during delivery, low birthweight, and a higher chance that the newborn will not survive.

Pregnancy-related deaths are the leading cause of mortality for 15–19 year-old girls (married and unmarried) worldwide. Mothers in this age group face a 20 to 200 per cent greater chance of dying in pregnancy than women aged 20 to 24. Those under age 15 are five times as likely to die as women in their twenties. The main causes are haemorrhage, sepsis, pre-eclampsia/eclampsia and obstructed labour. Unsafe abortion is the other major risk for teenage women—most of those affected are unmarried. . . . For every woman who dies in childbirth, 30 more suffer injuries, infections and disabilities, which usually go untreated and some of which are lifelong.

Part of this heavy toll has more to do with poor socio-economic status and lack of ante-natal and obstetric care than physical maturity alone. However, physical immaturity is the key risk for the under 15s. High rates of Vesico-Vaginal Fistula (VVF) are clearly identified with marriage and childbearing in the 10–15 year old age group; in one study in Niger, 88 per cent of women with fistula were in this age group at marriage. Mothers whose pelvis and birth canal are not fully developed often endure very prolonged labour. Unless the mother receives emergency obstetric care, relentless pressure from the baby's skull can damage the birth canal, causing breakages in the wall, allowing uncontrollable leakage from the bladder into the vagina. The same problem may also occur in relation to the rectum, with leakage of faeces ([R]ecto-[V]aginal [F]istulas, or RVF).

Fistula conditions are permanent without surgical intervention to re-seal the tissues[;]such intervention may not be sought or may be hard to access. . . . The prevalence of VVF/RVF is not fully known, but WHO estimates that there are two million women living with fistulas and an additional 50,000–100,000 new cases every year, many of which go untreated. A girl with the condition is usually ostracized as unclean, and is often divorced. In Nigeria, where the condition affects around 150,000 women, 80–90 per cent of wives with VVF are divorced by their husbands. . . .

Infant and early childhood care. . . .

A stronger likelihood of low birth-weight in the infant has been recorded among adolescent mothers than among older peers. This is mainly associated with poor maternal nutrition, reinforcing the point that adolescents are unready for childbirth. Low birth-weight babies are 5–30 times more likely to die than babies of normal weight. If a mother is under 18, her baby's chance of dying in the first year of life is 60 per cent higher than that of a baby born to a mother older than 19. . . .

Future maternal health and childbearing

Finally, early marriage extends a woman's potential childbearing capacity, which itself represents a risk to mothers. . . .

How Common Is Early Marriage?

The practice of marrying girls at a young age is most common in Sub-Saharan Africa and South Asia. However, in the Middle East, North Africa and other part of Asia, marriage at or shortly after puberty is common among those living traditional lifestyles. There are also specific parts of West and East Africa and of South Asia where marriages much earlier than puberty are not unusual, while marriages of girls between the ages of 16 and 18 are common in parts of Latin America and Eastern Europe.

Percentage of Women Aged 25–29 Married before Age 18

Latin America		Sub-Saharan Africa		Middle East and North Africa	
Guatemala	39	Niger	77		
Dominican Republic	38	Mali	70	Yemen	64
Paraguay	24	Burkina Faso	62	Egypt	30
		Mozambique	57		
South Central and Southeast Asia		Malawi	55		
Bangladesh	81	Cote d'Ivoire	44		
Nepal	68	Cameroon	43		
Pakistan	37	Benin	40		
Indonesia	34				

One problem in assessing the prevalence of early marriage is that so many are unregistered and unofficial and are not therefore counted as part of any standard data collection system. Very little country data exist about marriages under the age of 14, even less about those below age 10. An exception is Bangladesh, where the Demographic and Health Survey (DHS) of 1996–97 reported that 5 per cent of 10–14 year-olds were married. . . .

Married Adolescents: Percentage of 15–19 year-olds married

Sub-Saharan Africa	boys	girls	Middle East	boys	girls
Dem. Rep. of Congo	5	74	Iraq	15	28
Niger	4	70	Syria	4	25
Congo	12	56	Yemen	5	24
Uganda	11	50			
Mali	5	50	**Latin America and Caribbean**		
Asia			Honduras	7	30
Afghanistan	9	54	Cuba	7	29
Bangladesh	5	51	Guatemala	8	24
Nepal	14	42			

Early Marriage: The Causes. . . .

Early marriage as a strategy for economic survival

Poverty is one of the major factors underpinning early marriage. Where poverty is acute, a young girl may be regarded as an economic burden and her marriage to a much older—sometimes even elderly—man, a practice common in some Middle Eastern and South Asian societies, is a family survival strategy, and may even be seen as in her interests. In traditional societies in Sub-Saharan Africa, the bride's family may receive cattle from the groom, or the groom's family, as the brideprice for their daughter. A recent study of five very poor villages in Egypt found young girls being married off to much older men from oil-rich Middle Eastern countries via brokers. In Bangladesh, poverty-stricken parents are persuaded to part with daughters through promises of marriage, or by false marriages, which are used to lure the girls into prostitution abroad. . . .

In West Africa as a whole, a recent UNICEF study shows that economic hardship is encouraging a rise in early marriage, even among some population groups that do not normally practise it. Men are postponing marriage because of lack of resources, and parents have become anxious about the danger of their daughters becoming pregnant outside marriage. Thus any early opportunity for marriage may be seized upon. There are also reports from HIV/AIDS researchers in Eastern Africa that marriage is seen as one option for orphaned girls by caregivers who find it hard to provide for them. . . .

Other pressures can promote early marriage in societies under stress. Fear of HIV infection, for example, has encouraged men in some African countries to seek young virgin—and therefore uninfected—partners.[E] . . .

Protecting girls

Early marriage is one way to ensure that a wife is 'protected', or placed firmly under male control; that she is submissive to her husband and works hard for her in-laws'

[E] In addition to seeking virgins because they are uninfected, many men believe that sex with a virgin will cure them of HIV/AIDS. The propagation of this myth has led to the rape and

household; that the children she bears are 'legitimate'; and that bonds of affection between couples do not undermine the family unit. . . .

One important impetus for marrying girls at an early age is that it helps prevent premarital sex. Many societies prize virginity before marriage and this can manifest itself in a number of practices designed to 'protect' a girl from unsanctioned sexual activity. In effect, they amount to strict controls imposed upon the girl herself. She may, for example, be secluded from social interaction outside the family. She may be told what she can and cannot wear. In North-East Africa and parts of the Middle East in particular, control may also include the practice of . . . FGM . . . to restrict sexual pleasure and temptation. In some societies, parents withdraw their girls from school as soon as they begin to menstruate, fearing that exposure to male pupils or teachers puts them at risk. These practices are all intended to shield the girl from male sexual attention, but in the eyes of concerned parents, marriage is seen to offer the ultimate 'protection' measure. . . .

In some societies, the independent sense of self that a girl may develop during adolescence is seen as undesirable. . . . By the age of five, a girl in rural Pakistan has learnt to 'go outside' as little as possible, and adopt 'an attitude of care and service toward men.' Obviously, in Pakistan as elsewhere, the younger the bride, the more chance of conditioning her into the appropriate subservient behavior. . . .

TAKING ACTION. . . .

Education for empowerment and intellectual development. . . .

Both Sri Lanka and the state of Kerala in neighbouring India have relatively high age of first marriage. They also have something else in common that has contributed to this phenomenon: both have given high priority to education for women as well as men. This has changed the way men and women perceive their roles and potential, and has led to greater support for the rights of women than is found in many other parts of this region.

Where girls have lost out on formal education, non-formal programmes can help them catch up on the intellectual and personal growth offered by schooling. Such programmes can have a direct effect on early marriage: a programme from the 1990s among the people of the Samburu district in Kenya led to a fall in early marriage and helped women assert themselves. . . .

Formal Education: Bangladesh Secondary School Scholarships

On the assumption that financial constraints were the main reason for parents keeping their daughters out of school, a secondary school scholarship programme for girls was introduced in Bangladesh in the early 1990s.

---

prostitution of many young girls the world over. *See, e.g.,* Suzanne Leclerc-Madlala, *On the Virgin Cleansing Myth: Gendered Bodies, AIDS and Ethnomedicine,* 1 AFRICAN JOURNAL OF AIDS RESEARCH 87 (2002). The results: girls are 74% of "young people aged 15–24 living with HIV in sub-Saharan Africa," according to The Global Coalition on Women and AIDS, *Facts and Figures* (May 2006), *available at* http://womenandaids.unaids.org/publications_facts.html (last visited Aug. 28, 2007).

Fees and free books were provided for the students, and their parents were given some compensation for the loss of their daughters' agricultural and household work. The school timetable was also adjusted so that school days were shorter.

One of the most striking results was a sudden increase in marriage postponement, as parents were required to sign a bond that their daughters would not marry before age 18. Parents responded to the incentives, partly because they knew that daughters with a better education would marry men who are better providers. . . .

Support for improved economic status. . . .

A programme in Egypt for the girls of the Maqattam garbage settlement outside Cairo has enhanced their income-earning capacity while helping them resist early marriage. Rug making, paper recycling, and embroidery projects allow them to escape from garbage sorting and gain skills, an income and self-esteem. To encourage delayed and consensual marriage, a sum of E£500 (US$132.45) is offered to any girl who defers her marriage until age 19, and who enters marriage of her own free will. . . .

Legal change

Every year around 40 million births—one third of the world total—go unregistered. Without a birth certificate, a child has no defence against age-related rights abuses. In countries where the law on minimum age at marriage is ignored, the inadequacy of birth registration systems reinforces early marriage. . . .

Government action is required to review customary and civil law in light of internationally agreed human rights standards on marriage. . . .

Legislation and Change in Sri Lanka

In Sri Lanka, where age at marriage has traditionally been low, average age at marriage is now 25 years. This country's success in raising marriage age has been driven by the introduction of legislative reforms requiring that all marriages be registered and that the consent of both marriage partners be recorded. Moreover, Sri Lankan courts have ruled that specific cases of non-consensual marriages arranged by parents on behalf of their children are invalid. Underpinning these broad initiatives, which apply to Sri Lankan citizens of any religion, is a legal argument that Islamic law recognises the importance of consent to marriage. There are texts in Islamic law that indicate that parental authority in relation to the marriage of a daughter does not permit complete disregard of the child's welfare, and that accept the requirement of obtaining a child's consent to marriage. The positive impact of these legislative changes have been supported by social policies on health and education (including free education from primary to university level) to create an environment in which the practice of early marriage is in steep decline.

N O T E S

Does a Girl's Marriage Violate Her Reproductive Rights? Consider the different human rights treaties you have studied. Define which provisions provide reproductive rights. Does child marriage violate them? If so, why?

The Children's Rights Convention and CEDAW. Does a girl's early marriage—pursuant to a state statute permitting girls to marry at 15 with their parents' permission—violate the Children's Rights Convention? Article One defines a child as "every human being below the age of eighteen years unless under the law applicable to the child, majority is attained earlier." Does child marriage violate CEDAW? *See* Article 16(2), requiring states "to specify a minimum age for marriage." What weight should be given to the Children's Rights and CEDAW Committees' views that 18 is the right age? *See* General Comment No. 4, Adolescent health and development in the context of the Convention on the Rights of the Child, para. 9, and General Recommendation 21, Equality in marriage and family relations, para. 36.

The African Conventions. The only human rights treaties to require a minimum marriage age of 18 are the African Charter on the Rights and Welfare of the Child, Article 21(2), and the African Women's Rights Protocol, Article 6(b).

Child Marriage and Brideprice as Slave-Like Practices? The Supplementary Convention on the Abolition of Slavery, the Slave Trade, and Institutions and Practices Similar to Slavery prohibits practices where a "woman, without the right to refuse, is promised or given in marriage on payment of a consideration in money or in kind to her parents. . . ." To end this Article 1(c) practice, Article 2 requires that "States Parties undertake to prescribe, where appropriate, suitable minimum ages of marriage, [and] to encourage the use of facilities whereby the consent of both parties to a marriage may be freely expressed in the presence of a competent civil or religious authority. . . ." Many treaties require the "free and full consent of the intending spouses" to enter into marriage. *See, e.g.,* Article 23(3) of the ICCPR.

Child Marriage in the United States. A December 2004 Chicago Tribune article[F] notes that "even though early marriage is an issue overwhelmingly associated with the developing world—barely 2 percent of all American pregnancies, for instance, involve married girls under 18 . . .—the antique practice still survives in the United States. And it often sentences young American women to a lifetime of poverty and other problems. While they don't face the severe pregnancy-related injuries of young girls in the developing world, they risk increased rates of chronic anemia and obesity. . . . They tend to drop out of school at even higher rates than single mothers; their marriages usually don't last; and they face an increased risk of domestic violence. . . ." In the United States, a handful of states permit child marriages with parental consent. In Alabama, South Carolina, Texas, and Utah, girls can marry at 14; in New Hampshire, at 13; and in Massachusetts and Kansas, at 12. The article spotlights a Texan girl, who married her boyfriend of four years her senior at the age of 14 in order to keep him out of jail when the state of Texas was threatening to charge him with statutory rape. Should girls have a right to marry?

[F] Paul Salopek, *Early Marriage Survives in the U.S.,* CHICAGO TRIBUNE, Dec. 29, 2004.

What Other Rights Does Child Marriage Violate? The UNICEF article, *Early Marriage: Child Spouses,* answers: "Within a rights perspective, three key concerns are the denial of childhood and adolescence, the curtailment of personal freedom and the lack of opportunity to develop a full sense of selfhood as well as the denial of pychosocial and emotional well-being, reproductive health and educational opportunity. . . ."

Table of Cases

The principal cases are listed in bold. The references are to pages.

Glossary

Accession: "'Accession' is the act whereby a state accepts the offer or the opportunity to become a party to a treaty already negotiated and signed by other states. It has the same legal effect as ratification. Accession usually occurs after the treaty has entered into force. The Secretary-General of the United Nations, in his function as depositary, has also accepted accessions to some conventions before their entry into force." U.N. Treaty Collection, *Treaty Reference Guide*, "Glossary of terms related to treaty Action," para. 3, *available at* http:// untreaty.un.org/English/guide.asp [*Treaty Guide*] and RossRights.

Adoption: Adoption is the process by which the parties drafting a treaty agree to its text and thereby open the treaty for ratification or accession by potential states parties. *See* Vienna Convention, art. 9.

Entry into force: A treaty enters into force and becomes a legally binding document on all States Parties when the relevant treaty conditions are satisfied. Vienna Convention, art. 24, para. 1.

Reservation: A reservation is "a unilateral statement, however phrased or named, made by a State, when signing, ratifying, accepting, approving or acceding to a treaty, whereby it purports to exclude or to modify the legal effect of certain provisions of the treaty in their application to that State." Vienna Convention, art. 2, para. 1(d). A state cannot enter a reservation that is "incompatible with the object and purpose of the treaty." *Id.*, art. 19, para. c.

Self-Executing Treaty: A treaty that is self-executing can be applied by national courts without having a new law passed to implement the treaty. A treaty that is non-self-executing requires the legislature to first enact an implementing law before the courts apply the treaty, as expressed in the new statute, to the case at hand.

Shadow Reports: A shadow report supplements, or "shadows," the official state report to a human rights body. NGOs prepare these reports and meet with the treaty committee members.

Signature and Ratification: "Where the signature is subject to ratification, acceptance or approval, the signature does not establish the consent to be bound. However, it is a means of authentication and expresses the willingness of the signatory state to continue the treaty-making process. The signature qualifies the signatory state to proceed to ratification, acceptance or approval. It also creates an obligation to refrain, in good faith, from acts that would defeat the object and the purpose of the treaty." *Treaty Guide*, para. 23.

Ratification usually follows after signature and "defines the international act whereby a state indicates its consent to be bound to a treaty if the parties intended to show their consent by such an act." *Treaty Guide*, para. 18.

Special Rapporteur: A Special Rapporteur is an official appointed to take minutes or compile information on a specific issue for the use of the group making the appointment, usually on a temporary basis.

Travaux Préparatoires: The French term "travaux préparatoires"—meaning "preparatory works"—is the international law term to denote a concept similar to "legislative history" in the domestic law context.

Acronyms and Short Forms

ACHR	American Convention on Human Rights
AU	African Union
African Charter	African [Banjul] Charter on Human and Peoples' Rights
African Commission	African Commission on Human and Peoples' Rights
African Court	African Court on Human and Peoples' Rights
African WR Protocol	Protocol to the African Charter on Human and Peoples' Rights on the Rights of Women in Africa
CAT	Convention Against Torture and Other Cruel, Inhuman or Degrading Treatment or Punishment
CAT Committee	Committee Against Torture
CEDAW	Convention on the Elimination of All Forms of Discrimination Against Women
CEDAW Committee	Committee on the Elimination of Discrimination Against Women
CRC	Convention on the Rights of the Child
CRC Committee	Committee on the Rights of the Child
CRR	Center for Reproductive Rights
CSW	UN Commission on the Status of Women
DEDAW	UN Declaration on the Elimination of Discrimination Against Women
DEVAW	UN Declaration on the Elimination of Violence Against Women
EC	European Community
ECHR	European Court of Human Rights
ECOSOC	UN Economic and Social Council
EEC	European Economic Community
ESC Committee	Committee on Economic, Social and Cultural Rights
EU	European Union
FGC	Female Genital Cutting
FGM	Female Genital Mutilation
FSA	Female Selective Abortion
GAOR	UN General Assembly Official Records
HIV/AIDS	Human Immunodeficiency Virus/Acquired Immune Deficiency Syndrome
HRC	Human Rights Committee
HRO	Human Rights Organization

HRW	Human Rights Watch
ICCPR	International Covenant on Civil and Political Rights
ICESCR	International Covenant on Economic, Social and Cultural Rights
ICJ	International Court of Justice
ILO	International Labour Organization
Inter-American Court	Inter-American Court of Human Rights
Inter-American Commission	Inter-American Commission of Human Rights
Inter-American VAW	Inter-American Convention on the Prevention, Punishment and Eradication of Violence Against Women
NGO	Non-Governmental Organization
OAS	Organization of American States
OAU	Organization of African Unity
PHR	Physicians for Human Rights
UDHR	Universal Declaration of Human Rights
UN	United Nations
UNICEF	UN Children's Fund [originally UN International Children's Emergency Fund]
UNIFEM	UN Development Fund for Women
WHO	World Health Organization

Credits and Permissions

I would like to thank the following authors, publishers, and organizations for granting permission to reprint copyrighted materials.

A'Haleem, Asma Mohammed. *Claiming Our Bodies and Our Rights : Exploring Female Circumcision as an Act of Violence in Africa, in* Freedom from Violence: Women's Strategies from Around the World, 141–56 (Margaret Schuler ed., 1992). Copyright © 1992 by UNIFEM WIDBOOKS. Reprinted by permission of UNIFEM.

Abi-Mershed, Elizabeth A. H. *The Inter-American Commission on Human Rights: Prospects for the Inter-American Human Rights System to Protect and Promote the Human Rights of Women, in* Women and International Human Rights Law, Vol. 2, 417, 430–33 (Kelly D. Askin & Dorean M. Koenig eds., 2000). Copyright © 2000. Reprinted from Women and International Human Rights Law, Vol. 2, with the permission of Transnational Publishers, Ardsley, N.Y.

Adjetey, Fitnat Naa-Adjeley. *Female Genital Mutilation: Tradition or Torture?*, 57–59, 61–62. Unpublished LL.M. thesis, Georgetown University Law Center, May 2, 1994. Reprinted by permission of the author.

Adjetey, Fitnat Naa-Adjeley. *Religious & Cultural Rights: Reclaiming the African Woman's Individuality: the Struggle Between Women's Reproductive Autonomy and African Society and Culture*, 44 Am. U.L. Rev. 1351, 1359–1361, 1364 (1994). Copyright © 1994 by The American University Law Review. Reprinted by permission of The American University Law Review.

Al-Hibri, Azizah. *Who Defines Women's Rights? A Third World Woman's Response*, in The Center for Human Rights and Humanitarian Law, Human Rights Brief, Washington College of Law, The American University, Fall 1994. Reprinted by permission of the author.

American Law Institute. *Restatement (Third) Foreign Relations Law of the United States.* Copyright 1987 by The American Law Institute. Reprinted with permission of The American Law Institute. All rights reserved.

Amnesty International. *Pakistan: Insufficient Protection of Women*, April 16, 2002. Reprinted by permission of Amnesty International USA. *Available at* http://www.amnestyusa.org/countries/pakistan/reports.do

Amnesty International. *Pakistan: Violence Against Women in the Name of Honour*, September 21, 1999. Reprinted by permission of Amnesty International USA. *Available at* http://www.amnestyusa.org/countries/pakistan/reports.do

Babcock, Barbara Allen, Ann E. Freedman, Susan Deller Ross, Wendy Webster Williams, Rhonda Copelon, Deborah L. Rhode, and Nadine Taub. *Sex Discrimination and the Law: History, Practice, and Theory*, 425–27, 470, 484–89, 552–59, 1334–37 (2d ed. 1996). Copyright © 1996. Reprinted from Babcock/Freedman/Ross/Williams: *Sex Discrimination and the Law,*

2d ed. with the permission of Aspen Publishers. Reprinted by permission of Barbara Allen Babcock, Ann E. Freedman, Susan Deller Ross, and Wendy Webster Williams.

Bayefsky, Anne F. *General Approaches to Domestic Application of Women's International Human Rights Law, in* Human Rights of Women: National and International Perspectives, 351, 353–54, 359–60, 363–69 (Rebecca J. Cook ed., 1994). Copyright © 1994 by the University of Pennsylvania Press. Reprinted by permission of the University of Pennsylvania Press.

Bhagwati, P. N. *Bangalore Principles* (1988), 14 CLB 1196. Published by London, Commonwealth Secretariat. Reprinted by permission.

Boland, Reed and Jan Stepan eds. *Law No. 100 amending certain clauses in the law of personal status* (Summary). Annual Review of Population Law, Vol. 12, 320, 335–38 (1985). Copyright © 1985 by United Nations Population Fund (UNFPA). Reprinted by permission of UNFPA.

Burton, Barbara, Nata Duvvury and Nisha Varia. 2002. *Justice, Change and Human Rights: International Research and Responses to Domestic Violence.* Washington, D.C.: International Center for Research and Women and The Centre for Development and Population Activities. Reprinted by permission.

Butegwa, Florence. *Using the African Charter on Human and Peoples' Rights to Secure Women's Access to Land in Africa, in* Human Rights of Women: National and International Perspectives, 495–500 (Rebecca J. Cook ed., 1994). Copyright © 1994 by the University of Pennsylvania Press. Reprinted by permission of the University of Pennsylvania Press.

Carlson, Karen J., M.D., Stephanie A. Eisenstat, M.D., & Terra Ziporyn, Ph.D. *Breast Implants and Enlargement, in* The New Harvard Guide to Women's Health, 105–8 (2004). Reprinted by permission of the publisher from The New Harvard Guide to Women's Health by Karen J. Carlson, M.D., Stephanie A. Eisenstat, and Terra Ziporyn, 105–8, Cambridge, Mass.: The Belknap Press of Harvard University Press. Copyright © 1996, 2004 by the President and Fellows of Harvard College.

El Alami, Dawoud S. & Doreen Hinchcliffe. *Islamic Marriage and Divorce Laws of the Arab World,* 51–52. Copyright © 1996. Published for CIMEL SOAS by Kluwer Law International. Reprinted by permission of the authors.

El Alami, Dawoud S. *The Marriage Contract in Islamic Law in the Shari'ah and Personal Status Laws of Egypt and Morocco,* 129–35. Copyright © 1992. Published by Graham & Trotman. Reprinted by permission of the author.

Evatt, Elizabeth. *Finding a Voice for Women's Rights: The Early Days of CEDAW,* 34 Geo. Wash. Int'l L. Rev. 515 (2002). Copyright © 2002. Reprinted with permission from The George Washington International Law Review, Volume 34, Number 3, 2002.

Fitzpatrick, Joan. *The Use of International Human Rights Norms to Combat Violence Against Women, in* Human Rights of Women: National and International Perspectives, 532–40, 555–58 (Rebecca J. Cook ed., 1994). Copyright © 1994 by the University of Pennsylvania Press. Reprinted by permission of the University of Pennsylvania Press.

[Ghana] Law Reform Commission. *Abolishing Dehumanizing Customary Practices: Female Genital Mutilation* (Report No. 2), October 1997. Reprinted by permission.

Goodkind, Daniel. *Should Prenatal Sex Selection Be Restricted? Ethical Questions and Their Implications for Research and Policy,* Population Studies, Vol. 53, 49–53, 55–59. 1999. Reprinted by permission of Taylor and Francis Ltd. Copyright © 1999. Journal website: http://www.tandf.co.uk/journals.

Harrington, Julia. *The African Commission on Human and Peoples' Rights, in* Women and International Human Rights Law, Vol. 2, 455, 465–70 (Kelly D. Askin & Dorean M. Koenig eds., 2000). Copyright © 2000. Reprinted from Women and International Human Rights Law, Vol. 2, with the permission of Transnational Publishers, Ardsley, N.Y.

Hassan, Hossam, Rights-Egypt. *New Law Lets Women Divorce if They Waive Support,* International Press Service, March 28, 2000. Reprinted by permission. IPS website: http://ipsnews.net.

Howland, Courtney W. *The Challenge of Religious Fundamentalism to the Liberty and Equality Rights of Women: An Analysis Under the United Nations Charter,* 35 Colum. J. Transnat'l L. 271, 274–79,

282–324 (1997). Copyright © 1997. Reprinted from Columbia Journal of Transnational Law, Volume 35, Issue 2 by permission.

Human Rights Watch. *Divorced from Justice: Women's Unequal Access to Divorce in Egypt.* Copyright © 2004 by Human Rights Watch. Reprinted by permission.

Human Rights Watch. *Domestic Violence: Violence Against Women in Brazil, in* Human Rights Watch Global Report on Women's Human Rights, 348–60 (1995). Copyright © 1995 by Human Rights Watch. Reprinted by permission.

Human Rights Watch. *Honoring the Killers: Justice Denied for "Honor" Crimes in Jordan.* Copyright © 2004 by Human Rights Watch.

Martin, Lorna. *Waris Dirie is the desert flower who rebelled against the might of Somalian ritual. And for this beautiful warrior, the fight is just beginning,* The Herald (Glasgow), June 29, 2002, at 22. Reproduced with courtesy of The Herald (Glasgow), Newsquest (Herald & Times) Ltd.

Mayambala, Esther N. *Changing the Terms of the Debate: Polygamy and the Rights of Women in Kenya and Uganda,* 3 East African Journal of Peace & Human Rights, 200, 229–36, 238–39 (1997). Reprinted by permission of the author and journal.

Meekers, Dominique & Nadra Franklin. *Women's Perceptions of Polygamy Among the Kaguru of Tanzania,* 34 Ethnology 315–27 (1995). Reprinted by permission of Ethnology.

Miller, Barbara D. *Female-Selective Abortion in Asia: Patterns, Policies, and Debates,* American Anthropologist, Vol. 103, No. 4: 1083–95. © 2001, American Anthropological Association. Used by permission. All rights reserved.

Neft, Naomi and Anne D. Levine. *Where Women Stand: An International Report on the Status of Women in 140 Countries, 1997–1998.* Copyright © 1997 by Naomi Neft and Anne D. Levine. Used by permission of Random House, Inc.

Paisley, Sylvia. *Arms and the Man,* 38 NILQ 1987, 352, 364–66. Queen's University School of Law. Reprinted by permission.

Papua New Guinea National Court of Justice. *The State v. Kule,* 1991 PNGLR 405. Reprinted by permission.

Physicians for Human Rights. *The Taliban's War on Women: A Health and Human Rights Crisis in Afghanistan.* Reprinted by permission.

Posner, Richard A. *Sex and Reason.* Reprinted by permission of the publisher from Sex and Reason by Richard A. Posner, 253–60, Cambridge, Mass.: Harvard University Press. Copyright © 1992 by the President and Fellows of Harvard College.

Rahimi, Wali M., *Status of Women: Afghanistan,* 6–14, 62–65 (1991). Bangkok: UNESCO Principal Regional Office for Asia and the Pacific, 1991. Reprinted by permission of UNESCO.

Rahman, Anika, and Nahid Toubia, M.D. *Female Genital Mutilation: A Guide to Laws and Policies Worldwide.* Copyright © 2000. Zed Books Ltd.: London. Reprinted by permission of Nahid Toubia and RAINBO.

Ross, Susan Deller. *Legal Aspects of Parental Leave: At the Crossroads,* from Parental Leave and Child Care: Setting a Research and Policy Agenda, 94–98 (Janet Shibley Hyde & Marilyn J. Essex eds., 1991). Reprinted by permission of Temple University Press. Copyright © 1991 by Temple University. All Rights Reserved.

Ross, Susan Deller. *Polygyny as a Violation of Women's Right to Equality in Marriage: An Historical, Comparative and International Human Rights Overview,* 24 Delhi L. Rev. 22, 22–27, 34–36 (2002). Reprinted by permission of Delhi Law Review.

Sikkenk, Kathryn. *Historical Precursors to Modern Campaigns for Women's Human Rights: Campaigns Against Footbinding and Female Circumcision, in* Women and International Human Rights Law, Vol. 3, 797, 798–807 (Kelly D. Askin & Dorean M. Koenig, eds., 2001). Ardsley, N.Y.: Transnational Publishers, 2001. Copyright © 2001. Reprinted by permission of Koninklijke Brill NV.

Singh, Kirti. *Obstacles to Women's Rights in India, in* Human Rights of Women: National and International Perspectives, 377–81, 386–87 (Rebecca J. Cook ed., 1994). Copyright © 1994 by the University of Pennsylvania Press. Reprinted by permission of the University of Pennsylvania Press.

Toubia, Nahid, M.D. *Female Circumcision as a Public Health Issue*, New Eng. J. Med., 712–16 (Sept. 15, 1994). Reprinted by permission of New England Journal of Medicine.

Trebilcock, Anne. *ILO Conventions and Women Workers, in* Women and International Human Rights Law, Vol. 2, 301, 311–13 (Kelly D. Askin & Dorean M. Koenig eds., 2000). Copyright © 2000. Reprinted from Women and International Human Rights Law, Vol. 2, with the permission of Transnational Publishers, Ardsley, N.Y.

UNICEF Innocenti Research Center. *Early Marriage: Child Spouses.* Florence, Italy: UNICEF, 2001. Innocenti Digest. No. 7. Reprinted by permission of UNICEF.

Index

CPSIA information can be obtained
at www.ICGtesting.com
Printed in the USA
LVHW10s1320230918
591103LV00003B/116/P